ESTUARINE INTERACTIONS

Produced by

The Estuarine Research Federation
in cooperation with
The Marine Technology Society

Sponsored by

Army Corps of Engineers
Bureau of Land Management
Environmental Protection Agency
Fish and Wildlife Service
Geological Survey
  Land Information and Analysis Office
  Water Resources Divison
National Oceanic and Atmospheric Administration
  Marine Ecosystems Analysis Program
  National Marine Fisheries Service
  Office of Coastal Zone Management

Proceedings of the Fourth Biannual International
Estuarine Research Conference,
Mount Pocono, Pennsylvania, October 2–5, 1977

ESTUARINE INTERACTIONS

Edited by

MARTIN L. WILEY
University of Maryland
Center for Environmental and Estuarine Studies
Chesapeake Biological Laboratory
Solomons, Maryland

ACADEMIC PRESS   *New York   San Francisco   London*   *1978*
A Subsidiary of Harcourt Brace Jovanovich, Publishers

ACADEMIC PRESS, INC.
111 Fifth Avenue, New York, New York 10003

United Kingdom Edition published by
ACADEMIC PRESS, INC. (LONDON) LTD.
24/28 Oval Road, London NW1 7DX

Library of Congress Cataloging in Publication Data

International Estuarine Research Conference, 4th,
    Pocono, Pa., 1977.
    Estuarine interactions.

    Proceedings of the Fourth International Estuarine
Research Conference, Pocono, Pa., Oct. 2-5, 1977.
    Includes index.
    1. Estuaries—Congresses.   2.   Estuarine biology—
Congresses.   I.   Wiley, Martin L.   II.   Title.
GC96.5.I57 1977   574.5'2636   78-11110
ISBN 0-12-751850-9

PRINTED IN THE UNITED STATES OF AMERICA

78 79 80 81 82   9 8 7 6 5 4 3 2 1

CONTENTS

Interactions within Estuarine Communities: Primary and Secondary Productivity

Interactions within Estuarine Communities: Community Interactions

Land–Estuary Interactions: Natural Catastrophic Events

Land–Estuary Interactions: Freshwater Requirements of Estuaries

LIST OF CONTRIBUTORS

Aller, Robert C., Department of Geophysical Sciences, 5734 S. Ellis Avenue, University of Chicago, Chicago, Illinois 60637

Appan, S. G., Daniel Analytical Services Corp., 16821 Buccaneer Lane, Suite 202, Houston, Texas 77058

Armstrong, Neal E., Department of Civil Engineering, University of Texas, Austin, Texas 78712

Atkinson, L. P., Skidaway Institute of Oceanography, P.O. Box 13687, Savannah, Georgia 31406

Bahr, Leonard M., Jr., Department of Marine Sciences, Louisiana State University, Baton Rouge, Louisiana 70803

Bartsch-Winkler, Susan, U.S. Geological Survey, Branch of Alaskan Geology, 345 Middleford Road, Menlo Park, California 94025

Blanton, J. O., Skidaway Institute of Oceanography, P.O. Box 13687, Savannah, Georgia 31406

Buzas, Martin A., Department of Paleobiology, Smithsonian Institution, Washington, D.C. 20560

Carpenter, Roy, Department of Oceanography, University of Washington, Seattle, Washington 98195

Chamberlain, Charles F., Skidaway Institute of Oceanography, P.O. Box 13687, Savannah, Georgia 31406

Christian, Robert R., Department of Biological Sciences, Drexel University, Philadelphia, Pennsylvania 19104

Colwell, Rita R., Department of Microbiology, University of Maryland, College Park, Maryland 20742

Cross, Ford A., National Marine Fisheries Service, Southeast Fisheries Center, Beaufort Laboratory, Beaufort, North Carolina 28516

Crout, Richard L., Belle W. Baruch Institute for Marine Biology & Coastal Research, University of South Carolina, Columbia, South Carolina 29208

Day, John W., Jr., Department of Marine Sciences, Louisiana State University, Baton Rouge, Louisiana 70803

Dayal, R., Marine Sciences Research Center, State University of New York, Stony Brook, New York 11794

Duedall, Iver V., Marine Sciences Research Center, State University of New York, Stony Brook, New York 11794

Dunstan, William M., Skidaway Institute of Oceanography, P.O. Box 13687, Savannah, Georgia 31406

Elliott, A. J., Chesapeake Bay Institute, The Johns Hopkins University, Baltimore, Maryland 21218

Falk, Lloyd L., Engineering Service Division, Engineering Department, E. I. du Pont de Nemours & Co., Wilmington, Delaware 19898

Finley, Robert J., Bureau of Economic Geology, The University of Texas at Austin, Austin, Texas 78712

Fruh, E. Gus, Environmental Health Engineering Program, Department of Civil Engineering, The University of Texas at Austin, Austin, Texas 78712

Gallagher, John L., U.S. Environmental Protection Agency, Corvallis Environmental Research Laboratory, 200 S.W. 35th Street, Corvallis, Oregon 97330

Garside, Chris, Bigelow Laboratory for Ocean Sciences, McKown Point, W. Boothbay Harbor, Maine 04575

Greer, Jeffrey E., Belle W. Baruch Institute for Marine Biology & Coastal Research, University of South Carolina, Columbia, South Carolina 29208

Hanson, Roger B., Skidaway Institute of Oceanography, P.O. Box 13687, Savannah, Georgia 31406

Harris, Virginia M., Port Aransas Marine Laboratory, The University of Texas Marine Science Institute, Port Aransas, Texas 78373

Hayes, Miles O., Coastal Research Division, Department of Geology, University of South Carolina, Columbia, South Carolina 29208

Hedgpeth, Joel W., Dr., 5660 Montecito Avenue, Santa Rosa, California 95404

Heesen, Theadore C., Southern California Coastal Water Research Project, 1500 East Imperial Highway, El Segundo, California 90245

Herring, Janet P., Marine Sciences Institute, The University of Connecticut, Groton, Connecticut 06340

Hinson, Melvin O., Jr., Resources for the Future, Inc., 1755 Massachusetts Avenue, N.W., Washington, D.C. 20036

Hirschberg, D.J., Marine Sciences Research Center, State University of New York, Stony Brook, New York 11794

Hull, G., Bigelow Laboratory for Ocean Sciences, W. Boothbay Harbor, Maine 04575

Jackim, Eugene, U.S. Environmental Protection Agency, Environmental Research Laboratory, South Ferry Road, Narragansett, Rhode Island 02882

Jahnke, R. A., Department of Oceanography, University of Washington, Seattle, Washington 98195

Jan, Tsu-Kai, Southern California Coastal Water Research Project, 1500 East Imperial Highway, El Segundo, California 90245

Jones, K. W., Department of Physics, Brookhaven National Laboratory, Upton, New York 19973

Kamlet, Kenneth S., National Wildlife Federation, 1412 16th Street, N.W., Washington, D.C. 20036

Kaper, J., Department of Microbiology, University of Maryland, College Park, Maryland 20742

Kjerfve, Bjorn, Belle W. Baruch Institute for Marine Biology & Coastal Research, University of South Carolina, Columbia, South Carolina 29208

Kraner, H. W., Instrumentation Division, Brookhaven National Laboratory, Upton, New York 19973

Lake, Carol, Environmental Research Laboratory, South Ferry Road, Narragansett, Rhode Island 02882

Lambert, Walter P., U.S. Army Medical Bioengineering, Research & Development Laboratory, Fort Detrick, Maryland 21701

McCall, Peter L., Department of Earth Sciences Case Western Reserve University, Cleveland, Ohio 44106

Muller, Robert A., Department of Geography & Anthropology, Louisiana State University, Baton Rouge, Louisiana 70803

Ovenshine, A. T., U.S. Department of Interior, Geological Survey, Branch of Alaskan Geology, 345 Middleford Road, Menlo Park, California 94025

Parker, J. H., Marine Sciences Research Center, State University of New York, Stony Brook, New York 11794

Peterson, M. L., Department of Oceanography, University of Washington, Seattle, Washington 98195

Read, Luana M., Marine Sciences Institute, The University of Connecticut, Groton, Connecticut 06340

Rhoads, Donald C., Department of Geology & Geophysics, Box 2161, Yale Station, Yale University, New Haven, Connecticut 06520

Roels, Oswald A., Port Aransas Marine Laboratory, The University of Texas Marine Science Institute, Port Aransas, Texas 78373

Rogers, James A., Office of General Council, Water Quality Division (A-131), U.S. Environmental Protection Agency, Washington, D.C. 20460

Schroeder, William W., Dauphin Island Sea Laboratory, Box 386, Dauphin Island, Alabama 36528

Schubel, J. R., Marine Sciences Research Center, State University of New York, Stony Brook, New York 11794

Sharfstein, Bruce A., Port Aransas Marine Laboratory, The University of Texas Marine Science Institute, Port Aransas, Texas 78373

Sharp, James M., Gulf Universities Research Consortium, 16821 Buccaneer Lane, Suite 206, Houston, Texas 77058

Sherr, Barry, Department of Microbiology, University of Georgia, Athens, Georgia 30601

Shroy, R. E., Department of Physics, Brookhaven National Laboratory, Upton, New York 19973

Stone, James H., Department of Marine Sciences, Louisiana State University, Baton Rouge, Louisiana 70803

Sunda, William G., National Marine Fisheries Service, Southeast Fisheries Center, Beaufort Laboratory, Beaufort, North Carolina 28516

Taft, Jay L., Chesapeake Bay Institute, The Johns Hopkins University, Baltimore, Maryland 21218

Taylor, W. R., Chesapeake Bay Institute, The Johns Hopkins University, Baltimore, Maryland 21218

Tenore, Kenneth R., Skidaway Institute of Oceanography, P.O. Box 13687, Savannah, Georgia 31406

Tietjen, John H., Department of Biology, City College of The City University of New York, New York 10010

Ullman, William J., Department of Geophysical Sciences, University of Chicago, Chicago, Illinois 60637

Virnstein, Robert W., Harbor Branch Foundation, Inc., R.R. 1, Box 196, Fort Pierce, Florida 33450

Welsh, Barbara L., Marine Sciences Institute, The University of Connecticut, Groton, Connecticut 06340

Wetzel, Richard L., Wetlands Research, Virginia Institute of Marine Science, Gloucester Point, Virginia 23062

Yentsch, C. S., Bigelow Laboratory for Ocean Sciences, W. Boothbay Harbor, Maine 04575

Yingst, Josephine Y., Department of Geology & Geophysics, Box 2161, Yale Station, Yale University, New Haven, Connecticut 06520

Young, David R., Southern California Coastal Water Research Project, 1500 East Imperial Highway, El Segundo, California 90245

FOREWORD

Estuaries and adjacent environments are ecological systems that are subjected to continual stress by natural and man-induced perturbations. The goal of estuarine scientists is to gain knowledge of the structure and functioning of these complex interacting systems. It is hoped that this knowledge will be used by decision-makers when confronted with the awesome task of deciding the utilization and fate of these extremely valuable resources. Because of their dynamic nature and their societal importance, many scientific investigations dealing with estuaries are continuously underway. To facilitate the transfer of research information and to review the state of the art, a fundamental responsibility of the Estuarine Research Federation is to convene an international conference every two years dealing with advances in research. During the period of October 2–5, 1977, the Fourth International Estuarine Research Federation Conference was held at the Mount Airy Lodge, Mount Pocono, Pennsylvania at an elevation well above that of the high spring tide level. This volume includes the written form of the invited papers that were part of eight sessions. Although the excitement of the formal and informal discussions that took place at the meeting as a result of these papers is impossible to capture completely on paper, the rigorous reviewing by referees and the elegant editing by Martin Wiley have resulted in a volume that is of value not only to those estuarinists who were in attendance, but also to our colleagues who were unable to attend.

Based on the papers presented here, the objectives of the Estuarine Research Federation to review current research and to suggest new research directions have been accomplished, at least until our next meeting in 1979.

F. John Vernberg, President

ESTUARY–MAN INTERACTIONS: ESTUARINE MANAGEMENT NEEDS

AS BLIND MEN SEE THE ELEPHANT:
THE DILEMMA OF MARINE ECOSYSTEM RESEARCH

Joel W. Hedgpeth

Emeritus Professor of Oceanography
5660 Montecito Avenue
Santa Rosa, California

Abstract: We are beset in these days of impact assessments, environmental monitoring and all, with the problem of studying a complex system in some way that will convince us we know what is going on and that we can predict the effect of our actions on this system. Meetings on this subject tend to fragment into lobbyists for the various approaches. The Baconian ideal of compiling all knowledge and consigning it to the computer to tell us what to think about it all is the ultimate extreme on one side, and the notion that one (or perhaps two) numbers from a dying mussel may be all we need is the other extreme of the ancient problem of deducing the state of affairs from diverse concepts based on limited vision or perhaps no vision at all, but a disconnected set of tactile impressions of the elephant. Or, to put it another way, how we can be certain we are not still prisoners in Plato's cave?

During the 1976 International Marine Biology Symposium at Helgoland, I was asked to organize, or at lease convene, a discussion of the needs of marine ecosystem research. It turned out to be a frustrating experience for a number of reasons, and the discussion was not only inconclusive but also brought to mind the old story about the blind men trying to visualize an elephant from a disconnected set of tactile impressions (Hedgpeth, 1977d). Yet the need to develop research approaches that can provide us with predictive information and support conclusions on which to base management decisions in our pollution-ridden world are very much with us. In spite of the considerable body of knowledge that has been built up about the North Sea, for example, we still do not have the right information on which to base predictions for management. Here is a body of water lying between the highly industrialized and heavily populated continent of Europe and Great Britain, which has been treated ever since modern civilization developed as a waste disposal sink, yet does not seem to be dangerously polluted (Goldberg, 1973). After a century of research, we cannot manage this region as a natural interaction of biological and physical factors, and indeed the question was raised, appropriately, by a gentleman from Vienna: are ecosystems real entities, or concepts associated with the ordering nature of our mind?

Of course, all our concepts of nature are simplifications or abstractions and are "to some extent therefore a fairy tale," as the meteorologist Sir Napier Shaw said. This quotation, which introduces the chapter on the concepts of marine ecology that I wrote twenty years ago (and now is somewhat out of date), is the most important, and evidently least read, part of that attempt to summarize matters (Hedgpeth, 1957). The latest word for this process of simplification appears to be paradigm, which the dictionary tells me means "example, model or pattern," but which in some recent usage seems to mean something else, an exemplary abstraction arrived at by a process of "capsulization," which sounds like some idealization of abstract values and virtues. Perhaps some of the people who use this word these days have never looked it up in the dictionary and have it confused with paladin. In any event, according to the document, "An ecosystem paradigm for ecology" (P. L. Johnson *et al.*, 1977), the ecological paradigm is comprised of "statements and discussion." They do conclude, which is more to the point of this discussion, that "ecologically controlling variables are only partially within man's grasp." But do we need to "grasp variables"? An unfortunate word in this context, since it brings to mind grasping at straws. I am also afraid that this capsulogenous proclivity will not encourage those who have been exposed to an undergraduate course in ecology, and have since become bureaucrats and/or administrators (the terms are not necessarily synonymous), to keep up with the subject.

Whatever the ecosystem may be, or how complicated, or whether it is simply another word for the natural world we are part of, there are obviously too many things going on to study all of them or gather data on everything at once and ask the computer to tell us what it all means. Our concern is to understand the environment well enought to make predictions and hope to manage it, or at least control ourselves and our actions so that we will not find ourselves living on a vast dung heap beside a vaster cesspool. Such understanding and ultimate management is incompatible with political exigencies, the need for the quick fix. Things must be done, or at least appear to be done, between elections or budgets, to justify renewed incumbencies or refunded budgets. Most scientists refuse to consider this illogical approach to environmental management significant or even worth mentioning at all. Yet this sudden death urgency governs much of the demand for convincing data to support decisions, preferably by yesterday. And, of course, the sensible advice that if you do not know what the effect of an action or of a possible pollutant is going to be, you should not do it or use it, is unacceptable in our economic or political structure. We have to keep our hubristic, anthropocentric system going: "When it becomes a choice between ecology and people, people must go." A recent circular, soliciting subscriptions for a new magazine about the ocean, put this very clearly: "Our aim is to contribute to a wider public understanding of the oceans and to a greater appreciation of how they can serve us, today and in the future." Whoever wrote this bit of advertising copy has forgotton that even King Canute was unable to order the ocean to do his bidding. Nevertheless, it is a growing concern that if ecology goes, so will people, and hence our need for understanding the consequences of our acts and activities.

When we ask what part of nature our actions affect, without really understanding the entire ecosystem, we find ourselves among those blind men who touched various parts of the elephant without comprehending the nature of the whole animal. The inconclusive result of the discussion at Helgoland was inevitable because of the effort to represent various viewpoints, especially after the reservations expressed about the utility of complicated, all-encompassing models, both by myself (Hedgpeth, 1977b) and members of the panel discussion of the question "Can we manage the North Sea?" Models may be here to stay, but they should not be articles of faith. Modelers ought to get together and strive for a unified theory of modeling (Conway, 1977), and there should be more awareness of the difficulties involved: "It should be understood that modeling is an art for extremely qualified experts and that sophisticated numerical models are not a necessary part of every water quality plan. Models should be used only where they are really needed, and then only by persons with extensive familiarity with the model and its limitations" (Fischer, 1977).

This quotation refers to physical or hydrographic models rather than to those of natural systems, where the inferences and often the data are more subjective or involve increments of time and dimension not amenable to the requirements of the engineer. Some of these difficulties in modeling natural systems have been pointed out with special reference to managers and politicians: "Ecologists might best contribute to resource management by stressing the ambiguities in our knowledge about natural communities, and induce managers and politicians to make decisions that openly acknowledge that they are sometimes based on tentative information" (Hedgpeth and Obrebski, 1976). The same advice has been suggested for lawyers who should realize that "passing laws, adopting regulations, and even winning court cases do not necessarily resolve all the problems that may arise in understanding and coping with the consequences of action that may affect the natural environment" (Heikoff, 1977: p. 280). Lawyers should also be advised that models may be hypothetical or illustrated by trial runs of possible or even impossible conditions that cannot be used as factual evidence.

It is natural that each of us should consider our own limited approach to ecosystem research the best one, or at least the approach most useful in understanding the whole, because we are most familiar with it. This can produce a somewhat parochial approach to matters, like our east coast *Spartina* syndrome. This notion, actually a sort of model carried to its ultimate emphasis, is that the salt marshes are the key to productivity of the estuarine system because of the contribution of their detritus, and it follows that the best thing to do for an estuary system is to promote the growth of *Spartina*. In some California estuaries, however, the marsh is often separated from the deeper waters of the bay by extensive mud flats which are a significant component of the productivity and organic cycles in the estuary (Nichols, 1977). Similar conditions prevail in the

European Waddensee, where "detritus imported from salt marshes . . . is relatively unimportant and the secondary productivity from the tidal flats is more significant" (Wolff, 1977). Thus, recommendations that California estuaries need more *Spartina* marshes may actually result in interference with a natural system by accelerating sedimentation and accretion and consequent reduction of the mud flats.

Another danger is already apparent. In Oregon, where there is no native estuarine species of *Spartina* (there is a species associated with alkaline lakes), *Spartina patens* has become established in one locality, and appears to be rapidly crowding out the native high salt marsh vegetation. Spread of this plant into other coastal marshlands of the Pacific Coast may bring about drastic and unfortunate changes in the ecosystem.

Almost as dangerous as misplaced emphasis on individual species is misplaced faith in some magic number or symbol. Back in the innocent days of ecology, it was pH. There is the possibly apocryphal story of the professor on the dock at Woods Hole advising the field party embarking for a day of data gathering to leave all their gear behind except the pH kit. In our day, the magic number has been the diversity index. From the various ideas about the association of diversity with stability or "age" which have not withstood the judgment of time (Goodman, 1975), some sanitary engineers concluded, with innocent subjectivity, that diversity was an indication of "health": "In the field of ecology, it is generally accepted that an adverse environment will result in a decrease of the number of species, although the total number of organisms of a given species may increase because of reduced competition. Thus, an examination of the diversity of organisms may provide a measure as to the general health of the environment. In order to avoid subjective appraisals or measures, it is preferred to have a quantitative, mathematically defined concept of diversity" (Pearson *et al.,* 1967). Unfortunately, there was inadequate attention to the systematics of the organisms, and the totals of species identified varied from year to year because of varying standards of identification and identifiers, so that indexes developed according to this concept could not be compared. The diversity index approach is useful in determining the internal consistency of a sampling program, but objective application of diversity indexes for any purpose requires rigorous taxonomics and sampling control, as exemplified in such studies as those carried out in Tomales Bay by R. G. Johnson (1970; 1971). It is misleading when compiled from inadequately treated material and may be as uninformative as a series of random numbers, yet such diversity indices are acceptable and sometimes required in many pollution studies.

In Helgoland, we did try to discuss the essential needs for research in the marine ecosystem, but we were derailed for some time by a discussion of the utility of *Mytilus edulis* as an index organism by an indomitable person from Poland, a subject already considered at some length in a large book (Bayne, 1976). One species alone cannot tell us much about the ecosystem as such; when the canary dies in the mine, we know we should get out, but not necessarily why there is no air. *Mytilus edulis* is nevertheless a more or less accepted index species for certain substances, and such a popular species for pollution monitoring (Goldberg, 1976) that we now have a world-wide "mussel watch" program.

The other extreme is that we need to know, and to assemble as much data as possible from all available sources, about as many species as possible, and the best way to do this is to consign it all to a computer. A plan for some sort of master index of all species, all variables, all knowledge, is proposed by the EPA (for an applied example of the data bank approach, see Henderson *et al.*, 1976) as a sort of modern day fulfillment of Francis Bacon's ideal of assembling all knowledge and then attempting to understand the nature of the world from it. Bacon would have done well in this age of computers, but Aristotle would have learned more. It is useful to have all this information and to be able to arrange it in all possible sorts of ways, but we must not let it become an end in itself nor trust what the computer says, because the questions it answers are those we have asked of it. (Or one may not hhave to ask any questions at all: one supplier of black boxes that sense all variables claims that his "data logger . . . puts the entire environment within the reach of the computer." The ultimate result of this could be herds of black boxes wired to computers perpetually pouring out numbers.) And, whatever the question, the nature and reliability of the data are as critical as their quantity.

Then there is the approach that field studies or *in situ* observations will be the answer, and that in any event we need base line studies (which are of course field studies) to tell us what to expect of an ecosystem under stress. This approach, which involves asking questions before we know which ones to ask, can easily degenerate into the tedium of monitoring, i.e., repeated recording of the same information which may or may not be significant. Detailed monitoring, especially the identifying, counting, and measuring of innumerable species can be more time-consuming and expensive than the results justify, and is not very inspiring intellectually. One of the active practitioners of this type of before-the-event modeling recommends — in view of the limitations of base line studies because of our lack of knowledge of factors that govern recruitment, success, and mortality of littoral species in particular — that we use semi-quantitative methods and spend as little time as possible on such studies (Crapp, 1971). The shortcomings of sampling the bottom of the sea, especially in the days before diving spheres and frogmen, were fully realized by the founding father of quantitative sampling, C. G. J. Petersen, who not only reproduced the amusing drawing by Edward Forbes of the shortcomings of the dredge, but also made famous that comparison by his colleague, H. G. Jungersen: "A dredging ship may be compared with an air-ship towing a dredge over Copenhagen, catching a policeman in one street and a perambulator in another; and from these it draws conclusions as to the whole population of the town" (Petersen, 1914: p. 21).

Some paleoecologists have no qualms about the incomplete nature of their data. It has been suggested that a few dead shells may be better than the complexity of a living system: "Indeed, the assemblages of dead invertebrates appear to be more useful for environmental interpretations than the actual living assemblages, even when available" (Warme *et al.,* 1976). The inference from this would seem to be that we can take our sample, let all the soft stuff die, and then make deductions about the state of the community in the present as well as the past. This suggests that we might infer what killed the elephant from a handful (or perhaps bucketful) of metatarsals and phalanges. "This idea can certainly not be applied to the metastasizing field of environmental impact ecology," although it would, of course, "save us a lot of grubby sampling of worms and other creepy crawlies" (Hedgpeth, 1977b). The idea belongs in the same category as treating the fossil record as a sort of experimental diary of perturbations (Rosenzweig, 1977), which Mark and Flessa (1977) criticize from the viewpoint of the fossil record as "a risky undertaking."

Although concerned with the problems of studying freshwater ecosystems, the critical discussion by Hellawell (1977) is a more than adequate antidote for the reductionist approaches suggested by paleoecologists, modellers, and seekers of the mystic and magic number. This paper should be consulted by all of us concerned with ecosystem research:

> The ecosystem may conveniently be regarded as being built up from a series of sub-sets comprising individuals, species, biocoenoses, populations and communities, with each component contributing its properties to determine the character of the larger sets [Figure 1]. Surveillance may be undertaken at all organizational and trophic levels within an ecosystem, from the individual to communities, and each will contribute towards our understanding of the structure and function of the system. For example, the identities of species present can provide considerable information if their autecology and synecology are known. The proposition that many environmental insights would be derivable from consideration of a species list if tolerances, preferences and relationships of species were better known is attractive and has led to the concept of "indicator" species. Criticism of this concept has probably arisen from disappointment with the, as yet unrealized, premature aspirations of its proponents. In reality, few species are understood well enough to permit their use as ecological "litmuspaper" and the complexities of biological systems probably preclude such a simple approach. However, there appears to be no reason why, ultimately, all species should not be indicators, given sufficient knowledge of their ecology.
>
> The individual as a unit, ignoring its identity, seems to be one of the least useful components for consideration, although it possesses physiological attributes which might be of interest. Groups of individuals, whether mixed or single species populations, are more useful and can effectively be used to detect spatial or temporal change. An interesting example of the use of populations without detailed identification is the use of algal cell counts or chlorophyll determinations to estimate algal biomass and hence potable water quality.

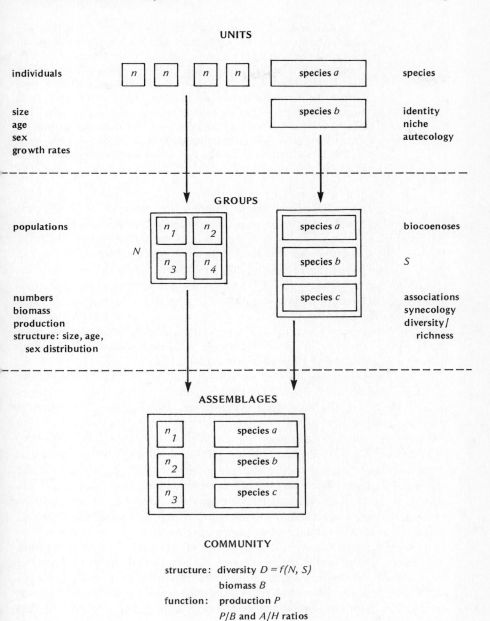

Figure 1. A conceptual framework of community organization and the structural or functional measures appropriate to each level (Hellawell, 1977).

Biocoenoses or groups of species occurring together are qualitative attributes of ecosystems which are probably more informative than indicator species, especially when the normal biocoenosis-habitat relationship is known. Assemblages of populations and biocoenoses form communities and provide quantitative measures of biocoenotic attributes. Studies at the community level ought to include all populations of organisms present within the area of the habitat but, in general usage, consideration is often restricted to particular taxonomic groups since resources or expertise are rarely sufficient to tackle the whole community (Hellawell, 1977: pp. 34-36).

This citation of a freshwater example is not intended to imply that little of value was said at Helgoland. On the contrary: the theme of the symposium was ecosystem research and there were many valuable contributions to this general problem, beginning with the opening papers of the proceedings (published as Volume 30 of Helgoländer wissenschaftliche Meeresuntersuchungen, in 735 pages!), notably those by Fishelson (1977) on stability and instability of marine ecosystems and by Oviatt *et al.* (1977) on studies of experimental marine ecosystems. A significant contribution to the modelling problem is Gary's (1977) paper on stability of benthic ecosystems, concerning once again the moot problem of succession in marine communities. The concept of neighborhood stability seems more realistic than that of global stability or succession-climax, but would require models "an order of magnitude more complex."

The Helgoland meeting was immediately followed by the 11th European Symposium on Marine Biology at Galway; the published proceedings of this symposium, *Biology of Benthic Organisms* (Pergamon, 1977) occupy 630 pages, and there are many contributions of direct significance to our problem. Earlier in this same year another symposium volume, *Ecology of Marine Benthos* (University of South Carolina Press, 1977) was published, although the conference at which the papers were presented was held in May of 1975. This volume, of 465 pages, has an index which may explain in part the delay in publication. It will take some time to assimilate and synthesize these three massive contributions which, if nothing else, testify to the extent of interest and research in problems all directly related to the analysis of marine ecosystems.

Some investigators, even though not blind, can walk right by an elephant and not see it at all and consequently may not even believe in its existence. For them, there is no question and no problem. It is possible to conclude like some blithe spirit that the absence of data means there is nothing to correlate, or that such data as there may be indicate no effect of A on B. Some data of this kind may sound imposing and authoritative, based on ten man-days of study which may mean that a group of twenty students spent half a day gathering the data. Whatever the nature of the information, it is certainly turning away from our troublesome elephant to conclude that a table showing nothing can be used to substantiate a claim that "no correlation" is discernible (Figure 2).

There were no correlations between the major species groups (Vermes, Crustacea, Echinodermata, Mollusca) in terms of biomass and total organics, silt, and water depth (Table 22). All species groups were found in sediments with high and low total organic content. This was in contrast to suggestions elsewhere that Crustacea are the most sensitive group to petroleum.

TABLE 22.

Relationship Between Biomass of Major Phyla and Total Hydrocarbons, Sediments (in terms of silt) and Depth

Phyla	Total Organics*	Silt	Depth
Vermes	−	−	−
	−		−
Crustacea	−	−	
	−		−
Echinodermata	−	−	
	−		−
Mollusca	−	−	
	−		−

*As determined by carbon tetrachloride analysis and infra-red analysis.

Figure 2. Q. E. D.: Where there are no data, there are no correlations (Straughan, 1976).

Nature is admittedly too complex for most of us, and some of us think we can do better in assessing potential effects of some environmental variables and pollutant substances by laboratory tests, especially on a suite of standardized test animals. There has been some confusion about exactly what is determined by testing tolerances with a small menagerie of almost invulnerable animals adapted to laboratory conditions and, in any event, not found in the sea. This use of standardized test animals has not been completely understood by the critics or, perhaps, adequately explained by the principal advocate of the method, as indicated by the running comments and discussions between European investigators and the chief keeper of "Tarzwell's Zoo" at a symposium on oil pollution (Hepple, 1971).

Of course, much of our knowledge about the reactions of organisms to various environmental variables has been derived from the standard procedures of physiology. Usually these involve testing a single factor while keeping the other environmental variables constant, and often it has been found that tolerances in nature may be different from those in the laboratory, primarily because of the interaction of several variables. It is not possible, for example, to discuss the effects of temperature in marine animals without also considering at least salinity and oxygen, as demonstrated by Kinne's masterful review of the subject (Kinne, 1970). Various ways of considering and representing combined effects are discussed by Alderdice (1972). Obviously, this type of treatment requires access to a computer, and interpretation of the curious graphs produced suggests again the need for that most subtle and indispensable of computers, the old-fashioned naturalist.

With some animals, especially perhaps well-known bivalves, it is possible to test field conditions in experimental apparatus (Bayne *et al.,* 1977). Insofar as polluted water is concerned, environmental or field conditions may be simulated in medium-sized experimental tanks and the potential effect of polluted water may be determined, although the exact effect of a particular component of the pollution may not be clearly identified (McIntyre, 1977). Here again, however, an essential aspect of nature has to be passed over lightly, i.e., the natural spacing and interactions of the organisms extracted from their environment and placed in the experimental containers. Even under experimental conditions in the environment, the results are sometimes difficult to interpret or may appear to lead us in the wrong direction (Arntz, 1977; Dayton, 1973).

The lesson of the blind man and the elephant is that the whole is greater than its parts and that a complex, most improbable animal like the elephant cannot be visualized as a summary of its parts. Perhaps the analogy is unfair; even with 20-20 vision, one cannot see all of the animal, especially what is going on inside. In this respect, our dilemma is that of the prisoners in the cave who can see only the shadows on the wall projected from the real world outside. But we, like Aristotle, cannot live with Plato's limitation, and we at least can look out of the cave and attempt to perceive the whole. "We have better means of information, however, concerning the things that perish, that is to say, plants and animals, because we live among them . . . . Let us now endeavor to describe the causes of all these things, particular as well as common; and, according to the principles laid down, we will begin with first things first (Aristotle, Parts of Animals, I.v.)."

Epilogue

Of course I did not think of quoting Aristotle at the necessarily brief presentation of some of these ideas in that honeymoon resort in the Poconos, but I did warn the audience that any resemblance between what I said and what I would write would be to some extent a coincidence.

It is difficult not to be somewhat negative when discussing the need to know everything in order to manage the environment in which we live (even or especially, to our own benefit), and when asked how would I go about the necessary studies if I were God, I could not resist the retort that I was being given six days for the job. When one looks at some of our fellow creatures, especially the elephant, one does wonder whether God (or Nature) is always practical. In any event I do not have a direct personal line of communication with Higher Authority on these matters, and the best I could recommend was that we do as much as possible as often as possible within our means and limitations. We should develop a simplified regime of measuring and sampling that would permit us to span at least a significant period of time with respect to the natural systems involved. This, of course, means that we must have more than six days, and it is we who must give ourselves that time. We hope for information that will enable us to make reasonably intelligent guesses about how to manage and protect our brief tenure on "this dark terrestrial ball." At best we will always have to accept uncertainty and inadequacy in both knowledge and environmental management, and to rely on subjective judgment, which in this context we prefer to think of as the experience and wisdom of the "old fashioned naturalist." The problem is cogently put in a retort to one of the innumerable critics whose remarks rise to the surface in the appendix to the draft of an environmental impact report: "The day that we have a 'thorough understanding of the population and community dynamics of . . . plankton . . . nekton and benthos,' as the reviewer suggests, is the day that all the speculations associated with environmental impact assessment will cease, and all marine ecologists can retire."

Retire from preparing impact assessments, indeed, but not from contemplation of the living world, preferably near some sunlit, shallow lagoon where they can see the bottom through the clear water and observe what is going on.

References

1. Alderdice, D. F. 1972. Response of marine poikilotherms to environmental factors acting in concert, pp. 1659-1722. *In* Otto Kinne (ed.), Factor Combinations in Marine Ecology, 1(3).

2. Arntz, W. E. 1977. Results and problems of an "unsuccessful" benthos cage predation experiment, pp. 31-44. *In* B. F. Keegan, P. O. Ceidigh and P. J. S. Boaden (eds.), Biology of Benthic Organisms. 11th European Symposium on Marine Biology. Pergamon Press.

3. Bayne, L. (ed.) 1976. Marine Mussels, their Ecology and Physiology. Cambridge University Press, 506 pp.

4. Bayne, B. L., J. Widdows and R. I. E. Newell. 1977. Physiological measurements on estuarine bivalve molluscs in the field, pp. 57-68. *In* B. F. Keegan, P. Ó Céidigh and P. J. S. Boaden (eds.), Biology of Benthic Organisms, 11th European Symposium on Marine Biology. Pergamon Press.

5. Connell, J. H. 1974. Field experiments in marine ecology, pp. 21-54. *In* R. N. Mariscal (ed.), Experimental Marine Biology. Academic Press.

6. Conway, G. R. 1977. Mathematical models in applied ecology. Nature 269: 291-297.

7. Crapp, G. B. 1971. Monitoring the rocky shore, pp. 102-113. *In* E. B. Cowell (ed.), The Ecological Effects of Oil Pollution on Littoral Communities. Institute of Petroleum, London.

8. Dayton, P. K. 1972. Toward an understanding of community resilience and the potential effects of enrichments to the benthos at McMurdo Sound, Antarctica, pp. 81-96. *In* B. Parker (ed. and inadvertent publisher), Proceedings of the Colloquium on Conservation Problems in Antarctica.

9. _____. 1973. Two cases of resource partitioning in an intertidal community. Making the right prediction for the wrong reasons. Amer. Nat. 107 (957):662-670.

10. Fischer, H. B. 1977. The effect of estuarine circulation on pollution dispersal, pp. 477-485. *In* Estuarine Pollution Control and Assessment. Proceedings of a conference, Vol. 2. Environmental Protection Agency, Washington, D.C.

11. Fishelson, L. 1977. Stability and instability of marine ecosystems, illustrated by examples from the Red Sea. Helgolander wiss. Meeresunters. 30:18-29.

12. Goldberg, E. D. (ed.) 1973. North Sea Science. NATO North Sea Science Conference, Aviemore, Scotland, 15-20 November 1971. MIT Press, Cambridge, Mass. 500 pp.

13. Goldberg, E. D. 1976. Strategies for marine pollution monitoring. John Wiley & Sons, New York.

14. Goodman, D. 1975. The theory of diversity-stability relationships in ecology. Quar. Rev. Biol. 50:237-266.

15. Gray, J. S. 1977. The stability of benthic ecosystems. Helgolander wiss. Meeresunters. 30:427-444.

16. Hedgpeth, J. W. 1957. Concepts of Marine Ecology, pp. 29-52. *In* Treatise on Marine Ecology and Paleoecology, Memoir 67, Geol. Soc. America, Vol. 1.

17. _____ . 1973. The impact of impact studies. Helgolander wiss. Meeresunters. 24:436-445.

18. _____ . 1977a. Seven ways to obliteration: factors of estuarine degradation, pp. 723-737. *In* Estuarine Pollution Control and Assessment. Proceedings of a conference, Vol. 2. Environmental Protection Agency, Washington, D. C.

19. _____ . 1977b. Review: Structure and classification of paleocommunities. Paleobiology 3(1):110-114.

20. _____ . 1977c. Models and muddles. Some philosophical observations. Helgolander wiss. Meeresunters. 30:92-104.

21. _____ . 1977d. Comments on an attempted discussion about the needs for marine ecosystem research. *Idem,* pp. 705-706.

22. Hedgpeth, J. W., and S. Obrebski. 1976. Ecosystem models and resource management. Bulletin The Coastal Society 1(2):5-10.

23. Heikoff, J. 1977. Coastal Resources Management. Ann Arbor Scientific Publications.

24. Hellawell, J. M. 1977. Change in natural and managed ecosystems; detection, measurement and assessment. Proc. Roy. Soc. London (B), 197:31-57.

25. Henderson, R. S., S. V. Smith and E. C. Evans III. 1976. Flow-through microcosms for simulation of marine ecosystems: development and intercomparison of open coast and bay facilities. U.S. Navy Undersea Center, San Diego. Report no. TP 519, 80 pp.

26. Hepple, P. (ed.) 1971. Water Pollution by Oil. The Institute of Petroleum, London (Elsevier, Amsterdam). 393 pp.

27. Holme, N. A., and A. D. McIntire (eds.). 1971. Methods for the Study of Marine Benthos. IBP Handbook No. 16. Blackwell Scientific Publications, Oxford & Edinburgh: 334 pp.

28. Johnson, P. L. (ed.) 1977. An ecosystem paradigm for ecology. Oak Ridge Associated Universities, 20 pp., April 1977.

29. Johnson, R. G. 1970. Variations in diversity within benthic marine communities. Amer. Nat. 104(937):285-300.

30. _____ . 1971. Animal-sediment relations in shallow water benthic communities. Marine Geol. 11:93-104.

31. Kinne, O. 1970. Chapter 3. Temperature, 3.3, Animals, 3.31, Invertebrates. *In* Marine Ecology, 1(1):407-514.

32. McIntyre, A. D. 1977. Effects of pollution on inshore benthos, pp. 301-318. *In* B. C. Coull (ed.), Ecology of Marine Benthos. University of South Carolina Press.

33. Mark, G. A., and K. W. Flessa. 1977. The fossil record is not an experimental diary. Paleobiology 3(3):324.

34. Nichols, F. H. 1977. Infaunal biomass and production on a mudflat, San Francisco Bay, California, pp. 339-357. *In* B. C. Coull (ed.), Ecology of Marine Benthos. University of South Carolina Press.

35. Oviatt, C. A., K. T. Perez, and S. W. Nixon. 1977. Multivariate analysis of experimental marine ecosystems. Helgolander wiss. Meeresunters. 30:30-46.

36. Pearson, E. A., P. N. Storrs, and R. E. Selleck. 1967. Some physical parameters and their significance in marine waste disposal, pp. 297-315. *In* T. A. Olson and F. J. Burgess (eds.), Pollution and Marine Ecology. Wiley, Interscience, New York.

37. Petersen, C. G. J. 1914. Valuation of the Sea II. The animal communities of the sea-bottom and their importance for marine zoogeography. Report Danish Biological Station, 21, 1913, 44 pp.

38. Rosenzweig, M. L. 1977. Does the fossil record provide for natural experiments? On interpreting the results of perturbation experiments performed by nature. Paleobiology 3(3):322-324.

39. Straughan, D. 1976. Sublethal effects of natural chronic exposure to petroleum in the marine environment. Final report submitted to The American Petroleum Institute, Environmental Affairs Department. API Publication no. 4280, 119 pp. (mimeo).

40. Warme, J. E., A. A. Ekdale, S. F. Ekdale, and C. H. Peterson. 1976. Raw material of the fossil record, pp. 143-169. *In* R. W. Scott and R. R. West (eds.), Structure and Classification of Paleocommunities. Dowden, Hutchinson, & Ross, Stroudsburg, Penna.

41. Wolff, W. J. 1977. A benthic food budget for the Grevelingen estuary, The Netherlands, and a consideration of the mechanisms causing high benthic secondary production in estuaries, pp. 267-280. *In* B. C. Coull (ed.), Ecology of Marine Benthos. University of South Carolina Press.

AN ENVIRONMENTAL LAWYER'S UNCERTAIN QUEST FOR LEGAL AND SCIENTIFIC CERTAINTY

Kenneth S. Kamlet

Counsel for National Wildlife Federation
1412 Sixteenth Street, N.W.
Washington, D.C.

Abstract: "Risk" is a mixture of probability and severity. What is an acceptable risk to you may be unacceptable to me, and a risk resulting from the actions of others is generally less acceptable than one of our own or of nature's making. Bureaucrats and legislators constantly make decisions which place the environment and human health at risk. Scientists and lawyers both have key roles to play in such decisions, despite differing concepts of causality and proof. Efforts to enhance the rationality of environmental decisionmaking should bear in mind the following principles: 1) unacceptable environmental risks cannot be avoided without placing limits on technological development and resource exploitation; 2) environmental risks cannot be properly assessed solely on the basis of cost-benefit analysis, because some costs are *per se* unacceptable, many costs cannot be adequately quantified, and because our ability to alter the environment surpasses our ability to predict the consequences of such alteration; 3) the burden of showing the absence of unacceptable risk should rest on those wishing to go forward with activities which may stress the environment, but in the case of existing activities, only after probable cause to expect such risk has been established; and 4) administrative standards and criteria represent an important, albeit imperfect, means of regulating existing risk-producing activities.

Introduction

Estuarine management, like man's efforts to manage the rest of his environment, presents a number of difficult — some would say, insoluble — problems. Everything man does affects his environment. The effects may be large or small, beneficial or adverse, reversible or irreversible, conscious or unconscious. Although this has been so since the advent of man, haphazard decisionmaking has become increasingly dangerous.

Man's capacity to alter the environment in large, adverse, and irreversible fashion has increased exponentially as a result of explosions in population growth and technological development. Irreplaceable wetlands are being drained for agriculture, filled in for housing, and paved over for highways. Inland and coastal waterways have been co-opted as conduits for human sewage and as substitutes for waste treatment. The landscape is dotted with factories which provide families with livelihoods and "better living through chemistry," but foul the air and water with noxious emissions, and all too often sow the seeds of future disease and premature death.

As environmental decisionmaking becomes ever more serious in its implications, it becomes increasingly vital to solve the fundamental dilemma of our times: How is "society" to decide how much in present benefits to trade for the avoidance of future risks, particularly where the benefits are palpable and the risks uncertain? What is the role of scientists and lawyers in this decisionmaking process?

That is the subject of this paper.

Estuaries at the Crossroads

Man's attitude toward estuaries illustrates our basic ecological predicament.

On the one hand, estuaries in their undegraded state represent a resource of unparalleled recreational, commercial, and ecological value. (Kalter, 1975; Bollman, 1975; Clark, 1975; Tihansky and Meade, 1975). For example, "approximately 65 percent of all commercial fish species and practically all of the sports fish species are dependent upon the estuarine zone for one or more phases of their life development" (Bollman, 1975).

On the other hand, as observed by Odum (1970), "the same mechanisms that make estuaries excellent nutrient traps and enhance their value to life also make them pollution traps" (Hedgpeth, 1975). Disproportionate numbers of the world's people cluster their habitations, their developments, and their pollution in and around estuaries. Cronin (1975) has tabulated a dozen "principal general uses of estuaries," including commercial shipping, shoreline development, mining, electricity generation, and waste placement. Many of these pose the risk of serious adverse environmental consequences. Hedgpeth (1975) places the major threats to estuaries in seven categories: ecological ineptitude, filling and dredging, diversion of fresh water, calefaction (thermal pollution), organic pollution (sewage), chemical pollution, and oil pollution.

Estuarine decisionmaking has tended to proceed in helter-skelter, generally destructive, fashion. Daily, the incursions continue: a power plant here, a sewage outfall there. To the extent consequences are considered at all, they are rationalized in terms of the public good and the gross national product.

Hedgpeth (1975) has characterized traditional cost-benefit balancing as "inept": ". . .An economist who suggests that we set a money value to the fish or amenity that may be destroyed by a power plant, and submit the cost-benefit ratio to a public vote, is proposing an evil and senseless procedure. This notion that we can assign money values to such diverse matters as clean water, fisheries, pleasing scenery, kilowatts, and parking lots is a recent contribution of man's hubris, especially when we make a decision on the basis of this arithmetic of apples and oranges that may extirpate other species from the scene and set irreversible ecological decay in motion; this notion is reprehensible. The idea of assigning a dollar and cents value to life — any life — can lead to the end of life on earth as it now does to the exhaustion of non-renewable resources, a mining out of life as if it were some raw material. This approach to the problem of environmental insult assumes that the processes of nature are simple and can be safely tampered with in terms of our idiotic anthropocentrism. . . ."

Yet this "inept" approach is the mainstay of this country's most far-reaching and important environmental law, the National Environmental Policy Act (NEPA). As elucidated by the U. S. Court of Appeals for the District of Columbia in the 1971 case of *Calvert Cliffs' Coordinating Committee v. Atomic Energy Commission* (a case involving a proposed power plant on the banks of an estuary):

> NEPA mandates a case-by-case balancing judgment on the part of federal agencies. . . . The particular economic and technical benefits of planned action must be assessed and then weighed against the environmental costs; alternatives must be considered which would affect the balance of values. . . . In some cases, the benefits will be great enough to justify a certain quantum of environmental costs; in other cases, they will not be so great and the proposed action may have to be abandoned or significantly altered. . . . The point of the individualized balancing analysis is to ensure . . . that the optimally beneficial action is finally taken.

For an in-depth analysis of the promises and failings of NEPA, see Anderson (1973).

Is NEPA then the most we are capable of? Are our estuaries and our global ecosystem doomed as a consequence of our "idiotic anthropocentrism"?

Assessing Risks in Environmental Management

It is axiomatic that no human activity is totally free of risks and that we constantly make decisions which expose us to risks which, however, we are quite prepared to accept. For example, we smoke cigarettes, drive automobiles, live in dwellings built on flood plains, play golf in thunderstorms, and do countless other things which expose us to readily calculable risks of death and serious injury. And despite the near certainty of death by cancer of workers in several occupations (Epstein, 1977), the workers voluntarily stay with their jobs.

It is not surprising, then, in light of this, that there has evolved a large and growing school of thought which regards it as possible and appropriate to specify a level of risk from industrial activity, for example, which can be considered socially acceptable and therefore unworthy of governmental regulatory attention. To cite an instance, Kletz (1977) concludes: "If the average risk to those exposed [to an industrial hazard] is less than one in 10 million per person per year, it should be accepted in the short term, and resources should not be allocated to its reduction." He bases this conclusion quite logically on the fact that people seem to accept risks from man-made events (except road transport) of about one in 10 million per person per year (e.g., floods in the United States, earthquakes in California, tornadoes in the mid-western states, storms in the United States., lightning in the United Kingdom, flooding of dikes in Holland, and bites of venomous creatures in the United Kingdom).

Implicit in this concept is its converse: that there are also activities that are so dangerous in the risks they present that they must be regarded as unacceptable *per se*. Since such an approach would minimize the need to balance incommensurable costs and benefits in evaluating inherently risky proposals to disrupt the environment, the concepts of "acceptable" and "unacceptable" risks warrant careful attention.

Let us first examine the notion of certain risks as being inherently "acceptable."

There are many obvious problems with this approach. For example, as argued by McGinty and Atherley (1977), "it is too much to expect that the ever-changing pattern of risks created by an innovatory industry can be measured with any real accuracy." It is simply unrealistic to assume that we are able to consider (much less quantify) all of the relevant risks of an activity. We may have a good idea of the likelihood of a worker's being mutilated by factory machinery, but absolutely no appreciation for the risk to the same worker of occupational disease twenty years after being exposed to the causative agent. If the best minds of our society — our archetypal "societal decisionmakers" — are unable to pin down the nature and magnitude of some of the most serious risks confronting the industrial worker, how can the worker himself be assumed to understand these risks and to have "knowingly" accepted them? Is society to make its conscious decisions on the basis of unknown risks unknowingly accepted by one or more of its members?

Indeed, even if the risks were known and there were those who consciously accepted them, must such risks be regarded as socially acceptable? McGinty and Atherley (1977) make the valid points that (1) there is no such thing as a single quantitative level of risk that is universally acceptable, since individual preferences vary considerable and must be respected in a democratic society, and (2) an evil is not justified by the mere existence of a greater evil. They conclude that "there is no quantitative, scientific methodology that will substitute for political acumen in reaching decisions about the allocation of resources for the regulation of risks." While it can be agreed that fundamental lifestyle choices should be made through the political process (i.e., by means of legislative enactments adopted by the legislative representatives of the public to be affected), to say that it is up to law-makers and politicians to make hard decisions does nothing to elucidate or improve the decisionmaking process. Other critics of the "acceptable risk" approach reach similarly unhelpful conclusions. Dunster (1977), for example, rejects the notion that any "non-trival detriment . . . is acceptable *per se*." Rather, according to this view, "to become acceptable, a non-trivial detriment needs to be outweighed by individual or social benefits." This means "society is undertaking (often unwittingly) cost benefit analysis in which costs include the probability of death and . . . effects on health" (Dunster, 1977).[1] This does not unduly disturb Dunster, who concludes that "there is 'virtue in compromise' " and that " 'Safety First' is a good slogan but a poor policy."

Unfortunately, this brings us right back to the flaws in cost-benefit balancing so eloquently bemoaned by Hedgpeth (1975).

Still further problems with the "acceptable risk" approach become apparent when this approach is applied in the context of environmental decision-making. How does one determine the "acceptability" of a risk, when the threatened risks must be borne by objects and organisms which lack a vote in determining what is acceptable? (Although such entities may play important roles in human ecosystems, so that activities which threaten them also indirectly threaten man, it can seldom be assumed that such interrelationships will be recognized and considered by human "risk-assessors"). Destruction of a wetland to make way for a housing development is unlikely to cause anyone illness or death. It may cost a bird-watcher the sight of some favorite birds or a fisherman some indeterminate drop in the size of his catch. But this activity poses no real "risk" to man in the same sense as industrial accidents or the discharge of toxic chemicals.

Moreover, the most important adverse consequences of wetland destruction (as of many other environmentally disruptive activities) are likely to be cumulative (i.e., the result of reducing the number of available wetland acres to a level below that necessary to support fish and wildlife) and delayed in their manifestation (i.e., it may take several breeding seasons before a decline in harvestable fish and shellfish species becomes apparent). In the context of pollution, if the DuPont Company is permitted to ocean-dump because overriding adverse consequences are not readily demonstrable, then so must Cyanamid, Allied Chemical, and NL Industries be permitted to ocean-dump — despite the fact that the consequences of the dumping activities of these companies in the aggregate may be decidedly adverse and unacceptable. A risk which is acceptable to an individual under a given set of circumstances should not necessarily be acceptable to society when cumulated over many individuals and many circumstances.

In short, the acceptable risk approach may have some utility in evaluating direct hazards to human life in an industrial or residential setting, where the hazards are well known, readily predictable, and easily comprehended. In the context of environmental decisionmaking, however, where sublethal and delayed effects, complex interactions, and cumulative and ecological impacts are the rule, the acceptable risk approach has little, if any, value.

What about the other side of the coin — the "unacceptable risk" approach?

At first blush, it would seem that the identification of risks which are *per se* unacceptable would suffer from at least the same limitations as the quest for acceptable risks. Incomplete (and often unobtainable) information and inadequate appreciation of risks will hamper individual evaluations of risks as unacceptable; so will lack of knowledge regarding cumulative and long-term impacts and the inability of valuable objects and lower organisms to articulate what is unacceptable to them. Furthermore, whereas it is possible to measure the acceptability of an activity to a person by whether or not he engages in the activity (if he engages in it, it is presumptively acceptable), one may not permissibly conclude from a person's abstinence from an activity that he abstained because the risk was too great. For example, Eskimos refrain from kissing and Mexicans from testing atomic weapons for reasons other than the perceived riskiness of the respective activities (perhaps more to the point, if A goes to work in a uranium mine, he can be assumed to accept the risk of radiation injury; however, the fact that B chose to work as a lawyer for the National Wildlife Federation implies nothing whatever about B's assessment of the risk of working in a uranium mine).

If risks defined as *per se* unacceptable are to play a role in environmental decisionmaking, therefore, it is clear that a mechanism other than the observed behavior of individuals must be used as the basis for selecting the activities regarded as displaying risks of this kind. Given the unreliability of individual preferences (as discussed above), this does not really leave us any worse off than we were in seeking to define acceptable risks (which, however, is not very well off).

The Case for **Per Se** *Unacceptability*

The American legal system is struggling at the present time to discard rules of evidence and proof that had their origins in 19th century attitudes about resource exploitation and property rights, which seem ill-suited to the resolution of present-day problems. Thus 19th century property rules often encouraged industrial development under a prevailing view of resource exploitation and technology growth as desirable objectives. "The risk of future injury was often found to be outweighed by the benefits of present exploitation because some new technology might eliminate the problem," and thereby minimize the risk (Gelpe and Tarlock, 1974; *see also* Anonymous, 1972). In a frontier wide-open-spaces setting, moreover, few risks seemed irreversible. If land was mismanaged or a stream polluted, there was always more land to occupy and more streams to despoil.

An early example of judicial encouragement of environmental degradation based upon the expectation that technology would come to the rescue before serious harm could occur was the English case of *Attorney General v. Corporation of Kingston* (1865), in which the court refused to enjoin the discharge of large quantities of sewage into the River Thames by the English township of Kingston. The court held that plaintiffs had to "establish the existence of an actual immediate nuisance," and not "a case of injury a hundred years hence, when chemical contrivances might have been discovered for preventing the evil" (Cited in Katz, 1975).

Today, although the courts (and scientists themselves) are less inclined to regard science as infallible, and new technology or new frontiers as universal rectifiers of human mistakes, they do continue generally to require those seeking to halt environmentally deleterious activities to "prove" their case. This amounts to a requirement that the plaintiff demonstrate that the risks presented by the activity outweigh the activity's benefits to society. While it is only fair in criminal cases and in many civil contexts that the accused be presumed innocent until proven guilty, I submit that such a presumption of innocence is inappropriate and, indeed, unconscionable in the context of activities which present serious risks of harm to man and the environment. In such cases, the notion of *per se* unacceptability plays a legitimate and vital role. It is possible that the very survival of life on this planet may depend upon the universal adoption of a presump- of "guilt" for certain unacceptably destructive categories of activities.

Scientists at Oregon State University (Bella *et al.,* unpublished) have gone even further in concluding that "environmental management must be directed towards securing life style needs which fall increasingly below our expanding capacities to apply technology and to exploit available resources," and that "the avoidance of environmental irreversibility is simply and plainly incompatible with increasing maximization of technology and resource use." In their view, any maximization of technology or resource use poses a risk which is unacceptable. They justify this rather extreme position on the basis of several principles: (1) that environmental management must protect the correctability of social and ecological systems, since man's power to alter such systems is increasingly outpacing his capacity to predict or correct the consequences of such alterations; (2) that environmental management must avoid significant environmental irreversibilities, since an undesirable ecosystem state is correctable only if the alteration which produced it is reversible; (3) that the direction of social change has been and continues to be toward a maximization of technological dependency and resource use, with society continuing to rely principally upon technological innovation for environmental protection; and (4) that the more dependent society becomes on technology and resource use, the greater is the potential for irreversible and uncorrectable ecosystem damage.

In essence, then, if this view of reality is accepted, what has been cited as the primary shortcoming of the "*per se* unacceptability" approach — often referred to as "shifting the burden of proof" — becomes its greatest justification: i.e., that the use of a shift in the burden of proof as the basis for making hard environmental decisions is to confront those seeking to alter the environment with an impossible proof problem (*see,* e.g., Gelpe and Tarlock, 1974). What better way to enforce a "non-degradation" policy than to require would-be degraders to surmount insurmountable obstacles?

As a conscious policy decision, however, and one with major resource allocation implications, where this sort of approach is followed it should be mandated by the legislative process. The statutory standard may take a variety of forms:

- *The absolute prohibition form*

Several existing statutes impose an irrebuttable presumption against certain activities once a specified threshold condition has been met. Examples are the Delaney amendment to the food and drug laws (which declares unsafe any food additive found to "induce cancer in man or animal") and the Endangered Species Act (which precludes federal agencies from taking actions which may jeopardize the continued existence of endangered species or destroy or modify their critical habitat).

- *The rebuttable presumption form*

Several statutes shift the burden of proof (in legal jargon, "the burden of persuasion") to the one seeking to embark upon a risky activity. Examples are the Marine Protection, Research, and Sanctuaries Act (which allows ocean dumping only when the dumping "will not" unreasonably degrade or endanger the marine environment); the Toxic Substances Control Act (which authorizes the EPA Administrator to limit the manufacture and distribution of substances which "may present unreasonable risk of injury to health or the environment"); the Federal Environmental Pesticide Control Act (which permits registration of a pesticide, once risk has been shown, only if the proponents can demonstrate that it will "not generally cause unreasonable adverse effects on the environment"); and the Federal-Aid Highway Act and the Department of Transportation Act (which allow highways to be constructed through parks and wildlife refuges only if (a) there is no "feasible and prudent" alternative, and then, only if (b) the project includes all possible planning to minimize harm to the park or refuge).

- *Miscellaneous forms*

The Federal Water Pollution Control Act Amendments of 1972 illustrate several other approaches (e.g., Section 316 (a) permits the relaxation of strict thermal discharge limitations if the applicant can demonstrate that such limitations are more stringent than necessary to assure a balanced, indigenous population of aquatic organisms; Section 403 precludes the issuance of an ocean discharge permit where insufficient information exists to apply guidelines established by the Administrator; Section 307 (a) requires the Administrator to set effluent standards for toxic pollutants which provide "an ample margin of safety"; and Section 404 (c) authorizes the Administrator to prohibit the disposal of dredged material which will have an "unacceptable adverse effect" on various aquatic values); as do the Coastal Zone Management Act, as amended (which requires activities in or affecting a state's coastal zone to be consistent with the state's approved coastal zone management program); and the Outer Continental Shelf Lands Act (which authorizes the Secretary of the Interior to regulate oil development on the outer continental shelf so as to conserve that area's living and non-living natural resources).

It can be seen from the diversity of formats available that it is possible to limit or preclude risky activities by adjusting the weight and nature of the proponent's burden of proof (ranging from insurmountable in a Delaney amendment situation to readily surmountable in certain water pollution situations). In cases involving "ultra-hazardous" activities (a term borrowed from classical tort law), particularly where the activity involves a new (as opposed to existing) assault on the environment, the use of an irrebuttable presumption may be indicated. In other cases, where the risk is less clear, the activity is already underway, and acceptable alternatives are not readily available, a different approach may be indicated, ranging from allowing the activity to continue under administrative standards which avoid further environmental degradation, to ordering the activity halted under a delayed phase-out schedule (to permit time to find an alternative), to requiring an immediate halt once a specified level of risk has been shown to be present.

Always, however, the lawyer and the scientist each have their roles to play: the lawyer, to settle disputes and assign responsibility for specific actions; the scientist, to draw inferences from observed to unobserved behavior and to establish objective "truth" based upon the systematic elucidation of natural laws. (*See* Gelpe and Tarlock, 1974; Abrams and Berry, 1977; Anonymous, 1972; Oakes, 1977; Leventhal, 1974; National Academy of Sciences, 1977).

Judge Harold Leventhal (1974) of the U.S. Court of Appeals for the District of Columbia, in endorsing the burden of proof approach, has described it as "nothing more or less than [a] device for controlling risks of error" in cases which require quick predictions and decisions, "lest a more conservative and deliberative study squander so much time as to generate irreversible damage to the environment."

The concluding portion of this paper provides a brief example of how these principles are applied in practice.

A Case Study: Sludge in the Ocean

In 1976, some 8.3 million tons of wastes, including sewage sludge (5.3 million tons), industrial waste (2.7 million tons), and construction and demolition debris (0.3 million tons) was ocean-dumped off United States coasts (limited to the Atlantic and Gulf coasts) (Environmental Protection Agency, 1977). An additional 65.5 million cubic yards of dredged material was ocean-dumped during the same period (along all United States coasts) (Department of the Army, 1977).

The environmental decisionmaker seeking a rational system for regulating the ocean disposal of a waste such as sewage sludge is faced at the outset with a dilemma that is increasingly typical of ecological systems: scientific information about the marine environment and the fate and effects of sewage sludge in it is not only largely unavailable, but it is also in any practical sense unobtainable. A complete description of ecological effects is impossible, given the impossibility of fully cataloging the resident species even within the assigned dumpsite. Anything less than a full catalog may cause the investigator to overlook the possibility of a devastating impact on an unstudied, but nevertheless vital, species. Indeed, even with respect to the few species that can be studied, it is beyond the powers of science to be certain, despite the absence of any gross impairment or accumulation of sludge constituents, that there have not been at work more subtle effects which may undermine the species' ability to survive, but which cannot be detected with the scientific tools available.

Moreover, even if effects could be detected, and even if they were recognized as signficant, it would be difficult or impossible to establish causal relationships between the sewage sludge dumped and the adverse impacts observed. This is so because cause and effect in ecological systems often follow convoluted paths. There may be a time lag, for example, between cause and effect; perhaps because time is required for enough of a given sludge constituent to accumulate to exceed a toxicity threshold; perhaps because the effect observed is not the primary effect but must await the consequences of prior impacts (e.g., on prey-predator relationships); or perhaps because the ecological system itself includes alternative pathways and buffering mechanisms which must fail before the system or certain of its components show visible signs of distress. Or the effect may be widely separated in distance from its cause. For example, sludge deposited at Point A may be transported by ocean currents to exert its effect on sensitive organisms at Point B, twenty miles away. Similarly, since marine ecosystems contain many highly mobile components, the major consequences of sludge dumping at Point A may be a fish that was there yesterday but is twenty miles away today at Point B, or on a sea bird that is fifty miles away at Point C, or on a vacationing fisherman who is three hundred miles away at Point B.

In short, the target of the marine scientist in this sort of situation is a moving one. The sludge is moving, the organisms potentially impacted by it are moving, and the scientists investigating it are moving. When one considers that limitations in scientific knowledge about normal ecological functions (let alone the effects of perturbations of such functions) amount to equipping our scientist-archer with a blindfold and a bent arrow, it is not too surprising that he often misses the target.

Faced with incomplete and inadequate information, who should bear the risk of the possible consequences of sewage sludge ocean dumping? In enacting the Marine Protection, Research, and Sanctuaries Act (MPRSA), Congress decided that those who wish to ocean-dump must bear the burden of demonstrating that the dumping will not cause unreasonable degradation and endangerment. It is not enough to justify the continuation of ocean dumping that land-based alternatives would be two to three times as costly, that ocean dumping has the virtue of "operational simplicity," or even that there is no clearcut evidence that ocean dumping is harmful (Guarino *et al.*, 1975;1977). As long as there is a plausible basis for anticipating that sludge in the ocean is harmful, the ocean-dumper's burden is to show that the harm likely to result is not "unreasonable" in light either of the benefits of continued dumping or the practical unavailability of acceptable alternatives.

What is "reasonable" is determined on the basis of administrative criteria which incorporate nine evaluation factors specified by MPRSA. Seven of these relate to the effects of the dumping; the other two concern the "need" for the dumping and the availability of "appropriate [alternative] locations and methods of disposal or recycling."

In the case of sewage sludge ocean dumping by the City of Philadelphia, for example, the decision of the Environmental Protection Agency in ordering the phased termination of the dumping was justified (and correctly so) because of a plausible risk of harm (based on the heavy metal and pathogen content of the sludge and the attendant potential impacts on marine organisms and human health) and the practical availability of preferable (albeit more costly) alternatives.

Significantly, the EPA Administrator, in affirming the phase-out order,[2] emphasized that it is not necessary under the MPRSA for there to be "significant evidence of actual harm at the [dumping] site," but that Congress intended to protect the ocean against potential as well as immediate harm. It was enough that Philadelphia's continued dumping might plausibly "contribute to a general deterioration of the ocean or that such deterioration [might] eventually cause adverse effects . . . ." Recognizing, however, that "there are degrees of potential harm, some calling for immediate action and others allowing more gradual implementation of remedial action," the Administrator upheld as appropriate the action of the Regional Administrator in allowing Philadelphia a reasonable time period in which to phase out its ocean dumping.

I suggest that there is nothing inappropriate in the burden of proof prescribed by the MPRSA or in EPA's application of this burden in the Philadelphia case. The decision represented a conscious allocation of society's resources and protected Philadelphia's right to a fair hearing and to be protected from arbitrary action.

Conclusion

In conclusion, unacceptable environmental risks cannot be avoided without placing limits on technological development and resource exploitation. Cost-benefit analysis generally is incapable of properly assessing environmental risks, because some risks are *per se* unacceptable and most of the rest are unquantifiable. The only rational alternative is to impose the burden of showing the absence of unacceptable risk on those wishing to go forward with risky activities.

Notes

1. The decision of the Eighth Circuit Court of Appeals in the case of *Reserve Mining Co. v. Environmental Protection Agency,* 514 F. 2d 492 (8th Cir. 1975), has been critized as being an example of just such an unwitting cost-benefit analysis. There the court refused to order an immediate halt to Reserve's polluting activities, despite a "reasonable medical concern" that Reserve's discharges produce human cancer. The court justified its approach of requiring Reserve merely to phase-out its activities on the basis that the evidence of adverse health impact wasn't strong enough to justify an immediate injunction. According to a perceptive commentator, what the court was really doing was predicting that the detrimental economic impact of an immediate injunction would be more severe than that of a shutdown following a transition period, and that the increase in economic benefits between immediate and postponed relief outweighed the thousands of lives at stake as a result of Reserve's continued discharges (Anonymous, 1975). It is easy to understand why the court studiously avoided saying that it was striking such a balance.

2. In Re Interim Ocean Disposal Permit No. PA-010 Granted to the City of Philadelphia, 5 Environmental Law Reporter 30003 (EPA, Sept. 25, 1975).

References

1. Abrams, N. E., and R. S. Berry. 1977. Mediation: a better alternative to science courts. Bull. At. Sci. 33(4):50-53.

2. Anderson, F. R. 1973. NEPA in the Courts: A Legal Analysis of the National Environmental Policy Act. The Johns Hopkins Univ. Press, Baltimore and London. 324 pp.

3. Anonymous. 1972. Imminent irreparable injury: a need for reform. S. Calif. Law Rev. 45:1025-10.

4. Anonymous. 1975. Reserve Mining — the standard of proof required to enjoin an environmental hazard to the public health. Minn. Law Rev. 59:893-926.

5. Bollman, F. H. 1975. The value of estuarine fisheries habitats: some basic considerations in their preservation, pp. 95-120. *In* U.S. Environmental Protection Agency, Estuarine Pollution Control and Assessment: Proceedings of a conference. Office of Water Planning and Standards, Washington, D.C.

6. Clark, J. 1975. Status of estuarine ecosystems in relation to sportfish resources, pp. 139-147. *Ibid.*

7. Cronin, L. E. 1975. Interactions of pollutants with uses of estuaries, pp. 739-756. *Ibid.*

8. Department of the Army. 1977. 1976 Report to Congress on Administration of Ocean Dumping Activities. U.S. Army Corps of Engineers, Washington, D.C.

9. Dunster, J. 1977. Virtue in compromise. New Sci. 74(1053):454-456.

10. Environmental Protection Agency. 1977. Ocean Dumping in the United States — 1977. Office of Water and Hazardous Materials, Washington, D.C. 65 pp.

11. Epstein, S. S. 1977. Cancer and the environment. Bull. At. Sci. 33(3):22-30.

12. Gelpe, M. R., and A. D. Tarlock. 1974. The uses of scientific information in environmental decisionmaking. S. Calif. Law Rev. 48:371-427.

13. Guarino, C. F., *et al.* 1975. Land and sea solids management alternatives in Philadelphia. J. Water Poll. Control Fed., 47(11):2551-2564.

14. _____ . 1977. Philadelphia sludge disposal in coastal waters. *Ibid.*, 49(5):737-744.

15. Hedgpeth, J. W. 1975. Seven ways to obliteration: factors of estuarine degradation, pp. 723-737. *In* U.S. Environmental Protection Agency, Estuarine Pollution Control and Assessment: Proceedings of a conference. Office of Water Planning and Standards, Washington, D.C.

16. Kalter, J. R. 1975. Recreation activities in the nation's coastal zone, pp. 83-94. *Ibid.*

17. Katz, J. M. 1975. In environmental cases involving scientific unknowns, risk-benefit analysis, rather than traditional standard of proof, will determine whether imminent health hazard exists. Cath. U. Law Rev. 25:178-191.

18. Kletz, T. A. 1977. What risks should we run? New Sci. 74(1051):320-322.

19. Leventhal, H. 1974. Environmental decisionmaking and the role of the courts. U. Penna. Law Rev. 122(3):509-555.

20. McGinty, L., and G. Atherley. 1977. Acceptability versus democracy. New Sci. 74(1051):323-325.

21. National Academy of Sciences. 1977. Decision Making in the Environmental Protection Agency. Commission on Natural Resources, National Research Council, Washington, D.C. 257 pp.

22. Oakes, J. L. 1977. Substantive judicial review in environmental law. Environ. Law Reptr. 7:50029-50033.

23. Odum, W. E. 1970. Insidious alteration of the estuarine environment. Trans. Amer. Fish. Soc. 99(4):836-847.

24. Tihansky, D. P., and N. F. Meade. 1975. Establishing the economic value of estuaries to U.S. commercial fisheries, pp. 671-684. *In* U.S. Environmental Protection Agency, Estuarine Pollution Control and Assessment: Proceedings of a conference. Office of Water Planning and Standards, Washington, D.C.

PROVING ENVIRONMENTAL COMPATIBILITY: SOUND REGULATORY REQUIREMENT OR INTELLECTUAL NONSENSE?

James A. Rogers

Associate General Counsel
United States Environmental Protection Agency
Washington, D.C.

Although I have been a government environmental lawyer for several years, I will be the first to admit that many of the basic federal water pollution laws on which we rely are unrealistic in what they appear to demand, in the way of proof, of all parties in major environmental regulatory decisions. I am thinking of those sections of the Federal Water Pollution Control Act and Ocean Dumping Act which require proof of precise environmental non-harm before regulatory approvals for an action may be given. For example, in the latter Act, one must address such Ph.D. thesis-worthy issues as species diversity, marine productivity and stability and bioconcentration potentials before the government can approve dumping of wastes. The person who bears the brunt of this lack of realism, is of course the one who has "to make a case," either that an activity will or will not endanger or harm the environment. Usually this person is the applicant for a government permit. *Who* bears the burden of proof becomes an all-important question.

One reason for impracticality in some of the laws' demands may be that environmental laws, as a sarcastic observer once put it, represent "applehood and motherpie" — the point being that the purposes are laudable but that the legislative draftsman's execution of the intent is often less than precise or practical. Certainly many lawmakers do not have adequate appreciation for the difficulty in diagnosing all but the most gross environmental degradation.

Having said that the requirements of factual proof in environmental laws may be unrealistic and probably based on a misunderstanding of what scientists can prove or disprove, I emphasize that in my opinion no one has developed a system that will work better and still allow a measure of case-by-case determination of environmental compatibility, for which industries so vehemently lobby. I will go further and say (at the risk of engendering substantial controversy) that my experiences with hard-fought scientific debates in courtrooms and hearing rooms lead me to believe that what one may call policy or legislative judgments made by lawyer-Congressmen, or lawyer-Administrators, many times in the absence of clear scientific "proof," often is the most reasonable way to resolve (or at least address) environmental problems.

We in EPA have found it much easier and certainly more efficient to have "legislative facts" to rely on rather than to be forced into a judicial fact-finding situation. Examples of legislative facts are Congressional rulings that cars must reduce NOx emissions by 90% before 1981 for public health reasons, or that ocean dumping of sludge endangers the New York Bight and therefore must be stopped by 1982. The other type of fact is, for example, one "found" by a judge on preponderance of evidence after a trial: the industrial plant discharged phenols in quantities which seriously affected fish reproduction in the estuary. "Judicial facts" usually result from a more rigorous examination of competing contentions, and I think that, in general, scientists are more comfortable with these than they are with legislative factual assumptions.

As most of you know, several of the major federal water pollution control laws require demonstration of environmental compatibility before a discharger can obtain federal approval for his discharges, or demonstration of environmental incompatibility before the government can sustain a set of regulations or a tough series of restrictions on an individual polluter. Examining the language in just a few of these laws (I have chosen examples for which estuarine scientists are often called on for assistance) can provide a more specific backdrop for analysis of the scientific proof problem.

● 1. The Ocean Dumping Act[1] allows the Administrator of EPA to issue a permit for the transportation and dumping of wastes only if the applicant can demonstrate (and thus the Administrator of EPA can make the statutorily mandated findings) that an activity will not unreasonably degrade the environment. The Congress has listed criteria which flesh out the "unreasonably degrade" language; these include consideration of the following:

> The effect of such dumping on marine ecosystems, particularly with respect to —
>
> (i) the transfer, concentration, and dispersion of such material and its byproducts through biological, physical and chemical processes,
>
> (ii) potential changes in marine ecosystem diversity, productivity and stability, and
>
> (iii) species and community population dynamics.[2]

● 2. In the Federal Water Pollution Control Act Amendments of 1972, there is a section devoted entirely to ocean outfalls, those pipes which discharge to marine waters outside the national baseline running along our shores.[3] Section 403 prohibits the granting of permission to discharge at all "where insufficient information exists on any proposed discharge to make a reasonable judgment on any of the guidelines" established by Congress and EPA. Those statutory criteria are much like the criteria quoted above under the ocean dumping legislation; parties again are asked to evaluate ecosystem diversity changes, productivity, and stability, among other requirements.[4]

● 3. Operators of power plants can obtain exemptions under Section 316 (a) from technology-based water pollution limitations if they can demonstrate that the limits are more stringent than necessary to assure "protection and propagation of a balanced, indigenous population of shellfish, fish and wildlife. . .."[5] (Technology-based standards are those that rely on installation of feasible pollution control devices rather than on the possible effects of the discharge on receiving water. The latter we call "effects-based" or "environmental-based" regulations.)

● 4. The Senate wants to expand greatly the use of the Section 316 (a)-type case-by-case ecological exemptions from basic technological standards. In proposed amendments to the Water Act, the Senate would allow less stringent discharge limitations for well over half of the nation's 42,910 dischargers if the permit application can show that there will not be an interference with "protection and propagation of a balanced, indigenous population of shellfish, fish, and wildlife. . .."[6] We all know that to respond to those statutory directives in a professionally responsible way takes a massive amount of data and perceptive interpretation. This piece of legislation will be known as the Biological Scientists Relief Act of 1977.

The point I wish to make is that seldom will parties to a major environmental dispute that hinges on questions of ecosystem diversity, for example, be confident that the facts clearly indicate the proper result, and that for the system to work (and by that I mean for large numbers of permits to issue and dischargers to accept limitations) one must grant to the EPA and other environmental regulatory authorities a great deal of discretion to act in an environmentally conservative manner in the face of scientific uncertainty. In the alternative we must move to reliance on legislative judgments and to general acceptance of pure technology standards as the prime regulatory tools.

Facts have been stated to be nothing more than risks, or statistical probabilities[7]; they are theories with high probabilities of validity.[8] But in the estuarine and marine pollution areas, we know that the probabilities inherent in certain facts are low, and that there is definitely little agreement on "second-order" facts (e.g., those facts which are one level more sophisticated than reading numbers off a gas chromatograph, such as that data on cadmium uptake in clams appear to reveal higher concentrations in the last few years) because we usually have fewer data points than we need, because analytical tools are crude, and because we simply don't understand much of the data that is generated.

A marine scientist at Woods Hole Oceanographic Institution once responded to a question during an EPA adjudicatory hearing with an answer that is representative of the scientific uncertainties with which we in the regulatory agencies must live. Asked about the possibility of environmental harm occurring at the ocean dumping site about 40 miles off Cape Henlopen, Delaware, where Philadelphia disposes of the sewage sludge he said, "In my opinion there are not data available anywhere which demonstrate sublethal effects of pollutants in the marine environment."[9] Dr. Donald Mount, Director of EPA's National Water Quality Laboratory at Duluth, Minnesota, once remarked that as much as the government has studied Lake Michigan, it would probably take a fifty percent change in the perch population in that lake before we could detect it.

We clearly are learning quickly about our environment, but we still know little. What is a regulatory official to do when there is so much uncertainty? I suggest that our duty is to "resolve" these major doubts in a conservative fashion, to attempt to find a solution which presumes to protect public health or ecological systems more than the alternatives do. Several courts have accepted this approach. In the famous case of *Ethyl Corporation* v. *EPA*,[10] involving EPA-mandated reduction in lead content of gasoline for health reasons, the United States Court of Appeals for the District of Columbia said:

> Questions involving the environment are particularly prone to uncertainty. Technological man has altered his world in ways never before experienced or anticipated. The health effects of such alterations are often unknown, sometimes unknowable. While a concerned Congress has passed legislation providing for protection of the public health against gross environmental modifications, the regulators entrusted with the enforcement of such laws have not thereby been endowed with the prescience that removes all doubt from their decision-making. Rather, speculation, conflicts in evidence, and theoretical extrapolation typify their every action. How else can they act, given a mandate to protect the public health but only a slight or non-existent data base upon which to draw? Never before have massive quantities of asbestiform tailings been spewed into the water we drink. Never before have our industrial workers been occupationally exposed to vinyl chloride or to asbestos dust. Never before has the food we eat been permeated with DDT or the pesticides aldrin and dieldrin. And never before have hundreds of thousands of tons of lead emissions been disgorged annually into the air we breathe. Sometimes, of course, relatively certain proof of danger or harm from such modification can be readily found. But, more commonly, "reasonable medical concerns" and theory long precede certainty. Yet the statutes — and common sense — demand regulatory action to prevent harm, even if the regulator is less than certain that harm is otherwise inevitable. *[Footnotes omitted]*

Because, at least in the view of the D.C. Circuit, the regulators must act even in the face of uncertainty as to crucial factual findings, administrators such as the head of EPA "must be accorded a flexibility, a flexibility that recognizes the special judicial interest in favor of protection of the health and welfare of the people."[11] And what has developed — explicitly in some decisions — is a rough correlation between health risks and tolerably (by reviewing courts) scientific uncertainty; when dealing with carcinogenic chemicals the courts are willing to allow flexibility in the government's analysis of slides of possible rat tumors.[12] In some cases of this type the reviewing courts have said they would have affirmed on the same record an opposite decision by the Administrator. That is, they would not have reversed a decision by the Administrator to refuse to ban a pesticide, and they would have allowed him to ban it. (This grant of substantial flexibility to the regulatory agencies has not met with uniform acceptance in the courts of appeals. In the *Ethyl* case, the dissenters said with respect to the Administrator's decision: "The result was, Hamlet-like, a blind stab through a curtain of ignorance, inflicting anguish, but in our judgment not solving any problem."[13])

In general rulemaking, EPA clearly has been afforded substantial discretion, especially when human health is involved. In cases involving individual permit appeals or ocean dumping applications, as examples, the Agency has often imposed restrictions or denied permission altogether, in the face of uncertain facts. Rarely have these actions been appealed to the courts, presumably because the industry's counsel have advised that the chances of success are small. But when EPA has had a burden of showing some environmental harm in individual situations, such as trying to draft effluent limits on the basis of receiving water quality, we have been more timid, in a large part due to the reasons the Congress in 1972 moved away from effects-based statutes to technology-based laws: the immense difficulties encountered when we attempt to model a receiving water system to derive end-of-pipe numbers.

There now seems to be a movement away from the technology-based "floors" on pollution and back to effects-based laws, as evidenced in the Senate-passed amendments quoted above. But the reasons for reliance on technology-based limits have not changed. There is still enormous uncertainty in "fine-tuning" effluent restrictions to meet — and just meet — water quality limits. And the ordeal of demonstrating lack of harm from a particular discharge before a permit can issue is a contest only the largest companies and the government can afford to enter. Because of the enormous data needs for an analysis of the environmental effects of a discharge it is a patently regressive approach, from an antitrust point of view, to allow environmental exemptions from technology standards. And it is an approach which in my view misconceives the state of the ecological sciences.

As I stated at the outset, I believe that if the system is to work, we have to allow for the great lack of knowledge of ecological effects of discharging pollutants into estuaries and other waters, by permitting the government a flexibility which recognizes not just the abstract intellectual difficulties in proving environmental effects, but also the practical problems of devoting much time to each of the thousands of petitions for case-by-case environmental analysis. If government is not to be accorded this flexibility in case-by-case determinations, we must move to use a firm technology-based regulatory system, which may indeed result, in some situations, in massive capital expenditures for little environmental gain, or we must rely more heavily on federal and state legislatures to define with specificity those practices and discharges which are unacceptable.

Notes

1. More formally known as the Marine Protection Research and Sanctuaries Act of 1972, as amended. P.L. 92-532, 33 U.S.C. § 1401 *et seq.*

2. Id., § 102 (a), 33 U.S.C. § 1412 (a). EPA published new regulations intended to carry out these statutory directions, on January 11, 1977. 42 *Federal Register* 2642, *amending* 40 C.F.R. Parts 220-228.

3. § 403, 33 U.S.C. § 1343 (c) (2).

4. § 403 (c) (1) requires the Administrator to publish guidelines which include consideration of the following:

   (A) the effect of disposal of pollutants on human health or welfare, including but not limited to plankton, fish, shellfish, wildlife, shorelines, and beaches;

   (B) the effect of disposal of pollutants on marine life including the transfer, concentration, and dispersal of pollutants or their byproducts through biological, physical, and chemical processes; changes in marine ecosystem diversity, productivity, and stability; and species and community population changes;

   (C) the effect of disposal of pollutants on esthetic, recreation, and economic values;

   (D) the persistence and permanence of the effects of disposal of pollutants;

   (E) the effect of the disposal at varying rates, of particular volumes and concentrations of pollutants;

   (F) other possible locations and methods of disposal or recycling of pollutants including land-based alternatives; and

   (G) the effect on alternative uses of the oceans, such as mineral exploitation and scientific study.

   EPA is preparing new criteria to implement this section.

5. § 316 (a) of the Federal Water Pollution Control Act Amendments of 1972, 33 U.S.C. § 1326 (a).

6. S. 1952, proposing addition of § 301 (d) (5).

7. Dr. Hume, *A Treatise of Human Nature,* I, pt. III, § 6 at 87, cited in *Ethyl Corporation* v. *EPA*, 544 F.2d 1, 25 n. 52.

8. *See* generally, T. Kuhn, *The Structure of Scientific Revolution, Ibid.*

9. Testimony at 2-246, *In Re City of Philadelphia Ocean Dumping Permit,* May 20, 1975.

10. 541 F.2d 1 (D.C. Cir., 1976).

11. 541 F.2d at 24.

12. *See,* e.g., 541 F.2d at 19.

13. 541 F.2d at 111.

ESTUARINE MANAGEMENT – USERS' NEEDS

Lloyd L. Falk

Engineering Service Division
Engineering Department
E. I. du Pont de Nemours & Co.
Wilmington, Delaware

Users of estuaries are not unique people or entities – they are all of us. Many, for example, use estuaries as laboratories to validate theories in aquatic biology, chemistry, or geology. Others use estuaries as sources of recreation, whether physical or aesthetic. Still others use estuaries to make a living – as do fishermen, navigators, transporters of goods – or even as researchers in estuarine ecology. Finally, we use estuaries as conveyors and assimilators of waste materials which we do not, cannot, or should not handle in other ways.

What is true of users of estuaries is equally true of users of rivers, oceans, land, and the atmosphere. What then can we, as users, say about how to manage estuaries, rivers, and the oceans? Such a broad subject needs narrowing. Therefore, I shall try to limit myself to consideration and management of the waste assimilative and conveyance capacities of such bodies of waters.

But before I go further, I need to point out that we live in a highly developed, integrated, and finely tuned technological society. As such we draw upon reservoirs of renewable and nonrenewable resources which occur in nature or which we cultivate. If we use these resources, laws of nature require those materials to be returned eventually to the oceans, to the air, or to the land whence they came. We may change the nature of the materials and how the deposition is distributed, but we cannot alter the ultimate requirement that deposition take place (Falk, 1975).

The natural law of the conservation of mass-energy says we can't make things disappear. Thus we see that the idea of total waste recycle within the confines of our technological society, or "zero discharge" – a concept with almost magical appeal to framers of our present Federal Water Pollution Control Act – cannot, in the long run, stand. Regardless of how many times we recycle material through our world society, once we take something from nature, we must somehow and eventually return it. The question really is: How do we make that return so as to be compatible with the environment we wish to maintain?

An excellent illustration of this is the major unsolved problem of acid precipitation. Our world society is a net acid producing one. Table 1 shows the world production of sulfur which was roughly estimated from 1974 data in the latest edition of the Minerals Yearbook (U.S. Bureau of Mines, 1976). I have omitted sulfur mined or extracted as neutral salts since this would not contribute to a world acid cycle.

The net total from nature shown in Table 1 is, then, about 130 million metric tons per year. Only about 18 percent of the sulfur involved is sulfur actually sought from nature. The rest is sulfur which actually gets in our way when we try to use fuels or recover certain metals.

Table 1

World-Wide Sources (1974) of Sulfur

Natural Source	*Sulfur Equivalent/Year (millions of metric tons)*
Sulfur Sought	
Native sulfur and pyrites	28.7
Sulfur Not Sought	
Copper, lead, zinc ores	4.9
Coal (@ 2 percent S)	62.6
Petroleum (@ 2 percent S)	56.2
Total	152.4
By-product S	22.9
Net Total From Nature	129.5

Looking at the 130 million metric tons of sulfur per year from an environmental standpoint, we see that sulfur almost entirely ends up in an oxidized state, either as sulfuric acid used in commerce or as an acid-forming gas released to the air. Since we get that sulfur from nature, we must eventually return it. If we, by positive action, do not neutralize the acid properties, nature will, by way of such phenomena as acid precipitation and soil leaching of minerals.

The problem facing users, then, is how can we return waste products to nature in a manner which is compatible with the environment we wish to maintain? In other words, what is the assimilative capacity of the world around us to accept the unavoidable, nonusable, or worn-out products (i.e., wastes) of our technological society? How much of the acid-producing sulfur products and by-products, for example, can our environment assimilate before we alter it more than we can tolerate?

Today, we use our waterways (rivers, estuaries, and the oceans) to accept our wastes. We shall continue to do so. Researchers of estuaries and other water bodies must tell us to what extent those waterways can be used. Put another way, users should determine what the assimilative capacities of waterways are for waste products.

I realize that even consideration of such a capacity is a "no-no" concept to many people. Perhaps we should euphemistically call it "carrying" capacity, or adorn the term in another way. We establish other capacities of waters as, for example, when we set quotas on the numbers of fish which may be taken or the whales and porpoises which may be killed. Many of us abhor the idea of killing animals for "sport," yet society sets waterfowl bag limits based on studies which determine the capacity of their populations to assimilate various degrees of hunting pressures.

When Congress amended the Federal Water Pollution Control Act in 1972, it established a "national goal that the discharge of pollutants into the navigable waters be eliminated by 1985" (U.S. Congress, 1972). My quarrel is not with the goal, but with how Congress defined "pollutant." Congress did not define it as something which causes pollution, i.e., a condition of waters which prevents or impairs their use for certain defined purposes. Rather, Congress defined pollutant as anything, including heat, discharged into water. All industrial, municipal, and agricultural wastes are included in the definition.

Our society cannot meet such a goal. Nor will it allow cessation of flows from municipal treatment plants, irrigation return flows, or even industrial effluents so long as these do not cause pollution. In other words, as long as appropriate constituents of these wastes are reduced to levels which our waters can assimilate, the goal of nonpollution will have been met. To require more is wasteful of our resources, indeed, of world resources. And since our society already uses a disproportionate share of the world's renewable and nonrenewable resources, the other nations of the world will not thank us for such wastefulness.

I believe that estuarine scientists have a duty to tell our society how we can use our estuaries (and other water bodies) most wisely. It is obvious we cannot, from energy resource as well as economic standpoints, continue down the road marked "zero discharge." Such a goal, which would have to be based on total recycle of all materials, is a will-o'-the-wisp, because the laws of nature require us to return to earth that which we take from it.

Obviously, we need to do a great deal more to learn how to control our use of natural resources so that usage is most efficient. But when we decide on a course of action — a course based on wise application of our knowledge of the scientific, economic, and social aspects of our society and their interrelationships — we can provide a high degree of stability to our efforts at managing our environmental impacts. That stability will result from our understanding of what impacts our environment can withstand and still be an environment in which we can function at the highest standard of living our society can support. That support must consider not only the assimilative capacities of waterways, but also their interrelationships with the assimilative capacities of the air, the ground, our economy, and that of the rest of the world. We must make certain that environmental regulations will indeed yield the least costly way to achieve the environmental management goals we have set for ourselves. But first, science and industry must find out what those least costly ways are.

References

1. Falk, L. L. 1975. Industrial viewpoint on ocean disposal. pp. 406-409. *In* T. M. Church (ed.), Marine Chemistry in the Coastal Environment. American Chemical Society Symposium Series 18, Washington, D.C.

2. U. S. Bureau of Mines. 1976. Minerals Yearbook 1974. Volume I. Metals, Minerals, and Fuels. U. S. Department of the Interior, Washington, D.C.

3. U. S. Congress. 1972. Federal Water Pollution Control Act Amendments of 1972. Public Law 92-500, 92nd Congress, S. 2770. October 18 (86 Stat. 816-904).

PANEL DISCUSSION
Following Estuarine Management Session

Convener's note: This discussion has been edited and transcribed from tape recordings. Some liberties have been taken with sequence in order to preserve context or to make certain passages meaningful. In addition, incomplete, inaudible, or garbled passages were deleted.

Andy McErlean

We have time for some questions.

Howard Sanders (WHOI)

Dr. Hedgpeth, I want you to play the role of God for a while, and so you have the total power to commandeer the resources of this world in the way you want. Now, what's your game plan? Being God, there is no need to concern yourself with bureaucracy or anything else.

Joel Hedgpeth

But then you are giving me only six days for the job? In view of this six-day time "constraint" as the bureaucrats are always calling it, everything cannot be done. In developing monitoring programs for San Francisco Bay, for example, they talked about replicate sampling. How many? They are not sure, but someone recommended at least twenty to work out somebody's theorem about diversity. Others thought three samples should be enough, and the argument went on. I suggested, as a believer in the doctrine of the mystery of numbers, let's use a magic number like nine. They actually accepted that, for a while.

Seriously, I did urge that the best procedure was to limit the sampling and data gathering to some manageable yet consistent minimum, say two bottom grabs (for internal consistency comparison), three plankton samples and some standard physical and chemical analyses, including chlorophyll, as often as we could possibly afford, and as long as possible. On the basis of such a simplified and limited plan we should come up with better information over a period of years than trying to do everything at once at every station possible within eighteen months. This kind of research is not like designing an atomic bomb. Biological processes require time.

We have been asked to comment, for example, on the first quarter's data from a monitoring program, to respond to such questions (put by some EPA person) as: "Does this data indicate that the outfall will have deleterious effects on the bottom fauna?" It takes years to establish natural variations, especially on an open coast such as Monterey Bay. It may not be the best answer to the question, but I think a simplified program of sampling and observations over an adequate period of time, carefully and consistently done, is better than a crash program set with arbitrary time limits according to a schedule set up by some distant bureaucrat. If God could set his own time, so should we.

Andy McErlean

I wonder if you mind expanding just a little bit on the point that you made that there is no effective baseline for San Francisco Bay. It confuses me a little bit since both the federal and state governments and other people have spent funds there and if that is true I'd like you to elaborate a little bit if you would, Joel.

Joel Hedgpeth

One of the most serious problems with baseline studies in San Francisco Bay is that there is no way to determine the natural baseline. During the days of hydraulic mining, much of the original bottom fauna was probably destroyed as parts of the bay were shoaled as much as two or three feet, and many of the common species in the bay are introduced, non-native. Often in the past these species, many of which are common east-coast Atlantic ones introduced during the days of oyster farming, were identified as "native" or confused with other species, so many of the older identifications are erroneous and there is now no way of confirming them. There was never a resident naturalist in the San Francisco Bay region to observe and identify these organisms before all the changes due to industrialization, filling, pollution, and ecological interactions among the species altered even the introduced species. In 1879, ninety-nine years ago, the striped bass (*Morone saxatilis*) was introduced, and almost immediately adapted itself. Now it is the principal sport fishery of the San Francisco Bay and Delta region and is a major management concern of the Fish & Game people of the state.

A few years ago, when pollution reached such a stage that action was obviously necessary, the State of California funded a three-million-dollar study by the Department of Sanitary Engineering of the University of California. These people however were neither zoologists, botanists, nor ecologists, but engineers, and engineers need numbers. They somehow hit upon the idea that the diversity of organisms was related to the "health" of the environment, and suggested the use of the diversity index in pollution studies, and by inference, in management of what are elegantly known as "receiving waters." Unfortunately the sampling was so inconsistent and the determination of the material so incompetent that most of this work is considered valueless and is now referred to only with embarrassment.

Baseline studies were attempted in 1911-1912 under the leadership of Professor C. A. Kofoid, who planned a series of monographs on the flora and fauna and hydrography of the bay. At the time the old U.S. Fish Commission steamer *Albatross* was available. However, she could only work in the deeper channels and did very little sampling in the shallows with her launch. Now we realize, thanks to the work of Fred Nichols and comparable studies of the tidal flats along the Dutch coast, that the broad shallow mud flat areas of San Francisco Bay are very highly productive and it is this aspect of the natural system that is as significant in this type of estuary as the *Spartina* marshes of the Atlantic estuaries are reputed to be.

Unfortunately the original baseline study of 1911-12 fell apart. For one thing the *Albatross* was withdrawn from the bay, and for another, members of the zoology faculties of Stanford and Berkeley agreed to part ways. Joseph Grinnell of Berkeley concentrated on upland birds and squirrels (he seemed to dislike waterfowl and the only aquatic bird he gave a second glance to was that aberrant wren, the water ouzel), and J. Otterbein Snyder of Stanford concentrated on freshwater fish. This famous gentleman's agreement had the unfortunate result that for decades aquatic biology was not studied at Berkeley and upland furred and feathered things were ignored at Stanford. Equally significant at the start was the defection of the field supervisor of the study, F. B. Sumner, who had just completed a similar task at Woods Hole and was not interested in doing the same thing twice, so he removed himself to La Jolla. There was a brief flurry of revived interest in the biology of the bay at Berkeley during the studies of the marine borer invasion associated with the drought years of the 1920's, but little more. No one, apparently, from either of the bay area universities was involved in the early discussions of the possible salt water barrier or the expanded use of upstream water that led directly to the California Water Plan and its devastating diversion plans. Decisions were made to change this environment before it was even realized that the San Francisco Bay-Delta system was an estuary. It has only been in the past few years that we have found out where the null zone in this system is.

We probably will never have a satisfactory "baseline" for San Francisco Bay. Things are being changed too fast. For example the null zone is in the narrow part of the bay system between Antioch and Carquinez Strait, and a few months ago the port development people suggested that a good site for a major container port facility would be the old town of Benecia on the north side of this site, and this could be achieved by a massive fill out to the middle of the channel. A development of this kind would alter the whole system irrevocably, but probably will not be sanctioned because of the considerable hydrodynamic changes induced in the current system and subsequent danger to the south side of the channel.

Andy McErlean

Just so there are no loose ends, I am not sure everybody understands the analogy of the title of your paper. Would you mind explaining that?

Joel Hedgpeth

This is the old story about the group of blind men who encountered an elephant, each restricted to one contact, who then compared notes to decide what it was. One who got the trunk said the elephant was like a serpent (or fire hose); the blind man who grabbed the tail thought the elephant was a rope, the one who bumped into its side thought it was a wall, and the last who grabbed an ear thought it was some sort of giant leaf. I am tempted to bring that all up to date by suggesting, after hearing a discussion by E. P. Odum of the significance of methane that another blind man stepped behind the elephant and made some conclusion about its gaseous state. And, of course, there are some, not even sightless, who can walk right by an elephant and conclude there is no problem at all.

Jim Rogers

I have a great deal of difficulty accepting an approach to environmental regulation that depends on determination of assimilative capacity of receiving waters. And I see that theme in Dr. Falk's statements and in repeated industry testimony on Capitol Hill. The problem is that you simply do not know with any degree of certainty what is happening in an estuary. Scientists rarely can tell you how much waste can be accepted without harm. We really know very little about the fate of most pollutants. In addition, many of the sources are changing their treatment systems, and there may be new industrial or municipal sources on the body of water which throw off previous calculations.

Lloyd Falk

The fallacy of that approach, Jim, is that, after a plant puts in best available technology by 1983, EPA, a governmental agency, or somebody will still have to answer the question: "What is the assimilative capacity of a receiving body of water?" The Federal Water Pollution Control Act says we must meet certain goals of fishable, swimmable, and other kinds of water. EPA can't tell me what technology-based standard we have to put in by 1983 to meet those water quality standards. So, we still have to determine the assimilative capacity to find out whether a plant, after putting in 1983 technology, has done enough. You must wait and make the effort. Perhaps you have to make a simultaneous effort to determine assimilative capacity; at the same time you require technology-based standards. I don't see that this is being done. There are people out in the audience who will be able to tell you.

Ken Kamlet

You keep emphasizing the need for determining assimilative capacity of the waterway for a particular beneficial use before going ahead and proposing more than minimum controls on industry. But you recognize, yourself, I think in your response to one of the questions, that there are certain materials — persistent non-biodegradable materials like pesticides and other chlorinated hydrocarbons — in relation to which the concept of assimilative capacity does not have terribly much meaning. What do you do for wastes of that type? If DuPont doesn't produce them, there are other chemical companies that do. What kind of approach is dictated where you have materials of this sort being put out? Can you afford to wait, and if you wait what are you waiting for?

Lloyd Falk

I think the answer is that you cannot apply the same kind of protocol to every individual kind of material. For example, what is the assimilative capacity of an estuary for a large community such as Philadelphia or New York? Why always come back to the fact that it's an industrial problem? It isn't. It's a problem for all of us. If you say we've got to cut down everything that goes to an estuary, then I ask "What do we do with it?" We take it out of the water and we have it in our grimy little hands; where do we put it? You know the city of Philadelphia is having a tremendous problem trying to figure out what in heaven's name to do with its sewage sludge.

Jim Rogers

At the same cost!

Lloyd Falk

It doesn't matter. Even if it costs three or four times as much. There are people who say: I don't want you to put that on the land next to my house, or I don't want that incinerator built in my neighborhood. The problems are not just the assimilative capacities of receiving bodies of water, but also the alternatives. How do you find a balance between all of these things when we do have a society that creates these waste materials?

Andy McErlean

I am going to intervene here to stop the argument on the assimilative capacity to pass on to another topic. I think perhaps you are being unfairly put on the spot, Dr. Falk, as the industry representative here, and I would like to stir the pot in a different direction.

A recent editorial contained in the Coastal Zone Management Journal has the provocative title: "Altruism, Selfishness and Coastal Resources." This article cites the real and apparent conflicts among the many uses of the estuarine and coastal area. What I found of interest in the article, and which the panel may wish to comment upon, is the following passage. This is a quotation:

"All of this leads to the conclusion [that] government regulation is not an altruistic endeavor. There is no public interest separate and distinct from selfish interest. The same competitors who previously made selfish demands in the marketplace are now making selfish demands on government. The job of public regulators is to arbitrate between conflicting selfish demands. If coastal zone managers can avoid the delusion and self-serving rhetoric of altruism, they can go on with their real jobs, which is to strike the appropriate social balance between productivity and preservation, amenity and efficiency."

Does the panel agree or disagree with this comment. Is there an identifiable public interest? Would the panel care to comment on this statement? I'd like to begin the commentary with Dr. Hedgpeth.

Joel Hedgpeth

Before I tackle that, I would like to say that I hope we will not extend Aldo Leopold's concept of carrying capacity to something like the processing capacity of receiving waters.

The problem of private and public interest and achieving social balance, productivity, and preservation at the same time and so on is exemplified by the California experience with coastal zone management. Hearings are held regularly and frequently, usually lasting until one a.m., about these matters. Much of it concerns the idea of private property, and the California Constitution is a little more explicit about the right of a property owner to thrive from his property; and so we must debate the public interest as opposed to those who assume they have the God-given right to sell and profit from their land (though this is contrary to Leviticus 25:23).

We almost came to the point of no return toward the end of 1977, the third year of drought. Indeed all the western states are near the eleventh hour in the matter of water use, and ultimately who can live where. Now that it has rained again, euphoria has returned, and with more water there will be more subdivisions, more intense agriculture with its resultant saline increment (some of it perhaps to be returned to San Francisco Bay) until there is the next drought, and should it last only a year longer, the entire system may be taxed beyond functioning and we will have a serious economic and social disaster. I predicted this ultimate condition forty years ago and founded The Society for the Prevention of Progress to that end. The idea is now philosophically and socially acceptable among many Californians.

Lloyd Falk

I don't really know what I can say about that specifically, but I often wonder about the matter of selfish uses of resources. Let's assume, for example, that an industry, through its actions, killed, say, two million ducks a year, year in and year out. I am sure that the wrath of the nation would be brought down upon its head. But I read an interesting statistic the other day. Every year approximately two million ducks are killed by lead poisoning *after* the duck hunting season. There is a very simple answer to solving that problem — stop hunting ducks. But

I am sure that if the National Wildlife Federation were to advocate such a thing, the wrath of the nation would be brought down on its head. So when you talk about selfish interests and who is knocking off whose resources, you have to recognize that we are a society, that there are many different points of view and many different interests, and one of the functions of government, I guess, is to try to put those interests together in such a way that we can still have a functioning society with minimum conflict.

Ken Kamlet

Dr. Hedgpeth suggested parenthetically that the answer to the lead shot problem is to use silver bullets.

But I do want to respond to Dr. Falk's comments about lead-shot mortalities in ducks. On another occasion, as I recall, just before I was about to testify at a congressional hearing against DuPont's ocean dumping of titanium dioxide waste, I think it was Dr. Falk and some other DuPont employee who came over to me and said, "You know we have analyzed the paper that *Conservation News*, one of our bi-weekly newsletters, is printed on and we found it's got titanium in it as its basic pigment." I don't know whether they mentioned that so I'd tone down my testimony, but I didn't. With respect to the lead shot problem, I am glad Dr. Falk used that example, because the National Wildlife Federation has spoken out on it very forcefully. Not against duck hunting, but against the use of lead shot. In fact, largely as a result of initiatives taken by our organization, the Fish and Wildlife Service has begun phasing out the use of lead shot and substituting not silver bullets, but steel shot in selected flyways around the country. There was that middle ground and we pressed for it even though it pitted us against the National Rifle Association with whom some of our members often are in sympathy. I was personally very gratified that we took that stand.

Let me comment though, as long as I have got the mike, on the question that Andy posed. I disagree that there is no public interest distinct from selfish interest. While one can define altruism in such a way that nothing anybody does is altruistic — even if somebody does something for purely public purposes he still derives gratification from it; in that sense, there is a self-interest or a selfish interest involved. But apart from that kind of trivial distinction, I think the marketplace and marketplace forces have their limits.

In a coastal zone, it is true that you have fishermen, sport fishermen, commercial fishermen, and others who derive their livelihoods from the coastal zone, and who are going to suffer economically if coastal areas are degraded. Their catches are reduced and their ability to market healthy seafood is reduced. That is true, and I suppose other users of the coastal zone would have an interest in protecting it. But after you accommodate all of their interests, it seems to me there remain interests which are unaccommodated by purely monetary and marketplace forces: interests in preserving ecosystems in a relatively undegraded state, in maintaining ecological diversity, and so forth, even if there is no obvious commercial species that is going to suffer as a result of destabiliztion of the ecosystem. This is true even if it is not possible to point to any adverse impacts that some definable economic interest is going to suffer. I think this really is an example of the "Tragedy of the Commons" which was alluded to earlier. Garrett Hardin's notion that marketplace factors really only work where you have competing property owners or competing owners each looking out for his own interests, and in doing so serving the public interest, which serves the interest of society.

In the ocean and in coastal areas, we don't have competing property interests. The oceans and the coastal environment belong to no one and belong to everyone and it is just like the people who graze their cattle in a common pasture. It's in everyone's individual economic interest to have his cattle eat up as much of the grass as possible because he gets fatter cattle and is able to market them and make bigger profits. The fact that if everybody overgrazes in that way, the carrying capacity of the pasture is going to be used up and next year nobody may get any profits out of that field doesn't really enter into it, because the individual ecnomic interest of the respective grazers lies in maximizing the market value that is returned for any given year from that field. That is precisely the kind of problem we have in the ocean and coastal environment. It seems to me that outside regulation and intervention is required because selfish interests won't do the job by themselves.

Jim Rogers

Andy said we will turn this over to questions and comments from the audience after my remarks, which are going to be very brief. I think I agree with Ken Kamlet. I don't find this a very convincing editorial. I find it kind of silly, written by someone who probably may not have been consulted on a decision and is now upset about it. It says that the job of public regulators is to arbitrate between conflicting selfish demands, and that this is all kind of a cynical game. I don't believe that is true. I think we were probably too hard on the government this morning. I think that most bureaucrats really do try to carry out what is called public interest. I think that most regulatory statutes set out in fairly clear terms the purpose which Congress considers to be most important in enacting the law, and I think by and large that there is a general public purpose, public interest, that can be recognized as distinct from simply competing private marketplace demands.

Andy McErlean

It is interesting that in terms of numbers the panel splits down the middle on that particular issue. Two for and two against. I would like to open the floor up to questions dealing with this particular topic, altruism and public usage. Please approach the microphone. Gene — did you have your hand up?

Gene Cronin (UMCEES)

I would like to propose policy and practice related to this discussion and ask the panel to comment on: (1) Is it legally possible? (2) Is it the most appropriate way to apply science? (3) Is it acceptable to environmental activists and industry? and (4) Do you think it would be a better way to go?

When we are trying to define the acceptable level of change in the estuary, I suggest that the available scientific knowledge about the effects of the proposed change be assembled. An assessment should then be made of the quality of our data and understanding on this problem. If that basis is strong, the decisions can be made with useful accuracy and we should have to be able to achieve both use of the resource and protection of the estuary. If the basis is weak, we must be highly conservative in permitting use or change in the estuary. For instance, the introduction of new exotic wastes or biologically indigestible materials would be highly controlled because precise knowledge is lacking but the values threatened are obviously large. As understanding grows, it will be possible to use increasingly the "assimilation capacity" responsibly.

This policy and practice would have several values:
1. It would permit decision to be made in each case.
2. It would emphasize the need that Joel has stated for the long-term studies and specific research required to produce a useful basis of knowledge.
3. It will permit some use of inherent capacities.
4. I think it will force industry, municipalities, and other users to speed up and intensify their efforts to recapture and recycle wastes and to explore again the problem of where to put irreducible residues.

Is this possible? Appropriate? Acceptable? Better?

Andy McErlean

This would seem to be a question that Jim Rogers should get the first shot at, being one of the two lawyers on the panel.

Jim Rogers

Well, as any good lawyer will do, I am not going to give you a direct answer. Is it legally acceptable right now? That is very difficult to answer. It may be. For example, in the Senate Amendments to the Clean Water Act, which are now pending joint house approval (these amendments were passed and signed by the President on December 27), many of these concepts will be embraced. Under the amended law, EPA and the states will write discharge permits for at least five-year terms, starting in a year or two, which will require compliance with effluent levels based on the use of best available control technology. These are technology-based standards. There will be a waiver provision or exemption provision with respect to controls on non-toxic water pollutants, and the industry will have an opportunity to demonstrate essentially what Dr. Falk was talking about — that there may be no need for those controls when one examines the receiving water body. (These provisions were enacted as section 301 (g) of the 1977 amendments.) The difference would be this: it would place the burden of showing that no controls are needed on the industrial discharger.

In effect, this system may work much like the system Dr. Cronin referred to, because it takes a category of pollutants, described largely by name, and for those the law says there are no exemptions from the technology-based standards. In a sense there has been a legislative determination that as to those persistent and highly toxic pollutants, we don't want to risk calculating that there is a carrying capacity of an estuary or other body of water. As to the other pollutants, which are essentially oxygen-demanding pollutants, there can be waivers to allow for carrying-capacity calculations.

The overall procedure Dr. Cronin talks about may be an ideal approach when you have enough money, time, and talented people to address a specific problem. But returning to my bureaucratic self, I must emphasize that we have thousands of dischargers in this country, all applying for permits every five years, and only a handful of scientists who can provide the necessary support for the deluxe modeling of an ecosystem or prediction of carrying capacity. The practical problems of running this enormous regulatory system with few people force the government into some approaches which may seem less than intellectual.

Ken Kamlet

I don't disagree with you on that, Jim. My basic response to the question would be that to a large extent, I think we have the kind of system you suggest in a handful of present environmental laws, some of which I mentioned in my talk. I think the system was intended to work in the way you described when the burdens of proof are placed on dischargers to show that their activities will not unreasonably degrade the environmental concerns that Congress intended to protect. Where sufficient information is available to make possible a demonstration that unacceptable impacts will not result, then yes, the activity can and should be allowed to proceed. If such information is not available and perhaps is not even obtainable, given limitations in our ability to understand ecosystems and interactions of pollutants within those ecosystems, then we really need to be conservative and not allow these activites to proceed.

I want to say in response to one aspect of your question as to whether that kind of system would be acceptable to environmental organizations, my answer is yes. We don't advocate, and I don't think any of our compatriot organizations around the country and throughout the world advocate, total cessation of industrial activity or industrial growth. We do recognize that there are assimilative capacities with respect to certain materials and certain activities in certain receiving waters. We also feel, very strongly, with respect to certain other receiving bodies and types of materials that the concept of assimilative capacity has no rational meaning. To rely on it is to attempt to delude ourselves.

Lloyd Falk (in response to Cronin's question)

I think the approach which you have outlined is reasonable. My problem is that it may be difficult to carry out but I think ultimately it's going to have to be carried out. Our society, hopefully, is going to be around here for many generations, and we talk about 1977 deadlines, 1983 deadlines. If our population and the world population continue to grow, we shall have to take those kinds of approaches in order to set upper limits as to what that growth will be. It cannot be infinite. So I think, fundamentally, industry would agree with it.

Andy McErlean

We have time for another question — the gentleman who's standing there.

Neil Savage

Neil Savage from Normandeau Associates, New Hampshire. I'd like to bring up this question again of the burden of proof and where it's placed on the applicant/user. Who decides when the burden of proof is sufficient? What I'm particularly concerned about is whether such a practice could become a tactical weapon to impede progress or to delay project activities. In other words, it's possible to construe that there's no limit to when something is proved and I'd like to have everybody's opinion there as to how we tackle the burden of proof so it doesn't become a fatal sledge hammer weapon that's used on industry.

Andy McErlean

Could we sharpen that up just a bit though? The point you're after is, when do we achieve enough information to make a decision. Is that right?

Neil Savage

Right, particularly responding to Ken's phrase "the burden of proof," as it applies to the permit process.

Andy McErlean

Mr. Rogers will attempt to answer.

Jim Rogers

Let me state a preface on this. Your firm's name rings a bell. Isn't it the one that supplied the data relative to the Seabrook nuclear station? Is that correct?

Neil Savage

That's correct.

Jim Rogers

I think your question is, what is there to protect the world from environmental groups constantly contending that there are possible dangers which have not been addressed, and placing the burden of proof on the discharger. In your mind, this procedure absolutely frustrates construction, for example, of a major nuclear facility. Is that right?

Neil Savage

Yes, but my question goes much beyond just the nuclear power issue.

Jim Rogers

Maybe Ken wants to comment in a general sense. I touched on this this morning. I think that if you read the statutes literally there always is an environmental question. The things that are mentioned as criteria are so pervasive that it's very difficult to come to a conclusion in any type of administrative process and be satisfied that you answered the questions. Indeed, I think we would be concerned if anyone said they answered all the questions, simply because we know there's so much uncertainty in science. That's why I said from the administrative point of view, great discretion has got to be allowed the administrator of an agency to do the best he can with the data that's available. I'll turn it over to Ken Kamlet. He may have a different view.

Ken Kamlet

There's a concept in tort law of what a "reasonable man" would do under the circumstances in trying to decide whether somebody responsible for injuring someone was negligent in his conduct. I think the reasonable man concept could and should have wider application. I think the question of when a burden of proof has been met is certainly a subjective one that reasonable decisionmakers can disagree on to some extent. But ultimately it is up to those decisionmakers, acting as reasonable men, to decide where those lines are drawn. And if somebody thinks the decisionmaker has been unreasonable in drawing this line, he has a recourse to court review. Then we have a judge second-guessing him and deciding whether he's been arbitrary and capricious in exercising the discretion that he has. That's far from a precise system, but it is the best we have; it's worked here and in England in the tort context for many years and I think it could serve here as well.

With respect to the Seabrook project, you had the EPA administrator who reviewed the record and decided on the basis of that record that it was reasonable to allow the thermal discharge and the design of intake structures carrying large amounts of water from the Seabrook estuary and the surrounding ocean. He decided that that was reasonable, that what needed to be determined had been determined, and that the risks were acceptable. That matter is now under review by the First Circuit Court of Appeals. I think the fact that the EPA administrator was able to decide, despite the absence of perfect and full and complete information about impacts, illustrates that it is possible to decide that the burden of proof has been met. I am not going to comment on whether I agree with Mr.

Costle's decision that the burden of proof had been adequately met in the Seabrook case, but I think it is possible in our system for industry and power plants and so forth to get the go-ahead even under the types of presumptions and statutory standards we talked about.

Andy McErlean

Are there additional questions from the floor? At this time we can go on to another prepared question for the panel or we can stay with questions from the floor.

Perhaps it would be best to go ahead with the direct questions from the floor.

Unidentified Person

The comment that I have I'd like to address to Jim Rogers since he touched on this. Both Hedgpeth and Sanders have adequately stated this morning that long-term study is required. On the other hand, we have the Environmental Protection Agency which is a regulatory agency, that is, I assume, responsible for the establishment of some of the statutes with respect to the laws that Congress hands down. My question is, why can't the EPA simply say there's not enough time within six months or 180 days to perform the task, even at the risk of being held in contempt of court?

Andy McErlean

We (EPA) haven't lost our virginity in that direction. Maybe Ken Kamlet would like to talk about it; I think he single-handedly has brought us to court suits more than other groups. Ken would you like to comment?

Ken Kamlet

The question basically is, if EPA feels it needs more time, why doesn't it just take more time and risk contempt of court citations, and so forth, if that's what it takes? Why doesn't it have the courage of its convictions? — to put it most favorably, I guess, to the questioner. Presumably, if we did this enough times, all of EPA's decisionmakers would be in jail for contempt of court and we wouldn't have to worry about the problem arising again. I have problems with the notion not only of agency officials disobeying the laws set by Congress, but particularly disobeying laws set by the courts. I'm not suggesting that it's inappropriate for individuals, where they conscientiously object to some policy of government to resist governmental action and risk the consequences. That's appropriate for some individuals but I think there's a difference between individuals and agency officials who are acting as representatives of the executive branch who are sworn to carry out the law and to apply the constitution and other things that are binding on them, for better and for worse. In our system, the way to correct bad laws is not for agency officials to disregard them or disobey them.

The way is to do the best that can be done to obey the laws, and if the laws are mistaken or inadequate or have undesirable consequences, then they ought to work to change the law. As a lawyer and officer of the court even if I personally saw things otherwise, which I don't, I think I'd have to say that.

Unidentified person

The question is: Does the EPA take an active role in trying to convince the courts and Congress that some of these studies require more time?

Jim Rogers

We do go to the Hill and we testify at some length and we send them documents, studies, outlines of resource constraints. The extent that they are considered in synthesizing the law is a different question. I'm not in a position to say how successful the Agency has been in convincing Congress of the great magnitude of the chore in regulating these difficult environmental problems. It is my personal view that we haven't been very successful. I am aware of the view that Congress has: that most administrative agencies, if allowed to go about their own ends, will take too long, that they need an occasional kick in the pants to get them going and the way you can do that is to give them deadlines. So yes, the answer to your first question is yes, we do try to participate fully before Congress. That is not a body in which you just go right up there and present your views. We have definite protocols as to how we approach Congress, how our views are presented. They don't appreciate various groups from the Agency coming up there and trying to lobby for certain positions. That is not accepted practice. There are statutes against lobbying on the part of the federal agencies. But we do try to give the practical realities in our views on pending legislation.

Let me just quickly go to the next question. That is, what do we do in court? We do go into court, and say to the judges that it's impossible for us to comply. We have said that; we've had Court of Appeals judges say that they realize our resource constraints and therefore they are going to give us additional time to do the jobs which Congress demanded but it is very rare for courts, in effect, to rewrite the statute by allowing additional time. It's something judges are very uncomfortable with. But as I have said, we have created a bit of a new law — they have given us relief in a couple of cases. We can't do that very often and we do not want to risk contempt of court. We try to abide by the law. So yes, to the extent that we are really in a bind we go in and plead that it is simply impossible for us to meet the deadline. But we usually try to convince the plaintiff to the lawsuit of that fact, before we get to that position. I don't know if we've answered your question.

Andy McErlean

If I can round that out with just one further point. I'd like to assure you that the EPA and other federal agencies do attempt to obtain funding for long-term research. I think this goes back to the question Dr. Alexander asked earlier.

It's very difficult in a regulatory mode to make a convincing case for long-term research. However, every opportunity we get we try to do this.

Ken Kamlet

As Jim has indicated, EPA often tries to persuade plaintiffs in environmental cases, where deadlines are unrealistic, not to hold the agency too strictly to account for missing the deadlines. I'd like to say from the standpoint of public interest plaintiffs in lawsuits against EPA that our organizations, and the National Wildlife Federation in particular, regard litigation as an extreme last resort. If there is any other way of working out the problem that we see, we will go to any length to obtain a solution in another way. Once we see that the agency is really doing a good faith job in attempting to meet its responsibilities under the statute, I can't imagine that we'd go to court to enforce against the agency the strict letter of the statutory deadline or some other rigid statutory requirement. I can't speak for all other environmental groups or potential plaintiff organizations, but I think the vast majority of them feel the same way. I don't want you to get the impression from what's been said that groups like ours are quick to leap into court the instant a statutory deadline or some other rigid statutory requirement looks as though it's not going to be met.

Andy McErlean

Thank you. Are there other questions from the floor? We are actually overtime by some twenty minutes at this point.

Herb Curl (NOAA)

I'll try to keep this short. I think we can get to one of the root problems. One of the problems seems to be that we have some bad environmental laws. It seems to me that our system of law is based on adversary procedures and therefore we end up with laws that express only one-half of the litigation. Take as an example the laws, statutes, and regulations that are used to combat cancer and at the same time we have some laws and statutes that support the production of cancer-producing substances. Now I wonder if it's feasible, possible, or desirable to attempt to get Congress to pass laws for agencies to produce regulations that address the potential litigants on both sides of a problem. That is, you try to balance off the cost of benefits of any particular action rather than simply producing a law that is for the benefit of either, let's say the environment or industry or something like that.

Andy McErlean

Who on the panel would wish to reply to this? Ken?

Ken Kamlet

I'll just venture one brief response to that and that is, by the nature of the legislative process it is rather rare that all kinds of competing interests do not go hand in hand into the process of enacting just about any statute. I think the problem that you referred to is a very real one but it arises not because competing interests are inadequately represented in the design of a given statute, as much as it is a problem of Congress tending to look at environmental and other problems in a compartmentalized kind of way. Congress is very good at responding to crises and individual cases and it is very seldom able to legislate with a broad overview. It often misses the forest for the trees. In the environmental area, Congress will often pass a Water Pollution Control Act, a Solid Waste Act, a Clean Air Act, regulating medium by medium and failing to recognize that there often, almost universally, are interactions that are very significant from one medium to another and the fact that although we control water pollution and prevent inputs into a fresh body of water, that the end products are going to wind up on land and in the air; there's carry-over and spill-over into other media. I think a large part of the problem that you identify, which is a very real one, is not that competing interests are not adequately represented, but rather that Congress tends to act in a very narrow focus rather than taking action in a broad overview to deal with the full problem, the kind of holistic approach that Gene Odum talks about. It's very difficult to get a legislator to think and legislate in that way.

Andy McErlean

Thank you very much, Ken. I would like to thank everybody for attending this session. I would be particularly interested in your reactions to this type of presentation which has been somewhat experimental for ERF; it's vastly different from the largely technical sessions that we've held in the past. It seems to blend a number of different interests together and I would be grateful to get your reactions to this. I would like, at this time, to thank Ken Kamlet, the general counsel for the National Wildlife Federation, Jim Rogers, the associate counsel for EPA, Dr. Lloyd Falk of the DuPont Company and Dr. Joel Hedgpeth, Professor of Marine Biology — thank you very much.

ESTUARY–MAN INTERACTIONS: IMPACTS OF COASTAL ENGINEERED SYSTEMS

CUMULATIVE EFFECTS OF OIL DRILLING AND PRODUCTION ON ESTUARINE AND NEAR-SHORE ECOSYSTEMS

James M. Sharp

Gulf Universities Research Consortium
16821 Buccaneer Lane, Suite 101
Houston, Texas

and

S. G. Appan

Daniel Analytical Services Corporation
16821 Buccaneer Lane, Suite 202
Houston, Texas

Abstract: The paper describes a two-year eight-season synoptic study to determine whether twenty-five years of intensive oil drilling and production had produced observable environmental or ecological change in Timbalier Bay and the adjacent offshore area in southern Louisiana. The primary approach involved comprehensive comparison of sites which were ecologically comparable and experienced natural variations in habitat conditions and inhabitant communities at essentially the same time and with essentially the same magnitude. Prior data, comparisons with other Gulf of Mexico ecosystem measurements, and accepted scientific causal relationships were also used to support interpretations. Biological, physical, chemical, and geological determinations made singly and in combination showed no evidence of significant ecological change and provided strong evidence of good ecological health.

Introduction

The Offshore Ecology Investigation (OEI) consisted of an integrated set of biological, chemical, geological, and physical field studies. The composite of these investigations was designed to comprise the minimal experimental program which could achieve the single objective of the program: "to determine whether long-term and intensive petroleum drilling and production has resulted in harmful environmental or ecological effects in offshore and adjacent estuarine ecosystems."

The 23-component scientific investigations conducted by competitively selected principal investigators were designed to describe the offshore and adjacent estuarine habitats, the general dynamics of those habitats, and the response of the inhabitant species and communities to either natural or man-induced variations in the habitats. These individual investigations were conducted during eight successive seasonal field studies, which extended from June 1972 through January 1974, with each seasonal cruise covering a period of seven to ten days.

Common measurement and sampling stations were used by the investigators. All investigations were adjusted to local habitat variabilities so that the measurements were synoptic. Thus, care was taken in program design to maximize the validity of temporal, spatial, or functional correlations among the approximately 250 basic descriptors which were used for total program analysis and for the development of a consensus interpretation.

Each investigator reduced and interpreted his own data and submitted his data and findings to a four-man Program Planning Council appointed by the Gulf Universities Research Consortium (GURC) Board of Trustees. Synthesis of the data and results, and the development of the consensus conclusions pertinent to the program objective based on an analysis of these 23 individual findings were carried out by that Council. Total program results were presented in GURC Report No. 138 in June 1974 — a 24-volume document covering all aspects of both the integrated program and its component investigations.

Scope of the OEI

The OEI was directed only to the stated specific objective and, in that regard, only to the acquisition of the minimum data set considered essential to achieving that objective. Because the objective emphasized *cumulative* effects, it was concerned principally with the effects of chronic low-level discharges of petroleum hydrocarbons, heavy metals, and the like, which might be attributed to drilling and production operations. While the program was designed to accommodate "rapid response" studies of major oil spills, no such spill occurred. Thus, the emphasis on the effects of long-term low-level discharges was even more pronounced. Bioaccumulation and possible carcinogenic, mutagenic, or oncogenic effects were not pursued because of the limited time and funds available for the field studies and associated laboratory analyses.

Once the Council had selected the area including Timbalier Bay and the adjacent offshore area for intensive OEI research, the program design was specific to determining cumulative effects in these "Louisiana Oil Patch" ecosystems. Operating within this constraint, the OEI was concerned with the end result of a maximum exposure of the ecosystem over a period of 25 years to low-level drilling and production discharges. That the cumulative impact should have been maximum is evident from the long period of exposure, from much of that exposure having preceded modern environmental control technology and practice, and from the experimental areas including some 400 active drilling and production operations. The idea that any possible ecological impacts should be observable is encouraged by the very large amount and diversity of the biota in the OEI area.

It is clear, then, that the OEI was not intended to provide a complete dynamic and functional description of ecosystem response to habitat variations throughout the 25-year period. Therefore, it was not intended to develop quantitative predictive bioenergetic or ecosystem models.

OEI Program Design Logic

An evaluation of possible cumulative effects of low-level discharges requires experimentation in an area of chronic long-term exposure to such discharges. In addition to the Louisiana Oil Patch, the OEI Council could have considered areas exposed to "natural seeps" of petroleum hydrocarbons. However, such seeps do not include all drilling and production effluents (e.g., heavy metals from paints, or sacrificial anodes). Also, according to determinations of the National Academy of Sciences in 1975 (NAS, 1975), natural seeps, on the average, contribute some 30 times more petroleum hydrocarbons to the world oceans than do normal drilling and production operations; hence they would, in general, not be representative of areas experiencing low-level discharges comparable to those of interest to the OEI. In no area suitable for the OEI studies have comprehensive environmental baselines been established prior to any drilling and production activity. OEI program design strategy, therefore, depended on developing a rationale in which such pertinent historical data as existed would be used, but in which comparisons with comprehensive baselines could not constitute the principal logic of the program plan.

A 1972 workshop involving some 125 university, agency, and industry scientists and petroleum technologists deliberated the questions of (1) OEI feasibility and (2) workable basic program strategy. The workshop, with subsequent refinements made by the Council, evolved the following "logic elements" as the basis for detailed OEI program planning and for subsequent synthesis of results and formulation of the consensus conclusions derived from the OEI:

- 1. *Point Source Discharge (Local Impact) Evaluations.* One aspect of the OEI plan required the investigation of selected individual drilling and production sites as point source discharges. Even without comprehensive baseline data, point source effects would be observable with a high level of confidence by:

  a. Making comparisons of complete physical, chemical, biological, and geological data sets taken synoptically at both (1) active platform sites having experienced maximum low-level cumulative exposure, and (2) "control" sites which have been determined to be ecologically comparable to the selected drilling and production sites, which have experienced no immediate drilling or production activity, and which should experience natural variabilities at essentially the same time as the selected platforms and with similar magnitudes;

  b. Seeking to identify significant gradients in both habitat and inhabitant descriptors in the radial direction from active platform sites; and

  c. Determining concentration levels of petroleum-related chemicals considered to be potentially damaging to the ecosystem.

Such comparisons and gradient determinations — which constitute a "spatial trajectory" investigation of environmental and ecological effects — were one principal method used in the OEI to answer such major questions as:

  □ Are there observable differences in key habitat descriptors and variabilities thereof between the platform and control sites?

  □ Is there evidence of significant point source discharge or accumulation of petroleum-operation-related chemicals having potential impacts on the health of the resident biological species and communities? And do platform-control comparisons indicate adverse cumulative ecological impact in terms of degradation of key biological descriptors which describe ecological health and stability?

● 2. *Dispersed Source Discharge (General Ecosytem Health) Evaluations.* Prolonged exposure to low-level discharges, particularly in an area with distributed multiple point sources, requires that an evaluation be made of the general ecosystem health of the entire experimental area; i.e., to view the problem as one of dispersed sources. Further, the absence of comprehensive pre-drilling baselines requires a suitable substitute for "time trajectory" comparisons. Therefore, in addition to the platform-control comparisons of key ecological descriptors, emphasis was placed on:

  a. Comparisons of OEI ecosystem descriptors with those for similar ecosystems in the Gulf of Mexico and other areas considered to be meaningfully similar as to habitat and inhabitants and as yet unexposed to chronic low-level petroleum discharges;
  b. Wherever pertinent historical data existed, the analysis of changes or trends indicating adverse or beneficial modification of the habitats or the inhabitant species and communities; and
  c. The exercise of independent scientific judgment based on the accumulated knowledge, data, and experience of the investigators.

These three approaches permit a valid comparison of ecosystem health within the OEI experimental area with the "end product" ecologies of similar systems not exposed to continuous low-level discharge from petroleum activities. Thus they provide a meaningful "time trajectory" substitute from which supportable conclusions can be drawn.

The controversial nature of such evaluations, including the use of biomass and of species composition and diversity as principal yardsticks for the measurement of ecological health or stability, is well known (COMS, 1977). However, the insufficiency of current ecosystem analysis, prediction, and modeling capabilities is equally well known (Levin, 1974; Russell, 1975). It is clear that improvements in the means for determining ecological health and stability are badly needed if determinations are to be entirely satisfactory and if impact assessment procedures are to become suitably precise and repeatable. However, in the OEI appraisals completed in 1974, species composition and diversity appeared to be the most useful basis for determinations, and, while the controversy continues and even grows, these still remain widely used indicators of ecological health.

- 3. *System Dynamics.* Scientifically conclusive comparisons as developed under the two preceding "logic elements" require the discrete identification of natural and man-induced differences in habitat and inhabitant descriptors between experimental and control sites. Thus, the third logic element in OEI planning consisted of monitoring natural variabilities in sufficient detail for such identification. Three major approaches were used in this regard:

    a. Synoptic measurements were made at the platform and control sites of key habitat descriptors so that ecosystem dynamics could be related to principal driving forces, such as tides, Mississippi River influences, and major current systems, and so that biological variations could be related to specific natural processes as necessary to separate such variations from the man-induced variations in the ecosystem being sought in the field studies.

    b. A series of four roughly parallel synoptic transects were made which were (1) generally perpendicular to the shoreline, (2) generally upstream from the platform and control sites offshore, and (3) remote from intensive petroleum production activities. These transects assisted in defining principal driving forces and system dynamics and also provided one basis for comparison of the OEI intensive study area of 400 square miles to assist in the appraisals of general ecosystem health.

    c. Since the intensive study area included both Timbalier Bay and the adjacent offshore area, it was important to determine whether exchange processes between the offshore and estuarine areas would result in significant offshore-to-bay ecological impacts. Hence, the program plan included the acquisition of high-density synoptic data along a 25-mile transect connecting the bay and offshore platform sites. Investigations of these data emphasized chemical and biological exchange processes so that at least a crude quantitative determination of this exchange could be made.

Program Rationale

- 1. *Habitat Variabilities.* Two reconnaissance experiments were conducted to obtain a preliminary evaluation of major variabilities in physical and geological conditions in order that the measurement and sampling operations in the first seasonal experiments could be adjusted appropriately to spatial and temporal density. As each of the successive seasonal experiments was conducted, physical and chemical variabilities were determined as repidly as possible — although not comprehensively — in order that further adjustments in measurement density and distribution could be made as considered necessary to maintain synopticity.

● 2. *Analysis of Inhabitant Response.* The set of eleven biological investigations was structured so that major biotic components representing many of the trophic levels were measured quantitatively as to biomass and species diversity. In general, species composition and, to a lesser degree, faunal affinity were used for platform-control comparisons and for comparing OEI area ecological health with similar ecosystems.

Among the species selected (of which a total of 673 are included in the OEI data base), care was taken to include: (1) both long- and short-lived species so that both long- and short-term effects could be observed and studied; (2) sessile, mobile, and planktonic species, in order that evaluations would cover observations of species which were immobile and of species which had varied levels of mobility and thus include a wide range of exposure to petroleum operations effluents and effects; and (3) species and communities which were considered to occupy "high-risk" niches in the ecosystem — such as the interstitial beach communities and the communities of fouling organisms on platform legs — where intensive exposure to petroleum operation effluents was expected.

The rationale for interpreting both species and community responses to natural and petroleum-related variabilities included the evaluation of biotic components in terms of life-times, position in the food web, and the occupation of high-risk niches. With regard to the latter, experiments emphasized metabolism, recruitment, and recolonization rates (in addition to biomass and diversity) of fouling communities on platform legs as being important in the assessment of possible cumulative ecological effects and of general ecosystem health.

Program Overview

Figure 1 shows the experimental area, including the drilling and production platforms used as experiment sites, the two control sites in Timbalier Bay, and the offshore control site. Also shown are the "synoptic transects" along which key descriptors were measured during each seasonal experiment.

Figure 2 shows the categories of inhabitant biotic components, the habitat descriptors, and the petroleum-related sources for which data were obtained during the field studies. The numbers in the functional diagram blocks refer to the principal investigators providing these data as identified on the left side of the figure. The previously mentioned emphasis on high-risk niches in the ecosys-

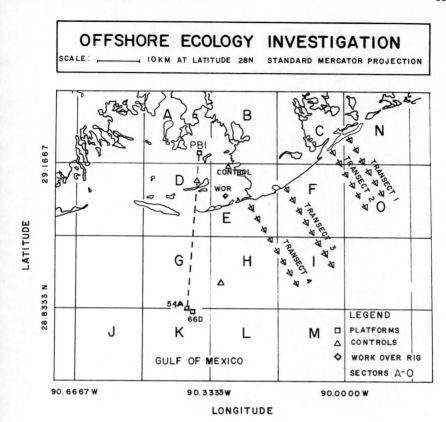

Figure 1. The region of the Offshore Ecology Investigation – the southern Louisiana "Oil Patch."

tem is evident from the numbers of biological investigators concerned with benthic and fouling organisms.

Figure 3 classifies the types of data taken by specific principal investigators and shows whether such data were obtained in Timbalier Bay and/or in the off-shore area, and whether data for drilling, production, and control sites were in-cluded by the specific investigator identified in the left column. Not all investiga-tors worked in both the bay and offshore because some of the vessels used for offshore could not operate in the shallow bay areas. Also, not all measurements were possible at all locations; e.g., a persistent nepheloid (high turbidity) layer detected during the field studies occupied the bottom of the water column off-shore, where it effectively eliminated light penetration to support the growth of benthic flora; hence biomass, diversity, and primary production from such sources could not be made for the control area (whereas their prolific growth on platform legs did permit their measurement at the platform sites).

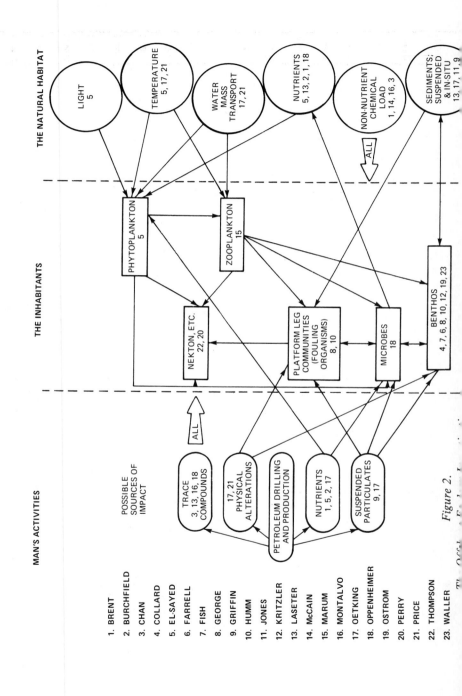

Figure 2.

THE NATURAL HABITAT

THE INHABITANTS

MAN'S ACTIVITIES

POSSIBLE SOURCES OF IMPACT

LIGHT
5

TEMPERATURE
5, 17, 21

WATER MASS TRANSPORT
17, 21

NUTRIENTS
5, 13, 2, 1, 18

NON-NUTRIENT CHEMICAL LOAD
1, 14, 16, 3

SEDIMENTS; SUSPENDED & IN-SITU
13, 17, 11, 9

ALL

PHYTOPLANKTON
5

ZOOPLANKTON
15

NEKTON, ETC.
22, 20

PLATFORM LEG COMMUNITIES (FOULING ORGANISMS)
8, 10

MICROBES
18

BENTHOS
4, 7, 6, 8, 10, 12, 19, 23

ALL

TRACE COMPOUNDS
3, 13, 16, 18

PHYSICAL ALTERATIONS
17, 21

PETROLEUM DRILLING AND PRODUCTION

NUTRIENTS
1, 5, 2, 17

SUSPENDED PARTICULATES
9, 17

1. BRENT
2. BURCHFIELD
3. CHAN
4. COLLARD
5. EL-SAYED
6. FARRELL
7. FISH
8. GEORGE
9. GRIFFIN
10. HUMM
11. JONES
12. KRITZLER
13. LASETER
14. McCAIN
15. MARUM
16. MONTALVO
17. OETKING
18. OPPENHEIMER
19. OSTROM
20. PERRY
21. PRICE
22. THOMPSON
23. WALLER

64

| | MAJOR ASPECT OF INVESTIGATION | | | | | | | LOCATION | | | | | |
| | | | | | | | | BAY | | | OFFSHORE | | |
PRINCIPAL INVESTIGATOR	PHYSICAL OCEANOGRAPHY	UPPER 10 CM SEDIMENTS	CHEMISTRY	BOTTOM ORGANICS	OTHER ORGANICS	BIOLOGY OF COMMUNITIES	REGIONAL STUDIES	CONTROL, UNDISTURBED	DRILLING	PRODUCTION	CONTROL, UNDISTURBED	DRILLING	PRODUCTION
1. BRENT			◆			◆	*	◆	◆	◆	◆	◆	◆
2. BURCHFIELD			◆				*	◆	◆	◆	◆	◆	◆
3. CHAN			◆				1, 2				◆	◆	◆
4. COLLARD					◆		1, 2, 3	◆	◆	◆	◆	◆	◆
5. EL-SAYED			◆		◆	◆	1, 2, 4				◆	◆	◆
6. FARRELL				◆	◆		*	◆	◆	◆	◆	◆	◆
7. FISH				◆	◆	◆	3	◆	◆	◆			
8. GEORGE					◆	◆	*	◆	◆	◆	◆	◆	◆
9. GRIFFIN	◆						*	◆	◆	◆	◆	◆	◆
10. HUMM				◆	◆	◆	1, 2, 3	◆	◆	◆	◆	◆	◆
11. JONES		◆	◆				1, 2, 3	◆	◆	◆	◆	◆	◆
12. KRITZLER				◆		◆	3	◆	◆	◆			
13. LASETER			◆				*	◆	◆	◆	◆	◆	◆
14. McCAIN			◆				*	◆	◆	◆	◆	◆	◆
15. MARUM					◆	◆	1, 2, 3	◆	◆	◆	◆	◆	◆
16. MONTALVO			◆				*	◆	◆	◆	◆	◆	◆
17. OETKING	◆	◆	◆				1, 2, 4				◆	◆	◆
18. OPPENHEIMER			◆		◆	◆	1, 2, 4	◆	◆	◆	◆	◆	◆
19. OSTROM				◆	◆	◆	3	◆	◆	◆			
20. PERRY					◆		*	◆	◆	◆	◆	◆	◆
21. PRICE	◆		◆				3	◆	◆	◆			
22. THOMPSON					◆		1, 2, 4				◆	◆	◆
23. WALLER				◆	◆		*	◆	◆	◆	◆	◆	◆

1: Bay-Offshore Transect; 2: Offshore; 3: Bay; 4: Four Synoptic Transects; *: All

Figure 3. Offshore Ecology Investigation, 1972-1974, Timbalier Bay, Louisiana, and offshore.

Some of the habitat descriptors selected by the OEI Council as being key indicators of habitat properties and processes were:

Stability
  salinity
  temperature
  dissolved oxygen

Nutrients
  ammonia nitrogen
  nitrite + nitrate
    nitrogen
  orthophosphate
  total phosphorus
  total nitrogen

Particulates
  suspended sediments

Oxygen
  biological oxygen
    demand

Heavy Metals
  lead
  zinc

Carbon
  organic carbon
  hydrocarbons

A total of 43 descriptors pertinent to the definition of natural physical properties and processes were measured. However, these 14 key descriptors were the principal indicators of habitat differences considered essential to the interpretation of biological data and the discrimination between biological variations resulting from natural processes and from petroleum drilling or production operations. With 1124 sampling stations being used, and measurements of the key descriptors being taken at an average of five depths for each station during each seasonal cruise, a very large number of displays of data could be generated that would be pertinent to such interpretations.

These three illustrations represent the several hundreds of "data browsing" displays which are now available. Thousands of displays are now easily and inexpensively obtained by the scientists presently engaged in the reexamination of OEI data and in evaluating the original conclusions using computer-assisted methods. Map displays, vertical and horizontal cross sections, X-Y plots, regression plots, and other displays are now being generated by direct English-language query of the OEI data base in this reexamination and reinterpretation exercise.

Summary of Biological Investigations

The set of eleven biological investigations and the identity of the investigators is included in the diagram shown in Figure 2. The following are highly compressed summaries of the appraisals of four of the eleven investigators relative to the OEI logic elements described previously, which are typical of those included in the entire set of eleven investigations:

- 1. *Phytoplankton Standing Crop/Primary Production.* Principal Investigator: Dr. Sayed Z. El-Sayed, Texas A&M University.

  Point source evaluations were made using primary production

determinations, from chlorophyll *a* concentrations, and species composition as the basis for platform-control comparison for the offshore area
only. Conclusion: No significant differences observable between platform and control sites.

General ecological health evaluations were made using comparisons
of OEI data as described above against similar data accumulated over a
twelve-year period for a large number of continental shelf sites in the
Gulf of Mexico.

Dynamics evaluations were made using comparisons of the data
taken for platform-control comparisons corresponding to seasonal and
episodic habitat variations. Conclusion: Natural variations have a much
greater impact on primary production and phytoplankton biomass than
do any of man's activities, including petroleum operations.

- 2. *Benthic Algae and Sea Grass/Primary Productivity*. Principal Investigator: Dr. Harold J. Humm, University of South Florida.

Point source evaluations were made using measurements of distribution, density, and diversity of benthic algae and sea grass, both in the
bay and on platform legs in the offshore field studies, with the former
being used for platform-control comparisons. Conclusions: No observable differences in the bay; benthic flora occur in the offshore ecosystem only on platform legs, so that comparisons are not applicable.

General ecological health evaluations were made, using comparisons
of benthic algae in the OEI intensive study area (bay and platform leg
communities) with similar data taken in Mississippi Sound, Chandeleur
Island, and inshore waters in Louisiana which were remote from petroleum operations. Conclusion: The same sets of algae species were found
in OEI as in the areas used for comparison; hence, diversity and therefore ecological health are comparable.

Independent scientific judgment was made, based on the flourishing sea grass community in Timbalier Bay (unexpected in such turbid
waters) and based on the flourishing platform leg communities and their
rapid rate of recolonization. Conclusions: General ecological health is
very good.

- 3. *Zooplankton/Secondary Productivity*. Principal Investigator: Dr. James
Marum, Florida State University.

Point source evaluations were made using copepod population
density, species diversity, and faunal affinity for platform-control comparisons. Conclusion: No significant differences between those determinations at the platform and control sites.

General ecological health evaluations were made, using (1) historical data taken in 1952, (2) comparisons with data from Chandeleur Island
and offshore Texas, and (3) independent scientific judgment in terms
of general comparisons with copepod species compositions as observed in

coastal waters of the northern Gulf of Mexico. Conclusions as regards (1), (2), and (3) respectively: No changes in species composition in the OEI area since 1952; high faunal affinity between OEI copepod community and those in Chandeleur Island and offshore Texas; and species composition in OEI is typical of those in other northern Gulf coastal waters.

Dynamics evaluations were made using platform-control comparison and offshore-to-bay transect data. Conclusion: The 1973 Mississippi River flood imposed much greater variation on copepod distribution, diversity, and composition than any other natural event. Faunal exchange between offshore and bay very limited due to shallow sill, low tidal amplitude, and barrier island; hence, offshore-to-onshore impacts should be insignificant.

● 4. *Benthic Polychaetes.* Principal Investigator: Professor Henry Kritzler, Florida State University.

Point source evaluations were made using polychaete species composition, species diversity, and biomass determinations. Conclusions: No significant differences in these determinations as made at platform and control sites.

General ecological health evaluations were made using comparisons with similar data from southern California and scientific judgment pertaining to the occurrence of indicator species. Conclusions: The genera found in the OEI are typical of healthy unpolluted fine sediment bottoms; there is no evidence of a "species wipe-out" nor opportunistic "species takeover" frequently observed in pollution-impacted coastal ecosystems.

The other seven biological investigations followed the basic program logic as indicated in the four examples cited. The results of the eleven investigations are presented in Figure 4. Figure 4 indicates the inclusion in the OEI of many important species at a number of trophic levels. The absence of significant differences between platform and control sites and the absence of any evidence of ecological damage or poor ecological health shows general agreement about conclusions among the investigators, based on their individual data and interpretations.

Information Synthesis and
Development of Consensus Conclusions

The synthesis of total program results involves more than the tabulation of individual findings against the logic elements. Additionally, it requires interdisciplinary comparisons among the habitat and inhabitant descriptors, the appraisal of the basic natural processes operating to control ecosystem dynamics: and thus the variability of habitat data; the summation of evidence relating to the 23 individual findings; and the weighting of the findings according to the program rationale. Figure 5 provides an indication of the complexity and magnitude of the synthesis effort for the OEI.

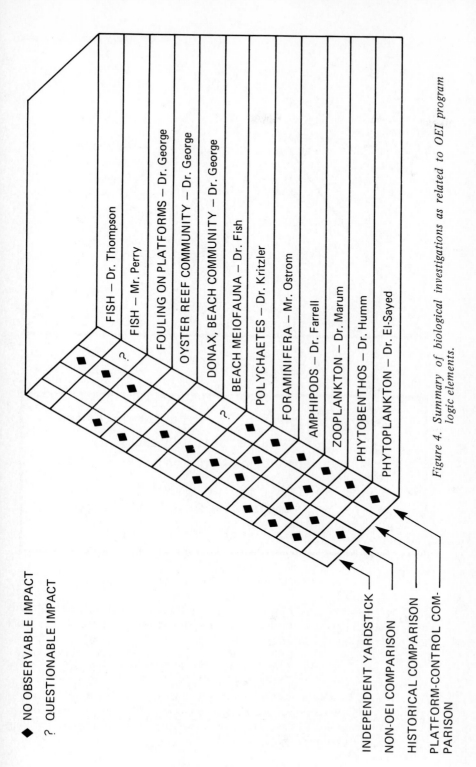

Figure 4. Summary of biological investigations as related to OEI program logic elements.

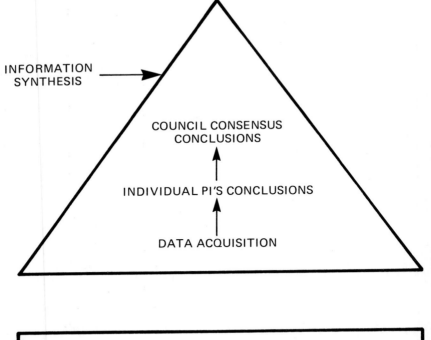

INFORMATION
SYNTHESIS

COUNCIL CONSENSUS
CONCLUSIONS

INDIVIDUAL PI'S CONCLUSIONS

DATA ACQUISITION

23 INVESTIGATORS   31 RELATIONAL FILES
250 ENVIRONMENTAL VARIABLES
HALF MILLION PIECES OF DATA
2 YEARS   8 SEASONS
400 SQUARE MILES
1124 STATIONS

Figure 5. Multidisciplinary Consensus Synthesis.

The consensus conclusions, as drawn by the OEI Council performing this synthesis and the subsequent interpretation of the totality of data and individual findings comprising the OEI were:

1. Timbalier Bay has not undergone significant ecological change as a result of petroleum drilling and production.
2. Every indication of good ecological health is present.
3. Natural phenomena such as floods and turbid layers have much greater impact upon the ecosystem than do petroleum drilling and production activities.

4. Concentrations of all compounds which are in any way related to drilling and production are sufficiently low to present no known persistent biological hazards.

This consensus of the OEI Council as to the interpretation of the total data and results combines the biological summary of Figure 4 with the results of physical, chemical, and geological studies and applies "weighting" factors based on the program rationale. As indicated in Figure 6, this aspect of program synthesis requires the appraisal of these results as they would apply at the several trophic levels; taking into account the probably greater importance of determinations involving organisms experiencing maximum exposure or occupying high-

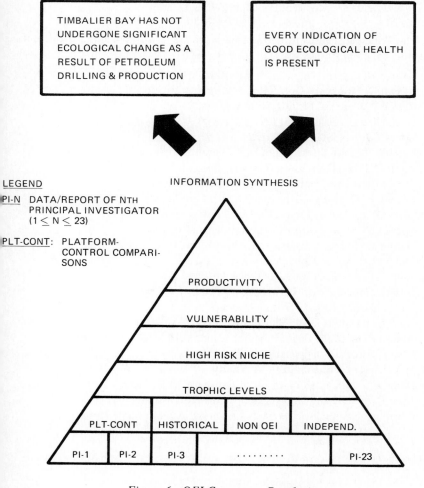

Figure 6. OEI Consensus Conclusions.

risk niches in the ecosystem; the appraisal of vulnerability of species on the basis of resistance, resiliency, and adaptability as well as exposure; and overall productivity of the food web as indicated by the investigations at the various trophic levels.

Acknowledgments

The OEI was planned, directed, and the results and conclusions developed by the OEI Council, consisting of:

James P. Morgan, Louisiana State University, Council Chairman
Robert J. Menzies, Florida State University, Chief Scientist (deceased)
Carl H. Oppenheimer, University of Texas at Austin
Sayed Z. El-Sayed, Texas A&M University

The Principal Investigators who conducted the 23 component investigations comprising the field studies were:

George M. Griffin, University of Florida
Joseph G. Montalvo, Gulf South Research Institute
Robert J. Menzies, Florida State University
Henry Kritzler, Florida State University
James I. Jones, State of Florida
Harry P. Burchfield, Gulf South Research Institute
Keith C. Price, Gulf South Research Institute
A. Geoffrey Fish, University of Southern Mississippi
Robert Y. George, University of North Carolina
Sayed Z. El-Sayed, Texas A&M University
Charles R. Brent, University of Southern Mississippi
Harold J. Humm, University of South Florida
Philip Oetking, Southwest Research Institute
John L. Laseter, University of New Orleans
Carl H. Oppenheimer, University of Texas at Austin
James Marum, Florida State University
Douglas Farrell, Florida State University
Allison Perry, Gulf Coast Research Laboratory
Sneed B. Collard, University of West Florida
Jeff Hanor, Louisiana State University
Douglas C. McCain, University of Southern Mississippi
John R. Thompson, University of Southern Mississippi
Enrique F. Mandelli, Universidad Nacional Autónoma de Mexico

References

1. Center for Ocean Management Studies. 1977. Ocean research in the 1980's.
    Recommendations from a series of workshops or promising opportunities in

large-scale oceanographic research. Prepared for National Science Foundation. COMS, University of Rhode Island, Kingston, R.I.

2. Levin, S. A., ed. 1974. Ecosystem analysis and prediction. Proceedings, Conference on ecosystems, Alta, Utah. Sponsored by SIAM-SIMS and supported by National Science Foundation. 337 pp.

3. National Academy of Sciences. 1975. Petroleum in the marine environment. Proceedings, Workshop on inputs, fates, and the effects of petroleum in the marine environment, May 21-25, 1973, Airlie House, Airlie, Virginia.

4. Russell, C. S., ed. 1975. Ecological modeling in a resource management framework. Proceedings, Symposium sponsored by National Oceanic and Atmospheric Administration and Resources for the Future, Inc., Washington, D.C. 394 pp.

AN EVALUATION OF ONGOING CHANGE
AFFECTING ENVIRONMENTAL GEOLOGIC MAPPING
IN THE TEXAS COASTAL ZONE

Robert J. Finley

Bureau of Economic Geology
The University of Texas at Austin
Austin, Texas

Abstract: Although the Texas Coastal Zone, an area of some 51,800 sq km, includes 6 percent of the total area of the state, approximately 34 percent of the state's economic resources are found adjacent to the Gulf of Mexico shoreline. This distribution of resources results, in part, from the abundance of hydrocarbon reserves, ground-water supplies, transportation facilities, fish and wildlife resources, and recreational opportunities in a region which includes 5,439 sq km of bays and estuaries.

Industrial growth, residential development, agriculture, and other activities continue to increase, and to change the area. In order to evaluate these changes, basic mapping and periodic assessments of the map data are required.

The Environmental Geologic Atlas of the Texas Coastal Zone, prepared by the Bureau of Economic Geology, includes environmental geologic maps dependent upon revised U. S. Geological Survey topographic maps, and upon black-and-white photographic mosaics dating from 1956-1959. These environmental geologic maps provide information on substrate materials, geologic processes, botanical zones, and man-made units.

Comparison of the gulfward half of each map with 1975 color-infrared aerial photography located 1,105 changes. Nearly one-half of these alterations involved channel dredging and spoil disposal, while other man-induced and natural alterations of coastal ponds and marshlands accounted for 25 percent of the changes. Such results suggest that thorough, detailed mapping, even when based on older photography, provides a viable, open-ended document which can then be supplemented by an evaluation of ongoing change.

Introduction

The Texas Coastal Zone, as defined for a major mapping project at the Bureau of Economic Geology, covers an area of approximately 51,800 km^2 along 591 km of Gulf coastline, and is subdivided into seven map areas (Figure 1). Some 5,440 km^2 of brackish to hypersaline bays and estuaries are included within this region. While containing only 6 percent of the total area of the state, about

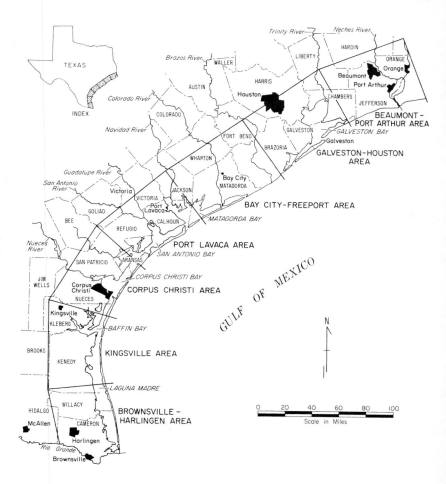

Figure 1. Index of the Environmental Geologic Atlas of the Texas Coastal Zone (from Fisher et al., 1972).

one-third of the state's population and one-third of its economic resources are found within the Texas Coastal Zone (Fisher *et al.,* 1972). Population growth along the Texas coast will continue and even accelerate above present trends. An increase of 24.8 percent occurred between 1960 and 1970 (Texas Coastal and Marine Council, 1977), and in 1972 total population within a 29-county coastal area was over 3.5 million (Texas General Land Office, 1975). By 1980, 4.1 million persons will reside in this region, with 80 percent of the increase expected in the Houston-Galveston area. Between 1970 and 1980 even the slowest-growing sections of the Texas coast are expected to experience population increases of at least 12 percent (Texas General Land Office, 1975).

The economic growth of the Texas Coastal Zone is stimulated by a great abundance and variety of natural resources. Oil, gas, and sulfur reserves, groundwater supplies, fish and wildlife resources, and recreational opportunities are found close to the major population centers, which enjoy good transportation facilities and a mild climate. Petroleum production and related activities alone are worth nearly $13 billion to the state's economy. The Texas coastal region contains over 25 percent of the nation's refining capacity, and 40 percent of the nation's petrochemical industry, much of which is located in the Houston-Galveston area (Texas General Land Office, 1975).

Economic development and coastal recreation bring both more tourists and more permanent residents to the Texas Coastal Zone each year. Development of barrier islands for permanent and seasonal residence also is increasing, as is the consideration of wetlands for industrial, residential, and dredged-material disposal sites. In order to evaluate both the rate and the direction of environmental change in man-modified areas as well as unmodified ecosystems, periodic mapping is a fundamental requirement (McGowen *et al.*, 1976). Such mapping must display coastal resource data in a meaningful way to help in the planning and management processes. The Environmental Geologic Atlas of the Texas Coastal Zone, a product representing over 30 man-years of research and analysis, serves both as a basic inventory of the coastal physical environment, and as a baseline against which to measure ongoing change.

Environmental Geologic Mapping

The Environmental Geologic Atlas of the Texas Coastal Zone (Brown, coordinator, in progress) includes seven folios (Figure 1), each consisting of a descriptive text, an environmental geologic map, and eight special-use maps (Figure 2). The Coastal Zone covered by each map extends from the inner continental shelf to about 64 km inland, and includes all estuaries, tidally-influenced streams, and adjacent wetlands. The environmental geologic units are based upon the physical, geological, and biological characteristics that define both the natural systems and the man-made components of the Texas coastal environment. The total of all natural characteristics of each land and water unit is therefore expressed as an environmental geologic map unit (Figure 3). Map units are flexible, and they are readily modified to account for variations in the coastal ecosystems between the humid northern section and the semi-arid southern section of Texas.

Aerial photos, in the form of both 1956-1959, 7.5-minute Edgar Tobin Aerial Surveys photomosaics, and U. S. Geological Survey topographic maps, were the basic materials from which the map units were delineated. Other primary data sources, in both map and text format, are shown in Figure 2. Field checking on the ground and from an aircraft at low altitude was carried out throughout the area, and approximately 150 specific environmental geologic units were recognized and mapped in the Texas Coastal Zone (Table 1). These units are grouped into natural associations, such as fluvial-deltaic, barrier-strandplain, and bay-estuary-lagoon systems (Figure 4), and include processes and environments which are

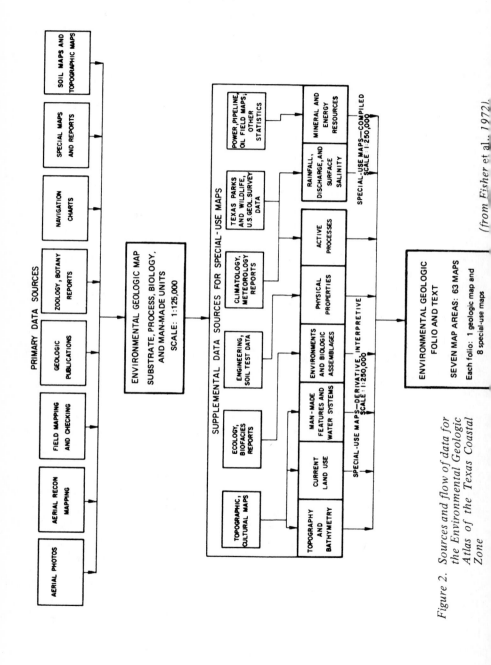

Figure 2. Sources and flow of data for the Environmental Geologic Atlas of the Texas Coastal Zone

(from Fisher et al., 1972).

78

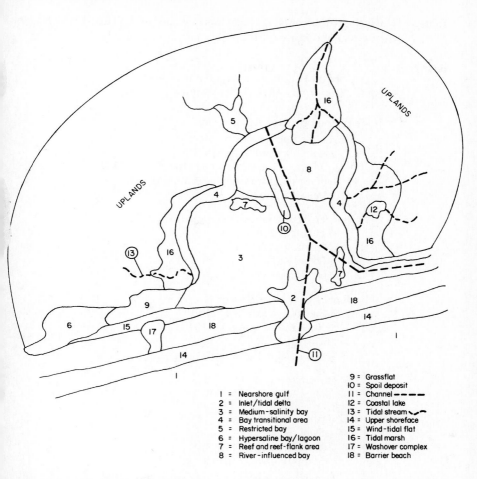

1 = Nearshore gulf	9 = Grassflat
2 = Inlet/tidal delta	10 = Spoil deposit
3 = Medium-salinity bay	11 = Channel – – –
4 = Bay transitional area	12 = Coastal lake
5 = Restricted bay	13 = Tidal stream ⌣⌢
6 = Hypersaline bay/lagoon	14 = Upper shoreface
7 = Reef and reef-flank area	15 = Wind-tidal flat
8 = River-influenced bay	16 = Tidal marsh
	17 = Washover complex
	18 = Barrier beach

Figure 3. Composite resource areas of coastal waters and shorelands (after Woodruff, in Texas General Land Office, 1976).

interrelated in both origin and distribution (Brown *et al.*, 1976). Man-made units relating to dredged material are grouped separately within the map explanation; navigation channels, jetties and groins, holding tanks, and cooling ponds were updated on a newly-compiled map base at the time when each of the Atlas folios was published. An individual environmental geology map, such as the Corpus Christi Sheet, contains 76 units designated by color and pattern on a 1:125,000-scale map base; photomosaics at 1:24,000 scale, on which the original photointerpretations were made, remain on open file at the Bureau of Economic Geology.

Specific Urban Impacts

St. Clair *et al.* (1975) expanded the concept of a resource capability unit

Table 1. Principal environmental geologic units mapped in the Texas Coastal Zone (from Groat and Brown, 1972).

Basic Environmental Geology Maps
(1:125,000 scale)

Modern-Holocene Age features
Fluvial-deltaic systems
Active stream units (14)*
Inactive, non-entrenched stream units (12)
Inactive, entrenched stream units (3)
Deltaic units (3)

Barrier-strandplain-chenier and shelf systems
Tidal delta units (9)
Storm units (5)
Other units (19)
Offshore units (2)

Bay-estuary-lagoon systems
Subaqueous units (12)
Reef and related units (5)
Tidal flat units (7)
Subaerial marginal units (5)

Marsh-swamp systems
Mapped units (7)

Eolian system
Dune field (2)
Base-leveled plain (3)
Stability characteristics (2)
Other units (3)

Pleistocene Age features
Fluvial-deltaic systems
Fluvial units (10)
Deltaic units (12)

Barrier-strandplain-chenier systems
Mapped units (7)

Man-made and other features
Mapped units (10)

*Number of specific features depicted on maps.

(from Brown *et al.*, 1971) to designate land- and water-resource units as "mappable entities, either natural or man-made, that are defined by the physical, chemical and biological characteristics or processes which govern the type or degree of use that is consistent with both their natural quality and productive utilization." In comparing these units to resource-related activities in the Texas Coastal Zone, Brown *et al.* (1971, 1976) developed a concise list of major activities, as shown in Table 2. Many of these activities are associated with urban development.

The basic environmental geologic units used during mapping for the Coastal Atlas were grouped into 34 major land- and water-capability units. The correlation of unit capabilities with twenty of man's activities in the Texas Coastal Zone (Table 2) suggests environmental guidelines which, while not dictating strict preservation, will indicate the degree of suitability between sections of the coastal environment and man's use of resources. A schematic distribution of land- and water-resource-capability units in the Corpus Christi area (Figure 5) illustrates how these components are distributed among the coastal environmental systems depicted by the environmental geologic mapping.

Many of the activities listed in Table 2 are readily assessed by analysis of the detailed data contained in the environmental geology maps. These include the most common coastal activities of excavating, filling, and channel dredging, as well as structural modifications including building jetties and seawalls. Land use, man-made features such as pipelines and disposal sites, active processes such as erosion and storm surge inundation, mineral and energy resources, physical properties including engineering characteristics, biologic assemblages, and stream discharge and salinity data are shown on the special-use derivative maps which accompany each environmental geology sheet. Urban impacts such as siting of additional sewage disposal plants, erosion due to new updrift shoreline structures, and increased residential development of barrier islands can be evaluated, using Coastal Atlas mapping as a comprehensive baseline.

Some of man's activities in the Texas Coastal Zone require data extraction and map display aimed at topics even more specific than those contained in the special-use maps. One of these topics involves the assessment of coastal natural hazards.

Coastal hazards

While man's activities may alter the natural coastal environment, there are a number of natural processes operating in coastal regions which can also radically affect man's intended resource use. These factors can be termed coastal hazards, and they result from the naturally dynamic and continually evolving nature of

Table 2. (overleaf) Coastal Zone land and water resource units: use and capability. Evaluations are based on natural capability which can be improved by special planning and construction methods. Definition of land- and water-resource units, including limiting use factors and undesirable uses, are discussed in Brown et al. *(1971) (from Brown* et al., *1976).*

Table 2

LAND AND WATER RESOURCE UNITS	LIQUID-WASTE DISPOSAL			SOLID-WASTE DISPOSAL	SHORELINE CONSTRUCTION		COASTAL AND INLAND CONSTRUCTION				COASTAL, INLAND, AND OFFSHORE CONSTRUCTION									
ACTIVITIES	Surface disposal of untreated liquid wastes	Shallow subsurface disposal of untreated liquid wastes	Maintenance of feed lots	Disposal of solid-waste materials	Construction of jetties, groins, and piers	Construction of storm barriers and/or seawalls	Light construction	Construction of highways (excluding causeways)	Heavy construction	Flooding as a result of dam construction	Construction of production platforms and other oil well development activities	Placement of pipelines and/or subsurface cables	Dredging of canals and channels, and spoil disposal	Excavation, including extraction of natural materials	Filling for development	Draining of wetlands	Devegetation	Traversing with vehicles, including marsh buggies, air boats, dune buggies, and motorcycles	Light recreational activities, including hiking, nature trails, and pleasure boating	Use of herbicides, pesticides, insecticides
WATER RESOURCE UNITS — BAYS, ESTUARIES, AND LAGOONS																				
River-influenced bay, including prodelta and delta front	×	×		×	o	×					o	o	×		×					
Enclosed bay	×	×		×	o	×					o	o	o	×	o					
Living oyster reefs and related areas	×	×		×	×	×					×	×	×	o	×					
Dead oyster and serpulid reefs and related areas	×	×		×	o	×					o	o	×		×					
Grassflats	×	×		×	×	×					×	×	×	×	×					
Mobil bay-margin sand	×	×		×	×	×					×	×	×		×		×	×		
Open bay, lower end with tidal influence	×	×		×	o	×					o	o	×		×					
Subaqueous spoil	×	×		×	o	o					o	o	o		o					
Inlets and subaqueous tidal deltas	×	×		×	×	×					×	×	×		×					
Tidal flats	×	×		×	o	o	×	×	×		o	o	o	×	×					

82

LAND RESOURCE UNITS

Category	Land resource unit
COASTAL WETLANDS	Salt-water marsh
	Fresh-water marsh
	Swamps
COASTAL BARRIERS	Beach and shoreface
	Fore-island dunes and vegetated barrier flat
	Washover areas
	Blowouts and back-island dune fields
	Wind-tidal flats
	Swales
MAN-MADE	Made land and spoil
COASTAL PLAINS	Highly permeable sand
	Moderately permeable sand
	Impermeable mud
	Broad, shallow depressions with variable substrate
	Highly forested upland areas
	Steep lands, locally high relief
	Stabilized dunes
	Unstabilized, unvegetated dunes
	Fresh-water lakes, ponds, and sloughs, and playas containing fresh water
	Mainland beaches
MAJOR FLOOD-PLAIN SYSTEMS	Areas of active faulting and subsidence
	Point-bar sand
	Overbank mud and silt
	Water

Legend

- ▨ (hatched) — Not applicable
- X — Undesirable—significant problems likely
- O — Possible problems
- ☐ (blank) — Significant problems unlikely
- + — Significant problems unlikely on vegetated barrier flat. Construction and recreation activities on fore-island dunes are undesirable.

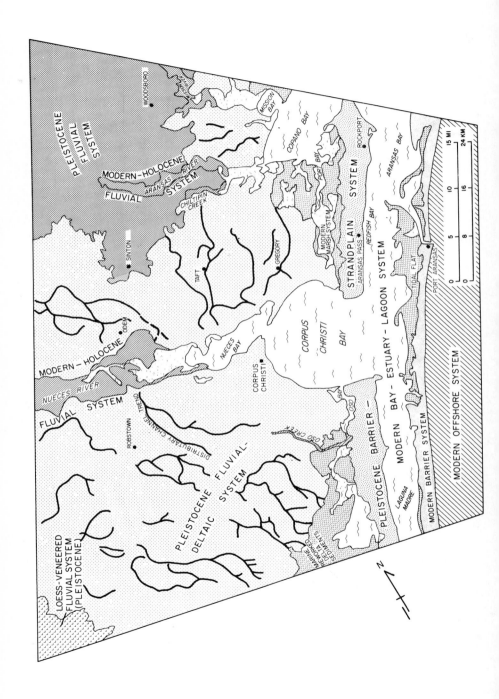

84

the coastal region. Population increases and urban development can bring severe imbalance to coastal ecosystems, as in the often-cited example of a marsh filled to create residential housing. Marshes, however, are in equilibrium with hurricane impact and have some natural capacity for self-rejuvenation; residential developments do not have this capacity. The impacts of short-term events such as hurricanes and flooding are quite dramatic and obvious. Long-term processes, such as erosion, land subsidence due to ground-water withdrawal, and surface faulting may be more difficult to recognize, but they are equally deleterious. Careful monitoring and historical studies, within the framework of thorough environmental geologic mapping, are required to document the occurrence and rate of these slower processes. Often the full potential effect is not evident until storm conditions and flooding occur, and for this reason historically documented map information must be used to appreciate, for example, the extent of 8,195 sq km of salt-water flooding caused by Hurricanes *Carla* (1961) and *Beulah* (1967).

Specific human activities can directly increase the effects of urban development in the coastal zone, with or without the longer impact cycle linked through ecological feedback (Clark, 1974), such as results from the destruction of wetland habitat. For example, the increase in human population on storm-vulnerable barrier islands also increases the risk to those who must evacuate the area using a limited number of access points. Major structures have been built in known washover channels. The cutting of boat channels from the bay sides of barrier islands, and the digging of borrow pits near the beachline increase the risk of disabling transportation routes by rising storm-surge waters. These man-made alterations of the coastal environment have a major potential impact on human life and property.

Significantly, much of the coastal population has never experienced a hurricane. The last major hurricane to strike the middle and upper Texas coast was *Carla*, in 1961, and since that time hundreds of thousands of new residents have entered the area. Since many of these people are unaware of the natural hazards of the coastal zone, efforts are underway to make hazard information generally available (Texas Coastal and Marine Council, 1977). Much of this effort at information dissemination, however, is dependent upon an understanding by the public of coastal process mechanisms and of the distribution of resource capability units acquired in the course of environmental geologic mapping.

Evaluation of Ongoing Change

When mapping for the Coastal Atlas project began in 1969, 1:24,000 scale photomosaics dating from 1955 through 1959 provided the only uniform cover-

Figure 4. (opposite) Natural systems defined by environmental mapping in the Corpus Christi area. These systems are composed of genetically related environments, sedimentary substrates, biologic assemblages, areas of significant physical processes, and man-made features. Simplified from the Environmental Geology Map *of the Atlas (from Brown et al., 1976).*

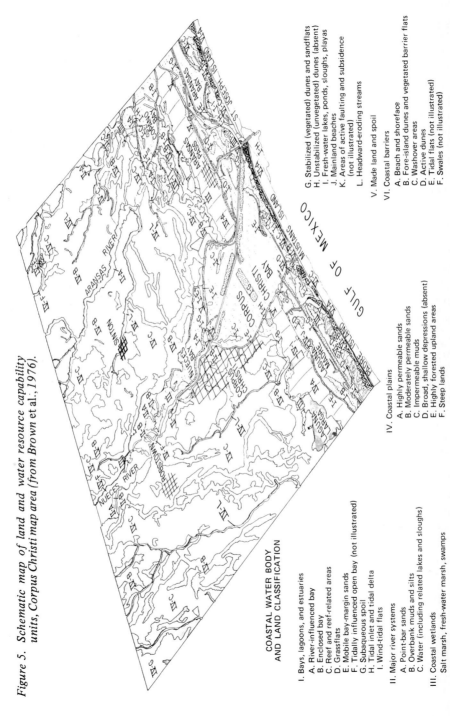

Figure 5. *Schematic map of land and water resource capability
units, Corpus Christi map area (from Brown et al., 1976).*

COASTAL WATER BODY
AND LAND CLASSIFICATION

I. Bays, lagoons, and estuaries

  A. River-influenced bay
  B. Enclosed bay
  C. Reef and reef-related areas
  D. Grassflats
  E. Mobile bay-margin sands
  F. Tidally influenced open bay (not illustrated)
  G. Subaqueous spoil
  H. Tidal inlet and tidal delta
  I. Wind-tidal flats

II. Major river systems

  A. Point-bar sands
  B. Overbank muds and silts
  C. Water (including related lakes and sloughs)

III. Coastal wetlands

  Salt marsh, fresh-water marsh, swamps

IV. Coastal plains

  A. Highly permeable sands
  B. Moderately permeable sands
  C. Impermeable muds
  D. Broad, shallow depressions (absent)
  E. Highly forested upland areas
  F. Steep lands

  G. Stabilized (vegetated) dunes and sandflats
  H. Unstabilized (unvegetated) dunes (absent)
  I. Fresh-water lakes, ponds, sloughs, playas
  J. Mainland beaches
  K. Areas of active faulting and subsidence
    (not illustrated)
  L. Headward-eroding streams

V. Made land and spoil

VI. Coastal barriers

  A. Beach and shoreface
  B. Fore-island dunes and vegetated barrier flats
  C. Washover areas
  D. Active dunes
  E. Tidal flats (not illustrated)
  F. Swales (not illustrated)

age of the entire area included in the seven atlas folios (Brown *et al.*, 1976). The environmental geologic mapping was assembled on a new 1:125,000 map base compiled from 7.5-minute U.S. Geological Survey quadrangle maps, on which updated cultural features and all paved roads were included. Whether or not the use of photomosaics now some twenty years old detracts significantly from the overall quality of the Environmental Geologic Atlas of the Texas Coastal Zone is a question which has been asked by potential users of the atlas data. An evaluation of the mapping should provide both an assessment of the ability of the Coastal Atlas to provide resource data for present needs, and some measure of man's impact in the coastal region.

The updating procedure

A recently compiled analysis of Landsat imagery of the Texas coastal region (Finley, 1976) used environmental geologic mapping as an aid in the interpretation of Landsat data. To insure that the atlas maps reflected current conditions, a part of each folio was compared with aerial photographs taken in February 1975. The photographs, in both color and color infrared, were flown by the National Aeronautics and Space Administration (Mission 300, 1:120,000 scale) to assist in the development of Landsat as a tool for the monitoring of Texas coastal resources. The area covered by the photography corresponds to approximately the seaward half of each environmental geology sheet, a coast-parallel strip some 32 to 40 km wide.

Changes in map units were compiled from these photographs on an overlay with line boundaries derived from the same negatives as the original map (Figure 6). A change labeled "addition" refers either to boundary expansion of an existing area, or to delineation and classification of a new area, all of whose boundaries are new. "Deletion" refers to areal contraction of an existing classified area. The sense of direction of most changes was considered as addition. For example, the emplacement of new dredge spoil was noted as dredge spoil addition, rather than as deletion of the bay bottom environment.

The revised overlays are intended for use with the color prints of the environmental geology maps from the Environmental Geologic Atlas of the Texas Coastal Zone (Brown, coordinator, in progress). A complete set of overlays will be available at the Bureau of Economic Geology in an open-file format for use by state agencies and interested individuals. By proper registration of the map and the overlay, the full extent of the originally mapped category and corresponding explanation, and the additions or deletions derived from the more recent photography, can be compared.

Alteration of coastal environments

A coastal region is highly dynamic, and it undergoes continous modification by daily processes of erosion and accretion, by passage of storms, by natural biologic processes, and by the presence of man. Most changes detected using the 1975 color-infrared photographs were expected revisions relating to man's indus-

*Figure 6.   An example of the overlay updating part of the Environmental Geology
Map, Corpus Christi Map area. The categories indicated are: 24 − wind-
tidal flat; 46 − stabilized blowout dune complex; 50 − washover distal
fan; 51 − fore-island blowout dunes; 63 − bay and lagoon mud; 73 −
subaerial spoil; 74 − subaerial reworked spoil; 75 − subaqueous spoil;
78 − dredged channel.*

trial, commercial, and residential activity. Operation of natural geologic and biologic processes characteristic of the coastal region, including wind, tidal and longshore currents, and colonization of new substrate by marsh vegetation, were also
evident. Table 3 specifically lists the most frequent types of changes that occur.

     The detected changes in no way detract from the Environmental Geologic
Atlas as a thorough coastwide analysis of natural resources and the total coastal
environment. The Atlas is intended to be open-ended and subject to updating
(Brown *et al.*, 1976), while serving as a prime historical reference from which

Table 3. Types of ongoing changes in the Texas Coastal Zone.

- *Dredging of navigation channels*
- *Spoil disposal in heaps or in creation of made land*
- *Boundary changes and drying up of lakes and ponds*
- *Creation of reservoirs for agriculture or industry*
- *Marsh succession over filled ponds*
- *Marsh destruction due to housing development*
- *Marsh-plant colonization of new substrate (washovers)*
- *Reworking of subaerial spoil*
- *Subaqueous spoil deposition*
- *Shoreline erosion and accretion, especially at tidal inlets and river mouths*
- *Changes in inlet flood- and ebb-tidal deltas*
- *Washover fan and channel development*
- *Grassflat, mudflat, and tidal flat alteration*
- *Sand-dune migration and wind deflation*
- *Alteration of barrier flats, fore-island and back-island dunes, and beach ridges*
- *Configuration changes of tidal channels and ephemeral streams*

rates and directions of change can be delineated. Man's impact, for example, on the areal extent of marsh vegetation could be easily evaluated in detail by checking changes in all four marsh units over the entire area of each environmental geology sheet.

Coastal changes delineated

Among the 1,105 changes detected within the area (Table 4) covered by the February 1975 photography, 43.6 percent were related to channel dredging and spoil disposal. This figure reflects the need for navigation channels across the shallow Texas bays and estuaries. Many of these channels are dredged to allow barge-mounted drilling rigs to reach a desired site, are of limited width and depth, and often are not maintained after initial use. Spoil deposited during these one-time operations is reworked by natural processes and becomes less evident with time. Along major ship channels, however, maintenance dredging and channel improvements generate material in large quantities, and disposal of this material can be monitored using Landsat imagery. The amount of dredged material and attendant requirements for disposal sites could increase greatly in areas where onshore terminals for deep draft vessels are under consideration. Increased residential development which includes the dredging of small boat channels also was noted. This type of environmental alteration is of particular concern on the Texas coast, where the low range of astronomical tide may lead to inadequate water circulation in these channels.

Table 4. Ten leading categories of change for all environmental geology maps within the Environmental Geologic Atlas of the Texas Coastal Zone. Units shown are the new categories at each location.

Category	Number of Changes[1]	Percent of Total
1. Spoil, subaerial	294	26.6
2. Lakes and ponds[2]	237	21.4
3. Dredged channel[2]	114	10.3
4. Spoil, subaqueous	51	4.6
5. Active blowout dune	48	4.3
6. Bay-margin sand, sandy mud	35	3.2
7. Active dune complex	32	2.9
8. Marsh, saline	28	2.5
9. Made land (spoil)	28	2.5
10. Bay mud and silt	26	2.4
Wind-tidal flat	26	2.4
Marsh, fresh to brackish	26	2.4
	945	85.2

[1] An additional 26 categories accounted for another 160 changes, amounting to the remaining 14.8 percent of the 1,105 environmental alterations which were detected.

[2] These units appear on the environmental geology sheets as part of the map base, rather than as environmental geologic units listed within the map explanation.

The man-induced and natural alteration of ponds and lakes on the Texas coastal region is an ongoing process which has minimal impact on a region-wide inventory such as the Coastal Atlas. While these changes are mappable at a 1: 125,000 scale, they relate to expected ranching, farming, and industrial activities, and to natural sedimentation and vegetation growth. The extent of man-induced alteration of coastal ponds may increase near urban centers, but it is likely to remain static where agricultural activities have reached a level, fully developed state.

The coastal marsh units were delineated by four categories on the environmental geology maps: salt-water marsh, brackish closed marsh (drainage courses limited), fresh- to brackish-marsh, and freshwater marsh. A summation of changes among these categories for all seven map folios indicates 59 deletions of marsh and 30 additions, suggesting that change does not necessarily mean loss of wetland habitat. In fact, in the Port Lavaca area (Figure 1), additions outnumbered deletions by fourteen to one as a result of grass colonization on overwash deposits of Matagorda Peninsula. Typically, however, marsh habitat is being lost to the creation of made land, especially along the more densely populated northeast Texas coast. A more precise evaluation of wetland loss awaits analysis of the area involved in each change.

Conclusions

1. Detailed environmental geologic mapping provides a baseline against which coastal environmental changes can be measured.

2. Ongoing alterations of the Texas Coastal Zone are related to expected natural processes, and to man's economic development of the region.

3. Of over 1,000 changes detected within an area covered by February 1975 aerial photography, nearly half were related to channel dredging, spoil disposal, reworking of existing spoil, and the creation of made land for economic development.

4. The environmental changes which have taken place since the Edgar Tobin Aerial Surveys photomosaics were made in 1955-1959 do not detract from the Environmental Geologic Atlas of the Texas Coastal Zone as a thorough, detailed, but open-ended compilation of resource information. The total area affected by the changes averages only 0.9 percent of the map area examined, that is, only 278 km^2 of a 30,614 km^2 area.

Acknowledgments

These results were obtained in the course of an analysis of Landsat imagery funded by the Texas General Land Office through Contract NAS5-20986 with the National Aeronautics and Space Administration. Peggy Harwood was Landsat project coordinator at the General Land Office, and Robert Baumgardner, Jr., and Sam Shannon served as project research assistants. The text was reviewed by W. E. Galloway and L. F. Brown, Jr.

References

1. Brown, L. F., Jr. project coordinator, in progress. Environmental Geologic Atlas of the Texas Coastal Zone: seven volumes. Univ. of Texas, Austin. Bureau of Economic Geology.

2. Brown, L. F., J. L. Brewton, J. H. McGowen, T. J. Evans, W. L. Fisher, and C. G. Groat. 1976. Environmental Geologic Atlas of the Texas Coastal Zone — Corpus Christi area. Univ. of Texas, Austin. Bureau of Economic Geology. 123 pp.

3. Brown, L. F., W. L. Fisher, A. W. Erxleben, and J. H. McGowen. 1971. Resource Capability Units — their utility in land and water-use management, with examples from the Texas Coastal Zone. Univ. of Texas, Austin. Bureau of Economic Geology Geol. Circ. 71-1. 22 pp.

4. Clark, J. 1974. Coastal Ecosystems. Washington, D. C. The Conservation Foundation. 178 pp.

5. Finley, R. J. 1976. Interpretation of unenhanced Landsat imagery for wet-
    land and land use delineation in the Texas Coastal Zone. Trans. Gulf Coast
    Assoc. Geol. Soc. 26:279-297.

6. Fisher, W. L., J. H. McGowen, L. F. Brown, Jr., and C. G. Groat. 1972. En-
    vironmental Geologic Atlas of the Texas Coastal Zone — Galveston-Houston
    Area. Univ. of Texas, Austin. Bureau of Economic Geology. 91 pp.

7. Groat, C. G., and L. F. Brown, Jr. 1972. Environmental Geologic Atlas of
    the Texas Coast: Basic data for coastal zone management, Feb. 14-15, pp. 1-
    15. In Tools for Coastal Zone Management, Proceedings of the conference.
    Washington, D.C. The Marine Technology Society.

8. McGowen, J. H., C. V. Proctor, L. F. Brown, Jr., T. J. Evans, W. L. Fisher,
    and C. G. Groat. 1976. Environmental Geologic Atlas of the Texas Coastal
    Zone — Port Lavaca Area. Univ. of Texas, Austin. Bureau of Economic Ge-
    ology. 107 pp.

9. St. Clair, A. E., C. V. Proctor, Jr., W. L. Fisher, C. W. Kreitler, and J. H.
    McGowen. 1975. Land and water resources — Houston-Galveston Area
    Council. Univ. Texas, Austin. Bureau of Economic Geology. 25 pp.

10. Texas Coastal and Marine Council. 1977. Hurricane resistant building stan-
    dards and natural hazards. Report to the 65th Legislature. Austin, Texas.

11. Texas General Land Office. 1975. The Coastal Economy: an economic re-
    port. Austin, Texas. 66 pp. + appendices.

12. Texas Teneral Land Office. 1976. Texas Coastal Zone Management Program:
    Report to the Governor and the 65th Legislature. Austin, Texas.

INTERACTIONS WITHIN
ESTUARINE COMMUNITIES PRIMARY
AND SECONDARY PRODUCTIVITY

INTERACTION BETWEEN SUBSTRATE, MICROBES, AND CONSUMERS OF *SPARTINA* DETRITUS IN ESTUARIES

Robert R. Christian

Department of Biological Sciences
Drexel University
Philadelphia, Pennsylvania

and

Richard L. Wetzel

Wetlands Research
Virginia Institute of Marine Science
Gloucester Point, Virginia

Abstract: A review of recent literature has indicated that the classic view of estuarine detritus food webs is simplistic. The dynamics of the detritus microbial complex is best understood when consideration is given to each component and its interactions, rather than merely considering the complex as a whole. This is true not only in determining the fate of the detritus substrate, but also in predicting the availability of microbes to consumers. Partitioning of detritus substrate, microbe, and consumer components was made in a simple, theoretical simulation model. The importance of the partitioning was demonstrated in 1) the energetics of trophic relationships between substrate, microbes, and the consumer sink; 2) the heterogeneity of microbial attachment in time and space; and 3) consumer requirements for energy and nutrients.

Introduction

W. E. Odum and Heald (1975) referred to detritus as ". . . a small ecosystem within a larger system." As such they have characterized the level of complexity inherent in detritus microecosystems as comparable to the macroecosystems of forests, estuaries, and oceans. The concept implies that detritus possesses such ecosystem properties as species diversity, succession, nutrient cycling, and energy flow. While this analogy may not hold for a conservative definition of an ecosystem, it does illustrate an important point: the internal structure and dynamics of detritus are complex and interactive. Therefore, a thorough understanding of detritus and its role in the larger ecosystem cannot be accomplished as long as detritus is conceptualized as a single black box.

In this paper we consider detritus as a "microecosystem" with trophic structure. The simplest structure of interaction is the detrital substrate being grazed by a heterotrophic microbial population which in turn is grazed by larger heterotrophic consumers. A theoretical simulation model of this food chain has been constructed and analyzed to examine the ramifications of various conditions of substrate, microbe, and consumer interactions. As with other ecosystems, the detritus food chain concept gives way to the food web when considering the natural system. A review of the recent literature is used to identify some emergent properties of detrital structure complexity. These properties include:

1. The energy flow related to microbial physiological ecology.

2. The temporal and spatial heterogeneity of detrital substrate and microbes.

3. The consumer requirements for nutrition, energy, and growth from detritus.

In this paper we shall deal primarily with the first topic. The topic of heterogeneity has been discussed to some degree by Biggs and Flemer (1972), Reimold *et al.* (1975), and Tenore (1977b). Recently, Tenore (1977c) and Heinle *et al.*, (1977) have discussed the consumer requirements.

While we have reviewed the recent literature on detritus to describe these emergent complexities, this report is not meant to supersede recent and more comprehensive reviews by others. Other contemporary reviews of the general subject include those by Riley (1970), W. E. Odum *et al.* (1972), Sieburth (1976), W. E. Odum and Heald (1975), and Lenz (1977). Melchiorri-Santolini and Hopton (1972) have edited the proceedings of an IBP-UNESCO symposium on detritus in aquatic ecosystems, and more recently Anderson and Macfadyen (1976) edited a book entitled *The Role of Terrestrial and Aquatic Organisms in Decomposition Processes.*

While Darnell's (1967) definition of detritus referred to the non-living organic constituents, a detritus particle may be closely associated with a living component. As such it includes the particulate substrate, sorbed dissolved substrates, and the residing microbial community. Within this general definition and subject area we will limit the scope of this report in two ways. First, we have considered primarily the dynamics of detritus within aerobic water columns. Detritus food webs are significant to the energetics of benthic systems (Tenore, 1977a). However, major differences exist between water column and sediment with respect to microbial attachment to particles (Wiebe and Pomeroy, 1972) and mode of microbial metabolism (Pomeroy *et al.,* 1977). Secondly, we will restrict ourselves to estuarine environments dominated by *Spartina* species as the major macrophytes and presumably major sources for detritus. This assumption, however, has recently been questioned in a Georgia estuary (Haines, 1977). For discussions of estuaries dominated by other macrophytes, see Odum and Heald (1975) and Mann (1972).

1. The energetics related to microbial numbers and particle size

The transformations of *Spartina* detrital substrates are largely dependent upon the number, nature, and activity of the resident microorganisms. The concepts of detritus put forth by Darnell, and E. P. Odum and de la Cruz in Estuaries (1967), suggested that the detritus substrates were coated with large quantities of microbes which could be grazed by animal consumers. However, direct microscopy has often failed to show large numbers of microbes on particles (Wiebe and Pomeroy, 1972; Sieburth, 1975; Marsh and W. E. Odum, 1978). Wiebe and Pomeroy (1972) found that more than 70% of the bacterial cells in water from the Duplin River watershed were non-motile and unattached. In subsurface water samples an average of less than one bacterium per particle was found. Only when samples from the interstitial waters of a *Spartina* raft were examined was a diverse and large microflora and microfauna seen. Even then, 50% of the particles were devoid of bacteria. Using scanning electron microscopy, Sieburth (1975) also found that most particles within the water column were devoid of bacteria. Marsh and W. E. Odum (1978) recently examined particles between 5 and 40 μm diameters from three sites in the York River estuary, Virginia. They also noted that many of the smallest particles were not colonized. The overall number of bacteria per μm^2 was 0.019 ± 0.023. This would represent no more than approximately 2% of the total surface area of a particle. In the studies by both Marsh and Odum (1978) and Wiebe and Pomeroy (1972), the major attached forms were bacteria. Denmark (1975) also found primarily bacteria attached to particles in a tidal creek in the Great Bay estuary of New Jersey, although he did not quantitate them.

These observations of few attached microbes is seemingly in contrast to metabolic studies. E. P. Odum and de la Cruz (1967) measured oxygen consumption by different detrital-size fractions in the Duplin River watershed. The oxygen consumption per g or g ash-free dry wt (AFDW) increased with decreasing particle size. Denmark (1975) also found an increase in oxygen consumption per g dry wt with decreasing particle size in detritus from a New Jersey estuary. Gosselink and Kirby (1974) found a similar trend in oxygen consumption per AFDW in laboratory studies. The general conclusions have been that the increased respiration rates with decreasing particle size are indicative of an increase in biomass of the microbial community in the smaller fractions.

Another method by which investigators have studied the microbial attachment to particles has been by the analysis of uptake of radioactive soluble organic substrates by various size fractions. This technique only measures that portion of the community capable of using the labelled substrate. Hanson and Wiebe (1977) examined the uptake of ^{14}C-glucose in estuarine waters of Georgia on various size particles. They concluded that more than 90% of the glucose uptake and respiration of labelled substrate was associated with particles greater than 3 μm. The percentage contribution of size fraction to total uptake varied with the stage of the tide.

An increase in microbial biomass with decreasing particle size and decomposition has also been inferred from organic nitrogen measurements of detritus (E. P. Odum and de la Cruz, 1967; Gosselink and Kirby, 1974). E. P. Odum and de la Cruz (1967) found an increase in protein (Kjeldahl N x 6.25) from approximately 7% AFDW in standing dead plants to 24% AFDW in the "nanno-detritus" fraction. Thus as particle size decreased, protein content increased. Gosselink and Kirby (1974) used the increase in organic nitrogen to calculate microbial biomass during decomposition of *Spartina* in laboratory experiments. They examined the decomposition of four fractions with median sizes of 67 to 213 μm diameters over 30 days in culture flasks. The organic nitrogen on a percent AFDW basis rose with time for all fractions: the smaller the size fraction, the greater the increase in "microbial" organic nitrogen. Based on the work of Lipinsky and Litchfield (1970), Gosselink and Kirby (1974) calculated g AFDW from g N using a conversion of 13% (i.e., g N x g AFDW^{-1}). Thus g AFDW microbial biomass per g AFDW detritus at day 30 ranged from 0.22 to 0.75. Using similar conversions for the data of Odum and de la Cruz (1967), the "nanno detritus" would contain 0.21 g AFDW microbial biomass per g AFDW detritus. Thus according to these calculations microbial biomass accounted for 21% to 75% of detrital biomass. If all of the microbes were bacteria and the AFDW of an average 1 μm^3 per bacterium [a conservatively large size (Ferguson and Rublee, 1976)] were approximately 2 X 10^{-13} g (Luria, 1960), one would expect a range of values of 1 X 10^{12} to 3.75 X 10^{12} bacteria (g AFDW detritus)$^{-1}$. This is orders of magnitude greater than anything seen in the water column. Even if many of the organisms were larger protozoans, fungi, or algae, the density of the community would be far greater than seen. Gosselink and Kirby's (1974) results were for culture flasks in the laboratory which might be expected to have larger populations than *in situ*. However, Odum and de la Cruz's (1967) results were from field sampling and must be reconciled with the results of others. It should be noted that while Denmark (1975) found an increase in respiration per dry wt with decreasing particle size, he found no concomitant increase in organic nitrogen. Hall *et al.* (1970) found a decreased amount of protein in seston as compared to *Spartina,* although ash content was not considered. One cautionary note should be added concerning sampling. Material after original fractionation was often filtered onto 0.45 μm or glass-fiber filters for analysis of N or respiration. This material may have contained many of the unattached microorganisms as well as those attached to particles. The magnitude of this error is unknown.

Several differences may be noted between the various studies. The first difference between the investigations cited above is in the median size classes studied. The size classes of the two tidal transport studies (Odum and de la Cruz, 1967; Denmark, 1975) were similar, and the median particle sizes of the laboratory study (Gosselink and Kirby, 1964) fell within the range of these medians. The investigations of Wiebe and Pomeroy (1972) and Marsh and Odum (1978) involved smaller-size particles, while Hanson and Wiebe (1977) studied the entire range of particle sizes. Another difference is in the denominator unit. Odum and de la Cruz and Gosselink and Kirby expressed respiration on a g AFDW basis.

Denmark expressed respiration on a g dry wt basis. Wiebe and Pomeroy used bacteria per particle, while Marsh and Odum used bacteria per μm^2 as well as bacteria per particle. Hanson and Wiebe expressed uptake of glucose on a per unit volume of water basis, as did Gosselink and Kirby in their calculation of microbial biomass increase.

Comparative interpretations must be based largely on the physical relationships of particle size, surface area, and weight. If we assume that particles are cubic and have a specific density near 1, the theoretical relationships of the several variables can be calculated. Larger particles have a greater surface area per particle than smaller particles with the surface area increase being related to the square of particle length. The surface area per unit weight, however, increases linearly with decreasing particle length. In terms of numbers of particles per unit weight, the numbers increase cubically with decrease in particle length. While the exact relationships will be altered by particle configuration the order of magnitude changes will hold. In fact these relationships were found to be generally true for *Thalassia testudinum* detritus by Fenchel (1970).

Other empirical findings must also come into play in comparative interpretations. The number of particles per unit volume and weight of particles per unit volume of water has been found to increase with decreasing particle size (Odum and de la Cruz, 1967; Denmark, 1975). Thus a large metabolic rate per unit volume of water associated with smaller particles may not be indicative of increased attachment on a per particle or per weight basis. Also, if the ash content increases with decreasing particle size, organic particulate detritus measurements on a g dry wt or g wet wt basis may be biased (Odum and de la Cruz, 1967). Thus the increase in activity per unit volume of water with decreasing particle size seen in Hanson and Wiebe's (1977) results may be accounted for on the basis of a proportionally larger number of small particles per unit volume.

When the relationships of particle size, surface area, number, and weight are taken into account, there is presently no evidence to suggest an overall increase in microbial attachment and activity on a per surface area or per particle basis with decreasing particle size. On a per weight basis the increases seen are probably due to the increased number of particles and surface area asssociated with smaller particles. Such interpretations are consistent with all of the available data as well as the findings for *Thalassia* detritus (Fenchel, 1970). Admittedly, the data are scanty and the interpretations premature, but the need for a concerted effort into the relationships of particle size, microbial attachment and microbial metabolism is striking. The initial theories of particles coated with microbes (Darnell, 1967) may need reevaluation. More emphasis should be placed on direct observation using epifluorescence and scanning electron microscopy. Also, results should be obtained on as many variables of the substrate (weight, volume, surface area) as possible.

2. The growth yield of the microorganisms

Respiratory losses by microorganisms during the transformation of substrate represent a significant loss of energy available to animal consumers. While true *in situ* measurements of microbial growth yields are available, estimates have been made in several ways. Gosselink and Kirby (1974) derived a growth yield

$$\frac{\text{g biomass produced} \times 100}{\text{g substrate consumed}}$$

of 24% to 66% through their laboratory experiments. The percent efficiency increased as initial particle size decreased. Fallon and Pfaender (1976) established growth yields

$$\frac{^{14}\text{C in particulate matter} \times 100}{^{14}\text{C in substrate consumed}}$$

of 54% to 82% for bacteria and fungi, respectively, feeding on soluble extracts of *S. alterniflora*. The short-term uptake of various organic compounds has been used to estimate growth yields by Williams (1973). However, short-term experiments may give erroneous results (Hanson and Wiebe, 1977).

The best information on growth yields comes from the microbial physiology literature. Payne (1970, 1972) reviewed the literature and derived amazingly constant values for aerobic growth. The gram dry wt yield of cells per kcal of substrate (Y_{kcal}) for many different species of organisms and types of substrates ranged from 0.075 to 0.164 with a mean of 0.121. Assuming the caloric content of bacteria to average 5.3 kcal (g dry wt)$^{-1}$ (Prochazka *et al.*, 1970), an average energy yield was derived in which approximately 60% substrate was converted to biomass, and 40% was lost through respiration. This holds for active aerobic growth of both bacteria and fungi under many conditions. Anaerobic growth yields would be dependent on the mode of electron acceptance, but anaerobic yields would be no greater than, and probably less than, aerobic yields. Thus in an aerobic water column with few anaerobic microsites, the expected maximum yield of microbial biomass from the transformation of detrital substrate would not exceed 60%. Animals capable of consuming or grazing the microbial trophic level would ingest 40% less energy in the form of microbial biomass than the amounts often proposed as "available to the estuary" (see Teal, 1962; Reimold *et al.*, 1975).

3. The complexity of the microbial community

The assemblage of microorganisms on the detrital substrate may represent a community level interaction rather than a population level. The particles may contain algae, fungi, bacteria, protozoans, and perhaps higher metazoans such as nematodes and rotifers (Sieburth, 1975; Wiebe and Pomeroy, 1972). Again, it should be stressed that not all particles contain all of these elements, and in fact many particles may be devoid of most (Wiebe and Pomeroy, 1972; Marsh and Odum, 1978).

The complexity of this community affects the trophic structure of detritus in several ways. First, diatoms may be found within detritus (Sieburth, 1975).

As primary producers an increase in their biomass does not require a loss of detrital substrate. This enhances the nutritional value per detrital particle available to consumers. Thus the more active the diatoms are within the detritus, the more energy and nutrients are available to consumers. The organic matter "available to the estuary" is thus augumented by this portion of the community.

The fungi and heterotrophic bacteria may serve as the major transformers of substrate. While some investigators have stressed the role of bacteria (Wiebe and Pomeroy, 1972; Hanson and Wiebe, 1977; Marsh and Odum, 1978), other studies have suggested the importance of fungi in the transformation (decomposition) process (Gessner *et al.*, 1972; May, 1974; Erkenbrecker, 1977). Scanning electron microscopy has been used to reveal that fungi were often the primary colonizers of standing dead material of *Spartina alterniflora*. Subsequently bacterial colonization occurred (Gessner *et al.*, 1972). Following primary colonization, protozoans and small microfauna were found. However, the small particles in the water column have a microflora that is largely bacterial (Wiebe and Pomeroy, 1972; Denmark, 1975; Marsh and Odum, 1978). Thus a successional sequence of microorganisms appears to occur from the standing dead *Spartina* through the development of small detritus particles. The nature of the microflora on detrital substrate may be a direct result of the state of succession. Such successional trends have been found in other particulate systems (Vargo *et al.*, 1975; Boling *et al.*, 1975).

Just as algae within detritus derive energy from external sources, so may heterotrophs such as fungi, bacteria, and protozoans. In this group dissolved organic matter (DOM) in the water column may be the dominant energy-carbon source (Darnell, 1967; Lenz, 1977). Hanson and Wiebe (1977) have characterized the activity of microbes on particles through the uptake of dissolved radioactive glucose. The implication is that microbes on particles will use this compound in a way similar to their use of the particulate substrate. In fact, for bacteria and fungi to use particulate organic matter (POM), they must first transform it to DOM (Pomeroy *et al.*, 1977). Thus the microbes may use the substrate as a raft, deriving some portion of their nutritional requirements from the pool of DOM within which they bathe (Darnell, 1967; Paerl, 1974; Lenz, 1977). Unfortunately, the relative portions of energy or carbon that are derived from DOM and POM are unknown. If much of the microbial nutritional requirement is fulfilled by DOM, then the animal consumers may be deriving a considerable portion of their requirements ultimately from sources other than dead macrophyte tissue. The DOM used by the microbes could come from photosynthate release of algae, living macrophytes, animal excreta, or through sediment release (Pomeroy *et al.*, 1977; Gallagher *et al.*, 1976).

In the detritus community with more than one trophic level, the community growth yield is less than for a population. The growth yields given for microorganisms in section 2 are for the population. Fallon and Pfaender (1976) found that a mixed microbial community had only a 21% growth yield during the uptake of labelled *Spartina alterniflora* extracts. The trophic structure and complexity of the detritus community will control the amount of energy actually available for higher order consumers.

While we have discussed detritus of *Spartina* origin, detritus in the estuary may have origins other than *Spartina*. Other origins of detrital particles would include decaying tissues of other marsh macrophytes, algae, animals, sedimentary material, fecal material, and perhaps non-estuarine material derived from terrestrial or freshwater environments or coastal waters (Woodwell *et al.*, 1977; Frankenberg and Smith, 1967; Tenore, 1977a; Haines, 1977; Darnell, 1967). The standing crop of particulate organic carbon in a Georgia salt marsh estuarine system has been studied using $^{13}C:^{12}C$ (Haines, 1977). The seston appeared to have carbon primarily of non-*Spartina* origin. If this work is confirmed, a thorough re-evaluation must be made of the role *Spartina* detritus has in the food web and the general function marshes have in the estuarine system as a whole. In fact the exemplification of salt marshes as a source of organic carbon to estuaries recently has been questioned (Woodwell *et al.*, 1977; Wiegert *et al.*, 1975; Heinle and Flemer, 1976; Shisler and Jobbins, 1977). Thus a heterogeneous composite of detrital particles is available at any given time to consumers. The structure of this composite is dependent in part on the time at which the initial substrate becomes available, the source of the substrate, as well as the speed with which the succession and transformations of detritus occur.

Consideration of the previous discussions leads one to few definitive conclusions regarding either the dynamics of the detrital complex or interactions that may control the availability of the detrital-microbial substrate to consumers higher in the trophic structure of the estuarine water column. We obviously have given little attention to such important physical parameters as temperature, salinity, tidal mixing, or transport with regard to these processes. However, we can make some general conclusions for *Spartina*-based estuaries from the information discussed; and some observations about them.

- Microbial attachment on a surface area or per particle basis appears small, and a significant portion of the microbes are not attached.

- Maximum microbial conversion efficiency (trophic level efficiency) is on the order of 60% and may decrease significantly (i.e., to about 20%) with an increase in the complexity of community structure.

- Growth yield appears amazingly constant for a variety of microbes with approximately 40% of assimilated substrate meeting respiratory demands.

- Detrital-microbe availability to consumers will in large part be controlled by the complexity of the attached microbial community. The numbers and types of microbes may reflect the successional state of the detritus. The successional rate is determined by origin of the detrital substrate, residence time in the system, history of the particle, and particle size.

Using the above observations, we have designed and constructed a theoretical material transport simulation model to evaluate the implicit interactions of detrital substrate, microbes, and consumers of estuarine detritus. In the following section we present the effects within the model boundaries of changes in, and consequences of, the above four postulates. A detailed discussion of the model and interaction equations are the subject of another presentation.

4. Model evaluation of substrate-microbe-consumer interactions

Simulation models of *Spartina*-dominated estuaries exist for Barataria Bay, Louisiana (Day *et al.*, 1973), Bissel Cove, Rhode Island (Nixon and Oivatt, 1973), the Duplin River Estuary, Georgia (Wiegert *et al.*, 1975; Wiegert and Wetzel, 1978), and the North Inlet, South Carolina (Dame *et al.*, 1977; Vernberg *et al.*, 1977). The first two of these treat detritus as a black box containing the respiratory activity of a biological compartment. The remaining two consider the detrital substrate as particulate organic carbon. The attendant microbial community is an undefined portion of the total heterotrophic water-column community, and is contained in a separate model compartment in the Duplin River model (Wiegert *et al.*, 1975). In the North Inlet model there is a separate decomposer compartment which includes attached and unattached microorganisms (Dame *et al.*, 1977). In all cases the energy, carbon or oxygen flow through the detrital pathway represents a dominant transfer within the model system. Yet, at least in the first two models, much of the effort of modeling and compartmentalization has been with the less significant energy transfer of higher trophic levels (e.g., blue crabs, birds, shrimp, and eels). Thus it seems that far less attention has been devoted to the detrital microecosystem in these models than would be warranted on the basis of energy flow.

We are familar with two specific simulation models of detritus dynamics, although neither was directed toward estuarine studies (Boling *et al.*, 1975; Clesceri *et al.*, 1977). Boling *et al.* (1975) constructed a state-space model for litter decomposition in a woodland stream. Emphasis was placed on the matrix interaction between particle size and "colonizing stages" of detritus, but the microbial community was not separated from the detrital substrate explicitly. Very recently, Clesceri *et al.* (1977) developed a general model of detrital substrate, microbial interaction for aquatic systems. This represented an advance in the compartmentalization of the detrital microecosystem.

An advantage of mathematical modelling is that systems may be simplified to their basis components. The interactions between these components may be studied in detail, at least within a theoretical framework. The number of components and interactions may then be increased in stages, and the ramifications of these increases in complexity assessed. We have thus developed a model that comprises the substrate, microbe, and consumer compartments of a detrital food chain. Some of the interactions of this food chain have been examined. Later stages of model development and analysis will include food web interactions and greater model complexity.

Model description. The five compartment non-linear model is shown in Figure 1. The central compartment is the microbial population or community

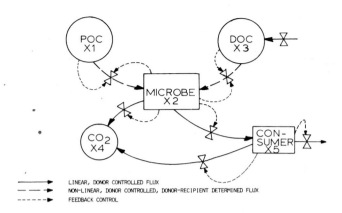

Figure 1. Conceptual model for interactions between substrate, microbes, and consumers of estuarine detritus.

which derives energy or carbon from both particulate substrate and dissolved organic material. The microbes are then grazed by the consumer population. The model has been designed to study Lagrangian dynamics, as a set quantity of particulate substrate and associated microbes move through a water column, rather than the Eulerian dynamics of a stationary compartmentalization through which water moves. The equations of state are shown in Table. 1 Although a detailed explanation of the mathematical structure and interaction equations is beyond the scope of this presentation, we present and discuss below a list of the parameters used in the simulation model:

- a) T_{ij}: the instantaneous rate of transfer via ingestion between compartment X_i and X_j (units of T^{-1}).

- b) R_{ij}: the instantaneous rate of transfer via respiration between compartments X_i and X_j (units of T^{-1}).

- c) A_{ij}: the density (mass x vol.$^{-1}$) below which the resource compartment, X_i, becomes limiting to the recipient compartment, X_j.

- d) G_{ij}: the refuge density of resource X_i at which the resource becomes unavailable to the recipient X_j.

- e) A_{iij}: the ratio of recipient density (X_j mass x vol.$^{-1}$) to donor density (X_i mass x vol.$^{-1}$) at which available space for attachment becomes limiting.

- f) G_{iij}: the ration, as above, where space for attachment becomes unavailable.

- g) A_{jj}: the density of X_j at which space becomes limiting.

- h) G_{jj}: the maximum attainable density by X_j due to space limitation.

Table 1. Equations of state for the model of substrate, microbe, and consumer interaction.

$$\dot{X}_1 = -F_{12}$$

$$\dot{X}_2 = F_{12} + F_{32} - F_{24} - F_{25}$$

$$\dot{X}_3 = F_{03} - F_{32}$$

$$\dot{X}_4 = F_{24} + F_{54}$$

$$\dot{X}_5 = F_{25} - F_{50} - F_{54}$$

where:

$$F_{12} = T_{12}X_2 \, (1 - FB_{12} - FB_{112} \, (1 - (((T_{12}/ \, (T_{12} + T_{32})) \, R_{24}) / T_{12})))$$

$$F_{32} = T_{32}X_2 \, (1 - FB_{32} - FB_{22} \, (1 - (((T_{32}/ \, (T_{12} + T_{32})) \, R_{24}) / T_{32})))$$

$$F_{25} = T_{25}X_2$$

$$F_{24} = R_{24}X_2$$

$$F_{25} = R_{54}X_5$$

$$F_{50} = EG_{50}F_{25}$$

$$F_{03} = F_{32}$$

and:

$$FB_{112} = (((X_2/X_1) - A_{112})_+ / (G_{112} - A_{112}))_+$$

$$FB_{12} = ((A_{12} - X_1)_+ / (A_{12} - G_{12}))_+$$

$$FB_{22} = ((X_2 - A_{22}) / (G_{22} - A_{22}))_+$$

$$FB_{32} = 0$$

i) EG_{ij}: the proportion of ingested material which is egested by X_i.

Several flows have been over-simplified at this stage, while others possess complex feedback structure. The flow of material from POC to microbes contains non-linear feedback terms for biochemical availability (metabolizable substrate) and spatial limitation (attachment). The DOC to microbes flow is linear, recipient controlled. The questions being asked through model simulation concern the ramifications of various DOC inputs and rates of utilization to the system, rather than evaluation of DOC dynamics. The microbe-to-consumer flow is linear-donor controlled, as model simulation questions concern microbial availability for con-

Table 2. Parameters varied for model experiments.

Experiment Number	Proportion of microbial uptake from POC $T_{12}/(T_{12}+T_{32})$	Microbial ingestion rate $(T_{12}+T_{32})$	Grazing pressure on microbes T_{25}	Microbial Respiration R_{24}	Spatial limitation (A_{122}, G_{122})
1	0.1 to 0.9	1.156	0.3	0.4	0.05, 0.1
2	0.5	0.116 to 1.156	0.1	$0.4\,(T_{32}+T_{12})$	0.05, 0.1
3	0.5	1.156	0.0 to 0.6	0.4	0.05, 0.1
4	0.5	1.156	0.1	0.2 to 0.8	0.05, 0.1
5	0.5	1.156	0.1	0.4	0.05 to 0.25, 0.1 to 0.5
6	0.1 to 0.9	1.156	0.0 to 0.6	0.4	0.05, 0.1

sumer growth, and assumes consumers are not limited by other factors. All other flows illustrated in Figure 1 are linear-donor controlled fluxes.

5. Model simulation experiments

To evaluate, within the modelled system context, the four generalizations presented before, a series of six model simulation experiments were done consisting of 24 computer runs. The parameter conditions for experiments are presented in Table 2. Model simulation experiments were done at the Virginia Institute of Marine Science (VIMS) Computer Center using an IBM 370/115 system. The methods of computer simulation and integration technique have been reported elsewhere (see Wiegert and Wetzel, 1974).

Generally, the simulation experiments fall in the following categories:

1. Effects of resource partitioning, turnover time, and conversion efficiency of POC and DOC utilization by the microbial compartment.

2. Effects of microbial attachment (spatial limitation) based on particle surface area.

3. Effects of grazing pressure on the microbial substrate.

4. Interactive effects of microbial resource utilization and grazing pressure.

Analysis of the simulation experiments was based on system stability and material allocation within compartments at steady state.

Parameter changes for the model experiments were made one at a time and thus do not reflect interactive effects on a per-run basis. Other than the parameter changes noted, nominal conditions for the simulation studies were as follows:

a) Initial conditions for the compartments were: $X1 = 1000$, $X2 = 10$, $X3 = 100$, $X4 = 0$, $X5 = 1$.

b) X3 (DOC) was held constant for all runs.

c) 90% of the POC was metabolically available.

d) Maximum compartmental standing stock for the microbes was 500, with limitation beginning at 250.

e) 10% of POC calculated as the ratio of X2/X1 was available for microbial attachment, with limitation (spatial) beginning at 5%.

f) Trophic level efficiency of the consumers was 30%.

As each parameter was varied through a given range; the conditions, except for the change in the given parameter value, were reset for each model simulation run. The above nominal conditions were chosen to reflect the information given previously. Absolute standing stocks of model predictions are completely arbitrary.

Table 3 summarizes those parameters sets and model conditions which resulted in compartmental steady state being achieved within 360 days of model simulation. Reading down the columns, increases in the parameter values reflect

Table 3. Parameter sets achieving steady state conditions within 360 days.

Resource Partition Exp. 1 $T_{12}/(T_{12} + T_{32})$		Generation Time Exp. 2 $(T_{12} + T_{32})$		Grazing Pressure Exp. 3 T_{25}		Growth Yield Exp. 4 R_{24}		Particle Attachment Exp. 5 (A_{122}, G_{122})	
0.1	S	0.116	NS	0.0	S	0.2	S	(0.05, 0.1)	S
0.25	S	0.230	NS	0.1	S	0.4	S	(0.1, 0.25)	S
0.5	NS	0.578	S	0.15	S	0.5	AS	(0.25, 0.5)	S
0.9	NS	1.156	S	0.2	AS	0.6	NS		
				0.3	NS	0.8	NS		
				0.6	NS				

S = steady state by 360 days
AS = approaching steady state by 360 days
NS = no steady state by 360 days

changes in resource partitioning by microbes (POC vs DOC: Experiment 1); decreases in potential doubling time or generation-time of the microbes (10 days to 1 day: Experiment 2); increases in grazing pressure by the consumer compartment (0.0 to 60% day^{-1}: Experiment 3); decreases in growth yield by the microbes (0.8 to 0.2 of assimilation: Experiment 4); and increases in potential particle attachment by microbes (10% to 50% of available space: Experiment 5). For the first four model experiments, system stability (defined for the purposes of this report as a parameter condition set leading to compartmental steady state within 360 model simulation days) was sensitive to parameter increases and showed abrupt changes in stability around defined parameter values with slight changes in the actual value. This suggests that the overall dynamics of the detritus-microbe system is extremely sensitive to the four basic parameters associated with resource partitioning, potential turnover rate, growth yield, and grazing pressure.

Figures 2 and 3 illustrate the compartmental dynamics of microbes under various conditions of grazing pressure and growth yield respectively. Optimum stability conditions for the complex in terms of the model would appear to be characterized by a microbial compartment that:

1) shows a high preference for dissolved substrate;

2) has the potential for rapid turnover;

3) has better than a 50% growth yield; and

4) is not grazed by consumers.

Increased grazing pressure decreases microbial biomass. This was also noted by

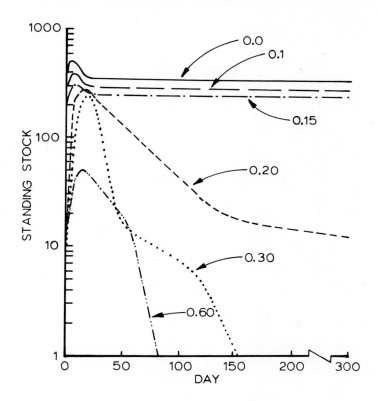

Figure 2. Dynamics of microbe compartment under various conditions of grazing pressure.

Barsdate *et al.* (1974) in their detritus, bacteria, protozoan microcosms using *Carex aquatilis* as their detrital substrate source. In fact, it appears from these first simulation studies that high or very efficient grazing of the detrital-microbial substrate tends to drive the system to an unstable condition. Although no rigorous treatment of the simulation results regarding sensitivity analysis has been completed yet, it appears that resource partitioning (i.e., knowledge of the actual rates of POC vs DOC utilization by microbes) and consumer grazing pressure are interactively determinate. With regard to higher order consumers of the detrital-microbe substrate, the simulation studies suggest that either the detrital-microbe substrate might be simple structurally (trophically), or if in fact the complex is diverse, grazing pressure by consumers relying solely on this water component might be low (see Experiment 4: growth yield by the complex).

Table 4 summarizes in terms of model stability the interactive effects of POC:DOC partitioning and grazing pressure. The results of the simulation studies and stability conditions are evident. Moderate grazing pressure can only be sustained under conditions of high DOC preference and constant DOC input. This

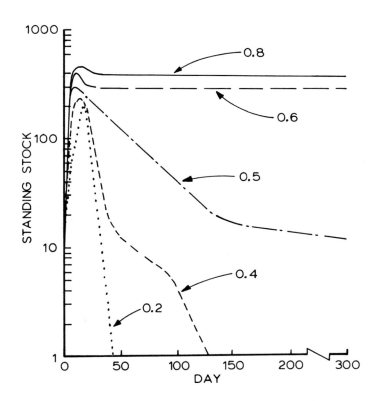

Figure 3. Dynamics of microbe compartment under various conditions of growth yield.

result argues strongly for the conclusion drawn by Pomeroy *et al.* (1977) that there is a close coupling between DOC supply and input and micro-heterotrophic utilization of dissolved substrates.

Although, as we stated before, the absolute standing stocks of the model compartments either initially or as predicted by model simulation are arbitrary, the ratios of the various predicted compartmental standing stocks at steady state for various parameter conditions should be indicative of overall system behavior. Table 5 summarizes the compartmental standing stock ratios for those simulation experiments that reached steady state. An interesting result of the comparisons is that for the various conditions used in the simulation, amazingly consistent compartmental standing stocks and ratios are predicted. It is particularly interesting to note that the POC:Microbe ratio indicates that a significant if not a major fraction of the microbes in the water column are unattached. Changing the available space for attachment (Experiment 5; Table 5) does not change the predicted steady state values or compartmental relations at steady state. This result suggests

Table 4. Interaction of microbial resource partitioning and grazing pressure.

			Grazing Pressure (T^{-1})		
$T_{12}/(T_{12} + T_{32})$	0.0	0.1	0.2	0.3	0.6
0.1	S	S	S	S	NS
0.25	S	S	S	S	NS
0.5	S	S	AS	NS	NS
0.9	NS	NS	NS	NS	NS

S = steady state by 360 days
AS = approaching steady state by 360 days
NS = no steady state by 360 days

Table 5. Ratios of microbes to POC and microbes to consumers at steady state.

Experiment	*Condition*	*POC*	*Microbes*	*Consumers*	*P:M*	*M:C*
1. Resource	0.1	198	375	338	0.53	1.11
Partitioning	0.25	198	324	291	0.61	1.11
2. Generation	0.578	214	307	92	0.70	3.34
Time	1.156	198	302	90	0.66	3.36
3. Grazing	0.0	198	368	0	0.54	--
Pressure	0.1	198	302	90	0.66	3.36
	0.15	198	269	121	0.74	2.22
4. Growth	0.2	224	395	119	0.57	3.32
Yield	0.4	198	302	90	0.66	3.36
5. Attachment	0.05, 0.1	198	302	90	0.66	3.36
	0.1, 0.25	198	302	91	0.66	3.32
	0.25, 0.5	198	302	91	0.66	3.32

that it would be worthwhile if not necessary to further compartmentalize the microbial component into attached and free-living forms, particularly if consumer interactions are important to the overall dynamics of the substrate-microbe system.

Acknowledgments

Ms. Priscilla Snelling, Beverly Holbrook, Nancy Hudgins and Carole Know for secretarial services. Mr. F. Degges, and Ms. Shirley Robbins and Glenda Owen for computing aid.

Contribution No. 855 from the Virginia Institute of Marine Sciences, Gloucester Point, Virginia.

References

1. Anderson, J. M., and A. Macfadyen. 1976. The Role of Terrestrial and Aquatic Organisms in Decomposition Processes. Blackwell Scientific Publ., London, 474 pp.

2. Barsdate, R. J., R. T. Prentki, and T. Fenchel. 1974. Phosphorous cycle of model ecosystems: significance for decomposer food chains and effect of bacterial grazers. Oikos 25:239-251.

3. Biggs, R. B., and D. A. Flemer. 1972. The flux of particulate carbon in an estuary. Mar. Biol. 12:11-17.

4. Boling, R. H. Jr., E. D. Goodman, J. A. Van Sickle, J. O. Zimmer, K. W. Cummins, R. C. Petersen, and S. R. Reice. 1975. Toward a model of detritus processing in a woodland stream. Ecology 56:141-151.

5. Clesceri, L. S., R. A. Park, and J. A. Bloomfield. 1977. General model of microbial growth and decomposition in aquatic ecosystems. Appl. Environ. Microbiol. 33:1047-1058.

6. Dame, R., F. Vernberg, R. Bonnell, and W. Kitchens. 1977. The North Inlet marsh-estuarine ecosystem: a conceptual approach. Helgolander Wiss. Meeresunters 30:343-356.

7. Darnell, R. M. 1967. Organic detritus in relation to the estuarine ecosystem, pp. 376-382. *In* G. H. Lauff (ed.), Estuaries. American Association for the Advancement of Science, Washington, D.C.

8. Day, J. W., Jr., W. G. Smith, P. R. Wagner, and W. C. Stowe. 1973. Community structure and carbon budget of a salt marsh and shallow bay estuarine system in Louisiana. Louisiana State Univ., Publ. No. LSU-SG-72-04, Baton Rouge.

9. Denmark, R. E. 1975. Particulate organic detritus in a New Jersey salt marsh-estuarine ecosystem. M.S. thesis. Rutgers University, Camden, N.J. 123 pp.

10. Erkenbrecher, C. W. 1977. Interactions among microbial populations and a fluctuating estuarine environment. Abst. Ann. Meeting Amer. Soc. Microbiol. 77:224.

11. Fallon, R. D., and F. K. Pfaender. 1976. Carbon metabolism in model microbial systems from a temperate salt marsh. Appl. Environ. Microbiol. 31: 959-968.

12. Fenchel, T. 1970. Studies on the decomposition of organic detritus derived from the turtle grass *Thalassia testudinum*. Limnol. Oceanogr. 15:14-20.

13. Ferguson, R. L., and P. Rublee. 1976. Contribution of bacteria to standing crop of coastal plankton. Limnol. Oceanogr. 21:141-145.

14. Frankenberg, D., and K. L. Smith, Jr. 1967. Coprophagy in marine animals. Limnol. Oceanogr. 12:443-450.

15. Gallagher, J. L., W. J. Pfeiffer, and L. R. Pomeroy. 1976. Leaching and microbial utilization of dissolved organic carbon from leaves of *Spartina alterniflora*. Estuar. Coastal Mar. Sci. 4:467-471.

16. Gessner, R. V., R. D. Goos, and J. McN. Sieburth. 1972. The fungal microcosm of the internodes of *Spartina alterniflora*. Mar. Biol. 16:269-273.

17. Gosselink, J. G., and C. J. Kirby. 1974. Decomposition of salt marsh grass, *Spartina alterniflora* Loisel. Limnol. Oceanogr. 19:825-832.

18. Haines, E. B. 1977. On the origins of detritus in Georgia salt marsh estuaries. Oikos 29:254-260.

19. Hall, K. J., W. C. Weimer, and G. F. Lee. 1970. Amino acids in an estuarine environment. Limnol. Oceanogr. 15:162-164.

20. Hanson, R. B., and W. J. Wiebe. 1977. Heterotrophic activity associated with particulate size fraction in a *Spartina alterniflora* Loisel salt marsh-estuary, Sapelo Island, Georgia, and the continental shelf waters. Mar. Biol. 42:321-330.

21. Heinle, D. R., and D. A. Flemer. 1976. Flows of materials between poorly flooded tidal marshes and an estuary. Mar. Biol. 35:359-373.

22. Heinle, D. R., R. P. Harris, J. F. Ustach, and D. A. Flemer. 1977. Detritus as food for estuarine copepods. Mar. Biol. 40:341-353.

23. Lenz, J. 1977. On detritus as a food source for pelagic filter-feeders. Mar. Biol. 41:39-48.

24. Lipinsky, E. S., and J. H. Litchfield. 1970. Algae, bacteria, and yeasts as food or feed. Chem. Rubber Co. Critical Rev. Food Technol. 1:581-618.

25. Luria, S. E. 1960. The bacterial protoplasm: Composition and organization, pp. 1-34. *In* J. C. Gunsalus and R. Y. Stanier (eds.), The Bacteria: A Treatise on Structure and Function, vol. I. Academic Press, N.Y.

26. Mann, K. H. 1972. Macrophyte production and detritus food chains in coastal waters. Mem. Ist. Ital. Idrobiol., 29 Suppl: 353-383.

27. Marsh, D. H., and W. E. Odum. 1978. The relationship between size of microdetritus particles and extent of microbial colonization. Limnol. Oceanogr. (In press).

28. May, M. S., III. 1974. Probable agents for the formation of detritus from the halophyte, *Spartina alterniflora*, pp. 429-440. *In* R. J. Reimold and W. H. Queen (eds.), Ecology of Halophytes. Academic Press, N.Y.

29. Melchiorri-Santolini, U., and J. W. Hopton (eds.) 1972. Detritus and Its Role in Aquatic Ecosystems. Mem. Ist. Ital. Idrobiol., 29 Suppl. 540 pp.

30. Nixon, S. W., and C. A. Oviatt. 1973. Ecology of a New England salt marsh. Ecol. Monogr. 43:463-498.

31. Odum, E. P., and A. A. de la Cruz. 1967. Particulate organic detritus in a Georgia salt marsh-estuarine ecosystem, pp. 383-388. *In* G. H. Lauff (ed.), Estuaries. American Association for the Advancement of Science, Washington, D. C.

32. Odum, W. E. and E. J. Heald. 1975. The detritus-based food web of an estuarine mangrove community, pp. 265-286. *In* L. E. Cronin (ed.), Estuarine Research, Vol. I, Academic Press, N.Y.

33. Odum, W. E., J. C. Zieman, and E. J. Heald. 1972. The importance of vascular plant detritus to estuaries, pp. 91-135. *In* R. H. Chabreck (ed.), Proceedings of the Coastal Marsh and Estuary Management Symposium. Louisiana State Univ. Division of Continuing Education, Baton Rouge.

34. Paerl, H. W. 1974. Bacterial uptake of dissolved organic matter in relation to detrital aggregation in marine and freshwater systems. Limnol. Oceanogr. 19:966-972.

35. Payne, W. J. 1970. Energy yield and growth of heterotrophs. Ann. Rev. Microbiol. 24:17-52.

36. Payne, W. J. 1972. Bacterial growth yields, pp. 57-73. *In* L. J. Guarraia and R. K. Ballentine (eds.), The Aquatic Environment: Microbial Transforma-

tions and Water Management Implications. Environmental Protection Agency 430/G-73-008.

37. Pomeroy, L. R., K. Bancroft, J. Breed, R. R. Christian, D. Frankenberg, J. R. Hall, L. G. Maurer, W. J. Wiebe, R. G. Wiegert, and R. L. Wetzel. 1977. Flux of organic matter through a salt marsh, pp. 270-279. *In* M. Wiley (ed.), Estuarine Processes, Vol. II. Academic Press, New York.

38. Prochazka, G. J., W. J. Payne, and W. R. Mayberry. 1970. Calorific content of certain bacteria and fungi. J. Bacteriol. 104:646-649.

39. Reimold, R. J., J. L. Gallagher, R. A. Linthurst, and W. J. Pfeiffer. 1975. Detritus production in coastal Georgia, pp. 217-228. *In* L. E. Cronin (ed.), Estuarine Research, Vol. I. Academic Press, N.Y.

40. Riley, G. A. 1970. Particulate organic matter in sea water. Adv. Mar. Biol. 8:1-118.

41. Shisler, J. K., and D. M. Jobbins. 1977. Tidal variations in the movement of organic carbon in New Jersey salt marshes. Mar. Biol. 40:127-134.

42. Sieburth, J. McN. 1975. Microbial Seascapes. University Park Press, Baltimore, Md. 216 pp.

43. _____. 1976. Bacterial substrates and productivity in marine ecosystems. Ann. Rev. Ecol. Syst. 7:259-285.

44. Teal, J. M. 1962. Energy flow in the salt marsh ecosystem of Georgia. Ecology 43:614-624.

45. Tenore, K. R. 1977a. Food chain pathways in detrital feeding benthic communities: a review, with new observations on sediment resuspension and detrital recycling, pp. 37-53. *In* B. Coull (ed.), Ecology of Marine Benthos. B. Baruch Library in Marine Science, No. 6. Univ. of South Carolina Press, Columbia, S.C.

46. _____. 1977b. Utilization of aged detritus derived from different sources by the polychaete, *Capitella capitata*. Mar. Biol. 44:51-56.

47. _____. 1977c. Growth of the polychaete, *Capitella capitata,* cultured on various levels of detritus derived from different sources. Limnol. Oceanogr. 22:936-941.

48. Vargo, G. A., P. E. Hargraves, and P. Johnson. 1975. Scanning electron microscopy of dialysis tubes incubated in flowing seawater. Mar. Biol. 31:113-120.

49. Vernberg, F. J., R. Bonnell, B. Coull, R. Dame, P. DeCoursey, W. Kitchens, B. Kjerfve, H. Stevenson, W. Vernberg, and R. Zingmark. 1977. The dynamics of an estuary as a natural ecosystem. Ecological Research Series, Environmental Protection Agency, 600/3-77-016.

50. Wiebe, W. J., and L. R. Pomeroy. 1972. Microorganisms and their association with aggregates and detritus in the sea: a microscopic study. Mem. Ist. Ital. Idiobiol., 29 Suppl.:325-352.

51. Wiegert, R. G., and R. L. Wetzel. 1974. The effect of numerical integration technique on the simulation of carbon flow in a Georgia salt marsh. Proc. Summer Computer Simulation Conference (Houston):575-577.

52. _____. 1978. Simulation experiments with a fourteen compartment model of a *Spartina* salt marsh. (In press) *In* R. Dame (ed.), Marsh Estuarine Simulation. Univ. of South Carolina Press, Columbia, S.C.

53. Wiegert, R. G., R. R. Christian, J. L. Gallagher, J. R. Hall, R. D. H. Jones, and R. L. Wetzel. 1975. A preliminary ecosystem model of a coastal Georgia *Spartina* marsh, pp. 583-601. *In* L. E. Cronin (ed.), Estuarine Research, Vol. I. Academic Press, New York.

54. Williams, P. J. Le B. 1973. On the question of growth yields of natural hetero-trophic populations. Bull. Ecol. Res. Comm. (Stockholm) 17:511.

55. Woodwell, G. M., D. E. Whitney, C. A. S. Hall, and R. A. Houghton. 1977. The Flax Pond ecosystem study: exchanges of carbon in water between a salt marsh and Long Island Sound. Limnol. Oceanogr. 22:833-838.

BOX MODEL ANALYSIS
OF CHESAPEAKE BAY AMMONIUM AND NITRATE FLUXES

J. L. Taft, A. J. Elliott, and W. R. Taylor

Chesapeake Bay Institute
The Johns Hopkins University
Baltimore, Maryland

Abstract: A kinematic box model using salt as natural tracer is employed as an analytical tool to estimate longitudinal and vertical transport of ammonium and nitrate in Chesapeake Bay. Both conservative behavior and non-conservative nutrient addition and removal are quantitated for the two layers of each segment in this partially mixed estuary. Results suggest the lower layer is an ammonium source year round. North of $38°53'N$ new nitrogen input may be significant in supporting phytoplankton productivity during winter, but south of this latitude nitrogen regenerated in the upper mixed layer is more significant to primary production. The most active regions for longitudinal flux are near the Potomac River mouth and near $39°00'N$.

Introduction

Nutrient retention is a principal contributing factor to the relatively high productivity of estuaries. The biochemical cycle consisting of nutrient uptake in seaward flowing surface water, sinking of particulate material and its remineralization in landward flowing deep water, and upward advection of remineralized nutrient is directly related to the physical circulation. In this paper we describe an effort to quantitate the flux of two combined forms of nitrogen through a major estuary.

A considerable body of nutrient data for the Chesapeake Bay has been accumulating since the 1940's. Much of the data was reliably collected and seems to be accurate because they are comparable to recent data, particularly those from two extensive nutrient surveys covering most of the bay in 1964--66 (Whaley *et al.*, 1966; Carpenter *et al.*, 1969) and 1969--71 (Taylor and Grant, 1977). Several years ago analysis of some of these historical data was attempted with a simple two-dimensional model developed by Pritchard (1969). However, the results were unsatisfactory because few data points had been collected in the appropriate spatial array. Therefore additional nutrient data were collected during 1975-76 to provide the required spatial resolution, sacrificing the closer temporal coverage provided in the 1964–66 and 1969–71 studies. During the recent study period, Pritchard's model was modified and automated by Elliott (1976a), increasing its utility for field-oriented chemists and biologists. This paper discusses some of the preliminary results obtained through the use of this model.

The questions for which we sought answers in the data are: 1) What are the longitudinal ammonium and nitrate flux rates in seaward flowing surface waters and landward flowing deep waters? 2) What are the nutrient loss rates to the coastal ocean and the input rates from the coastal ocean? 3) What are the rates of deep water ammonium accumulation observed in summer and what are the vertical flux rates to the euphotic zone? 4) Are deep waters and/or sediments year-round ammonium sources for the euphotic zone?

To begin answering these questions requires information about nutrient concentrations and about the physical processes of water motion. Diffusive processes are complex, so we chose not to differentiate between vertical diffusion and vertical advection. Diffusion can be differentiated from advection with the method used, particularly if dynamic measurements are made; but differentiation is not necessary for an initial description of the net nutrient flux.

In application of the model the bay was divided into boxes with vertical boundaries at lateral transects through the hydrographic stations (Figure 1) and horizontal boundaries at the upper edge of the pycnocline. Nutrient flux coefficients were calculated, using the observed salinity distribution and river flow. The nutrient concentrations at the vertical boundaries were weighted by the boundary surface area and a mean concentration was calculated for each upper and lower box. The nutrient flux across each boundary was then calculated. Nutrients are not conservative, so summing the inputs and outputs for each box revealed discrepancies due to non-conservative behavior. Since mass must be conserved, these discrepancies were accounted for as sources or sinks of nutrient in each segment. The advantages of this approach are that nutrient removal from the dissolved inorganic pool may be distinguished from nutrient dilution by mixing of high and low nutrient waters, and addition of nutrient to the upper layer or removal from the lower layer can be identified when this is not obvious by inspection of the concentration data. Disadvantages are that the relative significance of advection and diffusion (or turbulent diffusion) are not assessed as transport mechanisms, identification of nutrient addition and removal mechanisms are left to the investigator, and contributions of the lower layer cannot be distinguished from those resulting from sediment-water interactions.

Methods

Cruises (PROCON 16, 17, 21) of the R/V Ridgely Warfield were undertaken to previously established Chesapeake Bay stations (Figure 1) during February and

Figure 1. (opposite) Map of Chesapeake Bay showing station locations and box model boundaries.

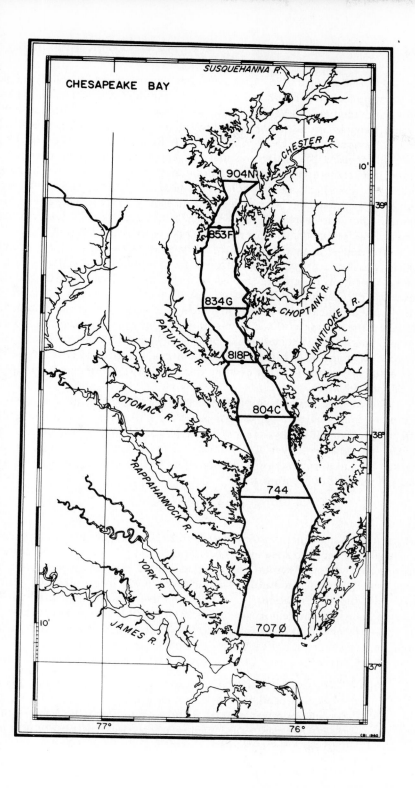

May 1975, and August 1976. A submersible pump was lowered to collect samples for constructing temperature and conductivity profiles (Schiemer and Pritchard, 1961), and simultaneous Van Dorn casts were made to five or six selected depths to obtain samples for nutrient analyses. In subdued laboratory light, immediately after collection, samples were passed through Reeve Angel 984H or Whatman GF/C filters using 25 cm Hg pressure differential. Filtrate was refrigerated or frozen in pyrex bottles for one to five hours prior to analysis for ammonium (Solórzano, 1969) and nitrate (Wood *et al.*, 1967) as described in Strickland and Parsons (1972). Methods were scaled to 5 ml sample volumes and phenol hypochlorite color was developed at $50°C$ (McCarthy *et al.*, 1977). The data were then analyzed, using the two-layered box model described in Elliot (1976a).

This model is an elaboration of the method given by Pritchard (1969), which considers a partially mixed estuary to be a two-layered system in which the salt balance is maintained through a combination of horizontal and vertical advection plus vertical diffusion. This type of model is kinematic, i.e., does not use dynamic principles, and does not include horizontal dispersion explicitly. However, the horizontal fluxes represent exchanges and are, in fact, the sum of advective and diffusive fluxes; as a result of this formulation the transport due to longitudinal horizontal diffusion is included in the horizontal advective terms. [Some inherent disadvantages of using this simple two-layered model are given in Elliott (1976b).]

The horizontal fluxes in the upper and lower layers are derived by use of the basin equations, and the vertical advection is deduced by continuity. The effective vertical diffusivity is then obtained by considering the salt balance for a portion of the upper layer of the estuary. A nutrient balance equation is then written for the upper and lower portion of each segment and this leads to a system of equations of the form

$$\underline{\underline{A}} \ \underline{c} = \underline{p}$$

where $\underline{\underline{A}}$ is a square matrix which characterizes the advection/diffusion processes, $\underline{c}$ is a column vector containing concentrations, and $\underline{p}$ is a column vector representing source terms. There are now two possibilities: either the source/sink terms are known (as in the simulation of a discharge) in which case the system can be solved for the concentrations; or, as in the present context, the concentrations may be known (from field measurements) and the system of equations can then be solved to obtain the source/sink terms. An error analysis indicated that the computed fluxes and sources will have a probable error of $\pm 9\%$.

The following sequence of steps was used while analyzing the data:

Step 1: The vertical salinity profiles were plotted for each station and the halocline depths were selected; since no current measurements were available, it was assumed that the depth of the halocline coincided with the depth of the interface between the upper and lower layers.

Step 2: The cross-sectional areas for the depth ranges between vertically adjacent sample points were found from Cronin (1975).

Step 3: The observed values of NH_4^+ and $NO_3^{\equiv}$ were averaged above and below the interfaces to estimate concentrations in the upper and lower layers at each station.

Step 4: The mean river flow was determined from monthly mean stream flow data during the study period provided by USGS, and additional inflow through the sides of the boxes other than major tributaries was considered to be negligible.

Step 5: The mean NH_4^+ and $NO_3^{\equiv}$ concentration data were fed into the model.

Results

The NH_4^+ and $NO_3^{\equiv}$ concentration data are represented in Figure 2.

Ammonium flux calculation for February 1975 (Figure 3) indicates ammonium removal in the upper layer between stations 904N and 818P, and addition in the lower layer of that region. If the removal was due entirely to phytoplankton uptake, then net uptake was the sum of the sink terms or 1081×10^5 μg atom $\cdot s^{-1}$. Net production in the lower layer was 668×10^5 μg atom $\cdot s^{-1}$ or 62% of net uptake in the surface layer. Vertical input to the upper layer was 450×10^5 μg atom $\cdot s^{-1}$ and input from upstream was 640×10^5 μg atom $\cdot s^{-1}$. These two fluxes provided 1090 μg atom $\cdot s^{-1}$, just exceeding the net uptake. Therefore, about 41% of the net ammonium loss from the upper layer was supplied from below the pycnocline and 59% was added from north of station 904N. Ammonium leaving the region in the upper layer at station 818P was approximately balanced by ammonium entering the lower layer at 818P.

The upper layer of the southern portion of the bay (stations 818P to 707ϕ) showed a net production of 1212×10^5 μg atom $\cdot s^{-1}$. Mechanisms for this contrast to the ammonium flux in the northern bay are not obvious. The Potomac River may have some influence near station 804C, but would not be expected to influence the region between stations 744 and 707ϕ. Ammonium output in the surface layer at station 707ϕ was balanced by ammonium input with the lower layer ocean water.

Dividing the source and sink terms by the volume of the box containing them yields input and loss estimates per liter of water, which is a more common way to compare nutrient flux values. Table 1 contains ammonium and nitrate flux values for winter normalized to μg atom $(liter \cdot day)^{-1}$. The source and sink terms for the southern bay (stations 818P and 707ϕ) reflect lower biological activity per unit volume of water, if *in situ* biota are largely responsible for the calculated nutrient inputs and losses. However, chlorophyll a and particuate nutrient data collected simultaneously (Taft, unpublished data) indicate consistent levels of phytoplankton biomass (< 35 μm) in northern and southern Chesapeake Bay. Particulate nitrogen levels in the upper layer of the northern bay

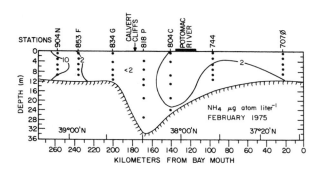

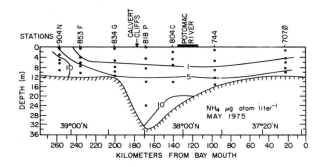

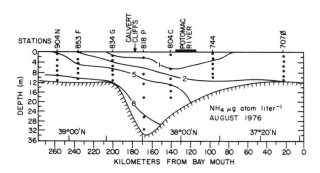

Figure 2a. Longitudinal ammonium distributions in February and May 1975 and August 1976.

were about 8 μg atom · liter^{-1}. Thus, the loss of ammonium plus nitrate in the upper layer of the 904N-853F segment could have yielded about one doubling of the phytoplankton per day. However, in the 853F-818P segments the net loss of ammonium and nitrate would have supported one phytoplankton doubling in

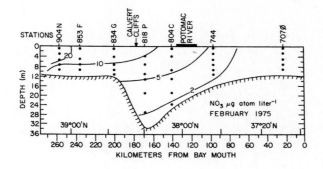

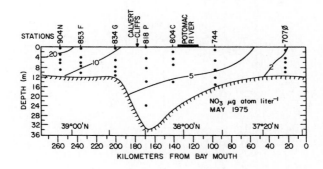

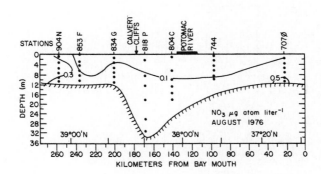

Figure 2b. Longitudinal nitrate distributions in February and May 1975 and August 1976.

about two weeks. This is contrary to ^{14}C measurements of phytoplankton growth in this area, which indicate 2- to 5-day winter doubling times (Flemer, 1970; Taylor, unpublished data), and suggests that the recycling of nitrogen within each upper layer segment, not the input of "new" nitrogen from adjacent segments,

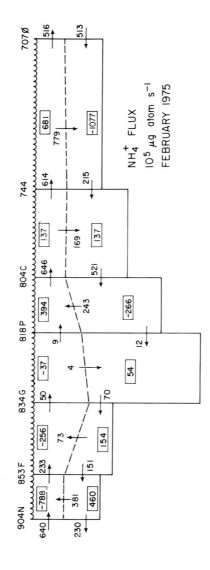

Figure 3. Ammonium flux for February 1975.

Table 1. Sources (+) and sinks (−) of ammonium and nitrate expressed as mass per liter per day for February 1975.

	Upper Layer μg atom $(\text{liter} \cdot \text{day})^{-1}$		Lower Layer μg atom $(\text{liter} \cdot \text{day})^{-1}$	
	NH_4^+	NO_3^-	NH_4^+	NO_3^-
904N				
	−6.2	−2.6	+8.4	+3.0
853F				
	−0.7	−0.3	+2.2	+1.7
834G				
	−0.1	+0.6	+0.5	+0.2
818P				
	+1.0	−0.9	−1.2	+0.8
744				
	+0.4	−0.1	−1.1	−0.4
707ϕ				

is the more significant process south of 853F.

Ammonium flux in May 1975 (Figure 4) was characterized by input of 225 x 10^5 μg atom $\cdot$s^{-1} in the upper layer from north of station 904N, 76% of which was lost from the water, presumably the result of phytoplankton uptake. About 15% was lost vertically to the lower layer and 8% was transported downstream. Loss from the upper layer between stations 904N and 818P (275 x 10^5 μg atom $\cdot$s^{-1}) was nearly balanced (82%) by the single 225 x 10^5 μg atom$\cdot$s^{-1} input from north of station 904N. The remaining 18% was contributed from the lower layer. Export from the northern bay across the boundary represented by 818P approximately equalled the vertical flux in segment 834G-818P. In contrast to the February ammonium flux, lower layer input to the northern bay was about three times the upper layer export.

The southern bay (818P-707ϕ) incurred a 395 x 10^5 μg atom$\cdot$s^{-1} ammonium loss which was nearly balanced by vertical flux of 376 x 10^5 μg atom$\cdot$s^{-1}. Ammonium input with the lower layer ocean water was more than three times the surface loss to the continental shelf waters. Landward ammonium flux increased to segment 818P-804C then dropped sharply across boundaries 818P and 834G. Excess net ammonium production was calculated for lower layer 804C-707ϕ but net loss was indicated in lower layer 834G-804C.

The nitrate flux calculations for May 1975 (Figure 5) indicate production in all lower layer segments. However, nitrate production was only 66% of ammonium loss in segment 834G-818P, so other processes could be involved.

Other characteristics of the nitrate flux are substantial input from north of station 904N (520 μg atom $\cdot$s^{-1}) as observed by Carpenter *et al.* (1969); loss in the surface waters, except in segment 818P-804C which showed a net nitrate

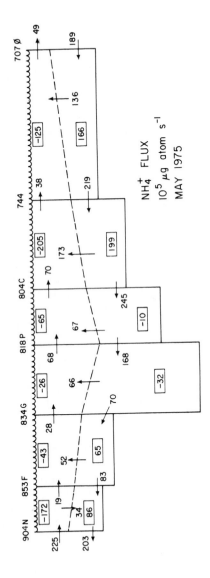

Figure 4. Ammonium flux for May 1975.

NH$_4^+$ FLUX
10^5 μg atom s^{-1}
MAY 1975

707 Ø   744   804C   818 P   834 G   853 F   904 N

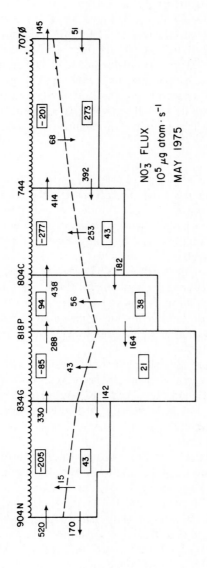

Figure 5. Nitrate flux for May 1975.

increase; significant downstream transport and net export in the upper layer; relatively low vertical flux rates except in segment 804C-744; and significant landward movement of nitrate in the deep water.

The most striking feature of the ammonium flux for August 1976 (Figure 6) was an excess production of 720×10^5 μg atom·s^{-1} in lower segment 853F-834G combined with a downward flux of 319×10^5 μg atom·s^{-1}, resulting in landward lower layer flux of 1126×10^5 μg atom·s^{-1}. Vertical flux from lower to upper segment 904N-853F accounted for 967×10^5 μg atom·s^{-1}. A physical ammonium cycle appears to have existed in the 904N-834G segment with seaward flux in the upper layer, downward flux in the 853F-834G segment, landward flux in the lower layer and upward flux in the 904N-853F segment. Downward flux in the 853F-834G segment was not observed in the previously discussed winter and spring calculation.

Discussion

The majority of estuaries along the east coast of the United States are partially-mixed, coastal-plain-type estuaries. These were formed by the drowning of river valleys during the most recent rise in sea level and are characterized dynamically by vertical salinity variations and by a net circulation pattern which is directed seaward in the upper layers and landward in the lower layers. This circulation pattern is the result of the interaction between two pressure distributions: one directed upstream and due to the horizontal variation in salinity; and the other directed downstream and due to the mean slope of the free surface. The interaction of these pressure forces with the tidally generated turbulence leads to the characteristic vertical variations in salinity and velocity which are observed in partially-mixed estuaries.

Superimposed on the physical circulation is a biochemical circulation (Redfield, 1955) in which nutrient elements incorporated into particles in seaward flowing surface waters sink and move landward, eventually being remineralized. Thus nutrients remain in estuaries and support the observed high production rates. In this paper we address the circulation of two soluble nutrients, NH_4^+ and $NO_3^=$, without the particulate phase.

The longitudinal ammonium flux rates in seaward flowing surface waters were higher in winter than in spring or summer, with peak values exceeding 600 $\times 10^5$ μg atom·s^{-1} in certain Chesapeake Bay segments. In general, the landward flux was less than seaward flux in winter and greater than seaward flux in spring and summer. Landward flux rates were frequently greater than 200×10^5 μg atom·s^{-1} and the peak exceeded 1000×10^5 μg atom·s^{-1} in the upper bay during summer. However, the seaward flux of nitrate in spring exceeded the landward flux by a factor of 2 or more at most boundaries.

Only the spring nitrate calculations indicate nutrient loss to the coastal ocean. Complex physical circulation and biological activity in southernmost Chesapeake Bay result in net ammonium retention and perhaps even ammonium gain from coastal ocean waters in spring and summer.

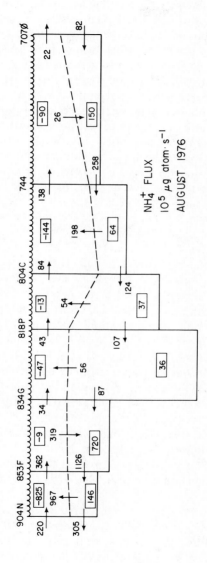

Figure 6. Ammonium flux for August 1976.

127

The sum of advective and diffusive vertical ammonium transports was temporally and spatially variable with the higher upward rates in the northern bay during winter and summer. Carpenter *et al* (1969) estimated negligible upward ammonium flux in the upper Chesapeake Bay compared to phytoplankton requirements during low flow conditions. Our results generally support their findings for the region south of 38°53'N. However, upward flux between 853F and 904N can periodically supply 50--100% of the phytoplankton nitrogen requirement (Figures 3 and 6). Except for segment 804C-744 (Figure 5), upward vertical nitrate flux was much less than longitudinal flux. Such results could be expected since the Susquehanna River is the primary nitrate source. However, the net upward vertical nitrate transport north of station 744 was somewhat surprising. With a known source at the surface, net downward movement was expected. Two possible explanations are: 1) Nitrate is being produced via ammonium oxidation in the deepwater/sediment as indicated by the net production values in Figure 5; or 2) Nitrate is mixed downward near shore and advected to mid-channel where the measurements were made. Results from experiments reviewed by Vaccaro (1965) suggest that ammonium oxidation is possible, yielding energy to those bacteria involved. But possibility 2 cannot be ruled out as a contributing factor without additional research.

Although substantial quantities of ammonium are moved by advective and diffusive processes, the non-conservative aspects, such as deepwater accumulation rates and sources, are perhaps more significant in plankton ecology. Spring and summer data (Figure 2) clearly show elevated deepwater ammonium concentrations but the winter data do not. However, Figure 3 does indicate net deepwater ammonium production between stations 904N and 818P, and between 804C and 744 in winter. The model quantitates net ammonium accumulation at 54 to 460 x 10^5 μg atom $\cdot$ s^{-1} in February, 65 to 199 x 10^5 in May, and 36 to 720 x 10^5 in August. Predominant sources should be excretion by protozoan and metazoan heterotrophs, and release from sediment interstitial water where ammonium is dissolved as a product of benthic bacterial activity and other heterotrophic metabolism. The well-oxygenated winter and spring deepwater should support animal activity and the resultant ammonium excretion, but the anaerobic summer deepwater containing hydrogen sulfide should not. Ammonium release by diffusion and tidal pumping from sediment interstitial water should be prevalent regardless of oxygen content in the overlying water (Hartwig, 1976; Rowe *et al.,* 1975).

Net ammonium loss from deepwater occurred in mid-bay and lower bay in February 1975 and mid-bay in May 1975. Mechanisms are not clear, but at least four possibilities exist. First, lateral water circulation could carry ammonium into the shallows and thereby induce vertical motion not accounted for in our averaging procedures. Second, uptake by bacteria or phytoplankton is possible, even at low light intensities (Eppley *et al.,* 1971; Bhovichitra and Swift, 1977). Third, ammonium could be oxidized by heterotrophic activity to nitrite or nitrate. Fourth, ammonium could adsorb to organic coatings on non-living particles, but it is unlikely such activity would be significant enough to cause net ammonium loss from the deepwater. One of the first two mechanisms is more likely.

Acknowledgments

This research was supported by ERDA Contract EY-76-S-02-3279, Document No. COO-3279-30, and by NSF Grants GA-33445 and OCE 76-11399. Chesapeake Bay Institute Contribution No. 252. We gratefully acknowledge the analytical assistance of R. Loftus, the help provided by the crew on the R/V Warfield and the data processing competence of J. Smith. We thank Drs. J. H. Carpenter and R. Ulanowicz for critically reading the manuscript.

References

1. Bhovichitra, M., and E. Swift. 1977. Light and dark uptake of nitrate and ammonium by large oceanic dinoflagellates: *Pyrocystis noctiluca Pyrocystis fusiformis*, and *Dissodinium lunula*. Limnol Oceanogr. 22:73-83.

2. Carpenter, J. H., D. W. Prtichard and R. C. Whaley. 1969. Observations of eutrophication and nutrient cycles in some coastal plain estuaries, pp. 210-221. *In* Eutrophication: Causes, Consequences, Correctives. Natl. Acad. Sci. Publ. 1700.

3. Cronin, W. B. 1975. Additional statistics on the dimensions of the Chesapeake Bay and its tributaries: Cross-section widths and segment volumes per meter depth. Ches. Bay Inst. Spec. Rept. 42.

4. Elliott, A. J. 1976a. Methods for determining the concentrations and sources of pollutants in estuaries. Ches. Bay Inst. Spec. Rept. 50.

5. _____ . 1976b. Estimates of advection and diffusion in the Potomac Estuary. J. Environ. Sci. Health — Environ. Sci. Eng. All (2):131-152.

6. Eppley, R. W., J. N. Rogers and J. J. McCarthy. 1971. Light/dark periodicity in nitrogen assimilation of the marine phytoplankters *Skeletonema costatum* and *Coccolithus hyxleyi* in N-limited chemostat culture. J. Phycology 7:150-154.

7. Flemer. D. A. 1970. Primary production in the Chesapeake Bay. Chesapeake Sci. 11:117-129.

8. Hansen, D. V. 1967. Salt balance and circulation in partially mixed estuaries, pp. 45-51. *In* G. Lauff (ed.), Estuaries, Amer. Assoc. Adv. Sci. Publ. 83.

9. Hartwig, E. O. 1976. The impact of nitrogen and phosphorus release from a siliceous sediment on the overlying water, pp. 103-117. *In* M. Wiley (ed.), Estuarine Processes, Academic Press, New York.

10. McCarthy, J. J., W. R. Taylor and J. L. Taft. 1977. Nitrogenous nutrition of the plankton in the Chesapeake Bay. 1. Nutrient availability and phytoplankton preferences. Limnol. Oceanogr. 22:996-1011.

11. Pritchard, D. W. 1967. What is an estuary: physical viewpoint, pp. 3-5. *In* G. Lauff (ed.), Estuaries, Amer. Assoc. Adv. Sci. Publ. 83.

12. _____ . 1969. Dispersion and flushing of pollutants in estuaries. J. Hydraulics Div. Amer. Soc. Civil. Eng. 95, No. HY 1, Proc. Paper 6344, 115-125.

13. Redfield, A. C. 1955. The hydrography of the Gulf of Venezuela. Deep-Sea Res. Suppl. to Vol. 3:115-133.

14. Rowe, G. T., C. H. Clifford, K. L. Smith, and P. L. Hamilton. 1975. Benthic nutrient regeneration and its coupling to primary productivity in coastal waters. Nature 255:215-217.

15. Schiemer, E. W., and D. W. Pritchard. 1961. An induction conductivity indicator. Ches. Bay Inst. Tech. Report 25.

16. Solórzano, L. 1969. Determination of ammonia in natural waters by the phenylhypochlorite method. Limnol. Oceanogr. 14:799-801.

17. Strickland, J. D. H., and T. R. Parsons. 1972. A practical handbook of seawater analysis, 2nd ed. Bull. Fish Res. Bd. Can. 167.

18. Taylor, W. R., and V. Grant. 1977. Plankton ecology project. Nutrient and chlorophyll data — Aesop cruises April 1969 to April 1971. Ches. Bay Inst. Spec. Report 61.

19. Vaccaro, R. F. 1965. Inorganic nitrogen in sea water, pp. 365-408. *In* J. Riley and G. Skirrow (eds.), Chemical Oceanography, Academic Press, London.

20. Whaley, R. D., J. H. Carpenter and R. L. Baker. 1966. Nutrient data summary 1964, 1965, 1966; Upper Chesapeake Bay (Smith Point to Turkey Point), Potomac, South, Severn, Magothy, Back, Chester, and Miles Rivers; and Eastern Bay. Ches. Bay Inst. Spec. Report 12.

21. Wood, E. P., F. A. J. Armstrong, and F. A. Richards. 1967. Determination of nitrate in sea water by cadmium-copper reduction to nitrate. J. Mar. Bio. Assoc. U. K. 47:23-31.

ESTUARINE ANGIOSPERMS: PRODUCTIVITY AND INITIAL PHOTOSYNTHATE DISPERSION IN THE ECOSYSTEM

John L. Gallagher

The University of Georgia Marine Institute
Sapelo Island, Georgia

Abstract: A number of species of angiosperms are adapted to high salinity wetland environments. They are organized into communities that form recognizable entities from the arctic to the tropics. Seagrass beds, marshes and mangrove swamps are systems which have largely detritus-based food webs. Mangrove swamps in the tropics represent the ecosystem equivalent of the marshes which are prevalent at higher latitudes. In the subtropics, the two intermingle and seagrass beds are adjacent to both in most waters where light penetration is sufficient. Beaches often derive their organic nutrition from detritus in adjacent marshes, swamps and seagrass beds.

Some representatives of these three systems rank among the most productive examples of natural or managed ecosystems. Most of the measurements available on primary productivity and initial photosynthate dispersion are limited to aerial production. Those data available on underground production indicate root system growth is often as great as shoot development.

In spite of the importance of detritus in these systems, relatively little emphasis has been placed on the early stages (senescence, organic material leaching, microbial colonization, and community metabolic activity) of that food web. As membranes lose their integrity during senescence it appears that organic carbon dispersion by leaching is quantitatively more important than gaseous respiratory losses. Later, when the dead plants become heavily colonized by bacteria and fungi, the microbes mediate the net leaching rate. Environmental conditions influence both the rates and the proportion of gases and larger molecules produced. Both physical and biological factors are important in determining the particle size of the detritus which is exported from these systems.

In addition to their role in primary production, the vegetation in these wetlands provides shelter for adult and young planktonic and pelagic organisms and forms a substrate for epiphytes. Furthermore, the plants slow water current velocities, thereby reducing erosion and promoting sediment accretion.

Introduction

Several hundred species of angiosperms are adapted to living in saline tidal wetlands. They are organized into wetland communities that form recognizable entities from the arctic to the tropics. McRoy and Helfferich (1977) recognize

131

49 species of seagrasses which live in shallow saline water from the tropics to the Arctic Circle. Higher in the intertidal zone more than 100 angiosperm species grow in saline marshes within this range. At the lower latitudes, marshes are largely replaced by mangroves. Although the number can change depending on what genera are included in the definition of mangroves, about 70 species are distributed world-wide (Chapman, 1976). These wetland plant systems have the potential for high productivity and in some locations rank among the world's most productive natural or managed ecosystems. As in many ecosystems, most of the photosynthate flows through the detritus rather than grazing food webs.

Perhaps the most significant aspect of all these systems is their interaction with each other and adjacent systems (Figure 1). A dense, moving, fluid medium with excellent solvent characteristics either constantly or periodically inundates them. The mechanism for exchange of soluble and particulate material is thus highly developed.

Because of the role of tidal waters in both the internal and external functions (interactions) of each of these wetlands they are extremely sensitive to substrate elevational alterations. Natural fluctuations in sea level due to changes in polar ice cap thickness, land subsidence or rising can affect inundation. Sedimentation rates may change as silt loads in rivers vary because of water velocity alterations or discharge volume changes. These changes may be natural as plant succession in the watershed causes differences in runoff rate and soil erosion. As dramatic as these changes may be on a geologic time scale, their short-term impact is likely to be small when compared to that caused by man's activities.

Each of these wetland types has internal functions affecting species of importance to man. Also, the systems interact extensively (external functions) with adjacent ecosystems involving species and functions whose roles are important to man. As a result, a large volume of literature has been produced about

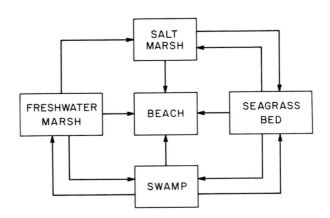

Figure 1. Movement of materials between wetland ecosystems.

some aspects of these wetlands. Until recently most of the work with these systems has involved their natural history. Work on the primary and secondary production and the flow of energy through these systems began early in East Coast marshes (Pomeroy, 1959; Teal, 1962; Odum and de la Cruz, 1967; Smalley, 1958) and has continued until the present (Woodwell and Whitney, in press; Pomeroy *et al.*, 1976). More recently, such studies have begun on Gulf Coast marshes (Kirby and Gosselink, 1976; Day *et al.*, 1973). Similar studies on West Coast marshes are just beginning (Mahall and Park, 1976; Eilers, 1974; Winfield and Zedler, 1977). Less research has been published on seagrass bed productivity (Zieman, 1968; Phillips, 1974) and quantitative estimates of their energy flow pattern (Thayer *et al.*, 1975) than on estuarine marshes. Chapman (1976) recently reviewed distribution and mangrove autecology. Heald (1971) presented production data on Florida mangrove swamps and Odum (1971) examined the role mangrove detritus played in the estuarine food web.

My purpose in this paper is to review briefly some of the work on primary production in these three wetland systems and to focus on some of the work we have done on the dispersion of photosynthate from saline-adapted angiosperms.

Primary Production

Marshes

In recent years there have been a number of reviews of salt marsh primary production (Keefe, 1972; Turner, 1976). Production values range widely depending on species, the intertidal elevation of a given species in the marsh, and the nature of substrate on which the plants are growing. Most of the estimates made thus far come from Atlantic Coast marshes. Typical values in Maine range from 485 g dry wt m^{-2} yr^{-1} for *Juncus gerardi* to 5163 g dry wt m^{-2} yr^{-1} for *Spartina patens* (Linthurst, 1977). Within species, variation can be seen when populations of creekbank and high marsh *J. gerardi* are compared. The creekbank produced approximately 3500 g dry wt m^{-2} yr^{-1} while the high marsh only produced 485 g dry wt m^{-2} yr^{-1} (Linthurst, 1977). Various methods have been used to estimate net primary production. Peak standing crop (Milner and Hughes, 1968), changes in living and dead biomass (Smalley, 1958), stem life and death (Williams and Murdoch, 1972), biomass changes plus corrections for death (Wiegert and Evans, 1964), and calculations from gas exchange data (Giurgevich, 1977) have all been used to estimate net primary production. Each method has its advantages and disadvantages for each species and each environmental setting. There seems to be no "standard method" suitable for all species and the procedure must be chosen from a series of tested methods depending on the type of marsh to be sampled. Results of studies on peak biomass of living marsh plants for salt marshes along the Atlantic, Gulf, and Pacific coasts are summarized in Table 1. At least 28 primary production studies have been or are currently being conducted on the Atlantic coast and a survey of the literature revealed 11 on the Gulf coast. The literature on the Pacific coast is not so voluminous and only five published primary production studies were located for these marshes. Species diversity in western

Table 1. Peak living biomass of marsh plants on the East and Gulf Coasts. (g dry wt m^{-2})

		Species		
State	Spartina alterniflora	Spartina patens	Juncus roemerianus	Distichlis spicata
ME	863t 887s[1]	3036[1]		
MA	300[2]			
NY		991[3] 503[4]		647[4] 985[5]
NJ	300[6]	724 623[7]		
VA	459[8] 1570t 695m[9]	805[9]	650[9]	306[9]
NC	455s 1752t[10]	1555 898[10]	2088[10]	
GA	3315t[12] 2182s 1966t 388s[13]	2304[1]	1538[15]	1718[1] 603[13]
DL	572[5]	1924[1]	1308[1]	2444[1]
LA	1906t 1544s [14] 1948t 1488s[16]	1685[15]		
TX	735 1551 1143[17] 1846			

References
[1] Linthurst, 1977
[2] Valiela, Teal, and Sass, 1975
[3] Harper, 1918
[4] Udell et al., 1969
[5] Morgan, 1961
[6] Good, 1965
[7] Nadeau, 1972
[8] Mendelssohn and Marcellis, 1976
[9] Wass and Wright, 1969
[10] Stroud and Cooper, 1968
[11] Waits, 1967
[12] Odum and Fanning, 1973
[13] Gallagher et al., 1972
[14] Kirby, 1971
[15] Payonk, 1975
[16] Kirby and Gosselink, 1976
[17] Turner and Gosselink, 1975
t = tall
s = short

Table 2. Peak living biomass (g dry wt m^{-2}) of marsh plants on the Pacific Coast.

Species

State	*Salicornia virginica*	*Spartina foliosa*	*Carex lyngbyei*	*Triglochin maritima*	*Distichlis spicata*	*Potentilla pacifica*	*Deschampsia caespitosa*
CA	2722 2000[18]	203 109 626[18] 401					
OR	184[19]		206[19]	130[19]	72[19]	60[20]	106[19]

References

[18] Mahall and Park, 1976
[19] Hoffnagle, 1976
[20] Eilers, 1974

marshes is high, particularly in the Northwest, and most of the marsh research in this geographical area has focused on understanding community structure and species distribution patterns.

At the U.S. Environmental Protection Agency Corvallis Environmental Research Laboratory we are currently conducting research on net primary production on the nine major salt marsh species found in the Pacific Northwest. Grasses *(Distichlis spicata)*, broad-leafed herbs *(Potentilla pacifica)*, sedges *(Carex lyngbyei)*, rushes *(Juncus balticus)*, and succulents *(Salicornia virginica)* represent a variety of growth forms. Because of this variation, a variety of sampling techniques are being used. Only on the west coast would further refinement of aerial primary production values seem to be needed for understanding the angiosperm input into the aerial part of the ecosystem. Underground production may be as great as or more than aerial although the documentation is not very extensive. Valiela *et al.* (1976) have estimated underground productivity in *S. alterniflora* in Massachusetts to be 3500 g dry wt m^{-2} yr^{-1}. Our estimates based on sampling 18 sites involving 10 species ranged from 100 to 1700 gC m^{-2} yr^{-1} (Gallagher *et al.*, in press). Our higher values are very close to those obtained by Valiela *et al.* (1976). In many areas where coastal marshes are adjacent to seagrass beds, there may be a significant exchange of organic material between the two systems.

Seagrasses

These inconspicuous wetlands (seagrass beds), like the marshes, are often very productive and highly variable in carbon fixation. Phillips (1974) reports values for *Zostera marina* ranging from 140 to 800 g organic matter m^{-2}. Assuming 40% carbon, data from Jones (1968) for *Thalassia testudinum* converts to 1500 g organic matter m^{-2}. There have been a few studies which have identified several factors that regulate primary production. Nutrient concentrations in both soil and water can be factors, since nutrients can be absorbed either through leaves or roots, at least in *Zostera* (McRoy and Barsdate, 1970). Irradiance levels are important in determining turion density and hence productivity in *Zostera* (Backman and Barilotti, 1976). Few data on the underground portions of the plants are available, although Jones (1968) reports a dry weight underground biomass of 1500 to 2500 g m^{-2} for *Thalassia*.

Mangroves

Estimates of mangrove productivity approximate 100 g dry wt m^{-2} yr^{-1} (Golley *et al.*, 1962; Miller, 1972). I was able to find no estimates of root productivity in the literature. Much remains to be done in evaluating mangrove primary productivity and the factors regulating it.

These brief considerations of primary production in various wetland types serve to show that the unperturbated systems are often among our most productive natural or managed ecosystems and how widely their primary production varies.

Dispersion of the Photosynthate

At the production site

Figure 2 shows the dispersion of net productivity from a generalized wetland system. In *Spartina* marshes net leaching losses from the leaves of living plants averaged 5 g C m^{-2} yr^{-1} (Gallagher *et al.*, 1976). Since this material is readily consumed by microbes it may represent a more important contribution than its small quantity indicates. Studies with *Thalassia* indicate that net losses from seagrasses to the estuarine water are somewhat higher than has been measured from marsh plants and a much smaller loss of photosynthate than is usually reported for algae (Thomas, 1970). Recently, however, Sharp (1977) has challenged the high values for phytoplankton.

Constant contact with tidal waters would be the norm for seagrasses. Marsh plants on the average are exposed to the atmosphere much more than they are inundated. As a consequence of these two immersion patterns, the pattern of DOC (dissolved organic carbon) release to the estuary from the two types of wetlands will be different in several respects. Since the seagrass beds are in constant interaction with the estuarine system, the DOC release will be continual. Marsh plants on the other hand will pulse the system with a frequency which will be a function of their intertidal elevation and the tidal wave characteristics of the basin. A second contrasting characteristic between seagrass and marsh plant DOC release is the influence of rainfall. Freshwater leaching is certainly of major importance in high marshes such as the *Juncus gerardi* marshes of the Northeast and the *Deschampsia caespitosa* marshes of the Northwest. Likewise, rainfall leaching is

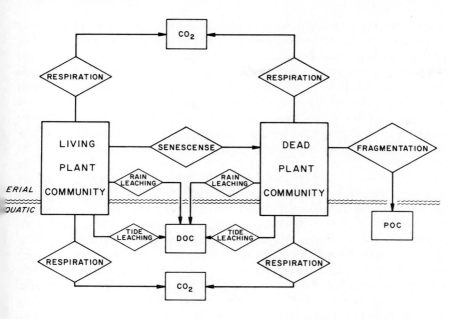

Figure 2. Conceptual model of dispersion of photosynthate from wetland plants. POC = particulate organic carbon, DOC = dissolved organic carbon.

the major type of leaching associated with living leaves in mangrove swamps, whereas it is of little significance in most seagrass beds.

DOC release from wetland plant roots may act to maintain a rhizosphere flora. We attempted to measure this type of release in *Spartina alterniflora* growing high on a sandy intertidal bar in Georgia. A pit was dug and roots carefully excavated, using a fine water jet from a squeeze bottle. At least an hour was required to obtain a root we were confident was undamaged. We were unable to detect a net release of DOC in any of the five root and three rhizome segments measured using the method described by Gallagher *et al.* (1976). Either the microbes attached to the tissue were acting as efficient filters or the tissues were not releasing DOC. Many questions regarding DOC release from living tissue remain unanswered or unasked for even the most studied of the estuarine angiosperms.

Respiratory release of CO_2 by the living plants represents a loss rather than an interaction between the plant and the estuary. The extent to which the photosynthate is respired rather than lost as DOC or stored for members of the detritus food web may be a function of the environment within the wetland.

The diversion of energy from growth to osmoregulation is one obvious area where environmental regulation of photosynthate dispersion occurs. The greater the salt stress the more energy may be directed to the excretion of salt by plant species such as *Distichlis spicata, Spartina alterniflora,* and *Sporobolus virginicus.*

In addition, the proportion of plant material directed above and below ground may likewise be altered by environmental conditions. Gallagher (1975), working with nitrogen enrichment of *Spartina alterniflora,* noted that a larger percentage of the photosynthetic resources were allocated to aerial portions of the plants in the fertilized marsh. In *Sporobolus virginicus,* high salinity reduced root growth more than aerial development (Gallagher, in press).

As the plant material senesces, the metabolism changes from that of the macrophyte to that of the colonizing microflora. Marsh plants are quickly colonized by fungi and bacteria (Gessner and Goos, 1973; Seliskar *et al.,* 1977). We have estimated rates of *Spartina alterniflora* leaf senescence by measuring the rate of advance of the death front; during the fall the rate averaged 5.5 mm/day (Gallagher and Seliskar, 1976). Respiratory rates of senescing plant leaves and the dead plant leaf communities were 51% and 31%, respectively, of the living plant tissue. Compared to the living leaf, the biomass of microbial tissue is probably very low in the case of the dead leaf communities. Dissolved carbohydrate release was highest from the dead plant community and lowest in the senescing leaves. Heald (1971) found leaf senescence and drop in *Rhizophora* to be greatest in June and July. Seagrass senescence and death is, of course, species and environment dependent. Temperate seagrass species such as *Zostera marina* drop to a very low biomass in winter. The tropic seagrass *Thalassia* by contrast maintains a relatively high biomass throughout the year.

Dead material from all these wetland types decays in either the estuarine water or in an intertidal zone where it is alternately wet and dry.

In those high areas in the marsh most decay is under aerial conditions while at the lower elevations much of the time the conditions are aquatic. Aerial respiratory rates of the dead plant community have a positive linear correlation with moisture content (Seliskar *et al.,* 1977) in marsh grass. With various species of mangrove and marsh plants those highest in the intertidal zone had lower respiration rates and higher DOC leaching rates than their lower elevation counterparts (Gallagher, unpublished data). Seagrasses decay in a totally submerged habitat and Fenchel (1977) gives an excellent review of the literature on their decomposition in the seagrass beds. While most of the seagrass biomass decays in the grass beds, a portion ends up on the beaches and decays there.

On the beach

There are three beach zones above the low tide mark which seem to have different major sources of organic nutrients. The zone below the mean high tide line is frequently bathed with water rich in dissolved organic compounds and fine organic particulate matter. Above the influence of all but storm tides the sand is normally vegetated by macrophytes. The attached plant input in the form of leached organics, leaf and stem litter, as well as dead roots and rhizomes, undoubtedly constitutes the major source of organic nutrition in that region. Between this vegetated zone and the one frequently inundated by the tides is a zone without living macrophytes or daily tidal input. This portion of the beach varies in width from a few meters in some profiles to 70 or more meters in others.

Wrack, transported by the spring tides, accumulates in this back beach zone and comprises the major organic input. Although some of this wrack in the estuarine environment consists of inert products of civilization, most of it is detritus exported from neighboring wetlands. The material imported from marshes has first been partially "processed" on the marsh surface (Gallagher and Pfeiffer, 1977) and in the tidal creeks (Odum and de la Cruz, 1967; Burkholder and Bornside, 1957). The most resistant macrodetritus (primarily whole stems) is transported out of the marsh and accumulates on the beaches. Figure 3 shows a conceptual model of the breakdown of this wrack. After the wrack is stranded, its moisture content decreases and the respiratory rate of the microbial community declines. Shifting sand covers the material and respiration rates once again rise but remain below rates in the marsh (20 vs $80 \mu g C \ m^{-2} \ hr^{-1}$). In the beach plant material, decay proceeds under much different environmental conditions than on the marshes where it was produced or in water which transported it to the beach. Beach temperatures are higher, water movement more rapid and the conditions more oxidizing than in the marsh. In January the standing crop of *Spartina alterniflora* detritus averaged 260 g dry wt m^{-2} over a 30-meter wide zone in an accreting beach on Sapelo Island, Georgia, where the tidal range is about 2.5 meters. In Santa Rosa Sound in Florida, where the tidal range was about 0.5 meters, *Thalassia testudinum* and *Halodule wrightii* averaged 52 g m^{-2} dry weight over a 2.5 meter wide band.

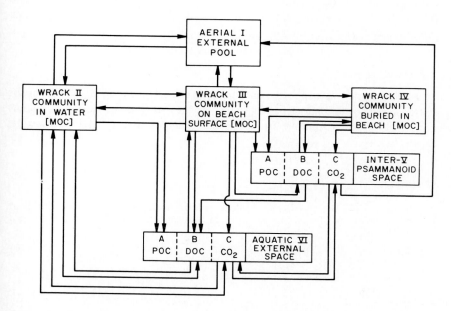

Figure 3. Conceptual model of decomposition of wrack on beaches. MOC = macro-organic carbon.

Since the most readily digestible material has been removed by earlier decay and the surface area decreased by removal of leaves, the respiratory rates for *Spartina* dead plant community would be expected to be lower at this stage of decay. Since the seagrass beds were only a few meters from the beach the material washing ashore was senescing or recently dead and community respiratory rates were high. The *Spartina,* on the other hand, had been partially decayed in the marsh and further degraded during its rather long transport from the marsh. C:N ratios for the seagrass wrack ranged from 8 to 15 while that for *Spartina* wrack were between 50 and 60. The DOC release rates from the two types of wrack indicate the seagrass wrack released 400 to 600 μgC^{-1} g dry wt hr^{-1} while the *Spartina* was less than 50 μgC^{-1} g dry wt hr^{-1}. The dynamics of wetland angiosperms transported to the beach is not well understood. The existence of feedback mechanisms from the beach to the adjacent wetlands is another matter for investigation.

Research needs

Refinement of aerial primary production estimates probably will not provide any further new insight into the functioning of saline marsh ecosystems, especially on the Atlantic and Gulf coasts. However, more data are needed on production for the above-ground portions of seagrasses and mangroves, and on the productivity of root systems of all three systems. Factors regulating productivity and photosynthate dispersion are generally not well understood, although the processes have been described. The interaction between wetland systems and the possibility of feedback mechanisms through tidal water has not been investigated to any extent.

Acknowledgments

This work was supported in part by grant DES72-016050-A02 from the National Science Foundation and grants from the Sapelo Island Research Foundation, Inc. Contribution 359 from the University of Georgia Marine Institute, Sapelo Island.

References

1. Backman, T. W., and D. C. Barilotti. 1976. Irradiance reduction: effects on standing crops of the eelgrass *Zostera marina* in a coastal lagoon. Mar. Biol. 34:33-40.

2. Burkholder, P. R., and G. H. Bornside. 1957. Decomposition of marsh grass by aerobic marine bacteria. Bull. Torrey Bot. Club 84:366-383.

3. Chapman, V. J. 1976. Mangrove Vegetation. J. Cramer, Germany. 447 pp.

4. Day, J. W., W. G. Smith, P. R. Wagner, and W. G. Stowe. 1973. Community structure and carbon budget of a salt marsh and shallow bay estuarine system in Louisiana. Louisiana State Univ., Baton Rouge. 79 pp.

5. Eilers, H. P. 1974. Plants, plant communities, net production and the tide

levels: the ecological biogeography of the Nehalem salt marshes, Tillamook County, Oregon. Ph.D. dissertation, Oregon State Univ., Corvallis. 368 pp.

6. Fenchel, T. 1977. Aspects of the decomposition of seagrasses, pp. 123-193. *In* C. P. McRoy and C. Helfferich (eds.), Seagrass Ecosystems. Marcel Dekker, Inc. New York. 314 pp.

7. Gallagher, J. L. 1975. Effect of an ammonium nitrate pulse on the growth and elemental composition of natural stands of *Spartina alterniflora* and *Juncus roemerianus*. Am. J. Bot. 62 (6):644-648.

8. _____ . In press. The influence of salinity on morphology, growth and element compositional responses of *Sporobolus virginicus* (L.) Kunth to substrate salinity and nitrogen status. Amer. Mid. Nat.

9. Gallagher, J. L., and W. H. Pfeiffer. 1977. Aquatic metabolism of the communities associated with attached dead shoots of salt marsh plants. Limnol. Oceanogr. 22:562-565.

10. Gallagher, J. L., W. J. Pfeiffer, and L. R. Pomeroy. 1976. Leaching and microbial utilization of dissolved organic carbon from leaves of *Spartina alterniflora*. Estuarine Coastal Mar. Sci. 4:467-471.

11. Gallagher, J. L., F. G. Plumley, and D. L. Wolf. In press. Underground biomass dynamics and substrate selective properties of Atlantic coastal salt marsh plants. Technical report. Office, Chief of Engineers, U.S. Army.

12. Gallagher, J. L., R. J. Reimold, and D. E. Thompson. 1972. Remote sensing and salt marsh productivity. Proc. 38th Ann. Mtg. Am. Soc. Photogrammetry. Washington, D.C. pp. 338-348.

13. Gallagher, J. L., and D. M. Seliskar. 1976. The metabolism of senescing *Spartina alterniflora*. Botanical Society of America Annual Meeting, Tulane Univ. New Orleans, La. (Abstr.).

14. Gessner, R. V., and R. D. Goos. 1973. Fungi from *Spartina alterniflora* in Rhode Island. Mycologia 65:1296-1301.

15. Giurgevich, J. R. 1977. Seasonal patterns of carbon metabolism and plant water relations of *Juncus roemerianus* (Scheele) and *Spartina alterniflora* (Loisel) in a Georgia salt marsh. Ph.D. dissertation, Univ. of Georgia, Athens.

16. Golley, F., H. T. Odum, and R. F. Wilson. 1962. The structure and metabolism of a Puerto Rican mangrove forest in May. Ecology 43:9-19.

17. Good, R. E. 1965. Salt marsh vegetation, Cape May, New Jersey. Bull. New Jersey Acad. Sci. 10 1:1-11.

18. Harper, R. M. 1918. Some dynamic studies of Long Island vegetation. Plant World 21:38-46.

19. Heald, E. J. 1971. The production of organic detritus in a south Florida estuary. Univ. of Miami. Sea Grant Technical Bulletin Number 6. 110 pp.

20. Hoffnagle, J. 1976. A comparative study of salt marshes in the Coos Bay estuary. Oregon Institute Marine Biology. 330 pp.

21. Jones, J. A. 1968. Primary productivity by the tropical marine turtle grass, *Thalassia testudinum* Konig, and its epiphytes. Ph.D. dissertation, Univ. of Miami, Miami, Fla. 196 pp.

22. Keefe, C. W. 1972. Marsh production: a summary of the literature. Contrib. Mar. Sci., Univ. of Texas 16:163-81.

23. Kirby, C. J. 1971. The annual net primary production and decompositon of the salt marsh grass *Spartina alterniflora* in the Barataria Bay estuary of Louisiana. Ph.D. dissertation. Louisiana State Univ., Baton Rouge. 74 pp.

24. Kirby, C. J., and J. G. Gosselink. 1976. Primary production in a Louisiana

gulf coast *Spartina alterniflora* marsh. Ecology 57 (5):1052-9.

25. Linthurst, R. A. 1977. An evaluation of biomass, stem density, net aerial primary production (NAPP) and NAPP estuarine methodology for selected estuarine angiosperms in Maine, Delaware and Georgia. M.S. thesis, North Carolina State Univ., Raleigh. 141 pp.

26. Mahall, B. E., and R. B. Park. 1976. The ecotone between *Spartina foliosa* Trin. and *Salicornia virginica* L. in salt marshes of northern San Francisco Bay. J. Ecology. 64:421-33.

27. McRoy, C. P., and R. J. Barsdate. 1970. Phosphate absorption in eelgrass. Limnol. Oceanogr. 15 (1):6-13.

28. McRoy, C. P., and C. Helfferich (eds.). 1977. Seagrass Ecosystems. Marcel Dekker, Inc. New York. 314 pp.

29. Mendelssohn, I. A., and K. L. Marcellis. 1976. Angiosperm production of three Virginia marshes in various salinity and soil nutrient regimes. Chesapeake Sci. 17:15-23.

30. Miller, P. C. 1972. Bioclimate, leaf temperature and primary production in red mangrove canopies in south Florida. Ecology 53:22-45.

31. Milner, C., and R. E. Hughes. 1968. Methods for the measurement of the primary production of grasslands. IBP Handbook No. 6. Blackwell Scientific Publ. Oxford. 70 pp.

32. Morgan, M. H. 1961. Annual angiosperm production on a salt marsh. M.S. thesis, Univ. of Delaware, Newark. 34 pp.

33. Nadeau, R. J. 1972. Primary production and export of plant material in the salt marsh ecosystem. Ph.D. dissertation. Rutgers Univ., New Brunswick.

34. Odum, W. E. 1971. Pathways of energy flow in a south Florida estuary. Univ. of Miami Sea Grant Technical Bulletin Number 7, 162.

35. Odum, E. P., and A. A. de la Cruz. 1967. Particulate organic detritus in a Georgia salt marsh estuarine ecosystem, pp. 753-88. *In* G. H. Lauff (ed.), Estuarines. Publ. AAAS. No. 83.

36. Odum, E. P., and M. E. Fanning. 1973. Comparison of the productivity of *Spartina alterniflora* and *Spartina cynosuroides* in Georgia coastal marshes. Ga. Acad. Sci. Bull. 31(1):1-12.

37. Payonk, P. 1975. The response of three species of marsh macrophytes to organic enrichment. M.S. thesis, Louisiana State Univ., Baton Rouge.

38. Phillips, R. C. 1974. Temperate grass flats, pp. 244-299. *In* H. T. Odum, B. T. Copeland, and E. A. McMahan (eds.), Coastal ecological systems of the United States. Conservation Foundation, Washington, D.C.

39. Pomeroy, L. R. 1959. Algal productivity in salt marshes of Georgia. Limnol. Oceanogr. 4:386-397.

40. Pomeroy, L. R., K. Bancroft, J. Breed, R. R. Christian, D. Frankenberg, J. R. Hall, L. G. Maurer, W. J. Wiebe, R. G. Weigert, and R. L. Wetzel. 1976. Flux of organic matter through a salt marsh, pp. 270-79. *In* M. Wiley (ed.) Estuarine Processes, Vol. II, Academic Press, New York.

41. Seliskar, D. M., J. L. Gallagher, and T. C. Pearson. 1977. Microbial colonization of leaves entering the detrital food webs in swamps and marshes. Fortieth Annual Meeting Am. Society of Limnology and Oceanography, Inc. Michigan State Univ., East Lansing (Abstr.).

42. Sharp, J. H. 1977. Excretion of organic matter by marine phytoplankton: Do healthy cells do it? Limnol. Oceanogr. 22:381-397.

43. Smalley, A. E. 1958. The role of two invertebrate populations, *Littorina*

irrorata and *Orchelimum fidicinum,* in the energy flow of a salt marsh ecosystem. Ph.D. dissertation, Univ. of Georgia, Athens, University Microfilms, Ann Arbor, 126 pp.

44. Stroud, L. M., and A. W. Cooper. 1968. Color-infrared aerial photographic interpretation and net primary productivity of a regularly flooded North Carolina salt marsh. Univ. of North Carolina Water Resources Res. Inst. Rept. No. 14. 86 pp.

45. Teal, J. M. 1962. Energy flow in the salt marsh ecosystem of Georgia. Ecoloy 43:614-24.

46. Thayer, G. W., S. M. Adams, and M. W. LaCroix. 1975. Structural and functional aspects of a recently established *Zostera marina* community, pp. 518-540. *In* L. E. Cronin (ed.), Estuarine Research. Academic Press, New York.

47. Thomas, J. P. 1970. Release of dissolved organic matter from natural populations of marine phytoplankton. Ph.D. dissertation, Univ. of Georgia, Athens.

48. Turner, R. E. 1976. Geographic variations in salt marsh macrophyte production: a review. Contrib. Mar. Sci. 20:47-68.

49. Turner, R. E., and J. G. Gosselink. 1975. A note on standing crops of *Spartina alterniflora* in Texas and Florida. Contr. Mar. Sci. 19:113-118.

50. Udell, H. F., J. Zairdshy, T. E. Doheny, and P. R. Burkholder. 1969. Productivity and nutrient values of plants growing in the salt marshes of the town of Hempstead, Long Island. Bull. Tor. Bot. Club. 96:42-51.

51. Valiela, I., J. M. Teal, and N. Y. Pearson. 1976. Production and dynamics of experimentally enriched salt marsh vegetation: belowground biomass. Limnol. Oceanogr. 19:152-153.

52. Valiela, I., J. M. Teal, and W. J. Sass. 1975. Production and dynamics of salt marsh vegetation and the effect of experimental treatment with sewage sludge. J. Appl. Ecol. 12(3):973-81.

53. Waits, E. D. 1967. Net primary productivity of an irregularly flooded North Carolina salt marsh. Ph.D. dissertation, North Carolina State Univ., Raleigh. 113 pp.

54. Wass, M. L., and T. D. Wright. 1969. Coastal wetlands of Virginia. Interim report to the Governor and General Assembly. Virginia Inst. of Mar. Sci. Spec. Rept. in Applied Mar. Sci. and Ocean Eng. #10.

55. Wiegert, R. G. and F. C. Evans. 1964. Primary production and the disappearance of dead vegetation in an old field. Ecology 45:49-63.

56. Williams, R. B., and M. B. Murdoch. 1972. Compartmental analysis of the production of *Juncus roemerianus* in a North Carolina salt marsh. Chesapeake Sci. 13:69-79.

57. Winfield, T. P., and J. B. Zedler. 1977. Grass and succulent productivity: a comparison in southern California salt marsh. Ecological Society of America annual meeting. Michigan State Univ., East Lansing. (Abstr.).

58. Woodwell, G. M., and D. E. Whitney. In press. Flax pond ecosystems study: exchanges of phosphorus between a salt marsh and the coastal waters of Long Island Sound. Mar. Biol.

59. Zieman, J. C. 1968. Growth and decomposition of the seagrass, *Thalassia.* M.S. thesis, Univ. of Miami, Coral Gables. 50 pp.

AN EVALUATION OF THE FEASIBILITY OF A TEMPERATE CLIMATE EFFLUENT-AQUACULTURE-TERTIARY TREATMENT SYSTEM IN NEW YORK CITY

Oswald A. Roels, Bruce A. Sharfstein, and Virginia M. Harris

Port Aransas Marine Laboratory
The University of Texas Marine Science Institute
Port Aransas, Texas

Abstract: From March 1972 to June 1977, a feasibility test of a pilot scale effluent-aquaculture-tertiary treatment system was operated at New York City's Tallman Island Pollution Control Plant. The system was designed to remove and recycle sewage-derived inorganic nitrogen and phosphorus-containing compounds via a phytoplankton-shellfish-phycocolloid producing seaweed managed food chain.

Nitrogen (nitrate, nitrite, and ammonia) removal by phytoplankton was generally close to 100%, but the combination of high nitrogen concentrations in the sewage, and productivities of the order of 0.7 g N m^{-2} day^{-1} resulted in a minimum culture area requirement of 5 hectares per MGD of sewage.

Shellfish grew at rates ranging from 22% to 118% per week, wet weight, and assimilated an average of 22% of the incoming phytoplankton protein-nitrogen, necessitating the removal of nearly 80% of the original incoming nitrogen by the seaweed-effluent polishing step of the system.

Seaweeds removed in excess of 90% of the dissolved inorganic nitrogen in the shellfish effluent. Maximum sustained growth rates averaged 10 g dry weight m^{-2} day^{-1}, but nitrogen fixation rates were only 0.1 g nitrogen m^{-2} day^{-1} giving a treatment area requirement of 28.6 hectares per MGD.

Based on these results, the potential feasibility of large-scale effluent-aquaculture-tertiary sewage treatment systems is discussed.

Introduction

One of the major uses of our estuaries is undoubtedly the disposal of sewage. For example, New York City alone discharges 4.35×10^6 m^{-3} day^{-1} of sewage effluents to the Hudson and East Rivers and New York Bay (New York City Department of Water Resources, 1972). This represents only 46% of the total volume of sewage discharged daily by the entire New York metropolitan area. Assuming that all of this sewage has a mean inorganic nitrogen content equivalent to that of New York City's Tallman Island Pollution Control Plant (which is itself very close to the national average reported by Weinberger *et al.* 1966), this discharge adds 160 metric tons of nitrogen day^{-1} to the local receiving waters. To date, this discharge has had little demonstrable effect on primary productivity in the New York Bight (Garside *et al.* 1976), although anoxic conditions have been reported for localized areas in the Bight during the summer of 1977 (G. Rowe, pers. commun.). Thus it would seem that the possibility for future eutrophication in parts of the estuary in response to decreasing turbidities resulting from the present city-wide upgrading of sewage treatment facilities cannot be entirely discounted. In view of this potential for eutrophication, an increasing government interest in mandating tertiary treatment for sewage discharges (PL-92-500), and the conceptual desirability of recycling wasted sewage nutrients, we conducted a feasibility test of a greenhouse enclosed phytoplankton → shellfish → macrophyte biological tertiary treatment system at New York City's Tallman Island Pollution Control Plant from March 1972 to June 1977. This report presents the results of this study.

Materials and Methods

New York City's Tallman Island Pollution Control Plant is located on the southern shore of the East River near its confluence with Long Island Sound. From March 1972 to June 1977, we operated a small-scale effluent-aquaculture system on this site in cooperation with the New York City Department of Water Resources. The system was designed to recycle nutrients from wastewater into useful products as well as to remove dissolved inorganic nitrogen and phosphate from secondarily treated sewage effluent before discharging it into the New York Estuary.

Raw sewage obtained from the main interceptor sewer at the Tallman Island Plant was passed through a 1,200 gpd Clow extended aeration secondary treatment plant. The secondarily-treated sewage effluent thus produced was diluted 1:1 with saline, 15μ filtered East River water, and used to culture the phytoplankter, *Nannochloris* sp. The choice of phytoplankton species was based on the observation that *Nannochloris* supports good shellfish growth, and can be maintained in sewage-based, unialgal continuous culture for periods of up to 80 days.

Phytoplankton was grown in white, epoxy-painted, rectangular concrete tanks of 80 cm depth. However, in practice, the tanks were never completely filled, and *Nannochloris* was grown either in 500-liter volumes at a depth of 25 cm, or in 1,000-liter volumes at a depth of 50 cm. Since maximum nutrient utilization was a goal of the aquaculture system, turnover rates of the phytoplankton cultures were adjusted on a weekly basis to the maximum flow rate that still gave a greater than 90% removal of dissolved inorganic nitrogen or orthophosphate, depending on which macronutrient was limiting at the time.

Nannochloris culture was diluted 1:2 with 15μ filtered East River water, and fed to populations of the blue mussel *Mytilus edulis*.

Mytilus edulis was chosen for use in our aquaculture system because it is relatively euryhaline, has potential as a human food and can be used to produce an excellent livestock feed protein supplement (Gregoire *et al.*, 1976) where its suitability for human consumption is in question.

Although a number of discrete populations of *Mytilus* have been raised in the system over the past five years, the data reported here are for a single population of artificially spawned shellfish which were maintained in the system from July 1976 to June 1977, and which were subjected to two intensive nitrogen balance studies. The earliest of these ran from August 1976 to May 1977 and followed a population of *Mytilus edulis* fed *Nannochloris* sp., from a length of 2.5 mm to a length of 25–30 mm. The later study ran from May to June 1977 and utilized portions of this population of 30 mm long *Mytilus* fed either *Nannochloris* sp. cultured in our laboratory greenhouse or the natural phytoplankton contained in unfiltered East River water.

During the first nitrogen balance, the shellfish were allowed to attach to a nylon mesh screen which was then suspended in a funnel equipped with inflow and outflow lines and a resuspension air-lift mechanism (Sorgeloos and Persoone, 1972). During the second experiment, a simple aerated tank was used, since previous work had demonstrated little difference between the growth rates and protein conversion efficiencies obtained in the two habitats.

In both cases, shellfish were weighed weekly, and culled back to the initial population weight to maintain a relatively constant food supply:weight ratio. Culled animals were used for shellfish protein determinations.

A portion of the effluent from the shellfish tanks was passed to 2,100 liter tanks (0.60 m diameter x 0.40 meters deep) each containing 750 grams of the agar-producing macrophyte *Gracilaria debilis* at the start of the experiment. Throughout the experimental period, the *Gracilaria* in culture was collected on a weekly basis, weighed and culled back to its initial weight. Figure 1 presents a flow diagram of the system.

Cell densities, flow rates, pH, molybdate reactive orthophosphate concentration and water temperatures were monitored on a daily basis to check for system stability. Daily irradiance was also measured with an International Light Plant Growth Photometer. Daily samples for nitrate, nitrite, ammonia, and particulate protein analysis were taken throughout the system. Nitrate, nitrite, and ammonia were measured by automated techniques modified from Strickland and Parsons (1972). Particulate protein was measured by a modification of the Lowry technique (Dorsey *et al.* 1976).

Results and Discussions

Environmental conditions, light, temperature, and nutrients

The dominant characteristic that sets temperate climate effluent systems apart from many other forms of aquaculture is the extreme degree of variability encountered in all environmental conditions. Total daily irradiance varies from a seasonal high of 220 ly day^{-1} to a low of 1 to 2 ly day^{-1}. Water temperatures,

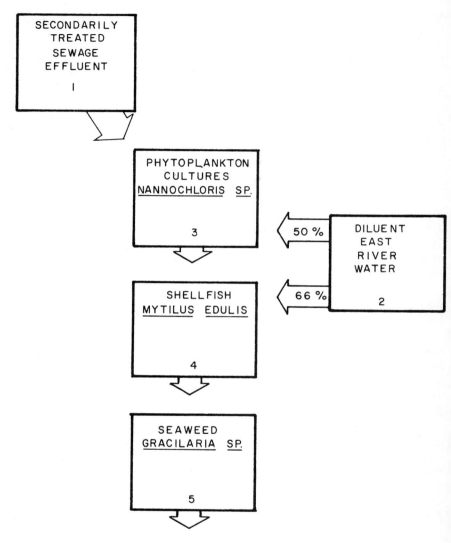

Figure 1.

even in our ventilated and heated greenhouse ranged from summer highs of 26°
to 28°C to a low of 8°C. Nutrient composition and concentrations in secondarily
treated sewage effluent and diluent East River water also showed wide fluctuations primarily related to treatment efficiency and storm water runoff. Secondary
effluent ammonia concentrations varied from 46 to 1600 μg at /1, nitrate concentrations from 1 to 9 μg at /1, and nitrite concentrations from 1 to 15 μg at
/1. Orthophosphate concentration also varied widely (20 to 180 μg at /1), and

Table 1. Partial nitrogen balance for the *Nannochloris* phase of the aquaculture system.

	INPUT					OUTPUT	
DIN* BAY	+	DIN EFFLUENT	+	PPN* BAY	+	PPN EFFLUENT	=
Week							
8/15/76	7.30	+	494.7	+	8.2	+	40.3
9/19/76	5.62	+	290.1	+	10.16	+	59.65
10/24/76	7.96	+	102.25	+	12.1	+	62.5

PPN OUT	+	RESIDUAL DIN	Percent Accounted For
= 530.75	+	0.51	97
= 326.26	+	0.96	90
= 208.8	+	0.91	113

μg-at N/liter   *DIN = Dissolved Inorganic Nitrogen   *PPN = Particulate Protein Nitrogen

more important, showed a constantly decreasing trend in response to progressively more stringent detergent-phosphate bans (Sharfstein *et al.*, 1977). Mean orthophosphate concentrations decreased from a high of 140 μg at/l in 1971, to a low of 50 μg at/l in 1974-1977. As a result, the mean N:P ratio of the 1:1 mixtures of sewage effluent and East River water used to culture *Nannochloris* increased from 9:1 in 1972 to 21:1 in 1977.

Primary production

Despite the observed fluctuations in input nitrogen and phosphate concentrations, the changing N:P ratio, and seasonal fluctuations in temperature and available light energy, regulation of culture flow rate proved a viable tool for regulating nutrient removal rates. Nitrogen depletion was generally close to 100%, and nearly all of the input inorganic nitrogen could be accounted for as phytoplankton protein (Table 1). Nevertheless, maximally attainable turnover rates (Figure 2), and rates of nitrogen fixation per unit area (Table 2) showed a strong seasonal dependency, but were generally higher than natural productivities measured in New York Bight at corresponding times of the year (Garside *et al.*, 1976).

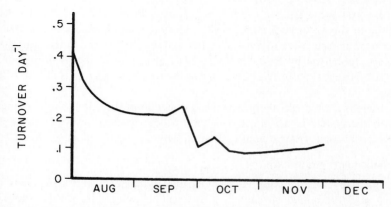

Figure 2. Turnover rates for Nannochloris *culture. August 8 to December 4, 1976*

Table 2. Rates of Nitrogen Fixation.

Production g N m^{-2} day^{-1}	Source of data
0.04	N.Y. Bight, winter
0.06	Tallman Island, Nov. 1976 20 cm tank
0.10	Tallman Island, Sept. 1976 20 cm tank
0.23	N.Y. Bight, summer
0.35	Tallman Island, Aug. 1976 20 cm tank
0.72	Tallman Island, June 1977 50 cm tank

Based on previous considerations of strategies for optimization of phytoplankton production (Roels *et al.*, 1976), it would appear that the value presented in Table 2 for a 50 cm deep tank (0.72 g N m^{-2} day^{-1}) is close to the maximum obtainable for *Nannochloris* in a greenhouse-enclosed culture system, in New York City, since at this depth, the 1% light level was reached at or near the bottom of the tank. Some slight increase over this value might be obtained in an open system where attenuation of light by a greenhouse roof is not a factor, but at present there is no way to estimate the degree of this improvement. Taking this value as a conservative maximum, the minimum area that would be required to treat the output from a 1-MGD plant is 5 hectares. Maximum area requirements (assuming a depth of one meter) during the winter months could be as high as 60 hectares. Even using Ryther's (1975) maximum productivity (1.2 g N m^{-2} day^{-1}) for the Woods Hole Oceanographic Institution's effluent aquaculture system, minimum area requirements for the phytoplankton phase of a 1-MGD system would be of the order of 3 hectares. Extrapolating the maximum productivities encountered in New York to the 4.35 x 10^9 gallons (160 metric tons of nitrogen) of sewage discharged by New York City daily gives a total area requirement of 2.2 x 10^4 hectares, more than one quarter the total land area of New York City proper.

There is little doubt that the area requirement for the initial photosynthetic phase of the system is the major constraint to the application of effluent aquaculture-tertiary sewage treatment systems in densely populated urban areas.

Secondary production

Since all available methods of mechanically harvesting microalgae are extremely energy intensive, we elected to use the bivalve mollusc, *Mytilus edulis,* as a biological filter for removing the sewage-effluent-grown *Nannochloris* from suspension. *Mytilus edulis* generally grew as well on *Nannochloris* as it did on natural populations of phytoplankton. Under both sets of conditions, weekly increases in live wet weight ranged from 22% to 118%. *Mytilus* was capable of ingesting more than 90% of the algal protein presented to it. However, protein retention by *Mytilus* ranged from 9% to 37% (Table 3), concomitantly decreasing the nitrogen-removal efficiency of the two-step tertiary treatment system. An average of 72% of the input phytoplankton nitrogen could be accounted for in our nitrogen balance studies (Table 4). Twenty-eight percent of this nitrogen ended up in shellfish protein (shell and meat), 63% appeared dissolved inorganic nitrogen, and 9% remained in the tank as feces or pseudofeces. The 28% of input nitrogen which was unrecoverable is presumed to be in the form of dissolved organic nitrogen, a fraction which we were unable to measure at the time.

Table 3. Protein Efficiency* of *Mytilus edulis*.

Organism Size (mm)	Condition	Protein Efficiency
2.5	Monoculture	12
7.0	Monoculture	15
12.5	Monoculture	34
30	Monoculture (dense feed)	19
30	Monoculture (dilute feed)	9
30	Natural feed	26
30	Natural feed	37
	$\tilde{X}$	22

$$\text{*Protein Efficiency} = 100 \times \frac{\text{Increase in secondary protein}}{\text{Primary protein ingested}}$$

Based on an average protein efficiency of 22%, a 1-MGD effluent aquaculture system would be capable of producing approximately 19 tons of animal protein per annum (sewage nitrogen x 0.22 x 6.25). Area requirements for this production are difficult to calculate since they are largely dependent on the spatial configuration of the chosen facility. However, based on reported mussel productivities of 600 metric tons of mussels ha^{-1} yr^{-1} for raft culture in Spain (Bardach *et al.,* 1972), the shellfish phase of a 1-MGD system would require an area of 0.1 ha, 3% of the *minimum* area requirement for the phytoplankton phase of the system.

The use of a filter-feeding shellfish as the phytoplankton filtering step in an effluent aquaculture system has the advantage of being potentially less energy-

Table 4. Output distribution of particulate protein ingested by *Mytilus edulis.*

Organism Size mm	Condition	PPN Ingested µg at/liter	% Recovered	Output DIN µg at/liter	Output PPN-SF µg at/liter Meat + Shell	Output PPN-Tank Deposit and Suspended µg at/liter
2.5	Monoculture	22.85	78	12.98	1.90 + 0.81	2.13
7.0	Monoculture	19.85	51	5.53	2.22 + 0.70	1.73
12.5	Monoculture	8.77	86	4.0	2.08 + 0.93	0.52
30	Monoculture: dense feed	78.0	60	28.05	9.95 + 4.72	4.46
30	Monoculture: dilute feed	28.98	66	15.54	2.6 + 0.13	0.942
30	Natural Feed	13.54	78	6.46	1.97 + 1.59	0.496
30	Natural Feed	10.04	81	3.94	2.2 + 1.51	0.481
	Mean	26.00	72	10.94	3.27 + 1.48	1.54
Average % of Recovered "N"				63	19 9	9%

PPN = Particulate protein nitrogen
DIN = Dissolved inorganic nitrogen
SF = Shellfish

152

intensive, and producing a higher value protein product when compared to conventional techniques for the direct harvest of microalgae. However, the use of shellfish also entails increased area and construction requirements, and makes a final photosynthetic nutrient-removal step a necessity if the tertiary treatment functions of the system are to be realized.

Production of agar containing macrophytes

Gracilaria debilis (identified by H. Humm) was introduced to the aquaculture system to provide nutrient removal of the dissolved inorganic nitrogen fraction of the shellfish effluent. Results of the nitrogen balance studies on the *Gracilaria* cultures indicate that they were consistently removing in excess of 90% of the residual dissolved inorganic nitrogen (Table 5). Maximum sustained growth rates averaged 10 g dry weight m^{-2} day^{-1}. This compares favorably with growth rates of 5 g m^{-2} day^{-1} reported for *Neoaghardella baileyii* cultured in 5% sewage at the Woods Hole Oceanographic Institution's effluent aquaculture system (DeBoer, 1976). However, rates of nitrogen fixation by *Gracilaria* were low, averaging only 0.1 g nitrogen m^{-2} day^{-1}.

Table 5. Partial nitrogen balance for *Gracilaria debilis* cultured in an effluent aquaculture system.

Week	DIN Shellfish Effluent	+	PPN Shellfish Effluent	=	DIN Seaweed Effluent	+	PPN Seaweed Effluent	+	Increase in Gracilaria PPN 1. Throughput
8/15/76	12.98	+	1.22	=	0.68	+	1.03	+	11.90
9/19/76	5.53	+	1.32	=	0.99	+	0.72	+	5.26
10/24/76	4.0	+	1.42	=	0.61	+	0.26	+	4.32

Week	% of Input Nitrogen Recovered	% of Input DIN Removed
8/15	92	92
9/19	102	95
10/24	96	108

Assuming an average 22% reduction in input sewage nitrogen resulting from the phytoplankton and shellfish phases of the system, the *Gracilaria* effluent polishing step would need to remove 28.7 kg of nitrogen for each million gallons of sewage processed by the system. This entails an additional area requirement of 28.6 hectares per MGD, or 1.2 x 10^5 hectares (1.5 times the area of New York City proper) to treat the entire 4.35 x 10^3 million gallons of sewage generated by New York City daily. Agar production in the system was low, averaging only 5% on a dry weight basis (Marine Colloids analysis). This is probably a result of the fast growth rates and elevated nutrient levels characteristic of the system (Neish and Shacklock, 1971). Potential economic value of the *Gracilaria* produced in the system would therefore tend to be low.

Conclusions

Without a detailed economic analysis, it is impossible to draw any conclusions about the cost-effectiveness of this type of biological tertiary treatment as compared to conventional mechanical-chemical methods. However, the results of this biological study alone lead to a number of conclusions as to the feasibility of phytoplankton → shellfish → seaweed effluent aquaculture systems.

Such systems have the potential to remove more than 90% of the dissolved inorganic nitrogen in secondarily treated sewage effluents, and to convert this nitrogen into potentially useful shellfish and seaweed products. Extrapolated summertime yields for a 1-MGD system would be on the order of 1.6 tons of animal protein and 4.3 tons of agar per month. However, in temperate climates, productivities have a strong seasonal dependency, and based on the response of the phytoplankton component alone, production in the winter months would probably be 5--10% of these values. More important, winter conditions would necessitate either a tenfold increase in system size, or a tenfold reduction in accepted removal efficiency to accommodate this decreased productivity.

The area required for an aquaculture system of this type is probably the single biggest restraint to its implementation. Based on results at Tallman Island, minimum area requirements for a 1-MGD system would be: phytoplankton 5 hectares + shellfish 0.1 hectares + *Gracilaria* 28.6 hectares = 33.7 hectares.

In retrospect, the use of a high-protein content, potentially valuable algal species such as *Spirulina* for the final effluent polishing step might have been advisable. *Spirulina* contains 10% nitrogen on a dry weight basis (Kosaric and Nguyen, 1974), and has shown productivities in excess of 12 g dry weight m^{-2} day^{-1} (Clement *et al.*, 1966). If these values could be obtained in continuous sewage-enriched culture, the area requirement for the final stage of the aquaculture system would be reduced to 2.4 hectares per MGD. However, even assuming a system with phytoplankton productivites of the order of those encountered at Woods Hole (1.2 g N m^{-2} day^{-1}) and a hypothetical *Spirulina* polishing step, area requirements for a 1-MGD system are 5.5 hectares. Given these values, it seems probable that effluent-aquaculture systems might provide a viable alternative to conventional tertiary treatment in areas with populations of up to 60--70,000 (10-MGD sewage production), where adequate land is available (Garside *et al.*, 1976), but they are certainly not applicable to densely populated urban areas.

Effluent-aquaculture-tertiary treatment systems may also have greater applicability in the southern United States where seasonal fluctuations in solar radiance and temperature are less extreme. However, since a warm-climate system would undoubtedly utilize different species, extrapolation of temperate climate results for such situations should be done with extreme caution.

Acknowledgments

The authors wish to thank the New York City Department of Water Resources for all the support and encouragement they have given us over the past five years.

We also wish to thank the Rockefeller Foundation, the Jesse Smith Noyes Foundation, and the Whitaker Foundation for their support of this work.

University of Texas Marine Science Institute Contribution No. 228.

References

1. Bardach, J., J. Ryther, and W. O. McLarney. 1972. Aquaculture. Wiley Interscience, New York, pp. 760-776.

2. Clement, G., M. Rebeller, and P. Trombouye. 1966. Utilisation massive du gaz carbonique dans la culture d'une nouvelle algue alimentaire, pp. 263-269. *In* New Contributions of Petroleum to Agriculture.

3. DeBoer, J. A. 1976. Effects of nitrogen concentration on growth rate and carageenan production in *Neoagardhiella baileyi*. *In* J. H. Ryther (ed.), Marine Polyculture Based on Natural Food Chains and Recycled Wastes. Woods Hole Technical Report #WHOI-76-92.

4. Dorsey, T. E., P. W. McDonald, and O. A. Roels. 1977. A heated biuret-Folin assay which gives equal absorbance with different proteins. Analytical Biochemistry 78:156-164.

5. Garside, C., T. C. Malone, O. A. Roels, and B. Sharfstein. 1976. An evaluation of sewage-derived nutrients and their influence on the Hudson Estuary and New York Bight. Estuarine Coastal Mar. Sci. 4:281-289.

6. Gregoire, R. J., G. J. Brisson, and O. A. Roels. 1976. Comparison of fresh and salt water mussel meals as a replacement of fish meal in broiler foods. Centre de Recherches en Nutrition, Laval University, Ste-Foy Quebec, Canada.

7. Kosaric, N., and H. T. Nguyen. 1974. Growth of *Spirulina maxima* algae in effluents from secondary waste treatment plants. Biotech & Bioeng. 16:881-896.

8. Neish, A. C. and P. F. Shacklock. 1971. Greenhouse experiments on the propagation of strain T4 of Irish moss. Natl. Res. Council of Canada, Atl. Reg. Lab. Tech. Rep. Ser. No. 14, 25 pp.

9. New York City Department of Water Resources. 1972. Environmental Protection Administration: Summary of plant operations.

10. Roels, O. A., S. Laurence, M. W. Farmer, and L. Van Hemelryck. 1976. Organic production potential of artificial upwelling marine culture. *In* H. G. Schlegel and J. Barnea (eds.), Microbial Energy Conversion. Erich Goltze KG, Gottingen.

11. Ryther, J. H. 1975. Preliminary results with a pilot plant waste recycling marine aquaculture system. Woods Hole Oceanographic Institution Technical Report #WHOI-75-41.

12. Sharfstein, B. A., V. Harris, V. L. Lee, and O. A. Roels. 1977. The influence of detergent legislation on the phosphorus concentration in sewage effluent and receiving waters. J. Water Poll. Cont. Fed. 49:2017-2027.

13. Sorgeloos, P., and G. Persoone. 1972. Three simple culture devices for aquat-

ic invertebrates and fish larvae with continuous recirculation of medium. Mar. Biol. 15:251-254.

14. Strickland, J. D. H., and T. R. Parsons. 1972. A practical handbook of sea water analysis. Bull. 167, Fish. Res. Bd. of Canada, Ottowa.

15. Weinberger, L. W., D. G. Stephan, and F. M. Middleton. 1966. Solving our water problems — water renovation and re-use. Ann. New York Acad. Sci. 136:131-154.

INTERACTIONS WITHIN ESTUARINE COMMUNITIES: COMMUNITY INTERACTIONS

THE EFFECTS OF ANIMAL-SEDIMENT INTERACTIONS ON GEOCHEMICAL PROCESSES NEAR THE SEDIMENT-WATER INTERFACE

Robert C. Aller

Department of the Geophysical Sciences
University of Chicago
Chicago, Illinois

Abstract: The construction and irrigation of permanent tube-dwellings by sedentary infaunal benthos result in complex patterns of chemical reactions and diffusion gradients in sedimentary deposits. These patterns are reflected in the three-dimensional distribution of pore water constituents, diagenetically mobile solid phases, biogeochemically important microorganisms, and meiobenthos. The quantitative effect of burrows on transport-reaction processes in sediments is analogous to the effect of roots on terrestrial soils. In contrast to factors which cause heterogeneity, mobile infauna rapidly homogenize sediment and presumably simplify internal gradients. The activities of both mobile and sedentary benthos increase the rates of certain metabolic reactions, such as sulfate reduction, which take place below the sediment-water interface. These same activities increase the flux of dissolved material between sediment and the overlying water to a greater degree than that accounted for by one-dimensional molecular diffusion. Increased exchange rates may obscure the presence of some reactions in sediments by preventing the depletion of reactants or buildup of reaction products. Because biogenic influences on particle and fluid transport in sedimentary deposits reflect the types of organisms present, bottom areas which are inhabited by macrobenthos of varying mobility and feeding type differ in their chemical characteristics. In environments having a large seasonal temperature range, biogenic control of sedimentary chemistry is replaced by abiogenic reaction-diffusion controls during winter periods.

Introduction

Animal-sediment interactions have been studied predominantly from the standpoint of relationships between benthos and physical properties of their sedimentary habitat (e.g. Grey, 1974; Rhoads, 1974). Consideration has been given to chemical properties of the bottom which might influence larval settling patterns (Crisp, 1965; Grey, 1974), but interactions of adult macrofauna with sediment chemistry have been largely ignored. Macrofaunal activities such as feeding, burrowing, tube construction, and irrigation result in particle and fluid transport within a deposit. These transport activities can be shown to have important effects on geochemical characteristics of sediments and overlying waters. Selected examples and discussion of such effects are given here with emphasis on the deposit-feeding infauna.

Many reactions occurring during early diagenesis are in some way associated with the decomposition of organic matter (e.g. Berner, 1976). Of the possible reactants or products of decomposition, ammonia is common, biologically important, and as the ammonium ion, relatively well-behaved chemically. Because of this it will be used here as a representative example of a dissolved species in sediment pore waters.

Ammonia is produced in sediments and released into pore waters by decomposition reactions such as (1) (Richards, 1965):

$$6(CH_2O)_x \ (NH_3)_y \ (H_3PO_4)_z \ + \ 3x(SO_4^=) \ \rightarrow \ 6x(HCO_3^-)$$
$$3x(HS^-) \ + \ 6y(NH_4^+) \ + \ 6z(HPO_4^=) \ + \ (3x \ + \ 12z \ - \ 6y)H^+$$

$$(1)$$

x, y, and z refer to the unknown stoichiometry of the source organic matter being remineralized at any given time or depth (e.g. Sholkovitz, 1973). NH_4^+ may subsequently undergo further biogenic or abiogenic reactions such as adsorption onto particles (Rosenfield, 1977), nitrification, or be released to overlying water where it is quickly reincorporated into organic material (e.g. Hartwig, 1974; Hale, 1975; Rowe et al., 1975; Nixon et al., 1976; Aller, 1977). Dissolved NH_4^+ is therefore a potentially useful tracer of the distribution of reactive organic source particles, transport processes internal to a sedimentary deposit, and exchange between sediment and overlying water.

Methods

Ammonia was determined in pore water and sea water aliquots passed through 0.4 μm pore-size Nuclepore or Millepore filters. Pore water separations were done in a N_2 atmosphere by either centrifuging or squeezing sediment samples. Analyses were made using phenolhypochlorite after fixing in phenol (Solorzano, 1969; Degobbis, 1973). Further details are given in the appropriate references for each specific example.

Discussion

Early studies of chemical diagenesis of sediments and nutrient regeneration were often done in anoxic basins where macrobenthos were scarce or in sediment zones well below the region of macrofaunal habitation (e.g. Rittenberg et al., 1955; Berner 1964). Under these conditions changes in pore water and solid phase chemistry were found to be adequately described by one-dimensional transport-reaction models such as (Berner, 1974):

$$\frac{\partial C}{\partial t} = D\frac{\partial^2 C}{\partial^2 x} - \omega\frac{\partial C}{\partial x} + R(x)$$

$$(2)$$

C = concentration of pore water constituent

t = time

x = space coordinate, origin fixed at sediment-water interface; positive axis into sediment (Cartesian system)

D = molecular diffusion coefficient modified for tortuosity and assumed constant

R(x) = reaction term

ω = sediment rate

Adsorption reactions and compaction are ignored in this present formulation. Normally steady state conditions are assumed and the equation solved for a given pore water constituent with $\frac{\partial C}{\partial t}$ = 0. In the case of NH_4^+ production, a reaction term of the form: $R(x) = R_o e^{-\alpha x}$ is often found adequate for defining the profiles (Berner, 1974; Rosenfeld, 1977; Aller, 1977).

It is possible to demonstrate within this conceptual framework how the presence of different kinds of macrobenthos affect basic transport-reaction processes near the sediment-water interface.

Particle transport

In the absence of macrofauna, reactive organic particles are deposited at the sediment-water interface and move into the sediment at the rate of net sedimentation, ω. When macrofauna are present, feeding, burrowing, and tube construction cause the redistribution of particles at a rate different from sedimentation. It is possible to quantify biogenic reworking in a particle diffusion coefficient, K, by analogy of particle mixing with eddy diffusion (Goldberg and Koide, 1963; Guinasso and Schink, 1975; Nozaki *et al.*, 1977; Robbins, 1977). The distribution of a particle-associated property, such as metabolizable organic matter, in the sediment is then determined by particle diffusion, net sedimentation, and reaction. The same mathematical formalism as used in equation (2) is applied to the property distribution. In the case of a nonexchangeable radionuclide whose source is at the sediment-water interface, C is replaced by A and R(x) becomes $(-\lambda A)$ where λ = decay constant and A = activity of the nuclide at depth x, giving:

$$\frac{\partial A}{\partial t} = K \frac{\partial^2 A}{\partial x^2} - \omega \frac{\partial A}{\partial x} - \lambda A \tag{3}$$

Vertical distributions in sediment of such radionuclides as ^{210}Pb or ^{234}Th are used to obtain quantitative measures of K.

Transport analogies to biogenic particle reworking other than diffusion have been proposed but are not extensively used at present (Berger and Heath, 1968; Goreau, 1977; J. B. Fisher, *et al.*, in prep.). It should not be assumed that diffusion is always the most appropriate description of particle reworking; for instance, some types of bioturbation are distinctly advective on short-time scales (e.g. Amiard-Triquet, 1974; Aller and Dodge, 1974). The diffusion analogue is particularly useful, however, in that it can be readily applied to the kinds of solid phase measurements normally taken and also allows comparisons between environments.

Most reported rates of biogenic particle diffusion are slower than molecular diffusion rates in sediments and range from about 10^{-9} cm^2/sec in the deep sea (Guinasso and Schink, 1975; Nozaki *et al.*, 1977) to 10^{-6} cm^2/sec in coastal areas (Guinasso and Schink, 1975; Aller and Cochran, 1976). This means that particle transport activities *per se* will not directly control diffusion rates of most dissolved ions in sediments (although resulting changes in particle shape and packing may influence tortuosity).

One major effect of reworking will be to redistribute reactive particles from the interface into the sediment body. The geometrical distribution of reaction rates in the sediment is thereby altered (i.e. R_0 and $\propto$ altered) although the total reactivity is not (i.e. $\int_0^\infty R(x)dx$ is constant). For example, fresh organic material which would otherwise be largely decomposed near the interface becomes subducted uniformly or along distinct shafts into the sediment where it is available for deeper-dwelling organisms. As a result, products of decomposition, such as NH$_4^+$, are released more rapidly at depth in a deposit than in the unmixed case. This could cause pore water concentrations to build up to higher levels, deep in a deposit, than they would have in the absence of mixing (Schink *et al.*, 1975). In the case of decomposition products subject to precipitation reactions (e.g. HPO$_4^=$), this hypothetical buildup might result in formation of an insoluble phase and permanent loss to sediments of regenerated nutrients. Even for ions which do not form insoluble phases the short-term (transient state) flux of regenerated nutrients to the overlying water following a pulse of organic material to the bottom could be decreased by particle mixing (at steady state the flux to overlying water will be identical in both the mixed and unmixed cases if $\int_0^\infty R(x)$ dx = constant). Such an alteration in the time dependence of sediment-water fluxes would have importance in seasonally productive environments. Although these consequences of redistributing reactive particles are possible, at the present time no evidence of either reduced fluxes or increased buildup of pore water concentrations resulting from biogenic particle reworking has been reported. The reasons for this are discussed later under fluid transport.

Mass balance requires the upward diffusion of particles toward the interface as well. Molecules, e.g. NH$_4^+$, reversibly adsorbed to particles at depth in the sediment, will be released to overlying water when placed at the interface. When packaged into distinct fecal pellets, material mixed upward may also retain active anaerobic organisms otherwise typical of deeper sediment (Jørgensen, 1977). Additional effects, such as oxidation of sulfides, are discussed in Aller (1977).

Fluid transport: Effects of sedentary infauna

When infauna which build permanent or semi-permanent tubes are present, a sediment deposit is not a homogenous body dominated by one-dimensional vertical diffusion as described by equation (2). Rather it is a body permeated by cylinders filled with sea water; this water is held by irrigation activity at ion concentrations close to those of overlying water. As illustrated by the case of an intertidal population of *Amphitrite ornata,* when irrigation ceases, concentrations of ions such as NH_4^+ in burrow water increase rapidly (Figure 1; after Aller and Yingst, 1978). This rate of increase represents the normal supply rate of NH_4^+ to the burrows from surrounding sediment and demonstrates the tapping of the surrounding dissolved ion reservoirs by the burrows. Direct excretion by the burrow inhabitants was negligible in this case.

All burrows will have the nonspecific effect of creating a cylindrical diffusion geometry in the sediment immediately surrounding them. There are also specific effects on diffusion-reaction distribution based on the way in which the burrow wall is constructed. *Amphitrite,* for example, extracts particles from surface sediment, manipulates them into mucus-laden bricks, and stacks them in the wall of its U-shaped burrow. The fresh organic matter in the surface sediment, the added mucus, and the abundant supply by irrigation of electron acceptors (e.g., O_2, NO_3^-, $SO_4^=$) in the core of the burrow provide ideal conditions for microbial activity in the burrow wall. The distribution of dissolved NH_4^+ in annular sample rings around one arm of an *Amphitrite* burrow demonstrates this (Figure 2; after Aller and Yingst, 1978). NH_4^+ is highest in sediment composing the wall and decreases both in the central core (sea water concentration) and surrounding sediment. In order to maintain these concentration gradients across the inner and outer surfaces of the burrow wall the rates of NH_4^+ production in the wall must be high. The diffusion-reaction symmetry is cylindrical and an appropriate model can be used to show that NH_4^+ production rates in the wall are much higher than ambient sediment and are comparable to those normally found in the upper 0-1 cm of nearshore marine sediments (Aller and Yingst, 1978). In this particular case sulfate reduction was found to be the most important decom-

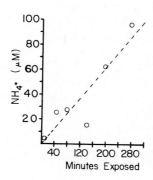

Figure 1. NH_4^+ *concentration in* Amphitrite ornata *(Leidy) burrows exposed on a tidal flat, versus time of exposure. Except for the first sample, each point represents the average concentration in two or more burrows (after Aller and Yingst, 1978).*

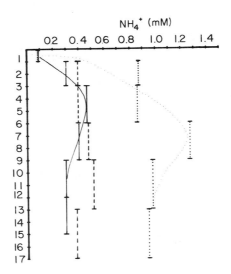

Figure 2. NH$_4^+$ *concentration in pore water from two concentric sample intervals around one arm of* A. ornata *burrow and from 30 cm away from burrow axis. Dotted line = 0.5--1.5 cm radial interval from burrow axis; dashed line = 1.5--3.75 cm radial interval; solid lines = surrounding sediment 30 cm from axis (after Aller and Yingst, 1978). Each bar represents the depth interval over which the sample was taken.*

position pathway, but this might differ depending on burrow wall structure. Tube linings, depending on their structure, may also greatly restrict exchange.

This example shows why products of decomposition do not build up at depth during reworking even though reactive particles are transported well beneath the interface: pore water decomposition products need not diffuse vertically toward the interface but can diffuse the very short distance laterally into the burrow core and be advected out of the sediment by irrigation (Aller, 1978). The geometry of pore water diffusion as well as solid phase reaction distributions has been altered by reworking. In fact, lateral concentration gradients may become greater than vertical onces (Figure 2).

In the general case where large numbers of burrows permeate the sediment, diffusion geometries become similar to those of terrestrial soils where roots permeate the soil body. Transport around randomly positioned burrows can be modeled in an analogous fashion to transport around roots (Aller, 1977). In some respects burrows also play a functional role similar to that of roots: sediment is tapped for dissolved nutrients and the nutrients advected into overlying water where active photosynthesis takes place. Only the xylem and phloem are missing.

The high rate of decomposition in some burrow walls and the resulting reducing conditions have important consequences for the distribution of sedimentary components other than NH$_4^+$. For instance, Fe becomes mobilized by both reduction in outer burrow walls and oxidation of Fe-sulfides along the inner burrow surfaces. This causes enrichment of inner burrow walls in Fe-oxides and creation of acid mine-like conditions in dwelling-tubes. The rich bacterial populations in burrow walls may also attract meiofauna, such as nematodes, capable of withstanding the reducing conditions (Aller and Yingst, 1978).

Fluid transport: Effects of mobile infauna

Unlike sedentary or permanent tube dwellers, mobile infauna do not remain stationary long enough to allow establishment of fixed diffusion-reaction geometries or at least to allow easy measurement of them. Radial diffusion plus vertical advection (by irrigation) of pore water still takes place around individuals but at a higher effective density of sites in the deposit. When animals of this type are restricted to near the sediment-water interface, their influence on pore water transport can be taken into account by use of an apparent or effective diffusion coefficient (Hammond *et al.*, 1975; Goldhaber *et al.*, 1977; Vanderborght *et al.*, 1977). This is similar in approach to that described for particle reworking. A biogenic diffusion coefficient in a zone of fixed thickness is adjusted to account for the observed pore water distributions (one dimension, vertical) or flux of material from sediment. Simple molecular diffusion is assumed to control transport in the sediment underlying the inhabited zone. The effective or stochastic pore water diffusion coefficient in a given case is generally larger than the corresponding biogenic diffusion coefficient for particles and on the average is $\sim$10 times the particle rate (Aller, 1977).

An example where this kind of description applies can be found in *Yoldia limatula*, a highly mobile deposit-feeding bivalve.

Yoldia restricts its activities largely to the upper 3--4 cm. Figure 3 (after

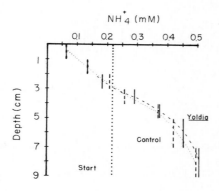

Figure 3. NH$_4^+$ *in pore water from laboratory tanks with and without* Yoldia limatula *(Say) (abundance = 300/m^2). The initial value in the sediment is given as* start; *other profiles represent values after 45 days (after Aller, 1978).*

Aller, 1978) shows vertical NH_4^+ pore water profiles from two laboratory tanks, one containing *Yoldia* and one without macrofauna (control). The rate of NH_4^+ production, R, is approximately constant with depth in both tanks due to initial homogenization of the substrate. It is assumed initially that R is not altered by reworking under these conditions. The salient points are that: (1) NH_4^+ concentrations are similar or lower in the upper 3 cm of the *Yoldia* tank than the control, and (2) NH_4^+ concentrations are slightly higher in the *Yoldia* tank than in the control below 3 cm. In addition, other data (both flux and pore water profiles of other dissolved species) from the same experiment indicate that the effective diffusion coefficient in the top few centimeters of the *Yoldia* tank is $\sim 0.9 - 1 \times 10^{-5} cm^2/sec$ (Aller, 1978). The expected molecular diffusion coefficient for NH_4^+ in this sediment is $\sim 7 \times 10^{-6} cm^2/sec$ (Rosenfeld, 1977).

A composite layer diffusion-reaction model can be constructed to describe conditions in the *Yoldia* and control tanks. In this model, NH_4^+ is transported vertically at $1 \times 10^{-5} cm^2/sec$ in the upper 3 cm of *Yoldia* tank sediment and at $7 \times 10^{-6} cm^2/sec$ in the lower 6 cm. An identical, constant rate of NH_4^+ production is assumed in both layers. The appropriate equations and boundary conditions describing the distribution of NH_4^+ in each zone are then:

Zone I:
$$\frac{\partial C_1}{\partial t} = \frac{D_1}{1+K} \frac{\partial^2 C_1}{\partial x^2} + \frac{R}{1+K}$$

$$(4)$$

Zone II:
$$\frac{\partial C_2}{\partial t} = \frac{D_2}{1+K} \frac{\partial^2 C_2}{\partial x^2} + \frac{R}{1+K}$$

$$x = 0, \ C = C_0$$

$$x = L_1, \ C_1 = C_2$$

$$x = L_1, D_1 \frac{\partial C_1}{\partial x} = D_2 \frac{\partial C_2}{\partial x}$$

$$x = L_2, \ \frac{\partial C_2}{\partial x} = 0$$

Where:
C_i = concentration of NH_4^+ in Zone 1 or Zone 2

D_i = effective diffusion coefficient in Zone 1 or 2

K = Langmuir adsorption constant for NH_4^+

R = constant production rate

L_1 = boundary depth between upper and lower zones

$$L_2 = \text{depth of sediment in tank}$$

Because of the nature of the experiment, sedimentation can be ignored. The concentration profiles of Figure 3 are not yet at steady state but for purposes of illustration steady state ($\frac{\partial C}{\partial t} = 0$) will be assumed.

The expected steady state distribution of dissolved NH_4^+ in such a tank compared with one in which the diffusion coefficients are $7 \times 10^{-6} cm^2/sec$ in both layers (i.e. the control) is shown in Figure 4 (see Aller, 1978 for detailed exposition of such models). This model predicts that because of mixing near the interface, the NH_4^+ concentrations should be lower throughout the *Yoldia* tank than the control unless the production rate of NH_4^+ is not equal in the two tanks. A conclusion consistent with all of the data (some not presented here) and the model, is that microbial production rates of NH_4^+ are greater below the mixed zone in the presence of *Yoldia* than in its absence. This conclusion is also consistent with additional studies showing increased microbial activity in the presence of macrofauna (Fenchel, 1970; Hargrave, 1970, 1976) but differs in that decomposition is stimulated in a sediment region *below* the zone of reworking. Although decomposition rates are increased, at the same time the higher exchange rates obscure this by preventing buildup of decomposition products.

Part of the microbial stimulation below the mixed zone may be caused by the provision of a nutrient source or a flushing from the sediment of an inhibitor

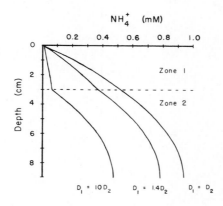

Figure 4. Hypothetical steady state pore water NH_4^+ profiles in tank experiments assuming two zone diffusion-reaction model; $R = 1.6 \times 10^{-7}$ mM/sec; $D_2 = 7 \times 10^{-6} cm^2/sec$. Profiles illustrate effect on pore water distributions of increasing the effective diffusion rate in Zone 1 relative to Zone 2 by different amounts relative to no burrowing case. D_1 ~1.4 D_2 is probably representative of values in the Yoldia tank experiment.

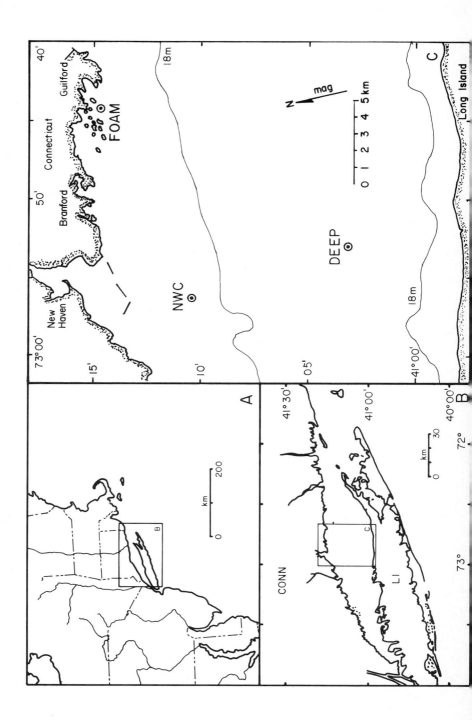

with a normal molecular $D \ll 1 \times 10^{-5} cm^2/sec$. Dissolved material with molecular diffusion coefficients $\ll 1 \times 10^{-5} cm^2/sec$ (the mixed layer rate) will be influenced to an even greater extent than NH_4^+ by the presence of a mixed layer. This type of effect is illustrated in Figure 4 where the case $D_1/D_2 = 10$ has also been plotted for the same NH_4^+ production rate as used for $D_1/D_2 = 1$ and 1.4.

Spatial changes in bottom chemistry
related to community composition

As is expected from the previous examples, spatial changes in the composition of bottom communities are reflected in sediment chemistry. This can be shown by data from the central basin of Long Island Sound, U.S.A. (see also Martens, 1976; Rhoads *et al.*, 1977). Three stations in three distinctly different depositional environments were chose for study (Figure 5). The stations represent an inshore-offshore environmental and depth sequence. The bottom fauna in the central Sound have distinct bathymetric patterns in distribution. These patterns are delineated by changes in the relative abundance of animals of certain sizes, life habits, life history, and feeding types in different regions of the bottom, and reflect depositional environment and severity-frequency of physical disturbances (McCall, 1977). This allows comparison, in an inshore-offshore transect, of diagenetic processes in sediment inhabited by animals of varied feeding groups, life habits, and life histories, all of which determine the ways in which animals interact with sediment.

The integrated rates of NH_4^+ production in the top 10 cm do not differ by more than a factor of 2 at the three stations and the concentration of organic matter is almost identical. The depth distribution of NH_4^+ production $[R(x)]$ changes only slightly from station to station with the highest rates found deepest in the sediment of DEEP. Despite these similarities, the buildup of decomposition products such as NH_4^+ is quite different (Figure 6). The differences arise because of the control of diffusion-reaction geometries at the three stations by macrofauna. The physically-disturbed station FOAM is characterized by small interface dwelling species such as *Ampelisca,* NWC by a *Yoldia-Nephtys* assemblage, and DEEP by deep-burrowing (> 20 cm) largely sedentary benthos such as cerianthids, maldanids, flabilligerids, and terebellids (McCall, 1976, 1977; Aller, 1977). Evidence of extensive deep-burrowing by crustaceans (probably *Squilla empusa*, A. Myers, pers. comm.) is also found at DEEP and to a lesser extent at NWC. Of the three sites, the sediment column at DEEP is the most open system, due to extensive burrow galleries, while FOAM is the most closed. The result is little buildup of decomposition products at DEEP because of three-dimensional diffusion into burrows, with successively greater buildup in areas where the fauna is more restricted to near interface regions. In essence, the bottom

Figure 5. (opposite) A. Location of Long Island Sound; B. Location of study area in the central Sound; C. Location of stations FOAM ($\sim$8 m), NWC ($\sim$15 m), and DEEP ($\sim$34 m).

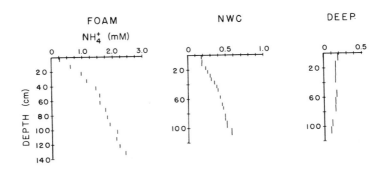

Figure 6. NH$_4^+$ *pore water profiles in gravity cores at three LIS stations (after Aller, 1977). Note* NH$_4^+$ *concentration scale change between FOAM and other sites.*

resembles a large sponge in its interaction with overlying water in regions with a well-established deep-burrowing infauna. The extensive chemical implications and detailed theoretical modeling of these and a range of supporting data are given in Aller (1977).

Temporal variation of sediment chemistry

In addition to the spatial changes in sediment chemistry in Long Island Sound there is a seasonal variation as well. The large annual temperature range (20°C) results in changing relative biological and physical contributions to bottom chemistry at various times of the year. This is exemplified in pore water profiles taken over a two-year period at NWC (Figure 7). The other stations follow similar patterns. During the spring and early summer, the increasing temperature, together with the input of fresh organic material from the spring phytoplankton bloom, causes rapid release of decomposition products in near interface sediments. Microbial production of NH$_4^+$ decreases exponentially with depth in these sediments (Goldhaber *et al.*, 1977; Rosenfeld, 1977; Aller, 1977), which in conjunction with diffusion into overlying water results in a maximum concentration value just beneath the interface. During the late summer and fall, macrofaunal reworking is the highest of the year (Aller and Cochran, 1976). A combination of rapid near-interface mixing by *Yoldia* and deeper three-dimensional diffusion due to polychaetes like *Nephtys* at NWC causes an equilibration of the sediment pore water with overlying water. This takes place through a combination of the mechanisms previously described. Concentrations of ions like NH$_4^+$ are depleted in the sediment down to depths > 15 cm at this time while ions whose source is overlying sea water, e.g. SO$_4^=$, are replenished. This represents a biogenic homeostasis of ion concentrations within the sediment. During the winter (2°C), microbial production and macrofaunal activity are greatly reduced. Pore water profiles take on a form typical of simple one-dimensional (vertical) molecular diffusion and represent diffusion-altered relicts of the fall profiles. Abiogenic reactions such as $HPO_4^=$ adsorption and $CaCO_3$ dissolution become evident at this time (Aller, 1977). The year can therefore be roughly broken into a period of biological control of bottom chemistry and a shorter period of predominately physical control. Within the time of biological control, microbially mediated reactions dominate initially, followed by biogenic transport control due to macrofauna.

Summary and Conclusions

For this conference I have highlighted some of the fundamental influences macrofauna have on sediment chemistry. Most of these influences derive from biologically changing a basically one-dimensional transport-reaction system into a three-dimensional one. The delivery of reactive particles to the sediment-water interface maintains the vertical dimension as the most important one, but lateral gradients cannot be ignored within the inhabited zone. The biogenic heterogeneity of the sediment has important implications for the distribution and ecology of infauna, particularly microorganisms and meiobenthos which respond to small-scale concentration gradients. The openness of the sediment deposit which results from reworking also lowers storage of nutrients such as NH_4^+ and increases interaction of benthic with overlying water communities. Geometrically, and perhaps functionally, the bottom resembles a root-permeated soil rather than a

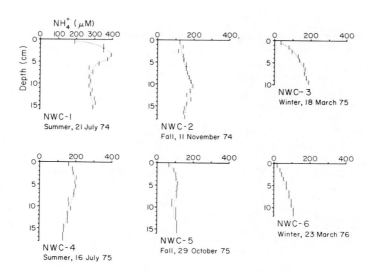

Figure 7. Seasonal pattern of change in NH_4^+ concentrations near the sediment-water interface over two-year period at NWC (after Aller, 1977).

relatively homogeneous slab. The position, scale, and density of burrows (roots) changes constantly at a rate reflecting the benthic community present and the temperature. In bottom areas inhabited by long-lived sedentary infauna, measurable horizontal as well as vertical gradients in sediment chemistry may develop. In regions inhabited predominately by mobile benthos, burrow positions change rapidly and horizontal gradients will be greatly reduced. For convenience, pore water solute transport can be modeled by an apparent or effective vertical diffusion coefficient although this obscures the three-dimensional nature of the system. Biological and geochemical sampling of sediment and interpretations should take these factors into account.

Acknowledgments

This work was supported predominately by ERDA grant no. EY-76-S-02-3573 (to K. K. Turekian), NSF grant no. GA-42-838 (to D. C. Rhoads), and an NSF fellowship while I was at Yale University. I thank my many colleagues who have aided over the years in the development of the ideas expressed here. I am grateful to J. B. Fisher and A. C. Myers for critically reading and commenting on the manuscript.

References

1. Aller, R. C. 1977. The influence of macrobenthos on chemical diagenesis of marine sediments. Ph.D. dissertation, Yale University (ERDA Report C00-3573-21), 600 pp.

2. ————. 1978. Experimental studies of changes produced by deposit feeders on pore water, sediment, and overlying water chemistry. Am. Jour. Sci. (in press).

3. Aller, R. C., and R. E. Dodge. 1974. Animal-sediment relations in a tropical lagoon, Discovery Bay, Jamaica. J. Mar. Res. 32: 209-232.

4. Aller, R. C., and J. K. Cochran. 1976. ^{234}Th/^{238}U disequilibrium in nearshore sediments: particle reworking and diagenetic time scales. Earth Planet. Sci. Letters 29: 37-50.

5. Aller, R. C., and J. Y. Yingst. 1978. Biogeochemistry of tube-dwellings: a study of the sedentary polychaete *Amphitrite ornata* (Leidy). J. Mar. Res. 36:201-254.

6. Amiard-Triquet, C. 1974. Etude experimentale de la contamination par le cerium 144 et le fer 59 d'un sediment a *Arenicola marina* L. (Annelide Polychete). Cahiers de Biologie Marine 15: 483-494.

7. Berger, W. H. and G. R. Heath. 1968. Vertical mixing in pelagic sediments. J. Mar. Res. 26:134-143.

8. Berner, R. A. 1964. Distribution and diagenesis of sulfur in some sediments from Gulf of California. Mar. Geol. 1:117-140.

9. ————. 1974. Kinetic models for the early diagenesis of nitrogen, sulfur, phosphorus, and silicon in axomic marine sediments, pp. 427-450. *In* E. D. Goldberg (ed.), The Sea, Vol. 5, Marine Chemistry. John Wiley and Sons, N.Y.

10. _____. 1976. The benthic boundary layer from the viewpoint of a geochemist, pp. 33-55. *In* I. N. McCave (ed.), The Benthic Boundary Layer. Plenum Publ. Corp., N.Y.

11. Crisp, D. J. 1965. Surface chemistry: a factor in the settlement of marine invertebrate larvae. Botanica Gothoburgensis 3: 51-61.

12. Degobbis, D. 1973. On the storage of sea water samples for ammonia determination. Limnol. Oceanogr. 18:146-150.

13. Fenchel, T. 1970. Studies on the decomposition of organic detritus derived from the turtle grass *Thalassia testudinum*. Limnol. Oceanogr. 15:14-20.

14. Goldberg, E. D., and M. Koide. 1962. Geochronological studies of deep-sea sediments by the ionium/thorium method. Geochim. Cosmochim. Acta 26: 417-450.

15. Goldhaber, M. B., R. C. Aller, J. K. Cochran, J. K. Rosenfeld, C. S. Martens, and R. A. Berner. 1977. Sulfate reduction, diffusion and bioturbation in Long Island Sound sediments: Report of the FOAM Group. Am. Jour. Sci. 277:193-237.

16. Goreau, T. J. 1977. Qantitative effects of sediment mixing on stratigraphy and biogeochemistry: a signal theory approach. Nature 265:525-526.

17. Grey, J. S. 1974. Animal-sediment relationships, pp. 223-261. *In*: H. Barnes (ed.), Oceanogr. Mar. Biol. Ann. Rev. 12.

18. Guinasso, N. L., Jr., and D. R. Schink. 1975. Quantitative estimates of biological mixing rates in abyssal sediments. J. Geophys. Res. 80:3032-3043.

19. Hale, S. S. 1975. The role of benthic communities in the nitrogen and phosphorus cycles of an estuary, pp. 291-308. *In* Mineral Cycling in Southeastern Ecosystems. Proc. Symp. at Augusta, Georgia. May 1-3, 1974, ERDA Symp. Series.

20. Hammond, D. E., H. J. Simpson, and G. Mathieu. 1975. Methane and Radon-222 as tracers for mechanisms of exchange across the sediment-water interface in the Hudson River Estuary, pp. 119-132. *In* T. M. Church (ed.), Marine Chemistry in the Coastal Environment. ACS Symp. Series 18.

21. Hargrave, B. T. 1970. The effect of a deposit-feeding amphipod on the metabolism of benthic microflora. Limnol. Oceanogr. 15:21-30.

22. _____. 1976. The central role of invertebrate faeces in sediment decomposition, pp. 285-299. *In* J. M. Anderson and A. Macfadyen (eds.), The Role of Terrestrial and Aquatic Organisms in Decomposition Processes. 17th Symp. Brit. Ecol. Soc.

23. Hartwig, E. O. 1974. Physical, chemical, and biological aspects of nutrient exchange between the marine benthos and the overlying water. U. of Calif. – Instit. of Marine Resources Ref. No. 74-14, Sea Grant Publication No. 40, 174 pp.

24. Jørgensen, B. B. 1977. Bacterial sulfate reduction within reduced microniches of oxidized marine sediments. Mar. Biol. 41:7-18.

25. Martens, C. S. 1976. Control of methane sediment-water transport by macroinfaunal irrigation in Cape Lookout Bight, North Carolina. Science 192: 998-1000.

26. McCall, P. L. 1976. The influence of disturbance on community patterns and adaptive strategies of the infaunal benthos of central Long Island Sound. Ph.D. dissertation, Yale University, New Haven, Connecticut. 198 pp.

27. _____. 1977. Community patterns and adaptive strategies of the infaunal benthos of Long Island Sound. J. Mar. Res. 35:221-266.

28. Nixon, S. W., C. A. Oviatt, and S. S. Hale. 1976. Nitrogen regeneration and the metabolism of coastal marine bottom communities, pp. 269-283. *In* J. M. Anderson and A. Macfadyen (eds.), The Role of Terrestrial and Aquatic Organisms in Decomposition Processes. 17th Symp. Brit. Ecol. Soc.

29. Nozaki, Y., J. K. Cochran, K. K. Turekian, and G. Keller. 1977. Radiocarbon and ^{210}Pb distribution in submersible-taken deep-sea cores from project FAMOUS. Earth Planet. Sci. Letters 34: 167-173.

30. Rhoads, D. C. 1974. Organism-sediment relations on the muddy sea floor, pp. 263-300. *In* H. Barnes (ed.), Oceanogr. Mar. Biol. Ann. Rev. 12.

31. Rhoads, D. C., R. C. Aller, and M. B. Goldhaber. 1977. The influence of colonizing benthos on physical properties and chemical diagenesis of the estuarine seafloor, pp. 113-138. *In* B. C. Coull (ed.), Ecology of Marine Benthos, Belle W. Baruch Library in Marine Science Number 6, University of South Carolina Press, Columbia, S. C.

32. Richards, F. A. 1965. Anoxic basins and fjords, pp. 611-645. *In* J. P. Riley and G. Skirrow (eds.), Chemical Oceanography, Vol. 1, Academic Press, N. Y.

33. Rittenberg, S. C., K. O. Emery, and W. L. Orr. 1955. Regeneration of nutrients in sediments of marine basins, Deep Sea Res. 3:23-45.

34. Robbins, J. A. 1977. Geochemical and geophysical applications of radioactive lead. *In* J. O. Nriagu (ed.), Biogeochemistry of Lead, Elsevier (in press).

35. Rosenfeld, J. K. 1977. Nitrogen diagenesis in nearshore anoxic sediments. Ph.D. dissertation, Yale University, New Haven, Conn. 191 pp.

36. Rowe, G. T., C. H. Clifford, K. L. Smith, Jr., and P. L. Hamilton. 1975. Benthic nutrient regeneration and its coupling to primary productivity in coastal waters. Nature 255:215-217.

37. Schink, D. R., N. L. Guinasso, Jr., and K. A. Fanning. 1975. Processes affecting the concentration of silica at the sediment-water interface of the Atlantic Ocean. J. Geophy. Res. 80:3013-3031.

38. Sholkovitz, E. 1973. Interstitial water chemistry of the Santa Barbara Basin sediments. Geochim. Cosmochim. Acta 37:2043-2073.

39. Solorzano, L. 1969. Determination of ammonia in natural waters by the phenolhypochlorite method. Limnol. Oceanogr. 14:799-801.

40. Vanderborght, J. P., R. Wollast, and G. Billen. 1977. Kinetic models of diagenesis in disturbed sediments: Part I. Mass transfer properties and silica diagenesis. Limnol. Oceanogr. 22:787-793.

COMMUNITY UNITY?
PATTERNS IN MOLLUSCS AND FORAMINIFERA

Martin A. Buzas

Department of Paleobiology
Smithsonian Institution
Washington, D.C.

Abstract: Organisms living together at the same time and place are often referred to as a "community." Few studies, however, have questioned whether changes in abundance by different-size members coincide. Here densities of molluscs and foraminifera in a tropical and a subtropical environment are compared.

Densities of bivalves and foraminifera were sampled monthly over a one-year period in Jamaica at a back-reef flat (less than 1 m depth), and at Discovery Bay (3 m depth). A significant difference in densities existed between the habitats for all species of bivalves. Two species also show periodicity with time. The total number of bivalve species found in the back-reef flat was six, and at Discovery Bay, 23. Of the 19 species of foraminifera analyzed, only six had density differences between habitats and seven had periodicity. The total number of foraminiferal species at the back-reef flat was 115 and at Discovery Bay, 117.

Molluscs were sampled inside and outside of a cage with 12-mm openings in December, 1975, and in February, April, June, 1976 at Linkport, Florida in the Indian River Estuary. Foraminifera were sampled inside and outside of the same cage during January, February, March, April, May, and June, 1976. In the same area, foraminifera were sampled inside and outside a cage with 1-mm openings during March, April, May, and June, 1976.

Of five species of gastropods analyzed, only one had a significant difference inside vs outside of the cage, with higher densities inside. Densities of four gastropod species had significant differences with time. The densities of total gastropods had no significant differences inside vs outside or with time. Densities of total bivalves were significantly higher inside the cage and differed significantly with time. The densities of three taxa of foraminifera tested and total foraminifera had no significant differences between inside and outside the 12-mm cage, but differed with time. The densities of all three taxa of foraminifera and total foraminifera were significantly higher inside the cage with 1-mm openings than outside, and differed with time. These results suggest only the cage with 1-mm openings provided an effective exclosure from foraminiferal predators. Foraminiferal densities were much greater inside vs outside the 1-mm cage than those for molluscs which had differences inside vs outside the 12-mm cage. Differences in foraminiferal densities were synchronous inside and outside of both cages. Molluscan densities differed with time among taxa.

The results suggest little integration in the response of these dominant members of the macro- and meiofauna to abiotic and biotic variables.

Introduction

A basic question of concern to ecologists and paleoecologists is whether or not various taxonomic groups react to habitat changes in a similar manner. If groups of organisms are regulated by the same physical-chemical variables, and have the same tolerances, similar patterns of biofacies should result. Similarly, if all organisms respond to the same environmental variables with time, similar periodicities should be observed. Understanding this unified behavior, or unison in time and space, is necessary to determine how "tightly-knit" are communities. Quantitative observations on two widely different-sized taxa made at the same time and place are, however, woefully scant.

In the present study, I examine patterns of density of molluscs and foraminifera in sea grass habitats in (1) Jamaica, West Indies, and (2) the Indian River, Florida. Three situations are analyzed: (1) different habitats, (2) periodicity with time, and (3) inside and outside of cages. The purpose is to see if the two groups act in unison.

I. Jamaica

Methods

Two homogeneous *Thalassia* habitats were sampled in Jamaica. The first, called Pear Tree Bottom, is located between Discovery Bay and Runaway Bay on the northern coast of Jamaica. The site is about 20 m from the mean-high water line on a back-reef flat. The water depth is about 10--15 cm at low tide (Station 1, Jackson, 1972). The second area, in Discovery Bay, is at a depth of 3 m (Station 3, Jackson, 1972). Samples of foraminifera and molluscs were collected simultaneously by Jackson (1972). Foraminiferal samples were taken by inserting plastic core liners into the sediment. Four replicate samples, each consisting of 20 ml of sediment, were taken each month for 12 successive months in 1969 and 1970. Buffered formalin was added to each sample in the field. All samples were washed over a 63 μ sieve and stored in alcohol within a few hours of sampling. In the laboratory samples were stained with rose bengal and floated in a mixture of bromoform-acetone. For laboratory details see Buzas *et al.* (1977).

Four replicate samples each of sizes .25 m^2 and 0.1 m^2 were taken for molluscs monthly for 12 months. The larger samples were sieved over a .64 mm sieve and the smaller ones over a 1 mm mesh sieve. For laboratory details see Jackson (1972).

At each sampling time, Jackson (1972) measured (1) bottom-water temperature, (2) sediment temperature, (3) bottom-water salinity, (4) bottom-water turbidity, (5) bottom-water particulate organic carbon, (6) bottom-water oxygen, (7) bottom-water pH, (8) sediment pH, (9) median sediment size, (10) sediment sorting, (11) sediment silt plus clay weight percent, and (12) dry weight *Thalassia*/ 0.1 m^2.

Results

A general linear model was constructed to analyze the Jamaican data; details are given by Buzas *et al.* (1977). In matrix notation the model is written

$$\Omega : \quad \underset{(N \times 1)}{x} \quad = \quad \underset{(N \times q)}{Z'} \quad \underset{(q \times 1)}{b} \quad + \quad \underset{(N \times 1)}{e} \quad .$$

The dependent variable, x, is a vector of $N = 96$ observed densities. The matrix Z' is composed of columns containing the 12 environmental variables and 10 instrumental variables given below. The vector b has $q = 22$ parameters to "explain" the observed species densities. The vector e is a vector of "residuals" not accounted for by the model. The composition of Z' is as follows. The vector z_1 is a column of units, and because each of the other z's add to zero, b_1 is the mean of the observations. The vector z_2 gives +1 values to Pear Tree Bottom and -1 to Discovery Bay, thereby contrasting them. The vectors $z_3, \ldots, z_{14}$ are the environmental variables. The vectors z_{15} and z_{16} are $\sin(m \times \frac{\pi}{6})$ and $\cos(m \times \frac{\pi}{6})$ where $m = 1, \ldots, 12$ respectively. The vectors z_{17} and z_{18} are $\sin(m \times \frac{\pi}{3})$ and $\cos(m \times \frac{\pi}{3})$ where $m = 1, \ldots, 12$ respectively. These vectors taken two at a time test for an overall periodicity in the observations. The vectors z_{19} and $z_{20} = z_2 \times z_{15}$ and $z_2 \times z_{16}$ respectively. The vectors z_{21} and $z_{22} = z_2 \times z_{12}$ and $z_2 \times z_{18}$ respectively. These vectors test whether or not the two localities have different periodicities, i.e., interaction.

To construct restricted ω models constaining s parameters, chosen b's are equated to zero. In this manner several hypotheses can be tested. To test the significance of an hypothesis the sum of squares of the residual, $\mathcal{L}_\Omega$, of the Ω model is compared with the sum of squares of the residual, $\mathcal{L}_\omega$, of an ω model. It can be shown that

$$\frac{\mathcal{L}_\omega - \mathcal{L}_\Omega \div (q-s)}{\mathcal{L}_\Omega \div (N-q)} = F_{(q-s)(N-q)}$$

$F_{(q-s)(N-q)}$ is called the F-ratio. Given the proper number of degrees of freedom we seek the probability α that a random variable z distributed as F exceeds the obtained F ratio z_α i.e. $Pr(z > z_\alpha) = \alpha$. In the present paper a value of $\alpha = .05$ was chosen as the significant α level.

The hypotheses tested are (1) sta diff (station differences), $b_2 = 0$, (2) envir var (environmental variables), $b_i = 0$ ($i = 3, \ldots, 14$), (3) $\pi/6$ overin (overall periodicity and interaction of $\pi/6$ type), $b_i = 0$ ($i = 15, 16, 19, 20$), (4) $\pi/3$ over-in (overall periodicity and interaction of $\pi/3$ type), $b_i = 0$ ($i = 17, 18, 21, 22$), (5) $\pi/6$ inter (interaction of $\pi/6$ type), $b_i = 0$ ($i = 19, 20$), (6) $\pi/3$ inter (interaction of $\pi/3$ type), $b_i = 0$ ($i = 21, 22$).

Most of the 143 species of foraminifera identified in Jamaica were relatively rare. Because of the extreme non-normality of species represented by only a few individuals, only those species with a grand mean of greater than two were statistically analyzed. Only 19 species met this criterion.

Table 1 shows the probability of exceeding the F ratio values for each hypothesis tested. For individual ANOVA's see tables in Buzas *et al.*, 1977. At the 95% (.05) level (values in bold type in Table 1), seven species exhibit periodicity and five a significant difference between localities, and environmental variables are not significant for any of the species. Results of analysis of the total living population (standing crop) are similar to those of the most abundant species, only overall periodicity is significant at the 95% level. Similarly, multivariate analysis (all 19 species considered simultaneously) using the same hypotheses showed only station differences and overall periodicity to be significant (Buzas *et al.*, 1977).

The trend in mean monthly density for the total live population of foraminifera was similar to that for most of the abundant species (Figure 1). May was a month of maximum densities at both stations. Most species had smaller peaks in November, February, August, or September. In summary, at the 95% level, six species, but none of the five most abundant, had significant station differences. An overall periodicity was exhibited by seven of the species studied. In no case were the hypotheses for environmental variables statistically significant. A total of 115 species were found at Pear Tree Bottom and 117 at Discovery Bay.

The same statistical model was used to analyze the bivalves. Table 2 shows the probabilities of exceeding the F ratios for four species of bivalves and the total number of individuals of all infaunal and semi-infaunal bivalves. All four species had significant station differences, two had overall periodicities and one of these also had different periodicities at the two sites. In no case were the hypotheses for environmental variables statistically significant, but the F values were higher than for the foraminifera. The total bivalve assemblage had a significant difference between stations, and periodicity differed between stations. The hypothesis for the set of environmental variables was significant at the 95% level. Figure 2 shows a plot of the mean total number of individuals by month. The maximum occurred in June at both stations. As the significance of the interaction hypothesis indicates, the pattern of minor peaks between stations was not similar. The total number of bivalve species observed is six at Pear Tree Bottom and 23 at Discovery Bay.

All four of the most abundant bivalve species had statistically significant station differences, while for foraminifera only about a third of the species did, and none of these are among the five most abundant. Two of four mollusc species and seven of 19 foraminiferal species had significant periodicities. As Figures 1 and 2 indicate, however, the times of maxima did not coincide. The total number of species observed at the two habitats was drastically different for molluscs while the number of foraminiferal species was quite similar. Evidently, the two habitats present vastly different environments for the molluscs, but were only slightly different for the foraminifera. Environmental variables, while not signficant at the 95% level for any of the molluscs, do have F values in three cases which are

Table 1. Probability that F ratio is exceeded for 19 foraminiferal species and total foraminifera in Jamaica. $\alpha \leq .05$ is in bold type. (See text for explanation of hypotheses.)

Species	Hypotheses					
	$\pi/3$ inter	$\pi/6$ inter	$\pi/3$ ovrin	$\pi/6$ ovrin	envir var	sta diff
Bolivina striatula	.99	.73	.73	**.02**	.11	.54
Bolivina subexcavata	.29	.62	.14	.07	.30	.69
Trifarina occidentalis	.22	.78	.47	.06	.16	.71
Ammonia beccarii	.33	.24	.62	.09	.93	.49
Rosalina globularis	**.02**	.72	.08	**.001**	.57	.19
Discorbis mira	.29	.08	.35	.11	.33	**.0005**
Rosalina subaraucana	.47	**.03**	.32	**.002**	.69	.10
Rosalina floridana	.29	.31	.52	.57	.40	**.03**
Amphistegina gibbosa	.66	.09	.82	.11	.65	**.0002**
Cymbaloporetta squammosa	**.01**	.25	**.05**	.19	.73	.78
Cymbaloporella tobagoensis	.36	.25	.28	.40	.09	.50
Cymbaloporetta atlantica	.20	**.02**	.06	**.0003**	.12	**.02**
Asterigerina carinata	.41	**.004**	.57	**.0008**	.22	.70
Bolivina doniezi	.99	.86	.97	.80	.66	.21
Planorbulinella acervalis	.22	.46	.35	.80	.40	.12
Nonionella auricula	.40	.82	.72	.42	.41	.08
Cyclogyra planorbis	.41	.15	.72	.10	.34	.21
Discorbis murrayi	.36	.98	.70	.77	.20	**.04**
Fursenkoina pontoni	.08	.16	**.05**	.27	.78	**.02**
Total Foraminifera	.24	.15	.57	**.002**	.07	.89

much higher than for the foraminifera. These analyses coupled with the great difference in species diversity between the habitats for the molluscs indicate that the molluscs were more abiotically controlled in these habitats than the foraminifera.

II. Indian River

Methods

Several square wire cages (12 mm mesh) 2 m on a side, were set up at Linkport for various experimental treatments in a seagrass bed of *Halodule wrightii*. The cages were placed in a subtidal flat and had no tops or bottoms. The present analyses utilized data from a plain cage (no treatment) and a nearby control area (no cage). Of the many Phyla collected (Young and Young, 1977) only the molluscs and foraminifera are treated here.

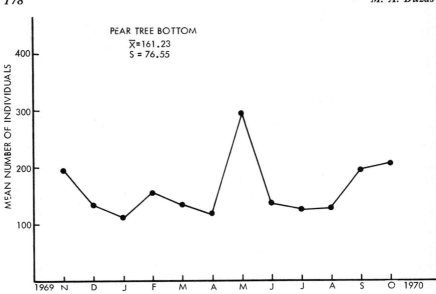

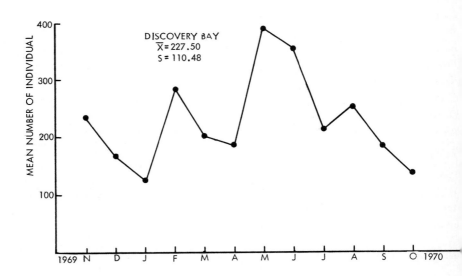

Figure 1. Monthly variations in density of foraminifera at Jamaica.

Macrofaunal sampling consisted of four replicate box cores (15 cm x 15 cm x 20 cm) taken inside and outside the cage during the months of December, 1976, and February, April, June, 1977.

The samples were washed through a 1 mm screen, narcotized, fixed, and preserved for later enumeration. For details see Young and Young (1977).

The foraminifera were sampled by inserting Phleger core liners into the sediment and removing the top 2 cm (20 ml) of sediment. The sediment was immediately fixed with neutralized formalin, washed over a 63 μ sieve, stored in alcohol, stained with rose bengal, floated in bromoform-acetone, rewetted, and enumerated while wet. Four replicates were taken inside the macrofaunal cage and four outside in the control area during the months of January, February, March, April, May, and June, 1976.

In addition to the macrofaunal cage, a foraminiferal cage was constructed by cutting four windows of 35 cm on a side 15 cm from the bottom of a large PVC trash can. The windows were covered with 1 mm nylon mesh screens to exclude predators. The screens were replaced about twice a week to prevent fouling. In February, the cage was placed in a 15 cm hole and 30 l of "sterile" sand was placed inside. Four replicate (20 ml) samples were taken inside and four outside the cage in an undisturbed area in March, April, May, and June, 1976. The samples were treated in the same manner as the foraminiferal samples from the macrofaunal cage.

Results

All of the experiments were designed to analyze differences in mean densities by a two-way analysis of variance with interaction. The three hypotheses are (1) an overall difference with time, (2) an overall difference between inside and outside the cage, and (3) interaction (differences inside and outside the cage with time). Only the more abundant species were analyzed. A minimum grand mean of about two was used as a cutoff (see Jackson, 1972; Young *et al.*, 1976). The original counts were transformed to 1n (x + 1) to normalize the data and to stabilize the variance.

Table 3 gives the probability of a random variable distributed as F exceeding the calculated F ratio for five species of gastropods, total gastropods, and total

Table 2. Probability that F ratio is exceeded for four bivalve species and total bivalves in Jamaica. $\propto \leq .05$ is in bold type. (See text for explanation of hypotheses.)

Species	$\pi/3$ inter	$\pi/6$ inter	$\pi/3$ ovrin	$\pi/6$ ovrin	envir var	sta diff
Codakia orbicularis	.96	**.03**	.69	**.05**	.07	**.001**
Ctena orbiculata	.56	.17	.31	.39	.14	**.0000**
Diplodonta punctata	.16	.73	**.05**	.90	.16	**.05**
Parvalucina costata	.65	.81	.52	.75	.60	**.005**
Total Bivalves	.93	**.03**	.74	.09	**.03**	**.04**

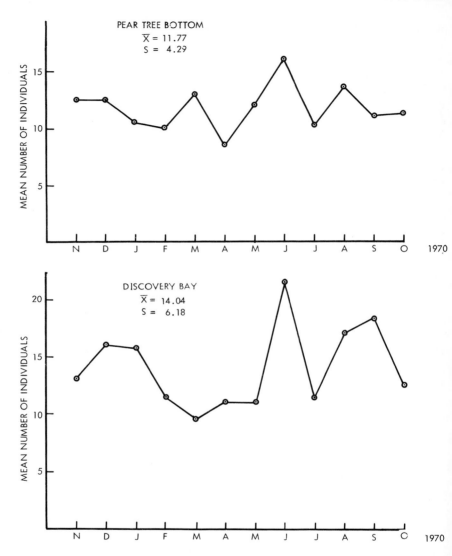

Figure 2. Monthly variations in density of bivalves at Jamaica.

bivalves (no bivalve species was abundant enough to be included in an individual analysis).

The mean numbers of individuals of *Diastoma varium* showed litttle difference inside and outside of the cage for the four sampling times. The only statistically significant hypothesis was for differences with time; maximum densities occurred in February (Figure 3).

The mean number of individuals of *Mitrella lunata* inside and outside of

Table 3. Probability that F ratio is exceeded for molluscs at Linkport. $\alpha \leq .05$ is in bold type.

Species	time	Hypotheses in vs out	interaction
Diastoma varium	**.02**	.66	.06
Mitrella lunata	.09	**.005**	.20
Crepidula fornicata	**.02**	.67	.43
Cerithium muscarum	**.0001**	.12	.19
Modulus modulus	**.0000**	.06	.19
Total Gastropods	.06	.35	.29
Total Bivalves	**.01**	**.005**	.49

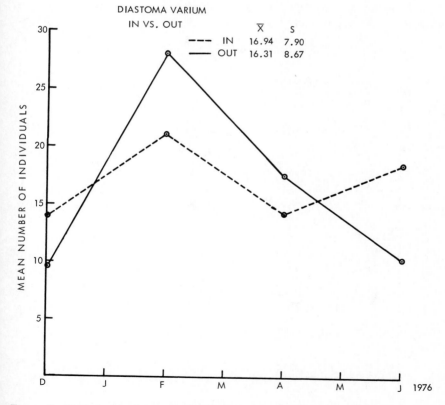

Figure 3. Variation in density of Diastoma varium *inside vs outside cage at Link-port, Florida.*

the cage for the four sampling times is shown in Figure 4. Table 3 indicates a significant difference between inside and outside, which is apparent in the plot for the months February, April, and June. This species was the only one tested that lacked a statistically significant difference with time.

The mean number of individuals of *Crepidula fornicata* inside and outside of the cage at the sampling times is shown in Figure 5. Little difference was observed inside vs outside of the cage, but as Table 3 indicates, there was a significant difference with time. The maximum density was in December.

The mean numbers of individuals of *Cerithium muscarum* per sampling time is shown in Figure 6. Little difference was observed between inside and outside, and a maximum density occurred in December. Table 3 indicates a statistically significant difference in density with time. The maximum density occurred in December.

The mean number of individuals per sampling time for *Modulus modulus* is shown in Figure 7. Again, the hypothesis for time is significant (Table 3). The maximum density occurred in April.

In summary, only *Mitrella lunata* was affected by the cage, having higher densities inside, and this was the only species showing no difference with time.

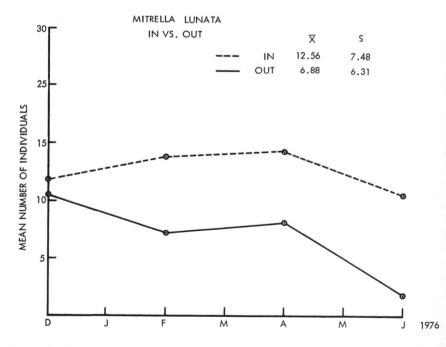

Figure 4. Variation in density of Mitrella lunata *inside vs outside cage at Linkport, Florida.*

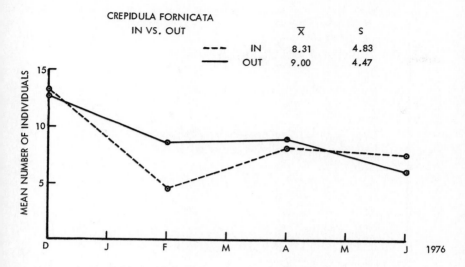

Figure 5. Variation in density of Crepidula fornicata *inside vs outside cage at Linkport, Florida.*

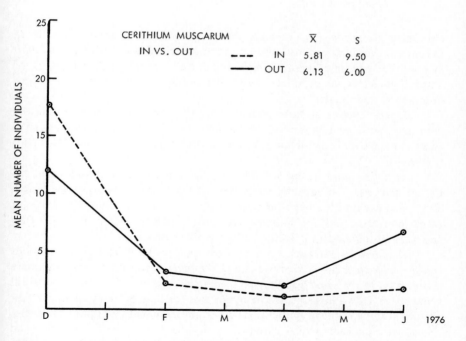

Figure 6. Variation in density of Cerithium muscarum *inside vs outside cage at Linkport, Florida.*

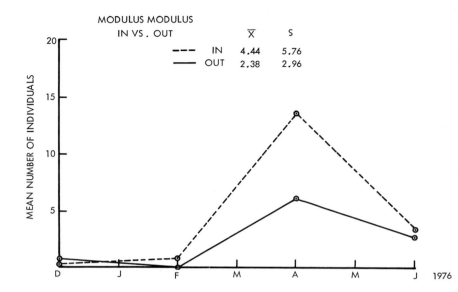

Figure 7. Variation in density of Modulus modulus *inside vs outside cage at Linkport, Florida.*

Cerithium muscarum and *Crepidula fornicata* both had maximum densities in December. *Diastoma varium* had a maximum in February and *Modulus modulus* in April. The pattern of densities inside and outside was similar for all species. As Table 3 indicates, no significant difference exists inside vs outside with time (interaction hypothesis).

Because species of gastropods do not have the same pattern of densities with time, we cannot expect the total number of gastropods to reflect the differences cited above. None of the hypotheses were significant for total gastropods (Figure 8).

As stated above, no species of bivalve was abundant enough to warrant statistical analysis. Consequently, only the total number of bivalves was tested. Table 3 shows that the hypothesis for inside vs outside and time was significant while interaction was not. Bivalves were always more abundant inside the cage and were most abundant in December and April (Figure 9).

The foraminiferal taxa *Ammonia beccarii, Elphidium mexicanum,* miliolids (mostly *Quinqueloculina impressa* and *Q. seminula*), and total foraminifera were enumerated at the same macrofaunal macrocage as the molluscs. The statistical summary is shown in Table 4. The hypothesis for time is highly significant for all four taxa. No other hypothesis is significant. Examination of plots of density against time indicates similar patterns for all taxa. Consequently, only the total foraminiferal densities are shown here (Figure 10). Densities of all taxa of foraminifera have maxima in April. As one would expect, the lack of a large difference between inside and outside indicates that a cage with 12 mm openings does not exclude predators of the foraminifera.

The hypotheses for time and inside vs outside are statistically significant for all taxa (Table 5). In addition, the interaction hypothesis is significant for *Ammonia beccarii*. As observed with the macrofaunal cage and control treatments, foraminifera had a maximum density in April. Figure 11 shows the pattern of density for the total living population. The differences between inside and outside are most striking with a maximum mean of about 5,000 individuals per 20 ml of sediment inside and 1,000 outside in April. Foraminiferal density patterns inside and outside were similar at the macrofaunal and meiofaunal sites (Figures 10 and 11). The synchrony observed is further assurance of adequate sampling and demonstrates that foraminifera respond to an overall rhythm at the Linkport site which, at present, is unexplainable.

Discussion

The results of this study indicate that densities of foraminifera and molluscs are not controlled in different habitats or with time in similar fashion. In Jamaica,

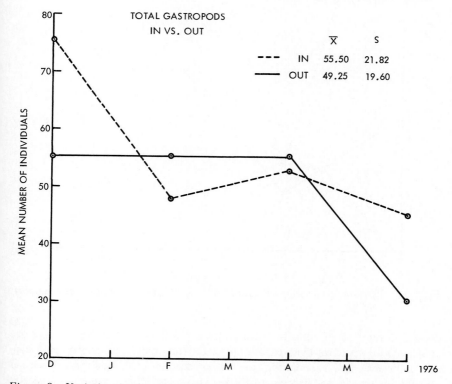

Figure 8. Variation in density of total gastropods inside vs outside cage at Link-port, Florida.

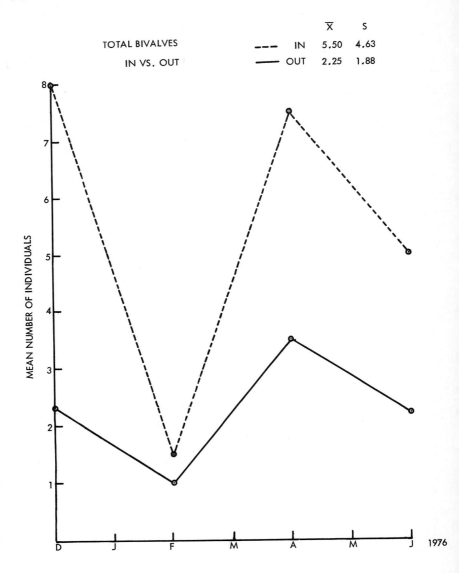

Figure 9. Variation in density of total bivalves inside vs outside cage at Linkport, Florida.

density differences of animals collected from a shallow subtidal habitat and one at 3 m are dramatic for bivalves, but not so for foraminifera. Similarly, periodicities of bivalves and foraminifera are not synchronous. Subtidal bivalve species also live in the deeper habitat, but never vice-versa. Most foraminiferal species occur in both habitats. These observations and the significance of the hypothesis

Table 4. Probability that F ratio is exceeded for foraminifera at Linkport (macrofaunal cage). $\alpha \leq .05$ is in bold type.

Species	time	Hypotheses in vs out	interaction
Ammonia beccarii	**.0004**	.07	.69
Elphidium mexicanum	**.0001**	.49	.94
Miliolids	**.0000**	.08	.86
Total Foraminifera	**.0000**	.38	.63

for environmental variables for total bivalves suggest that abiotic variables are more important for bivalves than for foraminifera. At Linkport in the Indian River, Florida, patterns of periodicity for individual species of gastropods differ widely, but not for foraminifera. While there is a significant difference of densi-

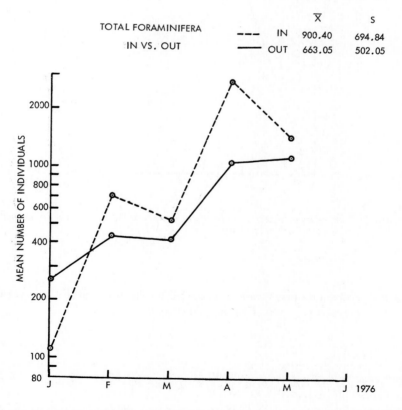

Figure 10. Variation in density of total foraminifera inside vs outside macrofaunal cage at Linkport, Florida.

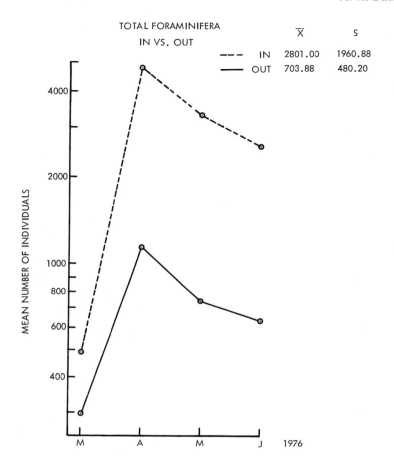

Figure 11. Variation in density of total foraminifera inside vs outside meiofaunal cage at Linkport, Florida.

Table 5. Probability that F ratio is exceeded for foraminifera at Linkport (meio-faunal cage). $\alpha \leq .05$ is in bold type.

Species	Hypotheses		
	time	in vs out	interaction
Ammonia beccarii	**.0000**	**.0000**	**.02**
Elphidium mexicanum	**.0000**	**.0000**	.23
Miliolids	**.0001**	**.0000**	.22
Total Foraminifera	**.0000**	**.0000**	.15

ties between inside and outside of a cage for bivalves, the differences are not nearly as large as for the foraminifera. Clearly, foraminifera and molluscs do not "see" the environment in the same way.

The results of this paper are not in agreement with Warme *et al.* (1976) who regarded as minor the differences between mollusc and foraminiferal biofacies identified through cluster analysis. They believed foraminifera and molluscs cluster into similar areally-distributed communities that reflect major habitats in Southern California and the eastern Yucatan. They suggested that foraminifera and molluscs are regulated by similar physical-chemical factors. There are, however, some difficulties with their comparisons. The mollusc data were clustered from correlation coefficients based on relative abundance and the foraminifera data were clustered from a simple matching coefficient using presence or absence. To further complicate matters, several other coefficients were used, and the one giving the best fit with the physical environment was chosen, a poor statistical procedure. Even so, there are many samples among the two groups that do not cluster in the same biofacies, and goodness of fit is a matter of opinion. In such analysis, much depends on whether you are looking for similarities or differences. Foraminifera and molluscs can probably be used to delimit the same biofacies on a relatively gross scale, but the data presented here, and I believe the data of Warme *et al.* (1976), indicate these organisms do not act as a simple unit.

Some ecologists and paleoecologists, e.g. Kauffman and Scott (1976), have suggested that all species should be included in community studies. With great difficulty a team of researchers could possibly survey and catalogue the fauna and flora of an estuary or similarly bounded area. This resulting community matrix containing abundances of all organisms could be stored in a large computer, but I have no idea what could be done with it. The wide discrepancies between patterns of density of molluscs and foraminifera as demonstrated here indicate that little can be learned by subjecting them jointly to sophisticated mathematical manipulation.

This study does not demonstrate that interactions between foraminifera and molluscs do not exist. Recently, K. Carle (personal communication) discovered two species of a small gastropod belonging to the genus *Acteocina* and a small fish *Gobionellus boleosoma* which eat foraminifera at Linkport, but most snails and fish do not. Consequently, we should not analyze all gastropods and foraminifera, but only those species whose life histories are sufficiently known so that specific hypotheses can be tested. Such an approach is in keeping with Young *et al.* (1976) who analyzed feeding types rather than taxonomic groups. We are still ill-prepared to tackle an entire community and must instead be content with studying parts for which we can formulate and test specific hypotheses.

Acknowledgments

Special thanks to K. Carle who did most of the field and laboratory work at Linkport. Thanks also to R. Bronson, K. D. Cairns, L. B. Ishman, M. A. Capone,

L. A. Hayek, J. E. Miller, D. H. Mook, R. W. Virstein, R. T. Wolcott, D. K. Young, and M. W. Young, who all helped in various ways.

References

1. Buzas, M. A., R. K. Smith, and K. A. Beem. 1977. Ecology and systematics of foraminifera in two *Thalassia* habitats, Jamaica, West Indies. Smithsonian Contrib. Paleo., no. 31, 139 pp.
2. Jackson, J. B. C. 1972. The ecology of the molluscs of *Thalassia* communities, Jamaica, West Indies. II. Molluscan population variability along an environmental stress gradient. Marine Biol. 14:304-337.
3. Kauffman, E. G., and R. W. Scott. 1976. Basic concepts of community ecology and paleoecology, pp. 1-28. *In* R. W. Scott and R. R. West (eds.), Structure and Classification of Paleocommunities. Dowden, Hutchinson, and Ross, Inc.
4. Warme, J. E., A. A. Ekdale, S. F. Ekdale, and C. H. Peterson. 1976. Raw material of the fossil record, pp. 143-169. *In* R. W. Scott and R. R. West (eds.), Structure and Classification of Paleocommunities. Dowden, Hutchinson, and Ross, Inc.
5. Young, D. K., M. A. Buzas, and M. W. Young, 1976. Species densities of macrobenthos associated with seagrass: a field experimental study of predation. Jour. Marine Res. 34:577-592.
6. Young, D. K., and M. W. Young. 1977. Community structure of the macrobenthos associated with seagrass of the Indian River estuary, Florida, pp. 359-381. *In* B. C. Coull (ed.), Ecology of Marine Benthos, vol. 6, University of So. Carolina Press.

SPATIAL-TEMPORAL DISTRIBUTIONS OF LONG ISLAND SOUND INFAUNA: THE ROLE OF BOTTOM DISTURBANCE IN A NEARSHORE MARINE HABITAT

Peter L. McCall

Department of Earth Sciences
Case Western Reserve University
Cleveland, Ohio

Abstract: Field experiments demonstrated a characteristic response of Long Island Sound infauna to substratum disturbance. Relatively opportunistic and equilibrium adaptive strategies were discerned. Three grab sample surveys were made during 1971-1973 to test the hypothesis that benthos spatial and temporal distributions result from differential adaptation to bottom disturbance.

Opportunistic species were patchily distributed in space and time; equilibrium species were evenly distributed. Opportunist-dominated stations were found on all bottom types, but in depths of less than twenty meters. Analyses of variance and canonical variate analyses of benthos samples showed that while faunal differences among bottom types do exist, depth-associated differences were most pronounced. Wave hindcasts and observation of storm effects showed that disturbance frequency and intensity were also depth-dependent. The distribution and effects of benthos predators remain unknown.

Eighty-five percent of the bivalve species sampled decreased in abundance from 1972 to 1973, while only twenty percent of the polychaetes declined. Three fourths of those species possessing lecithotrophic larvae or brood protection were unaffected or increased in abundance between 1972 and 1973; only 30–40% of the species with long-lived planktotrophic larvae were unaffected. While many benthos distribution patterns appear to result from differential adaptation to bottom disturbance, others are most clearly related to plankton phenomena.

Introduction

Nearshore marine habitats are characterized by species populations that are highly variable in space and time. At the same time, this variability is not characteristic of all shallow water species — some species manage relatively uniform distributions in the face of changes occurring about them.

Field experiments on the colonization by infaunal benthos of defaunated substrata indicate that differential adaptation to local bottom disturbance may account for such patterns, a result predicted by Johnson (1972). Although Johnson concerned himself primarily with disturbances resulting in an alteration of sediment grain size, his ideas apply to a whole variety of bottom disturbances. Here we take a disturbance to be any alteration of resources (food, space) by some agent extrinsic to the population. Common alterations are mortality events caused by storms or predators and alterations in sediment food content by bottom currents. Experimental results have been published (McCall, 1977) and will not be emphasized. Here the spatial-temporal abundance patterns of central Long Island Sound infauna will be examined in order to discern some factors important in controlling nearshore benthos distribution and abundance — of special concern is the importance of bottom disturbance relative to substratum type — and to begin to construct an ecologically significant habitat and taxa classification for nearshore marine benthos.

Study Area

Long Island Sound is a tidal embayment on the northeast coast of the United States. It is divided into two basins by the Mattituck Sill, which runs in a north-south direction near the eastern boundary of the study area (Bokuniewicz *et al.,* 1976). The estuarine circulation of the western basin is driven by the Housatonic and East River, and is superimposed on a strong tidal stream described by Gordon and Pilbeam (1975). The seasonal salinity range during the 1972-1973 period of study was about 3 °/oo (25--28 °/oo). Annual temperature range of the surface water was 20°C (3--23°C). Bottom and surface temperatures usually differed by less than 0.1°C (R. B. Gordon and C. C. Pilbeam, unpubl. data). The distribution of sediment types in the study area has been studied by McCrone *et al.* (1961), Buzas (1965), and Bokuniewicz *et al.* (1976) and is shown in Figure 1.

Methods

The colonization experiment

To determine the response of the infauna to a local bottom disturbance, defaunated substratum was placed on the bottom and colonization of this new microenvironment monitored. Four colonization experiments were conducted in 1972-1973 at two sites in Long Island Sound (Figure 2). One experiment at site A (14 m water depth) will be described here. Mud was collected from the harbor of the Yale Biological Field Station and defaunated onshore by dehydration, heating, and addition of fresh water to the mud. Defaunated mud was placed into wooden trays (3.1 m x 3.7 m x 1.5 m) containing one hundred 0.1 m² plastic sample boxes. Individual sample boxes were covered with plastic prior to the start of the experiment. Wooden trays were fitted with flotation collars, towed to site A, and sunk to the bottom. The experiment began on July 27, 1972 when divers removed the covers from the boxes. Colonization was monitored by collecting at least two sample boxes at each of nine intervals over a 384-day period. Collected samples were preserved in a 3% formalin-seawater solution and washed through a 297 micron sieve; animals were picked from sieve residue under a dissecting microscope.

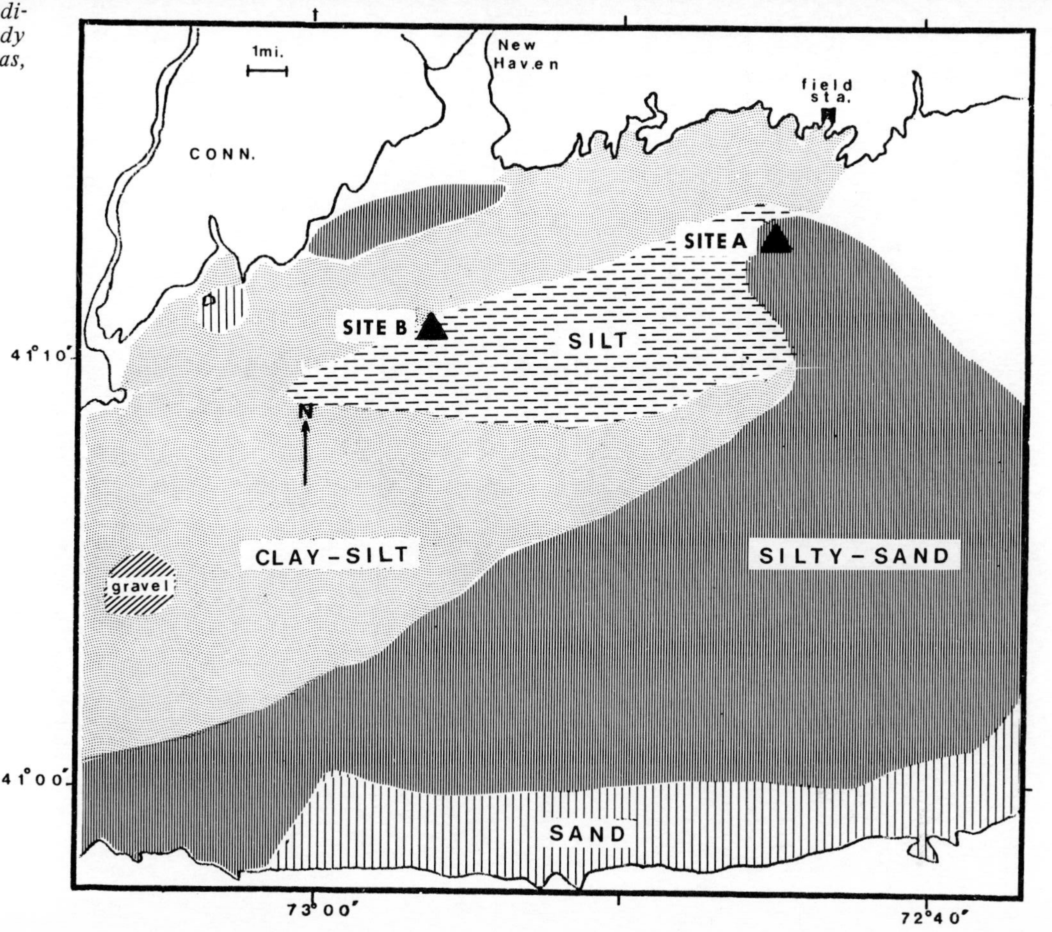

Figure 1. Distribution of sediment types in the study area (after Buzas, 1965).

193

The field surveys

If disturbance of the bottom (due say to storms or predation) is important in Long Island Sound and if there is a characteristic response to disturbance by benthos, then distribution patterns found in faunal surveys may be the result of frequency or recency of local disturbances. To test this idea and to identify other factors important in controlling benthos distribution and abundance, faunal surveys were conducted in central Long Island Sound in the summer of 1972 (8/16--8/21), winter of 1972–73 (2/17--3/30), and summer of 1973 (8/9–9/15). A total of 33 stations were occupied (Figure 2), although not all were visited in both summer and winter. In the summer of 1972 only stations A1 to A10 were visited. In the 1973 surveys a minimum of two .041 m^2 Van Veen grab samples were collected at each locality. In 1972, a .147 m^2 Van Veen was used. All survey samples were passed through a 1 mm sieve. The same preservation and counting methods were used here as in the colonization experiment.

Statistical analyses

A total of 136 samples were collected from 33 stations in three seasons, yielding 66 infaunal species. Most species were represented by only a very few individuals and the 15 most abundant species accounted for nearly 95% of the

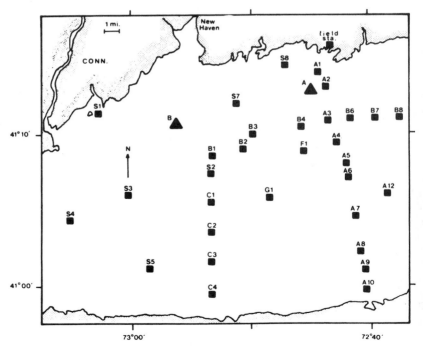

Figure 2. Grab sample survey station locations visited in 1972 and 1973.

individuals collected. Although plots of species density were constructed for the three surveys, a more parsimonious method of analysis and presentation of results was sought. The distribution of species groups defined by the colonization experiment was analyzed by multivariate analysis of variance. Number of species, H diversity (Pielou, 1966), and $1n (x + 1)$ transformed total abundance were calculated for all stations. Three separate univariate analyses and one multivariate analysis were performed on these variates using the general linear model. In addition, a multivariate analysis of species composition was made using the $1n (x + 1)$ transformed abundance of the 15 most abundant species as variates.

The general linear model has been described in detail by Seal (1964), Morrison (1967), and Finn (1974), and has been used in analysis of benthic data by Buzas (1969, 1971) and Young et al. (1976), among others. All notation used here follows that of Seal (1964). Briefly, in matrix notation a general model was formed, so that

$$\underset{(N \times p)}{X} = \underset{(N \times q)}{Z'} \underset{(q \times p)}{B} + \underset{(N \times p)}{E}$$

$\underline{X}$ was the matrix of p-variate observations (1, 2, 3, 4, or 15 in this case); $\underline{Z}'$ a "design" matrix of instrumental variables which explained the data (in this case a vector of observation means and seasonal, sedimentary, and depth differences); $\underline{B}$ a matrix of fitted coefficients describing the importance of the design variables; and $\underline{E}$ a matrix of residuals assumed to be $N(\underline{O}, \underline{\Sigma})$. The importance of design variables — the hypotheses about the relationship among the various observations — was tested in the univariate case by comparing the residual variance under Ω with that under ω, the linear model with the appropriate $(q\text{-}s)$ rows of $\underline{B}$ equated to zero.

The appropriate test statistic

$$\frac{(S_\omega - S_\Omega)\ (N-q)}{(S_\Omega)\ (q-s)}$$

where S is the number of fitted parameters, is distributed as $F_{(q-s),\ (N-q)}$ (Seal, 1964). In the multivariate case, comparison of full Ω and reduced ω models was effected by calculation of the determinant ratio U of their variance-covariance matrices (Seal, 1964):

$$U_{p,\ (q-s),\ (N-q)} = \frac{|(N-q)\,\underline{\Sigma}_\Omega|}{|(N-s)\,\underline{\Sigma}_\omega|}$$

Bartlett (1938) showed that the test statistic

$$[1/2 \, (q-p+s+1) \; - \; (N-q)] \; \ln U \approx X^2_{p(q-s)}.$$

Critical values for the F ratio and chi-square distributions were taken from Owen (1962). A succinct description of the differences in species composition in different seasons and depth zones on different substrata was obtained by displaying the multivariate means of stations so grouped on canonical axes. Canonical variates were produced by a transformation of the original multivariate means which restricted the new canonical variates to unit variance and zero covariance. In addition, the first variate accounted for greatest variability between the means of the groups; the second the next greatest, and so on. In this way, multivariate differences among groups could be displayed along canonical axes in fewer dimensions than in the untransformed case. Seal (1964) and Hope (1968) describe the calculation of canonical variates; Buzas (1967, 1970) has shown the utility of the method in analyzing faunal survey data. The chi-square approximation of Bartlett (1947, 1965) described also by Seal (1964),

$$[(N-1) \; - \; (p+h)/2] \; \ln \, [\overset{m}{\underset{j=k+1}{\pi}} \, (1+\phi_j)]$$

where N is the number of observations, p the number of variates, h the number of groups or universes, and m the smaller of p and $(h-1)$, was used to test the roots (eigenvalues) of a determinental equation used in calculating the transformation matrix. The correction described by Pearson and Hartley (1972) for this approximation was used when the value of the criterion was near the critical ($p < .05$) chi-square value. The non-significance of a root meant that differences among group means projected onto the canonical variate axis were small relative to differences within a group. With larger samples, groups may be significantly different along this same axis.

Equality of the p-variate normal variance-covariance matrices of the h groups is required. This could not be tested with this data since in all cases either the number of observations in a group was less than (p+1) or else the determinant of the test matrix was equal to zero. Hope (1968) and Reyment (1962) showed that the method is insensitive to some departure from normality or homogeneity of the matrices.

Results

Colonization experiment review

The experiment began on July 27, 1972. The number of species found in experimental samples equilibrated with surrounding natural bottom species number 50--84 days after the start of the experiment (Figure 3). Experimental tray populations subsequently experienced a more severe winter decline and more rapid spring increase to become again equal to natural bottom species number about a year after the start of the experiment. Species composition of experimental trays and natural bottom did not become similar until almost a year after the start of the experiment (Figure 4). It is this difference in species composition that is of special interest.

The time course of abundance of the seven species commonly encountered in the experimental trays and natural bottom samples is shown in Figure 5. Species were placed into one of three groups based on differences in peak abundance, time of peak abundance, and death rate. The large differences in species abundance patterns among these species are perhaps not so obvious in logarithmic plots, but are clearly seen in Table 1. The three groups erected on the basis of abundance patterns also possessed life habits in common. Group I species *Streblospio benedicti, Capitella capitata,* and *Ampelisca abdita* are small ($<$ .5 mg), sedentary, tube dwelling, near surface deposit feeders with rapid development and many reproductions per year. During reproduction few eggs per female are produced ($10-10^3$), but all species have some form of brood protection. Group II species *Nucula proxima* and *Tellina agilis* are intermediate between Groups I and III in size, mobility, number of eggs per female (10^3-10^4) and length of pelagic larval phase. Group III species *Nephtys incisa* and *Ensis directus* are large (30--300 mg), mobile, and relative to Group I species exhibit slow development and few reproductions per year. They do not brood developing young, but produce large numbers of planktotrophic larvae (10^3-10^6 per female). More complete life history descriptions have been presented by McCall (1975, 1977). Subsequent colonization experiments yielded similar patterns with *Owenia fusiformis* substituting for the eçologically similar *Streblospio benedicti.*

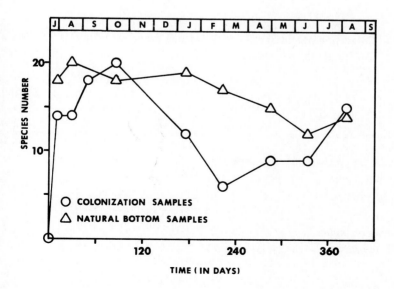

Figure 3. Total number of species found in experimental trays and surrounding untreated bottom 7/27/72 to 8/10/73.

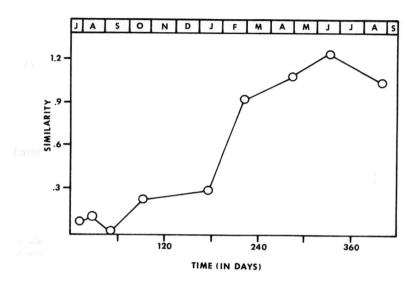

Figure 4. Similarity of experimental tray and bottom samples. A similarity of 1 represents the average similarity of any 2 natural bottom samples. A modification of Sorenson's index was used to calculate sample similarity; see McCall (1977) for details.

Table 1. Colonizing potential of benthic infauna found from July, 1972 -- March, 1973 in samples from tray experiment.

	Peak Abundance ($\#/m^2$)	Time at Peak Abundance (days)	Final Abundance ($\#/m^2$)
Group I			
Streblospio benedicti	418,315	10	335
Capitella capitata	80,385	29-50	955
Ampelisca abdita	9,990	29-50	0
Group II			
Nucula proxima	3,735	50	50
Tellina agilis	1,400	86	0
Group III			
Nephtys incisa	220	175 ($\approx$ constant)	120
Ensis directus	30	50-223 ($\approx$ constant)	0

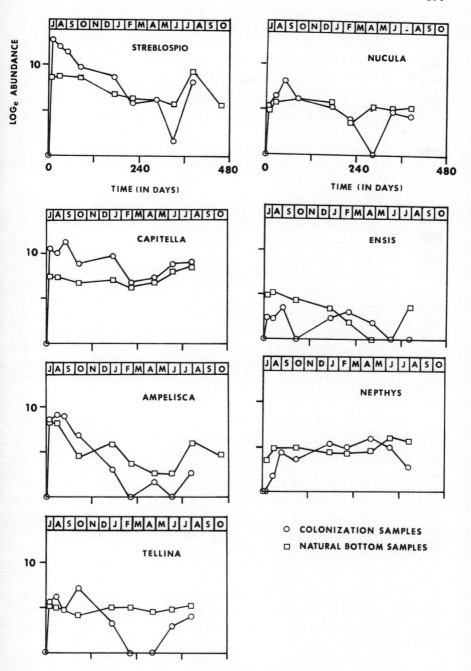

Figure 5. Log$_e$ abundance of the seven species commonly found in experimental trays with their abundance on untreated bottom.

Group I species are restricted to a sedentary life near the sediment-water interface and so are subject to more frequent mortality from disturbances they cannot escape. These species thus devote their energies to rapid reproduction and dispersal under favorable conditions at the expense of competitive abilities or physiological tolerance. Such species are called "opportunists" or "r-strategists" (MacArthur and Wilson, 1967; Wilson and Bossert, 1970; Grassle and Grassle, 1974). Group I species discovered newly created habitats quickly, only to suffer high subsequent mortality. Infauna able to escape interfacial sources of mortality either by possession of a shell (Group II) and/or by deep burrowing (Group III) are more likely to employ a converse "equilibrium" or "K-strategy" and have no need for the colonizing abilities of Group I species.

Faunal survey hypotheses

The elucidation of infaunal adaptive strategies in the colonization experiments suggested several hypotheses testable by benthos surveys and raised some interesting questions. Specifically, one expects that heterogeneous bottom disturbance ought to generate a relatively patchy distribution of Group I species while Group III species remain uniformly distributed by comparison. Opportunistic Group I species should be most abundant in high stress regions where new microhabitats are being generated continually. Group III species may be uniformly distributed over much of a stress gradient (if one exists). One can ask, what are the relative roles of substratum type and bottom disturbance in determining benthos distribution? Are there other important controlling factors? Are there "communities" in the sense of co-occurring species in Central Long Island Sound; if so, what controls their distribution?

Determination of stress gradients

Bottom disturbance was suspected to be a major control of benthos distribution. Both storm-generated waves and predators were likely sources of bottom disturbance. Wind records from the period 1965-1977 showed that Long Island Sound is subjected to several storms a year, winter storms being more frequent and intense than summer storms (Table 2). The period just preceding and during this study (1971-1973) was exceptionally windy. The effect of these storms on the bottom was roughly estimated, using wave hindcasting techniques of Bretschneider (1958), suitably modified for shallow water waves, small amplitude wave theory, and the quadratic stress law to produce the depth distribution of bottom stress as a function of wind speed (Figure 6). Most fine-grained natural sediments are entrained from the bottom at stresses from 0.5 to 1 dynes cm^{-2} (Fukuda, 1978; Rhoads *et al.*, 1977), so we may estimate that the combined stress effects of storms and the tidal stream have little influence on the bottom below about 20 m.

X-ray radiographs made from box cores taken at three depths on August 16, 1976 one week after Hurricane Belle showed the effects of storm-generated currents on the bottom (Figure 7). At the 13 m station an obvious erosional sur-

Table 2. Distribution of storm days 1965--1976. A storm is here defined as a nine-hour record of winds greater than 25 knots.

YEAR	J	F	M	A	M	J	J	A	S	O	N	D	Annual number of storm days
1977	1		2	1	2								
1976					1					1	1		3
1975				2									2
1974		1	3							2	1		7
1973	2		3	2	1					1	2		10
1972			3	1	1	1					3	4	13
1971	1	2	2	2	1			1		1	1	1	12
1970		2		1								3	6
1969	1	2										3	6
1968	1	2	1									3	7
1967		1	1	2		1			1				6
1966	5		1					1			1		8
1965	3	2	2						1	2	2	2	12
Average storm days per month	1.1	1.0	1.3	.8	.3	.2	0.0	.2	.2	.6	.8	1.4	

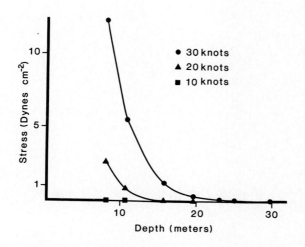

Figure 6. Calculated average bottom shear stresses as a function of wind speed along a transect from New Haven, Conn. to Port Jefferson, N.Y.

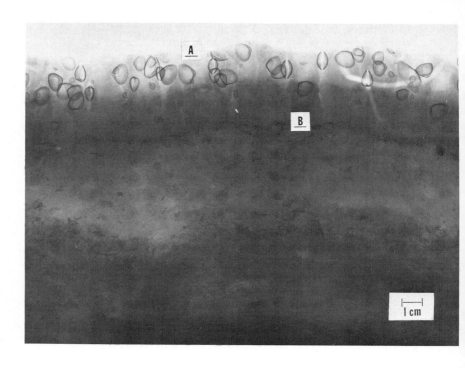

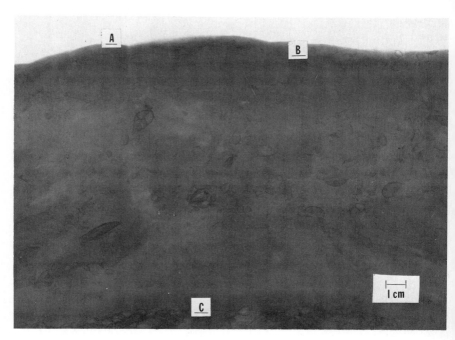

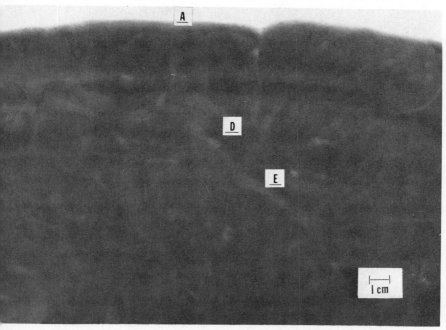

Figure 7. X-ray radiographs of box cores taken following Hurricane Belle at: (a: opposite, top) Lat. 41°11.8'N, Long. 72°56.7'W, depth 13 m; (b: opposite bottom) 41°8.1'N, 72°56.4'W, depth 20 m; (c: above) 41°5.7'N, 72°56.4'W, depth 27 m. A = sediment water interface, B = base of recent storm deposit, C = old storm layer, D = maldanid tube, E = Nephtys burrow.

face was found at a depth of 4.5--5 cm underlying storm-deposited graded bedding. The molluscan opportunist *Mulinia lateralis* (Levington, 1970) was abundant, along with the bivalves *Nucula proxima*, small *Yoldia limatula*, and small polychaetes. At the 20 m station recent storm effects were more difficult to see below 0.5 cm. It is possible that no sediment was redeposited on top of the erosional surface, making the real storm effect indeterminate. Also, winds were primarily from the north at this time and had only a short fetch, so effects at this depth may have truly been small. Effects of past storms however were clear in this radiograph. At the 27 m station no storm effects of any kind were seen. Deep living maldanid worms and deep burrowing *Nephtys* burrows were abundant here.

Effects of predators were not determined in this study. To date, all attempts to assess the effects of predation on infaunal abundance in Long Island Sound by exclosure of predators from the bottom have failed, principally because of the large amount of solids suspended in the tidal stream and the baffle effects of predator screens on the settling of particulates. The depth distribution of predators is poorly known. The starfish *Asterias forbesi* is the most abundant and pro-

Table 3. Composition of the design matrix Z'.

	VECTOR	INTERPRETATION
z_0	= a vector of units	
z_1	= +1 for winter samples, -1 for summer samples	seasonal differences
z_2	= -1 for sand stations, 0 for silty sand stations, +1 for silt, clay stations	
z_3	= +1 for sand stations, -2 for silty sand stations, +1 for silt, clay stations	substratum differences
z_4	= z_1 x z_2	season-substratum
z_5	= z_1 x z_3	interaction
z_6	= +7 for stations 20 m depth, -11 for stations 20 m depth	contrast of 11 shallow and 7 deep stations
z_7	= z_1 x z_6	depth-season interaction
z_8	= z_2 x z_6	depth-substratum
z_9	= z_3 x z_6	interaction

ductive benthic predator, and it preys primarily on molluscs, although a few polychaetes are also taken (Richards and Riley, 1967). Although substratum effects were not controlled, Burkenroad (1946) and Richards and Riley (1967) found standing crops five to ten times larger in shallow ($<$ 40 feet) than in deep water. The winter flounder *Pseudopleuronectes americanus* is the most abundant demersal fish predator in Long Island Sound (Richards and Riley, 1967). Adults, which feed on larger polychaetes (*Nephtys*) and crustaceans, comprise most of the offshore population; juveniles, which feed on small near-surface polychaetes and amphipods, are most abundant in shallow water (Pearcy, 1962; Richards, 1963). The exact food preferences and regional distribution of decapod, xiphosuran, and molluscan predators remain unknown. Predators may be more abundant in the shallower parts of the Sound, but until their distribution and effects are better known, the placement of a dividing line between high and low stress environments at the 20-meter isobath must remain provisional.

Analyses of variance

A single design matrix, Z', was used in the linear models to explain differences among the stations sampled in 1973 (Table 3). All the z_1 are zero sum vec tors except for z_0, so that β_0 is the overall mean of all observations used in the model. Interpretation of the design vectors is shown in the table. The concept of interaction is shown by the vectors z_4 and z_5, which describe the season-substratum interaction; i.e., the equality of substratum type differences in different seasons. Six ω models were constructed to test the significance of the relationships described by Z'. The one full and six reduced models were run on eight sets of variates whose composition is shown in Table 4. Results of these analyses are shown in Table 5.

Group I species showed no significant difference in distribution in different seasons on different sediment types or in different depths. The same is true for the Group III species *Nephtys incisa*. This does not mean however that Group I and III species behave the same in similar sedimentary environments or depth zones. Analyses of species density maps (McCall, 1977) already suggested that Group I species were patchily abundant in shallower areas. The linear model analyzes differences in *mean* behavior. The group mean varied little among environments for opportunists and equilibrium species; their dispersion about this mean changed significantly. The Siegel-Tukey test for relative spread in paired samples (Siegel and Tukey, 1960) showed that all Group I species had a greater spread (= patchy distribution) than the Group III species *Nephtys incisa* (p < .001). By the same test, two of the four Group I species showed greater patchiness in shallow than in deep water; *Nephtys incisa* showed no differences. These results agree with variance/mean ratio differences reported earlier (McCall, 1977). Group II species showed differences among sediment types and a depth effect that was different on different substrata. Linear contrasts among the beta coefficients showed that Group II species were most abundant on silty-sand bottoms and in shallow water (< 20 m). Species density maps showed the greatest density near the 20 m isobath.

Variations in species diversity, log total station abundance and species number were analyzed singly and also, since the three measures were highly correlated

Table 4. Variates used in models.

x_1 = log abundance of *Strebospio benedicti, Ampelisca abdita, Capitella capitata,* and *Owenia fusiformis*   (p = 4)

x_2 = log abundance of *Nucula proxima* and *Tellina agilis*   (p = 2)

x_3 = log abundance of *Nephtys incisa*   (p = 1)

x_4 = log total station abundance   (p = 1)

x_5 = number of species   (p = 1)

x_6 = diversity   (p = 1)

x_7 = (x_4, x_5, x_6) (p = 3)

x_8 = log abundance of 15 most abundant species   (p = 15)

Table 5. Analyses of Variance for Survey Data.

MANOVA OF GROUP I SPECIES (p = 4)

Hypothesis	Variability Accounted For	Determinant Ratio	Bartletts Criterion	D.F.	p
$\beta_1 = 0$	seasonal differences	.7899	6.01	4	NS
$\beta_2 = \beta_3 = 0$	substratum differences	.6746	10.23	8	NS
$\beta_4 = \beta_5 = 0$	substratum-season interaction	.6277	10.69	8	NS
$\beta_6 = 0$	depth differences	.8275	4.82	4	NS
$\beta_7 = 0$	depth-season interaction	.8226	4.98	4	NS
$\beta_8 = \beta_9 = 0$	depth-substratum interaction	.8524	4.15	8	NS

Residual determinant = 181.73213

MANOVA OF GROUP II SPECIES (p = 2)

Hypothesis	Variability Accounted For	Determinant Ratio	Bartletts Criterion	D.F.	p
$\beta_1 = 0$	seasonal differences	.9882	0.31	2	NS
$\beta_2 = \beta_3 = 0$	substratum differences	.6963	9.59	4	$.025 < p < .05$
$\beta_4 = \beta_5 = 0$	substratum-season interaction	.8941	2.97	4	NS
$\beta_6 = 0$	depth differences	.9215	2.17	2	NS
$\beta_7 = 0$	depth-season interaction	.9781	0.59	2	NS
$\beta_8 = \beta_9 = 0$	depth-substratum interaction	.5868	13.86	4	$.005 < p < .01$

Residual determinant = 203.7524

ANOVA OF GROUP III, *NEPHTYS INCISA*

Hypothesis	Variability Accounted For	D.F.	Sum of Squares	F	p
$\beta_1 = 0$	seasonal differences	1	.0243	.06	NS
$\beta_2 = \beta_3 = 0$	substratum differences	2	.0366	.04	NS
$\beta_4 = \beta_5 = 0$	substratum-season interaction	2	.0782	.19	NS
$\beta_6 = 0$	depth differences	1	.0969	.24	NS
$\beta_7 = 0$	depth-season interaction	1	.0462	.11	NS
$\beta_8 = \beta_9 = 0$	depth-substratum interaction	2	.0725	.18	NS
	Residual	36	10.4923		

ANOVA OF STATION ABUNDANCE

Hypothesis	Variability Accounted For	D.F.	Sum of Squares	F	p
$\beta_1 = 0$	seasonal differences	1	2.6274	2.36	NS
$\beta_2 = \beta_3 = 0$	substratum differences	2	6.8847	3.08	NS
$\beta_4 = \beta_5 = 0$	substratum-season interaction	2	2.4355	1.54	NS
$\beta_6 = 0$	depth differences	1	0.2845	0.25	NS
$\beta_7 = 0$	depth-season interaction	1	0.57	0.51	NS
$\beta_8 = \beta_9 = 0$	depth-substratum interaction	2	4.8533	2.18	NS
	Residual	26	28.9806		

Table 5. Analyses of Variance for Survey Data *(cont.)*.

ANOVA OF SPECIES NUMBER

Hypothesis	Variability Accounted For	D.F.	Sum of Squares	F	p
$\beta_1 = 0$	seasonal differences	1	65.8196	6.32	.01 < p < .025
$\beta_2 = \beta_3 = 0$	substratum differences	2	61.4745	2.95	NS
$\beta_4 = \beta_5 = 0$	substratum-season interaction	2	16.1666	1.55	NS
$\beta_6 = 0$	depth differences	1	3.5556	.34	NS
$\beta_7 = 0$	depth-season interaction	1	3.3327	.32	NS
$\beta_8 = \beta_9 = 0$	depth-substratum interaction	2	3.1945	.31	NS
	Residual	26	270.5835		

ANOVA OF SPECIES DIVERSITY

Hypothesis	Variability Accounted For	D.F.	Sum of Squares	F	p
$\beta_1 = 0$	seasonal differences	1	1.7740	3.58	NS
$\beta_2 = \beta_3 = 0$	substratum differences	2	.9724	0.98	NS
$\beta_4 = \beta_5 = 0$	substratum-season interaction	2	.7676	0.77	NS
$\beta_6 = 0$	depth differences	1	.0606	0.12	NS
$\beta_7 = 0$	depth-season interaction	1	0.642	0.13	NS
$\beta_8 = \beta_9 = 0$	depth-substratum interaction	2	1.8679	1.88	NS
	Residual	26	12.8952		

MANOVA OF COMMUNITY PARAMETERS (p = 3)

Hypothesis	Variability Accounted For	Determinant Ratio	Bartletts Criterion	D.F.	p
$\beta_1 = 0$	seasonal differences	.7623	6.65	3	NS (.05 < p < .10)
$\beta_2 = \beta_3 = 0$	substratum differences	.6230	11.83	6	NS (.05 < p < .10)
$\beta_4 = \beta_5 = 0$	substratum-season interaction	.8370	4.45	6	NS
$\beta_6 = 0$	depth differences	.9661	0.84	3	NS
$\beta_7 = 0$	depth-season interaction	.9265	1.87	3	NS
$\beta_8 = \beta_9 = 0$	depth-substratum interaction	.7972	5.67	6	NS

Residual determinant = 24480.969

MANOVA OF SPECIES COMPOSITION (p = 15)

Hypothesis	Variability Accounted For	Determinant Ratio	Bartletts Criterion	D.F.	p
$\beta_1 = 0$	seasonal differences	.0902	44.51	15	p < .005
$\beta_2 = \beta_3 = 0$	substratum differences	.0682	51.02	30	.005 < p < .01
$\beta_4 = \beta_5 = 0$	substratum-season interaction	.0656	51.76	30	.000 < p < .01
$\beta_6 = 0$	depth differences	.4760	13.73	15	NS
$\beta_7 = 0$	depth-season interaction	.1677	33.03	15	p < .005
$\beta_8 = \beta_9 = 0$	depth-substratum interaction	.0774	48.62	30	.01 < p < 0.25

Residual determinant = .66484932E13

with one another, as a single trivariate station measurement. The only significant difference found among those tested was an increase in the mean number of species per station from winter to summer of 3.14 ± 2.2 species.

The linear model of Table 3 was not applicable to the summer 1972 data. Too few stations were visited and different sampling equipment was used. However, there was a substantial difference between the two years; the distribution-free median difference in number of species per station between summer 1972 and summer 1973 with 95% confidence interval was 10 ± 3 species (sign test; Owen, 1962). In spite of the sampling differences, these results correspond well with the results at Site A, where a drop of six species was found between 1972 and 1973 using the same sampling procedure throughout. D. C. Rhoads and A. Michaels (unpubl. data) observed similar changes in another part of Long Island Sound.

Analysis of variance of species composition using the fifteen most abundant species showed larger heterogeneities than the aggregate parameters of species number, diversity, and log total station abundance. Highly significant seasonal and depth-season interaction effects were found. The multivariate mean of different sediment types was also significantly different; substratum differences changed from winter to summer. To display these differences, canonical variates of the significantly different groups were calculated.

Canonical analyses

Five canonical analyses were performed. Results are shown in Tables 6 to 9 and Figures 8 and 9. (Since the variates are of unit variance, the circles around the means, with radius $1.65/n^{1/2}$, represent rough 90% confidence intervals.)

The first analysis was of the six groups defined by sand, silty sand, and clay facies in summer and winter 1973 (Figure 8). Only the first two canonical variates were significant. The first canonical variate, which accounted for 44% of the total variability, separated the groups on the basis of seasonal differences. The second variate accounted for 28% of the total variability and roughly separated the groups on the basis of sediment type. Note that the configuration of the three group subsets changed seasonally. Sand stations seemd to change the least from winter to summer.

When the stations were regrouped into shallow (less than 20 meters) and deep (greater than 20 meters) groups, a canonical analysis of the four groups defined by season and depth again had two significant variates accounting for 70% and 23% of the variance, respectively. The first most important variate contrasted shallow and deep stations (Figure 9); the second, winter and summer differences. Shallow areas experienced larger faunal fluctuations than deep areas.

Abundances of species were not strictly comparable from summer to summer for reasons mentioned above. However, Buzas (1971) showed that much information on faunal differences could be obtained from analysis of presence-absence data. Accordingly, species collected at nine stations on the transect visited in summer 1972 and summer 1973 were recorded as present or absent (Table 7).

Table 6. Species used in canonical analysis with vectors of mean abundance in three sediment types.

Species	Mean log$_e$ abundance vectors		
	WINTER		
	sand	silty sand	silt-clay
1. *Nucula proxima*	.28	1.07	1.27
2. *Yoldia limatula*	0.00	.33	.19
3. *Tellina agilis*	.32	.26	.19
4. *Nassarius trivittatus*	1.33	.89	1.16
5. *Nephtys incisa*	1.11	1.73	1.96
6. *Sigambra tentaculata*	0.00	0.00	0.00
7. *Capitella capitata*	0.00	.23	0.00
8. *Maldanid A*	.19	1.76	1.18
9. *Maldanid B*	0.00	.72	.19
10. *Owenia fusiformis*	1.22	.24	0.00
11. *Streblospio benedicti*	1.05	.19	0.00
12. *Polydora* sp.	.19	0.00	0.00
13. *Ninoe nigripes*	.87	.76	.23
14. *Pherusa affinis*	1.01	1.33	.73
15. *Ampelisca* sp.	.83	1.01	.23
	SUMMER		
1. *Nucula proxima*	.94	1.04	1.00
2. *Yoldia limatula*	.66	.19	.68
3. *Tellina agilis*	.47	.23	.37
4. *Nassarius trivittatus*	1.18	1.60	1.13
5. *Nephtys incisa*	1.65	2.31	1.88
6. *Sigambra tentaculata*	.50	1.73	1.42
7. *Capitella capitata*	.23	.87	.19
8. *Maldanid A*	1.25	1.76	.96
9. *Maldanid B*	.88	1.18	.63
10. *Owenia fusiformis*	2.04	1.45	1.63
11. *Streblospio benedicti*	0.00	.23	.45
12. *Polydora* sp.	.73	.61	.79
13. *Ninoe nigripes*	.23	.19	.19
14. *Pherusa affinis*	.96	.42	.98
15. *Ampelisca* sp.	1.40		.94

All logs are to the base e. Means listed are mean logs of the same stations used in the MANOVA.

Table 7. Presence and absence data for stations visited in both summer 1972 and summer 1973.

1972

Station	Species														
	01	*02*	*03*	*04*	*05*	*06*	*07*	*08*	*09*	*10*	*11*	*12*	*13*	*14*	*15*
A1	1	0	1	1	1	1	0	1	1	1	0	1	0	1	1
A2	1	1	1	1	1	0	0	1	1	0	1	1	1	0	1
A4	1	1	1	1	1	0	0	1	1	1	0	0	1	0	1
A5	0	1	1	1	1	1	1	1	0	1	1	1	1	1	1
A6	0	1	1	1	1	1	0	1	1	1	1	0	1	1	1
A7	0	1	1	1	1	1	1	1	1	1	0	0	1	0	1
A8	1	1	1	1	1	0	0	1	1	1	0	0	1	1	1
A9	1	1	1	1	1	0	1	1	1	1	0	0	1	1	1
A10	1	1	1	1	1	0	0	1	1	1	0	0	1	1	1

1973

Station	Species														
	01	*02*	*03*	*04*	*05*	*06*	*07*	*08*	*09*	*10*	*11*	*12*	*13*	*14*	*15*
A1	1	0	1	1	1	0	1	0	0	1	0	0	0	0	1
A2	1	1	1	1	1	0	0	0	0	1	1	0	0	1	0
A4	1	0	0	1	1	1	0	1	1	1	0	0	1	1	0
A5	0	0	0	1	0	0	0	1	1	1	0	0	1	0	1
A6	0	0	0	1	1	0	0	1	1	1	0	0	0	0	0
A7	0	0	0	1	1	0	0	1	1	1	0	1	0	1	0
A8	0	0	0	1	1	0	0	1	1	1	0	0	0	0	0
A9	1	1	0	1	1	0	0	1	1	1	0	0	0	1	0
A10	1	1	0	1	1	0	0	1	1	1	1	1	0	0	0

Canonical analysis showed that the difference between the multivariate mean abundances of the fifteen most common species was highly significant.

There was a decline in the number of species found on the bottom in winter 1973, and there was no subsequent rise in the summer of 1973 to the previous year levels. Moreover, Tables 6 and 7 show that not all species were affected identically. Inspection of species density maps makes it clear that some species were greatly reduced in abundance and occurrence while others were little affected; still others increased from 1972 to 1973. Results of this inspection are shown in

Table 8. Eigenvalues and percent of total variability accounted for in five canonical analyses.

Order Eigenvalue	Percent Variability	Cumulative Percent Variability
Groups by sediment type		
1. 1.6645	44.0214	44.0214
2. 1.0522	27.8112	71.8326
3. .5934	15.6859	87.5184
4. .3324	8.5219	96.0404
5. .1498	3.9596	100.0000
Groups by depth		
1. 3.0264	69.5609	69.5609
2. .9819	22.5687	92.1296
3. .3424	7.8704	100.0000
Comparison of two summers		
1. 875.9375	100.0000	100.0000
Groups by species: winter		
1. 1.4746	70.8676	70.8676
2. .4443	21.3552	92.2228
3. .1618	7.7772	100.0000
Groups by species: summer		
1. 1.4149	82.7764	82.7764
2. .2195	12.8404	95.6172
3. .0749	4.3828	100.0000

Table 10. It is interesting that 85% of the bivalve species decreased in abundance, while only 20% of the polychaete species experienced such decline. Relatively rare species were affected more than common species. Three-fourths of those species possessing lecithotrophic larvae or brood protection were unaffected or increased in abundance over the year; only 30--40% of the species with known long-lived planktotrophic larvae remained unaffected.

An attempt to group species into "communities" based on their co-occurrence and abundance in sand, silty sand, and silt-clay was made by performing canonical analyses with h = 15 species groups and p = 3 sediment types (Figure 10). No very tight species groups were present along the one significant canonical axis. No clear biologic significance could be attached to this canonical variate, although widespread and abundant species seemed to be contrasted with those that were rare and spotty in occurrence. There are no species *groups* however that

Table 9. Significance tests of canonical roots.

$$[(N-1) - (p+h)/2] \cdot \ln\prod_{j=k+1}^{m} (1+\phi_j), \text{ distributed as chi-square with}$$
$$(p-k) \times (h-k-1) \text{ d.f.}$$

Groups by sediment type

N = 59	j	ϕ	$\pi(1+\phi)$	47.5 · ln$\pi(1+\phi)$	chi-square d.f.	significance
	1	1.6654	13.2516	122.7458	75	p < .005
	2	1.0521	4.9717	76.1790	56	p < .05
	3	.5934	2.4220	42.0330	39	NS
	4	.3342				NS
	5	.1498				NS

Groups by water depth

N = 59	j	ϕ	$\pi(1+\phi)$	53.5 · ln$\pi(1+\phi)$	chi-square d.f.	significance
	1	3.0263	10.7120	126.8679	45	p < .005
	2	.9819	2.6605	52.3505	28	p < .005
	3	.3424	1.3424	15.7535	13	NS

Comparison of two summers

N = 18	j	ϕ	$\pi(1+\phi)$	8.5 · ln$\pi(1+\phi)$	chi-square d.f.	significance
	1	875.9375	876.9375	57.5760	15	p < .005

Species groups: winter

N = 90	j	ϕ	$\pi(1+\phi)$	80 · ln$\pi(1+\phi)$	chi-square d.f.	significance
	1	1.4745	4.1521	113.8890	42	p < .005
	2	.4443	1.6780	41.4076	26	p < .05
	3	.1618	1.1618	11.9976	12	NS

Species groups: summer

N = 90	1	1.4149	3.1779	92.4981	42	p < .005
	2	.2195	1.3159	21.9616	26	NS
	3	.0791				NS

(·) = non-significant variate

Table 10. Abundance changes from summer 1972 to summer 1973. Species marked with (L) possess lecithotrophic larvae or brooded larvae.

Decrease 1972-1973	Unaffected	Increase 1972-1973
Molluscs	Molluscs	Molluscs
Yoldia limatula (L)	*Nucula proxima* (L)	
Pitar morrhuana	*Nassarius trivittatus*	
Mulinia lateralis	*Retusa obtusa*	
Tellina agilis		
Ensis directus		
Pandora gouldiana (L)		
Polychaetes	Polychaetes	Polychaetes
Cirratulid sp.	*Phyllodocid* sp.	*Sigambra tentaculata*
Ninoe nigripes	*Glycera dibranchiata*	*Owenia fusiformis*
Ampharete acutifrons	*Nephtys incisa*	*Polydora* sp. (L)
	Capitella capitata (L)	
Amphipod	*Scalibregma inflatum*	
Ampelisca abdita (L)	Maldanid A (L)	
	Maldanid B (L)	
	Streblospio benedicti (L)	
	Maldanopsis elongata (L?)	

were clearly associated with sediment type. Neither was there a constancy of configuration of species from season to season.

Discussion

Substratum and distribution

There are some inadequacies in the data that should be pointed out. The first concerns the substratum classification used. Knowledge of a substratum type is not the same thing as knowledge of the whole grain size distribution. Substratum effects might be more precisely measured by replacing the vectors describing categorical differences with vectors containing percent sand, silt, or clay, say, or some other sedimentological variables. Sanders (1956) concluded as much in some early work in the region, but the variance of his data was large and the conclusion untested. The areal patterns of weight percent sand and silt clay in the study area reported by Bokuniewicz *et al.* (1976) suggest that the use of these variables would not alter the conclusions reached here. Second, in a variable environment, a two-year data run is not very long. The number of species collected during the years 1973-1974 seems abnormally low. Failure of recruitment by planktotrophic larvae may have eliminated differences between areas that may exist in other years. Many of the eliminated species were suspension-feeding bi-

SEDIMENT TYPE GROUPS

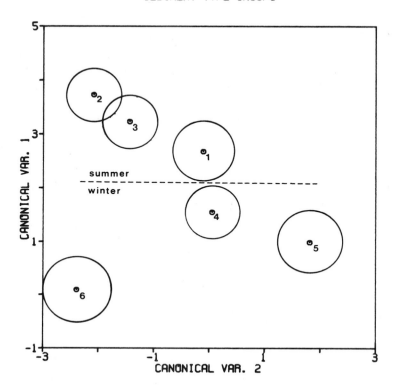

Figure 8. Canonical variate plot of stations grouped by substratum type. 1, 2, 3 = summer sand, silty sand, and silt clay stations; 4, 5, 6 = winter sand, silty sand, and silt clay stations.

valves that would be sensitive to substratum differences. Still, we are left with the conclusion that over this period of time at least, depth (and therefore disturbance) differences are overall much more important than substratum type in governing benthos distribution.

Disturbed bottoms appear to be patchily distributed in waters less than 20 m deep. While it is clear that heterogeneous predation may easily generate such a pattern, it is less obvious how storm-generated waves would act in a similar fashion. Patchiness in substratum mass properties constitutes a part of the answer to this problem. I have detected 10% differences in substratum water content over the space of a few meters at 15 m depths in the Sound. Postma (1967) and Fukuda (1978) determined that entrainment of fine-grain muds is strongly dependent on substratum water content. Fukuda (1978) found that sediment entrainment is non-linear with increasing bottom stress. Small differences in stress may produce large differences in sediment entrainment from the bottom. In addition, the bottom is biologically heterogeneous and this can also lead to differences in the susceptibility of the bottom to erosion (Rhoads *et al.,* 1977; Rhoads, this volume). Storms may affect the bottom not only by producing mortality among the benthos, but also by translocating animals or altering sediment microbial and geochemical characteristics as surface sediments are eroded in one place and deposited in another. All of these storm-related "disturbances" may initiate the characteristic benthic response described here. Benthos distribution will be patchy depending on the frequency and distribution of the disturbance and initial heterogeneity of the substratum.

Plankton phenomena

Some temporal patterns of benthos abundance seem unrelated to the disturbance gradient in Long Island Sound. Suspension feeding bivalves and species with planktotrophic larvae are disproportionately represented in the failure of recruitment in 1973. The period November, 1972 to April, 1973 was abnormally

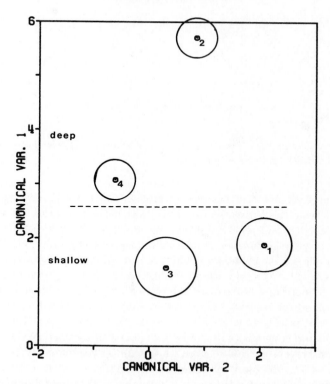

Figure 9. Canonical variate plot of stations grouped by water depth. 1, 2 = summer shallow (20 m); 2, 3 = winter shallow and deep stations.

SPECIES GROUPS-SUMMER

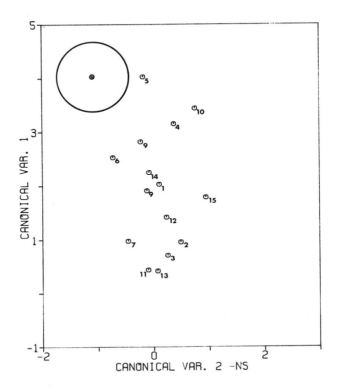

Figure 10. Canonical variate plot of species abundance. Species identifiers are identical to those in Table 6.

windy and suspension feeders may have diverted energy normally devoted to reproduction to combating increased turbidity. Alternatively, benthos fluctuations may have been the result of larval planktonic mortality. Physical factors such as light and temperature are known to influence the species composition and standing crop of phytoplankton communities, which in turn influence zooplankton standing crop. Deevey (1956) found large annual differences in the zooplankton standing crop of central Long Island Sound. Standing crop of the copepod, larval invertebrate, and larval fish components of the zooplankton in May-June 1952 were twice as large as in May-June 1953. Conover (1956) reported that total phytoplankton standing crop was the same in both years. In summer 1952, however, low light and temperature and increased nitrate in early summer favored the development of a large diatom crop relative to dinoflagellates, while in 1953 higher incident radiation and water temperature favored a large crop of dinoflagellates. Analogous weather conditions prevailed in the summers of 1972 and 1973 (June,

1972 cloud cover was 76% and air temperature 2.7°F below the 40-year monthly mean; June, 1973 cloud cover was 71% and air temperature 2.4°F above the 40-year mean). While copepods favor diatoms as a food source, the relative food value of natural populations of diatoms and dinoflagellates for bivalve and polychaete larvae are unknown. Bivalves are known to eat small diatoms and naked flagellates in culture; polychaetes utilize a larger size and wider range of food particles (Loosanoff and Davis, 1963; Thorson, 1946). While most authors feel that larval death seldom results from starvation, reduced food supplies can prolong life in the plankton and subject the population to increased predation (Thorson, 1946). (Fluctuating abundance of larval predators, of course, can produce the same effect.) Davis (1969) reported that when large numbers of dinoflagellates (*Peridium* sp., the same organisms involved in the 1953 dinoflagellate increase) are found in plankton samples, no straight-hinged bivalve larvae will occur. A toxic external metabolite of these organisms was believed to prevent bivalve larval development, although the possibility that the dinoflagellates subtract some necessary larval growth substance from the water remains untested. Yet another cause of larval mortality, epizootic infection by bacteria and fungi, remains a possibility. There is no available evidence at present to determine the relative importance of these hypotheses.

Conclusion

Heterogeneous bottom disturbance exerts a major control on benthos distribution and abundance in central Long Island Sound. As a result of the experiments and surveys described here we now understand why certain species (opportunists) fluctuate greatly in space and time while certain other (equilibrium species) in the same habitat do not. Still, not all patterns are interpretable in the light of opportunistic-equilibrium adaptive strategies. Adaptations to substratum type account for some spatial patterns and larval planktonic mortality for some temporal fluctuations. Finally, in view of the large and ecologically significant differences in benthos life histories and habits, it appears that detailed long-term studies of the entire life cycle of small groups of functionally similar species groups will yield a far higher dividend in the understanding of benthos distributions than occasional large-scale counts of all species retained on a particular size sieve.

Acknowledgments

I would like to thank J. B. Fisher and Michael Tevesz for their assistance in collecting the bottom samples and identifying the infauna. D. C. Rhoads provided valuable advice and the facilities of the Yale Biological Field Station during the course of the project. R. C. Aller and D. C. Rhoads collected the box cores and supplied the X-ray pictures. Y. P. Sheng kindly provided the Long Island Sound bottom stress calculations. J. F. Grassle and E. G. Driscoll provided valuable critical reviews of the manuscript.

References

1. Bartlett, M. S. 1938. Further aspects of the theory of multiple regression. Proc. Camb. Phil. Soc. 34:33-40.

2. _____ . 1947. Multivariate analysis. J. Roy. Stat. Soc. Suppl. 9:176-197.

3. _____ . 1965. Multivariate statistics, pp. 201-224. *In* T. H. Waterman and H. J. Morowitz (eds.), Theoretical and Mathematical Biology. Blaisdell Publ., New York.

4. Bokuniewicz, H. J., J. Gebert, and R. B. Gordon. 1976. Sediment mass balance of a large estuary. Long Island Sound. Estuarine Coastal Mar. Sci. 4:523-536.

5. Bretschneider, C. L. 1958. Revisions in wave forecasting. Deep and shallow water. Proc. 6th Conf. Coastal Engineering. pp. 30-67.

6. Burkenroad, M. D. 1946. General discussion of problems involved in starfish utilization. Bull Bingham Oceanogr. Coll. 9:44-58.

7. Buzas, M. A. 1965. The distribution and abundance of foraminifera in Long Island Sound. Smithsonian Misc. Coll. 149:1-89.

8. _____ . 1967. An application of canonical analysis as a method for comparing faunal areas. J. Animal Ecol. 36:563-577.

9. _____ . 1969. Foraminiferal species densities and environmental variables in an estuary. Limnol. Oceanogr. 14:411-422.

10. _____ . 1970. Spatial homogeneity: Statistical analyses of unispecies and multispecies populations of foraminifera. Ecology 51:874-879.

11. _____ . 1971. Analyses of species densities by the multivariate general linear model Limnol. Oceanogr. 16:667-670.

12. Conover, S. A. M. 1956. Oceanography of Long Island Sound, 1952-1954. IV. Phytoplankton. Bull. Bingham Oceanogr. Coll. 15:62-112.

13. Davis, H. C. 1969. *In* J. D. Costlow (ed.), Marine Biology, Vol. 5, Proc. 5th Interdisciplinary Conf. Mar. Biol., Gordon and Breach, N.Y. 606 pp.

14. Deevey, G. B. 1956. Oceanography of Long Island Sound, 1952-1954. Zooplankton. Bull. Bingham Oceangr. Coll. 15:113-155.

15. Finn, J. D. 1974. A General Model for Multivariate Analysis. Holt, Rinehart, and Winston, Inc., New York. 423 pp.

16. Fukuda, M. K. 1978. The entrainment of cohesive sediments in freshwater. Unpublished Ph.D. dissertation. Case Western Reserve University.

17. Gordon, R. B., and C. C. Pilbeam. 1975. Circulation in central Long Island Sound. Geophys. Res. 80:414-422.

18. Grassle, J. F., and J. P. Grassle. 1974. Opportunistic life histories and genetic systems in marine benthic polychaetes. J. Mar. Res. 32:253-284.

19. Hope, K. 1968. Methods of Multivariate Analysis. Univ. London Press, London, 165 pp.

20. Johnson, R. G. 1972. Conceptual models of benthic communities, pp. 148-159. *In* J. M. Schopf (ed.), Models in Paleobiology. Freeman Cooper Co., San Francisco.

21. Levinton, J. S. 1970. The paleoecological significance of opportunistic species. Lethaia 3:69-78.

22. Loosanoff, V. L. and H. C. Davis. 1963. Rearing of bivalve molluscs, pp. 2-136. *In* F. S. Russell (ed.), Advances in Marine Biology, Academic Press, New York.

23. MacArthur, R. H., and E. O. Wilson. 1967. Theory of Island Biogeography. Princeton University Press, 203 pp.

24. McCall, P. L. 1975. The influence of disturbance on community patterns and adaptive strategies of the infaunal benthos of central Long Island Sound. Ph.D. dissertation. Yale University.

25. _____ . 1977. Community patterns and adaptive strategies of the infaunal benthos of Long Island Sound. J. Mar. Res. 35:221-266.

26. McCrone, A. W., B. F. Ellis, and R. Charmatz. 1961. Preliminary observations on Long Island Sound sediments. New York Acad. Sci., Ser. 2, 24:119-129.

27. Morrison, D. F. 1967. Multivariate Statistical Methods. McGraw-Hill, New York, 415 pp.

28. Owen, D. B. 1962. Handbook of Statistical Tables. Addison-Wesley. Reading, Mass. 508 pp.

29. Percy, W. G. 1962. Ecology of an estuarine population of winter flounder, *Pseudopleuronectes americanus* (Walbaum). Parts I-IV. Bull. Bingham Oceanogr. Coll. 15:5-78.

30. Pearson, E. S., and A. O. Harley. 1972. Biometrika Tables for Statisticians, Vol. II. University Press, Cambridge. 385 pp.

31. Pielou, E. C. 1966. The measurement of diversity in different types of biological collections. J. Theor. Biol. 13:131-144.

32. Postma, H. 1967. Sediment transport and sedimentation in the estuarine environment, pp. 158-179. *In* H. Lauff (ed.), Estuaries, Amer. Ass. Adv. Sci. Publ. 83.

33. Reyment, R. A. 1962. Observations on the homogeneity of covariance matrices in paleontologic biometry. Biometrics 18:1-11.

34. Rhoads, D. C., R. C. Aller, and M. B. Goldhaber. 1977. The influence of colonizing benthos on physical properties and chemical diagenesis of the estuarine seafloor, pp. 113-138. *In* B. C. Coull (ed.), Ecology of Marine Benthos. Univ. of North Carolina, Chapel Hill.

35. Richards, S. W. 1963. The demersal fish population of Long Island Sound I. Species composition and relative abundance in two localities, 1956-1957. Bull. Bingham Oceanogr. Coll. 18:5-31.

36. Richards, S. W. and G. A. Riley. 1967. The benthic epifauna of Long Island Sound. Bull. Bingham Oceanogr. Coll. 15:113-155.

37. Sanders, H. L. 1956. Oceanography of Long Island Sound. X. The biology of marine bottom communities. Bull. Bingham Oceanogr. Coll. 15:245-258.

38. Seal, H. L. 1964.. Multivariate Statistical Analysis for Biologists. Methuen & Co., London. 209 pp.

39. Siegel, S., and J. W. Tukey. 1960. A nonparametric sum of ranks procedure for relative spread in unpaired samples. J. Amer. Stat. Assoc. 55:429-445.

40. Thorson, G. 1946. Reproduction and larval development of Danish marine bottom invertebrates with special reference to the planktonic larvae in the Sound (Oresund). Medd. Kamm-Havunderog., ser. plankton, 4:1-523.

41. Wilson, E. O., and W. H. Bossert. 1970. A Primer of Population Biology. Sinauer Assoc., Stamford, Conn., 192 pp.

42. Young, D. K., M. A. Buzas, and M. W. Young. 1976. Species densities of macrobenthos associated with seagrass: A field experimental study of predation. Jour. Mar. Res. 34:577-592.

SEAFLOOR STABILITY IN CENTRAL LONG ISLAND SOUND:
Part I. Temporal Changes
In Erodibility of Fine-Grained Sediment

Donald C. Rhoads, Josephine Y. Yingst

Department of Geology-Geophysics
Laboratory for Benthic Research
Yale University
New Haven, Connecticut

and

William J. Ullman

Department of Geophysical Sciences
University of Chicago
Chicago, Illinois

Abstract: This preliminary study documents temporal changes in seafloor erodibility at a 14-meter-deep mud bottom station in central Long Island Sound over a 29-month period.

The mean critical rolling and saltation velocities of the bottom were determined in the laboratory with a specially constructed flume containing salt water. A removable 45-cm length of the 10 cm by 10 cm closed flume channel was used as a box core. A removable bottom on the core box allowed scuba divers to obtain relatively undisturbed samples of the seafloor. Samples were returned to the laboratory in thermally insulated containers and critical erosion velocities were determined within a few hours.

In 1974 and 1975, minimum annual mean rolling velocities were measured in July (16--19 cm sec^{-1} at z = 100 cm). Maximum mean rolling velocities were recorded in November 1974 and October 1975 (respectively 28 cm sec^{-1} and 23 cm sec^{-1} at z = 100 cm). The observed change in mean critical velocities in 1976 was different from that observed in 1974 and 1975. The minimum mean rolling velocity in 1976 was recorded in October (19 cm sec^{-1} at z = 100 cm) and the peak threshold velocity was measured in July (28 cm sec^{-1} at z = 100 cm).

We propose tentatively that two opposing biogenic processes influence the observed changes in critical velocities; stabilization by sediment binding and destabilizaton by bioturbation.

An estimate of the influence of microbial growth and mucus binding on bottom erodibility was obtained by culturing microorganisms on beds of glass beads of various sizes in the flume. Critical rolling velocities of glass beads increased 25% to 60% after 3–15 days related to mucus production and binding of the beads.

Seafloor stabilization by sedentary polychaetes was also studied in the laboratory by comparing mean critical rolling velocities of natural sediment without tube-forming polychaetes with mean rolling velocities of the same sediment after introducing dense aggregations of *Heteromastus filiformis*. Critical rolling velocities increased by 80% over a period of 11 days.

Introduction

Tidal resuspension of fine-grained and organic-rich sediment into the water column is an important factor for sedimentological, biological, and geochemical processes. The transport, dispersion, and deposition of silt and clay-sized particles is largely determined by tidal resuspension (Van Straaten and Kuenen, 1958; Postma, 1961; Groen, 1967). This phenomenon results in a near-bottom turbidity maximum related to resuspension of bottom muds and may occur over a major fraction of the estuarine seafloor (e.g., Postma, 1967; Schubel, 1968; Young, 1971; Rhoads, 1973).

Measurements of the turbidity structure above the bottom on a time-scale of a few hours shows a close correlation between thickness of the bottom turbidity maximum, total concentration of suspended solids, and the tidal curve (Van Straaten and Kuenen, 1958; Postma, 1961; Groen, 1967; Schubel, 1968; Rhoads, 1973; Rhoads *et al.*, 1975). Longer-term resuspension cycles encompassing several months or several seasons are poorly documented.

The physical stability of the muddy seafloor is an important factor influencing water transparency and hence photosynthetic compensation depth. Also, the settlement and survival of many benthic invertebrate species is controlled by seafloor stability (e.g., Rhoads and Young, 1970). Near-bottom sediment suspensions containing microbially coated particles are probably important food resources for both zooplankton and benthic organisms (Riley, 1959; Baylor and Sutcliffe, 1963). In the future, these particle suspensions may be important nutrient sources for detritus-based *in situ* aquaculture systems (Rhoads, 1973; Rhoads *et al.*, 1975; Tenore, 1977). Suspended sediment is also important to estuarine chemical processes like sorption and desorption of trace metals and radionuclides (e.g., Benninger, 1976; Aller and Cochran, 1976; and Turekian, 1977).

Two categories of biogenic processes are important in sediment transport: stabilization and destabilization. These terms are used here to describe respectively a net increase or decrease in the critical erosion velocity related to the interplay of these two opposing biogenic processes. Stabilization processes physically bind particles to the seafloor. Particle to particle agglutination (sediment cohesion) can be accomplished by mucus exudates secreted by microorganisms and larger benthic invertebrates (e.g., Schwarz, 1932; Frankel and Mead, 1973; Newman, 1974; Corpe, 1974; Hopkins, 1975). In well illuminated water, plant polysaccharides also bind particles (e.g., Bathurst, 1967; O'Colla, 1962; Fogg, 1962; Holland *et al.*, 1974). Dense concentrations of worm tubes, algal filaments, or aquatic vascular plants may similarly stabilize the bottom by elevating the viscous sublayer (e.g., Ginsburg and Lowenstam, 1958; Marshall and Lukas, 1970; Neuman *et al.*, 1970; Scoffin, 1970). Destabilization processes decrease critical erosion velocities by increasing boundary layer roughness. The importance of the activities of deposit-feeding organisms in lowering critical erosional velocities of marine muds by changing particle size composition and water content has been documented in both laboratory and field studies (Rhoads and Young, 1970; Southard *et al.*, 1975; Young, 1977; Young and Southard, 1978). If we assume that the relative importance of these two biogenic processes is controlled by seasonal changes in organism recruitment patterns, growth and production of bacteria, water temperature (metabolic rates) and nutrient inputs, then one might expect a seasonal change in erodibility of the seafloor and near-bottom water turbidity. This assumption serves as a working hypothesis for our ongoing study. Part I (this paper) documents temporal changes in seafloor stability at a benthic station in central Long Island Sound over a three-year period. We further examine in the laboratory the importance of mucus production and tube binding on critical erosion velocities. Part II (Yingst and Rhoads, this volume) is a preliminary attempt to explain the observed temporal change in seafloor erodibility in central Long Island Sound in terms of seasonal changes in organism abundances and metabolic activities of bioturbating organisms.

Study Area

Because this study involves biogenic alteration of boundary conditions, we were careful in choosing a study site. Ideally, one would like to make measurements of seafloor erodibility in a biofacies that is relatively predictable in both organism abundance and species composition: attributes of a mature successional stage. In fine-grained sediments of Long Island Sound, the mature infaunal community is composed of subsurface deposit-feeders (Rhoads, McCall, Yingst, in press). Sanders (1956) described such an assemblage in an extensive silty-clay deposit south of New Haven below depths of approximately 10 meters. It was called the *Nucula proxima-Nephtys incisa* assemblage. In earlier studies we were successful in locating a patch of the *Nucula-Nephtys* assemblage at a station called Northwest Control (NWC) (Figure 1). This station is located in 14 meters of water about 5.0 km southwest of the channel entrance to New Haven Harbor. All of our flume data comes from this station. A complete description of the biology of station NWC is given in Yingst (in press) and Yingst and Rhoads (this volume).

Methods

Measurement of sediment transport was made on samples in a closed-channel salt water flume (Figure 2). A 45-cm-long section of the channel is removable. This section is located 100 cm behind the flume channel intake. The cross section of the channel above the bed is 10 cm x 10 cm. The removable section serves as a box core. Internal dimensions of the plexiglass core are: 45 cm

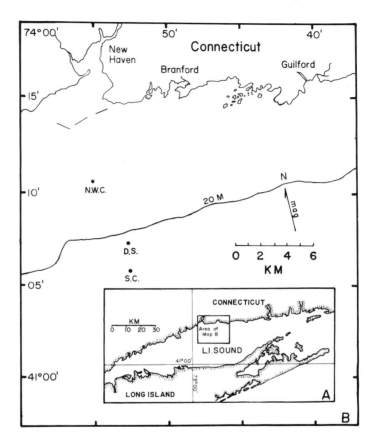

*Figure 1. Location of study sites. A) Inset of study area relative to Long Island
           Sound. B) Station NWC is the location of sampling of all flume box
           cores and benthic faunal data. Stations DS and SC are locations of
           bottom current meters (z = 100 cm).*

long, 10 cm wide, and 17.5 cm high. The ends of the box core, when not coupled
to the flume channel, are sealed by watertight covers. The bottom of the core
box is open and the edges are sharpened to facilitate coring. A water-tight base
plate covers the bottom after a diver has taken a core. This plate is held in place
by clamps.

    Divers push the box core into the bottom to a depth of about 7–8 cm.
Vent holes in the top of the box are then plugged and the sediment scooped away

*Figure 2. (opposite) A) Diagrammatic cross section of a closed channel salt-water
           flume used to measure bottom erodibility. A. Water supply pumped
           from reservoir. B. One meter high head-tank. C. A spill-over tank re-
           ceives excess water from head-tank and returns this water to the reser-
           voir. D. One meter long approach channel with a 100 m² cross-sectional*

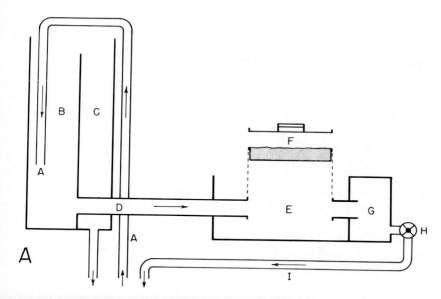

area. E. *Water bath tank in which the flume box core is inserted into the channel.* F. *Flume-box core shown in removed position.* G. *Valve chamber.* H. *Calibrated PVC ball valve.* I. *A discharge pipe returns effluent water to the reservoir (from Rhoads, Aller, and Goldhaber, 1977).* **B)** *Photograph of flume channel with a box core in place. Flow is from left to right. The microscope and illuminator have been removed from the viewing point to show an unobstructed view of the box core.*

from the box core by hand so that the watertight base plate can be inserted under the bottom of the box. The core is withdrawn to the level of the bottom surface, the base plate is clamped in place, and the sample returned to the sea surface.

At each sampling date two replicate box cores were taken at station NWC. Bottom sediment temperatures were measured in cores upon retrieval and then returned to the laboratory. Careful transport of the cores does not normally disturb the interface (Yingst and Rhoads, this volume). Samples were transported to the laboratory in thermally insulated containers. Changes in temperature during transport were less than 2°C. In the laboratory the box core was inserted into the flume channel after adjusting the height of the sediment surface to match that of the approach and exit channels. We did not attempt to adjust flume water temperature to the temperature of Long Island Sound bottom water. Flume measurements were completed within a maximum period of six hours; in most cases within three hours of collection. We believe that the period cores were exposed to flume water temperatures (about 20°C), and salinities (32–35 °/oo) did not significantly change biogenic boundary conditions. Nevertheless, we plan to do future work in a temperature-regulated flume.

In some cases, only one box core was run in the flume. We were careful not to run cores that experienced resuspension or water loss while being transferred to the laboratory. In some cases, cores were only used for quantifying macrofaunal numbers if laboratory preparation caused changes such as resuspension or 'slumping' of the core surface. One to 2% of our samples were not run for the above reasons.

We have not defined the grain-size distribution of surface sediment. Sedimentary particles at the surface of the muddy facies in the Sound consist of loosely bound organic-mineral aggregates (Riley, 1963; DiSalvo, 1973; Rhoads, 1973). Some of these particles can be identified as the feces of benthos. The dimensions of many of these fecal pellets, as well as organic-mineral aggregates, change in size in relation to decomposition and disintegration processes. Because of the difficulties encountered in sizing the particles, we chose to use their transport properties to characterize the bottom. However, it may be helpful to state that most of these aggregates fall within the size range of medium sand to coarse silt (Wentworth grade scale).

Particle transport was measured in the flume in the following way (refer to Figure 2): The operator observes particle behavior through a stereomicroscope (3.5x), viewing the sediment surface at an oblique angle of about 20°. The flow rate of water over the sediment surface was controlled by opening a calibrated PVC ball valve on the downstream side of the flume channel. Flow velocities up to about one knot are possible in this flume. Flow is defined in this study as the cross-sectional (100 cm^2) mean flow velocity. Flow accelerations, controlled manually, are on the order of 0.1 cm sec^{-2}. Measurements of particle motion are made at 1-cm intervals, starting at a distance of 22 cm from the upstream end of the box core (n = 10 unless otherwise noted). This is called a transect.

As the flow is accelerated from zero, three different critical velocities are recorded. First, a mean excitation velocity ($\bar{V}_e$) is noted. This is the velocity at which a population of particles vibrate in place but no net displacement is observed. In this case, shear stress acting on the bottom is not high enough to overcome grain inertia and adhesive forces. We do not report $\overline{V}_e$ values in this paper. As flow is accelerated above the excitation velocity, the mean rolling velocity ($\overline{V}_r$) is recorded. This is commonly referred to as the critical erosion velocity (e.g., Bagnold, 1966; Carson, 1971; Raudkivi, 1967). We have arbitrarily chosen to define V_r as the velocity where a particle population of 10 or more in the field of view initiates continuous horizontal rolling motion in contact with the bed (bed creep). We have found by experience that an observer is able to follow the individual behavior of up to 10 particles. Larger sample sizes do not allow the flume operator to keep track of the population of interest because of the numbers of particles moving into the field of view from upstream. At the $\overline{V}_r$, some particles on the bed surface still adhere to the bottom and therefore remain in an excitation state.

After a transect of 10 measurements of excitation and rolling velocity are made (transect 1), the transect is repeated recording the mean suspension velocity ($\overline{V}_s$) (transect 2). This is defined as the velocity at which a particle population of 10 or more leave the bed and are placed into suspension. This is probably equivalent to the saltation velocity (Bagnold, 1966), but because the scale of our measurements is so small, the total trajectory of a particle cannot be seen. It is necessary to defer measurement of the suspension velocity (transect 2) until all excitation and rolling velocities are determined (transect 1) because extensive surface erosion takes place at transect 2 velocities, completely changing initial biogenic boundary conditions.

The suspension velocity is the most difficult to estimate accurately. Particles tightly bound to the bottom suddenly jump. Such particles pass directly from an excitation state into suspension, bypassing the transitional rolling field. Such "break-away" behavior can occur over a wide range of velocities, depending on the degree of binding. This phenomenon makes it difficult for the operator to estimate accurately the critical velocity boundary between the rolling and suspension fields.

Our definition of erodibility, therefore, involves describing the change in the response of the seafloor to a controlled flow regime. We have chosen the mean rolling velocities ($\overline{V}_r$) as the flow parameter to characterize erodibility.

In some instances we have given flume velocity measurements as one-meter velocity equivalents. This extrapolation was done by first calculating turbulent boundary shear stress for the flume wall at a given discharge velocity. Using the flume wall shear stress value, a time-averaged velocity at $z = 100$ cm was then calculated, using Keulegan's vertical velocity distribution equation (e.g., Raudkivi, 1967, p. 47).

Laboratory experiments on microbial binding were done by introducing glass microbeads used in blast-polishing applications (Waldron Co. Inc., North Haven, Ct.) into flume core boxes. The beads are spheroidal in shape and contain not more than 15% irregularly-shaped particles (fused spheres or globules). These particles are reasonably free of surface abrasions and surface angularities. Densities range from 2.42 to 2.99 gm cm^{-3}. Bead densities exceed organic-aggregate densities. In the microbial binding experiments we were not attempting to replicate natural particle conditions. Five size classes of beads were used: 5-53, 44-74, 74-149, 149-250, and 300-350 microns.

Several time-series transects were run in the glass bead experiments. Mean critical velocity values are based on sample sizes of between 20 and 40.

The growth of microbial organisms on bead surfaces was followed by measuring the quantity of adenosine-triphosphate (ATP) present. We use the ATP assay as an indirect measure of the quantity of binding exudate present on bead surfaces.

In the 74-149μ glass bead experiments where ATP measurements were made (referred to later in Figure 6), two replicate box cores were used. One box core was coupled to the flume channel for periodic measurement of critical velocities. The second box was placed in the circulating reservoir tank of the flume. Bead samples were removed for ATP analysis from the replicate in the reservoir tank. It was not desirable to remove bead samples directly from the box attached to the channel because this process alters the bedform. Between runs, the boxes were covered to exclude light (plant production) and the water was aerated. Extractions of ATP from glass beads were made immediately after weighing, using the method of boiling NaHCO$_2$ (Christian *et al.*, 1975). ATP in the extracts was assayed by adding a 10μl sample to a 100μl reaction mixture of luciferase and luciferin (DuPont) and measuring the resulting light flash with an ATP photometer (DuPont 760 Luminescence Biometer). The efficiency of ATP recovery was determined by a two-point standard addition. All ATP values were corrected to 100% yield based on 10 samples averaging 93% ± 12% recovery.

In those glass-bead experiments where ATP was not measured (summarized in Figure 4), the box core containing beads was uncoupled from the flume channel between runs and placed into a small salt-water holding tank. A growth medium for heterotrophic marine bacteria (STP) (Tatewaki and Provasoli, 1964) was added to the holding tank after each run in concentrations of 5 ml/l to stimulate bacterial growth. The boxes were also covered to exclude light. The bath was continuously aerated to mix the nutrient medium. Because of the high pO$_2$ environment, the surficial bacteria in culture were most likely gram-negative aerobes. Although bacteria are present in flume water and on flume surfaces, we wanted to work with microbial populations present on the seafloor at NWC. Therefore, after making an initial $\overline{V}_r$ measurement, the surface of the bed was inoculated with milligram quantities of surface mud from station NWC. This introduced microorganisms onto the bed of glass beads. In the course of the bead experiments, water temperature ranged from 18–26°C and salinity from 32–35°/oo.

Results

Sediment erodibility at Station NWC

The seasonal change in $\overline{V}_r$ and $\overline{V}_s$ over a 29-month period is shown in Figure 3A. Data points are distributed unequally in time because of the difficulty of obtaining samples by diving in winter months. The spring, summer and fall months are documented best.

In all of our observations, the thickness of the eroded surface is on the order of 1–2 mm. This study does not address the problem of erosion of muds below this depth interval.

In 1974 and 1975, minimum critical velocities were observed in July. Values of $\overline{V}_r$ (flume) were 6 cm sec^{-1} and 7 cm sec^{-1} respectively. Minimum $\overline{V}_s$ values in both years were about 10 cm sec^{-1}. The period of greatest resistance to erosion and transport is difficult to determine because of the paucity of winter data. However, in 1974-1975, the period between November and April appears as if it may represent a time of relatively high bottom stability. If we compare seasonal values between 1974 and 1975, a significant difference is found, although the seasonal pattern of change between the two years appears qualitatively similar.

The relationship between bottom erodibility and seasonal bottom temperature over the three-year period is seen by comparing Figure 3A and 3B. If $\overline{V}_r$ is regressed against seasonal water temperature, the correlation is poor ($r = 0.18$). However, if we compare periods of increasing or decreasing $\overline{V}_r$ in 1974 and 1975 with changes in bottom water temperature, times of peak or increasing water temperature appear to coincide with relatively low, or decreasing trends in, $\overline{V}_r$. This qualitative trend does not hold for 1976.

The difference between the observed minimum and maximum $\overline{V}_r$ values in 1974 is 5 cm sec^{-1} (July and November), a 92% change in $\overline{V}_r$. The measured difference in 1975 is less, about 3 cm sec^{-1} (March and July), a change of about 70%. Because of the poor data base for winter months, these percentage changes are probably conservative.

Temporal changes in critical velocities in 1976 are different from those recorded in 1974 or 1975. We have chosen to consider the 1976 data set separately from the preceeding two years because of unique biological events observed in 1976 (*see* Yingst and Rhoads, this volume). Critical velocities in 1976 were highest in July and low in May and October.

Mucoid binding of particles

The effect of microbial mucus binding on $\overline{V}_r$ was explored by exposing beds of initially aseptic glass spherules to seawater enriched with a microbial nutrient (STP) for periods of from 19 to 26 days. The beds of glass spherules were periodically run in the flume and the change in $\overline{V}_r$ noted (Figure 4).

The initial flume measurements in 5-54μ and 74-149μ experiments yielded spurious $\overline{V}_r$ values. This was caused by difficulties in wetting glass bead surfaces. Interstitial air bubbles produced abnormally high $\overline{V}_r$ values because of surface tension effects. These bubbles dissolved after a day or two. In these two experiments we discount the initial data points. We do not know why this problem was not encountered in the 44-74μ size fraction. A summary of changes in $\overline{V}_r$ for the five experiments is given in Table 1.

The trend for all bead size-classes is for $\overline{V}_r$ to increase within a period of 3 to 15 days. The rate of increase in $\overline{V}_r$ does not appear to be related to grain size. The percentage change in $\overline{V}_r$ over the initial period of particle binding similarly appears unrelated to particle size or particle surface area.

After an initial period of particle-to-particle adhesion, values of $\overline{V}_r$ level off or decline. This decline can be reversed by the addition of a bacterial growth

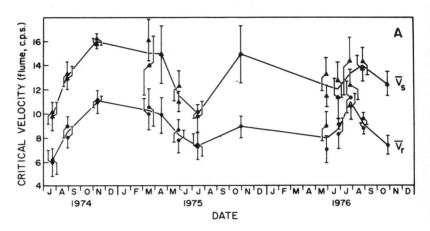

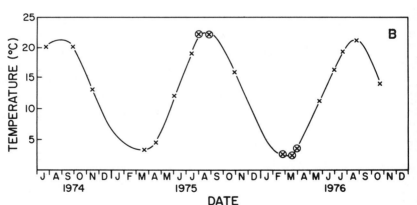

Figure 3. *A) Seasonal change in mean critical rolling velocity ($\overline{V}_r$) and mean suspension velocity ($\overline{V}_s$) at station NWC. Vertical bars represent one standard deviation. Curves fitted to the average of two replicate samples except for April and October 1975, and October 1976, when data points were determined from single box cores. Data points are significantly different at 0.95 level if separated by $\geq$ 0.8 velocity units on the Y axis.*
B) Seasonal change in bottom sediment temperature at station NWC. Circled data points are times when bottom temperatures were taken without sampling with flume cores.

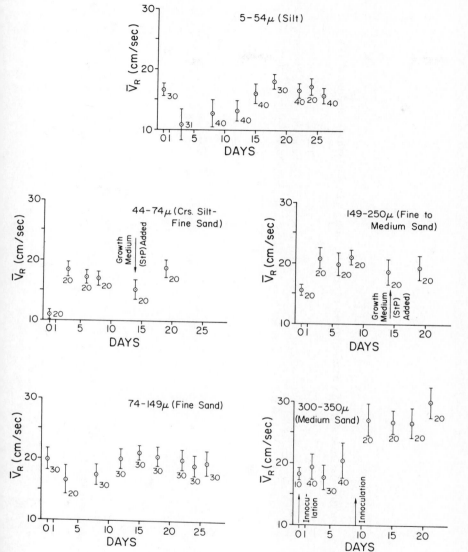

Figure 4. Laboratory flume experiments of five size classes of glass beads exposed to microbial growth over periods ranging from 19–26 days. The mean rolling velocity ($\overline{V}_r$) is given ± one standard deviation. The number of measurements is noted by each data point. A microbial growth medium (STP) was added to the 44–74µ and the 149–250µ experiments after about 14 days to stimulate microbial growth. Natural sediment inoculation was introduced onto the bed of the 300–350µ experiment to increase microbial binding (Figure modified from Ullman, 1974).

Table 1. Changes in $\bar{V}_r$ for four size classes of glass beads cultured in seawater with a microbial growth medium (STP).

Sediment size (μ)		lowest* $\bar{V}_r$ (cm sec^{-1})	highest* $\bar{V}_r$ (cm sec^{-1})	$\Delta \bar{V}_r$ (cm sec^{-1})	Time Interval (days)	rate of change in $\bar{V}_r$ (cm sec^{-1}/day)	Percentage change in $\bar{V}_r$
5-3	fine to coarse silt	11	18	7	15	0.47	56
44-74	coarse silt-fine sand	11	19	8	3	2.67	59
74-149	very fine sand	16	21	5	9	0.56	25
149-250	fine to medium sand	15	21	6	3	2.00	31
300-350	medium sand	18	30	12	11	1.09	60

*Values rounded to the nearest cm sec^{-1}

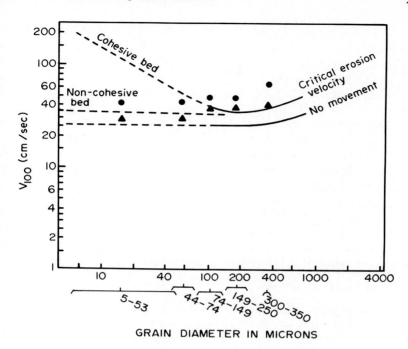

Figure 5. The maximum observed change in mean rolling velocity ($\overline{V}_r$) of five glass bead experiments following exposure to microbial growth (replotted from Ullman, 1974). Flow data converted to z = 100 cm and plotted on a competency diagram (Sundborg diagram as modified by Allen, 1965). Triangular symbols are initial (aseptic) bead $\overline{V}_r$ values; circles are $\overline{V}_r$ values after microbial binding (data from Table I). Microbial binding displaces threshold $\overline{V}_r$ values above the quartz critical erosion velocity boundary.

medium (STP) to the holding tank. This was done in the 44–74μ and 149–250μ experiments; a slight, but statistically insignificant, increase in $\overline{V}_r$ was also observed in the 149–250μ experiment.

The decline in $\overline{V}_r$ after an initial increase may be caused by microbial self-inhibition by a buildup of interstitial metabolites (decreased mucus production). Alternatively, over time, microbial mucus cements glass beads together into bead aggregates. These aggregates project above the bed surface and are easily moved relative to individual grains. Because both microbial inhibition and grain aggregation may be operating, we are presently unable to separate their relative effects on $\overline{V}_r$

The 300–350μ experiment did not show significant change in $\overline{V}_r$ over the first week after inoculation. On day 9 the bed was again inoculated; by the following day $\overline{V}_r$ increased by 35%.

The effect of mucus binding on $\overline{V}_r$ for the five size classes of glass spheres is plotted on a modified Sunborg competency diagram (Figure 5). The Sundborg diagram is constructed from experimental data using quartz particles of uniform size covered with fresh water. Our glass bead experiments do not conform to these experimental conditions; however, we use this diagram as a means of comparison.

The quantitative relationship between microbial ATP and $\overline{V}_r$ for fine sand-sized glass spheres is shown in Figure 6A. Within a day and a half, $\overline{V}_r$ increased by 50% at a rate of 2 cm sec^{-1} day^{-1}. From day 3 through day 8, $\overline{V}_r$ values continued to increase, but at a slower rate. Over the 8-day period, microbial ATP extracted from bead surfaces showed an increase at a constant rate (Figure 6B). The regression of $\overline{V}_r$ against microbial ATP shows these two variables to be positively correlated (Figure 6C). The initial period of microbial growth and its associated mucus appears to have an almost immediate binding effect. Once this thin layer of mucus joins particles at point contacts, continued microbial growth apparently contributes little to increasing interparticle binding.

Polychaete tube effects

Dense aggregations of small tube-dwelling organisms are sometimes found on mud bottoms, especially in early stages of colonization following seafloor disturbance (e.g., McCall, 1977). We have made a preliminary study of the effects of a polychaete, *Heteromastus filiformis* (Capitellidae), on $\overline{V}_r$ and $\overline{V}_s$.

A diver-taken box core of ambient NWC sediment was run in the flume to determine critical velocities on July 21, 1974 (Figure 7). Five days later, the surface of the core was "seeded" with *H. filiformis*. Within a few days *H. filiformis* formed vertical tubes constructed of mucus-bound mud; the upper ends of the tubes extended about 0.5 cm above the sediment-water interface. The spatial dispersion of the tubes was patchy but, in general, tubes were spaced less than 1 cm apart. On the fifth, sixth, and tenth day after seeding, $\overline{V}_s$ and $\overline{V}_r$ values were determined. $\overline{V}_s$ doubled and $\overline{V}_r$ increased by 80% after seeding.

Several phenomena may contribute to the observed increase in critical velocities after the appearance of polychaete tubes: 1) the vertical tubes may have decreased the efficiency of bioturbation by acting as "barriers" to the lateral movements of burrowing infauna; 2) activities of *Heteromastus filiformis* may have stimulated microbial production and binding; 3) feeding activities of *H. filiformis* may have changed particle size, or mucus secretions used in tube construction or feeding may have bound the bottom; and 4) the tops of the tubes may have acted as points of flow detachment. Reattachment of the free shear layer onto nearby (downstream) tubes would effectively increase the thickness of the viscous and buffer sublayers (*sensu* Allen, 1970). Qualitative observations of the sediment surface under magnification indicate that (4) is, in fact, an im-

Figure 6. (opposite) The relationship between mean critical rolling velocity and microbial ATP using a bed of glass beads with a grain size range of 74—

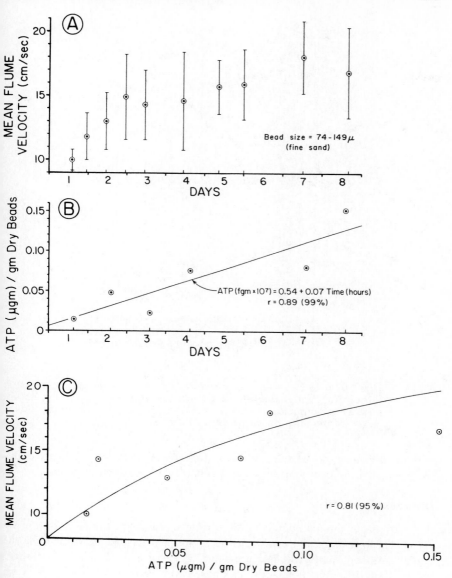

149μ. A) Increase in mean rolling velocity ($\overline{V}_r$) of glass beads exposed to microbial growth over an eight-day period. Each mean based on 20 measurements. B) Adenosine triphosphate, a measure of microbial biomass, extracted from bead surfaces over the eight-day period. Values are means of three replicate measurements. C) Regression of microbial ATP against $\overline{V}_r$ over the eight-day period. The origin of the curve placed at $ATP^{(x)} = 0$, $\overline{V}_r^{(y)} = 8$ cm sec^{-1} is arbitrary and may be inaccurate.

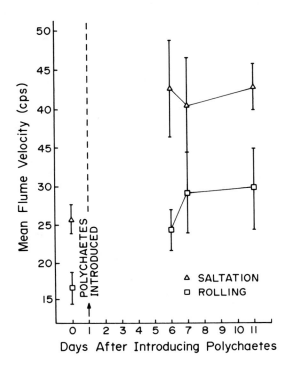

Figure 7. *The effect of dense tube aggregations of the polychaete* Heteromastus
filiformis *(Capitellidae) on mean critical rolling and suspension velocities. Data points are means (N = 10) ± one standard deviation. Day 0
values represent polychaete free critical velocities.*

portant mechanism for stabilizing the bottom. We are presently unable to evaluate the relative contributions of the other (1 to 3) proposed mechanisms.

Discussion

From our limited number of observations at a single sampling station we
are unable to make generalizations about patterns of change in $\overline{V}_r$ or $\overline{V}_s$ in the
Sound. Although biological data presented in Yingst and Rhoads (this volume)
suggest that 1976 was biologically an unusual year relative to 1974 or 1975, we
are unable to say that 1974 or 1975 represent the typical pattern of seafloor
erodibility. It is entirely possible that, with an extended data base, erodibility
will be found to be random with respect to season.

Our initial hypothesis that seasonal changes in seafloor erodibility should
be observed in seasonally variable coastal waters remains unanswered. We have
been able to show that significant changes in seafloor erodibility exist yet these
changes are not closely correlated with water temperature. This might be expected
a priori, in an environment where benthic recruitment is highly variable from

season to season and year to year (Yingst, in press).

It is interesting to speculate on the potential importance of temporally changing boundary conditions on fine-grained sediment transport in the Sound. For example, velocity-frequency histograms of both tidal and non-tidal currents measured one meter above the bottom (z = 100 cm) are shown in Figure 8. Currents at station DS were measured April–June 1973 and at station SC September–October 1973. Both of these hydrographic stations are located 5.5 to 6.0 km southeast of station NWC. On the velocity-frequency histograms is plotted the maximum range in $\overline{V}_r$ from the flume data for 1974; also given as a velocity at one meter height above the bottom. If we assume that the measured velocity-frequency distributions are representative of average flow regimes, currrents in this part of the Sound are subcritical (≤ 16 cm/sec) at least 43% of the time at station SC, and 53% of the time at station DS.

During early summer, when $\overline{V}_r$ values ranged between 16 and 21 cm/sec, V_r would have been exceeded about 47% of the time at both stations. Assuming a mean winter value of 28 cm sec^{-1}, $\overline{V}_r$ would have been exceeded only about

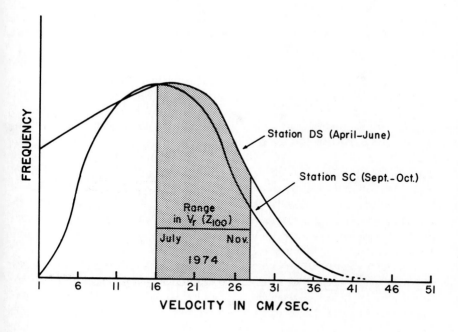

Figure 8. Velocity-frequency diagrams for two stations in central Long Island Sound (see Figure 1 for locations). Current measurements made at z = 100 cm with a Savonius rotor current meter. Station DS was measured from April–June (N = 3744); station SC was measured from September–November (N = 4896). Mean velocity was recorded once every 20 minutes. The maximum range of erodibility recorded in 1974 is superimposed on these velocity distributions.

20% of the time at both stations.

These data suggest that, if one had made time-averaged measurements of bottom turbidity, early summer turbidity levels should have been over twice those of winter months. McCall (1977) measured sediment resuspension rates with a sediment trap located 15 cm above a mud bottom at a benthic station in 13 meters of water near the Connecticut coast of Long Island Sound. He recorded mean summer resuspension rates of 250 mg cm^{-2} day^{-1}. Mean resuspension rates in the winter were less than half of the summer rates (121 mg/cm^2/day).

The temporal resuspension differences are interesting when compared to seasonal storminess in the Sound. The general level of turbulence in the Sound, as measured as the variance of the non-tidal water level, has been calculated for each month of the year over a 38-year period (Bokuniewicz *et al.*, 1977). The period October through May has the greatest variance in non-tidal water level: a period of storm-generated turbulence. This added energy apparently may do little work in resuspending bottom muds during winter months if erodibility is low.

We have made measurements of $\overline{V}_r$ and $\overline{V}_s$ in flume box cores taken from a newly dumped dredge spoil deposit located 5.5 km southeast of station NWC over the period June 5, 1974 through April 10, 1975. The temporal trends in critical velocities were found to be similar to trends observed at station NWC over the same time interval (Rhoads *et al.*, 1977).

Benninger (1976) sampled seston from the surface of Long Island Sound with a 35μ mesh net over a period of one year. He characterized the bulk chemistry of the samples by three end members: amorphous silica (diatom), non-opaline ash ("dirt"), and organic matter (loss on combustion). Figure 9 shows that most samples fall within the 75% "dirt" apex. In the autumn and winter months, pelagic production is reflected in the bulk composition; values migrate toward either the diatom (opaline SiO_2) apex or zooplankton (organic matter) apex. In early spring and summer, bulk seston composition migrates toward the "dirt" apex. The bulk composition of seston in the month of June, a period of low $\overline{V}_r$ and $\overline{V}_s$ values, falls within the sediment field. Microscopic examination of the non-living seston component shows a dominance of mineral particles and fecal pellets of benthos. The above indirect evidence suggests that seasonal changes in water column particulates may reflect changes in bottom erodibility.

Careful interpretation is required of seston data. Suspended aggregates in seawater have at least three origins. Aggregates can form at, or near, the sea surface from complexing of dissolved high molecular weight organics (Riley, 1963; Baylor and Sutcliffe, 1963) or from associations of organics and mineral grains (Kranck, 1973; 1975). Organic aggregates may also be produced in the estuary at the mixing region of fresh and salt water (Kranck, 1974). After organic aggregates settle to the seafloor they are mixed into the ambient sediment and their bulk composition changes (e.g., Riley, 1963). These "metamorphosed" aggregates can then be resuspended.

The phenomenon of biogenic destabilization of the seafloor in coastal em-

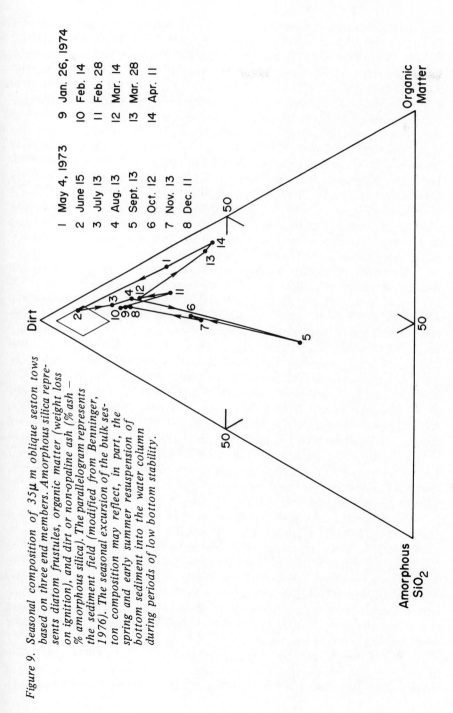

Figure 9. Seasonal composition of 35 μ m oblique seston tows based on three end members. Amorphous silica represents diatom frustules, organic matter (weight loss on ignition), and dirt or non-opaline ash (% ash — % amorphous silica). The parallelogram represents the sediment field (modified from Benninger, 1976). The seasonal excursion of the bulk seston composition may reflect, in part, the spring and early summer resuspension of bottom sediment into the water column during periods of low bottom stability.

bayments has received most intensive study in Buzzards Bay, Massachusetts (Young, 1971; Rhoads and Young, 1970; Rhoads, 1973; Rhoads *et al.*, 1975; Tenore, 1977; Young, 1977; Young and Southard, 1978). An annual cycle in particulate-phase nitrogen and carbon has been measured in bottom water of Buzzards Bay (Young, 1971; Rhoads *et al.*, 1975; Tenore, 1977). An annual minimum occurred in March. In early spring, both particulate organic nitrogen and carbon increased in bottom suspensions. An annual maximum was observed in June. Near-bottom values of particulate nitrogen and carbon were consistently higher than at the sea surface. These data are consistent with changes in seafloor erodibility as measured at station NWC in central Long Island Sound in 1974-1975. The importance of resuspended particulates for estuarine nutrient recycling is discussed in Rhoads *et al.* (1975) and Tenore (1977).

Summerhayes *et al.* (1977) also studied seasonal resuspension of fine-grained sediment in western Buzzards Bay with optical transmissometry. They showed near-bottom resuspension values to be high in early spring and summer. Suspended sediment was found to be in the form of fecal pellets and "agglomerates."

Measurements of the threshold erosion velocity of clayey silts in central Buzzards Bay have been made with an *in situ* flume (Seaflume) by Young (1977) and Young and Southard (1978). The measurements were made over the period August 1974–February 1975. If we convert Young's shear stress data to a one-meter velocity equivalent, the measured range of threshold values is within the range 8–24 cm sec^{-1} ($\bar{x}$ = 12 cm sec^{-1}). These values are generally lower than those recorded in our study of Long Island Sound sediment. The disparity in defining and measuring threshold velocities between the two studies may be related to differences in flow characteristics of our respective flumes. Alternatively, the differences may be real. The surficial layer of reworked sediment in Buzzards Bay is up to a centimeter thick (Rhoads and Young, 1970); in Long Island Sound the layer is commonly half as thick. This may be a structural manifestation of differences in biotrubation rates in the two embayments. Young and Southard (1978) were unable to identify a seasonal pattern in critical shear stress because spatial or short-term temporal patchiness in threshold velocities exceeded or masked possible long-term temporal differences.

Although the glass bead experiments give an insight into the magnitude of microbial binding effects on particle adhesion and critical velocities, the experiments need to be repeated under more controlled conditions. We did repeat the 74–149μ size class experiment (compare Figures 4 and 6A). Large differences in $\bar{V}_r$ values were observed between the two experiments. We believe that this is related to different microbial growth conditions. The fact that the observed binding effects cannot be correlated with textural differences between the five glass bead size classes (Table 1) further suggests that microbial growth conditions were not held constant in these experiments.

The factors of grain packing, porosity and exposure to flow should be explored in subsequent glass bead experiments. Mucus binding takes place only at grain-to-grain point contacts, hence sorting and grain packing are important variables. Also, the porosity of the bed is important for the molecular diffusion of microbial nutrients and metabolites. In addition, because microbial growth is stimulated by flowing water (advective diffusion) one can expect microbial growth to be sensitive to the frequency and duration of flume measurements.

Our experiments also lack satisfactory controls. We have used the initial data point to characterize a bacteria-free critical velocity. A more satisfactory experiment would consist of two box cores: one exposed to microbial growth and an identical control bed exposed to antibiotics or ultraviolet radiation.

Future Work

The results of our study show significant temporal changes in critical velocities. The period of greatest change in critical velocities appears to be spring, summer, and autumn. This period should be intensively studied to determine if flume measurements of erodibility are, in fact, coupled with changing turbidity of bottom water. It is unclear whether erodibility is solely a function of seasonal differences in binding efficiency or a reflection of temporal changes in the availability of newly produced (and unbound) aggregates. Future measurements of erodibility should therefore be accompanied by turbidity profiles of the water column over several tidal cycles. We recommend in addition that the experimental approach be pursued further using natural sediment. The rate of bioturbation and the efficiency of sediment binding are variables that can be controlled in the laboratory. Such manipulative experiments should go far in helping to explain the underlying processes controlling observed temporal changes in seafloor erodibility.

If sediment destabilization in spring and early summer is related to increased bioturbation rates, can recruitment success of deposit feeders be inferred from the turbidity structure of bottom water? As noted earlier, deposit-feeding communities in central Long Island Sound are patchily distributed. This patchiness suggests that the bottom erosion may be similarly localized. Is this patchiness manifested in localized origins of near-bottom turbidity plumes or erosional features?

Also, assemblages of subsurface bioturbating deposit-feeders appear to be characteristic of high-order successional stages, while sedentary suspension feeders and surface grazers form pioneering assemblages (Rhoads, McCall, Yingst, in press). Does the turbidity of the water column reflect a successional sequence of trophic types following disturbance of the seafloor?

Acknowledgments

Much of this work involved diving under adverse weather and visibility conditions. We wish to thank fellow divers Peter McCall, J. Berton Fisher, Page Hiller, Robert Aller, Mike Pimer. Rose Petrucca, and Dwight Muschenheim. Robert Wells assisted us on shipboard, assisted in construction of the flume, and attended to equipment details. The flume box cores were skillfully constructed by Art Goodhue. Advice in growing plant-free microbial populations in the flume was provided by Luigi Provasoli. We also thank him for providing the microbial growth medium. R. Gordon and H. Bokuniewicz provided us with current meter data. J. Southard and R. Young provided us with an instructive review of this manuscript. Many of their comments have been included in the final draft. Parts of this study were supported by NSF grant GA-OCE 42838 and Army Corps of Engineers contract DACW 33-74-M-035.

References

1. Allen, J. R. L. 1965. A review of the origin and characteristics of recent alluvial sediments. Sedimentology 5:89-191.

2. _____ . 1970. Physical Processes of Sedimentation. American Elsevier, New York. 248 pp.

3. Aller, R. C., and J. K. Cochran. 1976. ^{234}Th/^{238}U disequilibrium in near-shore sediment: particle reworking and diagenetic time scales. Earth Planet. Sci. Lett. 29(1):37-50.

4. Bagnold, R. A. 1966. An approach to the sediment transport problem from general physics. U.S. Geol. Survey Prof. Paper 422-I.

5. Bathurst, R. G. C. 1967. Subtidal gelatinous mat, sand stabilizer and food, Great Bahama Bank. J. Geol. 75:736-738.

6. Baylor, E. R., and W. H. Sutcliffe. 1963. Dissolved organic matter in sea-water as a source of particulate food. Limnol. Oceanogr. 8:369-371.

7. Benninger, L. K. 1976. The uranium-series radionuclides as tracers of geochemical processes in Long Island Sound. Ph.D. thesis, Yale University. 151 pp.

8. Bokuniewicz, H. J., J. Gebert, R. B. Gordon, P. Kaminsky, C. C. Pilbeam, M. Reed, and C. Tuttle. 1977. Field study of the effects of storms on the stability and fate of dredged material in subaqueous disposal areas. Final report, Dredge Material Res. Program, Environ. Effects Lab., U.S. Army Engineer Waterways Exper. Sta., Vicksburg, Miss. 86 pp.

9. Carson, M. A. 1971. The Mechanics of Erosion. Pion Ltd. 174 pp.

10. Christian, R. R., K. Bancroft, and W. J. Wiebe. 1975. Distribution of microbial adenosine triphosphate in salt marsh sediments at Sapelo Island, Georgia. Soil Sci. 119(1):89-97.

11. Corpe, W. A. 1974. Periphytic marine bacteria and the formation of microbial films on solid surfaces, pp. 397-417. *In* R. R. Colwell and R. Y. Morita (eds.), Effect of the Ocean Environment on Microbial Activity. Univ. Park Press, Baltimore, Md.

12. DiSalvo, L. M. 1973. Contamination of surfaces by bacterial neuston. Limnol. Oceanogr. 18:165-168.

13. Fogg, G. E. 1962. Extracellular products, pp. 475-489. *In* R. A. Levin (ed.), Physiology and Biochemistry of Algae, Academic Press, New York and London. 929 pp.

14. Frankel, L., and D. J. Meade. 1973. Mucilaginous matrix of some estuarine sands in Connecticut. J. Sed. Petrol. 43:1090-1095.

15. Ginsburg, R. N., and H. A. Lowenstam. 1958. The influence of marine bottom communities on the depositional environment of sediments. J. Geol. 66:310-318.

16. Groen, P. 1967. On the residual transport of suspended matter by an alternating tidal current. Netherlands J. Sea Res. 3(4):564-574.

17. Holland, A. F., R. G. Zingmark, and J. M. Dean. 1974. Quantitative evidence concerning the stabilization of sediments by marine benthic diatoms. Mar. Biol. 27:191-196.

18. Hopkins, J. 1975. A biochemical analysis of the mucus secreted by *Polynices duplicatus* including a review of its significance as a marine exudate. Unpublished senior thesis, Department of Geology and Geophysics, Yale University, New Haven, Conn. 24 pp.

19. Kranck, K. 1973. Flocculation of suspended sediment in the sea. Nature 246:348-350.

20. _____. 1974. The role of flocculation in the transport of particulate pollutants in the marine environment, 41-46. *In* Proc. Int. Conf. on Transport of Persistent Chemicals in Aquatic Ecosystems. Ottawa, Ont. May 1-3.

21. _____. 1975. Sediment deposition from flocculated suspensions. Sedimentology 22:111-123.

22. Marshall, N. K. and Lukas. 1970. Preliminary observations on the properties of bottom sediments with and without eelgrass, *Zostera marina*. Proc. Nat. Shellfisheries Assoc. 60:107-111.

23. McCall, P. L. 1977. Community patterns and adaptive strategies of the infaunal benthos of Long Island Sound. J. Mar. Res. 35:221-266.

24. Neuman, A. C., C. P. Gebelein, and T. P. Scoffin. 1970. The composition, structure and erodibility of subtidal mats, Abaco, Bahamas, J. Sed. Petrol. 40:274-297.

25. Newman, H. N. 1974. Microbial films in nature. Microbios 9:247-257.

26. O'Colla, P. S. 1962. Mucilages, pp. 337-356. *In* R. A. Lewin (ed.) Physiology and Biochemistry of Algae, Academic Press, New York and London, 929 pp.

27. Postma, H. 1961. Transport and accumulation of suspended matter in the Dutch Wadden Sea. Neth. J. Sea Res. 1:148-190.

28. _____. 1967. Sediment transport and sedimentation in the estuarine environment, pp. 158-179. *In* G. H. Lauff (ed.) Estuaries. Publs. Am. Assoc. Advmt. Sci. no. 83, Washington, D.C. 757 pp.

29. Raudkivi, A. J. 1967. Loose Boundary Hydraulics. Pergamon Press New York, 331 pp.

30. Rhoads, D. C. 1973. The influence of deposit-feeding benthos on water turbidity and nutrient recycling. Am. J. Sci. 273:1-22.

31. Rhoads, D. C., R. Aller and M. Goldhaber. 1977. The influence of colonizing benthos on physical properties and chemical diagenesis of the estuarine seafloor, pp. 113-138. *In* B. C. Coull (ed.) Belle Baruch Symposium on the Ecology of Marine Benthos. University of S. Carolina Press, Columbia, S. Carolina. 467 pp.

32. Rhoads, D. C., P. L. McCall and J. Y. Yingst. In press. The ecology of seafloor disturbances. Am. Scientist.

33. Rhoads, D. C., K. Tenore and M. Browne. 1975. The role of suspended bottom mud in nutrient cycles of shallow embayments, pp. 563-579. *In* L. E. Cronin (ed.) Estuarine Research I. Chemistry, Biology and the Estuarine System. Academic Press, New York. 738 pp.

34. Rhoads, D. C., and D. K. Young. 1970. The influence of deposit-feeding organisms on sediment stability and community trophic structure. J. Mar. Res. 28:150-178.

35. Riley, G. A. 1959. Note on particulate matter in Long Island Sound. Bull. Bingham Oceanogr. Coll. 17:83-85.

36. _____ . 1963. Organic aggregates in seawater and the dynamics of their formation and utilization. Limnol. Oceanogr. 8:372-381.

37. Sanders, H. L. 1956. Oceanography of Long Island Sound 1952-1954. X. The biology of marine bottom communities. Bull. Bingham Oceanogr. Coll. 15:345-414.

38. Schubel, J. R. 1968. Turbidity maximum of the Northern Chesapeake Bay. Science 6:1013-1015.

39. Schwarz, A. 1932. Der Tierische Einfluss auf die Meeressedimente. Senckenbergiana 14:118-172.

40. Scoffin, T. P. 1970. The trapping and binding of sub-tidal carbonate sediments by marine vegetation in Bimini Lagoon, Bahamas. J. Sed. Petrol. 40: 249-273.

41. Southard, J. B., C. D. Hollister, R. A. Young, and P. F. Lonsdale, 1975. Dynamics of small-scale interaction between marine bottom currents and mud substrate (Abstract). EOS 75.019:372.

42. Summerhayes, C. P., J. P. Ellis, P. Stoffers, S. R. Briggs, and M. G. Fitzgerald. 1977. Fine-grained sediment and industrial waste distribution and dispersal in New Bedford Harbor and western Buzzards Bay, Massachusetts. Woods Hole Oceanogr. Inst. Tech. Rept. pp. 76-115. Unpublished manuscript. 110 pp.

43. Tatewaki, M., and L. Provasoli. 1964. Vitamin requirements of three species of *Antithaminion*. Botanica Marina 6:193-203.

44. Tenore, K. R. 1977. Food chain pathways in detrital feeding benthic communities: A review, with new observations on sediment resuspension and detrital recycling, pp. 37-53. *In* B. C. Coull (ed.), Belle Baruch Symposium on the ecology of marine benthos. The Belle Baruch library in marine science no. 6. University of S. Carolina Press, Columbia, S. Carolina. 467 pp.

45. Turekian, K. K. 1977. The fate of metals in the oceans. Geochim. Cosmochim. Acta 41:1139-1144.

46. Ullman, W. J. 1974. The stabilization of the water-sediment interface by the presence of extracellular products of microorganisms. Unpublished senior thesis, Department of Geology and Geophysics, Yale University, New Haven, Ct. 41 pp.

47. Van Straaten, L.M.J.U., and P. H. Kuenen. 1958. Tidal action as a cause of clay accumulation. J. Sed. Petrol. 28:406-413.

48. Yingst, J. Y. In press. Patterns of micro- and meiofaunal abundances in marine sediments measured with the adenosine triphosphate assay. Mar. Biol.

49. Yingst, J. Y., and D. C. Rhoads. In press. Seafloor stability in central Long Island Sound. Part II. Biological interactions and their potential importance for seafloor erodibility. Fourth Biennial Estuarine Research Conference, Mt. Pocono, Pa. Oct. 2-5, 1977.

50. Young, D. K. 1971. Effects of infauna on the sediment and seston of a subtidal environment. Vie et Milieu. supp. 22:557-571.

51. Young, R. A. 1977. Seaflume: a device for *in-situ* studies of threshold erosion velocity and erosional behavior of undisturbed marine muds. Mar. Geol. 23: M11-18.

52. Young, R. A., and J. B. Southard. In press. Erosion of fine-grained marine sediments: seafloor and laboratory experiments. Bull. Geol. Soc. Am.

SEAFLOOR STABILITY IN CENTRAL LONG ISLAND SOUND:
Part II. Biological Interactions
And Their Potential Importance for Seafloor Erodibility

Josephine Y. Yingst and Donald C. Rhoads

Department of Geology-Geophysics
Laboratory for Benthic Research
Yale University
New Haven, Connecticut

Abstract: Temporal variation in the stability of the seafloor in central Long Island Sound can be qualitatively related to changes in water temperature, sediment surface organic content, sediment surface water content, and numbers of micro-, meio-, and macrofauna. Control of temporal changes in stability appears to result from biological processes which influence sediment stabilization and sediment destabilization.

At station NWC, which is below photosynthetic compensation depth, polysaccharides produced by heterotrophic microorganisms bind the sediment. The reworking activities of meio- and macrofauna break up the bound layer of organic-mineral aggregates and cause destabilization of the sediment surface. The stabilization process probably reflects the combined effects of chemical, physical, and biological changes on the formation, stability, and decomposition of polysaccharides in the sediment. We propose that the binding potential of microbially produced polysaccharides is always present. Mucopolysaccharides produced by some meio- and macrobenthos may also be important to the binding process.

Although rates of sediment reworking depend on the number of bioturbating macro- and meiofauna and temperature-related seasonal variations in activity, the processes which result in destabilization cannot be adequately explained by these two factors alone. Changes in metabolic activity of all size groups of organisms are related to temperature, but there appears to be a phase lag between temperature, input of organic matter, sediment binding, and bioturbation of the sediment by the benthos.

Seasonal changes in biological activities and interactions may contribute to the temporal variations in seafloor stability through their influence on the chemistry of binding as well as the physical characteristics of the sediments.

Changes in turbidity levels in the water overlying the bottom resulting from a cycle in seafloor stability may affect the seasonal compensation depth for planktic and benthic plants and probably controls the recruitment success of some groups of benthic larvae.

Introduction

Temporal changes in seafloor erodibility of subtidal Long Island Sound sediments have been described by Rhoads, Yingst, and Ullman (this volume). The processes that control changes in erodibility are complex. The observed stability of fine-grained sediments is probably the net result of two biological processes: sediment binding and sediment destabilization. These animal-sediment relations probably involve the actions and interactions of micro-, meio- and macrofaunal benthic organisms.

The laboratory experiments described by Rhoads, Yingst, and Ullman (this volume) show that microbial organisms and dense aggregations of tube-building polychaetes are important sediment binding agents. Laboratory experiments by Rhoads and Young (1970) and Young and Southard (1975, 1978) have also shown that bioturbation by macrofauna reduce the physical stability of the sediment surface.

In this paper, we discuss biogenic processes which might be important in changing boundary conditions to enhance stabilization or erodibility of the bottom. From our preliminary results, we suggest how subsequent studies should be designed to explore these problems. Because our research on these processes is incomplete, our conclusions are tentative.

Study Area

The study site (indicated in NWC in Figure 1, Rhoads, Yingst, and Ullman, this volume) is located 5 km southeast of the New Haven, Connecticut harbor breakwater on a topographically flat, silty-clay seafloor in 14 m of water and is below the compensation depth (Wasman and Ramus, 1973).

The macrofauna at station NWC (Northwest control) are typical of the fauna in many silt-clay bottoms in shallow subtidal areas of the northeastern United States. The dominant infauna are the deposit-feeding protobranch molluscs, *Nucula annulata* and *Yoldia limatula* and the errant polychaete *Nephtys incisa*. The upper 2 cm of the intensively bioturbated silty-clay bottom tends to be physically homogenous as a result of reworking activities. The errant macrofauna in these muds tend to be randomly dispersed (Sanders, 1960; Levinton, 1971).

Methods and Sampling

Bottom samples were taken by scuba divers using hand-held plexiglass box cores. On each sampling date, divers took a 0.022 m^2 box core (25 cm high, 30 cm long, 7.5 cm wide) in addition to the 2 flume cores (Rhoads, Yingst, and Ullman, this volume). Bottom sediment temperatures were measured in cores upon retrieval. The box cores were kept in the dark to prevent plant growth, at temperatures approximating those at which they were collected, until processed three to five hours after collection.

Because the core boxes are watertight and contain their initial overlying water, careful transport of the cores does not normally disturb the interface. The small amount of resuspension of the interface which may occur during transport of the cores to the laboratory is trivial compared with the natural level of resuspension by tidal currents at this station (Rhoads, Tenore, and Brown, 1975).

Although only one box core was taken at each sampling date for the determination of meio- and microorganism biomass (based on ATP measurements) and meiofaunal densities, the corers sampled a surface sediment area of 220 cm². This area is more than 20 times that sampled by round tube corers (Wieser, 1960; Coull, 1968; Tietjen, 1969; Fergusen and Murdoch, 1975) and comparable to the total area sampled by the Reineck box core used by Coull *et al.* (1977) in the quantitative estimate of deep sea meiofauna.

The term meiobenthos refers to organisms < 1 mm in size, but usually > 0.04 to 0.1 mm, and includes species which will remain within the size category throughout their life-span, as well as juveniles of larger forms (*sensu*, McIntyre, 1969). Microorganisms are less than 0.1 mm in diameter.

Preparation of the cores for the various analyses consisted of first removing water overlying the sediment using a vacuum; second, removing the sediment at 1-cm intervals using sterile spatulas; third, placing the sediment from each 1-cm depth interval in sterile plastic containers. The sediment from each depth interval was homogenized by gentle hand mixing and subdivided for analyses. Only data from the top first and second cm (in the case of microorganism standing stocks) are reported in this paper.

Meiofaunal densities were determined from 3 to 6 gm aliquots of wet sediment. These sediment samples were weighed, preserved with 10% buffered formalin and stained with rose bengal. Within two weeks, samples were transferred to 70% isopropyl alcohol to which rose bengal was added. Prior to counting, the sediment was passed through a sieve with a mesh opening of 0.062 mm. Only organisms retained on the 0.062 mm mesh screen were counted, although silt passing through the screen was collected and examined for larval organisms. No organisms were found.

After removing sediment from the box cores, the ATP content of the sediment and meiofauna was determined immediately, using the boiling bicarbonate extraction method of Christian *et al.* (1975). ATP in the extracts was assayed by adding a 10 μl sample to a 100 μl reacton mixture of luciferase and luciferin (DuPont) and measuring the resulting light flash with an ATP photometer (DuPont 760 Luminescence biometer). The efficiency of ATP recovery was determined by a single point standard addition. All ATP values were corrected to 100% yield, based on an average recovery of 108.0% ± 23.9% (n = 48 samples). A complete description of extraction procedures for both sediment and meiofaunal ATP, error estimates, determination of meiofaunal densities and estimation of the contribution of meiofauna and microorganisms to the total sediment ATP content is provided by Yingst (1978). Meiofaunal abundances are given as numbers per 10 cm². Biomass estimates of microorganisms are given as μg ATP per cm².

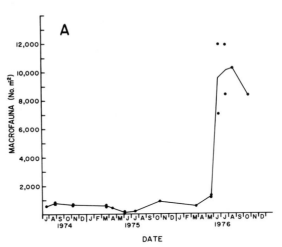

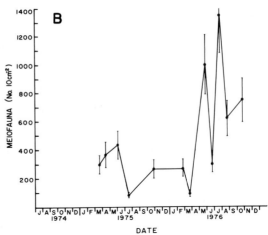

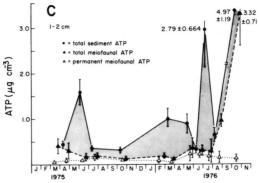

As some organisms may have been lost during flume runs, meiofaunal densities were determined from the 0.022 m² box cores instead of flume boxes.

Sediment water content was determined by weight losses of known weights of sediment dried at 100°C. In order to convert weight to volume, dry bulk sediment densities were determined for the cores from weight losses of known volumes of wet sediment dried at 100°C. Dry bulk sediment densities for 1975 are taken from Aller and Cochran (1976) from cores taken at the same study site at approximately the same dates as were the cores analyzed in this study.

A portion of each sample was ashed at 475°C for six hours to determine percent organic matter by weight loss.

The organic content of surface sediments at each sampling date is plotted against sediment water content at that same time in Figure 2B. A regression slope has been fitted to these data by least square methods. Formulas for the calculation of the least squares linear regression line (y = ax + b) and the corrrelation coefficient (r) in Figure 2B are given in Sokal and Rohlf (1969).

After completing a set of flume measurements, flume box cores were uncoupled from the flume channel and the sediment was washed through a 1-mm mesh sieve. Retained organisms, defined as macrofauna, were counted and standardized to numbers per m².

Results

Sediment binding

Seasonal changes in standing stocks of microorganisms, as measured by ATP concentrations, are shown for subsurface sediment (1-2 cm) in Figure 1C. Subsurface rather than surface ATP concentrations are used because, during summer and fall months especially, the small fraction of microbial ATP concentration at the sediments surface is masked by the ATP concentration contributed by meiofauna (Yingst, 1978). Large numbers of newly settled bivalves and ju-

Figure 1. (opposite) Seasonal abundance patterns of macro-, meio-, and microorganisms in surface sediments at station NWC over a three-year period.

A) Macrofaunal abundances reported as numbers per m². The range and average density at each sampling date are plotted (n=2).

B) Meiofaunal abundances reported as numbers per 10 cm². Bars indicate magnitude of error (21%) based on analysis of five replicate aliquots of sediment from the top 1 cm taken on one sampling date at NWC station (see Yingst, 1978).

C) The biomass of microorganisms (indicated by shading) is equal to the difference between total sediment ATP concentrations (solid circles) and the ATP contribution by all meiobenthos (solid triangles) at each sampling data. Bars for total sediment ATP concentration indicate the magnitude of error (24%). Bars for the contribution of meiofauna represent a cumulative error estimate based on variations in densities and variations in the ATP content of individual organisms. The cumulative error ranges from 33% in March 1976 to 88% in July 1976 (see Yingst, 1978).

Table 1. Seasonal distribution of meiobenthos in the top cm of sediment from Station NWC, Long Island Sound, during 1975 and 1976. Values are in numbers cm^{-3}.

Depth 0-1 cm	1975					1976						
Taxa	3/19	4/15	6/3	7/16	10/29	2/24	3/23	5/26	6/23	7/21	8/24	10/25
Foraminifera	7.56	4.76	5.23	1.12	2.31	9.98	5.37	6.47	--	1.67	1.87	1.09
Nematoda	4.29	0.30	1.91	0.37	2.11	8.87	1.38	13.26	3.88	8.33	20.14	24.57
Kinorhyncha	--	--	--	--	--	2.22	--	0.12	--	--	0.37	0.55
Platyhelmintha	--	--	--	--	--	--	--	1.24	--	--	--	7.09
Polychaeta												
Owenia fusiformis	--	--	--	--	--	--	--	--	--	--	9.70	2.18
Nephtys incisa	0.26	--	0.195	--	--	--	--	--	2.23	39.97	0.37	--
Pectinaria gouldii	--	--	--	--	--	2.22	--	--	--	--	0.37	--
Streblospio benedicta	--	0.15	--	0.12	0.11	--	--	--	--	--	--	1.64
Uniden. juveniles	--	--	--	--	--	--	--	2.28	--	--	--	.55
Crustacea												
Amphipoda												
Ampelisca spp.	0.12	--	--	--	--	--	--	--	--	--	--	--
Copepoda (harpacticoid)	4.29	5.48	13.95	2.71	12.97	3.33	1.21	21.79	21.42	51.63	15.29	18.02
Ostracoda	1.01	1.19	0.195	0.37	0.96	1.11	0.171	1.05	0.556	--	0.37	--
Nauplii larvae (principally harpacticoid copepods)	--	--	--	--	--	--	--	48.60	--	28.31	4.10	3.82
Mollusca												
Bivalvia												
Yoldia limatula	10.24	24.31	19.33	3.79	7.56	--	0.35	3.37	0.56	1.61	0.75	4.37
Nucula annulata	1.65	0.89	1.95	0.12	1.16	--	1.04	--	--	3.33	3.36	--
Mulinia lateralis	--	--	--	--	--	--	--	1.47	1.95	1.67	2.24	10.38
Pandora gouldiana	--	--	--	--	--	--	--	--	--	--	0.37	--
Gastropoda												
Rictaxis punctostriatus	0.17	--	0.195	--	0.11	--	--	--	--	--	--	--
Retusa obtusa	0.26	--	--	--	--	--	0.171	--	--	--	--	--
Odostomia sp.	--	--	--	--	--	--	--	--	--	--	--	--
Turbonilla sp.	--	--	0.77	0.12	--	--	--	--	--	--	--	--
Polinices duplicatus	--	--	--	--	--	--	--	--	--	--	0.37	--
Eggs	NC	--	--	--	--	--	--	2.83	1.16	18.32	2.24	6.55
Total Individuals	30.27	37.23	43.68	8.716	27.27	27.73	9.70	100.21	30.60	136.58	62.28	74.81
Total permanent meiobenthos	18.13	11.88	22.21	4.68	18.45	25.53	8.31	43.93	25.31	61.63	40.65	51.87

Table 2. Seasonal distribution of macrofauna at station NWC, Long Island Sound, from July 1974, through October 1976. Values are in numbers m^{-2}.

Taxa	1974			1975					1976					
	7/21	8/29	11/11	3/19	4/15	6/3	7/16	10/29	3/23	5/26	6/23	7/22	8/24	10/25
Polychaeta														
Nephtys incisa	289	211	211	144	89	151	--	215	236	269	555	499	66	333
Owenia fusiformis	--	--	11	--	22	--	65	108	--	33	--	--	--	--
Pherusa affinis	--	--	--	--	--	65	--	--	--	--	333	11	--	--
Pectinaria gouldii	--	--	--	--	--	--	--	22	--	--	--	22	--	--
Clymenella torquata	--	--	--	--	--	--	--	--	--	--	--	--	--	--
Spiochaetopterus oculatus	--	--	--	--	--	--	--	--	--	--	222	--	--	--
Maldane sarsi	--	--	--	--	--	--	--	--	--	--	56	44	--	22
Potamilla neglecta	--	--	--	--	--	--	--	--	--	--	11	33	--	--
Bivalvia														
Pitar morrhuana	--	22	33	100	89	--	43	--	--	--	155	66	111	--
Macoma tenta	--	--	--	--	--	22	22	--	34	11	244	222	66	44
Yoldia limatula	200	356	265	67	67	--	86	452	279	774	2,153	2,264	1,687	200
Nucula annulata	--	155	156	217	110	--	--	22	--	22	4,040	3,952	7,037	6,172
Mulinia lateralis	--	--	44	--	--	--	--	--	--	11	688	1,132	666	1,110
Tellina agilis	--	--	--	--	--	--	--	--	--	22	--	--	--	--
Anadara sp.	--	--	--	--	--	--	--	21	--	--	--	--	--	22
Gastropoda														
Nassarius trivittatus	--	--	11	22	--	--	--	--	--	--	--	--	--	--
Retusa obtusa	--	--	--	11	44	--	--	--	--	--	577	1,199	799	89
Scaphander punctostriatus	--	--	--	--	--	--	--	--	--	--	222	311	--	222
Turbonilla sp.	--	--	--	--	--	--	--	--	--	--	44	44	--	44
Rictaxis punctostriatus	--	--	--	--	--	--	--	--	--	--	--	11	--	11
Crustacea														
Amphipoda														
Ampelisca spp.	67	33	11	--	--	--	--	--	--	--	--	--	--	--
Gammarus sp.	--	--	--	--	--	--	--	--	--	76	11	--	--	--
Decapoda														
Crangon septemspinosus	--	--	--	--	--	--	22	--	--	--	--	--	--	--
Carcinus maenas	--	--	--	--	--	--	--	--	--	11	--	--	22	--
Isopoda (*Ancinus* sp.?)	--	--	--	--	--	--	--	--	--	--	11	11	--	--
Mysidacea	--	--	--	--	--	--	--	--	--	--	--	11	--	--
Total Individuals	556	777	742	561	421	238	238	840	549	1,229	9,322	9,832	10,454	8,269

251

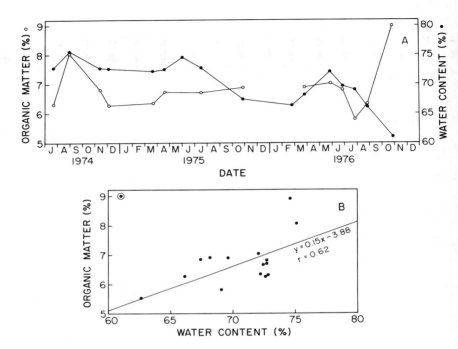

Figure 2. A) Seasonal variation in surface sediment water content and organic content at station NWC over a three-year period.
B) Regression of organic content against water content of surface sediments at station NWC. Slopes determined by least-squares fit. Circled value was not included in the calculation of the slope or of r.

venile polychaetes in the topmost 1 cm during these months dominate the total biomass of organisms < 1 mm in size and make it difficult to distinguish the relative contribution of microorganisms versus meiofauna, using ATP as a biomass measure. The standing stocks of microorganisms increase during the late spring-early summer and decline again by late summer (Figure 1C).

Densities of meiofaunal-sized *Owenia fusiformis* at the sediment surface (0-1 cm) reached 399 individuals per 10 cm^2 and averaged 456 individuals per 10 cm^2 over a depth interval of 1 to 3 cm in July 1976 (Table 1). By the end of August, numbers of *O. fusiformis* decreased to approximately 10 individuals per 10 cm^2 in the 0-1 cm depth interval. Sediment stability also declined in this period (Rhoads, Yingst, and Ullman, this volume).

Sediment destabilization

Seasonal abundance patterns of macro- and meiofauna are presented in Tables 1 and 2 and shown in Figures 1A and 1B. Macrofaunal abundances ranged between 161 and 882 individuals per m^2 during 1974 and 1975 and increased during the spring of 1976, reaching a peak density of 10,456 individuals per m^2

during August 1976. Throughout the spring, summer and fall of 1976, densities increased between 87% and 98% over the two previous years. The greatest increases were in numbers of bivalves; *Yoldia limatula* reached densities of 2236 individuals per m^2 in July, but decreased again in August and continued to decrease throughout the fall. *Nucula annulata* reached densities of 6993 individuals per m^2 in August and remained higher than 6000 individuals per m^2 throughout the fall.

Meiofaunal densities were markedly higher during 1976 than during 1975, reaching 1366 individuals per 10 cm^2 in the top 1 cm during July 1976 compared to 87 individuals per 10 cm^2 in the topmost 1 cm during July of 1975. Copepods were more abundant during July 1976 than at any other time during the 24-month period (516 per 10 cm^2), as was the tube dwelling polychaete *Owenia fusiformis* (400 per 10 cm^2).

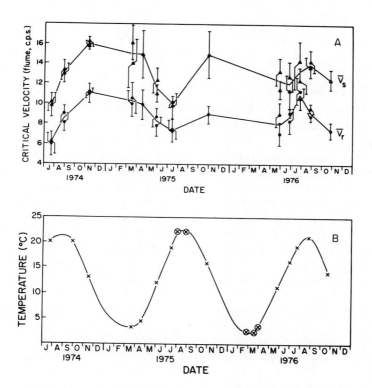

Figure 3. A) Seasonal change in mean critical rolling velocity ($\overline{V}_r$) ± 1 Std. dev. N=10) and mean suspension velocity ($\overline{V}_s$) ± 1 Std. dev. (N=10) at station NWC. Curves fitted to average of two replicate samples except for April and October 1975 and October 1976, when data points were determined from single box cores. Mean $\overline{V}$ values are significantly different at 0.95 level if separated by ≥ 0.8 velocity values on the Y axis.

Sediment water content is an indirect, yet sensitive indicator of biogenic reworking (Rhoads, Aller, and Goldhaber, 1977). Water content of the topmost 1 cm of sediment varied seasonally from 61% to 75% and tended to be lower in the fall (66%) and winter (69%) than spring (72%) and summer (71%), although these seasonal values are not significantly different at $P_{0.95}$ (Figure 2A).

The organic content of the surface sediments showed an increase of 2--3% in early summer over winter values, followed by a subsequent decrease of about the same magnitude in late summer (Figure 2A). Ignition loss measurements varied over the year from 6--9%.

Sediment water content was positively correlated with surface sediment organic content (Figure 2B). Both water content and organic matter increased as the temperature increased in the spring-early summer and decreased in the late summer-early fall (Figure 3B). The one exception to the general trend was seen in October 1976 when concentrations of organic matter were higher than had been measured during the three-year period (9%) and sediment water content was lower than had been previously recorded (61%).

Discussion

Stabilization processes

The seafloor at station NWC in 1974-1975 appeared to be most resistant to erosion from fall to winter (November-April) and most easily eroded in the late spring and early summer (March-May) (Figure 3A) (Rhoads, Yingst, and Ullman, this volume). The increased stability of the bottom qualitatively coincides with periods of decreasing water temperatures, low sediment organic content, decreased sediment water content, and lower numbers of micro-, meio-, and macrofauna. The glass bead experiments outlined in Part I (Rhoads, Yingst, and Ullman, this volume) demonstrate that mucus (polysaccharide) production associated with microbial growth was effective in binding individual glass beads at low concentrations of microorganism ATP (0.05 μg/gm dry beads), two orders of magnitude lower than concentrations found in natural sediment at station NWC (Yingst, 1978). Continued microbial growth contributed little to increasing interparticle binding.

Polysaccharides, the principal chemical binding agents of soil particles (Harris *et al.*, 1966; Martin and Aldrich, 1955) are common constituents and metabolic products of bacteria (Stacey and Barker, 1960). We have no data on polysaccharide concentrations in our sediments. However, we proposed that the binding potential by mucus or polysaccharide production is always present, and that the destabilization process is largely dependent on the nature and rate of bioturbation: the rate in which bound surface sediment is broken up into organic-mineral aggregates. These data (presented in this paper and in Part I, Rhoads, Yingst, and Ullman, this volume) suggest that maximum bottom stability during the winter is the result of decreased meiofaunal and macrofaunal bioturbation.

Measurements using either laboratory flumes (Rhoads, Yingst, and Ullman,

1978; Young and Southard, 1975, 1978) or *in situ* flumes (Young, 1977) tend to integrate all the physical, chemical, and biological events taking place at the sediment surface, within sediments, and in the overlying water. These integrative measurements appear, however, to be very sensitive to apparently random biological changes. Two examples of nonpredictable biological changes which affected threshold velocities are: first, the appearance of dense aggregations of tube-dwelling polychaetes in late June of 1976; and second, the increase in numbers of juvenile bivalves and nematodes in the fall of 1976 over summer densities (Table 1).

In contrast to 1974-1975 when the sediment surface was easily eroded in mid-July, the seafloor was tightly bound in July of 1976 following settlement in the previous month of the opportunistic Owenid polychaete, *Owenia fusiformis* (Figures 1B and 3A). The presence and reworking activities of harpacticoid copepods in densities of 516 per 10 cm^2 in the topmost cm and over 500 per m^2 macrofaunal-sized protobranch molluscs were apparently overshadowed by the binding effect of *O. fusiformis*. Dense aggregations of tube-dwelling polychaetes, in themselves, may stabilize the bottom by elevating the laminar sublayer. In addition, the presence of the tubes may pose physical barriers to the lateral movements of bioturbating deposit-feeders, resulting in reduced reworking rates. Perhaps because of the inhibitory effects of densely spaced tube-dwelling organisms, tubicolous organisms are rarely encountered together with errant deposit-feeders (Woodin, 1976).

Destabilization processes

With the warming of the water column in late May in central Long Island Sound and with the input of fresh organic matter from the January-February and May-June plankton blooms (Conover, 1956; Riley, 1963; Benninger, 1976; and Rhoads, Yingst, and Ullman, this volume), the abundance and presumably the metabolic activity of the benthic infauna increases. During this period the sediment surface is easily eroded.

The reworking activites of macrofauna have been shown to influence directly the erodibility of surface sediments in laboratory experiments by Young and Southard (1975, 1978). Young and Southard used a laboratory flume to measure the surface stability of trays filled with silty-clay sediments from Buzzards Bay, Massachusetts. The trays contained deposit-feeders typical of silty-clay sediments along the northeast coast of the United States. As the number of deposit-feeders increased, and the length of time the animals were allowed to rework the sediments increased, sediment stability decreased.

The small-scale reworking activities of various meiofaunal groups also may have a significant effect on the destabilization of surface sediments. Cullen (1973) found that traces and tracks produced by macrofauna were erased by the activities of interstitial meiofauna, particularly ostracods and nematodes. Burrowing ostracods, in fact, were observed to move sediment grains and aggregates actually several times their own size (Cullen, 1973). Some copepod species also appear to break up particle aggregates and "kick" them into suspension at the sediment surface (Marcotte and Coull, personal communication). We have noted similar surface "fluffing" in our flume observations. Nematodes, on the other hand, appear to secrete mucus and may, in spite of their reworking activities, help to bind sediment and particles (Riemann and Schrage, in press).

The relationship between the critical rolling velocity and the activities of the macro- and meiofauna are examined in Figure 4. The densities of macro- and meiofauna per m^2 have been multiplied by an activity coefficient which assumes a temperature dependence of activity or Q_{10} of 2.5 between maximum summer $(22°C)$ and minimum winter $(2°C)$ temperatures. With each $10°C$ change in temperature, the metabolic rate is assumed to increase (or decrease) by a factor of 2.5. This is a reasonable estimate of physiological temperature responses for benthic invertebrates (e.g., Mangum, 1963).

Processes affecting net seafloor stability

The correlation of $\overline{V}_r$ and the processing coefficients for both macro- and meiofauna is poor (respectively $r = 0.08$ and 0.17). The poor correlation between

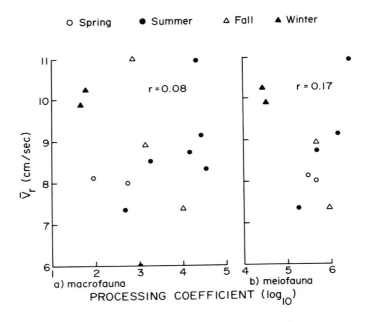

Figure 4. Relationship between the critical rolling velocity $(\overline{V}_r)$ and a processing coefficient for the macrofauna (a) and meiofauna (b). The processing coefficient is based on densities of macro- and meiofauna per m^2 multiplied by an activity coefficient which assumes a Q_{10} of 2.5 between maximum summer and minimum winter temperatures.

erodibility and our processing coefficient indicates that the number of bioturbators and temperature alone are inadequate to explain the seasonal cycle of seafloor stability. Difficulties in relating water temperature and bioturbation may be related to phase lags between increasing water temperature and peak bioturbation rates. It is not clear whether this phase lag affects the macrofauna to a greater extent than the meiofauna and microorganisms. The phase lag phenomenon between temperature and bioturbation has been observed by Aller (1977) and Aller and Cochran (1976), who used measurements of $^{234}Th/^{238}U$ disequilibrium to measure biologic mixing rates in sediments at the NWC station. They found that sediment reworking rates were highest within the period September-to-November, following the peak in sediment temperature in July-August, and that spring-early summer and late fall-winter rates are similar and approximately half those of the late summer-fall rates.

Temperature changes affect the metabolic activities of microorganisms and the production of polysaccharides in soils (Martin and Craggs, 1946; Harris *et al.*, 1966). The diverse types of microorganisms found in soils have been shown to produce chemically different binding agents (Aspiras *et al.*, 1971) which may differ in their biodegradability as well as physical properties they confer on soil aggregates. The effect of environmental variables such as temperature on the binding of sediment particles by microorganisms may involve the production of agents of different biodegradability (Martin and Craggs, 1946). Aspiras *et al.* (1971) found that maximum stability of microbially bound soil aggregates was reached sooner at high temperatures, but was maintained longer at lower temperatures once maximum stability was reached.

The extent of binding in soils by microbially-produced polysaccharides has been shown to depend on other factors which vary along with seasonal temperature changes; the nature of the microorganisms, their growth rates, the physical makeup of the soil, and the nature of the organic matter available (Martin and Waksman, 1940). Unfortunately, comparable information about sediment-bound polysaccharides is not available for marine environments.

Between 5% and 25% of soil organic matter is represented by carbohydrates (Swincer *et al.*, 1969) and polysaccharides may account for up to 20% of carbohydrate concentrations (Mehta *et al.*, 1961; Gupta, 1967). A multiple sequential extraction procedure for quantifying soil polysaccharides appears to give better than 80% recovery in most soil types (Swincer *et al.*, 1968). The applicability of this method for quantitatively measuring polysaccharide concentrations in our Long Island Sound sediments has yet to be determined.

In conclusion, seasonal changes in the activities and interactions of the micro-, meio-, and macrobenthos may contribute to changes in sediment surface erodibility through their influence not only on the physical, but on the chemical characteristics of the sediments (for examples, see Aller, 1977; Rhoads, Aller, and Goldhaber, 1977; Aller and Yingst, 1978). Although temperature, organic matter, and recruitment patterns of the benthos qualitatively follow similar seasonal patterns, we are unable to correlate temporal changes in $\overline{V}_r$ in any predictable way. We have attempted to identify processes which affect the stabilization and destabilization of surface sediments and to relate them to the observed erodibility patterns. In addition, we elucidate some factors requiring further work. These include: 1) the phase lag between temperature, organic matter inputs, sediment binding, and the reworking activities of the benthos; 2) direct measurements of polysaccharide concentrations in sediment and the effect of chemical as well as physical and biological changes on the formation, stability, and decomposition of the binding agents; 3) changes in the formation, characteristics, and stability of organic-mineral aggregates with time; 4) the relationship between the formation of organic-mineral aggregates at the sea surface, their sedimentation to the seafloor, and the erodibility of the sediment surface; and 5) the relationship between aggregate formation on the seafloor and the erodibility of the sediment surface.

Temporal changes in erodibility have far-reaching implications for the estuarine ecosystem. If increased stability is related to decreases in turbidity levels in the overlying water, for example, then the photosynthetic compensation depth may vary during the year, allowing benthic micro- and macroscopic plants to extend to deeper depths subtidally during the winter, or planktonic forms to occupy a thicker column of water. The presence of plants may in turn influence the sediment surface stability, as polysaccharides produced by plants have been shown to bind soil particles along with microbially produced binding agents (Martin and Craggs, 1946; Martin and Aldrich, 1955; Harris et al., 1966).

Increases in turbidity levels in the water overlying the seafloor as a result of decreases in seafloor stability may also influence the recruitment success of recently settled larvae. This effect would be expected to be most apparent in late spring and early summer. Biological interactions including trophic group amensalism would also be expected to be most effective during the times of maximum recruitment and at a time when the seafloor is least stable.

Acknowledgments

We wish to thank R. C. Aller, W. J. Ullman and M. Pimer, who accompanied the first author on dives and assisted in the collection of samples; R. A. Wells for help aboard ship and in the laboratory; and D. K. Muschenheim, J. Davis, R. C. Aller and W. J. Ullman for assistance in picking and identifying macrofauna. We are also grateful to S. W. Watson, Woods Hole Oceanographic Institute, for use of his Luminescence biometer and H. Quinby for her technical assistance in the ATP analyses. R. C. Aller also contributed valuable comments and suggestions throughout the course of this project. This study was supported by NSF grant GA-OCE 42838.

References

1. Aller, R. C. 1977. The influence of macrobenthos on chemical diagenesis of marine sediments. Ph.D. dissertation, Yale University. 600 pp.

2. Aller, R. C., and J. K Cochran. 1976. ^{234}Th/^{238}U disequilibrium in nearshore sediment: particle reworking and diagenetic time scales. Earth Planet Sci. Lett. 29 (1):37-50.

3. Aller, R. C., and J. Y. Yingst. 1978. Biogeochemistry of the tube-dwelling of *Amphitrite ornata* (Leidy), a sedentary polychaete. J. Mar. Res. 36(2): 201-254.

4. Aspiras, R. B., O. N. Allen, R. F. Harris, and G. Chesters. 1971. The role of microorganisms in the stabilization of soil aggregates. Soil Biol. Biochem. 3:347-353.

5. Benninger, L. K. 1976. The uranium-series radionuclides as tracers of geochemical processes in Long Island Sound. Ph.D. dissertation, Yale University, 151 pp.

6. Christian, R. R., K. Bancroft, and W. J. Wiebe. 1975. Distribution of microbial adenosine triphosphate in salt marsh sediments at Sapelo Island, Georgia. Soil Science 119:89-97.

7. Conover, S. A. M. 1956. Oceanography of Long Island Sound, 1952-1954. VI. Phytoplankton. Bull. Bingham Oceanogr. Coll. 15:62-112.

8. Coull, B. C. 1968. Shallow water meiobenthos of the Bermuda platform. Ph.D. dissertation, Lehigh University, Bethlehem, Pa. 189 pp.

9. Coull, B. C., R. L. Ellison, J. W. Fleeger, R. P. Higgins, W. D. Hope, W. D. Hummon, R. M. Rieger, W. E. Sterrer, H. Thiel, and J. H. Tietjen. 1977. Quantitative estimates of the meiofauna from the deep sea off North Carolina, Mar. Biol. 39:233-240.

10. Cullen, D. J. 1973. Bioturbation of superficial marine sediments by interstitial meiobenthos. Nature 242:323-324.

11. Fergusen, R. L., and M. B. Murdoch. 1975. Microbial ATP and organic carbon in sediments of the Newport river estuary, North Carolina, pp. 229-250. *In* L. E. Cronin (ed.), Estuarine Research, v. 1. Academic Press, New York.

12. Gupta, U. C. 1967. Carbohydrates, pp. 91-118. *In* A. D. Maclaren and G. M. Petersen (eds.), Soil Biochemistry, Marcel Dekker, New York.

13. Harris, R. F., G. Chesters, and O. N. Allen. 1966. Dynamics of soil aggregation. Adv. Agron. 18:107-169.

14. Levinton, J. S. 1971. The ecology of shallow water deposit feeding communities. Ph.D. dissertation, Yale University, 284 pp.

15. Mangum, C. P. 1963. Studies on speciation in maldanid polychaetes of the North American Atlantic Coast III. Intraspecific and interspecific divergence in oxygen consumption. Comp. Biochem. Physiol. 10:335-349.

16. Martin, J. P., and D. G. Aldrich. 1955. Influence of soil exchangeable cation ratios on the aggregating effects of natural and synthetic soil conditioners. Proc. Soil Sci. Soc. Am. 19:50-54.

17. Martin, J. P., and B. A. Craggs. 1946. Influence of temperature and moisture on the soil-aggregating effect of organic residues. J. Am. Soc. Agron. 38:322-339.

18. Martin, J. P., and S. A. Waksman. 1940. Influence of microorganisms on oil aggregation and erosion. Soil Sci. 50:29-47.

19. McIntyre, A. D. 1969. Ecology of marine meiobenthos. Biol. Rev. 44:245-290.

20. Mehta, N. C., P. Dubach, and H. Deuel. 1961. Carbohydrates in soil. Advan. Carbohydrate Chem. 16:335-355.

21. Rhoads, D. C., and D. K. Young. 1970. The influence of deposit-feeding organisms on sediment stability and community trophic structure. J. Mar. Res. 28(2):150-178.

22. Rhoads, D. C., R. C. Aller, and M. Goldhaber. 1977. The influence of colonizing benthos on physical properties and chemical diagenesis of the estuarine seafloor, pp. 113-138. *In* B. C. Coull (ed.), Ecology of marine benthos, Symp. Belle Baruch Inst., 1975. Belle W. Baruch library in marine science no. 6., University of So. Carolina Press, Columbia.

23. Rhoads, D. C., K. Tenore, and M. Brown. 1975. The role of resuspended bottom mud in nutrient cycles of shallow embayments, pp. 563-579. *In* L. E. Cronin (ed.), Estuarine Research, v. 1. Academic Press, New York.

24. Rhoads, D. C., J. Y. Yingst, and W. Ullman. 1978. Seafloor stability in central Long Island Sound: I. Seasonal changes in erodability of fine-grained sediments, pp. 221-244. *In* M. Wiley (ed.), Estuarine Interactions, Academic Press, New York.

25. Riemann, F., and M. Schrage. In press. On the aquatic nematodes: sedimentological and ecological aspects of the continuous mucus secretion. Oecologia (Berl.).

26. Sanders, H. 1960. Benthic studies in Buzzards Bay. III. The structure of the soft bottom community. Limnol. Oceanogr. 5:138-153.

27. Sokal, R. R., and F. J. Rohlf. 1969. Biometry. W. H. Freeman and Co., San Francisco, California, 776 pp.

28. Stacey, M., and S. A. Barker. 1960. Polysaccharides of Microorganisms. Oxford Univ. Press, London. 228 pp.

29. Swincer, G. D., J. M. Oades, and D. J. Greenland. 1968. Studies on soil polysaccharides. I. The isolation of polysaccharides from soil. Aust. J. Soil Res. 6:211-224.

30. _____. 1969. The extraction, characterization, and significance of soil polysaccharides. Adv. Agron. 21:195-235.

31. Tietjen, J. H. 1969. The ecology of shallow water meiofauna in two New England estuaries. Oecologia (Berl.) 2:251-291.

32. Wasman, E. R., and J. Ramus. 1973. Primary production measurements for the green seaweed *Codium fragile*. Mar. Biol. 21(4):289-297.

33. Wieser, W. 1960. Benthic studies in Buzzards Bay. II. The meiofauna. Limnol. Oceanogr. 5:121-137.

34. Woodin, S. A. 1976. Adult-larval interactions in dense infaunal assemblages: patterns of abundance. J. Mar. Res. 34(1):25-41.

35. Yingst, J. Y. (Submitted) Patterns of micro- and meiofaunal abundance in marine sediments measured with the adenosine triphosphate assay. Mar. Biol.

36. Young, R. A. 1977. Seaflume: A device for *in situ* studies of threshold erosion velocity and erosional behavior of undisturbed marine muds. Mar. Geol. 23:M11-18.

37. Young, R. A., and J. B. Southard. 1975. Field and laboratory experiments on the erosion of marine sediments. (Abstract) EOS 75:370.

38. _____. 1978. Erosion of fine-grained marine sediments: seafloor and laboratory experiments. Bull. Geol. Soc. Am. 89:663-672.

PREDATOR CAGING EXPERIMENTS IN SOFT SEDIMENTS: CAUTION ADVISED

Robert W. Virnstein

Harbor Branch Foundation
R.R.1, Box 196
Fort Pierce, Florida

Abstract: Field experiments in which predators were excluded from soft-sediment communities have been done in the York River, Virginia, the Indian River, Florida, and the shallow continental shelf off southeast Florida. The York River experiments revealed that predators on infaunal macrobenthos are important in determining community structure and population densities. There appeared to be only two major predators in shallow water — the blue crab *Callinectes sapidus* (Crustacea: Portunidae) and the spot *Leiostomus xanthurus* (Pisces: Sciaenidae). The same experiments in the Indian River, a coastal lagoon, showed no differences in infaunal densities inside and outside exclosures. The differences between results in the two geographic areas are attributed to the greater abundance in the Indian River of small decapod predators which were not excluded by the cages. These decapod predators actually increased in abundance in exclosures. Preliminary results from experiments on the shallow sandy shelf indicate that decapods and fishes are probably important here also as predators on the macrofauna. One must not assume the only effect of caging to be predator exclusion or inclusion. Cages may alter the physical environment or attract large predators; caging studies must be carefully planned and cautiously interpreted. This paper reviews problems of caging experiments encountered in the design, field, and interpretation stages. Consideration of all these potential problems is a necessity for a successful caging experiment.

Introduction

Manipulative field experiments are valuable tools for the study of biological interactions. Past work on marine rocky intertidal areas (see reviews by Connell, 1972, 1975) has demonstrated the importance of biological interactions (i.e., competition and predation) in controlling community structure and species abundances. If predation is a controlling factor limiting prey density, then removal of predation should permit an increase in the prey density. Recently, there has been a large increase in predator caging experiments in soft sediments. (By "soft sediment" I mean as opposed to hard substrate; the term would include sand as well as mud bottoms.) In this environment, however, manipulations, maintenance, observations, and sampling are much more difficult than for populations on hard substrates. Such field experiments must be interpreted cautiously, since cages frequently affect the sedimentary environment (Virnstein, 1977; McCall, 1977).

The objective of this paper is to present an overview of caging experiments in soft-sediment environments, based on my own experiences as well as others'. I suggest some possible reasons why the same or similar experiments in different habitats have yielded completely different results. Consideration of pitfalls discussed in this paper will lead perhaps to a more consistent and realistic approach to the design and interpretation of future experiments.

Methods

Predator exclusion experiments were conducted in the York River, Virginia (37° 15'N., 76° 30'W), in the Indian River, Florida (27° 32'N., 80° 21'W), and on the shallow shelf off southeast Florida (27° 33'N., 80° 03'W). The York River studies were reported in Virnstein (1977). The shallow shelf data are preliminary. In all three studies, 0.5 m by 0.5 m by 15 cm high predator exclosure cages covered with 12 mm mesh wire were set out in spring. The infauna was then sampled after 2 months or more. All samples were washed through a 0.5 mm mesh sieve, unless noted otherwise.

Sampling was either by $0.007 \, m^2$ (York River grass bed data) (Orth, 1975; 1977), or $0.005 \, m^2$ cores (Virnstein, 1977), or $0.0225 \, m^2$ "post-hole" samplers (from large cages in the Indian River) (Young et al., 1976; Young and Young, 1977), or with a $0.1 \, m^2$ hand-held scoop (shallow shelf experiment). The 31.6 cm wide scoop sampler was pushed 5 cm into the sediment and pushed horizontally through the sediment 31.6 cm. The sampler was then tilted up, dumping the sample into an attached cloth bag closable by a drawstring. Table 1 summarizes the number of samples, sample sizes, and dates for each experiment.

Table 1. Sampling schedule, number, and size at each of three sampling areas.

	Date set out	Date sampled	Number of replicate samples	Area of each sample
York River, Va.	July 73	Sept 73	10	$0.005 \, m^2$
	May 74	July 74	10	$0.005 \, m^2$
	August 74	Oct. 74	10	$0.007 \, m^2$
	April 75	June 75	5	$0.005 \, m^2$
Indian River, Fla.	Sept. 76	Nov. 76	4	$0.005 \, m^2$
	Sept. 76	Nov. 76	4	$0.0225 \, m^2$
	April 77	June 77	4	$0.005 \, m^2$
Florida shelf	April 77	July 77	1	$0.1 \, m^2$

Results

York River, Virginia

The area studied was a subtidal fine sand bottom, 1.5 m deep at mean low water, in the lower York River, a sub-estuary of the temperate Chesapeake Bay.

Infaunal densities in exclosure cages increased within two months (Figure 1), especially in cages set out in spring (reported in Virnstein, 1977). Densities in some cages were extremely high (to 233,000/m²), as compared to a yearly mean density in 1974 of 11,000/m² outside cages. At these high densities inside cages, competitive interactions presumably became important, but since

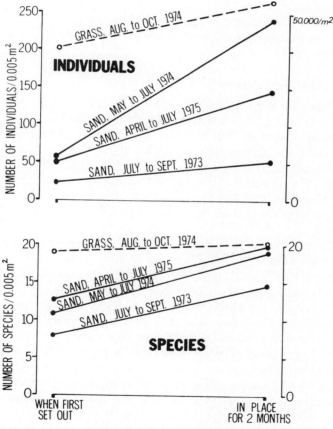

Figure 1.   Mean numbers of individuals and species per 0.005 m² within 0.5 m by 0.5 m cages in place for two months. Dates of setting out exclosure cages are given in 1973, 1974, and 1975. York River, Virginia. Densities outside cages are not plotted, but remained relatively constant from start to finish during the course of each separate experiment.

no species declined in abundance inside cages, it was assumed that competition did not play a significant role in the natural community. Shown to be of major importance were two species of large motile predators, the blue crab *Callinectes sapidus* (Crustacea: Portunidae) and the spot *Leiostomus xanthurus* (Pisces: Sciaenidae).

In a nearby *Zostera marina* seagrass bed, infaunal densities were normally much higher than in adjacent bare sand patches (Orth, 1977). Infaunal densities inside cages within the seagrass bed increased significantly (Figure 1; Orth, 1977); however, this increase was smaller than that in the sand, implying that predation on infauna is less important in seagrass beds than in bare sand. Predation pressure on epifauna of seagrass beds is probably greater than on infauna.

Infaunal densities and species richness inside cages on sands with initially low infaunal density increased to levels similar to those found in nearby seagrass beds.

Indian River, Florida

The Indian River is a bar-built subtropical coastal lagoon on the southeast Florida coast. Except for the Intracoastal Waterway, the Indian River is shallow (mean depth < 1.5 m) with extensive seagrass beds. Salinity is near marine except during the summer-fall rainy season when salinities may drop to 17⁰/oo. This study and previous work (Young and Young, 1977; Young *et al.*, 1976) were done in pure stands of the seagrass *Halodule (=Diplanthera) wrightii*.

This earlier work had found no differences in density inside and outside cages, but small decapod crustaceans were suggested as important predators on the infauna.

The experiment using the large 2 m x 2 m cages was duplicated in bare sand as well as in the seagrass bed, and no differences were found inside and outside cages (Figure 2), nor were any differences found using the smaller 0.5 m x 0.5 m cages in the sand (Figure 3).

To test the hypothesis that small decapod crustacean predators found refuge and increased in density inside cages, cages were initially set up in both sand and grass and the entire 2 m x 2 m area sampled for decapods by dip-netting, digging out grasses and sediments to a depth of 15 cm, and dip-netting again until no further organisms were obtained. These entire cage contents were sieved through 12 mm mesh. Then after two months the experimental cages were dug up and sampled in the same manner. The number of decapod crustaceans increased by at least a factor of 3 inside cages (Figure 4). Approximately half of these decapods were blue crabs, *Callinectes sapidus*, shown to be an important predator on infauna in Chesapeake Bay (Virnstein, 1977; Woodin, 1978). These cages were obviously not effective in keeping out major predators.

In essentially the same experiment repeated in the spring, the smaller cages were used in both seagrass and sand. In this more carefully controlled experiment, predators were searched for and removed from the cages. However, because of the refuge provided by the seagrasses, it was difficult to find the predators in the cage in the seagrass bed.

At the start of the experiment, the infaunal density in the seagrass bed was 2 x that in the bare sand. After two months, the reverse was true: the density in the cage in bare sand was 2 x that in the cage in the seagrass bed (Figure 5). This disparity was apparently still due to the decapods, which were more effectively removed from the cage in sand than from the cage in grass. There were no decapods in any of the samples from the sand cage, whereas every sample from the seagrass cage contained at least two species of decapods.

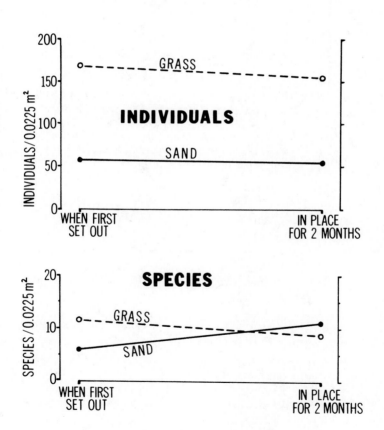

Figure 2.   Mean numbers of individuals and species per 0.0225 m² within 2 m by 2 m cages set out in September and sampled in November 1976. Indian River, Florida.

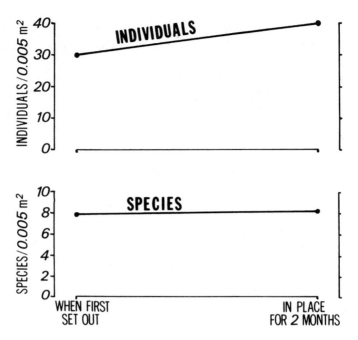

Figure 3.   Mean numbers of individuals and species per 0.005 m² within 0.5 m
by 0.5 m cages set out in September and sampled in November 1976.
Sand bottom in the Indian River, Florida.

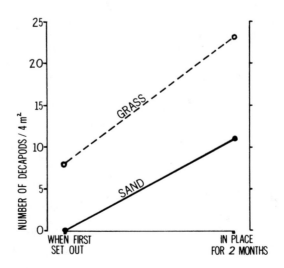

Figure 4.   Number of decapod crustaceans within 2 m by 2 m cages initially
(September) and after two months (November 1976). Indian River,
Florida.

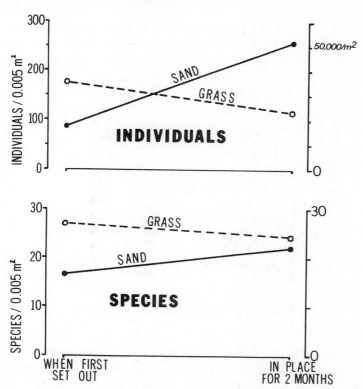

Figure 5. Mean numbers of individuals and species per 0.005 m² within 0.5 m by 0.5 m cages set out in April and sampled in June 1977. Indian River, Florida.

Shallow continental shelf

The study area was a sandy plain in 33 m of water 25 km offshore from Fort Pierce, Florida. Data are preliminary and are presented merely to illustrate the problems encountered.

After two and a half months, infaunal density inside the cage did not increase (Figure 6). Because cages were lowered from a surface ship, the bottom edge of the mesh could not be pushed into the sediment; therefore, animals could easily burrow under the edge of the cage and thus get into it. After cages had been in place 20 weeks, I was able to observe these cages from one of Harbor Branch Foundation's submersibles, the *Johnson-Sea-Link I*. The cages were obviously serving as miniature artificial reefs, providing structure and, I assume, refuge for fishes, crabs, and starfish. Within 2 m of each of the four cages, I counted 20 to 35 fish. Each cage had at least two fish inside it. After one of the cages was picked up with the submersible's manipulator arm and moved 1 m away, within two minutes two fish managed to get back inside the cage by wriggling under the edges. The cages were obviously not effective predator exclosures.

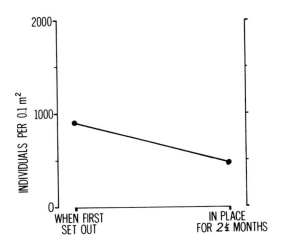

Figure 6.   Number of individuals per 0.1 m² within 0.5 by 0.5 m cages set out in April and sampled in July 1977. In 33 m off the southeast Florida coast.

Problems Encountered

Besides the problem mentioned in the above paragraph, there are many other problems in field caging experiments. Many of these problems are related to the presence of a physical structure that has effects other than keeping out predators.

The unnatural presence of a physical structure can alter the physical nature and hydrodynamics of the caged area. Depending on currents, sediment load, and cage shape and orientation, cages can induce either scouring or increased sedimentation. Scouring around cages has been observed in Monterey Bay, California (L. Hulberg, pers. commun.) and on the shallow (33 m) shelf off southeast Florida (personal observation). D. Cunningham (pers. commun. from P. McCall) found increased densities of infauna near cage walls, both inside and outside of cages on an intertidal mud flat in Long Island Sound.

Cages may slow down currents within the cage, allowing suspended sediments to settle out. This increase in sedimentation may be small (Virnstein, 1977), or in waters with a high sediment load may be sufficiently large that the entire cage is filled with sediment (Naqvi, 1968; McCall, 1977; R. J. Diaz, pers. commun.). Large cages (3 m on a side) as used by A. F. Holland and N. Mountford (pers. commun.) may have avoided this problem, but presented other problems associated with handling such a large structure in the field. I am not convinced that larger cages have smaller physical effects, although a large cage would have a smaller ratio of cage surface area to area enclosed.

Planktonic larvae encountering a cage may be induced to set within the cage ("larval entrapment") due to: 1) a decrease in current velocity; 2) a different sediment composition within the cage; or 3) contact with the cage surface. However, this effect may not be real and may instead be due to the increased survival of settling larvae inside the cage due to lack of predation. The 3 mm mesh cages used by Woodin (1974) selectively kept larvae of tube-building polychaetes from setting inside the cage because the larvae set and built tubes on the mesh of the cage.

The build-up of fouling organisms on cages can be expected to increase physical effects of the cage: change in currents and sedimentation, shading, and attraction of larger animals to feed on these fouling organisms. During summer in the York River, Virginia, cages needed scrubbing weekly. Instead of scrubbing, regular changes of the mesh on cages would be more satisfactory for the following reasons: 1) to temporarily remove fouling organisms; 2) to slow down fouling by providing new unconditioned surfaces; 3) to remove corroding surfaces; and 4) to avoid increasing the organic input into the cage (i.e., fouling organisms removed from the cage by scrubbing probably settle onto the sediment surface inside the cage). Reise (1977b) avoided fouling problems by adding several *Littorina littorea* to each cage; the snails grazed preferentially on the mesh.

Just as a natural reef provides structure and habitat for many animals, the presence of a cage in a generally structureless soft-sediment environment similarly attracts larger motile animals (also noticed by P. McCall, pers. commun.). The problem with the cages offshore was mentioned above. Arntz (1977) had a similar problem with cages on a mud bottom in the Baltic Sea. Starfish, crabs, and gobies were much more abundant inside his cages than outside. In a *Zostera marina* seagrass bed in the Chesapeake Bay, Orth (1975) had severe problems with oyster toadfish *(Opsanus tau)* digging next to cages, stakes, or any physical structure he set out. In the York and Indian Rivers, I have found that blue crabs are exceedingly difficult to keep out of cages, even when the bottom edge of the cage is pushed 5 cm into the sediment. S. A. Woodin (pers. commun.) has had this same problem with juveniles. When blue crabs molt, they are themselves temporarily very susceptible to predators and must seek cover at this stage. Small crabs may enter through the mesh, but after molting once, they may be too large to leave. The solution to complete exclusion of predators would seem to be the use of smaller mesh size, but: 1) there would be more problems of fouling and current effects; and 2) predators could still enter as juveniles or larvae and subsequently be protected from *their* predators during this critical phase, thus resulting in increased densities of predators inside cages. The existence of seasonal breeding migrations of predators and the use of appropriate seasonal timing may avoid this latter problem.

If seagrasses, marsh grasses, and drift algae are present, they may be trapped against the sides of cages, inhibiting current flow to the extent that Arntz (1977) found anaerobic conditions inside some of his cages. A fence surrounding the caged areas was proposed as a solution to the accumulation of drifting algae. I doubt that there is any caging study without problems; it is hoped that sufficient prior knowledge and careful planning will avoid many of these hazards.

Experimental Design Considerations

In designing a field caging experiment, there are several factors and choices that must be considered concerning predators, sampling schemes, type environment, and the cage itself. Some environments and communities are more amenable to caging experiments than others. Prior knowledge of the habitat and community is a prerequisite for anticipating field problems and limitations and for formulating testable hypotheses regarding potential predators and prey.

The cage itself should be designed to produce a minimum of disturbance effects other than the exclosure of predators. For example, if the predator size is known, then the mesh size should be just small enough to exclude this predator. Besides mesh size, the overall size, shape, and location of the cage need to be considered. To decrease edge effects and cage effects, bigger may be better, but the effect of cage size has never been tested. Larger cages could be sampled repetitively, but sampling disturbance would be too great in a cage less than several times the sample size. If cages are to be sampled over a time period, either repetitive samples can be taken from large cages, or enough smaller cages can be set out at the start of the experiment so that some cages are sampled after the first time interval, others sampled successively.

Replication of treatments is superior to replicate samples from only one replicate of the treatments. It has been my experience that variation between replicates is greater than the variation of samples within a replicate. This large between-treatment variability is likely due to the vagaries of initial colonization, and whether or not a small predator managed to get into the cage.

A "control" cage must be considered and attempted, although it is difficult to conceive of a cage that has all the physical effect of a cage but does not keep out predators. This control is essential to separate the effect of the cage from the effect of the predator. Topless, sideless, and two-sided cages have been used, but one must know their effects on animals and physical parameters to interpret them correctly.

The season during which a cage is in place can play a large role in determining the results (Virnstein, 1977). Many species spawn and recruit at certain times of the year only. If a cage is set out during this period, the larvae of these species are protected upon settlement and could successfully recruit within the cage at this time of the year but not at another time. Seasonal migration or activity patterns of major predators are common in estuaries. In Chesapeake Bay during the winter, when blue crabs and spot were absent from the system, cages produced no change in infaunal densities; during spring and summer, densities became much greater inside the cages (A. F. Holland and N. Mountford, pers. commun. of unpublished data).

If predators are to be enclosed inside cages, then the number of individuals, species, size, and possibly sex of the predator must be chosen. Some prior knowledge of the predator's normal range, behavior, and seasonal activity must enter into this choice. The behavior of a very active or swimming predator is probably altered by enclosure within a cage. A larger cage probably allows more normal behavior. The density of predators within a cage can be adjusted both by the number of predators within a cage and the size of the cage. Combinations of more than one species might be considered in order to approach the more complex natural situation. Especially in the tropics, predation may be extremely important without there being one or two species which are major predators. In such a situation where many species of predator play an individually small role, caging any one species of predator in or out would have a small effect although the sum of all predators has a major effect.

A more restricted use of cages could be the enclosure of a specific predator with a patch of potential prey to observe whether the predator will feed on that prey, and to estimate feeding rates.

In all cases where cages are used, some measurements of physical cage effects should be made to compare inside to outside, e.g., sediment size distribution, seston flux, current velocity, and incident light.

I recommend that extra cages be set out at the start of an experiment to allow for inevitable losses due to vandalism, human curiosity, snagging by hook and line or a vessel's anchor, and the occasional predator that somehow manages to get inside a cage.

As an alternative to caging, predators might be excluded by other means, e.g., chemical or scent barriers, or by periodically removing them by hand if they are slow-moving (e.g., gastropods and asteroids). If feasible, this method would be preferable to caging because the treatment involves only the removal of predators without any cage structure. A more artificial but more controlled method than field caging would be to transfer intact cores of sediments and animals into aquarium systems, and then to add predators to some cores but not to others. This method allows the use of a control treatment, but suffers from its artificial environmental constancy. It is not valid to assume that such experimental results also apply under natural field conditions.

Interpretation Considerations

The same caging experiment cannot be expected to produce the same effect in widely different situations. The results will depend on several factors. Manipulating predator density can produce changes other than changes in total abundance, e.g., there could result changes in species composition, relative abundance, size-class distribution, growth or reproductive rates, and total structure and function. For example, if resources are limiting and predation is selective on the dominant species, removing predators may result in competitive exclusion of non-dominant species (Paine, 1974). Removal of predators cannot be expected to result in an increase in total abundance when resources are limiting. At increased population densities inside cages, resources may become limiting, causing the observed subsequent decline in abundance of opportunistic deposit-feeding species (Virnstein, 1977; Commito, 1976; D. K. Young and M. W. Young, pers. commun.). Such high density assemblages inside cages may provide a good opportunity to study competitive interactions. In harsh, physically controlled systems, predation may never be given the opportunity to limit populations; the physical stresses may predominate, or the predators may be more sensitive than the prey and be preferentially eliminated (suggested by Young and Young, 1977).

Seasonal effects can largely alter results, especially in temperate regions. From caging experiments during the winter in Chesapeake Bay, one would conclude that predation is not important; such is not the case (Virnstein, 1977; Holland and Mountford, pers. commun.). Various aspects of seasonal effects include: when cages are set out and sampled, when species are spawning and recruiting, when predators are present and active, and when physical stresses are important. One must be aware of all these factors.

The mesh size decided upon might keep out major predators, but it cannot be automatically assumed that this mesh size will keep out all species of predators. My cages in the Indian River and Arntz's (1977) cages in the Baltic did keep out larger fishes, but provided access and refuge for smaller predators. Operationally defining a predator as an animal above a certain size obviously is improper without prior knowledge showing this to be true. Thus, adopting this limited definition would have falsely led Arntz and me to conclude that predators were not important in the communities studied. Reise (1977b) found significant density increases inside cages only with mesh sizes ≤ 5 mm, because the important predators on the community were small shore crabs, shrimp, and gobies.

One cannot assume that the only effect of a cage is the exclusion or inclusion of predators. The extent of these cage effects has not been adequately resolved in any soft-sediment habitat. If densities increase inside cages, does this occur because of "larval entrapment" (Nichols, 1977) or because the settling larvae survive better inside cages? If cages affect sediments within the cage, is any resulting density increase inside cages the result of the sediment change or the decrease in predation pressure? If this increased density is due to animals that aggregate fine sediments into tubes or fecal pellets, is the increase in sediment accumulation due to this biodeposition or to the physical effect of the cage? These are questions that must be considered and solutions attempted by careful measurement of physical parameters in conjunction with the use of adequate controls.

Although not without problems, caging studies, when planned, carried out, and interpreted with care, are a valuable tool for studying ecological relationships, particularly the role of predation.

Acknowledgments

D. F. Boesch advised throughout the duration of the York River work. D. K. Young's previous work and advice were invaluable for the Indian River experiments. The Florida work could not have been completed without the able and abundant assistance of M. A. Capone, J. E. Miller, and K. D. Cairns. My wife Elisabeth helped in all phases. I thank A. F. Holland for an extensive review of an earlier draft of the manuscript. All errors, speculations, and suppositions are mine.

References

1. Arntz, W. E. 1977. Results and problems of an "unsuccessful" benthos cage experiment (western Baltic), pp. 31-44. *In* B. F. Keegan, P. O. Ceidigh, and P. J. S. Boaden (eds.), Biology of Benthic Organisms. Pergamon Press, New York.

2. Commito, J. A. 1976. Predation, competition, life-history strategies, and the regulation of estuarine soft-bottom community structure. Ph.D. dissertation, Duke University, Durham, North Carolina 201 pp.

3. Connell, J. H. 1972. Community interactions on marine rocky intertidal shores. *Ann. Rev. Ecol. Syst.* 3:169-192.

4. _____. 1975. Some mechanisms producing structure in natural communities, pp. 460-490. *In* M. L. Cody and J. M. Diamond (eds.), Ecology and Evolution of Communities. Belknap Press of Harvard University Press, Cambridge, Massachusetts.

5. McCall, P. L. 1977. Community patterns and adaptive strategies of the infaunal benthos of Long Island Sound. *J. Mar. Res.* 35:221-266.

6. Naqvi, S. M. Z. 1968. Effects of predation on infaunal invertebrates of Alligator Harbor, Florida. *Gulf Res. Rpts.* 2:313-321.

7. Nichols, F. H. 1977. Dynamics and production of *Pectinaria koreni* in Kiel Bay, West Germany, pp. 453-464. *In* B. F. Keegan, P. O. Ceidigh, and P. J. S. Boaden (eds.), Biology of Benthic Organisms. Pergamon Press, New York.

8. Orth, R. J. 1975. The role of disturbance on an eelgrass, *Zostera marina*, community. Ph.D. dissertation, Univ. of Maryland, College Park. 97 pp.

9. _____. 1977. The importance of sediment stability in seagrass communities, pp. 281-300. *In* B. C. Coull (ed.), Ecology of Marine Benthos. Univ. of South Carolina Press, Columbia.

10. Paine, R. T. 1974. Intertidal community structure. Experimental studies on the relationship between a dominant competition and its principal predator. *Oecologia* 15:93-120.

11. Reise, K. 1977a. Predation pressure and community structure of an intertidal soft-bottom fauna, pp. 513-519. *In* B. F. Keegan, P. O. Ceidigh, and P. J. S. Boaden (eds.), Biology of Benthic Organisms. Pergamon Press, New York.

12. _____. 1977b. Predator exclusion experiments in an intertidal mud flat. *Helgoländer wiss. Meeresunters.* 30:263-271.

13. Virnstein, R. W. 1977. The importance of predation by crabs and fishes on benthic infauna in Chesapeake Bay. *Ecology* 58:1199-1217.

14. Woodin, S. A. 1974. Polychaete abundance patterns in a marine soft-sediment environment: the importance of biological interactions. *Ecol. Monogr.* 44:171-187.

15. _____. 1978. Refuges, disturbance and community structure: a marine soft-bottom example. *Ecology* 59 (In press).

16. Young, D. K., M. A. Buzas, and M. W. Young. 1976. Species densities of macrobenthos associated with seagrass: a field experimental study of predation. *J. Mar. Res.* 34:577–592.

17. Young, D. K., and M. W. Young. 1977. Community structure of the macrobenthos associated with seagrass of the Indian River estuary, Florida. pp. 359-382. *In* B. C. Coull (ed.), Ecology of Marine Benthos. Univ. of South Carolina Press, Columbia.

LAND–ESTUARY INTERACTIONS: NATURAL CATASTROPHIC EVENTS

PORTAGE, ALASKA: CASE HISTORY OF AN EARTHQUAKE'S IMPACT ON AN ESTUARINE SYSTEM

A. T. Ovenshine and Susan Bartsch-Winkler

U.S. Geological Survey
345 Middlefield Road
Menlo Park, California

Abstract: Regional tectonic subsidence and differential sediment consolidation during the 1964 Alaska earthquake (Richter mag.=8.5) lowered the Portage area into the intertidal zone of Turnagain Arm, forcing abandonment of the town of Portage. Ground subsidence amounted to as much as 2.4 m, and subsequent deposition deposited an estimated 20 million m³ of silt over 18 km² of land previously above tide water. Most of these post-earthquake sediments were deposited by tidal action rather than by the major streams that flow into Turnagain Arm in the vicinity of Portage. The layer of post-earthquake sediment is 1.5 m thick seaward of a highway embankment and thins landward to 0.9 m, with an areal distribution reflecting preexisting channel patterns. All samples landward of the highway contain less than 10% sand, whereas those seaward of the highway average over 20%. With minor exceptions, minerals in the sediment did not originate in the graywacke terrane of the surrounding Chugach Mountains, but ultimately must come from the plutonic and volcanic terranes west and north of Turnagain Arm and from coal beds of the Cook Inlet Basin.

Preliminary studies of a 93-m core taken at Portage indicate rapid deposition for the past 8,000 years, perhaps caused by repeated episodes of subsidence associated with tectonic activity. The sediment accumulation at Portage from 1964 to 1974 is a striking result of one such episode.

Introduction

The Portage area (Figure 1), about 77 km southeast of Anchorage, was within the area of maximum shaking and damage related to the Alaska earthquake of 1964. Land subsidence in the area amounted to at least 2.4 m; of this, approximately 1.6 m resulted from regional tectonic subsidence, and 0.8 m was from local subsidence (McCulloch and Bonilla, 1970). Because of the subsidence, high tides inundated 18 km² of land previously above sea level, and deposited more than 20 x 10⁶ m³ of silt. The small roadside settlement of Portage was abandoned; present habitation is limited to one house and several mobile homes associated with a service station.

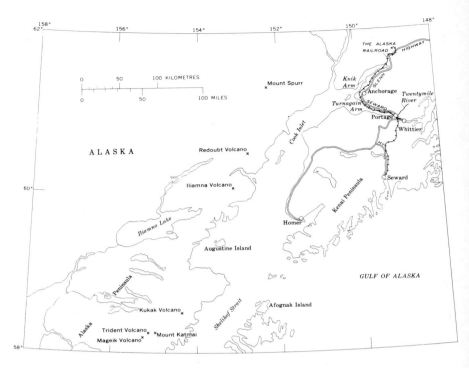

*Figure 1. Location of the Portage area in Alaska. Active volcanoes on the west
side of Cook Inlet indicated by an X (Ovenshine and others, 1976).*

Portage is situated at the mouths of three broad alluviated valleys–
Twentymile, Portage, and Placer–separated by steep bedrock ridges that rise
1,200 m above the valley floors. The valleys are underlain by Holocene sands
and gravels interfingered with tidal silts. Groundwater is within 1.5 m of the
ground surface throughout the Portage area. Large fast-flowing streams, with
headwaters in low-lying glaciers of the Chugach and Kenai Mountains, are
flanked by well-drained natural levees. In some places, between the levees and
the bedrock valley walls, are grassy or sparsely forested freshwater marshes and
bogs. Regional bedrock is Jurassic(?) and Cretaceous, consisting of graywacke,
siltite, and argillite of the Valdez(?) Group (Clark, 1972).

The streams reach tidewater at the head of Turnagain Arm, a southeast-
trending, 72-km-long embayment at the northeast end of Cook Inlet (Figure 1).
Turnagain Arm has a dramatic sedimentological system marked by a high tidal
range (11 m), swift tidal currents, a twice-daily tidal bore, and seasonal input
from rivers draining the surrounding glaciated mountains. The streams as well as
Turnagain Arm are frozen several months of the year and, during this time, very
little sedimentation occurs in the Arm.

The Placer River Silt: Portage Surface Study

The deposits of intertidal origin resulting from the Alaska earthquake of 1964 make up a recognizable geologic unit that has been mapped in the Portage area, and named the Placer River Silt (Ovenshine, Lawson, and Bartsch-Winkler, 1976). Exposures of the silt are found in banks of the three large rivers and in the banks of smaller channels that cross the tidal flat.

The Placer River Silt overlies a buried soil layer containing yellowish-orange and yellowish-brown oxidized zones encapsulating rootlets, twigs, and other plant debris. The soil horizon that underlies the Placer River Silt ranges in thickness from a few centimeters to about 30 centimeters, and varies according to the type of plants living there at the time of the earthquake. In areas of forest or alder thicket the soil is a centimeter or more of black leaf duff overlying 1 to 10 cm of brown root-bearing silt; in areas of bog or marsh, the soil is from 1 to 5 cm of spongy black malodorous peat composed of partially decayed grasses, sphagnum moss and rootlets; in areas that were grassland, as much as 30 cm of compacted silt is bound by a lacework of grass roots. In areas of spruce and cottonwood forest and willow/alder thicket, the plants were buried upright and intact. Ten years after the 1964 earthquake, the projecting parts of plants are dried and brittle and are being eroded away; parts below the silt horizon have retained their bark, fresh wood color, and much of the strength of living plant tissue. Ten years after burial, a few of the apparently dead willows have sprouted new growth.

Thickness measurements of the silt were obtained by hand-augering to the 1964 soil horizon underlying the Placer River Silt (Figure 2). The thickness of the formation reflects the geometry of the three major valleys and five streams which intersect tidewater at Portage; the effects of the highway embankment are also reflected.

Seaward of the highway the silt averages about 1.5 m in thickness; landward of the highway it averages about 0.9 m. Although factors such as greater subsidence, proximity to the source of sediment, and proximity to tidal channels would cause more accumulation seaward of the highway embankment, without doubt the single most important factor is the containment effect imposed on the flood tide by the gravel highway embankment. Flow through the embankment is restricted to five culverts at the bridges that cross the major rivers. Seaward of the embankment the Placer River Silt is tabular-shaped and of relatively even thickness. Levees along channel banks are non-existent, but tidal channels are as large as 2 m deep and 25 m wide.

Landward of the highway, the thickness distribution of the Placer River Silt is controlled by the stream geometry and, to an unknown extent, the amount of differential subsidence. Levees and crevasse splays are typical features of the Placer River Silt landward of the highway.

The sediment on the surface of Portage Flats is primarily silt, with admixtures of sand and a paucity of gravel and clay. A ternary plot of surface

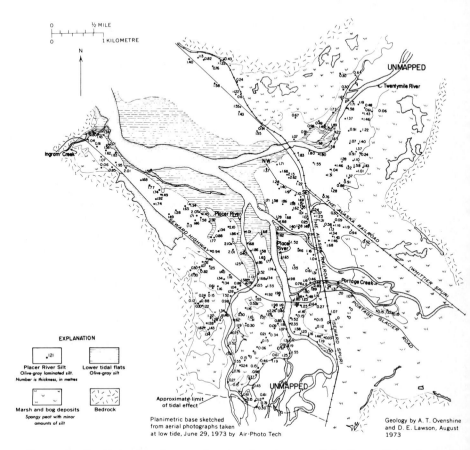

Figure 2. Geologic sketch map showing distribution of the Placer River Silt and depositional framework of the Portage area (Ovenshine and others, 1976).

sediments (Figure 3) shows them to be primarily silt and sandy silt. The sediment at Portage Flats contains more silt than is found elsewhere in Turnagain Arm (Ovenshine, Bartsch-Winkler, O'Brien, and Lawson, 1976): an average sample contains 0.3% gravel, 16.9% sand, 82.3% silt, and 0.5% clay (Bartsch-Winkler *et al.*, in press).

The highest percentages of sand (greater than 40%) are nearest the tidal channels (Figure 4). In a few isolated areas on the channel edges, gravel may occur. Flats near the channels contain 30–40% sand, and localities farthest from the channels and in topographically high areas on the tidal flat seaward of the highway embankment contain 10–20% sand. The most striking feature of the textural map is the general restriction of coarser sand and silt to seaward of the highway embankment (Figure 4). Tidal currents landward of the barrier are

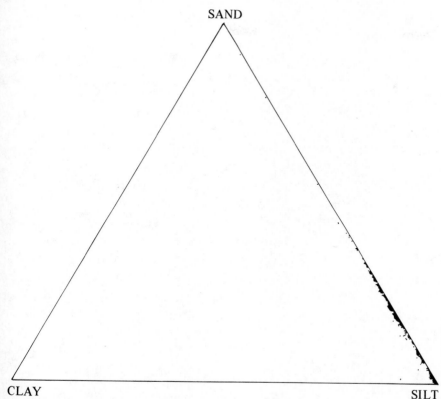

Figure 3. Ternary plot of analyzed surface sediments from Portage Flats (after Bartsch-Winkler and others, in press).

inhibited, since tidal waters have access to this area only through the five culverts where the highway crosses the main rivers. With few exceptions, the samples landward of the highway contain over 90% silt. Clay is a minor constituent in these samples, although one sample did contain 8% clay.

Bedforms

X-radiography reveals the typical bedding features at Portage to be planar bedding with some areas containing small-scale cross laminae and some disruption by grass rootlets. Notably absent are shells or burrowing structures left by intertidal creatures which are typical of many high tidal flat areas (Evans, 1965; Klein, 1963; Straaten, 1954). At no place in the Portage area was evidence of sediment infauna found. Small *Macoma* sp. shells up to 1 cm long are transported from Turnagain Arm and rarely are incorporated into the formation. Cavernous silt, formed by entrapment and burial of air as tidewater encroaches over dried sediment surfaces, is typical of the higher, grass-covered tidal flats at Portage.

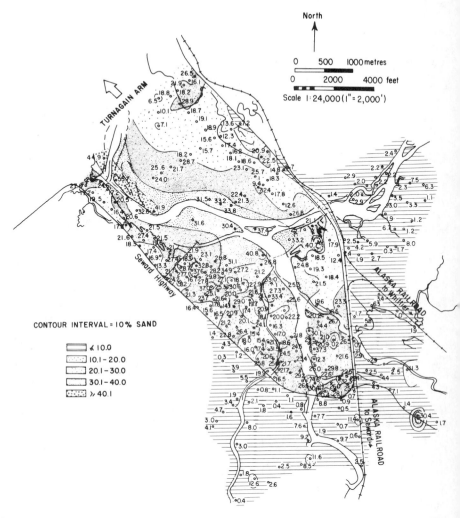

Figure 4. Percent sand of surface samples from Portage Flats (after Bartsch-Winkler and others, in press).

Source of the Placer River Silt

The accumulation of new sediment at Portage, which is generally thicker offshore and thinning landward, signifies offshore sources for the Placer River Silt. Thus, the probable immediate source of the new deposit is the extensive system of silty sand bars within Turnagain Arm. On the basis of the mineralogy of the grains making up the deposit, the sediment must ultimately originate outside of Turnagain Arm, but still within the Cook Inlet Basin.

Detailed studies of the mineralogy of the Placer River Silt indicate three possible source terranes within the Cook Inlet Basin (Figure 1). The rock fragments, flakes of chlorite, and the milky quartz grains are all consistent with derivation from the surrounding Chugach graywacke terrane, although they could also originate elsewhere in the Cook Inlet watershed. Grains of pumice, volcanic glass, and euhedral hornblende, however, could not have this provenance and probably are originally derived from the volcanic rocks of the southern Alaska Range, northwest of Cook Inlet. Abundant biotite and plagioclase grains probably originate in the Talkeetna Mountains batholith north and northeast of Knik Arm. Coal is plentiful in the Placer River Silt and most likely comes from Tertiary coal seams and glacial deposits that occur on the northwestern and western sides of Cook Inlet, and on the Kenai Peninsula.

Portage Core: Subsurface study

Ten years after the earthquake, the layer of new intertidal silt had commonly reached a thickness exceeding 1.5 m in the Portage area; up to 2.35 m of new sediment was measured (Figure 2). At this level very little sediment was still being added, and new surface vegetation was beginning to take hold. The sequence of events (subsidence, inundation, vegetation kill, deposition, revegetation) and available field evidence (two possible pre-1964 vegetation layers below the 1964 soil horizon) prompted us to drill in search of further cycles of earthquake-caused sedimentation in Portage's past that could be dated by carbon-14 methods. Accordingly, a 93-meter hole was drilled at Portage in February, 1975.

Preliminary studies show that nine distinct facies can be recognized from the core (Figure 5). About 1 m of artificial gravel pad caps the core and was not sampled. The pad overlies about 7 m of pre- and post-earthquake intertidal silts (Unit 1). Unit 2 (7 to 16 m depth) consists of stream-rounded gravel and sand. Sand, silt, and minor amounts of gravel make up Unit 3 (16 to 20 m depth). Spherical inclusions of sand up to 4 cm in diameter are found in several of the silty layers. At the 20-meter depth a gas pocket was intersected during drilling, and plant debris was carried to the surface by the gas and drilling mud (Reuben Kachadoorian, oral commun., 1975). Apparently all the plant material was carried out of the hole by the drilling fluid because no plant material was recovered in this portion of the core. A silt layer making up Unit 4 (20–33 m depth) contained several spherical sand inclusions like those described in Unit 3. The silt appears more compacted and more cohesive than the silt of Unit 1. At the top of Unit 4, abundant pumice was found and at the base of the unit (from 28–33 m depth), sand-size pumice laminae and pelecypod remains were observed in the radiographs. A sudden rise in the population of foraminifers apparently occurred in this laminated section (Figure 5). Unit 5 (33–45 m depth) is predominantly sand with minor amounts of gravel. The average sand content is 50%. Unit 6, from 45–50 m depth, is comprised of sand and inclusions of silt and

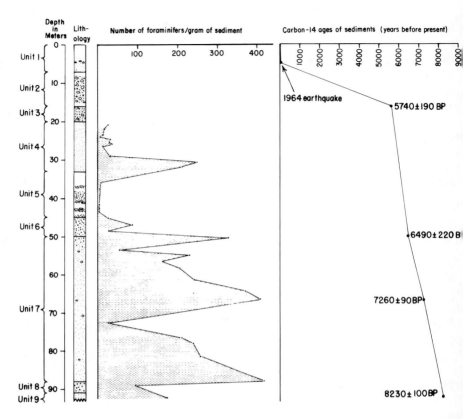

Figure 5. Diagram of lithologic units, foraminiferal abundance, and age/depth
relationships of the 93-meter core obtained at Portage, Alaska.

mud. The sand is not laminated as is the sand in Unit 5. The average sand content
is 63%. Unit 7, from 50 to 88 m depth, is the thickest sequence in the core. It is
comprised of well-laminated, fine-grain silt with layers of sand near the top.
Foraminifers are most abundant in this unit, especially at 67 m and 86 m depth.
Plant debris is abundant at 55 m depth, and is concentrated in laminae. At 84 m
depth, organic material is concentrated into definite layers 0.5 cm thick. Isolated
shells and pebbles are found throughout. Unit 8 (89–91 m depth) is made up
mainly of sand with some silt and mud. Unit 9 (91–93 m depth) is composed of
silt, with laminae of sand. Sand content is 32%.

    The radiographs indicate that laminated bedding was, by far, the most
prevalent bedding style throughout the core. Occasional small-scale crossbeds
1 cm in height occur in the finer-grain sand and silt, and two examples of
herringbone crossbeds, indicative of tidal environments, were observed near the
top of Unit 7 . Some larger-scale atypical crossbeds in Unit 7 are 3 cm in height.
A convoluted interval 46 cm thick is present in Unit 6.

Four samples of concentrated organic debris representing 2–3 m intervals were submitted for age-dating by the carbon-14 method. The resultant dates are plotted against depth on the graph shown in Figure 5. The nearly straight line plot indicates that a net rapid rate of sediment deposition took place at Portage between about 8,230 and 6,490 years B.P., suggesting that filling of a Turnagain Arm fiord embayment occurred from early to mid-Holocene time.

Below about 50 m depth, the sediments are composed of fine-grain silt and clay; foraminiferal populations increase in the core sediments below this depth, probably indicating deepwater environment with normal salinity, conditions which are more favorable for growth of these species. From 35 to 50 m depth, an interval of sand and gravel predominates: the clasts are of graywacke and siltite of Chugach provenance. This interval may represent subareal stream deposits, which drained the Portage area possibly during a period of stillstand or short-'term uplift resulting from a series of earthquakes. The silt underlying the gravel and sand contains herringbone crossbeds indicative of an intertidal environment. The silt units above the 35 m depth, including those on the surface today, contrast with the silts below the 50 m depth; they have almost no clay, and have only rare foraminifers (fewer than 20/gram of sediment). These silt units nearer the top of the core probably represent a shallower, more brackish water environment than those below the 50 m depth. Since 5,740 ± 190 years B.P., an apparent reduction in the net rate of sediment deposition is coupled with a probable nearshore textural regime. Near the surface, from 7 to 20 m depth, well-washed stream gravels occur. These are overlain by 7 m of intertidal silt of the present-day system, approximately 2.0 m of which were deposited after the 1964 earthquake.

Earthquake Effects

Direct short-lived engineering effects of the earthquake in the Portage area include destruction of buildings, bridges, and the railroad and highway embankments. Longer-term consequences are still being felt in the area at the present time. These effects, caused by the resultant inundation and sedimentation of the area, include human abandonment of the area, destruction of flora and associated esthetic deterioration, localized erosion, and development of quicksand hazards and other environmental effects.

High tides still inundate much of the area lowered into the intertidal zone, although there is evidence that sedimentation has slowed to a minor amount and revegetation is beginning; ten years after the catastrophe, grasses of several types had returned and a few apparently dead willows had sprouted new growth. The Portage landscape is being restored to its pre-earthquake condition, and may some day soon be habitable. A mathematical estimate of the rate and duration of sedimentation at Portage shows that the rate of post-earthquake sedimentation has decreased; by the early part of the next century, sedimentation is expected to cease (Ovenshine and Kachadoorian, 1976).

Ebb and flood currents focus localized erosion in the tidal channels. As a major result of this headward erosion of the channels, access is provided to the low-lying freshwater marsh, bog, and lake areas that rim the active intertidal zones. The continued progradation of salt water into these areas leads to further destruction of the plant communities. Quicksand hazards have developed over the entire Portage area; because of the uncompacted nature and the predominance of silt, the new sediment is readily liquefiable when saturated, as it is immediately following high tide. The instability of the sediment is well-known to local sportsmen, who shun foot travel in the region (Ovenshine, Lawson, and Bartsch-Winkler, 1976).

Environmental consequences of the 1964 earthquake at Portage were severe, but apparently not permanent. The cycle of earthquake, deposition, and the start of rejuvenation of the land surface took only ten years at Portage, an instant in geologic time. The sedimentary record at Portage indicates that earthquakes have occurred there in the past and will undoubtedly occur in the future. Knowledge of the recurrence of earthquakes and their consequences will have a critical bearing on the future development of Portage, of the greater Anchorage area, and other coastal areas subjected to sudsidence during an earthquake.

References

1. Bartsch-Winkler, S., and A. T. Ovenshine. In press. Coastal modifications at Portage, Alaska, resulting from the Alaska earthquake of March 27, 1964. In H. J. Walker, (ed.), Symposium on Research Techniques in Coastal Environments Proceedings, Louisiana State Univ., Baton Rouge, Louisiana.

2. Bartsch-Winkler, S., A. T. Ovenshine, and J. Rupert. In press. Sedimentological report on the silt of Portage Flats: U.S. Geol. Survey Misc. Field Inv. Map.

3. Clark, S. H. B. 1972. Reconnaissance bedrock geological map of the Chugach Mountains near Anchorage, Alaska: U.S. Geol. Survey Misc. Field Studies Map MF-350, scale 1:250,000.

4. Evans, G. 1965. Intertidal flat sediments and their environments of deposition in the Wash. Geol. Soc. London Quart. Jour., 121:209-245.

5. Klein, G. D. V. 1963. Bay of Fundy intertidal zone sediments. J. Sed. Petrology 33 (4):844-854.

6. McCulloch, D. S., and M. G. Bonilla. 1970. Effect of the earthquake of March 27, 1964, on the Alaska Railroad. U.S. Geol. Survey Prof. Paper 545-D, 161 pp.

7. Ovenshine, A. T., S. Bartsch-Winkler, N. R. O'Brien, and D. E. Lawson. 1976. Sedimentation of the high tidal range environment of Upper Turnagain Arm, Alaska, pp. M1-M26. In T. P. Miller, (ed.), Recent and Ancient Sedimentary Environments in Alaska. Anchorage, Alaska Geol. Soc. Symposium Proc.

8. Ovenshine, A. T., and R. Kachadoorian. 1976. Estimate of the time required for natural restoration of the effects of the 1964 earthquake at Portage, pp. 53-54. In E. H. Cobb (ed.), The United States Geological Survey in Alaska; accomplishments during 1975. U.S. Geol. Survey Circ. 733.

9. Ovenshine, A. T., D. E. Lawson, and S. Bartsch-Winkler. 1976. The Placer River Formation; inter-tidal sedimentation caused by the Alaska earthquake of March 27, 1964. U.S. Geol. Survey J. Research 4 (2):151-162.

10. Van Straaten, L. M. J. U.. 1954. Composition and structure of recent marine sediments in the Netherlands. Leidse Geol. Meded. 19:1-110.

ESTUARINE GRAVEYARDS, CLIMATIC CHANGE, AND THE IMPORTANCE OF THE ESTUARINE ENVIRONMENT

J. R. Schubel and D. J. Hirschberg

Marine Sciences Research Center
State University of New York
Stony Brook, New York

Abstract: Climatic variations and sea level fluctuations control the origin and distribution of estuaries. Interglacial ages lasting approximately 10,000 years each, and followed by a glacial maximum, have occurred on the average every 100,000 years during at least the past million years. Corresponding sea level variations have been on the order of 100 m. During highstands of sea level, estuaries are abundant and relatively large; during lowstands, rare and small. Estuaries are ephemeral on a geological time scale; lifetimes are usually limited to a few thousands of years and at most to a few tens of thousands of years. Weather events, such as hurricanes and floods, can accelerate the evolution of an estuary and shorten its life span appreciably. Estuaries have been abundant during only 10--20% of the last million years. The biological importance of estuaries to the survival of organisms and to the maintenance of the total marine ecosystem appears to have been exaggerated.

Estuarine deposits rarely can now be delimited unequivocally from other shallow water marine deposits in the geologic record, particularly those laid down more than a million years ago, because of their limited areal extent, their ephemeral character, and their lack of distinctive features. The estuarine graveyard is a palimpsest and most of its tales have been obliterated.

Introduction

Estuaries are common features of our coastline and have been during the last several thousands of years. According to Emery (1967), estuaries and lagoons now make up 80 to 90% of our Atlantic and Gulf coasts and 10 to 20% of our Pacific coast. Because of their abundance, their high primary productivity, the large populations of commercially and recreationally important species of fishes and shellfishes they support, and the varied uses man makes of them, a very important, sometimes even crucial, role in maintaining a well-balanced marine ecosystem has been attributed to estuaries.

In this paper we do three things:

(1) We review the processes by which an estuary is born, lives, and dies.

(2) We discuss the fluctuations in the abundance of estuaries during the last million years or so.
(3) We assess the importance of the estuary, per se, for the survival of species and the maintenance of the marine ecosystem.

The Birth, Life, and Death of an Estuary

The term "estuary" has been defined in many ways (Caspers, 1967; Schubel, 1971). The definition most commonly used by oceanographers, physical and geological, is that an estuary is a semi-enclosed coastal body of water which is freely connected with the ocean and within which seawater is measurably diluted with freshwater from runoff (Pritchard, 1967). From the geological viewpoint, Pritchard (1967) identified four kinds of estuaries: drowned river valleys, fjord estuaries, bar-built estuaries, and estuaries formed by tectonic processes.

The origin of estuaries is controlled primarily by those climatic events that control eustatic sea level changes—glaciations and deglaciations. The distribution of estuaries is determined by the interplay of climatic events and regional and more local geological processes. Estuaries are relatively large and abundant after periods of rising sea level, particularly where continental margins are broad and relatively flat, along epeirogenic coasts such as the Atlantic and Gulf coasts of the United States. Estuaries are smaller and less abundant during lowstands and where continental margins are narrow and the coast has high relief, along orogenic coasts such as the Pacific coast of the United States.

Once formed, estuaries are rapidly destroyed. On geological time scales they are ephemeral features having life spans measured in thousands of years to perhaps a few tens of thousands of years. They fill rapidly with sediments. Characteristically, sedimentation rates are highest near their heads where an estuarine delta usually forms in the upper reaches near the new river mouth (Schubel, 1971). The delta grows progressively seaward within the estuary to extend the realm of the river and force the intruding sea from the semi-enclosed coastal basin. In some estuaries lateral accretion by marshes and deposition of marine sediments near the mouth may be important (Schubel, 1971). Eventually, the intruding sea is displaced from the semi-enclosed coastal basin, the river reaches the sea through a broad depositional plain, and the transformation is complete. We can find estuaries in various stages of development around the coasts of the world (Schubel, 1971).

Emery and Uchupi (1972) estimated that if all the suspended sediment discharged by rivers, other than the Mississippi, into lagoons and estuaries of the Atlantic and Gulf coasts of the United States were deposited in these coastal basins they would be filled in 9,500 years on the average, assuming sea level remains constant.

Before the Quaternary, the life spans of estuaries could have been considerably longer if sea level were relatively constant or if periods of highstand were longer. Under these conditions, continents with broad flat continental shelves may have been the sites of persistent estuaries which advanced or retreated in response to local sea level changes produced by the balance of isostatic adjustment, sedimentation, and small changes in eustatic sea level. Until recently, it was generally held that from about two million years ago to 200 million years ago eustatic sea level was relatively constant. Vail *et al.*'s (1977) data, however, indicate that fluctuations of sea level during this period may have been of the same order as in the Quaternary, but that the frequency of highstands was probably lower and the frequency of lowstands higher. These conditions would increase neither the frequency nor the persistence of estuaries.

All present-day estuaries are very young geologically. They were formed during the most recent rise in sea level, which began about 15,000 years ago (Figure 1), and approached their present positions and configurations only within the past few thousand years. At the lowest stand of sea level, about 15,000 years ago, the level of the sea was approximately 95–125 m below its present position (Emery and Uchupi, 1972; Dillon and Oldale, 1977) and the shoreline lay near the edge of the continental shelf. At that time estuaries were rare and small, being confined to the heads of valleys carved into the outer shelf and upper slope (Russell, 1967; Schubel, 1971). As the glaciers retreated the sea rose and advanced across the continental shelf. From about 15,000 to 6,000 years ago the rise in sea level was rapid, more than 1 m/century. The rate of transgression of the rising sea across the shelf may have been too rapid for the formation of extensive estuaries on the shelf, particularly bar-built estuaries (Emery and Uchupi, 1972). On the Texas-Louisiana shelf, barrier islands began to form about 6,500 years ago when the rapid postglacial rise of sea level slowed substantially (Figure 1) (Shepard, Phleger, and van Andel, 1960). According to Field and Duane (1976), the Quaternary stratigraphic record of the Atlantic inner continental shelf indicates that barrier islands existed in many places and that they migrated continuously and discontinuously in time and space toward the present shoreline.

Estuaries reached their peak development—in number, size, and complexity—approximately 3,000–5,000 years ago when the rise of sea level slowed perceptibly and the level of the sea had reached nearly its present height. Since then, sea level changes may be due primarily to the subsidence of continental margins under the increased weight of the added overlying water. According to Bloom (1971), local sea level changes in estuaries and salt marshes may be controlled by the balance between isostatic adjustment and buildup by sedimentation. This isostatic adjustment is greater where shelves are wide than where shelves are narrow.

Although estuaries were small and rare during the last lowstand of sea level, there were still extensive low salinity areas of the coastal ocean where estuarine-dependent organisms could, and apparently did, grow and reproduce. Over much of the eastern seaboard of the United States, at least as far north as 50°N, rainfall plus snow melt minus evaporation may have been greater during

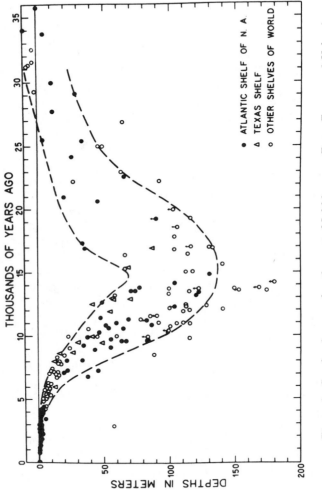

Figure 1. Sea level curve for the past 35,000 years. From Emery and Uchupi (1972).

the last glacial period than at present. According to Manabe and Hahn's model (1977), the excess of rainfall plus snow melt minus evaporation between glacial and interglacial periods was between 0.1 and 0.2 cm/day.

Figure 2 shows the percentage of the total area of the Atlantic continental shelf of the United States from Palm Beach, Florida (27°N) to Nantucket, Massachusetts (42°N) that has been submerged over the past 30,000 years. In making the determinations, the inshore boundary of the shelf has been taken as the present ocean shoreline, excluding estuaries. The data show that between about 17,000 years ago and 13,000 years ago the shelf was nearly completely emerged, and that for approximately 50% of the past 30,000 years, less than half of the continental shelf has been submerged, and therefore available for development of estuaries. For much of the past 30,000 years, sea level has either been too low or the rate of rise and fall so great that it is unlikely that there were significant estuaries on the Atlantic continental margin of the United States. And yet "estuarine" species have been with us for far longer times.

Sea Level and Estuaries During the Past Million Years

Sea level fluctuations are well documented over approximately the past 35,000 years, but levels before that time are poorly known. These older sea levels are most commonly inferred from paleotemperature indicators such as microorganisms (Ericson, Ewing, and Wollin, 1963; Bandy, 1967; and others),

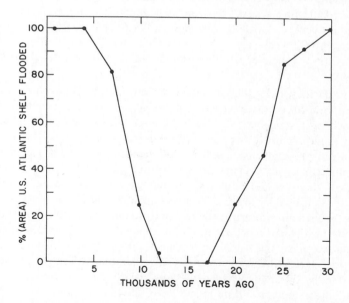

Figure 2. The percentage of the United States Atlantic Continental Shelf submerged over the past 30,000 years. The present ocean shoreline was taken as the inner boundary of the shelf.

and oxygen isotopes in the remains of calcareous organisms (Emiliani, 1955, 1964, 1966; Broecker, 1965; and others) and in ice cores (Dansgaard et al., 1971). Lack of any well-documented time scale is troublesome. Since the dates are beyond the range of radiocarbon, longer-lived isotopes (Broecker, 1965), magnetic reversals (Cox, Doell, and Dalrymple, 1964; Ericson and Wollin, 1968), and the Milankovitch curve of solar radiation must be used. The precision and accuracy attainable with these techniques are relatively poor.

Despite the uncertainties in the absolute time scale earlier than 35,000 years ago, the data indicate that for at least the past million years the earth's climate has been characterized by an alternation of glacial and interglacial episodes, marked in the northern hemisphere by waxing and waning of continental ice sheets, and in both hemispheres by rising and falling temperatures. These have been accompanied by large fluctuations in sea level (National Academy of Sciences, 1975).

The present interglacial period—the Holocene—which has now lasted for more than 10,000 years, represents a climatic regime that has been relatively rare during at least the past million years, most of which have been occupied by colder glacial regimes. During only about 8% of the past million years has the earth experienced climates as warm or warmer than the present. The most recent analog of the warm, ice-free conditions of the Holocene occurred about 125,000 years ago, the Eemian interglacial. The warmest part of that period lasted approximately 10,000 years and was followed by the abrupt onset of a cold glacial period lasting several thousands of years. The interval between this post-Eemian event (c. 115,000 years ago) and the most recent glacial maximum 15,000 to 18,000 years ago was characterized by marked fluctuation superimposed on a generally declining temperature (National Academy of Sciences, 1975).

Interglacial periods similar to the Holocene and the Eemian have occurred on the average approximately every 100,000 years over about the past million years. Each has lasted about 10,000 ± 2,000 years and has been followed by a glacial maximum. During this period of about one million years, fluctuations of northern hemisphere glaciers and the Antarctic ice sheet have caused variations in the position of sea level on the order of 100 m (National Academy of Sciences, 1975). There is no evidence to suggest that sea level has, in the past million years, been significantly lower than it was about 15,000 years ago.

At the present time the earth has an estimated $26 \times 10^6 \text{m}^3$ of glacial ice (Flint, 1969) which covers about 10% of the land. This ice is concentrated in the Greenland ice sheet, the Antarctic ice sheet, small glaciers in the Arctic, and small alpine glaciers. Approximately 10% of the total volume of glacial ice is contained in the Greenland ice sheet (Bauer, 1955), and less than 1% in Arctic and small alpine glaciers. More than 89% of the total is contained in the huge Antarctic ice sheet centered roughly on the South Pole (Bardin and Suyetora, 1967). If the Antarctic ice sheet were to melt entirely, sea level would rise by about 55 m. The actual rise would be less because the sea floor would adjust isostatically under the added weight of the meltwater. The time lag required for this eustatic readjustment may be several thousands of years.

Factors Controlling the Life Span of Modern Estuaries

Estuaries during the Quaternary originated and their distribution was controlled primarily by climatic changes associated with alternating glacial and interglacial periods and their resulting eustatic fluctuations in sea level. Once formed, the life span of an estuary is controlled by subsequent sea level changes which may be primarily local in nature, produced by a balance between isostatic adjustment and sedimentation. A rise in sea level prolongs the lifetime; a fall shortens it. However, if sea level remains relatively constant, as it has for the past several thousand years, the life span of most estuaries will depend upon sediment inputs controlled by the higher frequency climatic fluctuations associated with seasonal changes of annual period, and upon less frequent, but larger-scale weather events such as floods and hurricanes. If sea level were to rise, the lifetimes of existing estuaries would be prolonged, but in that case many large cities would be inundated if the rise exceeded a few meters. If sea level were to fall, estuarine lifetimes would be shortened, and many important ports would be inaccessible without major dredging projects. Substantial eustatic rises of sea level over a few decades could occur only from calving of large quantities of glacial ice from Antarctica into the Southern Ocean. Hollin (1969) estimated that a large surge of ice from Wilkes Land could raise sea level by as much as 17 m in less than a century. But, longer-term changes—changes over thousands of years are almost certain—and local changes due to isostatic adjustment are occurring.

Our estuaries and adjacent coastal areas literally live under the sword of Damocles. Even relatively minor changes in sea level would dramatically affect man's uses of estuaries. A 10 m drop in sea level would expose more than 75% of the area of the Chesapeake Bay estuarine system. On the other hand, a 10 m rise in sea level would inundate most of the world's major seaports. The future trend of eustatic sea level changes is unclear. But change is the order of nature and any change is almost certain to be bad for man.

The life span of an estuary is determined primarily by the stability of relative sea level—the resultant of local sea level changes and the sedimentation rate. The role of climate in the evolution of estuaries does not stop with sea level fluctuations. Climate also has a major effect on the rates of weathering of rocks, on sediment yields, and on sediment inputs to estuaries. Man's activities can also greatly affect sediment yields and, as a result, sediment inputs to estuaries. Streams that drain farmlands frequently carry more than 10 times as much sediment as streams that drain equivalent areas of forest land. Mining and urbanization can increase sediment yields by 10 to 1,000 times (Meade, 1969).

One of the best-documented case studies of sedimentary processes and the identification of the characteristic periods of those that control sedimentation of an estuary was made in upper Chesapeake Bay. During most years more than

70% of the total annual fluvial input of suspended sediment, which averages about 1 x 10^6 metric tons, is discharged by the Susquehanna River in a period of a few weeks during the normal spring freshet (Schubel, 1968a, b; 1972a, b; Biggs, 1970). This annual event occupies less than 10% of the year. Approximately 75% of this input of sediment is deposited in the upper 25–30 km of the estuary, above the limit of sea salt intrusion during the freshet (Schubel, 1968a, b; 1972b). During the rest of the year this material is reworked and redistributed by tidal currents and wind waves (Schubel, 1968a, c; 1972b). This pattern is also typical of the upper reaches of the larger tributaries of Chesapeake Bay (Nichols, 1972) and probably of many submerged river valley estuaries in temperate regions, although few have been studied in as much detail as the Chesapeake Bay estuarine system.

Infrequently this annual cycle of sedimentation is interrupted by an episode in which unusual weather conditions produce an extremely large river flow. Such "floods" can have a dramatic impact on the average sedimentation rate of estuaries. The only well-documented case study of the effects of a flood on an estuary is the chronicle of the effects of Tropical Storm *Agnes* (June 1972) on Chesapeake Bay and its subsequent return to normal conditions (Chesapeake Research Consortium, 1977). From measurements of the concentrations of suspended sediment in the mouth of the Susquehanna and river-flow data, Schubel (1974, 1977) estimated that during the 10-day period following passage of the storm, the Susquehanna discharged more than 31 x 10^6 metric tons of sediment into the upper bay—more than 30 times the average annual input. An analysis of X-radiographs of cores taken a few weeks after the flood indicated that the thickness of the *Agnes* layer in the upper 25–30 km of the Chesapeake Bay—Tolchester to Turkey Point—ranged from about 10 to 30 cm and averaged about 15 cm (Schubel and Zabawa, 1977). The average sedimentation rate in this region during normal years is about 0.7 cm/yr (Schubel, 1968a; Hirschberg and Schubel, in prep.). In 1972 the upper Chesapeake Bay "aged" by approximately 30 years in 10 days as a result of a flood with a recurrence interval of 200 years. Since estimates of recurrence intervals are based upon peak flows, they are not very diagnostic indicators of the geological importance of floods. The sediment discharge of a river in flood is dependent on a number of factors in addition to peak flow. These include the intensity and distribution of the associated rainfall, the season, and the total volume of water discharged during the event.

Using Pb^{210} dating, we have recently been able to confirm this estimate of the thickness of the *Agnes* deposit and have discovered a second even larger deposit that correlates well with the great flood of 1936. The 1936 flood was not the result of a major storm like *Agnes* but was caused by a combination of two smaller storms and the rapid melting of a deep snow and ice cover over much of the drainage basin of the Susquehanna. Our Pb^{210} data indicate a thickness of 30 cm for this deposit, almost twice that of the *Agnes* layer (Hirschberg and Schubel, in prep.). Although the peak flow in March 1936 was only 2.2 x 10^4 m^3/sec (Grover, 1937) compared with the peak flow during *Agnes* of 3.2 x 10^4

m³/sec, the total integrated discharge was greater because the 1936 flood extended over a longer time. The total discharge of the 1936 flood was 1.6×10^{10} m³ compared with 1.2×10^{10} m³ for *Agnes*. The larger freshwater input, combined with the possibility of ice rafting of sediment, may explain the larger sediment input in 1936.

These two episodes can account for at least half of all the sediment deposited in the upper Chesapeake Bay since 1900. Examination of the earlier stream flow data indicates that at least three more large floods occurred between 1787 and 1900 (Tice, 1968). These floods presumably had similar impacts on the upper bay, and probably discharged more sediment, because the lower reaches of the Susquehanna River were not dammed until 1900, and because sediment yields have decreased as a result of soil conservation practices. From these data and others, it is apparent that the infilling of the upper Chesapeake Bay is dominated by episodic floods (Figure 3). Episodic events can arise from a large

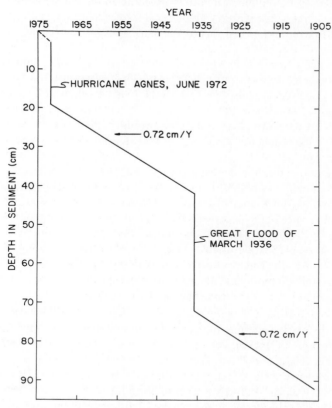

Figure 3. An interpretation of sedimentation at a site in the northern Chesa-peake Bay (39°23'N, 76°05'W) based upon the observed distribution of Pb²¹⁰ (not shown). The two storm events contributed about one-half of the total sediment accumulation since 1900.

variety of weather conditions and may range from the annual freshet to floods with recurrence intervals of from decades to centuries.

Estuaries in the Geological Record

Investigators who have attempted to identify estuarine deposits in the geological record have relied primarily upon paleontological and geomorphological criteria, although some attempts have been made to use geochemical indicators of paleosalinity, e.g., the boron content of clay minerals (Degens et al., 1957; 1958), calcium-to-iron ratio in phosphorite (Nelson, 1967), and iron-to-manganese ratio in ferromanganese nodules (Price, 1967). Using chemical criteria, investigators have sometimes been able to distinguish between freshwater, brackish water, and marine deposits (Eagar et al., 1969), but have failed to identify unequivocally true estuarine deposits (Müller, 1969; Gruber, 1969). Boron data, for example, when interpreted as an indicator of paleosalinity are only of relative value. Often a gradational sequence of increasing marine influence is discovered (Lerman, 1966) which is internally consistent, but can not be ''calibrated'' for freshwater and true marine conditions.

Primary depositional features such as ripple marks, laminations, and graded bedding, and secondary structures such as worm tubes, animal tracks, and gas cavities are also of little help (Van Stratten and Kuenen, 1958; Twenhofel, 1932; Moore and Scruton, 1957) in identifying estuarine deposits in the geological record. No primary or secondary depositional structures have been identified that are common to all estuarine deposits and are peculiar to estuaries.

Modern estuarine deposits are characterized by extremely variable and complex structures which form in response to complicated physical and biological processes (Moore and Scruton, 1957; Oertel, 1973; Howard and Frey, 1973). The spatial variability is sometimes so great that it is impossible to correlate features in X-rays of cores taken sequentially "at" the same station from an anchored vessel (Schubel and Zabawa, 1977; Hirschberg and Schubel, in prep.) where the only displacement is a result of swinging of the vessel on her anchor. The physical and biological processes that produce many, perhaps most, structures observed in modern estuarine deposits are obscure.

Composition and texture have little diagnostic value in delineating estuarine deposits. Attempts to use statistical parameters of grain size to distinguish features of ancient bar-built "estuarine" deposits have been somewhat successful (Hails and Hoyt, 1969), but in general the present is a poor key to estuaries of the past. A great many estuaries are characterized by fine-grained sediments, but the sediments accumulating in others are dominated by sands (Folger, 1972). Modern estuarine deposits are typically high in organic matter, but extremely variable (Folger, 1972). Reducing conditions are common, but not distinctive.

Perhaps the most diagnostic indicators of ancient estuarine deposits are the remains of "estuarine" organisms such as the common American oyster, *Crassostrea virginica,* and the clams, *Mercenaria mercenaria* and *Mya arenaria.* Today, these organisms are truly estuarine in the sense that they spend their entire lives within estuaries. In the past however, they must have lived and reproduced in shallow brackish open coastal areas. Some investigators (Hudson, 1963a, b; Williams, 1960) have been able to delimit brackish conditions in the geological record through application of "bio-facies maps" and "indicator species." These estuarine fossils have often not been in life position, and frequently occur in nearly mono-specific shell layers, indicative of a stressed environment in which there are many individuals of a few species.

Those areas identified in the geologic record as having low salinity conditions are estuaries only in the broad sense of nineteenth century geologists (Judd, 1873, 1878) where brackish implies low and fairly stable salinity, but never as stable as in the open sea. The Great Estuarine Series (Middle Jurassic) of the inner Hebrides is an example. The primary criteria for establishing its estuarine character were clear evidence of deposition in shallow water and a brackish water fauna that was impoverished in numbers of species, but very abundant in numbers of individuals (Hudson, 1963a). Many modern open coastal, brackish environments would meet these criteria, but are not *estuaries.*

Identification of estuarine deposits in the record is apt to be made even more difficult by post-depositional events. Not only are the clues few and equivocal, but if the deposits were formed while sea level was still rising, the deposits would have been vigorously reworked on the next fall of sea level. The alternating transgressions and regressions of the sea tend to obliterate most near-surface strandline deposits. The deeper the burial of the deposits before the next pass of the oscillating sea, the greater the chances of preservation in the record. The Holocene sedimentary deposits of Lavaca Bay, Texas (Wilkinson and Byrne, 1977) are made up of a transgressive fluvial-deltaic-estuarine sequence deposited during the past 10,000 years. Whether or not these deposits will be preserved is moot.

A considerable amount of controversy surrounds the fate of barrier islands and bar-built estuaries formed during previous lowstands of the sea (Field and Duane, 1976; 1977; Otvos, 1977). There is little agreement as to whether barrier islands formed attached to the mainland or as isolated bars, and whether or not they were able to migrate across the continental shelf in response to the transgressing sea. The only point that appears to be agreed upon is that no complete record has been found of any Holocene bar-built estuary on the continental shelf.

Relatively large-scale elongate depressions observed in sub-bottom profiling records of the Atlantic shelf are paleo-river channels that represent fluvial erosional features relict from a previous lowstand of the sea. The Hudson shelf valley is a good example, and is the locus of a series of estuaries of the Hudson River during the last rise in sea level. Sediments along the axis of the valley today are not estuarine, however (Emery and Uchupi, 1972), and the trough may be the site of active sediment transport. Some evidence of intact deltaic sequences at the outer edge of the shelf has been found (Emery and Uchupi, 1972). Here the rapid sea-level rise in relation to the steep topography may have aided preservation.

Clearly, it will be extremely difficult to delimit unequivocally estuarine deposits from other shallow marine and brackish deposits in the geological record because of their limited areal extent, the ephemeral character of estuaries, the paucity of distinctive sedimentological, geochemical, and paleontological features, and the locations of estuaries near the strandline where they are vigorously reworked by waves and currents. In 1967 Klein pointed out that the details for comparing modern and ancient sedimentary sequences of estuaries were lacking. More than a decade later, this observation is still true. Emery and Uchupi (1972) are correct in pointing out that far more effort has gone into making detailed studies of the sediments of individual estuaries than into either comparing results from a variety of estuaries with similar physical and geological characteristics, or into critical evaluations of processes.

The estuarine graveyard is a palimpsest and most of its tales have been obliterated.

Importance of Estuaries to the Marine Ecosystem

It has been pointed out by a variety of investigators (Hedgpeth, 1957; McHugh, 1966, 1967; Kutkuhn, 1966; Lyles, 1965; Smith, 1966; Tabb, 1966; Talbot, 1966; and many others) that many commercially and recreationally important finfishes and shellfishes are estuarine-dependent. According to McHugh (1966) most of the United States' domestic marine fishery harvest is taken in estuarine waters. Lyles (1965) estimated that twelve kinds of fishes made up more than 81% of the total value of the commercial catch in 1963, and more than 78% of its total weight. Most of these species spend considerable parts of their lives in estuaries, and for the most part, are caught in estuarine waters. Using the same basic data, McHugh (1966) estimated that of the first six generic kinds—by landed value—of marine animals landed by U.S. commercial fishermen in 1963, five were predominantly estuarine, or estuarine-dependent. Shrimp, salmon, oysters, menhaden, and crabs accounted for more than 50% of the total landed value and about 55% of the landed weight of all marine and fresh water commercial landings. However, McHugh cautioned that not everything included in these statistics is estuarine. Crabs, for example, included Alaskan king crabs which are neither estuarine, nor estuarine-dependent.

Almost two-thirds of the total value of the 1966 U.S. commercial catch and much of the marine sport catch was composed of species that "... spend at least part of their lives within land-bound estuaries" (McHugh, 1966). In 1970, 70% (by weight) of the total U.S. commercial and recreational fisheries landings of 6.5 billion pounds were estuarine-dependent (McHugh, 1976). These included shrimp, salmon, oysters, clams, menhaden, and flounders. In the Gulf of Mexico, estuarine-dependent species accounted for 98% (by weight) and 93%

(by value) of the commercial catch in 1970 (McHugh, 1976). According to Smith (1966), "...at least 65% of our Nation's commercial fish and shellfish and most marine sport species inhabit the estuarine environment during all or part of their life cycle."

In a more recent paper McHugh (in press, a) questioned the basis from which he and others had inferred estuarine-dependence. He pointed out that most migratory living resources of estuaries spend considerable parts of their lives also in the open sea, and thus could also be classified as ocean-dependent. He showed that fishery resources of an important estuary like Chesapeake Bay can be classified overwhelmingly either as estuarine-dependent or as ocean-dependent, depending upon which criterion is applied. He remarked that these results supported the often-repeated assertion that statistics can be used to prove anything. In the same paper McHugh also showed that marine fishery production along parts of the United States coasts that lack major estuaries can be equally as large as in Chesapeake Bay or the Gulf of Mexico, where estuarine and salt-marsh development are very great.

McHugh (in press, b) noted the dynamic, ever-changing characteristics of estuaries, and the evolutionary processes that eventually might lead to their demise. He pointed out that at least one author had questioned the merits of management of estuarine fishery stocks, like the hard clam (*Mercenaria mercenaria*), which were fated to diminish greatly in abundance, if not to disappear entirely, in the normal course of events.

The primary importance of estuaries in the life histories of many fishes seems to be as nursery areas. They appear to be less important as spawning grounds (Haedrich and Hall, 1976). However, as Walford (1966) has pointed out, the presence of large numbers of larval and juvenile fishes in estuaries is not conclusive evidence that estuaries are essential as nursery grounds for these species.

Much of the difficulty in assessing the importance of estuaries for the origin, survival, and maintenance of fish and shellfish populations stems from the lack of precision in the use of the terms estuary and estuarine environment. McHugh (1966), defining any area with surface salinity below 33.5 ‰ as estuarine, distinguished between inshore and offshore estuaries. Ketchum (1951) defined an estuary as "...a body of water in which the river water mixes with and measurably dilutes sea water." Smith (1966) defined the estuarine zone as an "...environmental system consisting of the estuary and those transitional areas consistently influenced or affected by water from the estuary." All of these definitions lead to the inclusion of large areas of open coastal waters within the estuarine zone. McHugh's (1966) definition even includes much of the North Pacific as an offshore estuary.

The number of kinds of truly estuarine organisms must be small. According to Hedgpeth (1957), truly estuarine organisms "...are those that seem to require the fluctuations of the estuarine environment for their optimum development." McHugh (1966) has pointed out that some sessile organisms are truly estuarine, but that "... hardly any fish is an estuarine animal in the conventional narrow sense."

It is clear that many species of fishes and shellfishes are dependent on low salinity waters for spawning and development during early life stages. It has not been established unequivocally however, that these species are dependent on estuaries for survival. Quaternary estuaries have provided attractive sites for the concentration of large numbers of individuals of a relatively small number of species, many of which are very important to man.

The importance of estuaries in the evolution of life has also been controversial. Opinions range from Annandale's (1922) contention that estuaries are the last refuge of spent species to Bernal's (1961) statement that life may have originated in estuaries. Both of these views are probably too extreme. According to Hedgpeth (1966), it is not only unlikely that life originated in the estuary, but the fluctuating estuarine environment may have provided a braking mechanism that retards the evolutionary process. There is no compelling evidence to indicate that estuaries have played an important evolutionary role for marine species. This is not surprising in view of the ephemeral character of individual estuaries and their low frequency of occurrence, at least during the Quaternary. One might argue that estuaries may have played a more important role in the evolution of freshwater organisms since they provide the only continuous transition zone between marine and freshwater environments.

Conclusions

Estuaries have probably been relatively rare during the past million years, and perhaps for much longer. According to Russell (1967) "... estuaries have been uncommon features during most of the earth's history." Not only are individual estuaries ephemeral features on geological time scales with lifetimes measured in scant thousands of years, but the conditions that favor the formation of estuaries have been relatively uncommon, at least over the past million years. Existing data do not support Hedgpeth's (1957) statement that although an individual estuary may be a transitory feature on a geological time scale, the estuarine environment as such has probably persisted throughout that part of time in which life has occurred. Estuaries have not been persistent geomorphological features throughout geological time; low salinity, open coastal areas have been.

Some well-intentioned but over-zealous environmentalists have laid great stress on the importance of estuaries for the survival of many important species of fishes and shellfishes. It would appear that such evaluations cannot be justified; which is not to say that estuaries are unimportant.

Estuaries are of the very greatest importance; not to the survival of species, or to the maintenance of the entire marine ecosystem, but to man. Of all the organisms which use estuaries, man makes the most varied demands on them. Man is clearly the most estuarine-dependent organism in the biosphere. The estuarine zone is approximately twice as densely populated as the rest of the nation. Man uses estuaries for activities which may be, and indeed frequently are, in conflict. He uses them for their extractable resources, both organic and inorganic; for shipping and transportation; for military activities; as a transient receiver for his human and industrial wastes; as a source of cooling water for power plants; and he uses them for recreation and re-creation.

Wise management of the coastal environment may have little effect on the span of time an estuary occupies in the geological record. That will be determined primarily by climatic events, although poor soil conservation practices throughout an estuary's drainage basin may increase the sediment yield and the rate of infilling of the estuary and shorten its lifetime by a factor of two or more. There are more serious consequences of the absence of sound estuarine management. Without effective management the biologically and recreationally useful life of an estuary can easily fall short of its geological life by an order of magnitude. Such negligent shortening of the useful life of an estuary may not spell disaster for estuarine-dependent shellfish and finfish, but for estuarine-dependent man it surely would be a serious loss.

Acknowledgments

We are indebted to B. Kinsman, J. L. McHugh, P. K. Weyl, and G. C. Williams for their helpful suggestions. Preparation of this report was supported by the Rockefeller Foundation and the New York Sea Grant Institute. David Hirschberg is a Jessie Smith Noyes Fellow of the Marine Sciences Research Center. Contribution 213 of the Marine Sciences Research Center, State University of New York.

References

1. Annandale, N. 1922. The Marine Element in the Fauna of the Ganges. Bijdr. Dierk (Feest Num. Max. Weber) pp. 143-154.

2. Bandy, O. L. 1967. Foraminiferal definition of the boundaries of the Pleistocene in southern California, U.S.A., pp. 27-49. *In* Mary Sears (ed.), Progress in Oceanography, v. 4, The Quaternary History of the Ocean Basins, Pergamon Press, New York.

3. Bardin, V. I., and I. A. Suyetora. 1967. Basic morphometric characteristics for Antarctica and budget of the Antarctic ice cover. Tokyo Nat. Science Mus. Jare Scientif. Repts., Spec. Issue 1:92.

4. Bauer, A. 1955. Über die in der heutigen Vergletscherung der Erde als Eis gebundene Wassermasse. Eiszeitalter Gegenwart 6:60

5. Bernal, J. D. 1961. Origin of life on the shore of the ocean; physical and chemical conditions determining the first appearance of the biological processes, pp. 95-118. *In* Mary Sears (ed.), Oceanography. Amer. Assoc. Adv. Sci. Pub. 67.

6. Biggs, R. B. 1970. Sources and distribution of suspended sediment in Northern Chesapeake Bay. Marine Geol. 9:187-201.

7. Bloom, A. L. 1971. Glacial-eustatic and isostatic controls of sea level since the last glaciation, pp. 355-380. *In* K. K. Turekian (ed.), Late Cenozoic Glacial Ages. Yale Univ. Press, New Haven, Conn.

8. Broecker, W. 1965. Isotope geochemistry and the Pleistocene climatic record, pp. 737-753. *In* H. E. Wright, Jr. and D. G. Frey (eds.), The Quaternary of the United States. Princeton Univ. Press, Princeton, N.J.

9. Caspers, H. 1967. Estuaries: analysis of definitions and biological considerations, pp. 6-8. *In* G. H. Lauff (ed.), Estuaries. Amer. Assoc. Adv. Sci. Pub. 83, Washington, D.C.

10. Chesapeake Research Consortium. 1977. The effects of Tropical Storm Agnes on the Chesapeake Bay estuarine system. CRC Publication No. 54, The Johns Hopkins Univ. Press, Baltimore, Md. 639 pp.

11. Cox, A., R. R. Doell, and G. B. Dalrymple. 1964. Reversals of the earth's magnetic field. Science 144:1537-1543.

12. Dansgaard, W., S. J. Johnson, H. B. Clausen, and C. C. Langway, Jr. 1971. Climatic record revealed by the Camp Century Ice Core, pp. 37-56. *In* K. K. Turekian (ed.), The Late Cenozoic Glacial Ages. Yale Univ. Press, New Haven, Conn.

13. Degens, E. T., E. G. Williams, K. L. Keith. 1957. Environmental studies of carboniferous sediments, Part I: Geochemical criteria for differentiating marine from fresh water shales. Bull. Am. Assoc. Pet. Geol. 41:2427-2455.

14. _____. 1958. Environmental studies of carboniferous sediments, Part II: Application of geochemical criteria. Bull. Am. Assoc. Pet. Geol. 42:981-997.

15. Dillon, W. P., and R. N. Oldale. 1977. Adjustment of the late Quaternary sea-level rise curve on the basis of recognition of large glacio-tectonic movements of the continental shelf south of New England, p. 951. *In* Ann. Meeting Geol. Soc. Amer. Abstracts with Programs, v. 9, no. 7.

16. Eagar, R. M. C., and D. A. Spears. 1969. Boron content in relation to organic carbon and to paleosalinity in certain British upper carboniferous sediments. Nature 209:177-181.

17. Emery, K. O. 1967. Estuaries and lagoons in relation to continental shelves, pp. 9-11. *In* G. H. Lauff (ed.), Estuaries. Amer. Assoc. Adv. Sci. Pub. 83, Washington, D.C.

18. Emery, K. O., and E. Uchupi. 1972. Western North Atlantic Ocean: Topography, rocks, structure, water, life, and sediments. Amer. Assoc. of Petroleum Geologists Mem. 17, Tulsa, Oklahoma. 532 p.

19. Emiliani, C. 1955. Pleistocene temperatures. Jour. Geology 63:538-578.

20. _____. 1964. Paleotemperature analysis of the Caribbean cores A254-BR-C and CP-28. Geol. Soc. Amer. Bull. 75:129-144.

21. _____. 1966. Paleotemperature analysis of the Caribbean cores P6304-8 and P6304-9 and a generalized temperature curve for the past 425,000 years. Jour. Geology 74:109-126.

22. Ericson, D. B., M. Ewing, and G. Wollin. 1963. Pliocene-Pleistocene boundary in deep-sea sediments. Science 139:727-737.

23. Ericson, D. B., and G. Wollin. 1968. Pleistocene climates and chronology in deep-sediments. Science 162: 1227.

24. Field, M. E., and D. B. Duane. 1976. Post-Pleistocene history of the United States inner continental shelf: significance to origin of barrier islands. Geol. Soc. Amer. Bull. 87:691-702.

25. _____. 1977. Reply to Otvos, E. G. Discussion Post-Pleistocene history of the United States inner continental shelf: signficance to origin of barrier islands. Geol. Soc. Amer. Bull. 88:735-736.

26. Flint, R. F. 1969. Glacial and Pleistocene Geology. John Wiley and Sons, Inc., New York. 553 pp.

27. Folger, D. W. 1972. Characteristics of estuarine sediments of the United States. U.S. Geol. Survey Prof. Paper 742. 94 pp.

28. Grover, N. C. 1937. The floods of March 1936; Part #2 Hudson River to Susquehanna River Region. U.S. Geol. Survey Water Supply Paper #799. 380 pp.

29. Gruber, A. L. 1969. Sedimentary phosphate method for estimating paleosalinity: a paleontological assumption. Science 166:744-746.

30. Haedrich, R. L., and C. A. S. Hall. 1976. Fishes and estuaries. Oceanus 19:55-63.

31. Hails, J. R., and J. H. Hoyt. 1969. The significance and limitations of statistical parameters for distinguishing ancient and modern sedimentary environments of the Lower Georgia coastal plain. Jour. Sed. Petrol. 39:559-580.

32. Hedgpeth, J. W. 1957. Estuaries and lagoons, Part II, Biological aspects, pp. 693-729 of Chapter 23. *In* J. W. Hedgpeth (ed.), Treatise on Marine Ecology and Paleoecology, vol. 1, Ecology. Geol. Soc. Amer. Memoir 67, Washington, D.C.

33. _____. 1966. Aspects of the estuarine ecosystem, pp. 3-11. *In* R. F. Smith, A. H. Swartz, and W. H. Massmann (eds.), A Symposium on Estuarine Fisheries. Amer. Fisheries Soc., Spec. Pub. No. 3, Washington, D.C.

34. Hollin, J. T. 1969. Ice-sheet surges and the geological record. Can. J. Earth Sci. 6:903-910.

35. Howard, J. D., and R. W. Frey. 1973. Characteristic physical and biogenic sedimentary structures in Georgia estuaries. Bull. Am. Assoc. Pet. Geol. 57:1169-1184.

36. Hudson, J. D. 1963a. The ecology and stratigraphical distribution of invertebrate fauna of the Great Estuarine Series. Paleontology 6:327-348.

37. _____. 1963b. The recognition of salinity controlled molluscan assemblages in the Great Estuarine Series (Middle Jurassic) of the Inner Hebrides. Paleontology 6:318-326.

38. Judd, J. W. 1873. The secondary rocks of Scotland. First paper. Quart. J. Geol. Soc. Lond. 29:97-194.

39. _____. 1878. The secondary rocks of Scotland. Third paper. The strata of the western coast and islands. Quart. J. Geol. Soc. Lond. 34:660-743.

40. Ketchum, B. H. 1951. The exchange of fresh and salt water in estuaries. J. Marine Res. 10:18-38.

41. Klein, G. de Vries. 1967. Comparison of recent and ancient tidal flat and estuarine sediments, pp. 207-218. *In* G. H. Lauff (ed.), Estuaries. Amer. Assoc. Adv. Sci. Pub. No. 83, Washington, D.C.

42. Kutkuhn, J. H. 1966. The role of estuaries in the development and perpetuation of commercial shrimp resources, pp. 16-36. *In* R. F. Smith, A. H. Swartz, and W. H. Massman (eds.), A Symposium on Estuarine Fisheries. Amer. Fisheries Soc., Spec. Pub. No. 3, Washington, D.C.

43. Lerman, A. 1966. Boron in clays and the estimation of paleosalinities. Sedimentology 6:267-286.

44. Lyles, C. H. 1965. Fishery statistics of the United States, 1963. U.S. Dept. Interior, Bureau of Commercial Fisheries, Statistical Digest 57. 522 pp.

45. Manabe, S., and D. C. Hahn. 1977. Simulation of the tropical climate of an ice age. Jour. Geophys. Res. 82:3889-3913.

46. McHugh, J. L. 1966. Management of estuarine fisheries, pp. 133-154. *In* R. F. Smith, A. H. Swartz, and W. H. Massman (eds.), A Symposium on Estuarine Fisheries. Amer. Fisheries Soc., Spec. Pub. No. 3, Washington, D.C.

47. _____. 1967. Estuarine nekton, pp. 581-620. *In* G. H. Lauff (ed.), Estuaries. Amer. Assoc. Adv. Sci. Pub. No. 83, Washington, D.C.

48. _____. 1976. Limiting factors affecting commercial fisheries in the Middle Atlantic estuarine area, pp. 149-170. *In* Estuarine Pollution Control and Assessment, Proceedings of a conference, vol. 1 U.S. Environmental Protection Agency, Washington, D.C.

49. _____. (In press, a). Living resources of the United States continental shelf. *In* Symposium on Ecology and Management of the Continental Shelf. 27th Ann. Meeting Am. Inst. Biol. Sci.

50. _____. (In press, b). Conference summary. Bi-State Conference on the Chesapeake Bay. Chesapeake Research Consortium.

51. Meade, R. H. 1969. Errors in using modern stream-load data to estimate natural rates of denudation. Geol. Soc. Amer. Bull. 80:1265-1274.

52. Milliman, J. D., and K. O. Emery. 1968. Sea levels during the past 35,000 years. Science 162:1121-1123.

53. Moore, D. G., and P. C. Scruton. 1957. Minor internal structures of some recent unconsolidated sediments. Bull. Am. Assoc. Pet. Geol. 41:2723-2751.

54. Müller, G. 1969. Sedimentary phosphate method for estimating paleosalintiy: limited applicability. Science 163:812-183.

55. National Academy of Sciences. 1975. Understanding climatic change, a program for action. U.S. Comm. for the Global Atmospheric Research Program, National Research Council, Washington, D.C. 239 pp.

56. Nelson, B. W. 1967. Sedimentary phosphate method for estimating paleosalinity. Science 158:917-920.

57. Nichols, M. M. 1972. Sediments of the James River Estuary, Virginia, pp. 169-212. *In* B. W. Nelson (ed.), Environmental Framework of Coastal Plain Estuaries. Geological Society of America Mem. 133, Boulder, Colorado.

58. Oertel, G. F. 1973. Examination of textures and structures of mud in layered sediments of the entrance of a Georgia tidal inlet. Jour. Sed. Petrol. 43:33-41.

59. Otvos, E. G. 1977. Post-Pleistocene history of the United States inner continental shelf: significance to the origin of barrier islands: Discussion. Geol. Soc. Amer. Bull. 88:734-736.

60. Price, N. B. 1967. Some geochemical observations on iron-manganese nodules from different depth environments. Marine Geol. 5:511-538.

61. Pritchard, D. W. 1967. What is an estuary: physical viewpoint, pp. 3-5. *In* G. H. Lauff (ed.), Estuaries. Amer. Assoc. Adv. Sci. Pub. No. 83, Washington, D.C.

62. Russell, R. J. 1967. Origins of estuaries, pp. 93-99. *In* G. H. Lauff (ed.), Estuaries. Amer. Assoc. Adv. Sci. Pub. No. 83, Washington, D.C.

63. Schubel, J. R. 1968a. Suspended sediment of the northern Chesapeake Bay. Chesapeake Bay Institute Tech. Rept. 35, Ref. 68-2, The Johns Hopkins Univ. Press, Baltimore, Md. 264 pp.

64. _____. 1968b. Suspended sediment discharge of the Susquehanna River at Havre de Grace, Md., during the period April 1, 1966 through March 31, 1967. Chesapeake Sci. 9:131-135.

65. _____. 1968c. Turbidity maximum of the northern Chesapeake Bay. Science 161:1013-1015.

66. _____. 1971. The estuarine environment; estuaries and estuarine sedimentation. Amer. Geol. Institute Short Course Lecture Notes, Washington, D.C. 324 pp. (not numbered consecutively).

67. _____. 1972a. Suspended sediment discharge of the Susquehanna River at Conowingo, Md., during 1969. Chesapeake Sci. 13:53-58.

68. _____. 1972b. Distribution and transportation of suspended sediment in Upper Chesapeake Bay, pp. 151-168. *In* B. W. Nelson (ed.), Environmental Framework of Coastal Plain Estuaries. Geol. Soc. Amer. Mem. 133, Boulder, Colorado.

69. _____. 1974. Effects of Tropical Storm Agnes on the suspended solids of the Northern Chesapeake Bay, pp. 113-132. *In* R. J. Gibbs (ed.), Suspended Solids in Water, Plenum Press, New York.

70. _____. 1977. Effects of Agnes on the suspended sediment of the Chesapeake Bay and contiguous shelf waters, pp. 179-200. *In* Chesapeake Research Consortium, Inc., The Effects of Tropical Storm Agnes on the Chesapeake Bay Estuarine System, The Johns Hopkins Univ. Press, Baltimore, Md.

71. Schubel, J. R., and C. F. Zabawa. 1977. Agnes in the geological record of the Upper Chesapeake Bay, pp. 240-248. *In* Chesapeake Research Consortium, Inc., The Effects of Tropical Storm Agnes on the Chesapeake Bay Estuarine System. The Johns Hopkins Univ. Press, Baltimore, Md.

72. Shepard, F. P., F. B. Phleger, and Tj. H. van Andel, eds. 1960. Recent sediments, northwest Gulf of Mexico. Amer. Assoc. Pet. Geol., Tulsa Oklahoma. 394 pp.

73. Smith, S. H. 1966. Effects of water use activities in Gulf of Mexico and South Atlantic estuarine areas, pp. 93-101. *In* R. F. Smith, A. H. Swartz, and W. H. Massman (eds.), A Symposium on Estuarine Fisheries. Amer. Fisheries Soc., Spec. Pub. No. 3, Washington, D.C.

74. Tabb, D. C. 1966. The estuary as a habitat for spotted sea trout, pp. 59-67. *In* R. R. Smith, A. H. Swartz, and W. H. Massman (eds.), A Symposium on Estuarine Fisheries. Amer. Fisheries Soc., Spec. Pub. No. 3, Washington, D.C.

75. Talbot, G. B. 1966. Estuarine environmental requirements and limiting factors for striped bass, pp. 37-49. *In* R. F. Smith, A. H. Swartz, and W. H. Massman (eds.), A Symposium on Estuarine Fisheries, Amer. Fisheries Soc., Spec. Pub. No. 3, Washington, D.C.

76. Tice, R. H. 1968. Magnitude and frequency of floods in the United States; Part 1-B: North Atlantic slope basins, New York to York River. U.S. Geol. Survey Water Supply Paper #1672. 585 pp.

77. Twenhofel, W. H. 1932. Treatise on Sedimentation. Williams and Wilkens Pub., Second Ed., 926 pp.

78. Vail, P. R., R. M. Mitchum, Jr., S. Thompson III, R. G. Todd, J. B. Sangree, J. M. Widmier, J. N. Bubb, and W. G. Hatlelid. 1977. Seismic stratigraphy and global changes in sea level, pp. 49-212. *In* C. E. Payton (ed.), Seismic Stratigraphy— Applications to Hydrocarbon Exploration. Amer. Assoc. of Petroleum Geologists Mem. 26, Tulsa, Oklahoma.

79. Van Straaten, L. M. J. U., and P. H. Kuenen. 1958. Tidal action as a cause for clay accumulation. Jour. Sed. Petrol. 28:406-413.

80. Walford, L. A. 1966. The estuary as a habitat for fishery organisms, Introduction, p. 15. *In* R. F. Smith, A. H. Swartz, and W. H. Massman, (eds.), A Symposium on Estuarine Fisheries. Amer. Fisheries Soc., Spec. Pub. No. 3, Washington, D.C.

81. Wilkinson, B. H., and J. R. Byrne. 1977. Lavaca Bay—transgressive deltaic sedimentation in a central Texas estuary. Bull. Am. Assoc. Petrol. Geol. 61:527-545.

82. Williams, E. G. 1960. Marine and fresh water folliliferous beds in the Pottsville and Allegheny Group of western Pennsylvania. Jour. Paleontology 34:905-922.

THE IMPACT OF POSSIBLE CLIMATIC CHANGES ON ESTUARINE ECOSYSTEMS

James H. Stone, John W. Day Jr., Leonard M. Bahr Jr.

Department of Marine Sciences
Louisiana State University
Baton Rouge, Louisiana

and

Robert A. Muller

Department of Geography and Anthropology
Louisiana State University
Baton Rouge, Louisiana

Abstract: Solar radiation ultimately controls the heat and water budgets of estuaries. These factors, in turn, determine the amount of sediments and water available to an estuary, the length of the growing season, and the amount of primary and secondary production. For example, full glacial periods have produced a drop in sea level of approximately 100 meters, and this has probably resulted in a reduction of the natural resource productivity (NRP) of estuaries owing to their decreased area, decreased capacity for nutrient entrapment, reduced overall production and capacity to act as a reservoir for freshwater and biota, and reduced ability to dampen environmental perturbations. Scenarios of short-term climatic changes are more relevant to management of estuaries. For example, the total water budget of Louisiana estuaries can vary between a dry and wet year by a factor of 3.5; and human activities, such as agricultural water use, can exacerbate the effects of drought.

Introduction

Our task was to determine the impact of possible climatic change on estuaries. This was difficult for several reasons. For example, predictions of climatic changes are as variable as the weather itself. Also, most scenarios have concentrated on long-term rather than short-term changes (Landsberg, 1976; Mason, 1976) while estuarine ecosystems are extremely ephemeral and change on a relatively short time scale. Despite these limitations, we believe that this effort is worthwhile for the following reasons. First, it indicates the importance of climate in determining estuarine functioning. Second, it identifies various possibilities for climatic change and their interactions with estuarine systems. Third, it helps to understand better how estuaries work. And finally, it should aid us in the management of estuaries because many natural changes reflect man-made changes.

Our predictions are based on a conceptual overview of an estuarine ecosystem in terms of its drainage basin. This overview allows us to identify those estuarine processes that are especially vulnerable to climatic forces and changes. From this we provide a brief description of the climatic background and illustrative data for estuarine basins. We then describe the impacts of future climatic changes by comparing selected estuarine ecosystems with our model and the climatic framework.

Conceptual Overview of Estuarine Ecosystems, and Climatic Influence on These Systems

From a management standpoint, estuarine ecosystems are most fruitfully considered at the conceptual level of the coastal drainage basin (Bahr *et al.* 1977). Thus, we consider an estuarine ecosystem to include bodies of open water, associated wetlands, terrestrial riverine inputs, and human influence within the basin.

It is possible to consider an estuarine basin as four linked components, each representing a different set of processes, and each in part responsible for the present state of a basin, and for the rate at which it changes. The four components are shown in Figure 1: (A) hydrologic processes, or water storage and flow through a basin; (B) natural resource productivity of a basin, or its capacity to support wildlife and fisheries and to perform other work services for man; (C) physiographic processes, particularly those resulting in loss or accretion of natural wetland; and (D) socioeconomic processes, or those human activities and

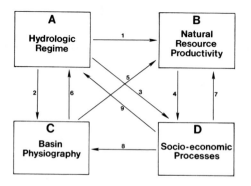

Figure 1. Conceptual overview of estuarine ecosystems.

management decisions impinging directly on natural processes in a basin. Each of these components is briefly described below. More detailed descriptions are given in Bahr *et al.* (1977).

A. Hydrology

The hydrologic regime at any specific site within an estuarine ecosystem basin is ultimately responsible for determining the kind of habitat that develops at that site. The role of hydrology in determining habitat type is primarily mediated via mean water levels and rates of change of water level, and by mean salinities and rates of change of salinity.

The estuarine hydrologic component includes the complex physiographic configuration of a basin, which, together with upstream and downstream water inputs, determines water level, water flow, salinity, and sediment regimes at any point in a basin. These variables in turn constrain the type of habitat which can develop at any site in question.

Short-term climatic changes impinge on the hydrologic regime via changes in precipitation. For example, significant increases or decreases in upstream input of water affect the salinity regime in a basin, causing habitats to shift seaward or landward, respectively.

B. Natural resource productivity (NRP)

Component B represents the natural work services of a basin, or the quality of a basin in terms of its ability to do such things as support important fishery and wildlife species, and to "purify" and store water, all at no cost to man. "Quality" refers to the fact that two areas having similar habitat types can vary greatly in their ability to support consumer organisms.

NRP consists of at least four subcomponents: producers, consumers, a refugium, and water storage. Producers and consumers include all organisms that occur naturally in all habitats within a basin. A particular habitat can be characterized by its carrying capacity for certain species; as its quality diminishes, so does its carrying capacity for organisms valued by man. Diminishing quality leads to changes in community structure, such as the development of populations of undesirable plant and fish species in eutrophic waters.

The natural resource productivity of a basin is thus a function of the particular mix of habitat types, especially the relative proportions of natural wetlands and water bodies, and the quality of each habitat type. Both factors are highly influenced by human perturbation.

Short-term climate changes, such as a change in mean temperature, could affect NRP by altering the water budget and salinity regime (change in evapotranspiration) or by altering the length of the growing season. Even a slight reduction in the growing season can induce drastic declines in agricultural productivity (Lieth, 1973); and the productivity of natural systems would presumably be similarly affected.

C. Physiographic processes

Component C represents the tradeoffs in habitat area that occur within a basin. Over the past several thousand years in coastal Louisiana the wetland habitat has grown, concurrent with deltaic deposition. During the past fifty years this trend has reversed with the loss of natural wetland, either to open water, or to impounded areas used for waterfowl and/or agriculture. Basically three processes cause loss of natural wetland; these are (1) hydrologic changes that result from canalling and impounding, (2) natural subsidence, and (3) erosion.

Short-term climatic change could affect physiographic processes, especially losses in wetlands, via a decline in precipitation over a relatively short time that could result in rapid landward movement of isohalines. In this scenario, swamp forest and freshwater marsh in the path of the encroaching salt water would die, and land would subside before colonization by salt-tolerant plants.

A long-term warming or cooling trend in climate causing positive or negative eustatic change would produce a change in the total area of coastal wetlands and estuaries. In Louisiana, a fall in mean sea level would reduce intertidal area.

D. Socioeconomic factors

Estuarine component D represents human effects at the basin level. Socioeconomic factors have been lumped into five categories:

- The total human population in a basin, its energy and material requirements, and its waste production.
- Commerce and industry such as manufacturing, refining, and retail sales, that occur in a basin, and concommitant waste release.
- Mineral resources in a basin, primarily petroleum and natural gas. Port and navigation facilities are included here. The extraction of minerals and maintenance of navigation channels entails release of waste, as well as extensive disruption of natural habitats (e.g., dredging).
- Fishery and wildlife resources harvested by man both commercially and for sports purposes.
- Finally, all agricultural activity, especially rice and cattle production. This activity also entails significant waste release, especially inorganic nutrients and pesticides.

A short-term climate change, especially a decline in precipitation or an increase in temperature, could reduce freshwater surplus and cause salinity intrusion. Agriculture, mineral extraction, and urban growth in Louisiana estuarine basins are all constrained by freshwater supply, as is habitat for many waterfowl and fish species.

E.   Basin synthesis

Interactions among the four estuarine components of a basin are briefly summarized in the following list of processes, numbered according to the arrows in Figure 1.

1) The hydrologic regime directly affects basin production. For example, water movement stimulates marsh production, and absence of movement due to impoundment inhibits production.
2) The hydrologic regime affects basin physiography, both on a long-term basis by controlling wetland elevation, and on a short-term basis via storm surges that rapidly alter channels and erode sediment.
3) The estuarine hydrologic regime provides "natural work services" in the form of dynamic forces and gradients that are valuable to man. A simple example is the use of flowing water as a sewer.
4) Primary production within a basin supports a food web at the top of which are a variety of extremely valuable wildlife and fishery species. Harvesting these species has a direct effect on the socioeconomic sector of a basin. In addition, water quality requirements of the socioeconomic sector depend on the capability of a basin to recycle and purify water.
5) Basin physiography, or the particular mix of habitat types and areas within a basin, controls total productivity of the system.
6) Basin physiography affects the hydrologic regime via a reciprocal relationship with process number 2. That is, land forms regulate water flow and are in turn altered by the flow.
7) The socioeconomic sector regulates natural resource productivity via management decisions that allow (or prohibit) a wide range of activities in the basin. These decisions range from regulating the harvest of wildlife and fishery species to authorizing the construction of pipeline canals in wetlands.
8) Socioeconomic effects on the physiography of a basin include dredging, filling, and various other construction activities in wetlands. Rapid loss of wetlands in Louisiana estuarine basins during the last fifty years includes direct removal of marsh and swamp, and indirect losses due to impoundment, and other occurrences.
9) Socioeconomic effects on the hydrologic regime of a basin are similar to process number 8, but refer specifically to alterations in water flow due to canal and channel construction and comparable projects.

Possible climate changes and their effects on each estuarine component ramify through an estuarine basin ecosystem via these nine major processes.

Our conceptual model suggests, in theory, that short-term changes in climate affect estuarine ecosystems more than do long-term changes. Potential long-term changes are too remote to be of interest for estuarine management; and estuarine systems presumably adapt to slow changes in climate. Nonetheless, having established our theoretical framework, it is now appropriate to consider the climatic background in order to establish whether long- and short-term patterns are evident, and to examine these data patterns in selected estuarine ecosystems.

Climatic Background: Long- and Short-Term Variations

Ideas about climatic variation have undergone spectacular changes over the last five to ten years. Quasi-periodic components of climatic variation with frequencies of about 100,000, 20,000, and 2,500 years have been tentatively identified, and there is confusing evidence of short-term climatic variation in terms of months, seasons, or a few years (U.S. Committee for the Global Atmospheric Research Program, USCGARP, 1975). Recent examples of the latter include the extraordinary cold winter of 1976-77 across the eastern United States, and the persistent severe drought during 1976 and 1977 over much of the western United States. This section briefly reviews recent ideas about quasi-periodic components of climatic variation, and then focuses on shorter-term climatic variation during the twentieth century, especially in the deltaic and estuarine coastal regions of Louisiana.

The main fluctuations of global climates over the past million years include the fundamental glacial-interglacial cycle with a wavelength of about 100,000 years and a quasi-periodic variability with a wavelength of about 20,000 years. The Eemian Interglacial (about 125,000 BP) was about as warm as the present interglacial (Holocene). There is also some evidence of an even shorter quasi-periodic variability with a wavelength of about 2,500 years. Variability at wavelengths of about 100,000 and 20,000 years has been related to systematic variations of the earth's orbit about the sun, producing seasonal and latitudinal changes in the distribution of global solar radiation income, but variability with a wavelength of about 2,500 years has not been similarly related to the earth's orbit. Since the full glacial conditions associated with the Wisconsin glacial stage about 18,000 BP, there has been very rapid warming beginning about 15,000 BP, a brief but very sudden Younger Dryas event at about 10,500 BP (when there was much forest destruction in Europe within less than a century), and the Hypsithermal Interval about 5,000 to 7,000 BP, with the mildest temperatures of the entire Holocene.

An elaborate computer model has been used to estimate global climates and vegetation patterns during full glacial conditions about 18,000 BP (CLIMAP Project Members, 1976). Sea level was 85 to 130 meters lower than at present, so the estuaries of southern Louisiana were shifted southward to the outer continental shelf where poorly dissected flat or gently sloping topography probably resulted in less estuarine area than at present. Surface-water temperatures of the northern Gulf of Mexico in summer were about 2°C lower than present. The climate of coastal Louisiana would probably have been classified as humid subtropical, but with harsher polar outbreaks during winter. During the Hypsi-thermal Interval, in contrast, sea level was somewhat higher, with the estuaries shifted toward the north. Mean temperatures were probably slightly higher than at present, but polar outbreaks must also have been less severe. The subtropical climate would still be considered humid, but precipitation during winter and spring was less than at present.

Temperature variation in Europe over the last 1,000 years is based on historical reconstructions of alpine glacier snouts and wine production. Two outstanding features have been identified. The first is the Little Ice Age which occurred between about 1400 and 1850; temperatures averaged about 1.5°C colder than the present. The colder climates of Europe undoubtedly resulted in widespread—but not very well understood—social and economic dislocations. The second feature is the thermal maximum of the 1940's with the highest average temperatures of the last 1,000 years. However, cooling probably began about 1945 and recent data suggest that this has leveled off.

Future projections are extremely controversial. They range from a "rapid" return to glacial or near-glacial conditions in a few hundred years, through periodic climatic variations but wih no significant trends, to increasing warmth due to the ever-increasing CO_2 atmospheric content. Because social and economic systems are based on present climatic patterns, almost any climatic trend toward warmer or colder should be considered dangerous in terms of global economic and political stability.

Shorter-term climatic variations also produce several environmentai and economic impacts. Figure 2 shows monthly temperature and precipitation varia-bility for southeastern Louisiana from 1911 through June 1977; the data repre-sent a regional or divisional average of about six to ten stations. The departure, or deviation, of each month from its respective mean for the 1931-1960 period is shown in Figure 2A; for example, in January 1940 the temperature was 6.7°C below the normal and in January 1950, it was 6.7°C above the normal. Figure 2B illustrates some of the short-term variation of temperature by a six-month running average; thus, for the six months ending with February 1932, the monthly temperature mean was about 2.8°C above the 1931-1960 normals, and in the six months ending with January 1977, it was 4.5°C below the same normals. There are two outstanding features in Figure 2B. One is the downward "step" of temperature beginning in the fall of 1957, persisting to the present with the exception of the winters of 1971-72 and 1973-74. The second feature is the tendency for clusters of months to be warmer or colder than normal, with the data series suggesting a frequency of about 10 to 14 months.

The frequency and duration of subfreezing temperatures are critical to certain vegetation species and biological activities. Figure 3A shows the number of freeze days across southern Louisiana during the winter of 1969-70, a winter with temperatures much below normal, and Figure 3B shows similar data for the winter of 1971-72, when temperatures were much above normal. The seasonal number of freeze days along coastal Louisiana ranged between 8 to 15 during the

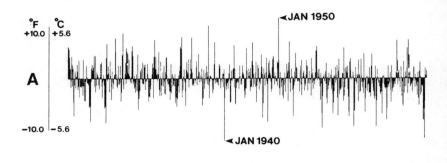

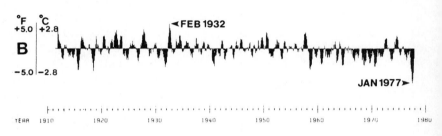

Figure 2.   Temperature and rainfall data for coastal Louisiana, Division Nine,
            1911-1976. A) Temperature departures from 1931--1960 norm. B)
            Mean of latest six months' temperature departures. For example, the
            mean departure for February, 1932, represents the sum of the indivi-
            dual monthly departures of September, October, November, and De-
            cember, 1931, and January and February, 1932, from their respective
            means, divided by six. C) Mean of latest six-month precipitation de-
            partures. Procedure used was same as for temperature. D) Precipitation
            departures from 1931--1960 norm (Muller and Willis, in press).

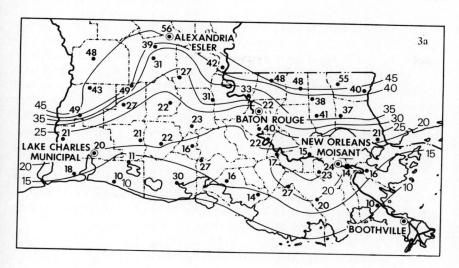

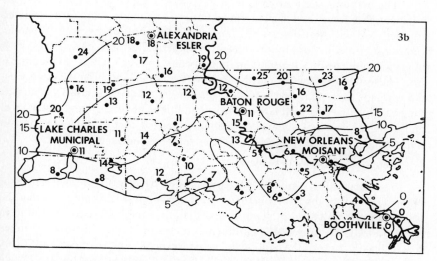

Figure 3. *Freeze days in southern Louisiana (Muller and Wax, 1978).*

cold winter, but only between 0 and 5 during the mild winter. For example, extreme air temperatures, down to about −12°C, occurred during January 1962; the previous occurrence of such temperatures was in February 1899.

The departures of monthly precipitation from the 1931-1960 normals are shown in Figure 2C, and the six-month running means of these departures are shown in Figure 2D. These data show shorter-term precipitation variability with a clustering of wetter and drier months and also over several years. Especially prominent are the dry periods of 1915-18, 1933-38, and 1951-55, all of which are related to drought periods on the Great Plains. Shorter-term but unusually intense dry periods also occurred during 1924-25, and 1962-63. The late 1920's and the late 1940's stand out as extended periods of excessive precipitation.

Drainage basins of the estuaries in Louisiana also show short-term variations (Muller, 1975). For example, during 1961, a wet year, the Louisiana wetlands generated about 2,500 m^3 sec^{-1} of freshwater on the average, but in 1962, a dry year, the wetlands generated only about 700 m^3 sec^{-1} on the average. Because runoff is largely the residual within the water budget, the environmental impact of precipitation variability, especially in terms of freshwater input and salinity, is considerable.

It is apparent that long- and short-term patterns can be identified in climatic data and the latter are particularly evident in estuaries. Indeed, it appears that these changes can be considerable. In the next section we address the impact of these changes in selected estuarine ecosystems.

Climatic Scenarios and Their Impact on Estuaries

The previous sections have related climatic change to estuarine systems and identified long- and short-term patterns in climatic data from selected estuaries. We will first discuss the impact of long-term changes on estuaries. Long-term climatic variation is related to estuaries in three basic ways: as it affects mean sea level, precipitation (both locally and regionally), and temperature. These three factors affect the extent, structure, and productivity of estuaries. In the case of sea level, existing data on depths and heights of the surface of the earth are used to postulate estuarine conditions under different water-level conditions. Existing gradients for precipitation and temperature are used to relate changes in these variables to predict future estuarine conditions.

Long-term changes in sea level

The total surface area of the earth is illustrated in Figure 4 in terms of heights and depths above and below sea level. From this it is apparent that the area between 0 to 200 m in depth is less than the area between 0 to 200 m in height. Indeed, the area of the continental plateau is approximately 1.7 times greater than the area of the continental slope; respective areas are 48 and 28.5 x 10^6 km^2. This means that a fall in sea level would probably reduce worldwide estuarine area, and might cause a decline in both primary and secondary production of estuarine ecosystems.

Long-term changes in precipitation

Precipitation affects estuarine ecosystems locally and regionally. The local area is the estuary itself and immediately adjacent areas; the regional area is the drainage basin of the estuary.

1. *Local*

In coastal areas with low rainfall much of the intertidal zone may consist of barrens. Smith and Monte (1975) have documented these conditions in the Gulf

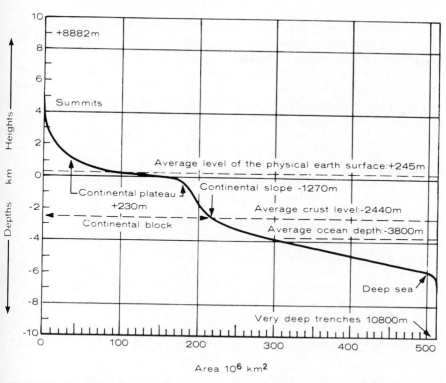

Figure 4. Surface area of the earth in terms of heights and depths above and below sea level (modified from Defant, 1961).

of Mexico. On the northwestern coast of the Yucatan peninsula, rainfall averages less than 500 mm and comes with a sharp seasonal peak (Figure 5). Extensive mangrove areas exist in the proximity of estuarine streams and lagoons. The higher parts of the tidal plain are barrens devoid of life except for a blue-green algal mat that may proliferate on the more frequently wetted parts. In Tabasco, Mexico, about 500 km southwest, the situation changes greatly. Rainfalls annually exceed 1,500 mm and mangrove communities cover the entire tidal area. At Tampico, the mangrove cover again becomes discontinuous, with barrens reflecting the generally drier and more seasonal climate. Northward toward Texas the coast becomes drier still, and in the Rio Grande delta, the barren tidal flats reach their maximum development. Small areas of salt marsh and mangrove exist on the more frequently wetted levels of the flats. Beyond Corpus Christi, on the Texas coast, rainfall increases in amount and frequency, and marshes gradually spread to cover the entire tidal plain. This trend culminates in the humid climate of the north central gulf coast (Louisiana, Mississippi, and Alabama) where marsh growth is luxuriant, particularly in Louisiana where the broad deltaic plain of the Mississippi River supports the largest tract of coastal marshlands in the United States. Macnae (1968) describes similar patterns for the Queensland coast in Australia, where precipitation changes significantly over short distances.

Areal extent of intertidal wetland area is strongly related to primary productivity and fisheries. Individual plants in arid areas are often stunted, and reduced plant coverage leads to lower overall wetland production. High fish catch is associated with intertidal wetlands. Shrimp catch in the Gulf of Mexico seems to be related to extensive wetlands in south Florida, Louisiana, and southeastern Texas, and the Laguna de Terminos in Mexico. Turner (1977) and Craig *et al.* (1977) have shown strong correlations between local intertidal wetland area and shrimp catch worldwide and total fisheries harvest in the Gulf of Mexico.

2. *Regional*

At the level of the drainage basin, riverine input of water, suspended sediments, and nutrients are strongly related to rainfall. (Other factors such as land use and soil type also affect riverine input.) The sediments form intertidal flats which can become vegetated. The nutrients increase productivity of the estuary, and water maintains estuarine salinity gradients.

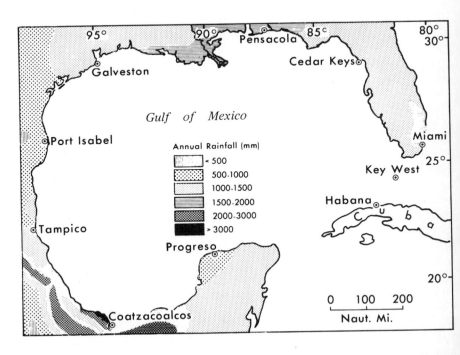

Figure 5. Average annual rainfall (mm) along Gulf of Mexico coast (Smith and Monte, 1975).

In the preceding section, we presented evidence that fisheries were related to intertidal wetland area. Other workers have shown that fisheries and fish production are also related to river discharge. (These two factors are highly interrelated.) Sutcliffe (1972) showed a positive correlation between runoff and the catch of four commercially important species in the Gulf of St. Lawrence. Gunter (1967) related fisheries in several areas of the Gulf of Mexico to estuarine area and river discharge. Moore *et al.* (1970) reported that the distribution of demersal fish off Louisiana and Texas correlated strongly with the discharge of the Mississippi River. Menhaden and shrimp catch in Louisiana are related to the flow of the Mississippi River and to regional rainfall (Stone, 1976).

The effect of decreased precipitation over a drainage basin can also be estimated from the effects of the Aswan High Dam on the Nile delta. The construction of this dam can be viewed as a large-scale experiment on the effect of decreased river flow on an estuarine ecosystem. George (1972) discussed the effect of the dam on fisheries in the Mediterranean Sea. Phosphorus concentrations in the eastern Mediterranean average about 0.1 μg at l^{-1}. Near the mouth of the Nine, 6.5 μg at l^{-1} have been measured. Lower salinity waters from the Nile extend along the coasts of Egypt, Israel, and Libya. During nonflood periods, Egyptian coastal waters contain about 35,000 phytoplankton cells per liter; at peak flood, concentrations reach 2,400,000 cells per liter. As a result of the dam, the discharge of water, nutrients, and sediments has practically ceased. George states that this marks "the dawn of a new nutrient regime for the southeastern Mediterranean." Egyptian fisheries in the Mediterranean dropped from 30,600 metric tons yr $^{-1}$ prior to dam construction to 12,600 metric tons yr $^{-1}$ afterwards, mainly because of the loss of the sardine fishery. Due to the loss of sediments, the shoreline of the delta is undergoing retreat (Kassas, 1972). Kassas states that in 1904 an average of 2,100 m² water per sec reached the sea, carrying 50–100 x 10^6 metric tons of suspended sediments yr^{-1}. Now sediments have been reduced to almost nil.

Long-term changes in temperature

Mean temperature at different places on the earth is used to characterize tropical, temperate, and arctic regions. A world map of terrestrial productivity shows that productivity is generally higher in lower latitudes (Lieth, 1973) and the distribution of productivity zones is particularly sensitive to rainfall. Lieth's map (*ibid.*) shows the coastal zones and major deltas (estuaries) are particularly productive.

Rosenzweig (1968) investigated the ability to predict net primary productivity of terrestrial climax communities from climatological data. He found that actual evapotranspiration (AE) was a highly significant predictor of net aboveground productivity in mature terrestrial plant communities. AE measures the simultaneous availability of water and solar energy (and hence temperature). For a given temperature regime, estuarine AE should approach potential evaporation because of abundant water. Rich nutrient supplies are also a factor in high productivity.

Turner (1976) showed a latitudinal gradient in salt-marsh production along the Atlantic and Gulf coasts. Since evapotranspiration approaches the maximum potential and nutrients are abundant, productivity is a function of increasing solar input and temperature at lower latitudes. Therefore, changes in temperature should lead to changes in productivity. To put this in perspective, during full glaciation the climate of the Gulf Coast region was probably similar to that of present New England. Live standing biomass of marsh grasses (end of season) ranges from 643 to 756 g m^{-2} in Gulf Coast salt marshes. By contrast, New England marshes averaged 413 g m^{-2}. Thus it is obvious that a change in temperature would cause productivity changes in estuaries.

Short-term changes

To this point, the discussion has been concerned with long-term effects of climatic change on estuaries. But it is appropriate to remember that one of our objectives is to determine how short-term climate change is related to human use and management of estuaries. For example, long-term sea level variation probably has little relevance to present coastal management, but short-term variation in local rainfall and temperature can be critical.

Short-term changes are usually not in one direction; thus, there are cycles of wet and dry years as well as warm and cool years. These periodic variations have effects on estuarine productivity. For example, Chapman (1966) demonstrated (Figure 6) a marked correlation between fish harvest and estuarine salinity in Texas by comparing the wet and dry year catch statistics. Thus, human use of estuaries can be strongly affected by short-term variation in the climate.

An understanding of short-term variation is very important in the management of coastal resources. For example, the Texas Basins project (Chapman, 1966) is part of a plan to develop water resources of Texas in the year 2010. Anticipated demands not related directly to the project, combined with project diversions, would reduce by 50 percent (75 percent during dry years) the average annual freshwater flow now reaching Texas estuaries. Reduction of tributary discharge and the introduction of toxic pesticides into estuaries could cause an annual loss of 60 percent of commercial fishery production and nearly 3 million man-days of sport fishing.

Another example of the effect of short-term variation is evidenced in rice production along the landward borders of estuaries in southwestern Louisiana. Growing rice requires about 100 cm (40 inches) of water per year; 45 cm from rain and 55 cm from irrigation sources (Kniffen, 1968). To do this, water has been drawn out heavily from streams, resulting in extensive saltwater intrusion. Salt water has also intruded into aquifers due to well pumping. In general there is usually a water surplus in southwestern Louisiana, but it varies considerably from year to year (Muller, 1975). During wet years the surplus is 50 to 88 cm;

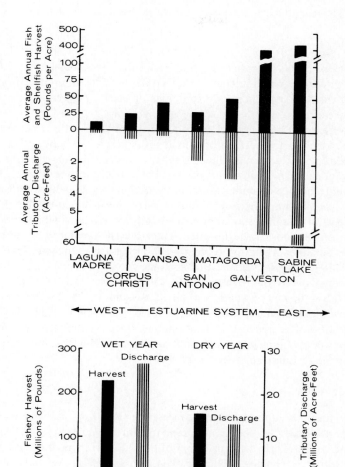

Figure 6.   Relationship between commercial fishery harvest and freshwater discharge into estuaries of the Texas coast (modified from Chapman, 1966 in Darnell et al. 1976).

however, during dry years it can be low as 25 cm, which is not enough to supply rice irrigation needs. In this case, we believe that poor management is leading to both lower estuarine productivity and lower rice yields, due to reduced freshwater input to the estuarine zone and increased salinity in irrigation water.

Implications

The theme of this paper has been to describe the effects of possible climatic changes on estuaries. We should now ask: Can we draw any inferences from our data and discussion? Are there any strategies or tactics for action that might mitigate these effects?

With regard to long-term changes there is probably little we can do. In order to plan for short-term effects of climate on estuaries, we believe that major efforts should be directed to modeling the water resources of each estuarine basin or region, as done for the Indus River basin in Pakistan (Ambroggi, 1977). These models should simulate climatic conditions as derived statistically from empirical data for each basin. The index conditions of those scenarios that predict adverse effects to estuaries should be made available to decisionmakers so that specific action programs can be designed. The effective transfer of this information to decisionmakers remains problematical, at least in Louisiana. At a stage before modeling, however, there is no substitute for an effective cost = benefit analysis of man's activities. For example, the proposed transfer of 8.5 x 10^6 acre-feet (10.5 x 10^9 m^3) of water from the Mississippi River to west Texas and eastern New Mexico would cost about \$330 per acre-foot (1,230 m^3) at a cost-benefit ratio of nearly 8 to 1. This estimate does not include costs for the additional power to operate the system nor the adverse environmental impacts to the coastal zone of Louisiana (Frederick, 1977).

Acknowledgments

Some financial support for this paper came from the Louisiana Sea Grant program, part of the National Sea Grant Program maintained by the National Oceanic and Atmospheric Administration of the U.S. Department of Commerce. We thank Robert E. Hinchee, William J. Wiseman Jr., Joe Poche, and Bobbie F. Young for their help and encouragement.

Figures 2, 3, and 5 are reprinted by courtesy of *Geoscience and Man*; Figure 4 by courtesy of *Permagon Press Inc.*; and Figure 6 by courtesy of *American Fisheries Society*.

References

1. Ambroggi, R. P. 1977. Underground reservoirs to control the water cycle. Scientific American 236(5):21-27.
2. Bahr, L. M., Jr., J. W. Day, Jr., and J. G. Gosselink. 1977. Conceptual modeling of coastal wetlands in southwestern Louisiana and southeastern Texas. Proc. Waubesa Conf. on Wetlands, Univ. Wisc., Madison, June 2-5.

3. Chapman, C. R. 1966. The Texas basins project. *In* R. F. Smith, A. H. Swartz, and W. H. Massmann (eds.), Symp. on Estuarine Fisheries. Am. Fish Soc. Spec. Publ. 3 (Suppl.), 95(4):83-92.

4. CLIMAP Project Members. 1976. The surface of the ice-age earth. Science, 191(4232):1131-1137.

5. Craig, N. J., R. E. Turner, and J. W. Day, Jr. 1977. Cumulative impact studies in the Louisiana coastal zone: land loss. Louisiana State University Center for Wetland Resources, Baton Rouge, La. Final Rept. to La. State Planning Office, Baton Rouge.

6. Darnell, R. M., W. E. Pequegnat, B. M. James, F. J. Benson, and R. A. Defenbaugh. 1976. Impacts of construction activities in wetlands of the United States. EPA, Environ. Res. Lab., Off. of Res. and Develop. Rept. EPA-600/3-76045, Corvallis, Ore.

7. Defant, A. 1961. Physical Oceanography, Vol. I. Pergamon Press, New York. 729 pp.

8. Frederick, K. D. 1977. Water uses and misuses: a world view. *In* Resources. Resources for the Future, April-June Issue No. 55, Washington, D.C.

9. George, C. J. 1972. The role of the Aswan High Dam in changing the fisheries of the southeastern Mediterranean, pp. 159-178. *In* M. Farvar and J. Milton (eds.), The Careless Technology. The Natural History Press, Garden City, New York.

10. Gunter, G. 1967. The relationships of estuaries to the fisheries of the Gulf of Mexico. *In* G. H. Lauff (ed.), Estuaries. Am. Assoc. for the Adv. Sci., 83:621-628.

11. Kassas, M. 1972. Impact of river control schemes on the shoreline of the Nile Delta, pp. 179-188. *In* M. Farvar and J. Milton (eds.), The Careless Technology. The Natural History Press, Garden City, New York.

12. Kniffen, F. B. 1968. Louisiana: Its Land and People. Louisiana State Press, Baton Rouge. 196 pp.

13. Landsberg, H. E. 1976. Whence global climate: hot or cold? An essay review. Bull. Am. Meteor. Soc., 54(4):441-443.

14. Lieth, H. 1973. Primary production: terrestrial ecosystems. Human Ecol., 1 (4):303-332.

15. Macnae, W. 1968. A general account of the fauna and flora of mangrove swamps and forests in the Indo-West-Pacific region. Adv. Mar. Biol., 5:73-270.

16. Mason, B. J. 1976. The nature and prediction of climatic changes. Endeavour, 35(125):51-57.

17. Moore, D., H. A. Brusher, and L. Trent. 1970. Relative abundance, seasonal distribution, and species composition of demersal fishes off Louisiana and Texas, 1962-1964. Contr. Mar. Sci., 15:45-70.

18. Muller, R. A. 1975. Freshwater potential in the Louisiana coastal marshes and estuaries. Geoscience and Man, 12:1-7.

19. Muller, R. A., and C. L. Wax. 1978. A comparative synoptic climatic baseline for coastal Louisiana. Geoscience and Man, 18.

20. Muller, R. A., and J. E. Willis. In press. Climatic variability of the lower Mississippi River valley. Geoscience and Man.

21. Rosenzweig, M. L. 1968. Net primary productivity of terrestrial communities: prediction from climatological data. The Am. Naturalist, 102(923):67-74.

22. Smith, W. G., and J. A. Monte. 1975. Marshes: the wet grasslands. Geoscience, 10:27-38.

23. Stone, J. H. 1976. Environmental factors related to Louisiana menhaden harvest. Louisiana State University Center for Wetland Resources, Baton Rouge, La. Final Rept. to U.S. Dept. Com., NOAA, Natl. Mar. Fish. Serv., St. Petersburg, Fla.

24. Sutcliffe, W. H. 1972. Some relations of land drainage, nutrients, particulate material, and fish catch in two eastern Canadian bays. J. Fish. Res. Bd. Canada, 29(4):357-362.

25. Turner, R. E. 1976. Geographic variations in salt marsh macrophyte production: a review. Contr. Mar. Sci., 20:47-68.

26. _____. 1977. Intertidal vegetation and commercial yields of Penaeid shrimp. Trans. Am. Fish. Soc. 106(5):411-416.

27. U.S. Committee for the Global Atmospheric Research Program (USGARP). 1975. Understanding climatic change: A program for action. Natl. Acad. Sciences, Washington, D.C.

IMPACT OF HURRICANES ON SEDIMENTATION IN ESTUARIES, BAYS, AND LAGOONS

Miles O. Hayes

Coastal Research Division
Department of Geology
University of South Carolina
Columbia, South Carolina

Abstract: Hurricane-generated processes that affect coastal sedimentation include storm surges which create strong currents and carry in suspended and bedload sediments, wave action, and flooding resulting from heavy rainfall. A single storm can cause more erosion and deposition in an estuary within a few hours than would occur in decades under normal conditions. The temperature-salinity stratification of the estuary may be drastically altered by the storm and remain so for weeks. The impact of a given storm will vary depending upon the size, speed of movement, and path of the storm, as well as upon certain characteristics of the affected coastal area, such as slope of adjacent continental shelf and shoreline configuration.

There are many documented cases in the literature of hurricane impacts on coastal water bodies, including: (1) building of washover fans into Texas bays; (2) formation of tidal inlets and building of tidal deltas and washover fans into mid-Atlantic estuaries; (3) storm sediment layers deposited in subtidal areas of the lagoons of the Great Bahama Bank and the Florida Keys; (4) widespread deposition of thin shell lag and laminated sand layers in mangrove-bordering bays of southwest Florida; (5) mud layers deposited over extensive areas of the supratidal flats of the Great Bahama Bank, Florida Bay, and South Texas; (6) growth of fan-deltas into Texas bays as the result of heavy rains affiliated with hurricanes; and (7) extreme modification of estuarine circulation and sedimentation patterns in Chesapeake Bay as the result of record flooding caused by Hurricane *Agnes* (1972).

Introduction

Tropical cyclones, or hurricanes, are catastrophic events that usually have important and lasting impact on the processes of sedimentation of the coastal water bodies that lie in their paths. High tides and waves generated by the storms and runoff from the associated rains carry into the estuaries, bays, and lagoons new sediments that may be permanently stored and little modified by normal, day-to-day processes. In some instances, sections of the estuaries, bays, and lagoons are swept clean of sediments by hurricane-generated waves and currents.

This paper summarizes studies conducted on fourteen separate storms that have occurred primarily within the past two decades. These findings are summarized briefly in Table 1. The paths of the fourteen storms studied are given in Figure 1.

In addition to the studies on the individual hurricanes listed in Table 1, Zeigler, Hayes, and Tuttle (1959; p. 330) briefly described the effects of three 1954 hurricanes, *Hazel, Carol* and *Edna*. These hurricanes caused flooding and severe shore-front erosion in the more enclosed sound and bay areas of New England, such as Naragansett Bay, Buzzards Bay, and Vineyard Sound, and battered the open coasts of the Carolinas. Shepard and Wanless (1971) in their book, *Our Changing Coastlines*, described hurricane-related changes on the east and Gulf coasts of the United States on the basis of aerial photographic interpretations. Notable among their many discussions of hurricane effects are the descriptions of the impact of Hurricane *Hazel* (1954) and *Helene* (1958) on the Outer Banks of North Carolina.

Hurricane Characteristics

Definitions

Technically, a hurricane is "a storm of tropical origin with a cyclonic wind circulation (counter-clockwise in the Northern Hemisphere) of seventy-four mph or higher" (>12 on Beaufort scale) (Dunn and Miller, 1960, p. 9). The hurricane is the North Atlantic member of the tropical cyclone family that includes the typhoon of the western North Pacific, the cyclone of the northern Indian Ocean, and the willy-willy of Australia (Tannehill, 1956). Tropical cyclones are the most powerful and destructive of all storms (Dunn and Miller, 1960; Tannehill, 1956). Tornadoes have higher wind velocities (central axis velocities may attain 640-800 km/hr), but tropical cyclones are also intense (winds may reach 250-300 km/hr) and cover a much larger area. At one stage, Hurricane *Carla*'s (1961) circulation enveloped the entire Gulf of Mexico, and fringe effects were felt by all Gulf Coast states (Cooperman and Sumner, 1962).

Tropical cyclones occur in the North Atlantic with a frequency of approximately 7.5 per year (Figure 2) and occur most often during the months of August, September, and October. The season of maximum occurrence of tropical cyclones corresponds roughly to the time when the ITC (intertropical convergence zone, or equatorial trough) has it maximum divergence from the equator (Hayes, 1967, p. 4).

Storm surge

The storm surge is "the rise or fall of the sea level caused by a meteorological disturbance" (Pore, 1961, p. 151). As used here, it refers to the hurricane

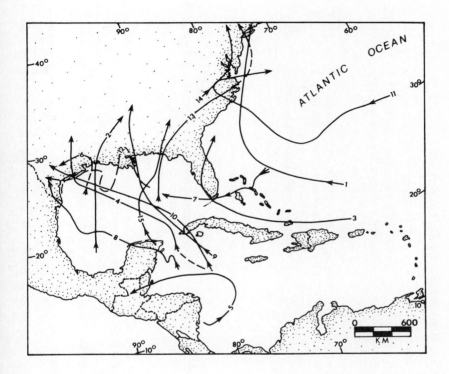

Figure 1. Tracks of hurricanes discussed in the literature with regard to their impact on coastal sedimentation (discussed in Table 1).

1. Sept. 1938
2. Audrey *(1957)*
3. Donna *(1960)*
4. Carla *(1961)*
5. Hattie *(1961)*
6. Cindy *(1963)*
7. Betsy *(1965)*
8. Beulah *(1967)*

9. Camille *(1969)*
10. Celia *(1970)*
11. Ginger *(1971)*
12. Fern *(1971)*
13. Agnes *(1972)*
14. Agnes' *secondary low (1972)*
15. Eloise *(1975)*

Table 1. Hurricanes discussed in the literature.

Hurricane (Date)	Landfall	Characteristics	Documented Effects	References
Sept. 1938	Long Island; Connecticut	**Large;** max. surge 4 m; winds 200 km/hr; heavy rains	Extreme shore erosion; formation of inlets and washovers; record flooding	Nichols and Marston (1939)
Audrey (1957)	Texas-Louisiana border	**Medium;** max. surge 4 m; winds to 130 km/hr	Shoreline retreat (25-30 m) in chenier plain area; mud deposition; shell berms deposited over marsh; numerous breaches through barriers and cheniers; mud flats not modified	Morgan, Nichols, and Wright (1958)
Donna (1960)	Florida Keys; southwest Florida	**Medium;** max. surge of 3 m; winds to 200 km/hr	Erosion of platform-edge reefs; mud layers deposited on supratidal flats; spillover lobes of coarse sediment deposited in breaks through reef fronts; beach erosion and inlet breaching in SW Florida	Ball, Shinn, and Stockman (1967); Perkins and Enos (1968); Tanner (1961)
Carla (1961)	Central Texas	**Large;** max. surge of 7 m; huge waves; winds to 200 km/hr	Eroded beaches; breached barrier islands; washover fans reactivated; mud layers and shell layers on tidal flats; sed. layer on inner shelf	Hayes (1967)
Hattie (1961)	British Honduras	**Large;** max. surge of 4 m; winds to 200 km/hr	Heavy destruction of reef corals; island overtopping and erosion; destruction of plant communities	Stoddart (1963; 1965)
Cindy (1963)	East Texas	**Small;** max. surge of 1 m	Only beach changes (mostly depositional)	Hayes (1967)
Betsy (1965)	Bahamas; Florida Keys	**Medium;** max. surge 3 m; winds 200 km/hr	Erosion of spillover lobes on Bahamas; deposition of spillover lobes at Cape Sable, Fla.; beach erosion in NW Florida; generally minor effects	Perkins and Enos (1968); Pray (1966); Warnke et al. (1966)

Storm	Location	Characteristics	Effects	References
Beulah (1967)	Texas-Mexico border	**Medium;** max. surge of 3 m; winds to 240 km/hr; heavy rains	Opened storm and tidal channels; deposited washovers; deltas formed on bay margins	Scott, Hoover, and McGowen (1969); McGowen (1970); McGowen and Scott (1975)
Camille (1969)	Louisiana; Mississippi border	**Large;** record storm surges > 7 m; heavy rains; winds 200 km/hr	Spit eroded at Miss. river mouth; islands eroded and washed over; sand washovers deposited on peats; deposition on natural levees	Wright, Swaye, and Coleman (1970); Sonu (1970)
Celia (1970)	Central Texas	**Medium;** max. surge 3 m; highly destructive winds to 150 km/hr; little rain; very fast moving	Minor breaching of barriers; minor beach erosion; heavy wind damage	McGowen *et al.* (1970)
Ginger (1971)	Outer Banks, N.C.	**Medium;** max. surges of 2.5 m; winds to 120 km/hr; heavy rains	Dune recession in man-modified areas; overwash processes and overwash deposition elsewhere	Dolan and Godfrey (1973)
Fern (1971)	Louisiana; south Texas	**Small;** slow moving; heavy rains	Mostly excessive rain and flooding	McGowen and Scott (1975)
Agnes (1972)	Northwest Florida; New York	**Medium;** winds to 120 km/hr; max. surge 2 m (in Fla.); large circulation; extremely heavy rains	Runoff produced by storm introduced as much sediment into upper 40 km of Chesapeake Bay in one week as would be normally deposited in fifty years	Schubel (1974); Zabawa and Schubel (1974)
Eloise (1975)	Northwest Florida	**Medium;** max. surge 5 m; winds to 210 km/hr; rains variable; fast moving	Mostly erosion related to storm surge and wave set up; wind damage and flooding minimal	Morton (1976)

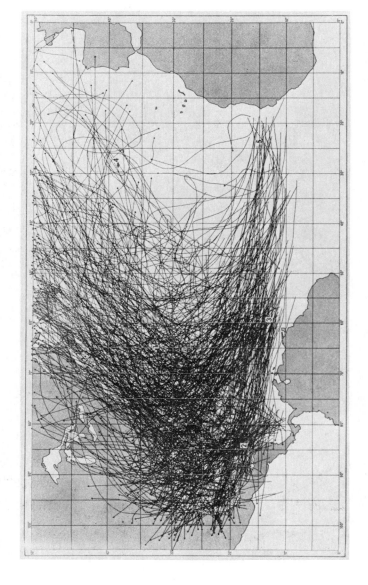

Figure 2. Computer plot showing the tracks of 680 recorded Atlantic tropical cyclones, 1886 through 1969 (from Neumann and Hill, 1976).

surge, or a "rapid rise in the water produced by hurricane winds and falling barometric pressure," and other factors (Dunn and Miller, 1960, p. 207).

Not only is the storm surge or storm tide the "primary cause of death and property damage in a hurricane" (Freeman, Baer, and Jung, 1957, p. 12), but it is also the characteristic of hurricanes most responsible for making them important geological agents. The rise in water level brought about by hurricanes inundates vast areas of low-lying coastal regions, producing widespread erosion and deposition of nearshore sediments.

The two most important factors in the generation of storm surges are the stress of wind on the sea surface (sometimes called wind set-up) and reduction of atmospheric pressure or inverted barometer effect. Winds of North Atlantic hurricanes have frequently reached velocities of 130 to 200 km/hr, and a few have attained 300 km/hr (Dunn and Miller, 1960). The width of the path of a single storm may sometimes extend 300 to 500 km. These factors, combined with the fact that a storm may last for several days, gives hurricanes the ability to pile up tremendous quantities of water against the coastline. Several other factors, such as shoreline configuration and shape and slope of continental shelf, may also tend to accentuate, or modify, the storm surge. Two hurricanes, *Carla* (1961) and *Camille* (1969), have generated surges on the order of 7 m on the Gulf Coast.

Waves

Probably the most spectacular geological effect of hurricanes is the erosion produced by breaking waves on an exposed shoreline. A cubic yard of water weighs about three-fourths of a ton, and a breaking wave may move forward at speeds up to 80–100 km/hr (Dunn and Miller, 1960). Their erosive effects are greatly increased when they ride the crest of a large storm surge, because much greater land areas are exposed to erosion. Some hurricane waves attain tremendous heights. Twelve to fourteen meter waves were reported by Coast Guard stations in New England during Hurricanes *Carol* and *Edna* of 1954 (Pore, 1957).

Although I know of no measurements of hurricane waves in bays, several observations of wave effects indicate that a significant increase in wave size occurs during storms, with an accompanying increase in shore erosion (McGowen and Scott, 1975; Perkins and Enos, 1968). Ball, Shinn, and Stockman (1967) gave the following description of wave effects in Florida Bay during Hurricane *Donna* (1960): "The increased chop soon whipped the shallow waters...in Florida Bay into a milky soup of suspended lime mud." Much of this suspended sediment made available by the waves was transported out of the bay by currents created by the storm.

Currents

Open ocean currents.   Sea conditions during hurricanes prohibit taking oceanographic measurements from a surface ship, so ocean currents generated by hurricanes are very poorly known. "In contrast to storm surge measurements, which are made routinely along populated coasts, no reliable current measurements have ever been made beneath a storm of hurricane intensity (Forristall, 1974; p. 2721)." Field measurements of currents produced by extratropical cyclones on the continental shelves of Washington and Oregon (Smith and Hopkins, 1972) and New England (Beardsley and Butman, 1974) indicate that these storms are the primary controls of both the current structure and sediment transport on those shelves.

Some indirect evidence indicates the the strong winds associated with hurricanes set up appreciable currents. Tannehill (1956, p. 34) described the effects of currents generated by the Texas hurricane of 1915 as follows: "...the current set up by the storm carried Trinity Shoals gas and whistling buoy nearly ten miles to the westward. This buoy weighed 21,000 pounds and was anchored in 42 feet of water with a 6,500 pound sinker and 252 feet of anchor chain weighing 3,250 pounds." Numerical and analytical models by Forristall (1974) and Sloss (1972) indicate that strong currents flow parallel to the coast during the approach and landfall of a hurricane, inasmuch as winds pile up water against the land to the right of the storm and push water offshore to the left of the storm.

Breaking waves, especially those breaking obliquely to the shoreline, generate strong longshore currents during hurricanes. Timbers and pilings from Bob Hall fishing pier on northern Padre Island, Texas, which was completely destroyed by Hurricane *Carla* (1961), were found for many miles south along the beach after the storm (Hayes, 1967, p. 7). Murray (1970) measured currents up to 160 cm/sec in 6.3 m of water off the coast of northwest Florida during the passage of Hurricane *Camille* (1969).

Strong currents flow in hurricane channels cut into Texas coast barrier islands during the high-water stage of the hurricane surge (Hayes, 1967; Scott, Hoover, and McGowen, 1969; McGowen *et al.* 1970). Ball, Shinn, and Stockman (1967) also made this observation in the passes between the Florida Keys during Hurricane *Donna* (1960), when currents washed out the interkey bridges and broke the pipeline supplying fresh water to the keys where the pipe crossed the bridges.

Currents in estuaries, bays, and lagoons. A recent paper by Gohren (1976) documented the currents generated by storm surges over the tidal flats of the German North Sea Coast. These storm surges are caused primarily by extratropical cyclones; however, the analogy seems apt. He found that during normal tides, current velocities were a relatively small 30–40 cm/sec (Figure 3A), with reversing directions. During storm surges, the currents increase as wind speed increases, usually exceeding about 1 m/sec at the peak of the surge. Data for 50 storm surges indicate modes at 50 and 90 cm/sec (Figure 3B). The data for a single surge are given in Figure 3B. During surges, the currents stop reversing, and unidirectional currents are set up in the direction of the wind. The residual current also increases from about 1 km per tide at normal tides to about 12 km per tide during larger storms. Therefore he concluded that

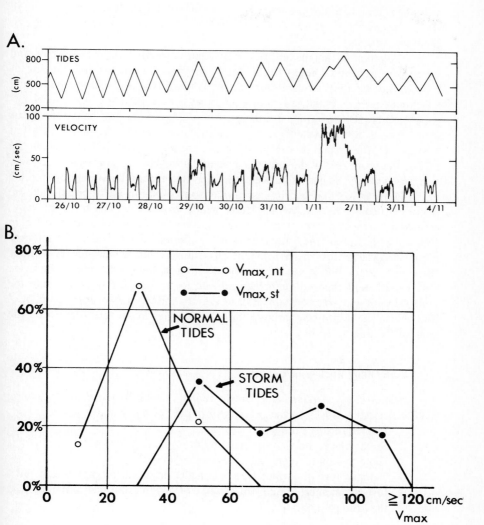

Figure 3. Effects of storm surges on current velocities over a tidal flat on the German North Sea coast (slightly modified after Gohren, 1976). A) Record of a current meter station that contains a storm surge. Note the dramatic increase in current velocity at the peak of the surge on 2/11. B) Frequency of maximum velocities. Based on data of 50 storm surges.

storms (a) double and triple maximum current velocities; (b) strongly increase the magnitude of the residual current; and (c) eliminate the reversing nature of the tidal currents.

It is probable that the only major circulation and flushing of many bays and lagoons in microtidal areas occur during storms. The pattern of flushing of Florida Bay during Hurricane *Donna* (1960) was described by Ball, Shinn, and Stockman (1967) (sketched diagrammatically in Figure 4). As *Donna* approached the keys from the southeast, the wind blowing out of the northeast across Florida Bay drove the shallow, muddy water out of the bay into the Gulf of Mexico. This decrease in water level inside the bay, coupled with a rise in the tide on the south side of the keys because of the impending storm surge, created currents through the passes between the keys that sent water streaming into the bay (Figure 4A). As the storm passed over southwest Florida after landfall, the winds shifted to the southwest. These winds drove water back into the bay, resulting in a rapid rise of the tide. At one tide station, the water level rose 4 m in 6 hours. Ball, Shinn, and Stockman (1967) estimated that currents of 2 knots or higher occurred within the central portion of the bay during that time. As the bay filled with water, the storm surge was receding on the ocean side of the keys. "Rivers of mud-charged water flowed out across the reef tract and into the northward-flowing Florida current (Ball, Shinn, and Stockman, 1967; p. 586)." The ebb of the storm tide through the inlets continued for three days after the peak of the tide in the bay.

Controlling Factors of Impact

Meteorological controls. McGowen et al. (1970) listed the following meteorological controls on the severity of impact of hurricanes:
1. Degree of low pressure
2. Stress placed on water surface by cyclonic circulation
3. Time available to generate wave turbulence
4. Temperature of surface waters contributing to the energy of the cell
5. Overall meteorological framework of North American circulation at the time of landfall

Geographical controls. Brown et al. (1976) listed the following geographical controls on the severity of impact of hurricanes:
1. Bottom slope and profile of the inner continental shelf and shoreface
2. Stage of the tide
3. Shape and orientation of shoreline
4. Degree of vegetative cover
5. Angle of storm approach

Life and death of a storm

Introductory statement. A succession of papers, including those of Price (1956), Hayes (1967), Scott, Hoover, and McGowen (1969), and McGowen *et al.* (1970), have outlined the various changes in storm effects that take place during the approach, landfall, and dissipation of hurricanes. All of these papers have dealt with storms striking the Texas coast. For purposes of discussion, the life and death of a Texas coastal hurricane can be divided into four stages: 1) approach, or storm-surge flood; 2) landfall; 3) early aftermath, or storm-surge ebb; and 4) late aftermath.

Approach. This is a period of rising tides, increased wind velocities, and increased wave heights. The slower the storm moves, the larger the storm surge. Some important effects during this period include erosion of shelf and shoreface, shore erosion, breaching of barrier islands and formation of washover fans, and mud deposition on supratidal flats (Hayes, 1967). During this phase, longshore currents are generated that flow from north to south (in this particular setting).

Landfall. "As the storm passes over the shore, the pattern of current and wave attack shifts into compliance with the direct influence of the counterclockwise winds of the hurricane (McGowen *et al.*, 1970; p. 5)." Water and sediment are pumped out of the bays on the south side of the storm, whereas water is still being pushed shoreward on the north side. This is the time of most severe coastal winds.

Early aftermath. As the storm moves inland, it becomes more diffuse and weaker. Winds blow either offshore or from south to north. This shift in wind direction and sudden rise in barometric pressure cause strong storm-surge ebb currents which scour out the hurricane channels and inlets and deposit bay and nearshore sediments on the barrier shoreface and inner continental shelf (Hayes, 1967). Wave erosion gradually diminishes with the falling water levels, and longshore currents flow from south to north (McGowen *et al.*, 1970).

As the storm moves further inland, it may be accompanied by tornadoes and heavy rains which produce large-scale runoff of flood proportions, inundating low-lying areas along stream courses and bay margins (Scott, Hoover, and McGowen, 1969). "Differences in the tracks of storms after landfall... greatly influence the extent of flooding and deltaic deposition [in the bays] (McGowen and Scott, 1975; p. 27)." For example, Hurricane *Beulah* (1967) stalled and went up the Rio Grande valley, producing rains in excess of 40 cm at many stations in south Texas (Scott, Hoover, and McGowen, 1969).

Late aftermath. During the weeks and months following the storm, longshore currents build bars across the mouths of the tidal passes cut by the storm (Hayes, 1967), waves restore the normal beach profile (Sonu, 1970; Morton, 1976), mud settles from suspension in the bays and in stranded ponds (Hayes, 1967), exposed fine-grain deposits are reworked by rain, dessication, and wind (McGowen *et al.*, 1970), and the wind blows some of the sand left exposed on the washover fans by the storm either back to sea or further into the bay (Andrews, 1970).

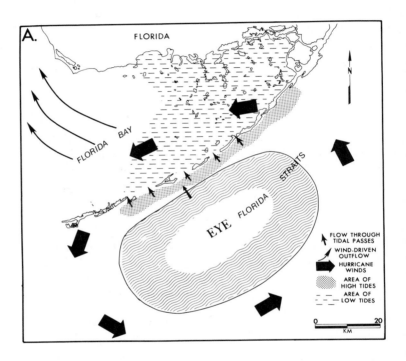

Figure 4A. Changes in flushing and circulation of Florida Bay during the passage
of Hurricane Donna *(1960). Based on descriptions in Ball, Shinn, and*
Stockman (1967). Hurricane approach accompanied by bay flushing.

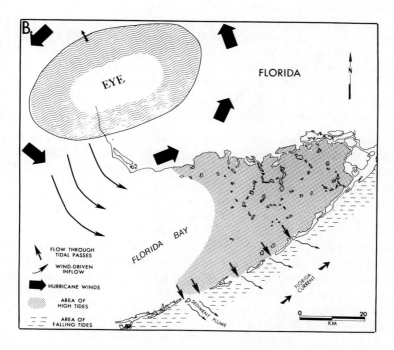

Figure 4B. Changes in flushing and circulation of Florida Bay during the passage of Hurricane Donna *(1960). Based on descriptions in Ball, Shinn, and Stockman (1967). Hurricane landfall accompanied by bay flooding.*

Documented Effects

Beach erosion

One of the more widely observed and documented effects of hurricanes is the erosion of shorefront property, beginning with Nichols and Marston's (1939) lucid descriptions of shore erosion in Rhode Island during the September, 1938 hurricane and ending with Morton's (1976) recent discussion of erosion along the northwest Florida coast during Hurricane *Eloise* (1975). Waves associated with Hurricane *Carla* (1961) removed a belt of foredunes 20 to 50 m wide from the seaward side of Padre Island and left the foredune ridge with wave-cut cliffs up to 3 m high. The post-storm beach usually has a flat and featureless profile. Further discussion of beach erosion during hurricanes is beyond the scope of this paper. (Consult references listed in Table 1 for more details.)

Inlets and washover fans

When a hurricane surge floods a barrier island, water flowing through breaks in the dunes is capable of scouring channels across the island. This is the mechanism by which many new tidal inlets are formed (El-Ashry and Wanless, 1965; Shepard and Wanless, 1971); however, most of the channels are closed off by swash-transported and wind-blown sand within a few weeks after the storm. As the surge waters fan out into the lagoon or onto the tidal flats behind the barrier, fan-shaped sediment bodies, called washover fans, are deposited (Figure 5). The magnitude of the overwash is directly proportional to the size of the storm surge (Leatherman, 1976). This process deposits large volumes of sediments into lagoons. Nordquist (1972), in a study of North Pass on St. Joseph Island, Texas, estimated that approximately 7.2 million cubic meters of sediment accumulated along the bay side of the pass as a consequence of hurricane activity between 1919 and 1971 (McGowen and Scott, 1975).

Numerous papers have discussed the formation of inlets and washover fans during hurricanes. Some of the more notable ones include the studies by: El-Ashry (1966), El-Ashry and Wanless (1968), and Dolan and Godfrey (1973) on the Outer Banks of North Carolina; Morgan, Nichols, and Wright (1958) and Wright, Swaye, and Coleman (1970) on the Louisiana coast; and Scott, Hoover, and McGowen (1969) and McGowen and Scott (1975) on the Texas coast. Process-response studies have been carried out on washover fans by Andrews (1970) on St. Joseph Island, Texas, Schwartz (1975) on the Outer Banks, and Leatherman (1976) on Assateague Island, Maryland. Andrews' conclusions about the nature of the washover deposits follow (p. 73):

"Deposition is rapid, and each washover sand [unit] consists of a one- to 2-inch shell- and clay-pebble placer at the base, grading up into mixed sand and small shells, then into relatively shell-free sand. The sedimentation unit is thus graded."

These deposits are mostly flat beds deposited under transitional and upper flow regime conditions. Schwartz (1975) showed that two dominant sedimentary

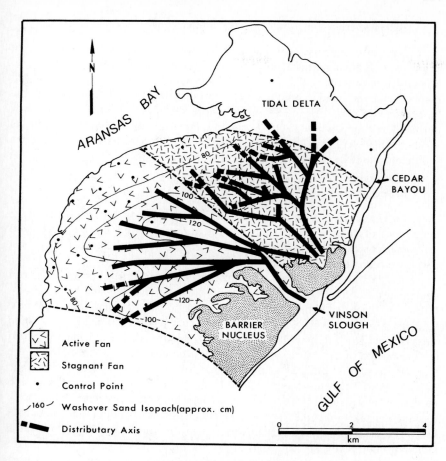

Figure 5. Hurricane washover fan, northern St. Joseph Island, Texas. After Andrews (1970) (slightly modified from McGowen and Scott, 1975).

structures occurred in the fans he studied: (1) flat-bed deposits in the landward and central portions of the fans; and (2) small delta-foreset strata along the landward margins of fans that build into a water body.

Andrews (1970) also pointed out that after the storm surge recedes, the newly deposited sand is reworked by eolian processes. Sand is blown across wind-tidal flats into the lagoon or, as Leatherman (1976) showed, back onto the beach. Price (1958) and Fisk (1959) emphasized that wind-transport of hurricane-deposited fan sediments is an important process of sediment infilling of the coastal lagoons of south Texas, as well as of the landward accretion of barrier islands (Scott, Hoover, and McGowen, 1969).

Shoreline erosion in estuaries, bays, and lagoons

Erosion of estuary, bay, and lagoon shorelines during hurricanes is not nearly so well documented as the erosion of ocean-front beaches. According to McGowen and Scott (1975; p. 40), cliff shorelines of south Texas bays and lagoons have retreated as much as 30 m during a single storm. Ball, Shinn, and Stockman (1967) described erosion and washover of islands inside Florida Bay during Hurricane *Donna* (1960). Strangely, however, the carbonate mud banks inside the bay were only slightly modified by the storm, apparently because the sediments were bound by grasses and organic slime.

Sediment layers

Introduction. A number of studies in recent years have pointed out the occurrence of discrete layers of sediments in otherwise homogeneous (mixed) sediments of various bay and lagoon subenvironments. These layers for the most part have been attributed to deposition during storms.

Subtidal layers. Layers of sediments deposited during storms have been described in subtidal environments of the Bahamas (Perkins and Enos, 1968), Florida Bay (Ball, Shinn, and Stockman, 1967; Perkins and Enos, 1968), lagoons of southwest Florida (Wanless and Rine, 1976), and the bays of south Texas (Scott, Hoover, and McGowen, 1969). Perkins and Enos (1968) described the deposition of 20 cm of soft lime mud in the nearshore environment of the Great Bahama Bank adjacent to the tidal flats of Andros Island during Hurricane *Betsy* (1965). This mud was probably washed off flats by the storm-surge ebb currents. They also described a thick mud deposit in the deeper parts of the back reef lagoon seaward of the northern Florida Keys. Ball, Shinn, and Stockman (1967) described two types of sediment layering in Florida Bay during Hurricane *Donna* (1960): redeposition on the bay floor of lime mud suspended by the storm; and accumulations of clean sand over mud produced by currents flowing across the mud banks.

Wanless and Rine (1976; p. 731) described sediment layers occurring in shallow mangrove-rimmed bays and channels in the Marco Island area in southwest Florida. The bottom sediments are composed of alternations of mud layers (10 to 50 cm thick) and quartz-sand and shell fragment layers (1 to 10 cm thick). The sand-shell layers are thought to originate by substrate winnowing and offshore-sediment influx during storms, whereas the mud layers are the result of settling of fine-grain sediments between storms. The uppermost sand-shell layer, which occurs at depths of 15 to 25 cm below the surface of the sediments, was attributed to Hurricane *Donna* (1960). The authors think the storm layers are preserved in this environment because: a) mud settling between storms buries the sand layers below the level of bioturbation; and b) the high turbidity of the bay reduces burrowing.

Supratidal layers. The most significant effect noted for several of the storms studied to date has been the stranding of large quantities of mud above the normal high-tide line on supratidal mud flats. This is especially true in carbonate depositional areas. Mud layers deposited by storms on the supratidal portions of Andros Island, the Bahamas, have been discussed by Shinn, Ginsburg, and Lloyd (1965); Roehl (1967); Shinn, Lloyd, and Ginsburg (1969); Ginsburg and Hardie (1975); and Wanless (1975). These deposits extend for 160 km along the western shores of Andros (Ginsburg and Hardie, 1975; p. 201). Similar mud deposition extended up to five miles inland at the south end of the Florida mainland after Hurricane *Donna* (1960) (Ball, Shinn, and Stockman, 1967; p. 591). The wind-tidal flats west of Laguna Madre, Texas were similarly covered with a terrigenous mud layer up to 10 cm thick after Hurricane *Carla* (1961) (Hayes, 1967). These layers are usually well-preserved because of lack of reworking by waves and currents and relatively small numbers of burrowing organisms. However in south Texas the layers sometimes dessicate and are eroded away by the wind.

These supratidal flat storm deposits have received considerable attention in carbonate sedimentation studies for two reasons: 1) they are widely recognized in the rock record (e.g. Roehl, 1967; Wanless, 1975), and 2) they represent the first step in the formation of penecontemporaneous dolomite deposits. According to Shinn, Ginsburg, and Lloyd (1965, p. 112), the mud layer is altered to dolomite in instances where tidal flooding and storm sedimentation is followed by many days of subaerial exposure. They think the mud in the storm layer is derived from offshore marine environments, because it is composed mostly of fecal pellets produced by the intertidal gastropod *Batillaria*, and because of visual observations of storm tides depositing mud on the supratidal flats. They referred to this process as a "river delta inside out," in that deposition occurs at the highest topographic elevation available to the water, rather than the lowest.

Impact of hurricane-induced rains

Introduction. An important impact of hurricanes on coastal sedimentation that is sometimes overlooked is brought about by the high run-off produced by the intense rains that fall during a storm. Important studies of this process have been carried out in Nueces Bay, Texas by McGowen and Scott (Scott, Hoover, and McGowen, 1969; McGowen, 1970; McGowen and Scott, 1975), and in Chesapeake Bay by Schubel and associates (Schubel, 1974; Zabawa and Schubel, 1974).

Gum Hollow delta. A small fan delta on the north shore of Nueces Bay, Texas, the Gum Hollow delta, was the subject of study for several years prior to the landfall of Hurricane *Beulah* (1967) by members of the geology department of the University of Texas (Scott, Hoover, and McGowen, 1969). *Beulah* raised the water level of the bay 1.5 m and dumped 40–60 cm of rain on the watershed of the delta (area of approx. 80 km²) in a two-day period. As reported by McGowen (1970), the flood resulting from these rains deposited 250,000 m³ of sand upon the previously-constructed fan plain (Figure 6). A layer of fine sand to 1.5 m thick, which terminated distally with a steep avalanche face having a maximum height of about 60 cm, was deposited (McGowen and Scott, 1975). All of this sand was deposited in less than one week and possibly in less than one day, providing another striking demonstration of the importance of hurricanes in the sedimentation processes of bays in the lower and middle latitudes.

Hurricane Agnes (1972) flood. Hurricane *Agnes* first came ashore at Panama City, Florida, on the afternoon of June 19, 1972 (De Angelis, 1973). The storm reached Norfolk, Virginia as a rejuvenated tropical storm on the night of June 21. At that time, a large extratropical low-pressure system formed just west of *Agnes* and paralleled her on the way north (Figure 1). *Agnes* generated an easterly flow of moist ocean air, which in conjunction with the sister storm, triggered torrential rains from South Carolina to New York on river basins already soaked by earlier June rains. The floods resulting from these low pressure systems caused the worst natural disaster ever to hit Pennsylvania, with total damage estimated at $2.12 billion (De Angelis, 1973).

The runoff from the *Agnes* rains resulted in record flooding throughout the drainage basin of northern Chesapeake Bay. Schubel (1974) reported the following effects of the storm on the hydrography of the bay:

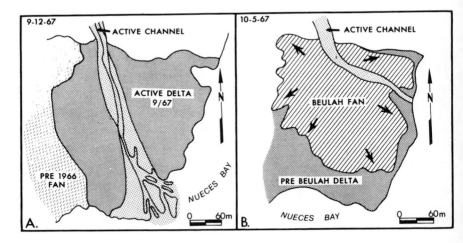

Figure 6. *Storm-related deposition on Gum Hollow delta, south Texas (slightly modified after McGowen and Scott, 1975). A) Delta prior to storm as mapped on September 12, 1967. B) The fan constructed on the delta within a 48-hour period as a result of rain produced by Hurricane Beulah (1967).*

1. On June 24, the day the Susquehanna River crested at its mouth, the daily average discharge of the river was 27,750 m³/sec (Figure 7A), which exceeded the previous recorded average high by 33%.

2. The salinities in the upper portion of the bay were the lowest ever observed.

3. On June 23, suspended solids at the river mouth exceeded 10,000 mg/1 (Figure 7B), a concentration more than 40 times greater than any previously recorded for the lower Susquehanna.

4. The tidal reaches of the estuary were pushed seaward more than 80 km from the mouth, which was more than 35 km further seaward than ever previously reported.

5. Vertical salinity gradients larger than any previously recorded were produced.

The impact on the sedimentation processes in the bay was also immense. During the week of June 22 to 28, the river probably discharged >50 x 10⁶ metric tons of suspended solids into the upper Chesapeake Bay. Normal yearly discharges of suspended solids range between 0.5 and 1.0 x 10⁶ metric tons. Schubel (1974; p. 121) concluded that the bulk of this sediment was deposited in the upper 40 km of the bay. Approximately 10 acres of new islands and several hundred acres of new intertidal flats were formed near Havre de Grace on a shoal area known as Susquehanna Flats. More than 38,000 m³ of new fill had to be dredged from one section of the main shipping channel. Post-storm coring of bottom sediments of the upper reaches of the bay (Zabawa and Schubel, 1974) revealed the presence of a Hurricane *Agnes* sediment layer up to 17 cm thick, which was estimated to contain 13 x 10⁶ metric tons of sediment. Following the assumption that estuaries are ephemeral features (in a geological sense) that are doomed to extinction by sediment infilling, Schubel concluded that Chesapeake Bay "aged" 50 years as a result of this tremendous input of sediments by a single storm.

Conclusions

Over twenty studies carried out on fourteen tropical storms and hurricanes in the past two decades have described dramatic effects on sedimentation in estuaries, bays, and lagoons brought about by these storms. Documented impact includes shoreline erosion, infilling of the seaward sides of estuaries by washover fan deposition, generation of new tidal inlets, deposition of both subtidal and supratidal sediment layers, and rapid sediment infilling and delta growth as a result of hurricane-caused rainfall and runoff.

At this point, it is difficult to outline a single scheme of hurricane impact, because no two storms behave exactly the same. This fact was made clear in Perkins and Enos' (1968) comparison of Hurricanes *Donna* (1960) and *Betsy* (1965), two storms of similar intensity but with greatly differing effects on the coastal environments of the Bahamas and South Florida. For example, *Donna*'s

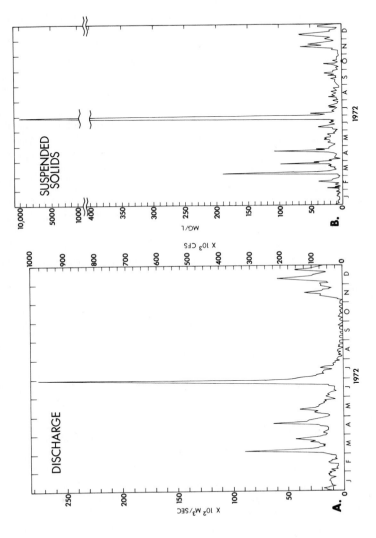

Figure 7. Changes in Susquehanna River at Conowingo, Maryland, as a result of flooding caused by Hurricane Agnes in June, 1972 (slightly modified after Schubel, 1974). A) Discharge. B) Suspended solids.

most striking influence was the deposition of supratidal mud layers, whereas *Betsy* was characterized by a lack of supratidal sedimentation (Perkins and Enos, 1968; p. 716). These differences were apparently the result of a combination of factors, including differences in tide levels and storm approach directions, as well as the fact that *Donna* (1960) had swept much of the area clean of friable reef rock and loose debris and sediments prior to the arrival of *Betsy* (1965). In some instances, smaller storms may be more effective than larger ones, if, for example, they stall in the coastal zone and produce heavy rainfall.

Most students of storms are much impressed by the magnitude with which coastal sedimentation patterns can be altered by a single storm within an instant of geological time. Tanner (1961; p. 2266) concluded that Hurricane *Donna* (1960) "appears to have done 100 years' work, considering the typical energy thought to prevail in the area" (southwest Florida); and as summarized above, Schubel (1974) concluded that an equivalent of 50 years of normal sedimentation occurred in Chesapeake Bay during one week as a result of Hurricane *Agnes* (1972). Thus, sedimentation in coastal areas appears to take place primarily as a series of energy bursts or spurts, a process that could be termed *quantum* sedimentation (Hayes, 1967).

References

1. Andrews, P. B. 1970. Facies and genesis of a hurricane washover fan, St. Joseph Island, central Texas coast. Bur. Econ. Geol., U. Texas. Rept. Inves. No. 67, 147 pp.

2. Ball, M. M., E. A. Shinn and K. W. Stockman. 1967. The geologic effects of Hurricane *Donna*. Jour. Geology 75:583-597.

3. Beardsley, R. C., and B. Butman. 1974. Circulation on the New England continental shelf: Response to strong wind storms, Geophys. Res. Lett. 1(4):181-184.

4. Brown, L. F., Jr., J. L. Brewton, H. J. McGowen, T. J. Evans, W. L. Fisher, and C. G. Groat. 1976. Environmental geologic atlas of the Texas coastal zone—Corpus Christi area. Univ. Texas. Bureau of Econ. Geol., Austin, Texas. 123 pp.

5. Cooperman, A. I., and H. C. Sumner. 1962. North Atlantic tropical cyclones, 1961. Mariner's Weather Log. 6(1):1-8.

6. De Angelis, R. M. 1973. North Atlantic tropical cyclones, 1972. Mariners Weather Log. 17(11):6-14.

7. Dolan, R., and P. Godfrey. 1973. Effects of Hurricane *Ginger* on the barrier islands of North Carolina. Geol. Soc. Amer. 84(4):1329-1334.

8. Dunn, G. E., and B. I. Miller. 1960. Atlantic Hurricanes. Louisiana State Press. 326 pp.

9. El-Ashry, M. T. 1966. Photointerpretation of shoreline changes in selected areas along the Atlantic and Gulf coasts of the United States. Univ. Illinois Ph.D. thesis in Geology.

10. El-Ashry, M. T., and H. R. Wanless. 1965. The birth and early growth of a tidal delta. Jour. Geol. 73(2):404-406.

11. _____ . 1968. Photo interpretation of shoreline changes between Cape Hatteras and Cape Fear (North Carolina). Mar. Geol. 6:347-379.

12. Fisk, H. N. 1959. Padre Island and the Laguna Madre Flats, coastal south Texas. Second Coastal Geography Conf., R. J. Russell, Chm. April 6–9, 1959. Louisiana State Univ., Baton Rouge, pp. 103-151.

13. Forristall, G. Z. 1974. Three-dimensional structure of storm-generated currents. J. Geophys. Res. 79(18):2721-2729.

14. Freeman, J.C., L. Baer, and G. H. Jung. 1957. The bathystropic storm tide. J. Marine Res. 16:12-22.

15. Ginsburg, R. N., and L. A. Hardie. 1975. Tidal and storm deposits, northwestern Andros Island, Bahamas, pp. 201-208. *In* R. N. Ginsburg (ed.), Tidal Flats, Springer-Verlag, New York.

16. Gohren, H. 1976. Currents in tidal flats during storm surges. Proc. 15th Coastal Eng. Conf., Honolulu, I:959-970.

17. Hayes, M. O. 1967. Hurricanes as geological agents: Case studies of Hurricanes *Carla* 1961 and *Cindy* 1963. Univ. Texas. Bur. Econ. Geol. Rept. 61. 56 pp.

18. Leatherman, S. P. 1976. Barrier island dynamics: Overwash processes and eolian transport. Proc. 15th Coastal Eng. Conf., Honolulu, I:1958-1974.

19. McGowen, J. H. 1970. Gum Hollow fan delta, Nueces Bay, Texas. Rept. of Inves. No. 69. Univ. Texas, Bureau Econ. Geol., 91 pp.

20. McGowen, J. H., C. G. Groat, L. F. Brown, W. L. Fisher, and A. J. Scott. 1970. Effects of Hurricane *Celia*, a focus of environmental geologic problems of the Texas coastal zone. Texas Univ. Bur. Econ. Geol. Circ. 70-3. 53 pp.

21. McGowen, J. H., and A. J. Scott. 1975. Hurricanes as geologic agents on the Texas coast, pp. 23-46. *In* L. E. Cronin (ed.), Estuarine Res. II., Geol. and Eng., Academic Press.

22. Morgan, J. P., L. G. Nichols, and M. Wright. 1958. Morphological effects of Hurricane *Audrey* on the Louisiana Coast. Baton Rouge, La., L.S.U. Coastal Studies Inst., Tech. Rept. 10. 53 pp.

23. Morton, R. A. 1976. Effects of Hurricane *Eloise* on beach and coastal structures, Florida Panhandle. Geology 4(5):277.

24. Murray, S. P. 1970. Bottom currents near the coast during Hurricane *Camille*. J. Geophys. Res. 75(24):4579-4582.

25. Nichols, R. L., and A. F. Marston. 1939. Shoreline changes in Rhode Island produced by hurricane of September 21, 1938. Geol. Soc. Amer. Bull., 50:1357-1370.

26. Neumann, C. J., and P. A. Hill. 1976. Computerized tropical cyclone climatology. Mariners Weather Log. 20 (5): 257-262.

27. Nordquist, R. W. 1972. Origin, development, and facies of a young hurricane washover fan on southern St. Joseph Island, central south Texas coast. M.S. thesis. Univ. Texas, Austin. 103 pp.

28. Perkins, R. D., and P. Enos. 1968. Hurricane *Betsy* in the Florida-Bahama area—geologic effects and comparison with Hurricane Donna. J. Geol. 76:710-717.

29. Pore, N.A. 1957. Ocean surface waves produced by some recent hurricanes. Monthly Weather Rev. 85:385-392.

30. _____ . 1961. The storm surge. Mariner's Weather Log. 5(5):1515-156.

31. Pray, L. C. 1966. Hurricane *Betsy* and nearshore carbonate sediments of the Florida Keys (abst.) Geol. Soc. Amer. Ann. Mtg.: 168-169.

32. Price, W. A. 1956. Hurricanes affecting the coast of Texas from Galveston to Rio Grande. Beach Erosion Board, U.S. Army Corps. Eng., 17 pp.

33. _____. 1958. Sedimentology and quaternary geomorphology of south Texas. Gulf Coast Assoc. Geol. Socs. Trans., 8:41-75.

34. Roehl, P. O. 1967. Stony Mountain (Ordovician) and Interlake (Silurian) facies analogs of recent low energy and subaerial carbonates, Bahamas. Am. Assoc. Petrol. Geol. 51:1979-2032.

35. Scott, A. J., R. A. Hoover, and J. H. McGowen. 1969. Effects of Hurricane *Beulah* 1967 on Texas coastal lagoons and barriers, pp. 221-236. *In* A. A. Castanares and F. B. Phleger (eds.), Coastal Lagoons: A Symposium. Mexico, Univ. Nac. Auton. de Mexico.

36. Schwartz, R. K. 1975. Nature and genesis of some storm washover deposits. CERC Tech. Memo. No. 61. 69 pp.

37. Schubel, J. R. 1974. Effects of tropical storm *Agnes* on the suspended solids of northern Chesapeake Bay, pp. 113-132. *In* R. J. Gibbs (ed.), Suspended Solids in Water, Plenum Press, N. Y.

38. Shepard, F. P., and H. R. Wanless. 1971. Our Changing Coastlines. McGraw-Hill Book Co., New York, 579 pp.

39. Shinn, E. A., R. N. Ginsburg, and R. M. Lloyd. 1965. Recent supratidal dolomite from Andros Island, Bahamas, pp. 112-123. *In* L. C. Pray and R. C. Murray, Dolomitization and Limestone Diagenesis, Soc. Econ. Paleon. Mineral. Spec. Pub. 13.

40. Shinn, E. A., R. M. Lloyd, and R. N. Ginsburg. 1969. Anatomy of a modern carbonate tidal-flat, Andros Island, Bahamas. Jour. Sed. Petrology 39:1202-1228.

41. Sloss, P. W. 1972. Coastal processes under hurricane action: Numerical simulation of a free-boundary shoreline. Ph.D. dissertation, Dept. of Geology, Rice University, Houston, Texas. 139 numbered leaves.

42. Smith, J. D., and T. S. Hopkins. 1972. Sediment transport on the continental shelf off Washington and Oregon in the light of recent current measurements, pp. 143-180. *In* D. J. P. Swift, D. B. Duane, and O. H. Pilkey (eds.), Shelf Sediment Transport: Process and Patterns, Dowden, Hutchinson, and Ross, Stroudsburg, Pa.

43. Sonu, C. J. 1970. Beach changes by extraordinary waves caused by Hurricane *Camille*. Louisiana State Univ., Coastal Studies Inst. Bull. 4:35-45.

44. Stoddart, D. R. 1963. Effects of Hurricane *Hattie* on the British Honduras reefs and cays. Atoll Res. Bull. 95:1-142.

45. _____. 1965. Resurvey of hurricane effects on the British Honduras reefs and cays. Nature 207:589-592.

46. Tannehill, I. R. 1956. Hurricanes. Princeton Univ. Press. 308 pp.

47. Tanner, W. F. 1961. Mainland beach changes due to Hurricane *Donna*. Jour. Geophys. Res. 66(7):2265-2266.

48. Wanless, H. R. 1975. Carbonate tidal flats of the Grand Canyon, pp. 269-278. *In* R. N. Ginsburg (ed.), Tidal Flats, Springer Verlag, New York.

49. Wanless, H. R., and J. M. Rine. 1976. Timing, character and preservability of sedimentation events in low energy coastal environments, southwest Florida: a contrast. Am. Assoc. Petrol. Geol. 60(4):731.

50. Warnke, D. A., V. Goldsmith, P. Grose, and J. J. Holt. 1966. Drastic beach changes in a low energy environment caused by Hurricane *Betsy*. J. Geophys. Res. 71(6):2013-2016.

51. Wright, L. D., F. J. Swaye, and J. M. Coleman. 1970. Effects of Hurricane *Camille* on the landscape of the Breton-Chandeleur Island chain and the eastern portion of the lower Mississippi Delta. Louisiana St. Univ. Coastal Studies Inst. Tech. Rept. 76:13-34.

52. Zabawa, C. F., and J. R. Schubel, 1974. Geologic effects of tropical storm *Agnes* on Upper Chesapeake Bay. Maritime Sediments 10(3):79-84.

53. Zeigler, J. M., C. R. Hayes, and S. D. Tuttle. 1959. Beach changes during storms on outer Cape Cod, Massachusetts. J. Geol. 67:318-336.

LAND–ESTUARY INTERACTIONS: FRESHWATER REQUIREMENTS OF ESTUARIES

RIVERINE INFLUENCE ON ESTUARIES: A CASE STUDY

William W. Schroeder

Marine Science Programs, University of Alabama System
P.O. Box 386
Dauphin Island, Alabama

Abstract: The Mobile Bay, Alabama estuary is a moderate-size, shallow, semi-enclosed coastal embayment with a simple triangular shape and a small tidal amplitude. It is also the terminus of the fourth largest river system in the United States, in terms of discharge, and the sixth largest on the North American continent. The average discharge of the Mobile River System is approximately 1,750 $m^3 sec^{-1}$ and the 10 and 90 percentile discharges are approximately 4,250 and 370 $m^3 sec^{-1}$, respectively. Waters from the system have a multi-faceted impact on the Mobile Bay. Discharges in excess of 7,000 $m^3 sec^{-1}$ are considered flooding and if they prevail over extended periods (10 to 15 days), can turn most of the bay into a near limnetic environment. Low-flow intervals, discharges less than 500 $m^3 sec^{-1}$, allow the upper bay waters to reach salinities > 26 ppt. Between these extreme conditions the river waters exhibit a variety of dispersion patterns as a function of specific discharge rate, local wind fields and amplitude of the astronomical tide, which results in significant longitudinal, lateral, and vertical salinity variations.

Introduction

Freshwater is an essential component of estuaries. The processes by which freshwater is made available to coastal bodies of marine waters vary. Land runoff, glacial melt and stream and river discharge are all prime examples. The broad variability that exists in both the sources of freshwater and the receiving basins has long been recognized. But often not enough emphasis is placed on the fact that this variability can lead to unique characteristics for individual estuaries. There has been a tendency among scientists, as well as administrators, to compare what is known about one estuary directly to another simply on the basis that they share some common general characteristic. This practice should be discouraged because it could result in the mismanagement of a vital resource. A multiple-year study was initiated in 1973 with this consideration in mind to characterize the riverine influence of the Mobile River System on the Mobile

Bay estuary. This paper deals with the first part of that study and presents a first-order descriptive characterization.

Mobile Bay, located in coastal Alabama, is a shallow submerged river valley with coastal barrier features that partially isolate it from the Gulf of Mexico. It is subjected to both periods of flooding which can render most of the bay almost limnetic, and periods of low flows which allow the upper bay waters to reach salinities >26 ppt. Hydrographic data have been collected in Mobile Bay utilizing a variety of platforms and instruments over different temporal and spatial regimes. These data have been incorporated into a physical environment atlas of coastal Alabama (Schroeder, 1976) and will serve as the major source of information for this paper.

Previous studies of hydrographic conditions in Mobile Bay have, in general, been limited. McPhearson (1970) presents average surface and bottom salinity and temperature patterns for bimonthly periods from May 1963 through October 1966. Consideration is given to variations in river discharge rates during the study period but only in a broad sense. Bault (1972) combines his monthly data from January 1968 through March 1969 with McPhearson's (1970) data, and also presents average bimonthly surface and bottom salinity and temperature patterns. Riverine influence is scarcely mentioned.

Schroeder (1977a) carried out an environmental characterization study of the surface waters of lower Mobile Bay utilizing time series salinity and temperature data during the fall of 1973 and the winter of 1973-74. The effect of river discharges ranging from low to high is discussed. A paper dealing with the impact of the 1973 spring flooding of the Mobile River System on Mobile Bay has recently been completed (Schroeder, 1977b).

The Study Area

Mobile Bay (Figure 1) is the terminus of the fourth largest river system, in terms of discharge, in the contiguous United States (Morisawa, 1968) and the sixth largest on the North American continent (Chow, 1964). Table 1 lists the average discharge and receiving basin of the largest North American river systems. The Mobile River System carries the combined flows of the Alabama and Tombigbee Rivers which account for approximately 95% of the freshwater input into Mobile Bay. The average discharge[1] of the system into the bay is approximately 1,750 m^3 sec^{-1} and the 10 and 90 percentile discharges are approximately 4,250 and 370 m^3 sec^{-1}, respectively. United States Geological Survey and U.S. Army Corps of Engineers data provide a 47-year record of the Mobile River System. Figure 2 compares average discharges (m^3 sec^{-1}) for each water year to the 47-year (1929–1976) average discharge (m^3 sec^{-1}). The maximum annual average discharge occurred in water year 1949 with 2,993 m^3 sec^{-1}, while the minimum annual average discharge is shared among water years 1931, 1934, 1941, and 1954, all ranging between 1,034 and 1,079 m^3 sec^{-1}. Water years 1973 through 1976 are all "wet" years, falling well above the 47-year average. The monthly average discharges for water year 1976 are

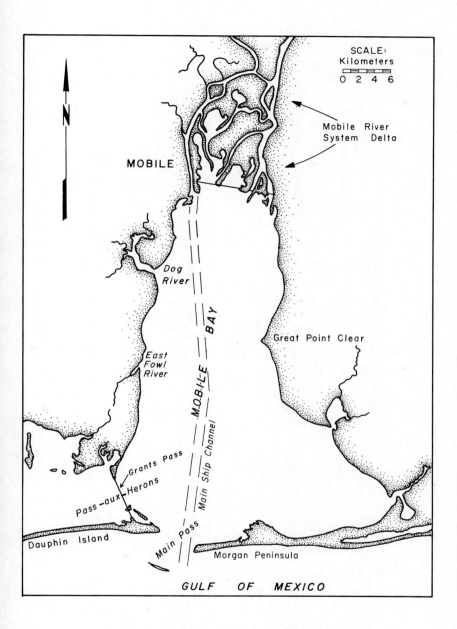

Figure 1. Map of the study area.

Table 1. North American River Systems

River System	Average Discharge (m³ sec⁻¹)	Receiving Basin
Mississippi	17,560	Gulf of Mexico ○
Mackenzie	12,740	Beaufort Sea ○
St. Lawrence	11,330	Gulf of St. Lawrence △
Columbia	6,650	Pacific Ocean □
Yukon	4,250	Bering Sea ○
→ Mobile	1,750	Mobile Bay △
Susquehanna	1,010	Chesapeake Bay △
Sacramento	740	San Pablo Bay △ (Greater San Francisco Bay)
Apalachicola	710	Apalachicola Bay △
Colorado	650	Gulf of California △

□ major ocean   ○ marginal sea   △ coastal embayment

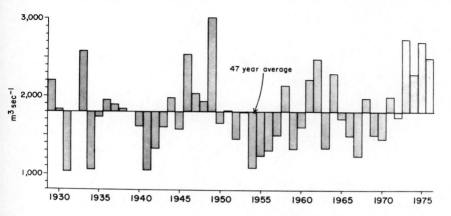

Figure 2. Mobile River System yearly average discharges for the period 1929-1976.

compared to the monthly average discharges over the previous 47 years in Figure 3. This 1976 water year curve is generally representative of the 1973 through 1975 water year curves. Above average discharges occur during both the normally low flow (August, September, and October) and normally high flow (February, March, and April) periods. This is consistent with the "wet" year concept. Figure 4 illustrates the daily average discharges for water year 1976. The striking feature of Figure 4 is the erratic fluctuation of the curve. This is principally a function of the sporadic and varied intensity of precipitation in the drainage basin. All other water years are also characterized by erratic fluctuations in their daily average discharge curves but the specific structure of each year is unique.

Mobile Bay (Figure 1) is triangular in shape with the apex to the north where the river delta interfaces and with the long axis (50 km) running perpendicular to the coastline. There are two openings in the southern portion of the bay: one to the Gulf of Mexico, Main Pass, and one to East Mississippi Sound, Pass-aux-Herons. Main Pass is responsible for approximately 85% and Pass-aux-Herons for approximately 15% of the exchange of waters in and out of Mobile Bay, respectively. The bay's average width is 17 km and maximum width is 38 km. The average depth at mean high water (MHW) is 3 m and the maximum depth, which occurs in East Main Pass, is 13 m. The volume of Mobile Bay is calculated to be 3.2×10^9 m^3 at mean high water (Crance, 1971). The replacement time for the MHW volume of the bay is approximately 21 days utilizing the 1,750 m^3 sec^{-1} average river discharge rate. A dredged ship channel, 120 m x 12 m, runs from Main Pass to the Port of Mobile. Mobile Bay is subjected primarily to a daily astronomical tide with an average tidal range <.5 m and a maximum tidal range of .8 m. Additional information on tides can be found in Marmer (1954) and McPhearson (1970).

The dominant wind fields over the bay are a northwest to northeast system during the late fall and winter and a southeast to southwest system in the spring

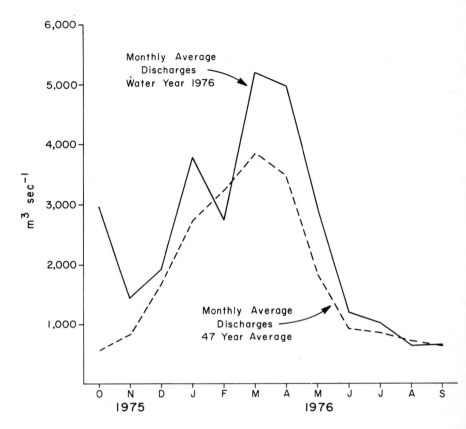

Figure 3.   *Mobile River System monthly average discharges for water year*
1976 compared to the 47-year average monthly discharges.

and summer. Often during the summer a land-sea breeze system prevails, and
during all seasons multiple day periods of light variable winds to calm may
occur. Detailed meteorological observations for lower Mobile Bay are presented
in Schroeder (1976).

Discussion

The effect freshwater input has on Mobile Bay will be examined for a
variety of river discharge rates.

Lower river discharge

Low flow conditions for this paper are defined as discharges <500 m^3
sec^{-1}. The lowest 7-day average flow on record for the Mobile River System is

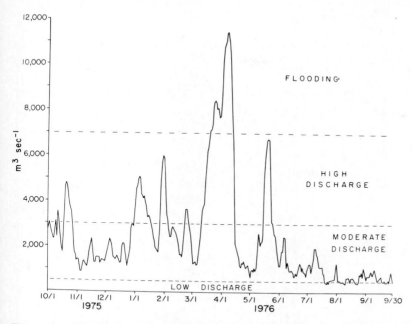

Figure 4. Mobile River System daily average discharges for water year 1976.

223 m³ sec⁻¹, which occurred in 1954 (Peirce, 1967). To illustrate the salinity structure of Mobile Bay during low river discharge the low flow periods of late summer through the fall of 1976 will be utilized. The lowest 7-day average flow during this period was 287 m³ sec⁻¹ recorded during October 13–19. Direct impact of low flow waters is totally confined to the upper bay. River waters quickly lose their absolute identity (salinity < 1.0 ppt) by mixing with upper bay waters to form salinities of 4 to 10 ppt.

An example of the salinity field structure of the upper bay is illustrated in Figure 5. These data were collected November 2, 1976, during a 7-day average low flow period of 370 m³ sec⁻¹. A pronounced salinity intrusion (wedge) with values > 22.0 ppt is depicted by the bottom salinity field. This feature resided in the center of the upper bay during high tide. Higher salinity values were observed in the ship channel but these are not considered here[2]. Slightly lower salinity waters prevailed on the bottom along the western (< 14.0 ppt) and eastern (< 18.0 ppt) shores and on the surface (8.0–13.0 ppt). Examination of the vertical profiles generated at selected stations indicates that a well-defined two-layer system existed with a major halocline present at 2.0 to 2.5 m in the 3.0 to 3.5 m water column. At low tide during the same survey the influence of river waters shifted 10 km southward in concert with a southward shift of the salinity intrusion. Winds during this survey varied between northwest to northeast at 1 to 12 k.

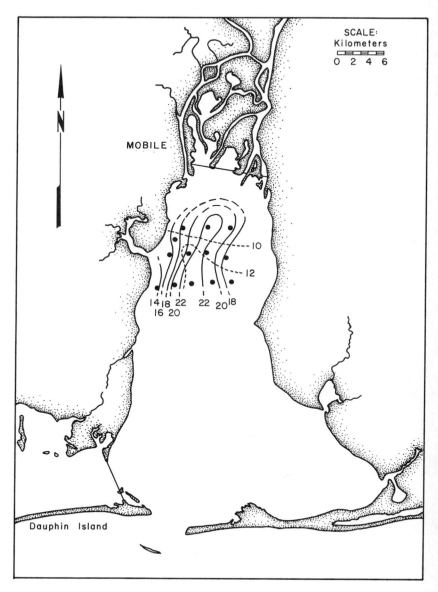

Figure 5. Surface (dashed lines) and bottom (solid lines) salinity (ppt) fields
in upper Mobile Bay, November 2, 1976, during low river discharge
and high tide.

Continuously recorded salinity data from 2 km off the mouth of East Fowl River, midway up the bay on the western shore, are presented in Figure 6. These data were collected from mid-August to mid-September 1976, at a 2.0 m depth in a 2.5 m water column. Data were recorded hourly. Daily average salinities ranged between 10.0 and 27.6 ppt and the absolute extremes were 6.0 ppt and 30.8 ppt. Over one-half of the daily averages exceeded 20.0 ppt and absolute maximum values > 26.0 ppt were common. The same type of data were collected during October 1976, 2 km off Great Point Clear, on the opposite side of the bay, at 2.5 m in a 3.0 m water column (Schroeder, 1976). Salinities of the same magnitude were observed there. All of these time series salinity curves are characterized by erratic fluctuations of significant proportions, similar to the daily average river discharge curves. Because of the obvious linkage between the two systems, this is not an unexpected relationship.

Bottom (4.0 m) salinities at Grants Pass during September and October 1976 ranged between 6.0 and 13.0 ppt (Schroeder, 1976). These salinities are

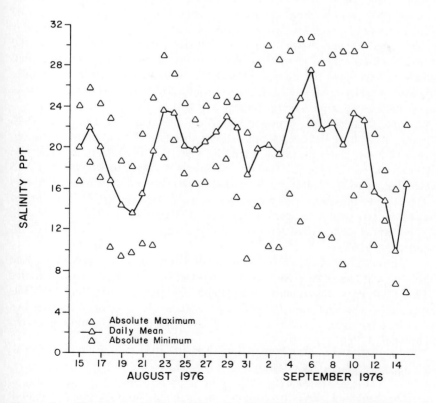

Figure 6.   *Time series bottom (2.0 m) salinity (ppt) structure off East Fowl River.*

considerably lower than the mid-bay values and an explanation to account for this is not apparent. Surface (1.0 m) salinities above 30 ppt have been reported for Grants Pass (Schroeder, 1976 and 1977a), which precludes the possibility that only moderate to low salinity waters are present in that area. The ranges of average surface (0–1.0 m) and bottom (7.0–9.0 m) salinities at East Main Pass for August through November 1976, generated from monthly 26-hour surveys, were 20.0 to 28.0 ppt and 31.0 to 32.0 ppt respectively (Schroeder, 1976).

Moderate river discharge

For this paper the range 500 to 3,000 m^3 sec^{-1} is defined as moderate discharge. The impact of moderate river discharge waters is felt into the middle of Mobile Bay. River waters easily maintain their identity (salinities < 1.0 ppt) in the upper bay, and can be observed at the surface as far away as Grants Pass. Generally, however, they are mixed with bay waters after moving into mid-bay. A typical salinity field structure during a moderate discharge is presented in Figure 7. The bottom salinity field, observed at high tide, depicts low salinity waters (< 6.0 ppt) present along the western and eastern shores and a moderate salinity (10.0 to 12.0 ppt) intrusion into the center of mid-bay. Surface salinities center around 4.0 ppt. A two-layer system is only apparent in the vicinity of the intrusion and even there the vertical profiles indicate the presence of only a weak halocline. Very little change was observed in the salinity structure at low tide. However, salinity values were decreased uniformly by 2.0 to 4.0 ppt. Winds during this survey were west to southwest at 1 to 10 k.

Data from off the mouth of East Fowl River during December 1976 (Figure 8) illustrate the time series salinity structure of west mid-bay bottom waters (2.0 m). Daily averages ranged between 3.0 to 13.0 ppt and absolute extremes were < 1.0 ppt and 19.4 ppt. At Grants Pass the ranges of surface (0.5 m) and bottom (4.0 m) salinities during late November and December 1976 were 1.0 to 9.0 ppt and 4.0 to 15.0 ppt, respectively (Schroeder, 1976). Salinities at East Main Pass over a complete tide cycle on December 7, 1976 were 16.0 to 22.0 ppt on the surface (0–1.0 m) and 25.0–32.0 ppt on the bottom (7.0–9.0 m) (Schoeder, 1976).

During July 1–2, 1975, 26-hour surveys were simultaneously run at East Main Pass and Grants Pass. Surface (0–1.0 m) and bottom (7.0–9.0 m) salinities at East Main Pass ranged between 18.0 and 29.0 ppt, and 31.0 and 33.0 ppt, respectively, while at Grants Pass salinities were nearly vertically homogeneous (0–4.0 m) but ranged between 6.0 and 20.0 ppt over the sampling period (Schroeder, 1976).

High river discharge

Discharges of 3,000 to 7,000 m^3 sec^{-1} are defined for this paper as high river discharge. During these periods the upper bay and upper-middle bay are totally under the influence of river waters while conditions in lower-middle bay

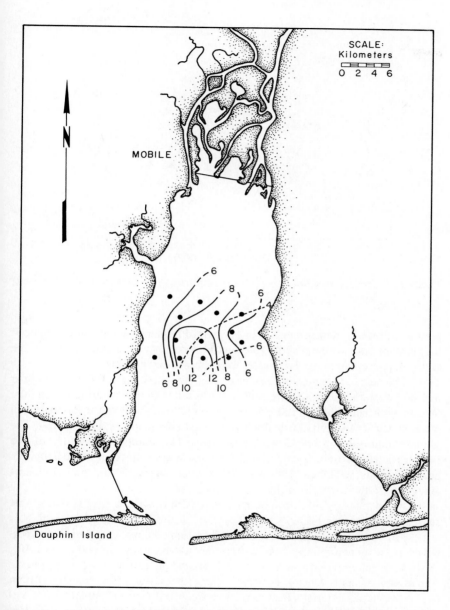

Figure 7. Surface (dashed lines) and bottom (solid lines) salinity (ppt) fields in middle Mobile Bay, March 1, 1977, during moderate river discharge and high tide.

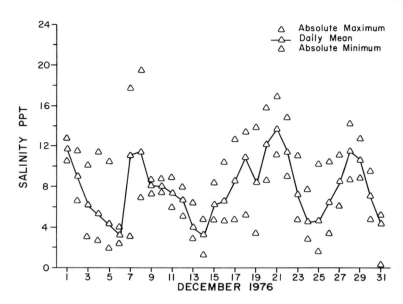

Figure 8.   Time series bottom (2.0 m) salinity (ppt) structure off East Fowl River.

are transitional between river and bay waters. Frequently the shoreward half of the western bay, all the way to Pass-aux-Herons, as well as the surface of the entire bay, is covered by river water for multiple-day periods.

The degree to which high river discharge waters can influence the upper half and western side of Mobile Bay is illustrated in Figure 9 during a high tide. Waters with salinities < 2.0 ppt are present throughout the upper half and western bay. The salinity intrusion is confined to the eastern side of the bay. The highest salinities observed were 15.2 ppt. The compact structure of the isohalines southwest of Great Point Clear demonstrates the force of the hydraulic head associated with the southward flowing river waters. Salinity measurements taken during the low tide of this survey indicated no significant shifting of the salinity structure and < 2.0 ppt changes in salinity values. Winds during this survey were variable.

The time series salinity structure of bottom (2.0 m) waters off East Fowl River is represented by the January-February 1976 survey interval (Figure 10). Daily averages centered around 2.0 to 4.0 ppt and the extremes were 0 ppt (river water) and 6.7 ppt. During February 1976, the surface (0.5 m) and bottom (4.0 m) salinities at Grants Pass ranged between < 1.0 to 7.0 ppt and 1.0 to 9.0 ppt respectively (Schroeder, 1976). The ranges of surface (0–1.0 m) and bottom (7.0–9.0 m) salinities observed at East Main Pass during the January and February 1976 26-hour surveys were 4.0 to 20.0 ppt and 14.0 to 36.0 ppt, respectively (Schroeder, 1976).

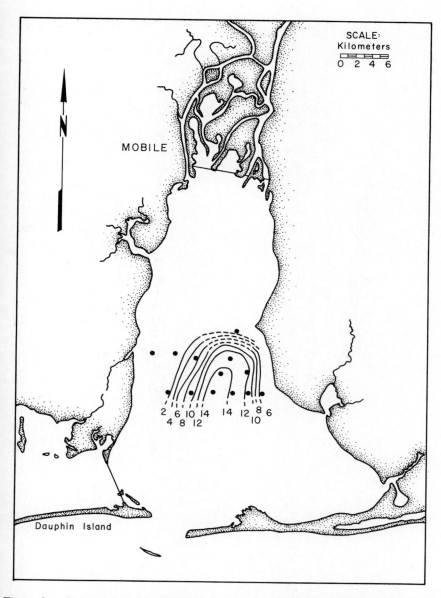

Figure 9.   Bottom salinity (ppt) field in middle Mobile Bay, March 16, 1977, during high river discharge and high tide.   Surface waters were all < 2.0 ppt.

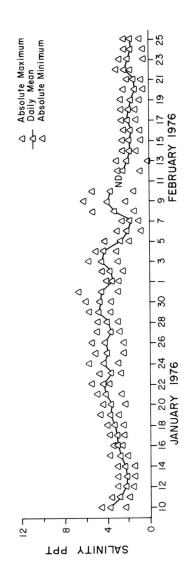

Figure 10. Time series bottom (2.0 m) salinity (ppt) structure off East Fowl River.

Flooding

Flooding conditions are defined as discharges $> 7,000 \text{ m}^3 \text{ sec}^{-1}$ following Peirce (1966). Flooding discharges can turn the greater part of Mobile Bay into a near limnetic system. The two areas which are only partially influenced by flooding are the region adjacent to Main Pass and the deeper portions of the main shipping channel. Figure 11 illustrates the bottom salinity field of lower Mobile Bay during the March and April floods of 1973 (20-day flood, maximum discharge 9,500 m^3 sec^{-1}). The intruding salinity wedge managed to move only 8 km into the bay. During this survey the tide was high and the winds were southeast. Therefore it is suggested that this is representative of the condition of maximum influence from the Gulf of Mexico during this flooding period. The steep vertical gradients of salinity associated with the salinity wedge (Figure 12) attest to the magnitude of the hydraulic head produced by the flooding river waters.

During the March and April floods of 1976, a 24-day flood with a maximum discharge of 11,500 m^3 sec^{-1}, the bottom (2.0 m) waters of East Fowl

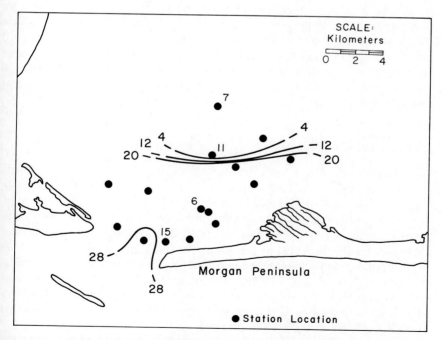

Figure 11. Bottom salinity (ppt) field in lower Mobile Bay, April 17, 1973, during flooding discharges. Surface waters were all < 4.0 ppt.

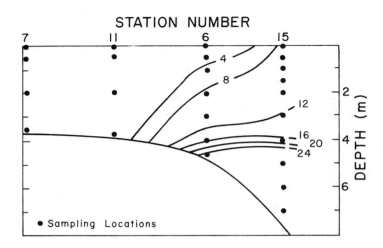

Figure 12. Vertical section of salinity (ppt) in lower Mobile Bay, April 17, 1973. See Figure 11 for station locations.

River were principally river waters (< 1.0 ppt), the surface (0.5 m) and bottom (4.0 m) waters at Grants Pass ranged between < 1.0 to 4.0 ppt and the surface (0–1.0 m) and bottom (7.0–9.0 m) waters at East Main Pass were < 1.0 to 2.0 ppt and 20.0 to 33.0 ppt, respectively (Schroeder, 1976). The replacement time for the MHW volume of Mobile Bay during both the 1973 flood (average flooding discharge 8,800 m³ sec⁻¹) and the 1976 flood (average flooding discharge 8,450 m³ sec⁻¹) is calculated to be approximately four days.

Summary and Conclusion

The Mobile Bay estuary is a moderate size (3.2×10^9 m³), shallow (average 3 m), semi-enclosed coastal embayment with a simple triangular configuration and a small tidal amplitude (average < .5 m). To date, the major man-made modification consists of a dredged ship channel, 120 m x 12 m, from the mouth to the head of the bay, a distance of 50 km. Approximately 95% of the freshwater input is provided by the Mobile River System, averaging 1,750 m³ sec⁻¹, through a single delta at the head of the bay. The pattern of average annual discharge has extremes of < 500 to > 7,000 m³ sec⁻¹. Therefore on an annual basis the influence of the Mobile River System on the Mobile Bay estuary can range from a simple source of freshwater at low discharges to near total dominance during high discharges and flooding.

The amount of freshwater discharged from the System can fluctuate rapidly. It is not uncommon, over a 10-day period, for discharges to change by ± 4,000 m³ sec⁻¹, which is equivalent to ± 2 to 3X in discharge rates; while over a 15-day period, changes of ± 10,000 m³ sec⁻¹ have been observed, which is equivalent to ± 5 to 10X in discharge rates. These freshwater input fluctuations, coupled with the triangular shape and shallow depth of the bay result in significant, non-symmetric, bay-wide salinity field fluctuations over generally the same periods. Longitudinal, lateral, and vertical variations in salinity are regularly observed.

Consistent with northern hemisphere conditions, river waters favor the western shore (right-hand side) as they move to the south while Gulf of Mexico waters favor the eastern shore (right-hand side) as they move to the north. However, movement of river waters down the eastern shore is not uncommon. At any given time portions of the bay can be highly stratified while other areas will be near vertically homogeneous. Two examples are, (1) during low river discharges a stratified system can exist in the upper bay while the high salinity lower bay waters can approach vertical homogeneity, and (2) during high river discharges the upper bay can be vertically uniform with river waters while the lower half of the bay becomes a stratified system.

Because of the bay's large surface area and shallow depth the wind can be both an important driving force and a modifying force. Winds with a northerly component complement river flow and move river influence toward the lower bay. The opposite condition occurs with southerly winds that move offshore waters into the bay and therefore move river influence up the bay. Winds with east or west components tend to push the surface waters to the opposite side of the bay and consequently there is often a complementary shift of the bottom waters to the windward side of the bay. Westerly winds are certain to play a role during some of the periods when river waters are moving south along the eastern shore. Multi-day periods of strong sustained winds can mix the entire bay vertically, except for the deeper areas. Data collected recently, particularly during moderate-to-high river discharge, suggest that the bay can begin to recover from this homogeneous condition in a matter of hours and re-establish a stratified system, salinity gradients of 8.0 to 16.0 ppt, in < 48 hours.

Daily astronomical tidal action, during maximum amplitude tropical tides, can shift the north-south position of the salinity intrusion in the bay as much as 15 to 20 km and thus can influence where river water and the salinity intrusion interface. On the other hand, during minimum amplitude equatorial tides, little or no movement of the river water-salinity intrusion interface is observed.

Acknowledgement

This research was supported in part by the USDI Office of Water Research and Technology through Alabama's Water Resources Research Institute of Auburn University (Project A-058-ALA), the USDC-NOAA office of Sea Grant through the Mississippi-Alabama Sea Grant Program (Grants 04-5-158-54 and 04-6-158-44060), and the National Aeronautics and Space Administration (Contracts NAS5-21876 and NAS8-30810). Technical assistance and field support were provided by R. Lysinger, G. Oakes, J. Shapiro and numerous staff and students of the Dauphin Island Sea Lab. Data processing was carried out by Ms. R. Horton and drafting was done by Ms. L. Lutz. A special thanks to Mr. H. Doyal, USACOE-Mobile, for teaching me about the Mobile River System.

Marine Environmental Sciences Consortium Contribution No. 16 and Contribution No. 6 from the Aquatic Biology Program of the University of Alabama.

References

1. Bault, E. I. 1972. Hydrology of Alabama estuarine areas—Cooperative Gulf of Mexico estuarine inventory. Alabama Mar. Res. Bull. 7:1-36.
2. Chow, V. T. 1964. Handbook of applied hydrology. McGraw-Hill, New York, 1467 pp.
3. Crance, J. H. 1971. Description of Alabama estuarine areas—Cooperative Gulf of Mexico estuarine inventory. Alabama Mar. Res. Bull. 6:1-85.
4. Marmer, H. A. 1954. Tides and sea level in the Gulf of Mexico, pp. 101-118. *In* Gulf of Mexico, its origin, waters and marine life. Bull. Fish and Wildl. Ser. 55. Washington, D.C.
5. McPhearson, R. M., Jr. 1970. The hydrography of Mobile Bay and Mississippi Sound, Alabama. Alabama Univ. Mar. Sci. Inst., J. Mar. Sci. 1:1-83.
6. Morisawa, M. 1968. Streams, their dynamics and morphology. McGraw-Hill, New York, 175 pp.
7. Peirce, L. B. 1966. Surface water in southwestern Alabama. Alabama Geol. Sur. Bull. 84:1-132.
8. _____. 1967. Seven-day low flow and flow duration of Alabama streams. Alabama Geol. Sur. Bull. 87 (Part A):1-114.
9. Schroeder, W. W. 1976. Physical environment atlas of coastal Alabama. Mississippi-Alabama Sea Grant Progam 76-034, 275 pp.
10. _____. 1977a. Sea-truth and environmental characterization studies of Mobile Bay, Alabama, utilizing ERTS-1 data collection platforms. Remote Sensing of Environment, 6:27-43.
11. _____. 1977b. The impact of the 1973 flooding of the Mobile River System on Mobile Bay and East Mississippi Sound. Northeast Gulf Sci. 1(2):68-76.

Notes

1. Mobile River System discharges are computed using U.S. Geological Survey Surface Water Records (Alabama) of the flows of the Tombigbee River at Coffeeville (02469761), Alabama, and of the Alabama River at Claiborne (02429500), Alabama. To calculate the discharge of the system, the flows at these two gauging stations are added together and multiplied by 1.07. Because of the distance between Mobile Bay and these gauging stations, a lag period for transit time of five to nine days is required.

2. Salinity values in the ship channel, because of its depth (12 m), are normally much higher than adjacent undredged bay bottom. Therefore the bottom salinity fields constructed for this paper will not utilize ship channel data but rather will consider, for ship channel stations, the two to four meter water column values depending on the depth of the bottom plain. This procedure is for drafting convenience and is not meant to suggest that the ship channel does not play a role in the hydrography of Mobile Bay, for it certainly provides an avenue for high salinity waters to move into the bay.

INFLUENCE OF FLOODING AND TIDES
ON NUTRIENT EXCHANGE FROM A TEXAS MARSH

Neal E. Armstrong

Department of Civil Engineering
The University of Texas at Austin
Austin, Texas

and

Melvin O. Hinson Jr.

Resources for the Future
Washington, D.C.

Abstract: The brackish water marshes of Lavaca Bay, Texas were investigated for the mechanisms of carbon, nitrogen, and phosphorus transport from the marsh to adjacent waters and for the magnitude of the areal exchange rates. This study, carried out in the summer of 1974, shows the importance of freshwater flooding and wind tides to nutrient exchange in contrast to the solunar tidal mechanism which dominates East Coast estuaries. In addition, the irregular cycle of inundation by floodwaters or wind tides, the growth of algae during inundation and the subsequent drying of these algae during dewatering with their physical transport out of the marsh during the next inundation period appear to provide as important a source of nutrients in the brackish marshes as the emergent plants.

Introduction

Saltwater marshes and grassflats have been shown to play an extremely important role in providing organic and inorganic food material to a variety of biota in estuaries. Numerous studies along the Atlantic coast of the United States and a few on the middle Gulf Coast have delineated the pathways of marsh-produced detritus, measured the productivity of the emergent vegetation and associated periphyton of the marsh, and shown the effect of organic waste and associated nutrients on the growth and species composition of the saltwater marsh system. Recent studies have attempted to quantify the amounts of carbon, nitrogen, and phosphorus reaching adjacent estuarine waters as a measure of the contribution of the marshes to the total productivity of the bay, and thus to assess the impact of human developments that fill in and replace marshes.

Attention in Texas, however, has been focused on those marsh systems which are dependent on freshwater flooding or other non-tidal flushing mechanisms to transport nutrients from the marshes to adjacent waters. Substantial marsh areas in southern Texas are located at the heads of estuaries away from tidal exchange, which is generally regarded as the major nutrient transport mechanism in East Coast estuaries. Also, the tidal range in the Gulf of Mexico is substantially less (about one foot or less in the marsh area) than along the East Coast, and freshwater flooding conditions and wind driven estuarine water exchange (wind tides) in the marshes may account for the major portion of nutrient exchange from these Texas marshes. To the date of this study, essentially no data on nutrient exchange rates from Texas estuaries were available, and because upstream water resource developments (impoundments) potentially could reduce flushing due to flooding, the Texas Water Development Board (now the Department of Water Resources) initiated studies to determine the importance of freshwater inflows to Texas estuaries. This was one of the studies, and its purpose was to provide initial data on the exchange rates of carbon, nitrogen, and phosphorus as a function of tidal exchange and freshwater flooding in one of the Texas marshes, since it was not known whether the nutrient-exchange-rate data from the tidal-exchange-dominated East Coast estuaries would apply to Texas marshes.

Methods

Study site

The site chosen for these studies was a bayou draining to Swan Lake which lies in the Lavaca River delta just northeast of the river before it empties into Lavaca Bay. Swan Lake drains to Lavaca Bay and is under tidal influence; it also receives floodwater from the river after it overbanks the marsh area and drains through the bayou. The area consisted of patches of emergent grass (primarily *Scirpus maritima*) and interspersed shallow pools of water, left at high tide, containing blue-green algal mats which can tolerate periods of dessication.

Sampling stations

A total of five sampling stations was utilized at various times (see Figure 1); four stations were located along the major bayou and its tributaries that drain the extensive marshes on the peninsula between Swan Lake and the Lavaca River, and a fifth was established in Swan Lake approximately 30 m from the mouth of the main bayou.

Station 1 was located on a well-defined section of the major marsh bayou where the channel sidewalls are steep and distinct and the entire bed composed of smooth clay scoured by rapid water movements. Here the bayou was 12 feet wide and 2 to 3 feet deep, depending on the prevailing tide stage. Station 2 was established on a small feeder channel that enters the main bayou between Station 1 and Swan Lake; however, this small and shallow (less than one foot deep)

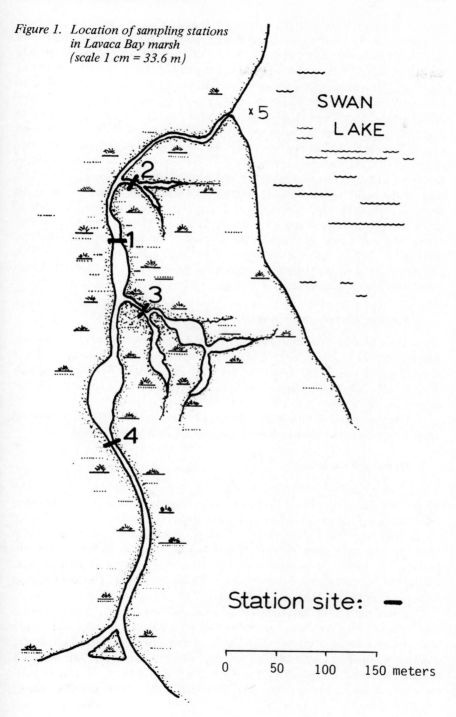

Figure 1. Location of sampling stations in Lavaca Bay marsh (scale 1 cm = 33.6 m)

SWAN LAKE

×5

2

1

3

4

Station site: —

0   50   100   150 meters

channel was abandoned after the first field trip when it became apparent that even a slight drop in overall water level would leave no water in the channel and completely isolate the algal mat pools that it drained. Station 3 was established on a small distinct bayou that drains a substantial vegetated area and a series of algae-rich pools between the major bayou and Swan Lake. A flooding tide often caused water to infiltrate into the marsh along the Swan Lake shoreline, flow through this channel, and supplement the water moving into the back reaches of the marsh upstream of the main bayou channel. Station 4 was situated on the main bayou channel after it narrows "downstream" from a large pool. From this sampling site, the channel continues inland toward a large bi-lobed pond and extensive slightly-vegetated mudflats which serve as the alternate water reservoir for the main bayou. Because a temporary bridge was erected to span the bayou at each station for sampling, water samples, flow measurements, and *in situ* water quality measurements could be taken at the same point each time. These sampling points were determined by rating the bayou at each sampling station over the tidal cycle, following U.S. Geological Survey procedures. This procedure revealed the particular location in the channel cross section where water velocities approximated the average velocity for the cross section.

Sampling periods and frequency

Three field investigations were conducted at two-week intervals during the summer of 1974 to define the hydrologic and water quality characteristics of the selected marsh area. The first two sampling runs lasted for 24 hours each (June 27–28, July 11–12), while the third trip continued for 48 hours (July 30–August 1).

Hydraulic and *in situ* physical-chemical measurements were made and water samples taken each two hours throughout the sampling period.

Hydrologic conditions

Flow measurements were taken with a manually-held Pygmy meter #R-720 at 0.2, 0.6, and 0.8 total depth. Velocity in feet per second was caculated using an equation based on the number of revolutions of the meter cone wheel that occur in 40–70 seconds. Water depth at the sampling points was taken regularly with the Pygmy meter staff which was marked with 0.1 foot (3 cm) graduations. Velocity measurements at Stations 1 and 4 in particular were well within the accuracy of the meter used. These measurements are given in Armstrong, *et al.* (1975).

Since the marsh bayou acted as an oscillating stream system, it was important to know the sources of the waters in the bayou, that is, whether the water moving through the bayou could have come in from Swan Lake or the standing waters of the upstream marsh. This was determined by calculating the cumulative distance traveled by a single water mass during the period of measurement, which extended over at least one tidal cycle. The period of measurement was divided into time intervals, Δt, and the distance, r, that a water mass would travel in that time interval was calculated at $r = v \cdot \Delta t$ where v was the average velocity of the water during the time interval. Cumulative sums were computed for the total distance traversed by the water mass from the start of the measurement period to the end of that period. Plots of the cumulative distance traveled revealed the total distance upstream and downstream that a water mass would have moved over the measurement period.

The mass flow of marsh water through each station (in liters per second) was calculated by multiplying the average water velocity of each time interval by the cross-sectional area of the stream channel at that particular time and water stage. The flows were then integrated over time to obtain total flows on the flood and ebb portions of the tidal cycle. Finally, the instantaneous flow values were used in conjunction with nutrient concentrations to calculate mass flows into and out of the marsh.

Measurement and analysis of water quality

During the field sampling, temperature, pH, conductivity, and dissolved oxygen were monitored *in situ* at the various stations. The dissolved oxygen levels were measured with a YSI model 51A Dissolved Oxygen Meter that has manual temperature and salinity compensation. The probe was submerged about 15 cm and moved continually to insure stable readings. Both air and water temperatures (°C) were measured using the thermistor in the oxygen probe. Readings were taken at the same point in the bayou cross section as the flow measurements.

Water samples for laboratory analyses were collected approximately 15 cm below the water surface when depth permitted and were taken to exclude organic surface films. Samples were normally collected in new one-liter Cubitainers (Hedwin Corporation), although acid-cleaned glass bottles were used for a short time. A portable Beckman pH Meter was used to measure pH in these containers immediately after sampling.

Both total organic carbon (TOC) and volatile suspended solids (VSS) were measured to show the relative proportion of dissolved and particulate carbon. TOC samples were collected in 50-ml Nalgene vials and stored on ice with no preservative added. Upon return from the field, these samples were stored in a 4°C cold room until they could be run on a Beckman Total Organic Carbon Analyzer Model 915. All TOC measurements were completed within two days of returning.

Volatile suspended solids (VSS) was determined by filtering a 100-ml aliquot through a tared Reeve Angel 934 AH glass fiber filter (0.75 to 1.25 μ porosity), drying the filter for 12 hours in a 100°C oven, reweighing, and then combusting in a furnace at 550°C for 20 minutes. The difference between dry and combusted weights represented VSS.

Phosphorus samples were collected in the liter-size Cubitainers, preserved by the addition of 2 ml chloroform to stop biological degradation and nutrient regeneration, then stored in a 4° cold room until delivery to the Texas State Health Department Laboratory for analysis of total phosphorus and orthophosphorus content. Nitrogen samples were handled the same way, except that 2 ml of concentrated sulfuric acid (36N) was used as preservative. All samples analyzed by the State Health Department Laboratory were kept at 4°C until analysis, and analyses were usually completed within one week but no longer than two weeks. Checks were made for sample deterioration, and the sample storage procedures proved satisfactory. The State Health Department Laboratory analyzed the water samples for organic nitrogen, ammonia, nitrite, and nitrate on a Technicon Autoanalyzer using the U.S. Environmental Protection Agency procedures for freshwater samples. Levels of detection were: organic and ammonia nitrogen 0.1 mg/1, nitrite and nitate 0.05 mg/1, and phosphorus 0.01 mg/1. Samples with known concentrations of each nutrient were submitted periodically as an external check on analytical accuracy. Multiple samples were also submitted for sampling error determination.

Changes in the chemical forms and concentrations of carbon, nitrogen, and phosphorus over the tidal cycle were analyzed to determine the mass nutrient exchange between the marsh and adjacent Swan Lake. Since the volume of water moving through each station was known, nutrient mass flows were calculated as the product of the nutrient concentration and the flow at any particular time. Mass flows during both flood (entering marsh) and ebb (leaving marsh) periods were compared to illustrate the overall mass balance, and this difference was indicative of the marsh's role as source or sink for the particular substance. Finally, areal nutrient exchange rates were calculated by dividing the net mass flow out of the marsh by the contributing area.

Results

Field and weather conditions

The first sampling period (June 27–28, 1974) followed a time of heavy precipitation in the Lavaca River drainage basin, which produced flooding in the marsh. The marsh area was still extensively inundated when sampling began; the bases of *Scirpus maritimus* were partially submerged during both flood and ebb tides. Weather conditions during this first field trip included clear skies, air temperatures between 20°C and 29.5°C, and a slight easterly breeze that never surpassed 16 kph.

By the July 11–12, 1974 sampling period, the water levels had receded from the high levels found in June, and the marsh vegetation was partially submerged during the flooding period and fully emergent during ebb slack. Clear weather was prevalent on July 11, but early morning cloudiness produced a short heavy rainstorm at 0900 near the end of sampling on July 12. Air temperatures ranged from 24.1 to 29.3°C and winds from the southeast blew at 24–32 kph during July 11, but fell off after sunset and were very light during the early morning hours (0–8 mph) of July 12.

By the final sample period on July 30–August 1, water levels had dropped below levels recorded during previous trips, and the bayou channels emptied almost completely during ebb tide. The marsh was almost dry, with the water mainly confined to the marsh channels and larger pools during both flood and ebb periods. Marsh vegetation was almost exclusively emergent. The weather during this 48-hour trip varied considerably from clear skies to imposing thunderhead formations. However, only a slight drizzle fell to break the normal summertime drought during the second day. Air temperatures reached a maximum of 32.8°C during the late afternoon, and winds were generally calm (slight breezes from the north) during periods of precipitation, but as skies cleared, they switched to the southeast with a velocity of 16–24 kph.

Hydrologic conditions

During the first sampling period (June 27–28, 1974), water velocities reached 21.3 cm sec^{-1} (0.7 fps) on both the ebb and flood tides as the tide range changed from a low stage of 0.61 m (2.0 ft) to a high of 0.85 m (2.8 ft) at Station 1. Water movement over this period reached a theoretical length of 5200 m (about 17,000 ft), which means that both Swan Lake and interior pond water was reaching Station 1 during the tidal cycle. Similar water velocities and water movement were observed during July 11–12 when flood conditions still prevailed, but to a lesser extent than the first period. Water stage at Station 1 ranged from 0.61 m (2.0 ft) to 0.82 m (2.7 ft). Between July 30 and August 1, water velocities were less than 9 cm sec^{-1} (0.3 fps) most of the time, and water movement was only 3050 m (10,000 ft), reflecting the dry conditions prevailing. Water stage at Station 1 ranged from 0.26 m (0.85 ft) to 0.64 m (2.1 ft), but almost all flow was confined to the channels only.

Water flows into and out of the marsh are given in Table 1. Note the small inflow and large outflow on June 27–28 produced by the flood waters leaving the marsh. The July 11–12 data reveal large flows into and out of the marsh but a small net exchange as the marsh water levels, though still in a flood condition, respond to solunar and wind tidal changes. During dry conditions on July 30–August 1, flows were very low but still permitted a net outflow. Such conditions would represent a normal tide-induced exchange situation in these particular marshes.

Water quality conditions

Temperature and dissolved oxygen concentrations followed normal diurnal patterns; the range of levels measured over the measurement periods are given in Table 2. Increasingly sharp changes in temperature and dissolved oxygen concentrations and a widening range of the latter paralleled the decrease in water stage from period to period. During the last sampling period, the combination of low water level and high community respiratory demand resulted in anoxic conditions which killed mullet and various sciaenid fishes in the area.

**Table 1. Water flows through Lavaca Bay marsh stations
during three different hydrologic conditions**

		Water movement (liters/tidal cycle)			
		Into Marsh	Out of Marsh	Net Out	
Date	Station	$(10^6 1)$	$(10^6 1)$	$(10^6 1)$	Comments
6/27-28/74	1	4.527	10.886	6.359	Marsh inundated
	2*	0.066	0.077	0.011	
	3	0.381	0.517	0.136	
	4**	—	—	—	
7/11-12/74	1	7.386	7.550	0.176	Marsh partially inundated
	3	0.454	0.891	0.437	
	4	7.010	5.199	-1.811	
7/30-8/1/74	1	3.116	4.447	1.361	Marsh dry
	3	0.749	0.419	-0.330	
	4	2.269	3.354	1.085	

*Station discontinued after first field trip
**Station not established until second field trip

Blue crabs adjusted to the oxygen depletion by migrating out of the water as the oxygen level dropped. When photosynthesis and reaeration produced a reasonable dissolved oxygen concentration after sunrise, the crabs moved back into the marsh waters.

Total organic carbon and volatile suspended solid concentrations were weakly correlated with water stage during the first two sampling periods but were strongly correlated with water stage during the last sampling period. On the flooding tide, concentrations were at the lower end of the ranges given in Table 2, while on the ebbing tide the concentrations were highest. Similar results were obtained for organic and ammonia nitrogen and total and orthophosphorus, although the concentrations of inorganic forms of nitrogen were almost always at or below the level of detection of the analytical methods used.

A summary of the mass flows of the carbon, nitrogen, and phosphorus forms monitored at the various stations is given in Table 3 in units of kg tidal cycle^{-1} which for these measuring periods is roughly equivalent to kg d^{-1}. The small values for Station 3 reflect its small drainage area and contribution to mass flows. The negative values for flow and nutrients at Station 4 and positive values at Station 1 during the July 11-12 sampling period indicate that materials were being lost from the portion of the marsh studied through another exit at this particular water stage. This "sink" for carbon, nitrogen, and phosphorus and the small net flow out account for the small export values of these materials from Station 1.

Calculation of areal exchange rates from these data was made difficult because the actual contributing areas during the periods of measurement were not known. Based on a topographic survey of the area, about 92.5 ha drain to Station 4 and 130.3 ha to Station 1. However, the area actually contributing to Station 1 on a given tidal cycle was less than that and was calculated as the rectangular surface of a water volume with an inverted triangle cross section whose height was equal to the change in water stage from flood to ebb. Based on this approximation, the contributing areas were estimated to be 8.92, 7.63, and 2.56 ha for the June, July, and July–August sampling periods, respectively. The net areal exchange rates estimated for the drainage areas for Station 1 are given in Table 4. As the mass flows given in Table 3 showed, the organic forms of carbon, nitrogen and phosphorus were exchanged to the greatest extent, but the exchange rates during the dry period were as high or higher than the fully inundated period. Also, all the rates are positive, indicating net export from the marsh. Most of the exchange rates for inorganic nitrogen forms were unreliable because of the levels of detection available and are not included in Table 4.

The original data for the hydraulic and water quality conditions described above may be obtained from Armstrong *et al.* (1975).

Table 2: Summary of temperature levels and dissolved oxygen and nutrient concentrations at Station 1

		Range for Sampling Period		
Analysis	*Units*	*June 27-28*	*July 11-12*	*July 30-August 1*
Temperature	°C	25.2-31.8	26.2-30.3	25.1-33.9
Dissolved Oxygen	mg/1	5.0-10.1*	1.2-8.8*	0.5-10.8
Total Organic Carbon	mg/1	13-27	11-22	20-57**
Volatile Susp. Solids	mg/1		10-21	18-240**
Organic Nitrogen	mg/1	0.7-1.3	0.8-1.7	0.8-4.3**
Ammonia-N	mg/1	0.1-0.2	<0.1	0.1-0.5**
Nitrite-N	mg/1	<0.5	<0.5	<0.5
Nitrate-N	mg/1	<0.5	<0.5	<0.5
Total P	mg/1	0.09-0.15	0.09-0.13	0.08-0.65**
Ortho P	mg/1	0.06-0.09	0.01-0.02	0.01-0.18**

* Weakly correlated with tidal exchange
** Strongly correlated with tidal exchange

Table 3: Summary of mass flows of nutrients from a Lavaca Bay marsh (units are kg tidal cycle^{-1})

Nutrient	June 27-28			July 11-12			July 30-August 1		
	1	2	3	1	3	4	1	3	4
Total Organic Carbon	112.10	0.26	3.80	7.15	2.74	-13.30	70.00	0.00	13.20
Volatile Susp. Solids				11.65	-0.15	-318.00	214.00	1.04	258.00
Organic N	10.96	0.04	0.08	1.59	2.16	0.18	2.85	0.01	2.44
Ammonia N	0.66	<0.01	0.04	-0.02	<0.01	-0.20	0.15	<0.01	0.04
Nitrite N	0.33	<0.01	-0.01	0.02	<0.01	-0.06	0.08	<0.01	0.06
Nitrate N	0.17	<0.01	<0.01	<0.01	<0.01	-0.08	0.04	<0.01	0.04
Total P	0.90	<0.01	0.04	0.06	<0.01	-0.12	0.41	<0.01	0.62
Ortho P	0.49	<0.01	0.01	-0.02	<0.01	-0.07	0.19	<0.01	0.13

Table 4: Summary of nutrient exchange rates for East Coast and Texas marsh systems (Units are kg ha^{-1} d^{-1})

	DOC	POC	VSS	Nitrogen		P
				Total	Organic	
Saltwater Marsh						
Pomeroy et al. (1967)						0.1
Reimold (1972)						6.3
Settlemyer and Gardner (1975)			18.4			0.18
Woodwell et al. (1977)	0.23	-1.7				
Odum and de la Cruz (1967)			2.28			
Brackish Marsh						
Stevenson et al. (1976)				0.029		0.005
Axelrad et al. (1976)	1.4	2.1		0.094	0.16	-0.024
This study						
Flood drainage (June 27-28)	12.6			1.3	1.2	0.1
Small net exchange (July 11-12)	0.94		1.5	0.21	0.21	>0.01
Normal w/drying (July 30-August 1)	27.3		83.6	1.2	1.1	0.16
Dawson and Armstrong (1975)						
Normal tidal exchange	2.3			0.39		0.08
Following drying	5.9			2.1		0.19

Discussion

The dense growths of algae and rooted vegetation in the marsh provide a rich source of nutrients. Decomposition of dead plant material provides various grades of particulate and dissolved organics and inorganic nutrients for support of marsh producers and consumers and transport to adjoining estuarine systems. Ambient concentrations of these degradation products fluctuated with the direction of flow, especially with low water levels in the marsh, decreasing when Swan Lake waters entered the marsh and increasing as ebb flows drained the area. Inorganic nitrogen forms (NO_2, NO_3) remained below levels of detection during all field trips regardless of the origin of water being sampled. Presumably these nitrogen forms are being removed by the algal mats and attached algae as they become available in the marsh through nitrification.

For the first two sampling periods when water levels were moderately high, orthophosphorus levels exhibited only slight variation in response to flow direction changes. Total phosphorus measurements, which include a sizeable organic-related component, responded more like other degradation products, increasing in concentration with the exodus of marsh water. When the rooted plants and attached algae were totally emergent during the July 30–August 1 sampling trip and completely reliant on soil-associated phosphorus, levels of both forms showed distinct pulses related to the stage of the tidal cycle. Thus, leaching of phosphorus from the sediments may be an important and major source of phosphorus for attached and benthic algae in this marsh.

Mass balances for the various nutrient species showed that the marsh under study acted as a source of nutrients for the Swan Lake and upper Lavaca Bay systems during the period of measurement. Although the quantity of outward material flow differs with marsh hydrologic conditions, water moving through Station 1 on the main bayou always carried more nutrients out during ebb flow than were brought in during the preceding flood period. This evidence appears to support the role of this brackish marsh as a net exporter of nutrients.

Comparison of the carbon, nitrogen, and phosphorus exchange rates measured in this study with those found by others is made in Table 4. Export rates for dissolved organic carbon (or TOC) are higher generally than those measured by Woodwell *et al.* (1977) and Axelrad *et al.* (1976) in tide-dominated East Coast systems while the export rates for VSS were in the range of those found by Settlemyer and Gardner (1975) and Odum and de la Cruz (1967). Similar comparisons can be made for total and organic nitrogen and for phosphorus.

The nutrient-exchange patterns in this marsh follow those found by Pomeroy *et al.* (1972), Gardner (1975), and others in East Coast marshes with the exception of periodic drying of epiphytic algae and benthic algal mats. In marshes where the tidal range is high and the marsh is inundated at least once and often twice per day, drying does not occur to the extent that it does in marshes with smaller solunar tides, wind tides, and variable drying periods. After these dry periods the attached algae and algal mats slough off and are transported easily out of the marsh even under low water conditions with minimum inundation. Such a situation was observed in this study. Flood conditions following a dry period would also be expected to dislodge and transport this material in large quantities out of the marsh.

Partial confirmation of this pattern was made by Dawson and Armstrong (1975) using portions of the *Scirpus* marsh in laboratory microcosm studies in which nutrient exchange was measured before and after a four-week drying period. During a two-week monitoring period following drying, it was found that TOC and phosphorus exchange rates increased over sixfold. Similar results were obtained for algal mat microcosms. The magnitudes of these exchange rates were in the same range as the field studies.

Further work on other Texas marshes using laboratory microcosms has produced comparable results for those marshes which experience periodic drying (Armstrong and Gordon, 1977a; 1977b; Armstrong, Harris, and Gordon, 1977).

Conclusions

1. Solunar tides, though small, may provide the prime mechanism for water movement through, and subsequently nutrient exchange from the marsh system studied, but river flooding and wind-tides altered this mechanism substantially during the period of study and would be expected to do so intermittently.

2. Various carbon forms (measured both as TOC and VSS), nitrogen as organic nitrogen and ammonia, and total phosphorus (organic component) produced rapidly during the decomposition of emergent vegetation or algal mats were exchanged in the largest quantities from the marsh and at rates which exceeded generally those measured in East Coast estuaries.

3. Periodic drying of the marsh area appears to be an important mechanism for enhancing organic nutrient release. Plants in this marsh, especially the algal mat, are adapted for periodic drying, high temperatures, and a widely varying salinity regime; high waters (flood or wind-driven inundation conditions) tend to flush sloughed mat materials from the marsh as well as to revive the mat, and normal tide water levels permit drying and sloughing.

Acknowledgments

The authors are indebted to a number of individuals for their help during the course of this project. First, the authors thank the Texas Water Development Board (now the Texas Department of Water Resources) funding under IAC (74-75)-0973 and Mr. Jack Nelson, formerly of the Board, for his guidance and help. Also, the assistance of Mr. Don Schwartz and Mr. Wiley Haydon of the Board and Mr. Gill Gilmore and Mr. George Clemens of the Texas Department of Parks and Wildlife, Coastal Fisheries Division, Seadrift Office, was appreciated. Next, the authors thank Mr. Robert Leshber and his staff of the Texas

State Health Department Laboratory for their chemical analysis of the samples collected. Finally, the authors are indebted to Dr. E. Gus Fruh, Mr. James Collins, Mr. Kenneth Aicklen, Mrs. Julie G. Collins, Mrs. Nadine Gordon, Mr. Frank Hulsey and Mr. Alan Goldstein for their able and unselfish assistance in the laboratory and field.

References

1. Armstrong, N. E., M. O. Hinson, Jr., J. H. Collins, and E. G. Fruh. 1975. Biogeochemical cycling of carbon, nitrogen, and phosphorus in saltwater marshes of Lavaca Bay, Texas. Report to the Texas Water Development Board by the Center for Research in Water Resources, The University of Texas at Austin, CRWR-121.

2. Armstrong, N. E., and V. N. Gordon. 1977a. Exchange rates for carbon, nitrogen, and phosphorus in Nueces and San Antonio Bay marshes. Report to the Texas Water Development Board by the Center for Research in Water Resources, The University of Texas at Austin, CRWR-152.

3. _____. 1977b. Exchange rates for carbon, nitrogen, and phosphorus in the Colorado River Delta marshes. Report to the Texas Water Development Board by the Center for Research in Water Resources, The University of Texas at Austin, CRWR-153.

4. Armstrong, N. E., S. E. Harris, and V. N. Gordon. 1977. Exchange rates for carbon, nitrogen, and phosphorus in the Trinity River Delta marshes. Report to the Texas Water Development Board by the Center for Research in Water Resources, The University of Texas at Austin, CRWR-154.

5. Axelrad, D. M., K. A. Moore, and M.E. Bender. 1976. Nitrogen, phosphorus and carbon flux in Chesapeake Bay marshes. Virginia Polytechnical Institute, Virginia Water Resources Research Center Bulletin 79, Blacksburg, 182 pp.

6. Dawson, A. J., and N. E. Armstrong. 1975. Exchange of carbon, nitrogen, and phosphorus in Lavaca Bay, Texas Marshes, Volume II, The role of plants in nutrient exchange in the Lavaca Bay brackish marsh system. Report to the Texas Development Board by the Center for Research in Water Resources, The University of Texas at Austin, CRWR-129.

7. Gardner, L. R. 1975. Runoff from an intertidal marsh during tidal exposure—recession curves and chemical characteristics. Limnol. Oceanogr. 20:81-89.

8. Odum, E. P., and A. A. de la Cruz. 1967. Particulate organic detritus in a Georgia salt marsh-estuarine ecosystem. *In* G. K. Lauff (ed.), Estuaries, American Association for the Advancement of Science, Publ. #83, Washington, D.C.

9. Pomeroy, L. R., R. E. Johannes, E. P. Odum, and B. Roffman. 1967. The phosphorus and zinc cycles and productivity of a salt marsh, pp. 412-419. *In* D. J. Nelson and F. C. Evans (eds.), *Symposium on Radioecology,* Proceedings of the Second National Symposium, Ann Arbor, Michigan, May 15-17, 1967, CONF-670503, Biology and Medicine (TID-4500), U.S. Atomic Commission.

10. Pomeroy, L. R., L. R. Shenton, R. D. H. Jones, and R. J. Reimold. 1972. Nutrient flux in estuaries, pp. 274-291. *In* G. E. Likens (ed.), Nutrients and Eutrophication: The Limiting-Nutrient Controversy, Special Symposium, Volume I, American Society of Limnology and Oceanography.

11. Reimold, R. J., 1972. The movement of phosphorus through the salt marsh cord grass, *Spartina alterniflora* Loisel. Limnol. Oceanogr. 17(4):606-611.

12. Settlemyre, J. L., and L. R. Gardner. 1975. A field study of chemical budgets for a small tidal creek—Charleston Harbor S.C., pp. 152-175. *In* T. M. Church (ed.), ACS Symposium Series, Number 18, Marine Chemistry in the Coastal Environment.

13. Stevenson, J. C., D. R. Heinle, D. A. Flemer, R. J. Small, R. Rowland, and J. Ustach. 1976. Nutrient exchanges between brackish water marshes and the estuary, pp. 219-240. *In* M. Wiley (ed.), Estuarine Processes, Vol. II, Academic Press, N.Y.

14. Woodwell, G. M., D. E. Whitney, C. A. S. Hall, and R. A. Houghton. 1977. The Flax Pond ecosystem study: Exchanges of carbon in water between a salt marsh and Long Island Sound. Limnol. Oceanogr. 22:833-838.

THE EFFECTS OF REDUCED WETLANDS AND STORAGE BASINS ON THE STABILITY OF A SMALL CONNECTICUT ESTUARY

Barbara L. Welsh, Janet P. Herring, and Luana M. Read

Marine Sciences Institute
The University of Connecticut
Groton, Connecticut

Abstract: Alewife Cove is a small (17 ha) receiving estuary for an 802-ha water-shed system in southeast Connecticut. Over the past hundred years, urban development has destroyed or functionally separated 50% of the system's former fresh watercourses and inland wetlands and 40% and 75% respectively of its estuarine basins and marshes. The estuary, no longer buffered against sporadic runoff, undergoes drastic salinity changes following rainstorms, causing the mixing zone to oscillate over fully one-half of its total area. Beneath this zone, flocculent silt-clay sediments (80-85% water) cover the bottom in a layer exceeding 2 m in places. Groundwater intrusion causes salinity gradients in the sediments which can exceed those in the water column, and sediment pH can be reduced to 3.5. The infaunal community lacks spatial or temporal integrity. Small opportunists (*Capitella, Streblospio*) dominate, representing an early sere. Biomass is low. Epibenthic forms are limited. Macrodetrital (> 0.5 mm) fragments, mostly freshwater and terrestrial material, outweigh living biomass by 10^1--10^3 and contribute to the conditions inhibiting macroinvertebrate processors large enough to handle them. This situation perpetuates organic loading to the area which sustains the stress. Depressed community structure beneath the mixing zone thus appears to result from a combination of factors which can be linked to the altered pattern of freshwater flow (flocculation, salinity stress, low pH and organic loadings). The proportionate influence of each of these factors, and also the extent to which other small estuaries are similarly affected await further study. These findings suggest that the maintenance of watershed storage capacity to buffer adequately against sporadic runoff is vital to maintaining healthy estuaries downstream from urbanized areas.

Introduction

Estuaries, as the transition zones between the world's freshwater and marine systems, are highly dynamic areas which have been classified in several ways with respect to their circulation patterns and salinity structure (Ketchum, 1951; Emery and Stevenson, 1957; Pritchard, 1967). The salinity regimes of particular zones within the estuary have also been classified by several schemes (Day, 1951; Rochford, 1951; Smith, 1956; Sanders *et al.*, 1965), all of which recognize a mixing or gradient zone at the freshwater-saltwater (FW-SW) interface which is characterized by steep spatial and temporal salinity gradients. The sediments beneath the mixing zone tend to accumulate flocculant silts and clays, although there is some disagreement over the nature of the depositional processes involved (Rochford, 1951; Schultz and Simmons, 1957; Meade, 1969, 1972).

As a consequence, despite the fact that estuaries are ranked globally as areas of high gross productivity (Odum, 1971), benthic secondary production beneath their mixing zones has been reported as extremely low (Conover, 1958; Phelps, 1964). Presumably the substrate is too soft to provide support and the continued deposition of loose floc smothers organisms that settle there.

The size, configuration, and location of the mixing zone is largely determined by the dynamic balance between FW discharge and tidal flow (Pritchard, 1967). The amount of FW inflow depends on the amount of rainfall, but the programming of its discharge reflects both the pattern of precipitation events and conditions within the watershed. When changes in the FW-SW ratio become great enough, the entire character of the FW-SW interface, as well as its location, will change. Frequent high amplitude variations could keep the mixing zone from becoming either structurally stabilized or localized, thus expanding the area of flocculation and converting areas of especially high benthic production into ones which are substantially lower.

Wetlands, lakes, and ponds in the FW portion of the system serve as storage basins during periods of heavy rains, preventing excessive discharge and erosion, and providing for the continued flow of water during later dry periods. If such storage facilities are lost, the discharge becomes highly variable, following short-term precipitation events rather than longer-term seasonal cycles. Erosion during periods of heavy flow increases the amount of suspended silts and clays carried into the estuary for deposition. Similarly, tidal basins and marshes serve to absorb tidal energies and trap suspended materials. Their losses would be expected to augment the intrusion of tidal water up-channel on the flood and its subsequent drainage on the ebb. This in turn would increase the deposition of marine-derived sediments in the channel and move them upstream, especially during periods when FW flow is too low to help flush the material out.

The present study was concerned with a small (17.1 ha) estuary and its watershed (802 ha), the Fenger Brook-Alewife Cove system in southeastern Connecticut (Figure 1). In the watershed, 50% of the fresh water courses and wetlands have either been lost or their surface discharge has been effectively blocked by urbanization (Welsh *et al.*, 1974). The system, in response, has adjusted by converting 9 ha of former lowland hardwood area into an overflow swamp. In the estuary, urban development has filled in 40% of the basins and 75% of the marshes over the last hundred years (Figure 2) which, combined with a general rise in sea level of 0.9 cm-yr^{-1} (Hicks, 1972), has increased tidal flow. A sizable sand bar has built up in the channel of the lower estuary in recent years,

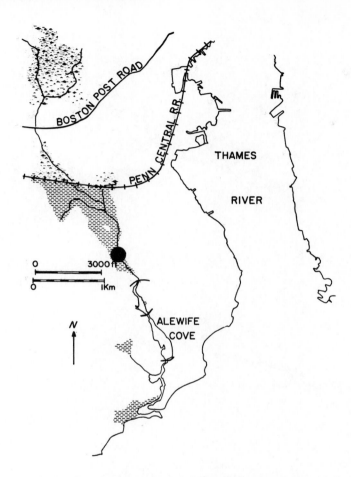

Figure 1. The Alewife Cove and Fenger Brook Watershed System. Wetlands are stippled. The darker portions above the railroad represent portions of the watershed functionally severed from the main system with respect to surface discharge. The dot marks a newly formed swamp area. Reprinted from Welsh et al. (1976), courtesy of Inst. Water Resources, Univ. of Conn.

and since 1968 it has expanded upstream a distance of 100 m. The major cause of this expansion is undoubtedly an increase in the import of suspended materials by flooding water from Long Island Sound. Changes in longshore transport characteristics in the vicinity of the cove can be traced historically as alternations between accretion and erosion of the baymouth bar (Figure 2), which is presently building beyond its 1962 configuration. However, the loss of a sustained FW flow, which normally helps to flush material out again, will contribute to the rate of filling.

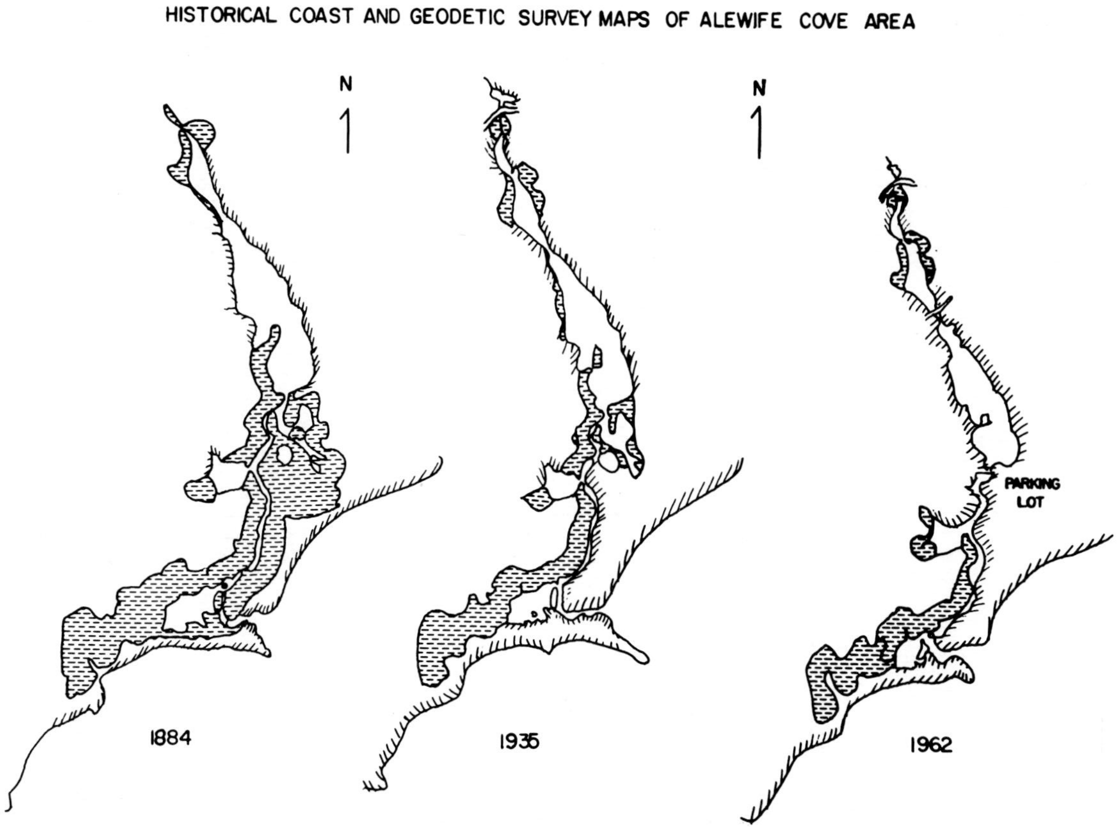

HISTORICAL COAST AND GEODETIC SURVEY MAPS OF ALEWIFE COVE AREA

Figure 2. *Historical charts of Alewife Cove reflecting the losses of wetlands (stipple) and tidal basins over the last hundred years. Reprinted from Welsh et al. (1976), courtesy of Inst. Water Resources, Univ. of Conn.*

Obviously, changes in configuration in both the tidal and freshwater portions of the system become integrated to affect flow characteristics and depositional regimes throughout the estuary. This study, however, focuses primarily on the FW effects in the mixing zone. Earlier work noted large salinity variations in the estuary (Welsh *et al.,* 1976). As a sequel, we wished to determine whether such losses of wetlands and storage basins had indeed destabilized the salinity structure; whether productivity of the benthos had been reduced as a consequence; and ultimately whether the functional value of the estuary as a self-maintaining system had been impaired. In so doing, we sought to demonstrate that man's modifications of watersheds must be approached holistically, because alterations in one area may have deleterious effects in another portion of the system.

Methods

Areas of various portions of the watershed and estuary were determined by planimetry, using USGS topographic maps and aerial survey photographs provided by the Connecticut Department of Environmental Protection (DEP). Bathymetric charts were prepared by selecting 58 cross sections along the estuary axis and measuring water depth across the section at 1-m intervals. Each section was standardized to mean low water (MLW) and related to sea level (SL) through a previous DEP survey at one of the stations. Volumes were determined by the method of Reid (1961, p. 33) for lake basins. These background data are summarized in Table 1.

Tidal prism data were determined by two independent methods. The volume of water flooding and ebbing through a cross-sectional area at the mouth was calculated from hourly current meter measurements. In addition, tide stake measurements of water level changes between high and low tide for various segments of the estuary were multiplied by the area of each segment. Results using the current meter were 9% higher than those using tide stakes on the spring tide, but the two could be reconciled by assuming that intertidal marshes which had not been included in the area measurements were flooded to an average depth of 5.6 cm. Therefore, the value derived from current meter measurements was used for the spring tide. On the neap tide the volume using the current meter was 6% lower than the tide stake volume. The latter was used because the current meter survey fell slightly short of a full tidal cycle.

Freshwater inflow from Fenger Brook was measured where it passed through three culverts beneath a roadbed at the head of the estuary. The diameter of each culvert and the depth of water within it were used to compute the cross-sectional area of the water (Posey, 1969, Table 104). This area was multiplied by flow velocity, determined by using Fluorescein dye tracer, to yield flow volume, which was summed over the three culverts.

Studies of the salinity structure within the water column of the estuary were conducted over a 14-day period in July and 10-day periods in October, February, and May, sampling at both high and low tide on each day. The twelve stations monitored in July were reduced to eight stations thereafter. Water samples were taken at 25-cm depth intervals. Salinity was measured using a Goldberg T/C Refractometer which can be read to $\pm 0.5\,°/oo$.

Depth profiles for sediment characteristics were obtained from sediment cores which were taken by diver, using acrylic core liners of 3.8 cm diameter O. D. Prior to core removal, *in situ* temperature and salinity measurements were made in the overlying water column, using a YSI Model 33-S-C-T probe and meter. Two cores from each of four stations were extruded vertically in the field and sectioned by scraping the extruded portion of sediment into separate containers, one for water and organic content of sediments and one for pore water salinities. Temperature and pH measurements were made by inserting a mercury bulb thermometer and a Corning combination glass pH electrode directly into each sediment section as it was extruded from the liner. In the laboratory, pore water salinity measurements were made on supernatant water after centrifuging the sediments at 2000 rpm for fifteen minutes. Water content was determined in the other samples by weighing the sediment before and after drying at $65°C$, and organic content was determined by combusting them at $550°C$ for three hours.

A bottom sediment survey at 20 stations in the estuary was conducted by Robert Tudor (unpublished). Sand, silt, and clay content were determined by the methods in Buchanan and Kain (1971). Organic content was determined on triplicates of Tudor's samples by one of the authors (Herring) using the aforementioned method. The depth of accumulation of the soft sediments was probed by pushing a 3-m length of 2-cm conduit pipe into the bottom until it met firm resistance.

Samples for benthic infauna were taken in December, 1975, and again in August, 1976, at eight stations in the estuary. In October, four stations were sampled to compare the lower cove with the upper cove. All samples were taken with a 0.073 m^2 Petersen grab, except in October when a 0.03 m^2 cyclindrical corer was used. The samples were washed through a 0.5-mm mesh screen and preserved in buffered 5% formalin with either Rose Bengal or Phloxine B stain added. For the winter collection, the entire sample was analyzed. Summer samples were split by pouring them over a wedge; the volumes of each portion were measured, and the larger animals were removed from both. Smaller animals were analyzed for one portion only and the proportionate volumes were used to estimate their numbers for the whole sample.

Results and Discussion

The mixing zone in Alewife Cove, as determined from salinity measurements made at the stations in Figure 3, migrated sharply in response to precipitation (Figure 4), switching the salinity structure from that of a homogeneous salt pond to that of a highly stratified estuary and back again over 10 to 14-day periods (Figure 5). During the October, February, and May observation periods, oscillations occurred which were similar to those shown for July in both magnitude and duration. Although the mean monthly rainfall tends to drop during the summer, it remains so variable that oscillating regimes may be considered a year-

Table 1. Some physical characteristics of the Alewife Cove-Fenger Brook System.

Watershed Area	Total (ha)	802
	Inland wetlands	70
	Lakes and ponds	4
Watercourses	Inland (km)	2.2[a]
	Tidal	2.2
Estuary Area	Total (ha)	17.1
	Upper basin	2.6
	Middle basin	8.8
	Lower reaches	5.6
	Tidal marshes	15.0
Depth	Upper basin:	
	Maximum/Predominant (m)	1.5/1.0
	Lower basin	2.0/1.0
	Lower reaches	2.5/0.5
Residual Volume	Total estuary (m^3)	201,145
Tidal Heights	MLW/MHW (m above SL)	0.5/1.3
Tidal Prism	Spring tide (m^3)	102,345
	Neap tide	44,910
Freshwater Discharge	Range ($m^3 \cdot day^{-1}$)	692-23,146
	Mean/Geometric Mean/Median	3102/1642/1879
	Coefficient of variation	107%
Tidal Volume: River Flow	(Boundaries of observed conditions):	
	Neap tide: Highest discharge (most stratified)	4:1
	Spring tide: Lowest discharge (most homogeneous)	300:1
Pritchard Model	(Boundaries of theoretical conditions):	
	Highly stratified estuary	1:1
	Moderately stratified estuary	10:1-100:1
	Vertically homogeneous salt pond	1000:1

[a]*Remaining area not functionally separated from system. Natural watershed contained 155 ha of inland wetlands, 5.3 km of inland watercourses (Welsh et al., 1974).*

[b]*Includes 4 ha impoundment (ibid.) and recently formed swamp area (see text Introduction).*

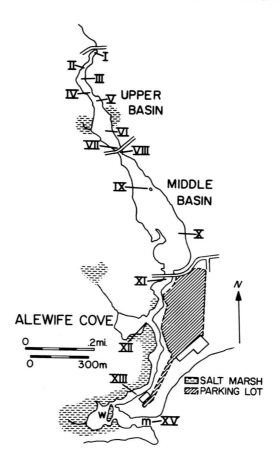

Figure 3. Alewife Cove showing sampling stations. The mixing zone covers roughly Upper and Middle Basins.

round phenomenon. We observed short-term responses to as little as 0.8 cm of rainfall.

   The alterations in structure and location of the mixing zone following rainstorms were far greater than those induced by the individual tidal cycles (Figure 4), and since their duration was much longer, they imposed considerably more stress than those in tidally fluctuating estuaries described by Sanders *et al.* (1965). On the other hand, the changes were too ephemeral to afford the seasonal stability described for gradient estuaries (Rochford, 1951). However, the observed changes in salinity structure in this cove relative to observed changes in FW discharge and tidal flow (Table 1) were consistent with Pritchard's (1967) models. They also indicate that the cove may be somewhat more sensitive than would be expected, probably due to its small size and shallow depths.

During its downstream migrations, the mixing zone expanded to occupy 50-70% of the estuary by area (Upper and Middle Basins) rather than the relatively narrow zones described in other studies (Rochford, 1951; Conover, 1958). The sediments beneath the zone contained up to 85% water at the surface. Their silt-clay and organic content were extremely high, but dropped off sharply both upstream and downstream, thus identifying the range of influence of the zone (Figure 6). These sediments formed a soft lens which extended to considerable depths, indicating that sedimentation rates have been very high within the area (Figure 7). The lens was thickest in the lower portion of the Middle Basin, where we probed to depths of 2 m without encountering firm bottom. This sediment was so soft that a 3.8-cm (O.D.) core liner inserted to a depth of 2 m yielded only 75 cm of core.

Such an accumulation may have occurred in earlier times when extensive marsh areas bordered the lower Middle Basin (Figure 2), or it may indicate that at that time the mixing zone was localized in this lower area when tidal basins and marshes occupied 2--4 times their present area and watershed storage areas were double their present size (Figure 1). The general rise in sea-level which has occurred would also have contributed to upstream encroachment of the salt water boundary over time. Test cores taken in the Upper Basin yielded an under-

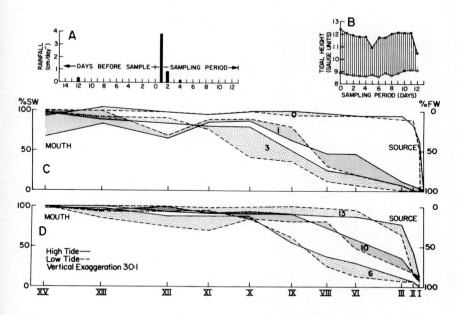

Figure 4. Precipitation events (A) and the resultant migration of the mixing zone (C and D) from Station I to Station XI on Days 0-6 and back again on Days 6-13 in July. Records from a tide gage 2 mi away in Long Island Sound (B) indicated that the daily tidal regime did not vary appreciably. Stippled areas depict tidally-induced changes.

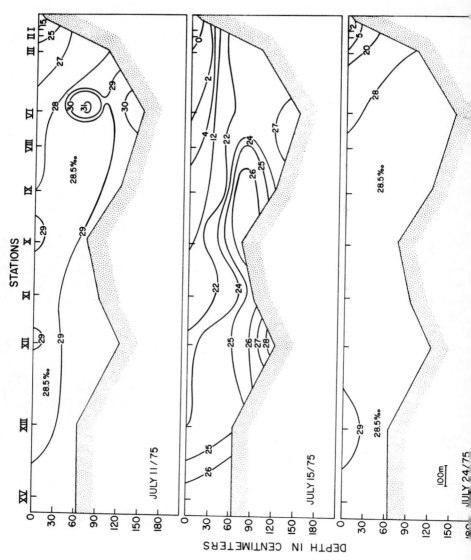

Figure 5. Salinity structure in Alewife Cove during alterations of the mixing regime in Figure 3, showing a salt pond structure on July 11 (Day 0), a highly stratified condition on July 15 (Day 6), and a return to nearly the original condition on July 24 (Day 13). Isohalines were constructed from vertical profiles sampled every 25 cm at 12 stations, only 11 of which are shown.

lying stratum of brown clay, suggesting a former FW condition there. The second thickest portion of the sediment lens was near the head of the cove, and may reflect the area of deposition under the low-flow conditions which predominate at the present time.

Modern benthic communities in the estuary would be most affected by conditions in the upper 10 cm of sediments. There, temporal changes in pore water salinity over a tidal cycle were negligible. However, negative vertical gradients of up to 9‰ over a 10-cm depth were found in Upper Basin (Figure 8), indicating considerable ground water intrusion. These profiles were all obtained during the summer (June-Aug.), which is a period of considerable drawdown in the aquifer (Thomas *et al.*, 1968), bringing the zone of diffusion (mixing zone between fresh ground water and SW) to its landward limit. In December, following partial recharge of the aquifer, similar gradients were found as far downstream as Station IX.

In addition to the salinity gradients, prevailing pH values in the pore waters were extremely low for marine sediments (Baas Becking *et al.*, 1960). During the summer months, a number of measurements dropped below the limits of the carbonate system (4.0), and may have resulted from the leaching of organic acids or iron from the large amounts of allochthonous material present (twigs and oak

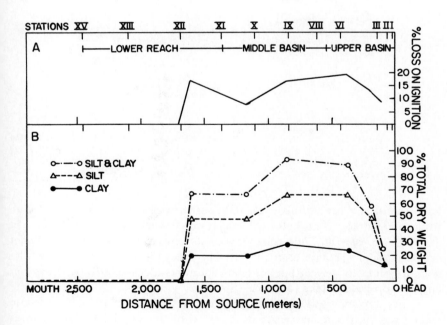

Figure 6. Organic content (A) and silt-clay content (B) for sediments along the axis of Alewife Cove. Both features decline sharply at either end of the expanded mixing zone.

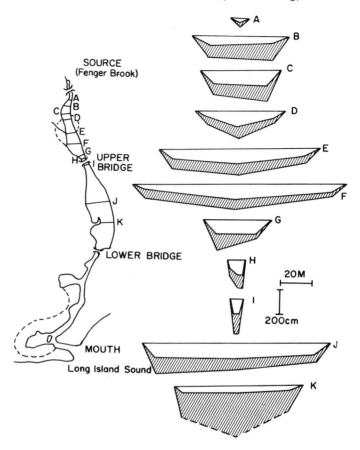

Figure 7. Subsurface profiles showing the depth of the lens of soft sediments (hatched areas) along transects A-K within the mixing zone. The edges were sampled 5--10 m from shore. Dashed boundary (Segment K) indicates no firm bottom found at maximum probe depth (2 m).

leaf fragments). Dissolved materials in the surface water and the groundwater intrusions could also contribute to low pH. Iron commonly exceeds 0.3 ppm in local streams, especially during low-flow conditions, and it is even more prevalent in groundwater (Thomas *et al.,* 1968). The decaying vegetation in the newly-formed swamp upstream should certainly constitute a local source. By December, however, pH had returned to normal (5.7--7.2).

Taken together, the low and variable values for salinity (more prevalent in winter) and pH (more prevalent in summer) within the upper 10 cm of sediment would impose irregular, multiple stresses for infauna which might reasonably be considered more lethal than either factor alone. Hence, the sediments could not provide the homogenous sanctuary for infauna described in Sanders *et al.* (1965).

At the lower pH values, even the microbial community would be limited to such forms as thio bacteria and iron bacteria (Baas Becking *et al.* (1960).

The infaunal community of the mixing zone reflected the highly-stressed

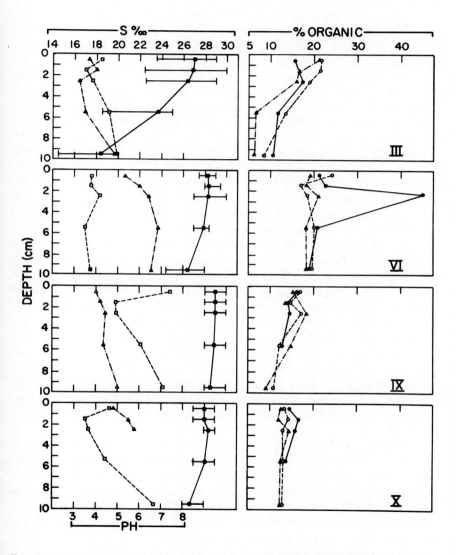

*Figure 8. Sediment profiles for 10-cm cores at selected stations (III-X), with sa-
linity and pH on the left and % organic by combustion on the right.
The solid squares with horizontal bars depicting the ranges summarize
7 salinity profiles (June-Aug.). For pH, △ = June and □ = July. Of
the 3 organic profiles, the solid bar was synoptic with the July pH
profile.*

nature of the area in several ways. Only 36 species were found over fifteen stations and two seasons (Table 2). Not only were they predominantly small species which could readily exploit micro-environments to avoid stressful gradients, but also most of the individuals were less than adult size, denoting recent settlement. In contrast, much larger individuals were found downstream (i.e., *Mya arenaria, Nassarius obsoletus*, large nereids, *Arabella iricolor, Scologlossus viridis, Spio setosa, Lumbrinereis acuta, Saccoglossus kowalewskii*), and there was a more even representation of major taxa (Table 3).

The faunal assemblages of Upper and Middle Basins lacked community integrity. The index of affinity (Sanders, 1960) for within-station replication over a 5-station series from Station XIII to Station III decreased progressively from 0.91--0.60 in the Lower Reach to 0.36--0.11 within the mixing zone. In addition, there was no spatial continuity between stations, such as would produce a gradually decreasing affinity between a station and its progressively distant neighbors (Sanders *et al.*, 1965). Finally, except for Station II at the upper limit of the zone, the similarity between winter and summer assemblages was low (0.15--0.48) reflecting a temporal heterogeneity which was not consistent by season, but typically involved an overwhelming dominance by opportunistic colonizers such as *Capitella, Streblospio* and *Scoloplos* (Table 4).

The assemblages resembled the chance associations described by Eagle (1975), resulting from whichever species happened to be available in a particular spot when conditions allowed them to survive there. Polychaetes accounted for 63--100% of the individuals at most stations, despite the fact that molluscs and crustaceans were available for recruitment from the mixed communities downstream (Table 3). Two amphipod species, *Microdeutopus* and *Corophium*, moved into stations in Middle Basin during the winter, but molluscs remained notably scarce, as would be expected under the combined stresses of salinity and pH. Only *Hydrobia*, whose epibenthic habits limit its contact with pore waters, reached any sizeable numbers. Of the dominant polychaetes, *Capitella* is especially well adapted to survive unstable conditions because it can exploit microhabitat refuges and reproduce rapidly once a tolerable environment is restored (Warren, 1977).

The heavy dominance by opportunists, which were characteristically small individuals, resulted in low diversity (Table 5), more particularly in low levels of living biomass, comparable to the heavily stressed areas of the Thames River. The numbers of individuals varied widely, reflecting the population explosions of the opportunists, but overall densities remained low, particularly in comparison to either the Pocasset River or to Charlestown and Flax Ponds (Table 6). Unlike Alewife Cove, perturbations in the Pocasset River were of shorter duration and the infaunal environment there remained constant (Sanders *et al.*, 1965), while in the salt ponds (Charlestown and Flax) even the salinities in the water column were relatively stable (Phelps, 1964; Koopman, 1973).

Two areas of Charlestown Pond, however, appeared to correspond well to our mixing zone: there were patches of flocculent sediments associated with two

Table 2. Species list for Alewife Cove. Size range of organisms encountered is given as mm in parentheses. Species numerically comprising more than 5% of any one sample are noted by * for summer and + for winter.

Cnidaria
　Anemone (3-5)

Nemertinea
　Tubulanus sp. (15-20)

Polycladida
　Euplana gracilis (1-3)

Polychaeta
　Eteone sp. (7-10)
　Parahesione luteola (9-12)
　Microphthalmus aberrans (2-6)
　**Nereis succinea* (10-100)
　*+*Capitella capitata* (2-32)
　Spio filicornis (8-10)
　*+*Streblospio benedicti* (3-13)
　*+*Polydora ligni* (13-23)
　Paraonis sp. (6)
　*+*Scoloplos fragilis* (5-55)
　Hypaniola grayi (5-10)
　Sabella microphthalma (4-5)
　Potamilla neglecta (2-5)

Oligochaeta
　Sp. A (2-3)

Gastropoda
　Sp. A (3)
　Hydrobia sp. (2-3)
　Mitrella lunata (3)
　Urosalpinx cinerea (5)
　*Opisthobranch sp. (1-10)

Pelecypoda
　Gemma gemma (2)
　Tellina sp. (3-10)
　Mya arenaria (5-10)
　*Sp. A (1-2)

Copepoda
　Harpacticoid sp. (1)

Ostrocod
　Sp. A (0.7-1.3)

Isopoda
　+*Edotea triloba* (7)

Amphipoda
　*+*Microdeutopus anomalus* (2-5)
　Micropropotus raneyi (2)
　**Jassa falcata* (2)
　+*Corophium insidiosum* (2)

Holothuria
　*Sp. A (1-5)

Sipunculida
　Sp. A (15)

small FW sources, where populations were so meager and the assemblages were so unpredictable and lacking in group structure that Phelps specifically excluded them from his study, interpreting them as permanently low seral stages. Fortunately for Charlestown Pond, such conditions pervaded only 5% of the total area, whereas in Alewife Cove they involved well over half of the system.

　Organic macrodetritus (>0.5 mm) was high, outweighing living biomass by one to three orders of magnitude, but the two were not correlated. These fragments were too large for *Capitella capitata* to utilize (Warren, 1977) and most probably they were equally unavailable to the rest of the individuals which represented the same size class, especially since macroheterotrophic processors such as amphipods or shrimp (Welsh, 1975) were notably absent. The breakdown of large

Table 3. A comparison of polychaetes, molluscs and crustaceans at stations in Upper and Middle Basins (VI and IX) with stations in Lower Reach (XIII and W) in October. Sp = species, Ind = individuals. Numbers are proportion of totals for these three groups only, by station.

Station	Polychaetes		Molluscs		Crustaceans	
	Sp.	Ind.	Sp.	Ind.	Sp.	Ind.
VI	.80	.95	.00	.00	.20	.05
IX	1.00	1.00	.00	.00	.00	.00
XIII	.50	.57	.06	.02	.44	.41
W	.63	.68	.32	.31	.05	.01

Table 4. Community dominants, in order of abundance. All groups represent more than 60% of total individuals.

Station	Summer	Winter
III	Streblospio, Capitella	Capitella, Streblospio
IV	Streblospio, Scoloplos	Capitella, Oligochaete
V	Streblospio	Capitella, Streblospio, Oligochaete
VI	(no data)	Streblospio, Capitella
VII	Capitella, Microdeutopus, Streblospio	Streblospio, Capitella
VIII	Streblospio, Scoloplos	Capitella, Streblospio
IX	Capitella	Microdeutopus, Capitella, Hydrobia
X	Capitella	Microdeutopus, Corophium, Capitella

fragments directly by microbes is slow under normal conditions, but may have been further depressed by the resistant nature of the material itself (oak leaves and twigs). Coincidentally, the detrital supply was lower by 50% at Stations IX and X where potential processors (amphipods) were found during the winter months, although these stations were also the farthest from the presumed source of the material (FW inflow).

At two of the stations (VI and X), the organic content did not diminish with depth (Figure 8), indicating that little decomposition occurred below the

Table 5. Comparison of communities between stations. All figures relate to g–m⁻² except species and H′. Living and detrital biomass are in g dry wt. W = winter. S = summer. SD = Standard deviation. CV = Coefficient of Variation. H′ = Shannon Weaver Index.

Station	No. Species		No. Individuals		H′		Living Biomass		Detrital Biomass	
	W	S	W	S	W	S	W	S	W	S
III	13	14	11522	2503	1.39	1.45	1.35	0.54	329	247
IV	10	14	13065	1358	1.23	1.85	2.04	0.15	335	243
V	6	12	2887	4225	1.33	0.95	0.61	0.97	140	132
VI	17	--	2791	--	1.68	--	3.22	--	122	--
VII	17	17	4437	4986	1.62	2.31	2.46	2.17	136	204
VIII	14	23	4499	8205	1.54	1.78	1.02	10.85[a]	250	453
IX	9	8	1207	604	1.72	0.87	0.16	0.10	70	63
X	8	12	665	19230	1.51	0.36	0.09	4.03	86	99
Mean	12	14	5134	5873	1.50	1.37	1.37	2.69[a]	184	206
SD	4.1	4.7	4637	6414	0.17	.68	1.12	3.86	106	130
CV	34%	34%	90%	109%	12%	49%	82%	143%	58%	63%

[a]*Unusually high due to large nereid. Mean biomass excluding VIII is 1.33*

Table 6. Comparison of numbers of individuals, biomass and diversity (H') for a number of soft-bottom areas. Units are no·m⁻² for individuals and g(dry wt)·m⁻² for biomass.

Location	No. Individuals		Biomass	H'	Source and (Mesh Size)
	Range	Mean			
Pocasset River	6,313 - 159,581	67,377	--	--	Sanders et al, 1965 (0.2)
Charlestown Pond[a]	0 - 95,000	10,200	--	2.1 - 2.8	Phelps, 1964 (0.5)
Flax Pond	0 - 132,300	12,800	14[b]	--	Koopman, 1973 (1.0)
Moriches Bay[a]	--	1,433	5.1[c]	4.6	O'Connor, 1972 (1.0)
Thames River[d]	41 - 4,897	1,680	--	1.2 - 1.8	Class Study, unpub. (1.0)
Alewife Cove					
Sta III-X	665 - 13,065	7,399	2.0	0.4 - 2.3	This Study (0.5)
Sta XIII	--	1,700	--[e]	2.9	
Sta W	--	4,717	--[e]	3.0	

[a]Fine sediment stations only

[b]Calculated as 10% of reported wet wt.

[c]Converted from ash free dry wt using our conversion factor (1.201)

[d]Heavily industrialized zone of lower river

[e]Biomass not measured but individuals large compared with Sta III-X

surface. Low pH regimes, potentially emanating from the detritus itself, may have been partially responsible for the absence of potential infaunal processors, thus impairing the recycling function of the consumer community and perpetuating organic loading in the area.

Conclusions

Alewife Cove represents the receiving estuary for a watershed which has lost much of its water storage capacity to urbanization. This loss has resulted in large, unpredictable variations in surface flow into the estuary and possibly also increases in groundwater intrusion due to forced filtration into the aquifer from areas where natural surface flow has been blocked. Strong pulses of freshwater, entering the estuary after heavy rains, destabilize the salinity regime there and spread the influence of the mixing zone over a substantial portion of the estuary. Fine sediments, presumably entrained by the heavy runoff, become deposited as a loose, flocculent layer beneath the expanded mixing zone, offering poor support for benthic macroorganisms and tending to smother those which settle there. Epifauna are further subjected to temporal salinity stresses imposed unpredictably by the oscillating regime, while infauna must contend with significant spatial gradients imposed by groundwater intrusion. Infauna may also experience extremely low pH, probably due to organic acids and iron, which may be brought in with the groundwater or leached from the terrestrial and FW debris introduced during heavy runoff.

There is too little information at present to determine the proportionate effects of the individual conditions resulting from the altered pattern of FW flow (flocculation, salinity stress, low pH, detrital loadings) on the dearth of organisms and impaired function of the heterotrophic community in the mixing zone. The combined effects indicate that they warrant further investigation, especially in small shallow estuaries which appear to be especially sensitive to alteration. Systems similar to Fenger Brook and Alewife Cove are common. In southern New England they are oriented north and south, while coastal urban development has been predominantly east and west along a system of highways and railroads, which has tended to cut off the estuaries from all or part of their watersheds. Intuitively, small shallow estuaries require predominantly healthy benthic communities to maintain their overall balance and their continued contribution to the coastal zone. A vital consideration in maintaining diverse and productive benthic communities in estuaries downstream from urbanized watersheds is the need for buffering against sporadic runoff by maintaining an adequate storage capacity.

Acknowledgments

This work was made possible by Grants No. 0000-564-22-5301-43-245, -262, -283, and -298 from the University of Connecticut Institute of Water Resources, and also from Grant No. 5.171-000-22-0202-35-705 from the University of Connecticut Research Foundation. The authors wish to thank R. Tudor for the use of his sediment study of Alewife Cove, and also L. Dunbar, P. Baillie, S. Edwards, K. Kaumeyer, and J. Tucker for help with sampling.

References

1. Baas Becking, L. G. M., I. R. Kaplan, and D. Moore. 1960. Limits of the natural environment in terms of pH and oxidation-reduction potentials. J. Geol. 68:243-284.

2. Buchanan, J. B., and J. M. Kain. 1971. Measurement of the physical and chemical environment, Chap. 3 *in* N. A. Holme, and A. D. McIntyre (eds.). Methods for the Study of Marine Benthos, IBP Handbook No. 16, Burgess and Son (Abingdon) Ltd. Abingdon, Berks, 334 pp.

3. Conover, J. T. 1958. Seasonal growth of benthic marine plants as related to environmental factors in an estuary. Publ. Inst. Mar. Sci., Univ. of Texas, 5: 97-147.

4. Day, J. H. 1951. The ecology of South African estuaries. I. A review of estuarine conditions in general. Trans. Roy. Soc. S. Africa 33:53-91.

5. Eagle, R. A. 1975. Natural fluctuations in a soft bottom benthic community. J. Mar. Biol. Assoc. U.K. 55:865-878.

6. Emery, K. O., and R. E. Stevenson. 1957. Estuaries and lagoons: I. Physical and chemical characteristics, p. 673-749. *In* J. W. Hedgpeth (ed.), Treatise on Marine Ecology and Paleoecology, Vol. I: Ecology. Geol. Soc. Amer. Mem. 67.

7. Hicks, S. D. 1972. Vertical crustal movements from sea level measurements along the east coast of the United States. J. Geophys. Res. 77:5930-5934.

8. Ketchum, B. H. 1951. The exchange of fresh and salt waters in tidal estuaries. J. Mar. Res. 10 (1):18-38.

9. Koopman, R. C. 1973. A benthic macrofauna study of Flax Pond, Old Field, New York. M.S. thesis, SUNY, Stony Brook, 73 pp.

10. Meade, R. H. 1969. Landward transport of bottom sediments in estuaries of the Atlantic coastal plain. J. Sed. Pet. 39:222-234.

11. _____ . 1972. Transport and deposition of sediments in estuaries, pp. 263-290. *In* Nelson, B. W. (ed.), Environmental Framework of Coastal Plain Estuaries, Geol. Soc. Amer. Mem. 133.

12. O'Connor, J. S. 1972. The benthic macrofauna of Moriches Bay, New York. Biol. Bull. 142:84-102.

13. Odum, E. P. 1971. Fundamentals of Ecology. W. B. Saunders Co., Phila. 574 pp.

14. Phelps, D. K. 1964. Functional relationships of benthos in a coastal lagoon. Ph.D. thesis, Univ. of Rhode Island.

15. Posey, C. J. 1969. Fundamentals of open channel hydraulics. Rocky Mountain Hydraulic Laboratory, Allenspark, Colo. 73 pp.

16. Pritchard, D. W. 1967. Observations of circulation in coastal plain estuaries, pp. 33-44. *In* G. H. Lauff (ed.), Estuaries. Am. Assoc. Adv. Sci. Pub. 83.

17. Reid, G. K. 1961. Ecology of inland waters and estuaries. D. Van Nostrand Co., New York. 375 pp.

18. Rochford, D. J. 1951. Studies in Australian estuarine hydrography. I. Introductory and comparative features. Australian J. Mar. Freshw. Res. 2:1-116.

19. Sanders, H. L. 1960. Benthic studies in Buzzards Bay. III. The structure of the soft-bottom community. Limnol. Oceanogr. 5:138-153.

20. Sanders, H. L., P. C. Mangelsdorf, Jr., and G. R. Hampson. 1965. Salinity and faunal distribution in the Pocasset River, Massachusetts. Limnol. Oceanogr. 10 Suppl:R216-R229.

21. Schultz, E. A., and H. B. Simmons. 1957. Freshwater-saltwater density currents: A major cause of siltation in estuaries. Committee on Tidal Hydraulics, Army Corps of Engineers, Tech. Bull. No. 2.

22. Smith, R. I. 1956. The ecology of the Tamar estuary. VII. Observations on the interstitial muds in the estuarine habitat of Nereis diversicolor. J. Mar. Biol. Assoc. U.K. 35:81-104.

23. Thomas, C. E., Jr., M. A. Cervione and I. G. Grossman. 1968. Water resources inventory of Connecticut. Part 3. Lower Thames and southeastern coastal river basins. Conn. Water Resources Bull. 15, 105 pp.

24. Tudor, R. A. (unpub.). Analysis of the sediment distribution of Alewife Cove. M.S.I. Student Report, Univ. of Connecticut.

25. Warren, L. M. 1977. The ecology of *Capitella capitata* in British waters. J. Mar. Biol. Assoc. U.K. 57:151-160.

26. Welsh, B. L. 1975. The role of the grass shrimp, *Palaemonetes pugio*, in a tidal marsh ecosystem. Ecology 56:513-530.

27. Welsh, B. L., D. Bessette, P. Clem and J. P. Herring. 1974. The importance of an holistic watershed approach to community planning. Waterford Planning and Zoning Commission Report, 21 pp.

28. Welsh, B. L., J. P. Herring, D. Bessette, and L. Read. 1976. The importance of an holistic approach to ecosystem management and community planning, pp. 16-33. *In* Lefor, Kennard and Helfgott (eds.). Proceedings: Third Wetlands Conf., Univ. of Connecticut. Inst. Water Res. Pub. 16. 26.

A METHODOLOGY FOR INVESTIGATING FRESHWATER INFLOW REQUIREMENTS FOR A TEXAS ESTUARY

Walter P. Lambert

*U.S. Army Medical Bioengineering Research
and Development Laboratory
Fort Detrick, Maryland*

and

E. Gus Fruh

*Environmental Health Engineering Program
Department of Civil Engineering
The University of Texas at Austin
Austin, Texas*

Abstract: A computer-oriented methodology was developed to provide a general, rational approach to the estuarine freshwater inflow problem without being dependent upon specific machines and computer programs. The methodology was demonstrated using existing computer models within an estuarine management scenario developed for Corpus Christi Bay, Texas. The methodology had a two-step structure. Step 1 translated qualitative, ecologically-oriented management policy goals for an estuary into a set of freshwater inflow requirements. Step 2 produced the set of freshwater release schedules required to satisfy those net inflow requirements. The test scenario demonstrated the viability of the methodology structure, but the specific data base and set of estuarine management policy options were too narrow to influence specific policy decisions for Corpus Christi Bay. The most important result from exercising the methodology for the Corpus Christi Bay scenario was the identification of several information gaps which were potential targets for further research.

Introduction

A structured, conceptual methodology was developed to determine freshwater inflow requirements for a Texas estuary. The methodology was developed within five principal constraints: (1) it was to be exercised on a digital computer but was to be neither machine-specific nor computer-program-dependent; (2) it was to be exercisable within existing computer hardware and software capabilities reasonably found within state-level water resource planning agencies; (3) it was to be responsive to ecologically-oriented freshwater management goals for an estuary; (4) an illustrative application was to be made within the context of a water resource scenario based on historical information from Corpus Christi Bay, Texas; and, (5) interpretation of implications drawn from the results of the illustrative application was to be for demonstrative purposes only. No attempt was made either to preempt the planning function of any Texas agency or to suggest specific policy decisions for Texas water management authorities. No bounds were placed on conceptualization of the methodology. It was formulated as an open structure into which available information and analytical techniques could be inserted on a problem-specific basis (Lambert and Fruh, 1975).

Freshwater Methodology

Figure 1 diagrams a four-step planning sequence for determining freshwater release schedules to an estuary. Step 1 and Step 2 are the technical portions of the planning sequence that comprise the freshwater methodology. Step Zero is the policy step and is likely to be executed or arbitrated by a public agency. Inputs to Step Zero include all the political, economic, bureaucratic, moralistic, scientific, and arbitrary factors which confuse public issues (Edmunds and Letey, 1973). The product from Step Zero is an estuarine management policy which must be translated into a set of management criteria before implementation is possible. Translation of qualitative policies into quantitative management criteria is one task within Step 1.

The objective of Step 1 is to determine the total net amount of freshwater necessary to meet the ecological goals stipulated or implied by the managerial policy. The total net freshwater inflow rate is defined as

$$
T_{fw} = \begin{matrix} \text{River} \\ \text{Inflows} \end{matrix} + \begin{matrix} \text{Local} \\ \text{Runoff} \end{matrix} + \begin{matrix} \text{Direct} \\ \text{Precipitation} \end{matrix}
$$

$$
+ \begin{matrix} \text{Return} \\ \text{Flows} \end{matrix} - \begin{matrix} \text{Evaporative} \\ \text{Losses} \end{matrix} \qquad \ldots (1)
$$

Step 2 produces freshwater release schedules for an estuary. Such schedules stipulate amount and timing and are defined as

$$
\begin{matrix} \text{Release} \\ \text{for} \\ \text{Estuary} \end{matrix} = \begin{matrix} \text{Total Net Fresh} \\ \text{Water Required} \\ \text{(Step 1)} \end{matrix} - \left[\begin{matrix} \text{Estimated} \\ \text{Local Runoff} \end{matrix} \right.
$$

$$
+ \begin{matrix} \text{Direct} \\ \text{Precipitation} \end{matrix} + \begin{matrix} \text{Accidental} \\ \text{River} \\ \text{Inflows} \end{matrix}
$$

$$
+ \left. \begin{matrix} \text{Estimated} \\ \text{Return} \\ \text{Flows} \end{matrix} \right] + \begin{matrix} \text{Evaporative} \\ \text{Losses} \end{matrix} \quad \ldots (2)
$$

STEP TASK

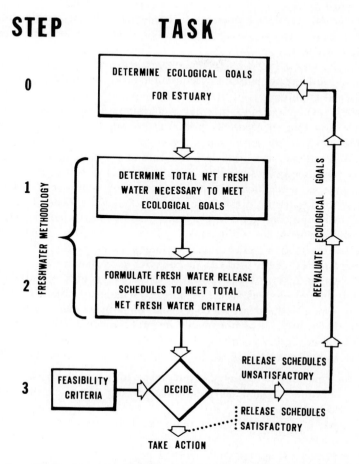

Figure 1. Freshwater release schedule planning sequence containing the freshwater methodology (after Lambert and Fruh, 1975:34).

Step 3 is a decision point outside the freshwater methodology. Input is made to Step 3 from the kinds of sources which made input to Step Zero. The form of the input is a set of specific feasibility criteria against which freshwater release schedules are evaluated. Such criteria might include the acceptable risk of freshwater shortage, the desired operating levels of upstream reservoirs, the projections of future water demands, or myriad other performance criteria which delineate the degree of acceptable conflict between traditional freshwater users and the estuary. If the release schedules are judged satisfactory, they become a basis for further managerial action. If not, a reevaluation of the ecological goals and of the feasibility criteria is in order. The planning sequence becomes iterative, and the four steps are repeated until the adjustable feasibility criteria of Step 3 and the adjustable ecological goals of Step Zero become mutually consistent.

The first task of Step 1 is to compile a detailed area study of the estuary and its environs. A degree of tailoring is required to make the area study conform to the analytical requirements of Step 2, but components of a typical area study contain, but are not limited to, (a) a comprehensive water resource inventory of the study area that incorporates historical stream flow records, historical meteorological and climatological records, ground water inventories, water resource use patterns and priorities, and current conflicts in water resources utilization; (b) supporting study area information such as demographic patterns, land-use patterns, perceptions of water resource requirements and conflicts, and legal structures governing freshwater appropriation and allocation; (c) projections for area population growth, per capita water demand coefficients, industrial freshwater demand coefficients, and trends in water legislation; and (d) specific information on the estuary including a biological profile, commercial characteristics, and hydrodynamic behavior and peculiarities.

A second task has two parts which are executed simultaneously: (a) identify one or more estuarine organisms as indicator organisms which in some way respond to the degree of compliance to the management policy of Step Zero, and (b) identify one or more environmental components which are responsive to freshwater inflows and to which the indicator organism(s) relate.

The environmental control component(s) chosen for Step 1 should:

a. be amenable to routine measurement with a time delay between sample acquisition and analysis results less than the estuarine system response time;
b. have a predictable effect upon the behavior of the indicator organism(s); and
c. be amenable to mathematical modeling.

The indicator organism(s) should:

a. be responsive to the environmental control component(s);
b. be in some way indicative of the desired biological state of the estuary, e.g., an oyster fishery as opposed to a blue crab fishery; and
c. be usable as an indicator without extensive, complex, or costly survey procedures.

The final task of Step 1 is the determination of the net freshwater requirements (T_{fw}) which quantitatively satisfy the qualitative goals of Step Zero. The key to the execution of this task is the formulation or availability of mathematical models which allow study of the behavior of the environmental control component(s) under a wide set of freshwater inflow conditions. Such a model, or group of models, should:

a. reflect observed and expected behavior of the environmental control component(s) over time and space;

b. be calibrated and verified with several sets of field survey data;

c. accept as input all the environmental variables significantly impacting upon the estuarine system under study;

d. be subjected to sensitivity analyses to determine the relative importance of the many variables involved;

e. be sufficiently inexpensive to operate so that a large number of computer experiments can be executed;

f. produce printed and graphics output understandable to both manager and expert;

g. be formulated in readable code according to accepted standards of programming style and structured programming so that mysteries encountered by new users can be easily investigated; and

h. be machine-independent so that transportation between computer facilities can be as painless as possible.

Freshwater release schedules are the product of another set of computer experiments. Information and data concerning freshwater utilization, which were compiled as part of the area study of Step 1, are input variables to water-system simulation models in Step 2. Control variables of a mathematical model of the study area water system are manipulated according to assumed or prescribed operation plans. The set of T_{fw} values produced by Step 1 become part of the operational constraints, and the capability of the area water system to fulfill the policy requirements of Step Zero is measured by the resulting freshwater release schedules. At a minimum, the water system simulation model should:

a. accept all pertinent hydrologic and meteorologic data;

b. operate within the specified study time interval;

c. simulate the water resource system for an unlimited number of consecutive time intervals;

d. handle all technical functions and constraints, including
1) diversions
2) return flows
3) power generation
4) flood control
5) minimum streamflows
6) maximum streamflows
7) flexible reservoir operation plans
8) priority systems for water utilization
9) local runoff
10) evaporation and rainfall
11) estuarine water demands
12) other functions necessary for the specific problem; and

e. provide output reports amenable to further analysis and to easy explanation.

Corpus Christi Bay Scenario

Corpus Christi Bay is a broad, shallow estuary on the lower Texas Gulf Coast fed by direct inflows from the Nueces River, return flows from the City of Corpus Christi and tributary industrial and agricultural operations, and by saline inflows from the Gulf of Mexico to the east, Laguna Madre to the south, and the Aransas-Copano estuarine system to the north.

The City of Corpus Christi is a dynamic community which has grown considerably since World War II. An important factor in the growth equation has been the availability of fresh water. Although the National Water Commission (1973:48-50) discounted water resource development as the sole motivator of regional growth, a potential for growth limitation still remains (Maxey, 1972). Corpus Christi is aware of the limiting potential of inadequate water resources because of its experiences during the drought of 1950-1957. Since the city desires to increase its population and industrial base in a reasonable manner, an adequate water supply must be guaranteed.

In response to area development goals, the Wesley E. Seale Dam was completed on the lower Nueces River in 1958, and a second reservoir was projected for an upstream site called Choke Canyon on the Frio River tributary of the Nueces River. Both reservoirs were designed primarily for water supply. Lake Corpus Christi, behind the Wesley E. Seale Dam, services the water requirements of the City of Corpus Christi, several outlying communities, and a number of industries along the shores of Corpus Christi Bay. Choke Canyon Reservoir was to have acted as a backup to Lake Corpus Christi. It was hoped that both reservoirs together would provide sufficient delivery capacity to meet municipal and industrial needs of the Corpus Christi area through at least the first third of the next century.

Along with potential increases in municipal and industrial water demands, however, was the likelihood that Corpus Christi Bay might itself become a legitimate freshwater customer. A trend existed in recent Texas water legislation indicating that such rights might be mandated for the purpose of protecting and preserving such a valuable natural resource. The result could mean a conflict between development goals of the city and ecological goals for the estuary.

To investigate the implications of such a conflict, an ecologically-oriented management goal for the Corpus Christi Bay System was hypothesized as "... the fresh and saline water resources of the Corpus Christi Estuarine System shall be managed in such a manner as to provide an estuarine environment conducive to the maintenance of current estuarine fisheries. . . ."

Two freshwater appropriation and allocation policies were identified as important for investigating the impact of the ecological goal. Water Allocation Policy 1 (P_1) was a traditional priority policy by which municipalities have first priority for acquisition of surface water with preemptive rights over other users. Irrigation and certain industries have next lower priorities. Traditionally, wildlife and wildlife systems have no water rights. Water Allocation Policy 2

(P$_2$) mirrored certain trends in recent Texas water law. The condition was imposed that after industrial demands were satisfied, it was mandatory to fulfill as much of the estuarine demand as possible without draining upstream reservoirs.

Two reservoir configuration policies within the Lower Nueces River Valley were considered important. Reservoir Configuration 1 (C$_1$) was the single reservoir system in existence within the study area as of 1973. Configuration 2 added Choke Canyon Reservoir to Lake Corpus Christi in 1985. The four combinations of two freshwater allocation policies and two reservoir configurations provided the basis for experimental designs of Step 1 and Step 2 for the demonstration scenario.

Execution of Step 1 for the Corpus Christi scenario required a series of simplifications which allowed demonstration of the methodology but which negated use of experimental results for actual policy decisions. A single indicator organism, the spotted seatrout, *Cynoscion nebulosus,* and a single environmental control component, salinity, were used to establish the net freshwater inflow criterion to satisfy the management goal. Lack of sufficient biological information and of available computer models necessitated such a constricted demonstration. Available data indicated a 27 parts per thousand preferred salinity ceiling for the spotted seatrout during the spawning season (Lambert and Fruh, 1975:61-69). Computer models HYDTID and LOTRAN (Brandes and Masch, 1972) were used to establish that the average net freshwater inflow satisfying the seatrout salinity constraint was -5.7 cubic meters per second (-201 cubic feet per second) during April through September of each year. This implied an accommodation of the spawning seatrout to net water losses during the summer months.

The net inflow requirement was one of three major data inputs to Step 2. Historical hydrologic, meteorologic, population, and water-use data constituted the second set. Statistically-generated synthetic data for streamflows, rainfall, evaporation, monthly diversion rates, and per capita freshwater demands were included in the third set. Historical data were used for Step 2 modeling of the Lower Nueces River System from 1973 through 2022 in a traditional sense. The historical data series comprised one possible data sample for the time period to be modeled. Synthetic data were used as a second sample. Results from Step 2 simulations for historical and synthetic input data sequences were regarded as experimental replicates.

Execution of Step 2 relied upon stochastic simulation of Lower Nueces River System behavior over the period 1973-2022 using the computer program HEC-3 (U.S. Army Corps of Engineers, 1974). The four policy options defined major system operating rules. P$_1$ assumed no inflow constraints. P$_2$ assumed the net inflow requirement of Step 1. When Choke Canyon Reservoir entered the system, it was used to support Lake Corpus Christi. Three population growth projections were used to determine population effects on freshwater system performance under the four primary policy options. Two performance criteria were established. End-of-month (EOM) storage in Lake Corpus Christi was used to indicate system stress. Reservoir level was inversely indicative of stress. The difference between supplied and required freshwater inflows, a quantity called Delta Q, was the measure of system effectiveness.

EOM storage in Lake Corpus Christi and Delta Q were tabulated and plotted for each of twenty-four simulation experiments (2 input data sequences x 4 policy options x 3 population growth projections = 24 experiments). Step 2 experiments conformed to a 2 x 2 x 2 x 3 full factorial design. The two performance variables were subjected to a two-way analysis of variance (ANOVA) to determine which of the four experimental factors, i.e., water allocation policy, reservoir configuration, population growth projection, and input data sequence, were statistically significant. ANOVA results implied that the estuary detected effects of freshwater allocation, reservoir configuration, and input data sequence independently. Population growth effects were apparently overshadowed by meteorologic and hydrologic effects. System stress appeared to be most sensitive to freshwater allocation policy.

Since ANOVA only identified statistically significant factors, comparative exceedence frequency analysis was used to clarify the nature of impacts on system performance. This meant identifying managerial significance in contrast to statistical significance. Factor effects on system performance were analyzed for managerial significance by comparing the frequencies of (a) at least meeting required net inflows; (b) EOM Lake Corpus Christi storages at or below distress level (70 feet mean sea level); (c) EOM Lake Corpus Christi storages at or below stress level (80 feet mean sea level); and (d) EOM Lake Corpus Christi storage at or above 90 percent of normal storage volume.

Results of the analyses implied that:

(a) Awarding Corpus Christi Bay a substantial freshwater allocation priority would increase Nueces River System effectiveness to satisfy net inflow requirements for maintaining the spotted seatrout fishery without a significant increase in persistent system stress. EOM storage levels in Lake Corpus Christi would be lower on a monthly, summer average, and two-summer running average basis, however, than under traditional freshwater allocations.

(b) Under either allocation policy, system effectiveness with Choke Canyon Reservoir would at most equal system effectiveness with only Lake Corpus Christi. This was apparently due to large evaporative losses from the surface of Choke Canyon Reservoir during the summer months.

Discussion

The statement of the freshwater methodology was deceptively simple. It reflected an engineering approach to one problem of estuarine management. The deceptive simplicity lay with a set of key assumptions which were needed to translate management goals into freshwater release schedules. Step 1 assumed the existence of: (a) a set of indicator organisms large enough to characterize the desired estuarine environment, small enough to be feasibly analyzed, and linked by known stimulus-response relationships to a set of control components; (b) a set of control components responsive to freshwater inflows, linked by known stimulus-response relationships to the set of indicator organisms, and amenable to mathematical modeling; and (c) mathematical models which accurately reflected control component responses to freshwater inflows. Background investigations for formulation of the demonstration scenario indicated that such an internally consistent body of information did not exist.

At the time of the study, reliable mathematical models were available only for estuarine hydrodynamics and for transport of conservative substances. This constrained the choice of control components to salinity. The control component constraint affected choices for indicator organisms. It necessitated the identification of organisms which showed relatively narrow salinity preferences and which were characteristic of the estuarine environment specified by the management goal. Circumstantial evidence for *Cynoscion nebulosus* indicated that it met the above two criteria and that is displayed its salinity preferences during the high-stress summer season.

The use of a single control component and a single indicator organism simplified the scenario, but such a condition would be unacceptable for actual inflow management. The shortage of information for an adequate definition of inflow requirements for Corpus Christi Bay dramatically illustrated that serious deficiencies existed in the ecological data base needed for scientific inflow management.

Assumptions underlying Step 2 included: (a) control points existed within the freshwater system which allowed management of estuarine inflows; (b) sufficient hydrologic and meteorologic data existed for use in water system simulations over some minimally acceptable planning period; (c) quantitative projections existed for detailing conflicts in freshwater demands over the planning period; and (d) mathematical models existed for simulating behavior of the upstream freshwater system under each policy option. These assumptions were more easily met for the demonstration scenario than were those for Step 1.

Step 3 of the planning sequence was not exercised for the Corpus Christi Bay scenario. Adequate, quantified feasibility criteria for Lower Nueces River System performance were not available, and development of such criteria was beyond the scope of this study.

Conclusions

In addition to meeting the five major constraints listed in the Introduction, the freshwater methodology proved useful in defining certain research requirements to meet the needs of estuarine managers. A greater number of better defined linkages needs to be identified between candidate estuarine indicator organisms and controllable estuarine water-quality components. A more detailed and better quantified definition of estuarine biotic structure is needed. The matrix of food web relationships needs to be studied for its content and for its behavior under various freshwater inflow stresses. Biotic structures reflecting desired and practically achievable estuarine environments need to be defined and quantified. Finally, a rational method for negotiating environmental goals for estuaries should be devised. The freshwater methodology developed in this study was conceptualized within an iterative planning procedure which assumed that negotiation techniques for management goals existed. They do, to some extent. The public forum and bureaucratic arbitration are two important elements of present methods. More rational techniques such as Delphi methods and objective ranking schemes need to be inserted so that long-term public welfare is not sacrificed to short-term private advantage.

Acknowledgments

This research has been supported by the National Science Foundation, Research Applied to National Needs Program, through Grant No. AEN74-13590-A01 and by the Office of the Governor of Texas through Interagency Agreement IAA—Division of Planning Coordination. The senior author was able to undertake this study through the U. S. Army Civil Schools Program.

Gratitude is extended to the many individuals of the Natural Resources Division in the Office of the Governor, Texas Water Development Board, U.S. Bureau of Reclamation, U.S. Geological Survey, City of Corpus Christi, Texas Parks and Wildlife Department, and Texas Coastal and Marine Council for their unselfish aid and assistance. Models utilized included those for the Corpus Christi estuary developed by Water Resources Engineers, Inc. and the Texas Water Development Board and for the Nueces River System by the Center for Research in Water Resources at The University of Texas at Austin and the Texas Water Development Board. Special thanks for advice and assistance is due to Mr. Roy Beard, Dr. Paul Jensen, Dr. Frank Masch, and Dr. Clyde Zinn of The University of Texas at Austin.

References

1. Brandes, R. J., and F. D. Masch. 1972. Tidal hydrodynamic and salinity models for Corpus Christi and Aransas Bays, Texas. A report to the Texas Water Development Board, Frank D. Masch and Associates, Austin, Texas.

2. Edmunds, S., and J. Letey. 1973. Environmental Administration. McGraw-Hill, New York.

3. Lambert, W. P., and E. G. Fruh. 1975. Methodology to evaluate alternate coastal zone management policies: application in the Texas coastal zone. Special Report III: A methodology for investigating fresh water inflow requirements of a Texas estuary. Austin, Texas: Research Applied to National Needs Program, National Science Foundation and Division of Planning Coordination, Office of the Governor of Texas, coordinated through the Division of Natural Resources and Environment, The University of Texas at Austin.

4. Maxey, G. B. 1972. The role of water resources development. *In* E. F. Gloyna and W. S. Butcher (eds.), Conflicts in water resources planning. Center for Research in Water Resources, The University of Texas at Austin.

5. National Water Commission. 1973. Water policies for the future. Final report to the President and to the Congress of the United States. U. S. Government Printing Office, Washington, D.C.

6. United States Army Corps of Engineers. 1974. HEC-3 reservoir system analysis for conservation computer program 723-X6-L2030 users' manual. The Hydrologic Engineering Center, Davis, California.

ESTUARY–NEARSHORE INTERACTIONS: POLLUTANT CYCLING AND WATER QUALITY

POLYNUCLEAR AROMATIC HYDROCARBONS IN ESTUARINE AND NEARSHORE ENVIRONMENTS

Eugene Jackim and Carol Lake

Environmental Research Laboratory
South Ferry Road
Narragansett, Rhode Island

Abstract: Polynuclear aromatic hydrocarbons (PNAH) are ubiquitous and are found in waters, soil, and bottom sediments throughout the world, although the concentrations are higher in industrialized locations. Interest in these compounds is generated by their carcinogenic and mutagenic properties. Although biosynthesis and petroleum spillages may be sources for PNAH's in localized areas, the major source of these compounds is pyrolytic. They tend to degrade by photo and biological oxidation. Like other hydrocarbons, they accumulate in most seafood, especially in bivalves. Generally, initial depuration is rapid; however, PNAH's might persist for years in some species.

Introduction

Polynuclear aromatic hydrocarbons (PNAH) are among the oldest known carcinogens. They were identified as the active carcinogens associated with soot which caused the first occupationally related cancer known as chimney sweep disease. They are ubiquitous and found in waters, soil, and bottom sediments throughout the world, although apparently in greater abundance in industrialized locations. Because of their carcinogenic, mutagenic, toxic, and ubiquitous nature it is important that the impact of these compounds on estuarine environments and ultimately on man be established.

In this review we will discuss primarily the aromatic compounds with more than two rings. A number of good review articles relating to this subject have been published and should be referred to: Suess, 1968, 1970; GESAMP, 1977; Blumer and Youngblood, 1975; Zobell, 1971; Hites, 1976; Andelman and Snodgrass, 1974. This review attempts to update briefly all the work on this subject and point toward some new conclusions.

Chemical and Physical Properties

PNAH's, typical of those found in the marine environment, are listed in Figure 1. Both the parent compounds listed and alkyl derivatives, containing

Figure 1. Typical PNAH's found in the marine environment.

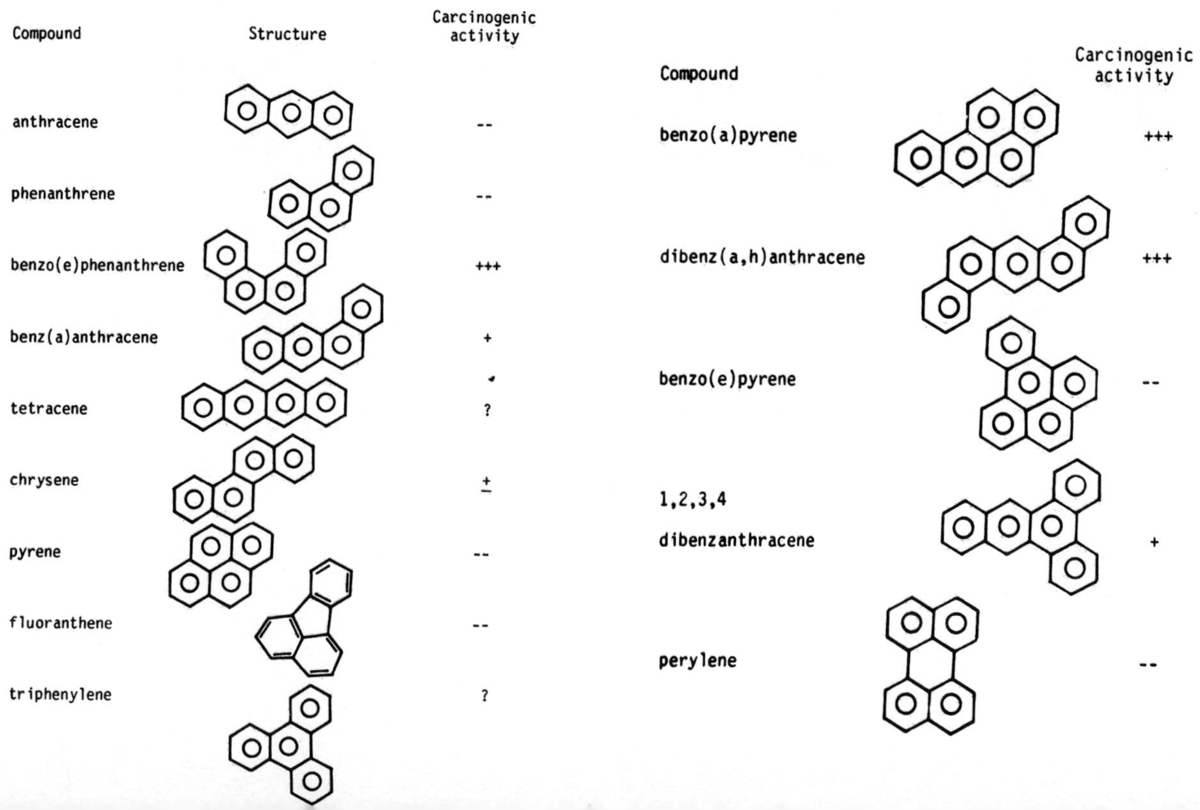

Compound	Structure	Carcinogenic activity		Compound	Carcinogenic activity
anthracene		--		benzo(a)pyrene	+++
phenanthrene		--		dibenz(a,h)anthracene	+++
benzo(e)phenanthrene		+++		benzo(e)pyrene	--
benz(a)anthracene		+		1,2,3,4 dibenzanthracene	+
tetracene		?		perylene	--
chrysene		+_			
pyrene		--			
fluoranthene		--			
triphenylene		?			

416

up to fifteen carbon atoms in the alkyl groups, have been isolated from estuarine sediments (Blumer and Youngblood, 1975; Youngblood and Blumer, 1975; Hites and Biemann, 1975; Giger and Blumer, 1974; Hase and Hites, 1976b). As shown in Figure 1, PNAH's are planar, condensed, multiring structures which exhibit many of the chemical and physical properties of one-and two-ring aromatic compounds, i.e., they absorb ultraviolet light, are oxidized by ozone, chlorine and ultraviolet light, and undergo electrophilic substitution in specific positions on the ring, depending on the structure and substituents present (Clar, 1964). PNAH's are potent mutagens and carcinogens, others are less active or suspected carcinogens. Some PNAH's, especially those of biological origin, are probably not carcinogens.

Carcinogenicity

No clear relationship between the electronic structure and carcinogenic activity of PNAH exists, although a hypothesis has been proposed (Pullman and Pullman, 1955).

In most, if not all, cases it appears that PNAH's have to be metabolically activated by tissue microsomes before they become biologically active (Miller and Miller, 1971). The activation mechanism occurs by hydroxylation or production of unstable epoxides of PNAH's which damage DNA and thus initiate the carcinogenic process (Ames *et al.*, 1972). It is well established that fish and, to a much lesser extent, crustaceans possess the enzymes necessary for activation. In contrast, it appears that mollusks lack the metabolizing enzymes and therefore, theoretically, should not activate PNAH's (Philpot *et al.*, 1976; Carlson, 1972; Lee *et al.*, 1972). However, very recently Robert Anderson at the Sloan Kittering Institute found evidence of low-level activation by shellfish (pers. commun.). Other invertebrates have a greatly reduced ability to metabolize hydrocarbons.

Hueper (1963), Yevich and Barszcz, (1976) and more recently Brown *et al.*, (1977) have demonstrated an increased incidence of neoplasia in the soft shell clam, *Mya arenaria,* from several oil-contaminated areas. It is tempting to speculate that PNAH's are the causative agents, except for the fact that shellfish have reduced enzyme-activating ability. A direct "cause and effect" relationship has not been established. The possibility exists that activation is not necessary in these animals or that certain benthic microorganisms might perform the necessary transformation. Other disturbing factors are that measurements of hydrocarbon body burden do not correlate well with neoplasia incidence (R. Brown, pers. commun.); and secondly, in spite of intensive efforts, the field observations of neoplasia have not yet been reproduced in the laboratory.

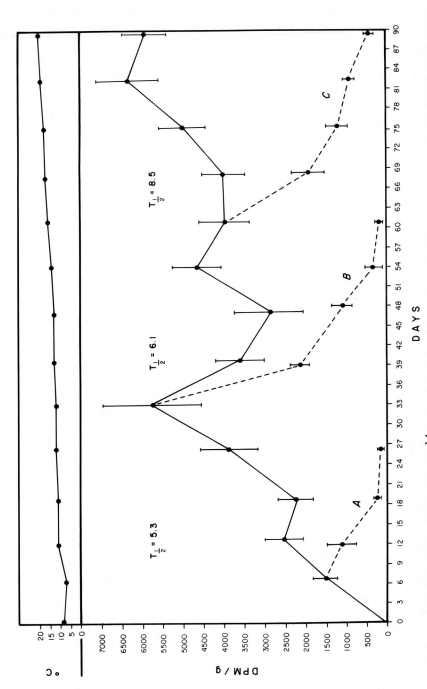

Figure 2. Accumulation and depuration of ^{14}C labelled benzo(a)pyrene in Mya arenaria. Curves A, B, and C indicate depuration starting at three different accumulation time periods.

Accumulation and Depuration

The accumulation of PNAH's in bivalves is considerable; for example, reported values range from non-detectable to over 1,675 μg/kg, from an industrial polluted area (Jackim and Wilson, 1977). Similarly, benzpyrene concentrations of up to 150 μg/kg have been reported in shellfish by GESAMP (1977). Since most of the carcinogenic hydrocarbons arise anthropogenically, it is not surprising that animal tissue concentrations fluctuate widely depending on the location from which the animals were obtained.

Fish apparently have the ability to avoid high concentrations of oil and other hydrocarbons. Nevertheless, benzpyrene concentrations of fifteen and sixty-five μg/kg were reported for cod from Greenland and sardine from Naples, respectively (Suess, 1970). Neoplasia have been reported in fish caught in waters contaminated by fuel oil or oil refinery wastes (Russell and Kotin, 1957). It is probable that PNAH's play a role in fish tumor development; however, the incidence of such tumors is likely to be too small to have much ecological significance.

In general, marine animals accumulate and depurate PNAH's much like other hydrocarbons, even though the rates for specific compounds differ somewhat. Alkylnaphthalenes followed by naphthalene accumulate to the greatest extent (Anderson *et al.*, 1974). The rate of PNAH accumulation in bivalves is also dependent upon water concentration and species type. Neff (1975) demonstrated that clams accumulate hydrocarbons more slowly than oysters.

It appears that most bivalves eliminate PNAH's rapidly, since PNAH's usually possess a biological half-life of between two and sixteen days (Jackim and Wilson, 1977). The only detailed report showing little or no depuration in bivalves is one concerning *Mercenaria mercenaria* by Boehm and Quinn (1977). This probably represents a different mechanism of elimination peculiar to this species, although other factors such as technical failure to resolve biogenic hydrocarbons or contamination could lead to this interpretation. Blumer, Souza, and Sass (1970) also reported on slow depuration in oysters. More recent work with oysters does not substantiate Blumer's findings (Neff, 1975). Stegeman and Teal (1973) demonstrated that about 90 percent of the accumulated hydrocarbons in oysters is released within two weeks of depuration, and the remaining 10 percent is released very slowly, suggesting that traces might remain indefinitely.

The turnover rate of hydrocarbons in fish and crustaceans is greater than in mollusks, due partly to the animals' ability to metabolize these compounds. A hypothesis was proposed, stating that with increased time of accumulation, hydrocarbon depuration rates decrease because the material becomes incorporated in slow turnover compartments. It was demonstrated, however, that increased accumulation time produced only a slight decrease in depuration rate in *Mya arenaria* (Jackim and Wilson, 1977) (Figure 2). It is still possible, however, that long-term chronic exposure as found in natural situations might decrease depuration rates and explain Blumer's observations. Benzpyrene and presumably other PNAH's tend to concentrate in the viscera and mantle; the abductor muscle and siphon accumulate only a small percentage of the total contaminant (Neff and Anderson, 1975; Jackim and Wilson, 1977).

Biomagnifications and Health Risk

Because of the relatively rapid degradation and depuration of PNAH's in most animals and low absorption by the intestinal tract in higher animals, it is unlikely that any significant biological magnification of PNAH concentration occurs up the food chain. The question of potential carcinogenic or mutagenic risk to man as a consumer of marine food does arise and is impossible to evaluate fully at this time because of the many unknowns concerning carcinogenicity. Among these are the unknowns concerning threshold levels, synergistic or co-carcinogenic effects and cellular recovery processes.

Looking at benzpyrene, we see that *Mya arenaria* from highly contaminated locations have upper values between 30 and 150 $\mu g/kg$. From clean areas the concentration generally drops to levels between trace and 1 to 5 $\mu g/kg$ (Mix *et al.*, 1977). Comparing these levels to that of other common foods, we find the non-polluted levels not extraordinarily high. For comparison, charcoal broiled meats range from 2.6 to 11.2 $\mu g/kg$, smoked ham or sausage 0.02 to 14.6 $\mu g/kg$, cooked fish 0.9 $\mu g/kg$, bread 0.1 to 4.1 $\mu g/kg$, margarine 0.2 to 6.8 $\mu g/kg$, and smoked fish 0.3 to 60 $\mu g/kg$ (GESAMP, 1977). We must remember that shellfish are not eaten in the quantities that some of the other foods mentioned above are, and also that they are generally not harvested from polluted areas. On the basis of existing evidence it appears that moderate consumption of shellfish from non-polluted waters presents little significant risk from PNAH's at this time. Shellfish from polluted areas might present risks from PNAH's as well as other pollutants. If necessary, a depuration period of several weeks in clean water should greatly decrease the PNAH levels in most seafood, with the possible exception of *Mercenaria mercenaria*. Fish and crustaceans present less of a problem than shellfish.

Distribution and Transportation

Polynuclear aromatic hydrocarbons are ubiquitous and are found in water, air, soil, and marine and lake sediment samples in small but detectable concentrations. In general, concentrations of PNAH are higher in samples taken near industrialized areas. It is well documented that PNAH's are found in marine sediment (Gearing *et al.*, 1976; Tissier and Oudin, 1973; Farrington and Quinn, 1973; Mallet *et al.*, 1963; Bourcart and Mallet, 1965; Lalou *et al.*, 1962; Bourcart *et al.*, 1961; Mallet *et al.*, 1960; Mallet and Le Theule, 1961; Piccinetti, 1967; Scarratt and Zitko, 1972; Vandermuelen *et al.*, 1977; Giger and Blumer, 1974; Hites and Biemann, 1975; MacLeod *et al.*, 1976; Orr and Grady,

1967; Aizenshtat, 1973), in water samples (Brown *et al.*, 1973) and manganese nodules (Thomas and Blumer, 1964).

Numerous routes exist for the transport of PNAH's into the marine environment. The high concentrations of PNAH's present in incomplete combustion products from vehicle exhaust and industrial smoke represent a major contributor of PNAH's to the marine waters, via atmospheric fallout. Inputs of sewage and industrial effluents, oil refinery effluent, urban runoff, shipping and harbor oil spillages, and harbor dredge spoils to estuarine and coastal waters contribute to the high concentrations of PNAH's found in localized areas.

The wide distribution of PNAH's in marine waters and sediment may be surprising in light of their limited solubility in water. Though the water solubility of PNAH's, especially those containing more than three rings, has been estimated at less than $10^{-10}M$ (Radding *et al.*, 1976), McGinnes and Snoeyink (1974) showed experimentally that 1,2 benzanthracene and 3,4 benzpyrene did not form a true solution with water but rather were present as a particulate suspension. Therefore the transportation and distribution of PNAH's in the marine environment is governed either by the movement of water containing solubilized PNAH's or by the movement, settling, and resuspension of particles to which PNAH's adhere. Radding *et al.* (1976) stated that, since the concentration of detergents in most coastal waters is generally less than that necessary for micelle formation, this mechanism of transport is of little importance to the marine environment. This may not be the case in estuarine and coastal water where the input of urban runoff, domestic sewage, and fulvic and humic acids may contribute high concentrations of detergents and surfactants which can solubilize otherwise insoluble organic compounds such as PNAH's (Schnitzer and Khan, 1972).

Laboratory studies have shown that PNAH's adsorb onto suspended estuarine material (Lee, 1977), kaolinite (McGinnes and Snoeyink, 1974), and calcite (Suess, 1968), and the movement of these contaminated particles is believed to be most important in the transport of PNAH's in the marine environment (Lee, 1977; Radding *et al.*, 1976; Suess, 1968; McGinnes and Snoeyink, 1974). Though UV and fluorescent identifications of specific PNAH's have been reported, the presence of numerous alkylated-homologous series of PNAH's in extracts of marine sediment (Hites and Biemann, 1975; Hase and Hites, 1976b; Youngblood and Blumer, 1975; Blumer and Youngblood, 1975; Giger and Blumer, 1974) can lead to bathochromic shifts in UV spectra and spectral overlap (Clar, 1964; Giger and Blumer, 1974). Due to the spectral problems with these complex mixtures, some researchers have stated that the assignment of specific peaks or areas of UV and fluorescent spectra to specific compounds is tenuous (Hargrave and Phillips, 1975). Others suggest that only through the combination of column chromotographic, GC/MS techniques, and UV and fluorescent spectrophotometric methods, can complete identification of compounds from complex mixtures be accomplished (Giger and Blumer, 1974; MacLeod *et al.*, 1976).

Sources

The ubiquitous distribution of PNAH's has led to a dispute regarding the source of these compounds. Niaussat (1970), Mallet and Tissier (1969), Niaussat and Attenwalder (1969), Zobell (1959, 1971), and Borneff *et al.*, (1968), to mention a few, reported endogenic synthesis of PNAH's by plants, algae, and bacteria; their findings have been disputed by researchers who believe the origins of these compounds were either pyrolytic (Hase and Hites, 1976a, b; Giger and Blumer, 1974; Youngblood and Blumer, 1975) or a result of petroleum pollution. Grimmer and Dueval (1970) used elaborate precautions to eliminate contamination by air-borne PNAH's and found that higher plants did not synthesize PNAH's. Hase and Hites (1976a) found that extracts of both test bacteria and reagent blanks contained comparable amounts of PNAH's (anthacene and/or phenanthrene, pyrene, chrysene, perylene). They concluded that bacteria are effective bioaccumulators of PNAH (by a factor of 500). In view of these findings, the results of earlier researchers (Mallet and Tissier, 1969; Niaussat and Attenwalder, 1969; Niaussant, 1970; Zobell, 1959, 1971) could be interpreted as bioaccumulation rather than biosynthesis. The use of GC/MS instrumentation (Youngblood and Blumer, 1975; Blumer and Youngblood, 1975; Hites and Biemann, 1975; Hase and Hites, 1976a; Giger and Blumer, 1974) demonstrated the great variety of PNAH and their alkyl homolog derivatives, the predominance of unsubstituted PNAH's and the presence of sulfur-containing compounds (benzothiophene, dibenzothiophene) in extracts from marine and marsh sediments. The likelihood that organisms could produce a similar complex mixture under a variety of environment conditions seemed remote (Youngblood and Blumer, 1975; Hase and Hites, 1976b). In addition, the low abundance of alkylated derivatives and the similarities with the distributions obtained in combustion products of fossil fuels strongly suggested a pyrolytic origin for these complex mixtures (Hase and Hites, 1976b; Youngblood and Blumer, 1975). Hase and Hites (1976b) and Blumer and Youngblood (1975) disagree as to the type of pyrolytic source. Blumer and Youngblood suggest that forest fires could be a major source of PNAH's since the wide range of combustion temperatures in forest fires could form the more alkylated derivatives of PNAH's found in marine sediment. On the other hand, Hase and Hites (1976b) state that the distribution of PNAH's is very similar regardless of the pyrolytic source and that the distribution of alkylated derivatives reflects the differential water solubility of higher alkyl homologs vs unsubstituted species.

The high concentration of perylene, as compared to that of other PNAH's found in rapidly accreting reducing sediments off California, Africa, and British Columbia, suggested a different origin for the perylene (Aizenshtat, 1973; Aizenshtat, *et al.*, 1973, Orr and Grady, 1967). Yen *et al.*, (1961) stated that the perylene found in oil was not synthesized under the same conditions as the other PNAH's present in oil, but rather was extracted from the sediment through which the oil migrated. The precursor of the perylene found in these basins was thought to be either from land biota (Aizenshtat, 1973) or from pigments of marine organisms (Orr and Grady, 1967). Since PNAH's are present in petroleum (Pancirov, 1974) and persist in sediments contaminated by oil spills (Vandermuelen *et al.*, 1977; Scarrat and Zitko, 1972; Blumer and Sass, 1972), the contribution of petroleum pollution as a major source of the PNAH's present in the marine environment has been analyzed. A recent report (GESAMP, 1977), however, reasons that the input of PNAH's into the sea from petroleum is greatly outweighed by other inputs, except in areas of major oil spills, since the concentration of PNAH's in oil is far less than that in other environmental contaminants (coal, atmospheric fallout, industrial sludge, domestic sewage, creosated wharf piles, and urban runoff). Furthermore, Hase and Hites (1976b) and Youngblood and Blumer (1975) reasoned that the deficiency of unsubstituted PNAH's and the prevalence of three and four carbon alkyl homologs in petroleum ruled out petroleum spillage as a major source of PNAH's in estuarine sediment. They felt that the distribution of PNAH's in the sediment more closely reflected that formed from an incomplete combustion of wood or fossil fuels.

Degradation

In the marine environment, degradation of PNAH's is primarily by biological metabolism or chemical oxidation. Chemical oxidation by ultraviolet light commonly occurs in coastal waters (McGinnes and Snoeyink, 1974), though oxidation by halogenation and ozonation could occur in waters near sewage treatment plants. The oxidation of 3,4 benzpyrene and benzanthracene to their quinones has been studied by Kuratsune and Hirohito (1962) and McGinnes and Snoeyink (1974), and reviewed by Radding *et al.*, (1976). The rate of decomposition of PNAH's in marine waters has been found to increase with UV light intensity (McGinnes and Snoeyink, 1974) and with absorption onto minerals present in suspended marine sediment, i.e., calcite (Suess, 1968) and kaolinite (McGinnes and Snoeyink, 1974). Nagata and Kondo (1977) studied the stability of PNAH's in water-acetone solutions and found that more than 90 percent of the PNAH's (chrysene, fluorene, pyrene, and 3,4 benzpyrene) remained after ten hours of radiation from a Hg lamp. This finding agreed with that of McGinnes and Snoeyink (1974) who found that a residue of 3,4 benzpyrene remained regardless of the duration of UV radiation. Suess (1968) found that twenty hours of daylight exposure degraded 90 percent benzpyrene in aqueous solution. Apparently, conditions other than light are important in determining the rate of photodegradation.

Research on the microbial degradation of PNAH's has been investigated by Gibson (1976). He and his coworkers have concentrated on the initial oxygenation reaction of PNAH's. Unlike mammalian oxidation of PNAH's to arene oxides, bacteria were found to oxidize phenanthrene, anthracene, benzo(a)pyrene, and benz(a)anthracene to a cis-dihydrodiol.

Lee (1977) examined microbial degradation of [14] C-labelled hydrocarbons in estuarine waters. Degradation rates were either zero or very small ($<0.012 \pm$

0.009 μg/liter day^{-1}) for PNAH's (anthracene, fluorene, 3,4-benzpyrene, benz(a)anthracene) in unpolluted and slightly oil-polluted waters. In highly oil-polluted waters, the degradation rate increased to 0.070 and 0.038 μg/liter day^{-1} for anthracene and fluorene, respectively. This rate, however, is still substantially less than that measured for other hydrocarbons. Lee also found that incubation of PNAH's with surface sediments indicated that sediment microbes are important in the degradation of these compounds.

Conclusion

In summary, research has focused on PNAH's because of their known relationship with carcinogenesis and mutagenesis. While research on the relationship between molecular structure and carcinogenic activity has been studied for many years, the distribution and source of PNAH's in the environment has only recently become the subject of considerable debate. The findings of research to date indicate that, although biosynthesis and petroleum spillage may be sources for PNAH's in localized areas, the major source of these compounds is pyrolytic. While some researchers feel that forest fires may be responsible for the ubiquitous distribution of these compounds (Blumer and Youngblood, 1975), strong evidence suggests that the combustion of fossil fuels and atmospheric transport are primarily responsible (Hase and Hites, 1976b). In the marine environment, the transport of PNAH's is limited by their low water solubilities and high tendency for adsorption onto particulate matter, and the movement of these contaminated particles is believed to be the dominant method of transport of these compounds. Although the degradation of these compounds may result from photochemical oxidation or through the microbial action, PNAH's appear to be quite persistent, especially in anaerobic sediments. Due to their carcinogenic and mutagenic activity, the extent of their distribution, and their persistence, more research on the fate and effects of PNAH's in the environment is greatly needed.

References

1. Aizenshtat, H. 1973. Perylene and its geochemical significance. Geo. et Cosmo. Acta 37:559-567.

2. Aizenshtat, Z., M. J. Baedecker, and I. R. Kaplan. 1973. Distribution and diagensis of organic compounds in JOIDES sediment from Gulf of Mexico and western Atlantic. Geo. et Cosmo. Acta 37:1881-1891.

3. Ames, B. N., P. Sims and P. L. Grover. 1972. Epoxides of carcinogenic polycyclic hydrocarbons are frameshift mutagens. Science 176:47-49.

4. Andelman, J. B., and J. E. Snodgrass. 1974. Incidence and significance of polynuclear aromatic hydrocarbons in the water environment. CRC Critical Reviews in Environmental Controls 4:69-83.

5. Anderson, J. W., J. M. Neff, B. A. Cox, H. E. Tatern, and G. M. Hightower. 1974. The effects of oil on estuarine animals: toxicity, uptake and depuration, respiration, pp. 285-310. *In* F. J. Vernberg and W. B. Vernberg (eds.), Pollution and Physiology of Marine Organisms.

6. Blumer, M., and J. Sass. 1972. Oil pollution: persistence and degradation of spilled fuel oil. Science 176:1120-2.

7. Blumer, M., G. Souza, and J. Sass. 1970. Hydrocarbon pollution of edible shellfish by an oil spill. Mar. Biol. 5:195-202.

8. Blumer, M., and W. W. Youngblood. 1975. Polycyclic aromatic hydrocarbons in soils and recent sediments. Science 188:53-55.

9. Boehm, P., and J. Quinn. 1977. Persistence of chronically accumulated hydrocarbons in the hard shell clam, *Mercenaria mercenaria*. Mar. Biol., in press.

10. Borneff, J., F. Selenka, H. Kunte, and A. Maximos. 1968. Experimental studies on the formation of polycyclic aromatic hydrocarbons in plants. Experimental Research 2:22-29.

11. Bourcart, J., C. Lalou, and L. Mallet. 1961. About the presence of hydrocarbons of type 3,4-BP in coastal muds and the beach sand along the coast of Villefranche (Alpes-Maritimes). Comp. Rend. 252:640-644.

12. Bourcart, J., and L. Mallet. 1965. Marine pollution of the shores of the central region of the Tyrrhenian Sea (Bay of Naples) by hydrocarbon polybenzenes of type 3,4-BP. Compt. Rend. 260:3729-3734.

13. Brown, R. A., T. D. Searl, J. J. Elliott, B. G. Phillips, D. E. Brandon, and P. H. Monaghan. 1973. Distribution of heavy hydrocarbons in some Atlantic Ocean waters, pp. 505-519. *In* Proceedings of Joint Conference on Prevention and Control of Oil Spills. March 13-15, 1973. Washington, D.C.

14. Brown, R. S., R. E. Wolke, C. W. Brown, and S. B. Suila. 1977. Hydrocarbon pollution on neoplasia in New England soft shell clam, *Mya arenaria*. Int. Symposium on Pathobiology of Environmental pollution. In press.

15. Carlson, G. P. 1972. Detoxicification of foreign organic compounds by the quahog, *Mercenaria mercenaria*. Comp. Biochem. Physiol. 43B:295-302.

16. Clar, E. 1964. Polycyclic Hydrocarbons. Vol. II. Academic Press, New York.

17. Farrington, J. W., and J. G. Quinn. 1973. Petroleum hydrocarbons in Narragasett Bay. I. Survey of hydrocarbons in sediments and clams. Estuarine Coastal Mar. Sci. 1:71-79.

18. Gearing, P., J. N. Gearing, T. F. Lytle, and J. S. Lytle. 1976. Hydrocarbons in sixty northeast Gulf of Mexico shelf sediments: a preliminary survey. *In* C. H. Thompson (ed.), Geo. et Cosmo. Acta 40:1005-1017.

19. GESAMP—Reports and Studies, No. 6. 1977. Human effects from oil discharge, Chap. 6. IMCO/FAO/UNESCO/WMO/WHO/IAEA/UN. Joint Group of Experts in the Scientific Aspects of Marine Pollution. Impact of Oil on the Marine Environment, pp. 91-116.

20. Gibson, D. T. 1976. Microbial degradation of carcinogenic hydrocarbons and related compounds, pp. 225-238. *In* F. T. Weiss (ed.), Sources, effects, and sinks of hydrocarbons in the aquatic environment. Amer. Inst. Biol. Sci.

21. Giger, W., and M. Blumer. 1974. Polycyclic aromatic hydrocarbons in the environment: isolation and characterization by chromatography, visible, ultraviolet, and mass spectrometry. Anal. Chem. 46:1663-1671.

22. Grimmer, G., and D. Duevel. 1970. Biosynthetic formation of polycyclic hydrocarbons in higher plants. 8: Carcinogenic hydrocarbons in human environment. Z. Naturforsch. 25B:1171-1175. Chem. Abstra. 74:57053.

23. Hargrave, B. T., and G. A. Phillips. 1975. Estimates of oil in aquatic sediment by fluorescence spectroscopy. Environ. Pollut. 8:193-215.

24. Hase, A., and R. A. Hites. 1976a. On the origin of polycyclic aromatic hydrocarbons in recent sediments: biosynthesis by anaerobic bacteria. Geo. et Cosmo. Acta 40:1141-1143.

25. _____. 1976b. On the origin of polycyclic aromatic hydrocarbons in the aqueous environment, pp. 205-214. *In* L. H. Keith (ed.), Identification and Analysis of Organic Pollutants in Water. Ann Arbor Science Pub.

26. Hites, R. A. 1976. Sources of polycyclic aromatic hydrocarbons in the aquatic environment, pp. 325-333. *In* F. T. Weiss (ed.), Sources, effects and sinks of hydrocarbons in the aquatic environment. Amer. Inst. Biol. Sci.

27. Hites, R. A., and W. G. Biemann. 1975. Identification of specific organic compounds in a highly anoxic sediment by GC/MS and HRMS. Adv. Chem. Ser. 147:188-201.

28. Hueper, W. C. 1963. Environmental carcinogenesis in man and animals. Ann. N. Y. Acad. Sci. 108:961-1038.

29. Jackim, E., and L. Wilson. 1977. Benzpyrene accumulation and depuration in the soft shell clam (*Mya arenaria*). Proceedings of tenth National Shellfish Sanitation Meeting. U.S. Dept. H.E.W. In press.

30. Kuratsune, M., and T. Hirohito. 1962. Decomposition of polycyclic aromatic hydrocarbons under laboratory illumination. National Cancer Inst. Monogr. No. 9. 117-125.

31. Lalou, C., L. Mallet, and M. Heros. 1962. Depth distribution of 3,4-BP in a core sample from the Bay of Villefranche-sur-Mer. Compt. Rend. 255:145-147.

32. Lee, R. F. 1977. Fate of petroleum components in estuarine waters of the southeastern United States, pp. 611-616. *In* J. O. Ludwigson (ed.), Proceedings 1977 Oil Spill Conference, March 8-10, 1977.

33. Lee, R. F., R. Sauerheber, and G. H. Dobbs. 1972. Petroleum hydrocarbons: uptake and discharge by marine mussel *Mytilus edulis*. Science 177:344-346.

34. MacLeod, W. D., D. W. Brown, R. G. Jenkins, L. S. Ramos, and V. D. Henry. 1976. A pilot study on the design of a petroleum hydrocarbon baseline investigation for northern Puget Sound and Strait of Juan de Fuca. NOAA Technical Memorandum ERL MESA-8. 53 pp.

35. Mallet, L., and Mme. Le Theule. 1961. Investigations of 3,4-BP in the muddy marine sands of the coastal regions of the Marche and the Atlantic. Compt. Rend. 252:565-567.

36. Mallet, L., L. V. Perdrian, and J. Perdrian. 1963. Pollution by polybenzene hydrocarbons of type 3,4-BP of the western region of the Arctic Ocean. Compt. Rend. 256:3487-9.

37. Mallet, L., M. Tendron, and V. Plessis. 1960. Investigation of carcinogenic hydrocarbons (Type 3,4-BP) in the waters and marine deposits of estuaries and their occurring biota. Ann. Med. Leg. 40:168-171.

38. Mallet, L., and M. Tissier. 1969. Biosynthesis of polycyclic hydrocarbons of the benzo(a)pyrene type in forest soil. C. R. Soc. Biol. (Paris) 163:63. C.A., 1970. 73:44301k.

39. McGinnes, P. R., and V. L. Snoeyink. 1974. Determination of the fate of polynuclear aromatic hydrocarbons in natural water systems. Univ. of Ill. Water Res. Cent. Project No. A-045-I11.

40. Miller, J. A., and E. C. Miller. 1971. Chemical carcinogenesis: mechanisms and approaches to its control. J. Natl. Cancer Inst. 47:5-14.

41. Mix, M. C., R. T. Riley, K. I. King, S. R. Trenholm, and R. L. Schuffer. 1977. Chemical carcinogens in the marine environment. Benzo(a)pyrene in economically important bivalve molusks from Oregon estuaries. *In* D. Wolf (ed.), Fate and Effects of Petroleum Hydrocarbons in Marine Organisms and Ecosystems. Pergamon Press, Elmsford, N.Y.

42. Nagata, S., and G. Kondo. 1977. Photo-oxidation of crude oils. Proc. 1977 Oil Spill Conf. March 8-10, 1977. 617-620.

43. Neff, J. M. 1975. Accumulation and release of petroleum-derived aromatic hydrocarbons by marine animals, pp. 839-849. Symposium on chemistry, occurrence, and measurement of polynuclear aromatic hydrocarbons, American Chemical Society, Chicago Meeting, Aug. 24-29, 1975.

44. Neff, J. M., and J. W. Anderson. 1975. Accumulation, release and distribution of benzo(a)pyrene C-14 in the clam *Rangia cunesta*. 1975 Conference on preventing and control of oil pollution, Proceedings. Amer. Petrol Inst., EPA, and U.S. Coast Guard.

45. Niaussat, P. 1970. Pollution, par biosynthèse "in situ" d'hydrocarbures cancerigènes, d'une biocoenose lagunaire réproduction "in vitro" de ce phénomène. Rev. Int. Oceanogr. Med. Carbon 17:87-98.

46. Niaussat, P., and J. Attenwalder. 1969. Apparition de benzo 3,4-pyrene dans des cultures "in vitro" de phytoplancton marin. Importance des souillures bactériennes associées. Rev. Hyg. et Med. Soc. 17:487-495.

47. Orr, W. L., and J. R. Grady. 1967. Perylene in basin sediments off southern California. Geo. et Cosmochim. Acta 31:1201-1209.

48. Pancirov, R. J. 1974. Compositional data on API reference oil used in biological studies: A #2 fuel oil, A Bunker C, Kuwart crude oil, and south Louisiana crude oil. Report No. AID. IBA. 74. 6 p.

49. Philpot, R. M., M. O. James, and J. R. Bend. 1976. Metabolism of benzo(a)pyrene and other xenobiotics by microsomal mixed-function oxidases in marine species, pp. 184-199. *In* F. T. Weiss (ed.), Sources, effects, and sinks of hydrocarbons in the aquatic environment. Amer. Inst. Biol. Sci.

50. Piccinetti, C. 1967. Diffusione dell idrocarburo cancerigeno benzo 3-4 pirene nell alto e media. Adriatioco. Arch. Ocenoagr. Limnol. Supplemento al vol. 15:169-183.

51. Pullman, A., and B. Pullman. 1955. Electronic structure and carcinogenic activity of aromatic molecules. Adv. Cancer Res. 3:117-167.

52. Radding, S. B., T. Mill, C. W. Gould, D. H. Liu, H. L. Johnson, D. C. Bomberger, and D. V. Tojo. 1976. The environmental fate of selected poly-nuclear aromatic hydrocarbons. Report EPA-560/5-75-009. 122 pp.

53. Russell, F. F., and P. Kotin. 1957. Squamous papilloma in the white croaker. Nat. Cancer Inst. J. 18:857-861.

54. Scarratt, D. J., and V. Zitko. 1972. Bunker C oil in sediments and benthic animals from shallow depths in Chedabucto Bay, N.S. J. Fish. Res. Bd. Canada. 29:1347-1350.

55. Schnitzer, M., and S. U. Khan. 1972. Humic substances in the environment. Marcel Dekker, Inc., New York. 327 pp.

56. Stegeman, J. T., and J. M. Teal. 1973. Accumulation, release and retention of petroleum hydrocarbons by the oyster *Crassostrea virginica*. Mar. Biol. 22:37-44.

57. Suess, M. J. 1968. Behavior and fate of 3,4 benzypyrene in aqueous systems. Ph.D. dissertation, Univ. of Pittsburgh.

58. _____. 1970. Presence of polynuclear aromatic hydrocarbons in coastal waters and the possible health consequences. Rev. Intern. Oceanogr. Med. tome XVIII-XIX. U.N. World Health Organization.

59. Tissier, M., and J. L. Oudin. 1973. Characteristics of naturally occurring and pollutant hydrocarbons in marine sediments, pp. 205-214. *In* Proceedings of Joint Conference on Prevention and Control of Oil Spills, March 13-15, 1973. Washington, D.C.

59. Tissier, M., and J. L. Ouding. 1973. Characteristics of naturally occurring and pollutant hydrocarbons in marine sediments, pp. 205-214. *In* Proceedings of Joint Conference on Prevention and Control of Oil Spills, March 13-15, 1973. Washington, D.C.

60. Thomas, D. A., and M. Blumer. 1964. Pyrene and fluoranthene in manganese nodules. Science 143:39.

61. Vandermuelen, J. H., P. D. Keizer, and W. R. Penrose. 1977. Persistence of non-alkane components of Bunker C oil in beach sediments of Chedabucto Bay and lack of their metabolism by molluscs. pp. 469-473. *In* Proc. 1977 Oil Spill Conference. March 8-10, 1977.

62. Yen, T. F., J. G. Erdman, and W. E. Hanson. 1961. Reinvestigation of densimetric methods of ring analysis. J. Chem. Eng. Data 6:443.

63. Yevich, P. P., and C. A. Barszcz. 1976. Gonadal and hematopoietric neoplasms in *Mya arenaria*. Mar. Fish. Rev. 38:42-43.

64. Youngblood, W. W., and M. Blumer. 1975. Polycyclic aromatic hydrocarbons in the environment homologous series of soils and recent marine sediments. Geo. Cosmo. Acta 39:1303-1314.

65. Zobell, C. E. 1959. Microbiology of oil. N. Z. Oceanogr. Inst. Mem. 3:39-47.

66. _____. 1971. Sources and biodegradation of carcinogenic hydrocarbons, pp. 441-451. *In* Proceedings of Joint Conference on Prevention and Control of Oil spills. Washington, D.C. June 15-17, 1971, American Petroleum Institute, Washington, D.C.

RELATIONSHIP BETWEEN
BIOAVAILABILITY OF TRACE METALS
AND GEOCHEMICAL PROCESSES IN ESTUARIES

Ford A. Cross and William G. Sunda

National Marine Fisheries Service
Southeast Fisheries Center
Beaufort Laboratory
Beaufort, North Carolina

Abstract: Accurate prediction of the biological impact of metallic contaminants in the estuarine environment, including return to man, requires identification and quantification of the ecological processes which control both the flux of metals through estuaries and their availability to biota. The extent of our knowledge has been limited somewhat by the lack of appropriate methods and techniques sufficiently sensitive or selective to measure metals at environmental levels or to distinguish among various chemical forms in water.

Recent research both on the bioavailability and estuarine chemistry of metals has led to a better understanding of (1) relative bioavailability of metals partitioned among major reservoirs (sediments, water, and biota); (2) the behavior of metals within various chemical regimes present in estuarine systems, particularly the mixing zone; (3) effect of chemical speciation of trace metals on bioavailability; and (4) environmental variables that control the chemical forms of trace metals in estuaries.

It is essential that the type of research information discussed in this paper be considered in the establishment of both water quality criteria needed to protect marine resources and regulatory levels which may be required to protect humans.

Introduction

This paper provides an overview of the possible influences that estuarine geochemical processes can have on the bioavailability of trace metals to estuarine organisms. [Bioavailability is defined for the purpose of this paper as the tendency of a trace metal to react with, or pass through, membranes of living cells and may be quantified by measuring either bioaccumulation or a biological response. The response of organisms to trace metals may be either positive (i.e., nutritional) or negative (i.e., toxic)]. Recent advances in estuarine geochemistry have been summarized (Burton and Liss, 1976) as has recent progress concerning the bioavailability of trace metals to aquatic organisms (Lockwood, 1976; Johnston, 1976; McIntyre and Mills, 1975). We believe that these two fields need to be drawn closer together.

When one examines the complex cycles of trace metals in estuaries, it becomes apparent that bioavailability of these metals probably differs significantly within and among estuarine systems. Until these differences are taken into account in both the design and interpretation of research on bioavailability and in the establishment of water quality criteria, we will not be addressing the potential problem of trace metals contamination in estuaries in a realistic manner. Mount (1975) provides an excellent discussion on this subject as it relates to trace metal standards in freshwater.

In this paper we discuss the relative differences that occur in bioavailability of trace metals as they are partitioned among major estuarine reservoirs (sediments, water, and biota) and then examine some geochemical processes that can alter both the partitioning and bioavailability of metals within an estuarine system. In the final section, some suggestions are offered for current research on biotoxicity of trace metals.

I. Bioavailability of Trace Metals Sorbed to Estuarine Sediments

When compared with water and biota, it has been well established that sediments represent the largest reservoir for trace metals within a estuarine system (Renfro, 1973). This reservoir obviously has the potential of conveying measurable quantities of trace metals to estuarine biota, particularly to benthic organisms which ingest sediment while feeding. This process of bioaccumulation would be of primary interest in areas where sediments were contaminated with metals from anthropogenic sources. In recent years, efforts have been made to assess the relative importance of trace metals associated with sediments as sources of metals to estuarine organisms as well as to determine what fraction of sediment-sorbed metal is "bioavailable". (For an in-depth review of this subject see Jenne and Luoma, in press.) These studies have taken place both in the laboratory and in the field, and a summary of recent research follows.

Laboratory studies

Several laboratory studies using radiotracers have been conducted in an effort to assess the capacity of benthic organisms to assimilate trace metals from ingested sediment. These experiments have shown limited but measurable rates of accumulation of sediment-sorbed [65]Zn, [54]Mn, and ^{51}Cr in polychaetes (Renfro, 1973; Renfro and Benayoun, 1976; Chipman, 1966; Chipman et al., 1968). With both [65]Zn and [54]Mn, radionuclide sorbed to organic detritus was accumulated at a faster rate than that associated with inorganic material.

Experiments that have been conducted to estimate bioavailable fractions of trace metals sorbed to sediments have encountered difficulties in both design and interpretation due to the fact that (1) metals in sediments will be present in different chemical forms, depending on the sediment type and chemical characteristics of the environment; (2) metals may exchange between sediment particles and water (both interstitial and overlying), thus confounding the direct source of metals to biota; (3) the rates of exchange reactions between particles and water are not well-known; and (4) rates of assimilation from the sediments could vary significantly among different species of animals. Luoma and Jenne (1976b and in press) have devised an experimental procedure that allows an estimation of the bioavailability of radiotracers (e.g., ^{60}Co, ^{65}Zn, ^{110m}Ag, ^{109}Cd) sorbed to particles of different chemical composition (iron oxide, manganese oxide, precipitated carbonates, biogenic carbonates and organic detritus) to the deposit-feeding clam *Macoma balthica*. The degree of bioavailability of each radiotracer was inversely related to the strength of binding between metals and particles: i.e., the capacity of the clams to accumulate ^{65}Zn, ^{60}Co and ^{110m}Ag from ingested sediments decreased as the particle-water distribution coefficient (K_{des}) for the radiotracers increased. Metals in natural mixed sediments will bind preferentially to particles having the highest sediment-water distribution coefficient and thus, the lowest metal bioavailability (Luoma and Jenne, in press). Accumulation of tracer from all of these particles was low, however, when compared to accumulation from solution (Jenne and Luoma, in press).

Luoma and Jenne (1976a) also used chemical extraction techniques to estimate the bioavailability of sediment-bound radiotracers. They compared concentrations of tracers in tissues of clams exposed to different labeled sediments to concentrations of tracers in several chemical extracts of the same sediments. Results of these comparisons indicated that a 70% ethanol or 1 N ammonium acetate extraction provided a good estimate of bioavailable ^{109}Cd or ^{60}Co and that extractions from sediments with either 1 N ammonium acetate or 1 N NaOH plus EDTA provided the best estimate of bioavailable ^{65}Zn. The development of extraction techniques such as these to estimate bioavailability of metals in sediments may prove useful in assessing the potential biological impact of trace metal contamination in estuaries and coastal areas.

Field studies

A number of surveys have been conducted in estuaries or coastal regions where sediments have been grossly contaminated with trace metals from either industrial and municipal wastewater discharges or mining operations, in an effort to assess the influence of sediments on trace metal content of biota. One of the most intensively studied areas relative to trace metal contamination has been the coastal region of southern California near the wastewater outfalls from Los Angeles. McDermott *et al.* (1976) and de Goeij *et al.* (1974) compared concentrations of thirteen trace metals in tissues of immature Dover sole (*Microstomus pacificus*) collected near the wastewater outfalls and from uncontaminated control areas. Although the enrichment of metals in sediments near the outfalls compared to the control area ranged from 3.2 for silver to 150 for cadmium, enrichment in the fish-tissues (flesh, gonads, and liver) was significant only for chromium in gonads and liver. Similarly, Eganhouse and Young (in press) were not able to relate concentrations of mercury in several species of benthic animals to elevated mercury levels in the sediment from this same geographical area. Additional data showing that concentrations of metals in benthic organisms do not appear to reflect concentrations in sediments have been reported by Halcrow *et al.* (1973), Valiela *et al.* (1974), Cross *et al.* (1970), Huggett *et al.* (1975), Luoma (1977), and Schell and Nevissi (1977).

A few studies, however, have shown that concentrations of metals in benthic invertebrates can reflect trace metal content of the sediments. Young and Jan (1976) observed elevated levels of several metals, particularly chromium, in tissues of rock scallops (*Hinites multirugosus*) collected near the Los Angeles wastewater outfalls compared with scallops from a control area. Bryan (1974) investigated the relationship between concentrations of copper and zinc in the polychaete *Nereis diversicolor* and concentrations of these two metals in estuarine sediment which had become contaminated with mining wastes during the past 200 years. He found that body burdens of copper in these worms reflected the concentrations of copper in sediments quite closely. Zinc, however, varied by only a factor of 3 in the worms, although the zinc concentration in the sediment varied by a factor of 30. Frazier (1976) reported that oysters placed in an estuary with sediments contaminated with copper and zinc accumulated these two metals to significantly higher levels than oysters in an uncontaminated estuary. He concluded that, although trace metal levels in sediments were not completely accurate predictors of levels in oysters, concentrations in the sediment can indicate the relative trend in availability of metals to biota.

The observations described above do not necessarily indicate direct cause and effect relationships, but do suggest that the bioavailabilty of metals in contaminated estuaries is highly variable and probably controlled by complex interactions of biogeochemical processes. The net effect of these processes will play an important role in determining bioavailability of metals and will be discussed later in more detail.

II. Bioavailability of Trace Metals in Food and Water

The apparent unimportance of sediment particles as a direct source of trace metals to estuarine macrofauna suggests that the two smallest reservoirs (food and water) contain the most readily bioavailable forms of trace metals for these organisms. Knowledge of the relative differences in bioavailability of metals between these two reservoirs and among chemical forms within each reservoir is essential before the consequences of metal additions, both in terms of bioaccumulation and toxicity, can be predicted.

Relative importance of food and water

At the present time, it has not been well established whether the major source of trace metals to marine fauna is through ingestion of food or from direct absorption from water across external surfaces such as the gill. Scientists seem split on this controversy and arguments for both points of view can be found in Polikarpov (1966) and Lowman *et al*. (1971).

Experimental studies, as yet, have not differentiated between these two sources quantitatively. Pentreath (1973a, 1973b, 1973c, and 1976d) has combined theoretical considerations and laboratory experiments with radiotracers to conclude that ingestion of food is the primary source (>95%) of manganese, iron, cobalt, and zinc in plaice (*Pleuronectes platessa*) and mussels (*Mytilus edulis*). In contrast to these findings, however, Renfro *et al*. (1975) found that accumulation of ^{65}Zn from food in shrimp, crustaceans, and fish was of less importance than reported in Pentreath's studies. For mercury, accumulation from water was considered to be of equal or greater importance than food for both methyl and inorganic forms in plaice and the thornback ray *Raja clavata* (Pentreath, 1976a, 1976b, 1976c).

In reality, the true pathways for the bioaccumulation of metals in estuaries is probably very complex and dependent upon a series of biological and chemical variables such as feeding type, composition of food, chemical behavior of the metal tested, and chemical characteristics of the water (pH, salinity, presence of complexing ligands, etc.). It is necessary, however, to obtain a more complete understanding of the sources of metals to estuarine animals, particularly those consumed by man, before accurate predictions can be made of the rate of bioaccumulation of trace metals for various trophic levels.

Dissolved metals: importance of free metal ion activity

Understanding the bioavailability of dissolved metals is a complex problem because some trace metals may exist in a variety of redox forms (e.g., Cr, Mn, Fe, Hg) and most have a tendency to form chemical associations with a variety of inorganic and organic ligands. Considerable progress, however, has been made in the past few years in determining the chemical forms of dissolved metals that are available to organisms. This progress, by and large, is a direct result of the application of thermodynamic theory to the problem of bioavailability.

Several recent experiments have demonstrated quantitatively that bioavailability (i.e., toxicity, nutritional availability, and cellular accumulation) of copper for unicellular algae is dependent on free cupric ion activity, and independent of the concentration of complexed copper (Manahan and Smith, 1973; Sunda and Guillard, 1976; Anderson and Morel, 1978). These experiments were conducted in culture media in which the chemical speciation of copper was varied systematically by varying the concentrations of model chelators—EDTA (Ethylenediaminetetraacetic acid) or Tris [(hydroxymethyl)aminomethane]—and total dissolved copper. By utilizing these chemically well-defined experimental media, it was possible to calculate the chemical activities of different dissolved species of copper from thermodynamic stability constants (see Stumm and Morgan, 1970). In experiments using an ion-selective electrode to measure cupric ion activities directly, Sunda and Lewis (in press) also demonstrated a direct relationship between cupric ion activity and toxicity of copper to an estuarine alga *Monochrysis lutheri*, in media where copper was complexed to different degrees by natural organic ligands present in river water. These experiments demonstrate that complexation of copper by natural organic ligands will reduce the toxicity of copper to phytoplankton by reducing the activity of cupric ion. Similar results have been found for bacteria (Sunda and Gillespie, unpublished data).

The importance of free metal ions in determining toxicity does not apply solely to unicellular organisms, to a single metal (copper), or to complexation by organic ligands. Andrew *et al.* (1977) found that mortality rates of the freshwater crustacean *Daphnia magna* were related to free cupric ion, but not to the concentrations of copper complexed to inorganic ligands (carbonate, orthophosphate, and pyrophosphate) or to copper present in particulate forms. In similar experiments with cadmium, the mortality of grass shrimp, *Palaemonetes pugio*, was shown to be a direct function of the measured cadmium ion activity, which in turn was controlled both by the total dissolved cadmium concentration and by the degree to which cadmium was complexed by chloride ion or nitrilotriacetate ion (Sunda *et al.*, 1978).

The above experiments show that relationships between toxicity and free metal activities can be quite independent of the degree of metal complexation or to the chemical nature of the complexing ligands. Also the dependency of acute metal toxicity on the free ion activities is probably not limited to copper and cadmium or to a few select species of aquatic organisms. In their discussion, Sunda *et al.* (1978) cite examples in the literature where chelation has reduced the bioavailability of copper, cadmium, manganese, zinc, and mercury to a variety of aquatic organisms.

From thermodynamic considerations, a dependency of bioavailability in general, and toxicity in particular, on free metal activities is not unexpected. The activity of a metal ion is a direct function of its free energy—the driving force of chemical reactions. For a trace metal to be bioavailable to an organism, it must invariably react chemically with molecular components of the organism. Thus, the tendency for the occurrence of such reactions will be directly related to metal ion activities. The situation with bioavailability of metals is analogous to that of hydrogen ions. It has been well accepted for a number of years that free hydrogen ion activity (pH) is the primary chemical factor that determines the availability of hydrogen ions to organisms. It should not be surprising, therefore, that trace metal ion activity should be the dominant chemical variable controlling bioavailability of trace metals.

Like all metal-ligand interactions, those of a particular trace metal with biological ligands such as proteins, nucleic acids, organic polyphosphates, and so on, will be determined not only by the activity of the metal ion in question, but also to varying degrees by the activities of other metal ions including hydrogen ions. This is due to the fact that most ligands possess the capacity to bind a variety of metal ions and thus, metal binding to ligands often involves competition among metals. The degree of competition is determined by relative magnitudes of metal ion activities and stability constants for metal-ligand associations. Competitive binding is reflected on an organismic level by metal antagonism—the ability of one metal to lower the availability of another. The accumulation of zinc by macroalgae, for example, is reduced by increased concentrations of copper, cadmium, and hydrogen ions (Gutknecht, 1963; Bryan, 1969). Increased concentrations of calcium significantly reduce the uptake of Zn by *Chlorella* (Matzku and Broda, 1970) and by the aquatic moss *Fontinalis antipyretica* (Pickering and Puia, 1969). Effects of metal competition may be particularly important in estuaries where changes in salinity are accompanied by order of magnitude changes in the concentrations of major cations (Ca^{2+}, Mg^{2+}, Na^+, and K^+). The influence of metal competition in controlling trace metal bioavailability in estuaries is at present poorly understood.

III. Relationship Between Estuarine Processes and Bioavailability

As trace metals move from rivers to estuaries, they enter a chemical regime which is highly variable due primarily to large differences in chemical composition between river water and seawater. The most conspicuous difference in estuarine water relative to river water is the large increase in the concentration of major dissolved ions (e.g., Na^+, K^+, Ca^{2+}, Mg^{2+}, Cl^-, and SO_4^-) which may cause the flocculation and deposition of metals associated with colloidal materials (e.g., hydrous metal oxides, metal-organic colloids, and clays). Large changes also may occur in pH, redox potential and the concentration and composition of organic ligands, all of which will influence the chemistry of trace metals. It is not surprising, therefore, that the distributional patterns of trace metals in estuaries often exhibit non-conservative behavior (Boyle *et al.*, 1974; Liss, 1976; MacKay and Leatherland, 1976; Evans *et al.*, 1977; Thomas and Grill, 1977).

This non-conservative behavior suggests that the chemical forms, and thus the bioavailability of metals, change substantially within and among estuarine systems. For example, "dissolved" iron is rapidly removed from most estuarine waters, apparently due to flocculation and precipitation of colloidal iron (Boyle *et al.*, 1974; Boyle, 1976; Holliday and Liss, 1976). Dissolved manganese, however, has been shown to be present at intermediate salinities in concentrations in excess of those predicted by conservative mixing of inflowing river and ocean water with subsequent loss from solution at high salinities (Evans *et al.*, 1977). The source of the excess dissolved manganese appears to be bottom sediments, and upstream recycling of particulate manganese from the lower to the upper estuary may resupply this reservoir (Evans *et al.*, 1977). Evidence also exists that zinc and copper may behave non-conservatively in estuaries, although deviations for these two metals from theoretical mixing curves are substantially less than for manganese or iron (Evans 1977; Holliday and Liss, 1976; Boyle, 1976).

Biological processes also may influence the spatial distribution as well as the bioavailable forms of trace metals in estuaries. Turekian (in press) discusses the role of burrowing animals in enhancing the exchange of trace metals between sediments and overlying water. Trace metals associated with suspended particulates may be removed from the water column by filter feeding invertebrates (Lowman *et al.*, 1971) and by juvenile fish (Cross *et al.*, 1975) via biodeposition of fecal material. In addition, biological processes are responsible either directly or indirectly for the production of dissolved organic ligands that may alter the chemical speciation of trace metals. At the present time, however, very little is known concerning the quantitative importance of these processes in controlling trace metal bioavailability in estuaries.

As mentioned earlier, the toxicity of at least two metals, copper and cadmium, to a number of different organisms has been shown experimentally to be directly related to free metal ion activity. Thus, processes that affect trace metal activities, such as complexation, adsorption, and precipitation, will also affect toxicity.

Laboratory experiments using ion-selective electrodes to measure free cupric ion activities directly have shown that dissolved copper is highly complexed (>90% bound at total copper concentrations $<10^{-6}M$) by dissolved organic ligands in water from coastal rivers in North Carolina (Sunda and Hanson, in press). Complexation to this material was found to increase with increasing concentration of organic matter, increasing pH, decreasing salinity and decreasing concentrations of calcium and magnesium. In estuaries of these rivers the complexation of copper should decrease in a seaward direction due to the combined effects of decreasing concentrations of organic matter and increasing salinity. Therefore, we would expect toxicity relative to total copper concentration to increase toward the mouth of the estuary. This prediction has been verified experimentally for the toxicity of copper to bacterial cultures (Sunda and Gillespie, unpublished data).

Recent experimental evidence suggests that in neritic or oceanic waters, where concentrations of dissolved organic matter are low and salinities are high relative to estuaries, naturally occurring cupric ion activities may be at or near those which are toxic to some marine organisms; e.g., phytoplankton (Davey *et al.*, 1973; Sunda and Guillard, 1976) and fish eggs (Engel and Sunda, in press). In addition, Anderson and Morel (1978) have found that the growth of *Gonyaulax tamarensis*, a red tide dinoflagellate, is completely inhibited at free cupric ion activities within the calculated range in seawater, assuming there is little or no organic complexation. This sensitivity to cupric ion is significantly higher than for several other algal species. Anderson and Morel hypothesize that the growth of this dinoflagellate may be inhibited by copper under natural conditions, and that increases in copper complexation, resulting from the introduction of increased concentrations of dissolved organic ligands into coastal waters during excessive runoff may reduce copper toxicity to this organism and trigger blooms. Results of CEPEX (Controlled Ecosystem Pollution Experiment) experiments, in which coastal seawater along with natural fauna and flora was placed in large plastic enclosures, have shown that as little as 5 ppb added total copper markedly altered phytoplankton species composition (Thomas and Seibert, 1977). The addition of copper caused the complete disappearance of more sensitive strains (dinoflagellates and centric diatoms), which were replaced by more copper-resistant pennate diatoms.

Measurements with ion-selective electrodes (Sunda and Lewis, 1976, Sunda *et al.*, 1978) and results of thermodynamic calculations (Zirino and Yamamoto, 1972; Stumm and Brauner, 1975) provide evidence that dissolved cadmium will be present predominantly as chloride complexes in coastal and estuarine waters. Thus, the level of cadmium complexation should be inversely related to chloride concentration (i.e., salinity) in estuarine waters. The effect of chloride complexation on free cadmium ion activities has been shown experimentally to account quantitatively for the observed inverse relationship between cadmium toxicity to grass shrimp and salinity (Sunda *et al.*, 1978). Chloride complexation probably also explains similar inverse salinity relationships that have been observed in cadmium toxicity and bioaccumulation experiments with a number of other organisms.

The above discussion leaves little doubt that bioavailability of metals is continually changing in estuaries as they are exposed to such biogeochemical processes as adsorption, precipitation, dissolution, complexation, and biological incorporation. The relative influence that these processes will have on bioavailability will depend to a large degree on the chemical composition of the river water, Eh and pH gradients within the estuary, physical characteristics of the estuary, and type and abundance of biota. The net effect of these processes on bioavailability of trace metals needs to be understood for different types of estuaries before the consequences of the addition of metals to these ecosystems can be predicted.

IV. Bioavailability, Bioassays, and the Real World

In this paper we have attempted to illustrate the interrelationships that exist between biogeochemical process in estuaries and bioavailability of trace metals. Knowledge gained relative to the complex behavior of metals in estuaries must be utilized in the interpretation of field observations of the distribution of metals in organisms and in the design of bioaccumulation and toxicity experiments in the laboratory, as evidence now exists that the bioavailability of trace metals can change substantially within and among estuarine systems. In addition, we must begin to consider the chronic as well as the acute consequences of metals additions to estuaries.

The utility of continuing to conduct bioaccumulation and toxicity experiments based solely on total dissolved concentrations in the water must be severely questioned. Experimental evidence suggests that food may contribute more than 95% of the total body burden for some metals at the higher trophic levels. Thus, biotoxicity experiments should be designed to assess the effect of ingestion as well as dissolved trace metals on physiological processes (Pentreath, 1973c). In addition, recent observations that acute toxicity of copper and cadmium in water is related to the free ion activities rather than total dissolved concentrations also should be reflected in the design of biotoxicity experiments, including a better understanding and control of those variables which regulate trace metal complexation (e.g., pH, salinity, and concentration, and composition of dissolved organic ligands). Bioavailability experiments with trace metals should be designed to present the metal to the organism under conditions similar to those that occur in nature. This will require more complex experimental designs in which animals would be exposed to elevated levels of metals in both food and water in a ratio indicative of the natural environment.

The establishment of water quality criteria must be more ecosystem specific. Toxicological information obtained for freshwater should not be extrapolated to marine ecosystems and should even address estuarine, neritic, and oceanic waters separately—because, as discussed previously, the toxicity of a metal at one total dissolved concentration will vary as a function of several environmental factors. Similarly, this knowledge should be used by decisionmakers in siting discharge points of metals into the estuaries and coastal waters and in the establishment of effluent guidelines to assess impacts on biota realistically. Obviously the estuarine chemist, the toxicologist, and the regulator need to become more interrelated.

Acknowledgments

We thank Drs. David Engel and Peter Hanson and Mr. James Willis for their helpful criticisms and discussion. This effort was supported by an Interagency Agreement between the National Marine Fisheries Service and the U.S. Department of Energy.

Contribution Number 78-27B, Southeast Fisheries Center, National Marine Fisheries Service, NOAA, Beaufort, North Carolina 28516.

References

1. Anderson, D. M., and F. M. M. Morel. 1978. Copper sensitivity of *Gonyaulax tamarensis*. Limnol. Oceanogr. 23(2):283-295.

2. Andrew, R. W., K. E. Biesinger, and G. E. Glass. 1977. Effects of inorganic complexing on the toxicity of copper to *Daphina magna*. Water Res. 11:309-315.

3. Boyle, E. A. 1976. The marine geochemistry of trace metals. Ph.D. dissertation, Massachusetts Institute of Technology and Woods Hole Oceanographic Institution. 155 pp.

4. Boyle, E., R. Collier, A. T. Dengler, J. M. Edmond, A. C. Ng, and R. F. Stallard. 1974. On the chemical mass-balance in estuaries. Geochim. Cosmochim. Acta 38:1719-1728.

5. Bryan, G. W. 1969. The absorption of zinc and other metals by the brown seaweed *Laminaria digitata*. J. Mar. Biol. Assoc. U.K. 49:225-243

6. _____. 1974. Adaptation of an estuarine polychaete to sediments containing high concentrations of heavy metals, pp. 123-136. *In* F. J. Vernberg and W. Vernberg (eds.), Pollution and Physiology of Marine Organisms. Academic Press, New York.

7. Burton, J. D., and P. S. Liss (eds.). 1976. Estuarine Chemistry. Academic Press, London.

8. Chipman, W. A. 1966. Some aspects of the accumulation of ^{51}Cr by marine organisms, pp. 931-941. *In* B. Aberg and F. Hungate (eds.), Radioecological Concentration Processes. Pergamon Press, London.

9. Chipman, W. A., E. Schommers, and M. Boyer. 1968. Uptake, accumulation and retention of radioactive manganese by the marine annelid worm *Hermione hystrix*. International Atomic Energy Agency Radioactivity in the Sea, Publ. No. 25, 16 pp.

10. Cross, F. A., T. W. Duke, and J. N. Willis. 1970. Biogeochemistry of trace elements in a coastal plain estuary: Distribution of manganese, iron and zinc in sediments, water, and polychaetous worms. Chesapeake Sci. 11:221-234.

11. Cross, F. A., J. N. Willis, L. H. Hardy, N. Y. Jones, and J. M. Lewis. 1975. Role of juvenile fish in cycling of Mn, Fe, Cu and Zn in a coastal-plain estuary, pp. 45-65. *In* L. E. Cronin (ed.), Estuarine research, vol. 1. Academic Press, New York.

12. Davey, E. W., M. J. Morgan, and S. J. Erickson. 1973. A biological measurement of copper complexation capacity of seawater. Limnol., Oceanogr. 18:993-997.

13. de Goeij, J. J. M., V. P. Guinn, D. R. Young, and A. J. Mearns. 1974. Neutron activation analysis trace-element studies of Dover sole livers and marine sediments, pp. 189-200. *In* Comparative studies of food and environmental contamination. International Atomic Energy Agency, Vienna. (IAE-SM-175/15).

14. Eganhouse, R. P., Jr., and D. R. Young. In press. Total and organic mercury in benthic organisms near a major submarine wastewater outfall system. Bull. Environ. Contam. Toxicol.

15. Engel, D. W., and W. G. Sunda. In press. The toxicity of cupric ion to the eggs of the spot, *Leiostomus xanthurus*, and the Atlantic silverside, *Menidia menidia*. Mar. Biol.

16. Evans, D. W. 1977. Exchange of manganese, iron, copper and zinc between dissolved and particulate forms in the Newport River estuary, North Carolina. Ph.D. dissertation, Oregon State Univ., Corvallis. 218 pp.

17. Evans, D. W., N. H. Cutshall, F. A. Cross, and D.A. Wolfe. 1977. Manganese cycling in the Newport River estuary, North Carolina. Estuarine Coastal Mar. Sci. 5(1):71-80.

18. Frazier, J. M. 1976. The dynamics of metals in the American oyster, *Crassostrea virginica*. II. Environmental effects. Chesapeake Sci. 17:188-197.

19. Gutknecht, J. 1963. Zn^{65} uptake by benthic marine algae. Limnol. Oceanogr. 8:31-18.

20. Halcrow, W., D. W. MacKay, and I. Thornton. 1973. The distribution of trace metals and fauna in the Firth of Clyde in relation to the disposal of sewage sludge. J. Mar. Biol. Assoc. U.K. 53:721-739.

21. Holliday, L. M., and P. S. Liss. 1976. The behavior of dissolved iron, manganese and zinc in the Beaulieu Estuary, S. England. Estuarine Coastal Mar. Sci. 4:349-353.

22. Huggett, R. J., F. A. Cross, and M. E. Bender. 1975. Distribution of copper and zinc in oysters and sediments from three coastal plain estuaries, pp. 224-238. *In* F. G. Howell, J. B. Gentry, and M. H. Smith (eds.), Symposium on Mineral Cycling in Southeastern Ecosystems. Augusta, Ga., 1974. Proceedings U. S. Environmental Research Development Administration Symposium Series (CONF-740513).

23. Jenne, E. A., and S. A. Luoma. In press. Forms of trace elements in soils, sediments, and associated waters: an overview of their determination and biological availability. Biological implications of metals in the environment, 15th Life Sciences Symposium, Richland, Washington, 1975.

24. Johnston, R. (ed.) 1976. Marine Pollution. Academic Press, New York. 729 pp.

25. Liss, P. S. 1976. Conservative and nonconservative behavior of dissolved constituents during estuarine mixing, pp. 93-130. In J. D. Burton and P. S. Liss (eds.), Estuarine Chemistry. Academic Press, London.

26. Lockwood, A. P. M. (ed.) 1976. Effects of Pollutants on aquatic organisms. Cambridge University Press, Cambridge. 193 pp.

27. Lowman, F. G., T. R. Rice, and F. W. Richards. 1971. Accumulation and redistribution of radionuclides by marine organisms, pp. 161-199. In A. H. Seymour (ed.), Radioactivity in the marine environment. National Academy of Sciences, Washington, D.C.

28. Luoma, S. N. 1977. The dynamics of biologically available mercury in a small estuary. Estuarine Coastal Mar. Sci. 5:643-652.

29. Luoma, S. N., and E. A. Jenne. 1976a. Estimating bioavailability of sediment-bound trace metals with chemical extractants, pp. 343-351. In D. D. Hemphill (ed.), Trace substances in environmental health—X. Univ. of Missouri, Columbia.

30. _____. 1976b. Factors affecting and availability of sediment-bound cadmium to the deposit-feeding bivalve, *Macoma balthica*, pp. 284-290, In C. E. Cushing (ed.), Radioecology and energy resources. Ecol. Soc. Amer., Spec. Pub. 1.

31. _____. In press. The availability of sediment-bound cobalt, silver and zinc to a deposit-feeding clam. Biological implications of metals in the environment, 15th Life Sciences Symposium, Richland, Washington, 1975.

32. MacKay, D. W., and T. M. Leatherland. 1976. Chemical processes in an estuary receiving major inputs of industrial and domestic wastes, pp. 185-218. In J. D. Burton and P. S. Liss (eds.), Estuarine Chemistry. Academic Press, London.

33. Manahan, S. E., and M. J. Smith. 1973. Copper micronutrient requirement for algae. Environ. Sci. Technol. 7:829-833.

34. Matzku, S., and E. Broda. 1970. Die zinkaufnahne in das innere von *Chlorella*. Planta. (Berl) 92:29-40.

35. McDermott, D. J., G. V. Alexander, D. R. Young, and A. J. Mearns. 1976. Metal contamination of flatfish around a large submarine outfall. J. Water Pollut. Control Fed. 48(8):1913-1918.

36. McIntyre, A. D., and C. F. Mills (eds.) 1975. Ecological Toxicology Research. Plenum Press, New York. 323 pp.

37. Mount, D. I. 1975. Research to develop heavy metal standards for fresh water, pp. 151-161. In international conference on heavy metals in the environment, symposium proceedings, vol. 1. Institute for Environmental Studies, Univ. of Toronto, Toronto.

38. Pentreath, R. J. 1973a. The accumulation and retention of ^{59}Fe and ^{58}Co by the plaice, *Pleuronectes platessa* L. J. Exp. Mar. Biol. Ecol. 12:315-326.

39. _____. 1973b. The accumulation and retention of ^{65}Zn and ^{54}Mn by the plaice, *Pleuronectes platessa* L. J. Exp. Mar. Biol. Ecol. 12:1-18.

40. _____. 1973c. The roles of food and water in the accumulation of radionuclides by marine teleost and elasmobranch fish, pp. 421-436. In Radioactive contamination of the marine environment. International Atomic Energy Agency, Vienna. (IAE-SM-158/26).

41. _____. 1976a. The accumulation of inorganic mercury from sea water by the plaice, *Pleuronectes platessa* L. J. Exp. Mar. Biol. Ecol. 24:103-119.

42. _____. 1976b. The accumulation of mercury by the thornback ray, *Raja clavata* L. J. Exp. Mar. Biol. Ecol. 25:131-140.

43. _____. 1976c. The accumulation of organic mercury from sea water by the plaice, *Pleuronectes platessa* L. J. Exp. Mar. Biol. Ecol. 24:121-132.

44. _____. 1976d. Some further studies on the accumulation and retention of [65]Zn and [54]Mn by the plaice, *Pleuronectes platessa* L. J. Exp. Mar. Biol. Ecol. 21:179-189.

45. Pickering, D. C., and I. L. Puia. 1969. Mechanism for the uptake of zinc by *Fontinalis antipyretica*. Physiol. Plant. 22:653-661.

46. Polikarpov, G. G. 1966. Radioecology of Aquatic Organisms. Reinhold, New York. 314 pp.

47. Renfro, W. C. 1973. Transfer of [65]Zn from sediments by marine polychaete worms. Mar. Biol. 21:305-316.

48. Renfro, W. C., and G. Benayoun. 1976. Sediment-worm interaction: Transfer of [65]Zn from marine silt by the polychaete *Nereis diversicolor*, pp. 250-255. *In* C. E. Cushing (ed.), Radioecology and energy resources, Ecol., Soc. Amer., Spec. Pub., No. 1.

49. Renfro, W. C., S. W. Fowler, M. Heyraud, and J. LaRose. 1975. Relative importance of food and water in long-term zinc[65] accumulation by marine biota. J. Fish. Res. Board Can. 32:1339-1345.

50. Schell, W. R., and A. Nevissi. 1977. Heavy metals from waste disposal in central Puget Sound. Environ. Sci. Technol. 11:887-893.

51. Stumm, W., and P. A. Brauner. 1975. Chemical speciation, pp. 173-239. *In* J. P. Riley, and G. Skirrow (eds.), Chemical Oceanography. Academic Press, New York.

52. Stumm, W., and J. J. Morgan. 1970. Aquatic Chemistry. Wiley Interscience, New York. 583 pp.

53. Sunda, W. G., D. W. Engel, and R. M. Thuotte. 1978. Effect of chemical speciation on the toxicity of cadmium to grass shrimp, *Palaemonetes pugio*: Importance of free cadmium ion. Environ. Sci. Technol. 12(4):409-413.

54. Sunda, W., and R. R. L. Guillard. 1976. The relationship between cupric ion activity and the toxicity of copper to phytoplankton. J. Mar. Res. 34(4):511-529.

55. Sunda, W. G. and P. J. Hanson. In press. Chemical speciation of copper in river water. Effect of total copper, pH, carbonate and dissolved organic matter. American Chemical Society Symposium on chemical modeling speciation, sorption, solubility and kinetics in aqueous systems. September 10-15, 1978. Miami, Fla.

56. Sunda, W. G., and J. M. Lewis. 1976. Determination of the binding of copper and cadmium in a coastal river-estuarine system using ion-selective electrodes, pp. 53-77. *In* Atlantic Estuarine Fisheries Center, Beaufort, N.C., Annual Report to the Energy Research and Development Administration, July 1, 1976.

57. _____. In press. Effect of complexation by natural organic ligands on the toxicity of copper to a unicellular alga, *Monochrysis lutheri*. Limnol. Oceanogr.

58. Thomas, D. J., and E. V. Grill. 1977. The effect of exchange reactions between Fraser River sediment and seawater on dissolved Cu and Zn concentrations in the Strait of Georgia. Estuarine Coastal Mar. Sci. 5:421-427.

59. Thomas, W. H., and D. L. R. Seibert. 1977. Effects of copper on the dominance and the diversity of algae: Controlled ecosystem pollution experiment. Bull. Mar. Sci. 27:23-33.

60. Turekian, K. K. In press. The fate of metals in the oceans. Geochim. Cosmochim. Acta.

61. Valiela, I., M. D. Banus, and J. M. Teal. 1974. Response of salt marsh bivalves to enrichment with metal-containing sewage sludge and retention to lead, zinc and cadmium by marsh sediments. Environ. Pollut. 7:149-157.

62. Young, D. R., and T. Jan. 1976. Metals in scallops, pp. 117-122. *In* Coastal Water Research Project, annual report for the year ended 30 June 1976. Southern California Coastal Water Research Project, El Segundo, California.

63. Zirino, A., and S. Yamamoto. 1972. A pH-dependent model for the speciation of copper, zinc, cadmium, and lead in seawater. Limnol. Oceanogr. 17:661-671.

DISTRIBUTION, SURVIVAL, AND SIGNIFICANCE OF PATHOGENIC BACTERIA AND VIRUSES IN ESTUARIES

R. R. Colwell and J. Kaper

Department of Microbiology
University of Maryland
College Park, Maryland

Abstract: The decline or "die-off" of enteric microbial populations in the sea has been intensively studied by researchers from a variety of disciplines. The observed rapid die-off of enteric bacteria has been related to several factors, viz. sedimentation, predation, toxicity of trace metals in seawater, nutrient deficiencies, or salinity. From results of microbiological studies of estuaries, it has been concluded that the incidence and survival of *Salmonella* spp., *Clostridium botulinum, Vibrio parahaemolyticus,* fecal streptococci, and fecal coliforms are significantly greater than suspected. Furthermore, the stability of human enteroviruses in estuarine and marine waters has been found to be such that infectious virus can be recovered after 46 weeks. Equally disturbing has been the isolation of antibiotic-resistant and heavy-metal-resistant coliforms in estuaries and in the ocean, i.e. in the New York Bight. A seasonal cycle of heavy metal and antibiotic-resistant bacteria in Chesapeake Bay has been noted and transfer of plasmid-mediated antibiotic resistance from *Escherichia coli* to *Vibrio parahaemolyticus,* an estuarine bacterium, has been documented. *Vibrio cholerae* has been discovered in the Upper Chesapeake Bay and appears to be ubiquitous in brackish water sites. These findings suggest that the autochthonous microbial flora of estuaries and coastal waters can be replaced by allochthonous species, many of which are pathogenic to man, under conditions of environmental stress and that the human pathogens, such as *Vibrio cholerae* may be part of the autochthonous flora of brackish water areas in estuaries.

Estuarine and coastal regions are increasingly subjected to the pressures of population growth, with associated demands on these ecosystems. Alterations in the physical structure of an estuary or coastline bring marked changes in the biota, including the microbial populations. One of the heaviest uses of the estuarine and coastal ecosystems is that of sewage disposal. Unfortunately very few studies have been carried out to assess the natural microbial community structure and function. Hence the assumption that estuaries and coastal waters can assimilate wastes has gone unchallenged, except in the most extreme cases where potential public health hazards were overt. Human enteric bacteria and viruses, in general, do not comprise the natural microbial flora of estuarine, coastal, and deep ocean waters. Only in areas of severe impact by sewage dumping, as in the case of the New York Bight (Koditschek and Guyre, 1974), are enterics readily isolated.

The universally applied indices of water quality of public health acceptance are the total and the fecal coliform tests. Because of the difficulty in isolating pathogenic microorganisms, the use of the coliforms as indicator organisms was developed, relating the presence of fecal contamination, i.e. the coliform index, to the possibility of disease transmission. Over the years to the present, refinement of the indicator concept has been accomplished. Unfortunately, methods for isolation and elucidation of the ecology of the pathogenic bacteria and viruses have been neglected. For the past several years, our work has focused on microbial pathogens present in the Chesapeake Bay. The indicator organism concept has been extensively reviewed and severely criticized; little more needs to be added (Colwell, 1975; Dutka, 1973; Cohen and Shuval, 1973). Therefore, in this paper, the distribution, survival, and significance of pathogenic bacteria and viruses in the estuarine environment are the points of focus.

Survival is of prime interest. If a pathogenic microorganism does not survive in nature, it will be of little significance as an environmental pathogen. For example, *Neisseria gonorrhoea,* the causative agent of gonorrhoea, apparently does not survive in the natural environment. Therefore it is not considered to be an environmentally significant pathogen. Many pathogenic bacteria do survive in estuarine and marine environments, however, and these have been extensively studied. Procedures employed to test for survival in estuarine and marine water and sediment include both laboratory and *in situ* studies. Experimental apparatus devised for such studies include the simple culture flask (Jamieson *et al.,* 1976), diffusion chamber apparatus (Vasconcelos and Swartz, 1976), and chemostat (Jannasch, 1968).

Many factors have been found to be involved in the "die-off" of coliforms and human pathogens in estuarine and marine water sediment, including dilution, bacteriocidal action of seawater, grazing by zooplankton, adsorption on estuarine and coastal sediments (Ketchum *et al.,* 1952), salinity, effect of heavy metals in seawater (Jones, 1963; 1971), lysis by indigenous marine bacteria, such as *Bdellovibrio* spp., and bacteriophages (Mitchell *et al.,* 1967; Mitchell, 1968; Carlucci and Pramer, 1960), low nutrient levels in seawater (Jannasch, 1968), production of toxins by plankton (Aubert *et al.,* 1964), sunlight (Pike *et al.,* 1970) and temperature. Unfortunately, it is not yet resolved whether any single factor is responsible for the die-off of terrestrial pathogens in estuarine or marine environments. In general, each of the factors cited above may act under appropriate conditions, both individually or synergistically, with any one or more of the other factors.

A variety of pathogenic microorganisms may be present in the feces of warm-blooded animals, viz., *Brucella, Salmonella, Shigella, Mycobacterium tuberculosis, Pasteurella, Leptospira, Vibrio cholerae, Entamoeba histolytica,* and various enteric viruses. Most of the genera noted are present in the feces of diseased animals. The principal factor is the occurrence of the pathogen in a human or animal population and the shedding of the microorganisms into water via feces. The density of pathogens in the aqueous environment is affected by a variety of factors: (a) type and degree of sewage treatment; (b) ability of microorganisms to survive the effects of antibiosis, predation, and chemical nature of the water; (c) dietary habits and socio-economic status of the community; (d) prevalence of specific disease in the community; (e) endemic conditions in the human and animal population; and (f) existing carrier rates in the population (Brezenski and Russomanno, 1969). Therefore, the introduction of specific pathogens, via sewage or runoff, into estuaries and coastal waters is not constant, but tends to be intermittent. With the uneven distribution of microorganisms in water, coupled with effects of dilution and environmental conditons such as temperature and salinity, it is understandable that the search for pathogenic microorganisms is usually accomplished by seeking an indicator organism rather than a specific pathogen.

Where the bacteriological quality of the water is poor, fecal coliforms and salmonellae can be isolated. Often in estuaries and coastal waters, waterfowl will contribute to the salmonellae population load (Strobel, 1968). *Salmonella,* in recent years, have been directly isolated from polluted tidal estuaries, but at low percentage recovery, e.g. 1 to 200 fecal coliforms (Brezenski and Russomanno, 1969). However, the prevalence of *Salmonella* is greater than previously believed and salinity, temperature, and other such factors associated with the marine environment cannot be depended upon to eliminate pathogens from the environment.

Studies in our laboratory have been directed toward: (1) improvement of methods for isolation of *Salmonella*; (2) elucidating the distribution of these organisms; and (3) determining factors affecting the incidence of *Salmonella* in estuaries and coastal waters. Initial efforts at isolating salmonellae from Chesapeake Bay were hampered by inefficient procedures and media. A new method was devised, utilizing an ambient temperature, a primary non-selective enrichment procedure which proved very effective in recovering *Salmonella* (Kaper *et al.,* 1977). Conventional methods for isolation of pathogens are designed for clinical samples and these methods employ highly selective enrichment and plating media that are often incubated at elevated temperatures (about 42°C) after inoculation. From our studies, we concluded that it was important to "resuscitate" such microorganisms as *Salmonella* that had undergone environmental stress. These organisms, although debilitated, remain potentially pathogenic for man. The procedure designed for environmental samples utilizes a primary nonselective enrichment media incubated at ambient temperature. By step-wise increase in media selectivity and temperature of incubation, a successful transition from the natural environment to the laboratory medium was provided for organisms otherwise not surviving. In a recently published study, the ambient-temperature primary nonselective method was used in parallel with conventional selective media for the isolation of salmonellae from the Chesapeake Bay (Sayler *et al.*, 1976). Serologically confirmed *Salmonella* spp. were recovered only when the non-selective enrichment method was employed. Hence appropriate methods are required for isolation and enumeration of pathogenic microorganisms in the estuarine and marine ecosystems.

Having appropriate methodology in hand, attention was turned to the distribution of *Salmonella* in the Chesapeake Bay. Statistical correlations with physical, chemical, and biological conditions were computed and the most important condition found to be related to the presence of salmonellae was the fecal coliform count (Kaper *et al.*, manuscript in preparation). *Salmonella* spp. were not isolated from samples collected in areas free of fecal contamination.

Salinity was not observed to be a restrictive factor, since salmonellae can be isolated from the harbor in Little Creek Virginia, where the salinity of the water is 21--22 ‰. Baltimore Harbor samples, as expected, revealed the highest counts of *Salmonella,* with the Most Probable Numbers (MPN) as high as 240 per 100 ml of water. Fecal coliform counts in Baltimore Harbor may be as high as 24,000/100 ml water. While no consistent ratio of *Salmonella* to fecal coliforms has been observed for Chesapeake Bay, the values ranged from 1 *Salmonella* per 100 fecal coliforms to 1 per 1000. Other investigators have reported ratios within these limits (Brezenski and Russomanno, 1969).

A total of 72 water and sediment samples have been examined, with 17, or 24 percent, yielding *Salmonella* spp. A seasonal effect has also been noted. *Salmonella* can be isolated in the fall, but no salmonellae are isolated in the winter, from December to March. In April, with the rise in water temperature, *Salmonella* spp. are isolated. If very large volumes of water are examined, it is possible that *Salmonella* could be isolated throughout the year. However, our results are consistent with those of other investigators who showed survival but no multiplication of *Salmonella* in polluted or unpolluted river water at temperatures below 10°C (Hendricks and Morrison, 1967). Presnell and Andrews (1976) examined estuarine water samples collected on the Gulf Coast and repeatedly isolated salmonellae from areas of high fecal coliform counts. Other investigators (Brezenski and Russomanno, 1969) examined samples collected from Raritan Bay and found that the frequency of isolation of *Salmonella* increased as the fecal coliform count increased. Salmonellae were detected in clams collected from 14 of the 50 stations sampled by Brezenski and Russomanno (1969). The shellfish invariably yielded *Salmonella* spp. when fecal coliform counts exceeded 1000 per 100 g. Interestingly, several of the shellfish samples were positive for salmonellae, but revealed low numbers of fecal coliforms, i.e. less than 20/100 g. Thus, even though fecal coliforms were isolated during the winter months, the hypothesis was advanced that at low water temperatures, salmonellae can exhibit increased survival in clams, compared with fecal coliforms. *Salmonella* isolations from shellfish were more likely to be positive when fecal coliform counts of the surrounding waters were high, i.e. 200 to 2000 per 100 ml. Thus the lack of correlation of incidence of *Salmonella* with that of fecal coliforms for samples collected during the winter months strongly suggests that fecal coliforms are a markedly inadequate indicator. Monitoring directly for *Salmonella* spp. appears to be preferable for samples collected from the natural environment.

In recent years, significantly greater attention has been paid to the anaerobic bacteria, viz. *Clostridium* spp., as indicators of pollution (Bonde, 1963). The predominant *Clostridium* species found in polluted marine sediments are *Clostridium perfringens, Cl. bifermentans* and *Clostridium novyi*. These species represent 58 percent of the anaerobic bacterial populations and are representative of the *Clostridium* spp. found in sewage (Matches *et al.,* 1974).

Cl. perfringens is a very important agent of food poisoning and can be readily isolated from soil and marine sediments (Yamagishi *et al.,* 1964). A significant relationship between the extent of pollution and number of *Cl. perfringens* has been reported, with low numbers found in upolluted samples (Bonde, 1967). Extensive studies of the incidence of *Cl. perfringens* in fish and sediment in Puget Sound revealed highest counts near the sewage disposal plant in Seattle (Matches *et al.,* 1974). Other less polluted stations in Puget Sound yielded mean counts of 1.7×10^3 per gram of sediment and 5.0×10^3 per gram of fish gut content.

Studies carried out in Chesapeake Bay were focused on the detection of *Cl. botulinum,* the agent of botulism, the toxin of which is among the deadliest known to man. The presence of *Cl. botulinum* in Chesapeake Bay was determined by indirect means, involving the detection of specific neurotoxin in sediments. Isolations were random and occurred at the mouths of the Susquehanna, Magothy, and Severn Rivers (Sayler *et al.,* 1976). In another study, *Cl. botulinum* was isolated from samples collected in the Rhode River, a sub-estuary of the Chesapeake Bay (Carney *et al.,* 1975), where, as in the Upper Bay study, 12 percent of the sediment samples were found to contain *Cl. botulinum* types B and E.

Vibrio parahaemolyticus

Salmonella and *Clostridium* spp. are human pathogens that are allochthonous to estuaries. *Vibrio parahaemolyticus,* on the other hand, is a pathogenic bacterium whose natural habitat is the estuarine environment (Colwell *et al.,* 1972). Its occurrence in estuaries is not correlated with fecal coliform counts, as in the case of *Salmonella* or *Clostridium*. The ecology of *V. parahaemolyticus* has been extensively studied and the distribution, seasonal cycle, and commensal associations have been elucidated (Kaneko and Colwell, 1973, 1975). Salinity has been found to have a significant influence on the distribution of *V. parahaemolyticus*. *V. parahaemolyticus* has not been isolated from the relatively fresh water areas of the Upper Chesapeake Bay. Full strength seawater will not support growth of the organism. The incidence of *V. parahaemolyticus* in Chesapeake Bay was found to be related to water temperature, and an association with zooplankton has also been established.

The annual cycle of *V. parahaemolyticus* in the Rhode River sub-estuary of Chesapeake Bay has been described (Kaneko and Colwell, 1978). The vibrios are not detected in the water column during the winter months, although they are present in the sediment. From late spring to early summer, when the water temperature is $14 \pm 1°C$, vibrios overwintering in sediment are released from the bottom communities and attach to zooplankton, proliferating as the temperature rises. When the water temperature reachs about 19°C, *V. parahaemolyticus* is easily detected in the water column. At this point, release of *V. parahaemolyticus* probably occurs, along with continual release from the sediment. During June and July, the first peak in bacterial counts, including counts of *V. parahaemolyticus* associated with plankton have been recorded between 10^7--10^8 per gram wet weight. The maximum numbers of *V. parahaemolyticus* occur in the summer months for plankton, water column, and sediment samples. Bacteria, including *V. parahaemolyticus*, associated with the proliferating plankton population, are involved in mineralization of the plankton, eventually breaking down and disintegrating the plankton subsequent to the plankton bloom. Mechanical action via water movement very likely assists in the release of bacteria into the water column, where the released bacteria are thereby capable of reattachment to other intact plankton. Some of the bacteria are brought back to the bottom via attachment to fragments of plankton which have been returned to the bottom by sedimentation.

  V. parahaemolyticus has been isolated from oysters, soft shell clams, and blue crabs in Chesapeake Bay (Colwell *et al.*, 1975), and it is through contaminated seafood that this organism exerts its pathogenicity. It is the leading cause of food poisoning in Japan and has caused several outbreaks of gastroenteritis in the United States. Undoubtedly, many cases of food poisoning due to *Vibrio parahaemolyticus* are not identified due to the inexperience of clinical microbiologists with the organism.

  Disease due to pathogenic *Vibrio* spp. is not limited to ingestion of contaminated seafood. Although uncommon, any open flesh wound exposed to estuarine or marine waters may be subject to infection by a halophilic *Vibrio* sp., such as *V. alginolyticus* or *V. parahaemolyticus* (Rubin and Tilton, 1975). Again, the incidence is probably greater than reported due to failure to consider these organisms as the infectious agent.

Viruses

  During the past decade, there has been worldwide interest and concern that significant levels of viruses are being transmitted through potable and recreational water. Conclusive evidence for the transmission of enteric viruses via this route lies in outbreaks of infectious hepatitis, where sanitary practice or water treatment has broken down, or contaminated shellfish have been consumed (Berg, 1973). The opinion that viruses in estuaries and coastal waters pose a threat to human health can be justified by the following facts. Most enteric viruses are more resistant than indicator bacteria to inactivation by water disinfectants. Infectivity tests have shown infection can be caused by one poliovirus TCD_{50} unit (Berg, 1971).

A consistently high endemic level of infectious hepatitis has occurred in the United States with the concomitant knowledge that the infectious hepatitis agent is relatively resistant to inactivation in the aquatic environment. Sporadic outbreaks of non-bacterial gastroenteritis suspected of being water-borne have occurred, coupled with a most likely high endemic level of the disease. Finally, surface-water domestic pollution has increased to the point that direct recycling of wastewater and reclamation of estuarine waters is very nearly a reality in the case of some water systems (Akin *et al.*, 1974). Clearly, the danger of water transmission of enteric viral disease is great enough to warrant the more careful consideration viruses are now receiving.

More than 100 new human enteric viruses have been described in the 25 years since the advent of viral propagation techniques using tissue cultures (Scarpino, 1974). All of these enteric viruses are known to be excreted in quantity in the feces of man, including enteroviruses (poliovirus, coxsackie virus, and echovirus), infectious hepatitis, adenoviruses, and reoviruses. Viruses do not multiply outside of living susceptible cells; hence, human enteric viruses can be expected to decrease in numbers with time, even when nutrient levels are high. However, the major question is, how long will human enteric viruses survive when discharged into estuarine and coastal waters? The presence of enteric viruses in estuarine and ocean waters has been amply documented (Metcalf and Stiles, 1965, 1968; Shuval, 1970). Survival of enteroviruses in the marine environment has been demonstrated by a number of investigators. Enteric virus survival in estuary and ocean waters has been shown to be dependent upon temperature, biotic flora, degree of pollution, and virus type (Metcalf and Stiles, 1968). A virucidal activity in seawater has been demonstrated, but it may have only a minor role in inactivating enteric viruses in estuarine and ocean waters.

Recent investigations at the University of Maryland have examined in detail the stability of human enteroviruses in estuarine and marine waters. Studies of the effects of temperature and salinity on the survival of polio and other viruses indicate that temperature, rather than salinity, is the crucial factor affecting their stability (Colwell and Hetrick, 1976; Lo *et al.*, 1976). In the laboratory studies, all of the viruses examined were stable at $4°C$, with infectious viruses still detectable after 46 weeks of incubation. This was the case for all salinities tested from $10°/oo$ to $34°/oo$. At $25°C$, infectious viruses were rarely detected after eight weeks of incubation. *In situ* studies, in free-flowing estuarine or marine water, confirmed laboratory predictions in that viruses persisted much longer in winter than in summer months. Although the viruses were more labile in natural waters than in the laboratory aquaria, coxsackie virus retained infectivity after 116 days of incubation. Other investigators have reached similar conclusions and have extended the work to virus survival in oysters (Metcalf and Stiles, 1965, 1967, 1968). Virus uptake and survival in oysters was also found to be related to temperature. When placed in virus-polluted waters of temperatures below $7°C$, virus-free oysters remained free from enteroviruses. Virus uptake occurred at temperatures above 7°C. Survival studies revealed that survival was inversely re lated to the depurative activity of oysters, with viruses surviving within oyster less than one week in the summer and more than two months during the winter.

While routine monitoring of shellfish and estuarine waters for viruses is not commonly performed, many isolations have been reported. Metcalf and Stiles (1965, 1968) have repeatedly isolated enteroviruses, such as poliovirus, coxsackie and echoviruses from water and oyster samples. The fact that isolates were ob tained from stations more than four miles from the nearest raw sewage outlet demonstrates the potential for widespread virus dissemination in an estuary.

The importance of enteric viruses is not in their numbers but in their in fectivity (Scarpino, 1974). One tissue-culture dose is considered to constitute an infectious dose, meaning that only a few virus particles are needed to initiate an infection in a susceptible host. Thus it has been necessary only to show the pres ence of viruses in water, with less emphasis placed on quantitation. Since entero viruses of human origin in estuarine and coastal waters may remain infectious for a significant period of time, depending on environmental factors, it has been sug gested that enteroviruses themselves may serve as the most valid indicator of pol lution. Poliovirus and infectious hepatitis virus (hepatitis A) have both been sug gested as indicator agents, although standard methods remain to be devised for their detection.

Methods for isolation of viruses from water samples are many and varied including gauze pads for pre-concentration *in situ* (Fattal and Katzenelson, 1976) membrane filter adsorption; electrophoresis; ultrafiltration hydro-extraction; pre cipitation, adsorption-elution; separation with two-phase polymers; soluble ultra filter; and ultracentrifugation (Foliguet *et al.*, 1973; Hill *et al.*, 1971). The main problem in virus isolation, namely, the large volumes of water that must be ex amined (up to 100 liters per sampling) appears to have been overcome (Hill *et al.*, 1972; Sobsey *et al.*, 1973). A virus concentration unit, designed by Melnick and co-workers, is being used for virus monitoring in water supplies throughout the world. At the International Conference on Viruses and Water, Mexico City 1974, it was clear that adequate methods for concentrating large volumes of water for enterovirus monitoring are now available.

Compared to the isolation and characterization of indicator bacteria, much work remains to be done for viruses. Perfecting the techniques for isolation and characterization of viruses is the main concern of research work underway. Still unknown is how widespread viruses are in estuaries and coastal waters. Also, the incidence of viral diseases transmitted via polluted estuarine and coastal waters is not known. New methods for viral detection should improve virus isolation and characterization; for example, the Australian antigen, a marker for hepatitis B virus, has been isolated from clams contaminated by untreated sewage from a coastal hospital (Mahoney *et al.*, 1974). Other such markers may be discovered as research on the enteroviruses progresses. Clearly, monitoring of estuarine and coastal waters for enteric viruses will eventually be commonplace, but for the present, routine monitoring of estuarine water for enteric viruses is yet to be accomplished on a large scale.

Antibiotic Resistant Bacteria

The increasing frequency of antibiotic-resistant bacteria is a cause for concern in hospitals around the world. Reports of antibiotic-resistant bacteria in the marine and estuarine environment are increasing and suggest that an environmental hazard, with respect to these bacteria, is developing. Studies in the Chesapeake Bay revealed the ubiquity of these resistant organisms (Colwell and Sizemore, 1976). A study carried out in the spring of 1975, employing water and shellfish samples collected from stations located near Baltimore and Annapolis, recovered a total of 479 organisms resistant to two antibiotics in combination (Morgan *et al.,* 1976). Resistant organisms were isolated from water, oysters, and clams. In Eastern Bay, one of the cleanest areas of the Chesapeake Bay and a productive shellfish harvesting site, antibiotic-resistant organisms were recovered, although at very low numbers and representing only small fractions of the total viable bacterial counts (usually about one percent). In Baltimore Harbor, an area with continual fecal coliform input, the population was considerably different, and extremely large numbers of antibiotic-resistant bacteria were found. Bacteria resistant to chloramphenicol were as numerous as 10^7 per gram of sediment. In terms of percent of the bacteria resistant to antibiotics, compared to the total heterotrophic bacterial population, the yearly mean of kanamycin-resistant bacteria approached 50 percent, while the proportion of bacteria resistant to the other antibiotics tested ranged from 10 to 20 percent (Allen, Kaper, and Colwell, manuscript in preparation).

It has been known for several years that the rapid increase in multiple-drug-resistant bacteria is due, in part, to the ability of these bacteria to transfer genes coding for resistance among the bacterial population by cell to cell contact (Anderson, 1968). The agent responsible for the transfer of resistance is an extra-chromosomal genetic element, termed an R-factor or R-plasmid. Transfer of plasmid-mediated antibiotic resistance is well known among members of the *Enterobacteriaceae,* which are not, however, microbial species common to unpolluted estuaries. Recently, R-plasmids were successfully transferred from *E. coli* to *Vibrio parahaemolyticus,* an autochthonous estuarine bacterium (Guerry and Colwell, 1977). Thus the possibility of *in situ* antibiotic resistance transfer from allochthonous fecal coliforms to autochthonous estuarine bacteria has been demonstrated.

The presence of antibiotic-resistant bacteria is not limited to Chesapeake Bay. Smith (1970) isolated large numbers of multiple-antibiotic-resistant bacteria from ocean bathing water in England. Koditschek (1977), working in the New York Bight, reported that about one percent of the sediment bacteria examined were consistently resistant to tetracycline, and/or mercury. In the same study, samples from a beach at Sandy Hook State Park contained very small numbers of coliforms, but larger numbers of bacteria resistant to seven or more antibiotics; the study suggests that antibiotic-resistant bacteria may be a useful indicator of recent or transient pollution in recreational waters. The relationship of heavy metal resistance to antibiotic resistance is also interesting, with potential selective pressure for antibiotic resistance in bacteria exposed to chronic heavy metal influx (Austin *et al.*, 1977).

Vibrio cholerae

An indication of how little is known about the incidence of pathogens in estuaries is the recent isolation of *Vibrio cholerae*, the causative agent of cholera from the Chesapeake Bay (Colwell and Kaper, 1977; Colwell *et al.*, 1977). Outbreaks of cholera were significant events in American history, but modern sanitary facilities and treatment of water supplies have virtually eliminated cholera in the United States. Because cholera is not widespread in North America, the organism was assumed by most microbiologists to be absent from U. S. waters. Owing to this *a priori* assumption, little attention was paid to *V. cholerae* as a potential pathogenic species in estuaries.

Our studies of *V. cholerae* in Chesapeake Bay began in fall, 1976 and are continuing. To date, a total of 54 isolates have been obtained and confirmed as *V. cholerae*. The initial isolations were made in Baltimore Harbor, an area where the numbers of fecal coliforms are large (see above). Subsequent work has shown, however, that there is no correlation between incidence of fecal coliforms and of *V. cholerae*, as was the case with *Salmonella*. Furthermore, *V. cholerae* is ubiquitous in Chesapeake Bay. Isolations have been made at several sites in the bay, including the mouths of the Chester, Magothy, Potomac, Patuxent and Choptank Rivers (Kaper *et al.*, manuscript in preparation). Salinity appears to be a controlling factor in the distribution of *V. cholerae*, since no isolations have been made at stations where the salinity of the water is below about 5°/oo or above 15°/oo. Of the 21 stations sampled to date, 13 stations revealed the presence of *V. cholerae*, and samples from eight stations were negative. Stations yielding *V. cholerae*, without exception, had salinities of 5 to 15 °/oo, whereas stations not yielding *V. cholerae* all had salinities $<$ 5°/oo or $>$ 15°/oo.

Isolates of *V. cholerae* have been obtained from water, sediment, and oyster samples; whether *V. cholerae* demonstrates a seasonal cycle is now being determined. Preliminary indications are that the distribution of *V. cholerae* in Chesapeake Bay does not resemble that of *V. parahaemolyticus*, with detection of the organism possible in the fall, spring, and summer, and also during the winter. All isolates of *V. cholerae* examined to date hydrolyze chitin, hence there may be an association of *V. cholerae* with plankton. For quantification of *V. cholerae* in Chesapeake Bay, an MPN technique is employed. The numbers of *V. cholerae* in Chesapeake Bay are very low, approximately one to two cells per liter of water, but may be as large as 46 cells per liter. Serological examination has shown that the serotypes of the Chesapeake Bay strains are of wide-spread geographical distribution, with serotypes of Chesapeake Bay strains isolated from various countries around the world, viz. Bangladesh, Yugoslavia, Iran, Japan, India, Hong Kong, and Hawaii, and from a variety of samples, including fresh water, brackish water, feces, sewage, shellfish, and packaged food (H. Smith, personal communication). The Chesapeake Bay strains have also been tested for toxin production, using animal cell cultures and *in vivo* tests, i.e. ligated ileal loops of rabbit intestines. Approximately 64 percent of the strains of *V. cholerae* tested to date produce toxin and can be considered potential human pathogens (Colwell *et al.*, 1977).

The discovery of *V. cholerae* in Chesapeake Bay is disturbing, but should not be interpreted as a serious epidemic threat. The *V. cholerae* strains isolated to date do not agglutinate in cholerae O Group I antiserum, and at the present time, only those strains of *V. cholerae* which agglutinate in Group I antiserum are recognized as an epidemic threat. However, many cases of cholera-like diarrhea resulting from the non-agglutinable, or NAG, vibrios have been documented (Finkelstein, 1973). Even if these strains were recognized as an epidemic threat, the numbers present in bay waters are not sufficient to cause disease, since large numbers of cells, about 10^8, are required to induce disease (Hornick *et al.*, 1971). However, the possibility of concentration by oysters or other shellfish exists and it would not be surprising if *V. cholerae* were to be isolated from diarrheal discharge of patients with symptoms of food poisoning. *V. cholerae* is rarely considered when food poisoning or non-specific diarrhea occurs. Clearly, there is a need for increased awareness of the autochthonous estuarine bacterial species, such as *V. cholerae* or *V. parahaemolyticus,* on the part of both ecologists and medical personnel.

In conclusion, enteric bacteria and viruses can survive in estuary and coastal water and sediments. The large numbers and many types of pathogens that have been isolated and enumerated in estuaries and coastal waters in recent years, with application of newer methods specifically designed for estuarine and marine samples, are a clear indication of adverse modification of these environments. Isolation and enumeration of indicator organisms are no longer useful for measuring public health safety. The pathogenic species themselves should be isolated and enumerated to assess risk or hazard. In fact, *Escherichia coli* is, itself, a pathogen under certain circumstances, i.e., enteropathogenic *E. coli* strains in food or water. The distribution and survival of *E. coli* varies from that of *Salmonella, Clostridium,* and other potential pathogens. Therefore, the individual pathogens should be the "indicators."

Aside from the allochthonous pathogens there are the autochthonous pathogens to be considered, as for example, *V. parahaemolyticus* and *V. cholerae*. With the indigenous pathogens, the greater risk is from alteration of these pathogens to antibiotic-resistance or toxin products by "uncontrolled bioengineering" being carried out in our estuaries and coastal waters via dumping of mixtures of sewage, sludge, industrial wastes, and other effluents into these waters. Reports of fish disease and/or evidence of contamination, with possible infection, of fish by human pathogens in areas of sewer outfalls and ocean dumpsites are disturbing

(Janssen and Meyers, 1968) and should be more closely studied to determine the hazards both to humans consuming these fish and to the fish populations themselves, in terms of loss of recruitment.

Newly developed methods of epifluorescence, ATP assay, LPS determination (Costerton and Colwell, in press), should be applied to studies of indicators and pathogens to assess the numbers of stressed, but viable, pathogens persisting in the environment but not appearing in the test results because of inappropriate media, temperature of incubation, or other factors affecting recovery of viable, potentially infective human pathogens persisting in the estuarine and coastal environments.

References

1. Akin, E. W., W. F. Hill, Jr., and N. A. Clarke. 1974. Mortality of enteric viruses in marine and other waters. Proc. Internat. Symp. Discharge of Sewage from Sea Outfalls, London, Paper No. 24.

2. Anderson, E. S. 1968. The ecology of transferable drug resistance in the enterobacteria. Ann. Rev. Microbiol. 22:131-180.

3. Aubert, M., H. LeBout, and J. Aubert. 1964. Role of plankton in the antibiotic activity of seawater. Annls. Inst. Pasteur, Paris 106:147-150.

4. Austin, B., D. A. Allen, A. L. Mills, and R. R. Colwell. 1977. Numerical taxonomy of heavy metal tolerant bacteria isolated from an estuary. Can. J. Microbiol. 23:1433-1447.

5. Berg, G. 1971. Integrated approach to problem of viruses in water. J. San. Engineering Div., Proc. Amer. Soc. Civil Eng. SA#6: 867-882.

6. _____ . 1973. Viruses in Waste, Renovated, and Other Waters. U.S. Environmental Protection Agency Publ. EPA-670/9-74-005, Cincinnati, Ohio.

7. Bonde, G. J. 1963. Bacterial indicators of water pollution. A study of quantitative estimation. Teknisk Forlag, 2nd ed., Copenhagen.

8. _____ . 1967. Pollution of a marine environment. J. Water Pollut. Cont. Fed. 39:45-63.

9. Brezenski, F. T., and R. Russomanno. 1969. The detection and use of salmonellae in studying polluted tidal estuaries. J. Water Pollut. Cont. Fed. 41: 725-737.

10. Carlucci, A. F., and D. Pramer. 1960. An evaluation of factors affecting the survival of *Escherichia coli* in sea water. IV. Bacteriophages. Appl. Microbiol. 8:254-256.

11. Carney, J. F., C. E. Carty, and R. R. Colwell. 1975. Seasonal occurrence and distribution of microbial indicators and pathogens in the Rhode River of Chesapeake Bay. Appl. Microbiol. 30:771-780.

12. Cohen, J., and H. I. Shuval. 1973. Coliforms, fecal coliforms and fecal streptococci as indicators of water pollution. Water, Air, and Soil Pollution. 2: 85-95.

13. Colwell, R. R. 1975. Bacteria and viruses — indicators of unnatural environmental changes occurring in the nation's estuaries, pp. 507-518. *In* Estuarine Pollution Control and Assessment. Proceedings of a conference, Vol. 2 USEPA, Washington, D. C.

14. Colwell, R. R., and F. M. Hetrick. 1976. Survival of microbial pathogens in the marine environment. Annual report submitted to the Office of Naval Research. Contract No. N00014-76-C.

15. Colwell, R. R., T. Kaneko, and T. Staley. 1972. *Vibrio parahaemolyticus* — an estuarine bacterium resident in Chesapeake Bay, pp. 87-94. *In* Marine Tech. Soc. Food — Drugs from the sea.

16. Colwell, R. R., and J. Kaper, 1977. *Vibrio* species as bacterial indicators of potential health hazards associated with water. *In* Bacterial Indicators/ Health Hazards Associated with Water, ASTM STP 645, A. W. Hoadley and B. J. Dutka, eds., American Society for Testing and Materials, pp. 112-125.

17. Colwell, R. R., J. Kaper, and S. W. Joseph. 1977. *Vibrio cholerae, V. parahaemolyticus,* and other vibrios: occurrence and distribution in Chesapeake Bay. Science 198:394-396.

18. Colwell, R. R., and R. K. Sizemore. 1974. Drug resistant bacteria in the marine environment. Proc. Marine Technol. Soc., pp. 427-430.

19. Colwell, R. R., T. C. Wicks, and H. S. Tubiash. 1975. A comparative study of the bacterial flora of the hemolymph of *Callinectes sapidus*. Marine Fisheries Rev. 37:29-33.

20. Costerton, J. W., and R. R. Colwell (eds). In press. Methods in Aquatic Microbiology. Proceedings of a conference, Minneapolis, June 1977. American Society for Testing and Materials.

21. Dutka, B. J. 1973. Coliforms are an inadequate index of water quality. J. Environ. Health 36:39-46.

22. Fattal, B., and E. Katzenelson. 1976. Evaluation of gauze pad method to recover viruses from water. Water Res. 10:1135-1140.

23. Finkelstein, R. A. 1973. Cholera. Chemical Rubber Company, Crit. Rev. Microbiol. 2:553-623.

24. Foliquet, J. M., J. Lavillaureix, and L. Schwartzbrod. 1973. Virus et eaux: II. Mise en évidence des virus dans le milieu hydrique. Mem. Origin. Rev. Epidem., Med. Soc. et Santé Publ. 21:185-259.

25. Guerry, P., and R. R. Colwell. 1977. Isolation of cryptic plasmid deoxyribonucleic acid from Kanagawa — positive strains of *Vibrio parahaemolyticus*. Infect. Immun. 16:328-334.

26. Hendricks, C. W., and S. M. Morrison. 1967. Multiplication and growth of selected enteric bacteria in clear mountain stream water. Water Res. 1:567-576.

27. Hill, W. F., Jr., E. W. Akin, and W. H. Benton. 1971. Detection of viruses in water: A review of methods and application. Water Res. 5:967-995.

28. Hill, W. F., Jr., E. W. Akin, W. H. Benton, and T. G. Metcalf. 1972. Virus in water. II. Evaluation of membrane cartridge filters for recovering low multiplicities of poliovirus from water. Appl. Microbiol. 23:880-888.

29. Hornick, R. B., S. I. Music, R. Wentzel, R. Cash, J. P. Libonati, M. J. Snyder, T. E. Woodward. 1971. The Broad Street pump revisited: Response of volunteers to ingested cholera vibrios. Bull. N.Y. Acad. Med. 47:1181-1191.

30. Jamieson, W., P. Madri, and G. Claus. 1976. Survival of certain pathogenic microorganisms in seawater. Hydrobiologica 50:117-121.

31. Jannasch, H. W. 1968. Competitive elimination of *Enterobacteriaceae* from seawater. Appl. Bacteriol. (G.B.) 16:1616.

32. Janssen, W. A., and C. D. Meyers. 1968. Fish: serologic evidence of infection with human pathogens. Science 159:547-548.

33. Jones, G. E. 1963. Suppression of bacterial growth by seawater. Symposium on Marine Microbiology. 53:572-579.

34. _____. 1971. The fate of freshwater bacteria in the sea. Devel. Ind. Microbiol. 12:141-151.

35. Kaneko, T., and R. R. Colwell. 1973. Ecology of *Vibrio parahaemolyticus* in Chesapeake Bay. J. Bacteriol. 113:24-32.

36. _____. 1975. Incidence of *Vibrio parahaemolyticus* in Chesapeake Bay. Appl. Microbiol. 30:251-257.

37. _____. 1978. The annual cycle of *Vibrio parahaemolyticus* in Chesapeake Bay. Microbiol. Ecology. 4:135-155.

38. Kaper, J. B., G. S. Sayler, M. M. Baldini, and R. R. Colwell. 1977. Ambient-temperature primary nonselective enrichment for isolation of *Salmonella* ssp. from an estuarine environment. Appl. and Environ. Microbiol. 33:829-835.

39. Ketchum, B. H., J. C. Ayers, and R. F. Vaccaro. 1952. Processes contributing to the decrease of coliform bacteria in a tidal estuary. Ecology 33:247-258.

40. Koditschek, L. 1977. Antimicrobial-resistant bacteria in the New York Bight. Am. Soc. Limnol. Oceanogr. Spec. Symp. 2:383-393.

41. Koditschek, L. and Guyre. 1974. Antimicrobial-resistant coliforms in New York Bight: Mar. Pollut. Bull. 5:71-74.

42. Lo, S., J. Gilbert, and F. Hetrick. 1976. Stability of human enteroviruses in estuarine and marine waters. Appl. Environ. Microbiol. 32:245-249.

43. Mahoney, P., G. Fleischner, I. Millman, W. T. London, B. S. Blumberg and I. M. Arias. 1974. Australia antigen: Detection and transmission in shellfish. Science 183:80.

44. Matches, J. R., J. Liston, and D. Curran. 1974. *Clostridium perfringens* in the environment. Appl. Microbiol. 28:655-660.

45. Metcalf, T. G., and W. C. Stiles. 1965. The accumulation of enteric viruses by the oyster, *Crassostrea virginica*. J. Infect. Dis. 115:68-76.

46. _____. 1967. Survival of enteric viruses in estuary waters and shellfish, pp. 439-447. *In* G. Berg (ed.), Transmission of Viruses by the Water Route. Interscience Publishers, New York.

47. _____. 1968. Enteroviruses within an estuarine environment. Amer. J. Epidemiol. 88:379-391.

48. Mitchell, R. 1968. Factors affecting the decline of non-marine microorganisms in seawater. Water Res. 2:535-543.

49. Mitchell, R., S. Yankofsky, and H. W. Jannasch. 1967. Lysis of *Escherichia coli* by marine microorganism. Nature 215:891-893.

50. Morgan. R. C., P. Guerry, and R. R. Colwell. 1976. Antibiotic-resistant bacteria in Chesapeake Bay. Chesapeake Sci. 17:216-219.

51. Pike, E. B., A. L. H. Gameson, and J. D. Gould. 1970. Mortality of coliform bacteria in sea water samples in the dark. Rev. Intern. Oceanogr. Med. 18-19: 97-106.

52. Presnell, M. W., and W. H. Andrews. 1976. Use of the membrane filter and a filter aid for concentrating and enumerating indicator bacteria and *Salmonella* from estuarine waters. Water Res. 10:549-554.

53. Rubin, S. J., and R. C. Tilton. 1975. Isolation of *Vibrio alginolyticus* from wound infections. J. Clin. Microbiol. 2:556-558.

54. Sayler, G. S., J. D. Nelson, Jr., A. Justice, and R. R. Colwell. 1976. Incidence of *Salmonella* sp., *Clostridium botulinum* and *Vibrio parahaemolyticus* in an estuary. Appl. Environ. Microbiol. 31:723-730.

55. Scarpino, P. V. 1974. Human enteric viruses and bacteriophages as indicators of sewage pollution. Proc. Int. Symp. Discharge of Sewage from Sea Outfalls, London. Paper No. 6.

56. Shuval, H. I. 1970. The detection and control of enteroviruses in the water environment, p. 47. *In* H. I. Shuval (ed.), Developments in Water Quality Research. Humphrey Science Publishers, Ann Arbor.

57. Smith, H. W. 1970. Incidence in river water of *Escherichia coli* containing R factors. Nature 228:1286-1288.

58. Sobsey, M. D., C. Wallis, M. Henderson, and J. L. Melnick. 1973. Concentration of enteroviruses from large volumes of water. Appl. Microbiol. 26: 529-534.

59. Strobel, G. A. 1968. Coliform-fecal coliform bacteria in tidal waters. J. San. Eng. Div., Proc. Amer. Soc. Civil Engineers. SA4:641-656.

60. Vasconcelos, G. J., and R. G. Swartz. 1976. Survival of bacteria in seawater using a diffusion chamber apparatus *in situ*. Appl. Environ. Microbiol. 31: 913-920.

61. Yamagishi, T., S. Ishida, and S. Nishida. 1964. Isolation of toxigenic strains of *Clostridium perfringens* from the soil. J. Bacteriol. 88:646-652.

SOURCES, SINKS, AND CYCLING OF ARSENIC
IN THE PUGET SOUND REGION

R. Carpenter, M. L. Peterson, and R. A. Jahnke

Department of Oceanography
University of Washington
Seattle, Washington

Abstract: The natural distribution of arsenic in the Puget Sound region is modified by a copper smelter which releases large amounts of arsenic in stack dust to the atmosphere and in liquid effluent directly into Puget Sound. This airborne material contributes arsenic to lakes and soils up to 50 km downwind, and supplies about the same amount of arsenic to Puget Sound as do rivers and the liquid effluent of the smelter. The major source of arsenic to Puget Sound is clearly the inflowing seawater. Most of the dissolved arsenic entering Puget Sound is removed by advection of surface waters out into the Strait of Juan de Fuca. Sedimentation processes including adsorption-desorption reactions with natural Puget Sound suspended matter remove less than 15% of the dissolved arsenic input. Hydrous iron oxides appear to dominate what removal of dissolved arsenic does occur. Both bell jar studies and analyses of arsenic in cores collected at the same station five years apart show there is no large flux of dissolved arsenic from the sediments back to the overlying seawaters. Vigorous tidal action quickly dilutes the anthropogenic arsenic; hence concentrations of arsenic in waters and organisms of most of the Sound are not elevated above natural concentrations.

Introduction

The natural distribution of arsenic in part of the Puget Sound region of western Washington is modified by a large copper smelter located on the shore of Puget Sound near Tacoma, Washington. This smelter, in operation since 1890, produces as a byproduct all the arsenic trioxide sold commercially in the United States.

Since 1970, increasing concern has been expressed over discharges by this smelter of large amounts of potentially harmful metals such as arsenic, lead, and cadmium into the environment. Arsenic is now recognized to have a complicated biogeochemical cycle that includes several methylated and inorganic forms which differ considerably in mobility, reactivity, and toxicity. Major features of the environmental cycling and effects of arsenic are reviewed by

Woolson (1977), Lunde (1977), Brinckman *et al.* (1977), Ridley *et al.* (1977), and Penrose *et al.* (1977).

Until 1974, the Tacoma smelter released arsenic into the environment in three ways: (1) as stack dust into the air, 1.5×10^8 g As/yr as fine arsenic trioxide particles; (2) as dissolved arsenic species (largely arsenite) in liquid effluent discharged directly into Puget Sound, 4×10^7 g As/yr; (3) as crystalline slag particles dumped directly into Puget Sound, 1.5×10^6 g As/yr. These figures are estimates compiled by Crecelius (1974), using limited data provided by regulatory agencies. Discharges of As by the smelter vary depending on smelter operations and type of ore being processed; hence it is hard to obtain reliable estimates of the total discharges.

Dumping of the slag material into Puget Sound ceased in 1974, but the other two types of discharges continued. Nelson (1977) gave the rate of As stack dust emissions by this smelter in 1976 as 400 lb/day, or $6-7 \times 10^7$ g As/yr. The installation of various new pollution control technologies supposedly greatly reduced the discharge of liquid effluent into Puget Sound during mid-1977 and was supposed to reduce the atmospheric emissions to about one-third the pre-1974 figure in February 1978. Tests of the effectiveness of these control measures are now underway.

Studies of arsenic in the Puget Sound region by our group were begun in 1972 by E. A. Crecelius. These studies have aimed at establishing a budget of arsenic fluxes, to determine the rate of movement of arsenic through Puget Sound and the processes controlling the ultimate fate of both natural and anthropogenic arsenic introduced into the Sound. This information is needed to predict the concentration of arsenic with time in different parts of Puget Sound, given various natural and anthropogenic inputs at different places around the Sound. Much of the data has already been published (Crecelius, 1974, 1975; Crecelius *et al.*, 1974; Crecelius *et al.*, 1975).

Crecelius (1974) found that the slag dumped into Puget Sound until 1974 by the smelter contains 1% As by weight. These slag particles are a major fraction of the sediments within one to two km of the smelter; hence these sediments contain up to nearly 1% As. However, Crecelius also found that strongly acid solutions were necessary to leach the As from the slag in the laboratory. His electron microprobe examinations of slag particles recovered from the sediments near the smelter did not reveal lower As concentrations near the outer edges than in the middle of the particles. This also suggests that the As in the slag is not being leached out in the environment; hence we have focused efforts on the fate of the arsenic discharged in the liquid effluent and in the stack dust.

Table 1 shows how dramatically the arsenic content of airborne dust collected in Seattle increases when the wind is from the south, from the Tacoma smelter area. Crecelius (1975) clearly documented that this arsenic-rich dust is a major source of arsenic to Lake Washington. His studies on arsenic concentrations in samples of atmospheric dust and precipitation collected in Seattle

Table 1. Concentration of arsenic, antimony, and aluminum (dry weight basis) in hivol dust samples (dust filtered from air) collected on the University of Washington campus, Seattle.

Date	Dust Weight (g)	As (ppm)	Sb (ppm)	Al%	As x 1000 / Al
Southerly Winds					
11-27-72	0.015	1000	190		
1-12-73	0.017	2050	300		
1-15-73	0.021	2410	360		
1-19-73	0.019	1610	216	1.1	150
3-02-73	0.025	1550	250	1.4	110
3-10-73	0.021	1550	240	1.5	100
5-23-73	0.010	1570	252	1.6	100
5-25-73	0.011	2610	333	2.0	130
12-12-73	0.011	1650	301		
12-15-73	0.018	352	78		
Mean		1640	250		
Northerly Winds					
1-08-73	0.018	46	12		
2-04-73	0.010	320	57		
2-06-73	0.040	100	21	3.3	3.0
2-20-73	0.028	450	94		
1-01-74	0.022	52	16	2.3	2.3
1-04-74	0.017	63	12	3.5	1.8
Mean		170	35		

From Crecelius (1974).

revealed that the second largest input of arsenic to Puget Sound was most likely atmospheric precipitation enriched in As from the smelter stack dust.

Crecelius *et al.* (1975) determined the fraction of the arsenic from various natural and anthropogenic sources removed by sedimentation in Puget Sound, and the fraction removed in the surface waters flowing out through Admiralty Inlet, in two ways. First, they compared the arsenic content of the suspended matter of rivers entering Puget Sound with the arsenic content of bottom sediments of Puget Sound. Second, they estimated the major inputs of arsenic and the removal in surface waters flowing out of Admiralty Inlet, and by difference estimated the importance of the sedimentation term for arsenic. Both approaches led to the conclusion that Puget Sound sediments are much less important sinks for arsenic than discharge to the Strait of Juan de Fuca. Their best estimate was that at most 15% of the dissolved arsenic entering Puget Sound is removed to the sediments.

Studies of arsenic in Puget Sound sediments were also summarized by Crecelius et al. (1975). It was clear from arsenic versus depth profiles in sediment cores that at least a portion of the arsenic introduced to Puget Sound by the Tacoma smelter has accumulated in bottom sediments of the area.

The similarity in arsenic content of river-suspended sediments and Puget Sound muds implies that the majority of the arsenic in Puget Sound sediments is supplied by the river particulates and that uptake or release of arsenic as the river particulates enter seawater can be of only minor importance in Puget Sound. This conclusion conflicts with the conclusion of DeGroot (1973), who suggested that 70% of the arsenic bound to Rhine River suspended matter was "mobilized" as the particles entered seawater. Possible reasons for this disagreement are summarized by Crecelius et al. (1975).

In this paper we extend the previous studies by (1) reporting and discussing data on the magnitudes of spatial and temporal variations in arsenic concentrations in seawaters within Puget Sound; (2) developing a more detailed evaluation of the relative importance of various sources of arsenic to Puget Sound, including a field study of the magnitude of any arsenic flux out of contaminated sediments back into the overlying seawater; (3) reporting results of an investigation to determine basic mechanisms controlling the extent, rate, and reversibility of adsorption/desorption reactions of dissolved arsenate ions with suspended matter from Puget Sound and with laboratory reference materials.

Analytical Techniques

We performed total arsenic analyses of sediments, organisms, and dust samples with instrumental neutron activation techniques. Irradiated samples were counted on a Ge(Li) detector that resolved the ^{76}As gamma ray peak at 559 kev from the adjacent peaks due to ^{82}Br and ^{122}Sb. Water samples were analyzed for total arsenic by neutron activation after the arsenic was concentrated by quantitative coprecipitation with ferric hydroxide. Determinations of the speciation of arsenic in solutions were made using the approach of Braman et al. (1977), modified somewhat to try to improve the reproducibility.

We have checked our procedures by analyzing standard reference materials including NBS orchard leaves, NBS tuna meal, USGS standard rocks and EPA trace metal solutions, and have shown that our techniques gives results within 10% of the certified or recommended values.

For studies of arsenate adsorption/desorption reactions, Puget Sound suspended matter was collected by pumping seawater from about two meters depth through a continuous flow centrifuge. Tests showed the centrifuge speed and flow rate employed collected 83% of the suspended particulates collected by a .45 μm millipore filter. Uptake of dissolved arsenate by the solids was followed by counting with a NaI detector the gamma activity in the liquid phase of a carrier-free [74]As arsenate spike (Amersham Searle #AJS.2). This spike had such a high activity that good count rates were obtained with arsenate concentrations only 1–2% above natural concentrations.

An [74]As labelled arsenate spike was added to seawater with 10–15 mg/l of particulates and adsorption of the radioarsenic onto the suspended matter was followed in 250 ml pyrex flasks kept in the dark in constant temperature baths set at 4° and 25°C. A control solution, prepared and sampled for counting similarly to the samples except for the omission of the solid phases, was maintained for each sample.

We investigated the rate and extent of adsorption of arsenate as a function of pH, temperature, total stable arsenic concentration, and solid phase composition. Two samples of natural Puget Sound suspended matter were used, one of predominantly inorganic material from Port Madison and one of predominantly organic material from Quartermaster Harbor. Experiments were also performed on three standard clays (illite API#35, montmorillonite API #23, kaolinite API #5) and on reagent Fe_2O_3 and MnO_2. These solids were aged in seawater for one month prior to use. The surface areas of the solids were measured using the single-point, continuous-flow BET method with N_2 as the adsorbing gas, introduced by Nelsen and Eggertsen (1958). Results were then normalized to available surface area and not just to the weight of solids used.

To test the reversibility of the adsorption reaction, desorption experiments were also performed on the [74]As labelled particles at the end of the uptake experiments by centrifuging them down and resuspending them in unspiked seawater. The pH and temperature were adjusted to the desired values and the [74]As activity in the water was monitored as in the uptake studies. Desorption of the [74]As from the particulates was followed at 4° and at 25°C for about three weeks. A predicted extent of desorption was calculated for each sample by assuming that the reaction was totally reversible, so the arsenate would partition itself between the solid and liquid in the same ratio as in the adsorption experiment.

We also used aerated bell jars in Quartermaster Harbor to make the first direct field measurements of the rate at which arsenic moves from contaminated sediments to the overlying seawater. The bell jars were constructed out of the top halves of 12-gallon pyrex carboys. When placed on the bottom by scuba divers, the jars covered an area of 1,240 cm² and contained about 20 liters of bottom water. Compressed air fed into the jars through a glass frit generated small bubbles to mix the water in the jars without disturbing the sediments and also prevented the water from becoming anoxic. Dissolved arsenic in the seawater enclosed above the sediments was monitored by analyzing 100 ml aliquots of water collected by divers from the jars at the beginning and periodically during the experiment through a septum in the sides of the jars. These samples were filtered through .45 μm filters before the arsenic analyses. Blank runs were made with the apparatus at the sea floor enclosing bottom seawater, but with a pyrex or teflon plate on the bottom preventing any influx from the sediments.

Sediment accumulation rates over the last 100 years were obtained by determining ^{210}Pb activity as a function of depth in cores by measuring the activity of the "granddaughter" ^{210}Po and using ingrowth curves to calculate the ^{210}Pb activities. The sediment samples were wet ashed and the ^{210}Po was spontaneously plated, together with ^{208}Po tracer for yield determination, onto silver discs. The two Po isotopes were then measured by alpha spectroscopy.

Results

Arsenic in Puget Sound waters

We established 11 seawater sampling stations at the major sills in Puget Sound (Figure 1). Vertical profiles of seawater samples were collected at these stations on nine cruises over a 20-month period. Analyses of seawater samples taken from the same sampling bottle gave a standard deviation of less than 5%. Samples collected from replicate hydrocasts on the same tidal cycle and on different tidal cycles gave total standard deviations of about 10%. The variability from sample to sample becomes much larger near the smelter, especially in the surface waters (Figure 1), due to incomplete mixing of freshwater from the Puyallup River, the smelter, and the seawater.

About 98% of the exchange of seawater between Puget Sound and the Strait of Juan de Fuca occurs through Admiralty Inlet (Figure 1). The circulation is typically estuarine, with less saline waters flowing outward into the Strait in the surface and with more saline waters flowing in at depth. The vigorous exchange of waters through Admiralty Inlet, driven mainly by strong tidal currents, replaces the waters of Puget Sound approximately twice a year and thus limits the time for reactions between dissolved and solid phases in the Sound. Barnes and Ebbesmeyer (1978) reported that inland of the Admiralty Inlet sill, the waters of the main Puget Sound channel mix in times of the order of weeks except for inside Whidbey Island, where a few months are required. Given this rapid mixing, it is not surprising to find the total As concentration (Figure 1) is nearly uniform at 1.5–2.0 ppb everywhere except within a few km of the smelter. No seasonal trends were noted.

The effects of the smelter discharges of As are most noticeable in the concentrations of As in the surface waters at the three stations north of the

Figure 1. (opposite) Average total arsenic concentrations in surface (numerator) and bottom (denominator) seawaters at 11 Puget Sound locations. The standard deviation about the mean is given, along with the number of samples averaged at each location (in parentheses). Replicate analyses of the same sample gave standard deviations of less than 5%, so most of the given standard deviation is due to variability in the samples. The average dissolved arsenic contents found in the 3 major rivers entering Puget Sound (Skagit, Stillaguamish and Snohomish) are also given, along with the standard deviation and number of samples indicated in parentheses.

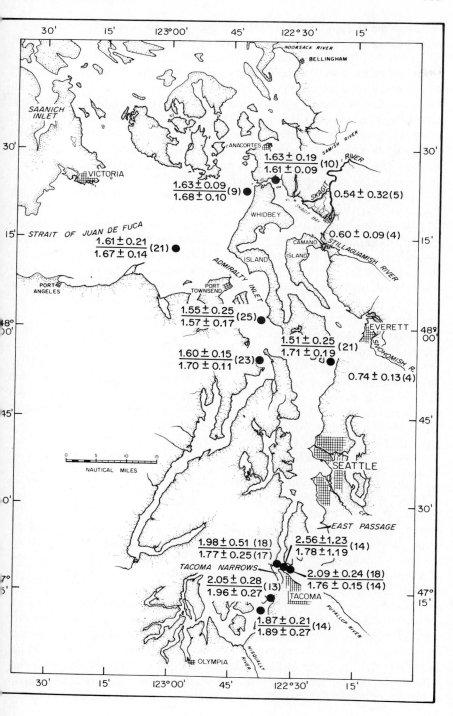

smelter in the channel between the mainland and Vashon Island (Figure 1). At these locations, 50 surface water samples averaged 2.2 ppb As, compared to values of 1.5–1.7 ppb everywhere north of Seattle. Bottom waters at these three stations contain 1.7 ppb As, the same as in Admiralty Inlet. Flood tides sweep the waters from east to west through this channel and then southward through the Narrows where a shallow sill promotes vigorous vertical mixing. At the two stations south of the Narrows, the As concentrations are vertically uniform at 1.9–2.0 ppb, slightly elevated compared to values in the northern Sound. The smelter discharges thus appear to raise the arsenic content of waters of the southern Sound by about 20% and do not have a measurable effect on arsenic concentrations in northern Puget Sound.

All the vertical profiles of total arsenic we determined at these locations (Figure 1), plus five others determined by Crecelius (1974), showed little change in arsenic concentration with depth in the water column. The somewhat higher arsenic concentrations in surface waters near the smelter have been noted. The slightly lower arsenic values in surface waters of northern Puget Sound compared with bottom water (Figure 1) probably reflect input of river waters lower in arsenic than the inflowing seawaters. No consistent changes which would suggest biological uptake of arsenic from surface water and release at depth were observed, even in vertical profiles collected during summer months.

Analyses of seven samples showed that particulate arsenic is generally less than 10% of the total arsenic in Puget Sound seawaters. Interaction with particulate phases is much less important for arsenic than for other elements such as lead and mercury. Analyses of a limited number of samples showed that most ($\geq$ 70%) of the dissolved arsenic in typical Puget Sound seawater is present as the thermodynamically stable form, arsenate, with varying amounts of arsenite and only a small amount ($<$ 10%) present in methylated forms.

Sources of arsenic to Puget Sound waters

In estimating fluxes of arsenic through Puget Sound, we have considered inputs from incoming seawater, river water, atmospheric precipitation and dustfall, the Tacoma smelter liquid effluent, sewage and industrial discharges of Seattle, and possible flux back out of contaminated sediments. Besides sedimentation, the only removal process to be estimated is the discharge of surface waters through Admiralty Inlet to the Strait of Juan de Fuca. Estimates of the quantities of arsenic entering Puget Sound from each of these sources are summarized in Table 2.

Figure 1 also shows average arsenic concentrations in the three rivers (Skagit, Stillaguamish and Snohomish) which supply over 75% of the fresh water to Puget Sound. We have analyzed 13 samples of these major rivers over a two-year period and find that they average 0.62 ppb dissolved As and 0.19 ppb particulate As. The effect of this freshwater input is to dilute the arsenic in the inflowing seawater, but note in Figure 1 that even the station near the mouth of the Skagit has surface and bottom seawater arsenic contents similar to the

Table 2. Summary of arsenic inputs to Puget Sound.

Arsenic Source	Input Rate 10^7 g As/yr
Inflowing seawater	$\geq 64 \pm 5$
Atmospheric precipitation	2.5
Atmospheric dustfall	1.1
Rivers	3 ± 1
Smelter liquid effluent	$4 \pm 1*$
Seattle sewage plant	.07
Seattle drydock operations	.09
Flux out of sediments	$\leq .2$

*Control measures instituted in mid-1977 are supposed to reduce this figure considerably.

rest of the northern Sound. Combining the average arsenic concentration for each river and its flow rate gives the river influx of arsenic to Puget Sound of $3 \pm 1 \times 10^7$ g As/yr.

This river imput is small compared with the As input from the seawaters flowing into Puget Sound at depth through Admiralty Inlet. We have measured an average of $1.67 \pm .14$ ppb As in 21 samples of these deep seawaters over a two-year period (Figure 1). The volume of seawater entering here is about $3.8-12 \times 10^{11}$ m^3/yr (Friebertshauser and Duxbury, 1972; Barnes and Ebbesmeyer, 1978) so the arsenic input from the incoming seawater is at least $64 \pm 5 \times 10^7$ g As/yr.

Studies of arsenic concentrations in samples of atmospheric dust and precipitation collected in Seattle performed by Crecelius (1974) revealed that the second largest input of arsenic to Puget Sound was most likely atmospheric precipitation enriched in As from the smelter stack dust. Crecelius found that 24 samples of unfiltered rain and snow collected in Seattle averaged 17 ± 8 ppb As, while a few samples collected west of the Olympic Mountains out of the influence of the smelter contained only $0.4 \pm .2$ ppb As. Thus, the effects of the atmospheric arsenic emissions from the Tacoma smelter are clearly evident in precipitation samples collected some 35 km downwind in Seattle.

The arsenic content of atmospheric dust and precipitation samples should thus be higher in the southern part of Puget Sound near Tacoma, and lower further north of Seattle. To better define the arsenic concentrations in precipitation over the Puget Sound basin we established rainwater collecting stations at the locations indicated in Figure 2. More than 200 samples collected over a two-year period at these locations have been analyzed, with the average arsenic concentration plus or minus one standard deviation shown for each location (Figure 2). There are large standard deviations at each location because the As

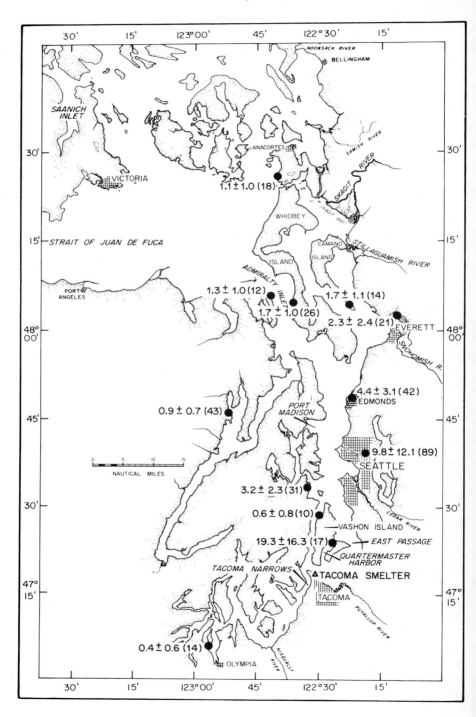

Figure 2. (opposite) Average arsenic content of rain and snow collected at 12 locations in the Puget Sound region, ± one standard deviation.

concentrations vary considerably with length of storm, type of precipitation, and so on, as do all components of precipitation.

These results confirm that arsenic concentrations in the precipitation samples decrease with distance north of the Tacoma smelter, consistent with the fact that southerly winds usually accompany rainstorms in this region. Arsenic concentrations still average 4 ppb at the Edmonds station north of Seattle, and 2 ppb even further north at Everett. Thus, elevated arsenic concentrations are still found at least 50 km downwind of the smelter. The average arsenic content measured in Seattle precipitation is likely to be an upper limit for the average in precipitation falling over the entire Sound. Using the Seattle average of 10 ppb and assuming 1 m/yr precipitation gives an arsenic input of 2.5×10^7 g As/yr.

A portion of the arsenic-rich dust observed downwind of the smelter will fall directly into Puget Sound. We have estimated the importance of this dustfall in the budget of arsenic fluxes to Puget Sound by determining the amount of dust falling each month on top of a three-story building on the University of Washington campus in Seattle, and its arsenic content, over an additional one-year period, using the same collection and analytical techniques as Crecelius (1974). By averaging our data with those of Crecelius (1974) and assuming that the concentrations of As and the magnitude of dustfall over Puget Sound average out the same as those in Seattle, we calculate the arsenic input via dustfall directly to Puget Sound to be 1.6×10^7 g As/yr.

The combined As inputs via atmospheric precipitation and dustfall amount to about one-fourth the arsenic emitted in stack dust by the Tacoma smelter during this time period. The remainder of the stack dust presumably falls onto land downwind, and Crecelius *et al.* (1974) have shown that soils downwind of the smelter are indeed enriched in smelter-derived arsenic and lead.

Other known arsenic inputs to Puget Sound are from Seattle's Metro sewage treatment plant and from the use of arsenite solutions in treating ship drydocks in Seattle's harbor. Our estimates of these inputs are $.07 \times 10^7$ g As/yr from the sewage plant and $.09 \times 10^7$ g As/yr from the drydock operations, both clearly negligible when compared with the other inputs. Later in this paper we estimate the arsenic flux from arsenic-contaminated sediments to be at most 0.2×10^7 g As/yr, also negligible compared with the other sources.

Given these estimates of arsenic inputs from various sources, the major source is clearly the inflowing seawater in this estuarine environment. We expect that this will be the case for arsenic in most other estuaries as well.

For Puget Sound with its rapid mixing, we propose, based on these arsenic results, the following generalization: unless anthropogenic discharges of a substance exceed those of arsenic, or unless the natural concentration of the substance in the inflowing seawater is much less than that of arsenic, elevated concentrations of the substance should not occur in the waters of the main Puget Sound basin.

Arsenate adsorption/desorption reactions

We have studied the extent and rate of adsorption/desorption reactions of dissolved arsenate ions with natural Puget Sound suspended matter and some laboratory reference materials. We studied arsenate adsorption/desorption as a function of temperature, pH, solution, and solid phase composition, to gain more insight into the basic mechanisms controlling the extent, rate, and reversibility of arsenate uptake by different kinds of suspended solids.

Many previous studies of adsorption/desorption reactions have been performed on single, pure solid phases at particle densities and/or dissolved ion concentrations much greater than those that naturally occur. We attempted to avoid the uncertain extrapolation of such studies to the natural environment, with its mixture of solid phases and much lower concentrations, by employing natural assemblages of Puget Sound suspended matter and by working at near-natural concentrations. We examined first the adsorption/desorption behavior of dissolved arsenate, the predominant form of arsenic in most natural waters.

A typical ^{74}As-arsenate adsorption versus time curve is shown in Figure 3, for runs at 4° and 25°C, normalized to constant surface area of the solids. The slower uptake rate at 4°C is obvious, but eventually the same amount of arsenate is sorbed at both temperatures. The extent of desorption was also only slightly affected by temperature in the range 2–25° C, if at all. From the very small temperature dependence of the "equilibrium" extent of adsorption, we calculate that the isosteric heat of adsorption onto natural Puget Sound suspended matter is small, probably less than 3 kcal/mole.

Muljadi et al. (1966) concluded that the isotherms describing the adsorption of phosphate onto kaolinite, gibbsite, and pseudo-boehmite could be divided into: (a) adsorption occurring at the edges of the surfaces with no measurable heat of adsorption, and (b) penetration of the phosphate into the solids with measurable (4–5 kcal/mole) heats of adsorption. We feel the small heat of arsenate adsorption plus the reversibility of the reaction to be discussed below favor the interpretation that the arsenate ions are sorbed predominantly on the surfaces and edges of the solid phases rather than penetrating into the crystal lattice.

We note that the two species which have been found to have the largest dependence of interstitial water concentrations upon temperature of squeezing are silicate and borate (Manheim, 1976 and references therein). These species may be entering the lattice of aluminosilicates, such as clays, rather than just remaining on the surfaces. One possibility suggested by our results is that the arsenate content of interstitial waters may not be very temperature-dependent if controlled by adsorption/desorption reactions.

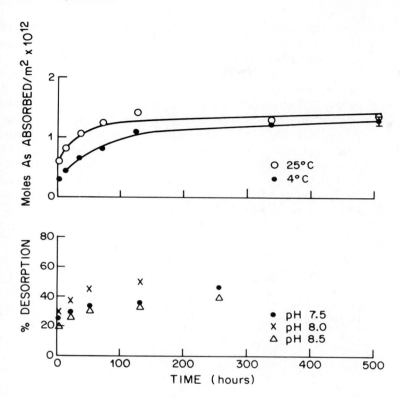

Figure 3. Rate and extent of arsenate adsorption and desorption by natural in-organic-rich Puget Sound suspended matter collected at Port Madison. The particulates contained 6.5% Al, 3.7% Fe, 0.44% Mn, 6.5% C, 1.0% N and had a surface area of 22 m²/g.

Our adsorption studies showed clearly that ferric hydroxides have the greatest affinity for dissolved arsenic. The manganese oxides were comparable to the inorganic-rich Puget Sound particulates from Port Madison and were much less effective at scavenging arsenic. Two marine ferromanganese nodules were also found to be extremely effective scavengers of dissolved arsenate. We also determined the total arsenic content of four deep sea ferromanganese nodules which contained 12–16% Fe. We found arsenic concentrations of 63, 277, 185, and 332 ppm dry weight, some ten times the arsenic concentrations of typical deep sea sediments. There is thus no doubt that these ferromanganese nodules are efficient scavengers of dissolved arsenic from seawater, probably due to their iron phases rather than their manganese phases. Samples of organic-rich suspended matter collected from Saanich Inlet and Quartermaster Harbor sorbed much less of the [74]As tracer than any of the other phases we studied.

We tried to fit the [74]As uptake data to both Langmuir and Freundlich isotherms. The Langmuir model assumes purely monolayer coverage, at sites of specific area and with a constant heat of adsorption of all sites regardless of the amount of surface covered. The Freundlich model allows the heat of adsorption to vary with the extent of adsorption.

Figure 4 gives examples of the Langmuir plots we obtained. We found that over a stable arsenate concentration range of less than a factor of ten, the systems investigated could be well described by the Langmuir isotherm. The natural, inorganic-rich Puget Sound suspended matter from Port Madison has adsorption affinities and capacities intermediate between pure Fe/Mn oxides and the clays. Of the clays studied, illite had the largest arsenate adsorption capacity, montmorillonite was intermediate, and kaolinite had the smallest capacity. Edzwald *et al.* (1976) found the same relative order for phosphate adsorption onto clays. It appears that the exposed surface of hydroxides in kaolinite is not where most of the arsenate uptake occurs. The organic-rich suspended particulates collected at Quartermaster Harbor displayed very small adsorption densities.

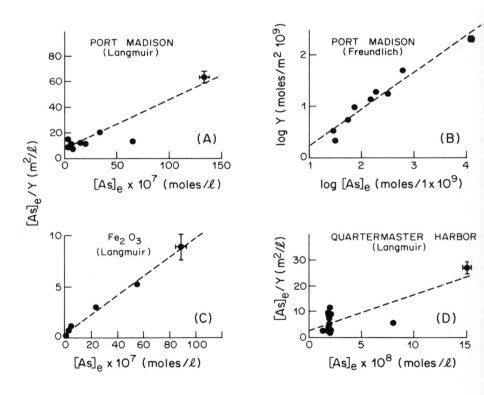

Figure 4. *Langmuir or Freundlich isotherms for arsenate adsorption from sea-water by the indicated solids.*

Combining the extent of adsorption we observed for these solids with assumed concentrations of 1.6–2.0 ppb dissolved arsenic and 3 mg/l suspended solids (values typical of Puget Sound and many other estuaries), we calculate that at "equilibrium" only 5–6% of the total arsenic in the seawater would be associated with the Fe/Mn oxides, and even less with all the other phases. This is in agreement with our observation that, in Puget Sound, particulate arsenic is less than 10% of the total arsenic in the water.

From the Langmuir isotherm, we calculate the theoretical maximum number of moles of arsenate that can adsorb onto one square meter of each solid surface and a constant, b, related to the binding strength of the arsenate-surface interaction by the equation:

$$\Delta G = -RT \ln b$$

(ΔG = Gibbs free energy of the adsorption reaction; R = gas constant; T = temperature).

Using this equation and the values of b obtained from the Langmuir isotherms, we calculate changes in free energy of 7–11 kcal/mole for arsenate adsorption by the natural Puget Sound suspended matter. The heat of adsorption was determined to be less than 3 kcal/mole from the small temperature dependence of the adsorption. Thus changes in entropy, probably due to the release of waters of hydration, significantly contribute to the overall free energy change on adsorption.

When we varied the stable arsenate concentrations over several orders of magnitude, our adsorption data were better fit by the Freundlich isotherm. This suggests that the adsorption energy is changing with surface coverage: that is, arsenate adsorbs onto the energetically more favorable sites first, leaving only less favorable sites for additional uptake. The adsorption intensities and capacities derived from the Freundlich isotherms are in the same order as those calculated from the Langmuir isotherms.

Examples of the important effect pH can have on adsorption are given by James and Healy (1972), Parks (1975), and O'Connor and Kester (1975) and references therein. Changes in pH may cause changes in the surface charge of the solid surface and/or may affect the form of the adsorbing species in solution. Changes in pH will certainly affect the relative amounts of $HAsO_4^{-2}$, $H_2AsO_4^{-}$, and AsO_4^{-3}. The extent of ion pairing of the arsenate species in seawater is not known. It might be expected to be similar to that of phosphate, and Atlas *et al.* (1976) calculated that in seawater at pH 8, the most important phosphate species should be: $MgHPO_4^0$, 41%; HPO_4^{-2}, 29%; $NaHPO_4^{-}$, 15%; $CaPO_4^{-}$, 8%; $CaHPO_4^0$, 5%.

We examined the pH dependence of arsenate adsorption only in the pH range of near-natural values. Figure 5 shows some of the results. We did not find a dramatic pH dependence for arsenate adsorption over the pH range studied, only a decrease of perhaps 25–50% in arsenate from pH 7.0 to 8.5.

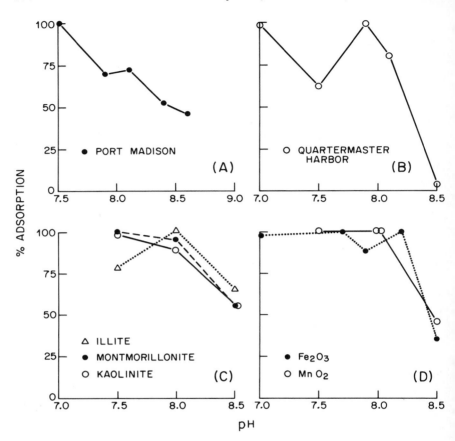

Figure 5. Dependence of arsenate adsorption from seawater by the indicated solids upon pH, normalized to the maximum adsorption observed at whatever pH for each solid.

Arsenate adsorption onto goethite was reported to decrease by 25% upon increasing the pH from 3 to 8 by Hingston *et al.* (1968). This pH dependency of arsenate adsorption onto goethite became less with increasing amounts of competing phosphate anions present. Our seawater had a salinity of 28 $^o/_{oo}$ and phosphate concentrations of about 2 micromolar, so this competition undoubtedly occurred. Anderson *et al.* (1976) found no pH effect on arsenate adsorption onto pure amorphous aluminum oxide from pH 4–8.5, and a moderate decrease in adsorption at higher pHs. The lack of strong pH dependence of arsenate uptake by natural suspended matter is thus supported by the available literature data on these two pure phases.

Figure 3 shows the result of one of the arsenate desorption experiments, giving the percentage of the calculated desorption reaction actually observed in the indicated time. In most cases these experiments had to be terminated due to decay of ^{74}As before the desorption reached "equilibrium." Over the time periods of 250–500 hours, we observed the following percentages of the desorption reaction: Port Madison suspended matter, 73 ± 15%; Quartermaster Harbor suspended matter, 59 ± 16%; Fe_2O_3, 63 ± 24%; MnO_2, 110 ± 34%; illite, 115 ± 12%; kaolinite, 96 ± 17%; and montmorillonite, 101 ± 7%.

We conclude that, over time scales of a few weeks, the arsenate adsorption reactions are largely reversible. This leads to the important implication that the suspended particulates may take up dissolved arsenate in one area of high As concentration, transport it with the solids to an area of lower As concentration, and then release the arsenic back into solution.

This reversibility of arsenate uptake could explain the difference in behavior of particulate arsenic between the Rhine and Puget Sound rivers referred to above. The Rhine was reported to contain 5.6 ppb total As, with two-thirds in particulate phases, while the Puget Sound rivers contain about 0.8 ppb total As with one-quarter in particulate phases. If the North Sea contains about the same arsenic concentration as Puget Sound, or 1.5–2.0 ppb, then the Rhine particles entering the sea are moving from a higher to lower arsenic concentration and, neglecting salt effects, should release some of their arsenic. In contrast, the particulates brought to Puget Sound by rivers enter an area slightly higher in dissolved arsenic and would be expected perhaps to take up a little As. This simple argument assumes the ionic strength, competing species, complexing agents, and so on of both seawaters to be the same. On the other hand, Müller and Förstner (1975) have claimed that the metal solubilization claimed by DeGroot could just be the result of mixing of relatively nonpolluted North Sea sediments with the polluted Rhine sediments.

Arsenic in Puget Sound sediments

It is clear from arsenic versus depth profiles in sediment cores such as those in Figure 6 that at least a portion of the arsenic introduced to Puget Sound by the Tacoma smelter has accumulated in bottom sediments of the area.

We believe the arsenic accumulating in the sediments of Quartermaster Harbor and East Passage (Figure 6) is derived from wind-transported stack dust. Both locations are about the same distance downwind of the smelter, yet the arsenic increase in the more recent sediments is much more evident in the Quartermaster Harbor core. Our ^{210}Pb-derived sedimentation rates show that the East Passage location is accumulating sediments some seven times faster than the Quartermaster Harbor site; thus there is greater dilution of the smelter-derived arsenic, so the concentration of arsenic in the surface sediments is less than in Quartermaster Harbor. Also, the East Passage core did not penetrate back prior to 1950; hence its arsenic concentrations at depth do not decrease to presmelter values. The Quartermaster Harbor core penetrates back to about 1850, so its sediments do record the increase in arsenic beginning around 1890 when the smelter began operating.

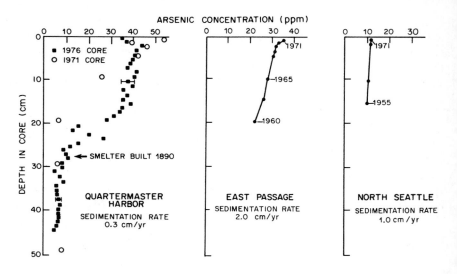

Figure 6. Total arsenic concentrations in sediment cores from Puget Sound which have the indicated ^{210} *Pb-derived recent sedimentation rates. The North Seattle core is from an area off Shilshole Bay believed out of the influence of the Tacoma smelter discharges.*

This is a good example of the value of ^{210}Pb-derived recent sedimentation rates in understanding the distributions of trace metals in estuarine sediments. From the ^{210}Pb activity versus depth profiles in the cores, we obtain estimates of the depths to which benthic organisms and bottom currents mix the surface sediments. The depth of this mixed layer will affect the depth of oxygen penetration into the sediments, the transport of chemicals across the sediment/water interface, and so forth. From the ^{210}Pb versus depth profiles beneath this mixed layer, we obtain the sedimentation rate during the past 100 years, which is needed along with the metal content of the sediments to determine the metal sedimentation rate in the area.

Having observed such increases in arsenic in some of the recent sediments of Puget Sound, we investigated the magnitude of any flux of arsenic out of the sediments back into the overlying seawater. Such a flux could lead to the sediments being a significant source of a metal long after the termination of the original pollutant source.

The Quartermaster Harbor sediments have the largest increases in arsenic likely to be reactive (i.e., arsenic not in slag particles) which we have found in Puget Sound; hence this site would be expected to have the largest flux of arsenic from the sediments to the overlying sea water. Figure 6 shows that cores collected at the same location in Quartermaster Harbor five years apart had essentially identical profiles of arsenic concentrations versus depth in the sediment. This suggests that either there is no significant flux of arsenic out of these sediments, or else it is balanced by the addition of the identical amount of smelter-derived arsenic.

We calculated the flux of arsenic expected from these sediments due to purely inorganic diffusion. We found 10–20 ppb As in filtered interstitial water from the 0–2 cm depth interval of several cores from Quartermaster Harbor, and 2 ppb As in the bottom seawaters. The diffusion coefficient for dissolved arsenic in the interstitial waters at about 5° C is most likely in the range 1–3 x 10^{-6} cm²/sec depending on the porosity/tortuosity of the sediment and what the diffusing As species is—uncomplexed arsenate or arsenite ions, or perhaps some ion pair with Mg. Assuming a diffusion coefficient of 2 x 10^{-6} cm²/sec, and As concentrations of 15 and 2 ppb in the interstitial and overlying seawaters:

$$\text{diffusive flux} = 2 \times 10^{-6} \, \frac{\text{cm}^2}{\text{sec}} \times 13 \, \frac{\mu g \, As}{\text{liter} \cdot 2 \, \text{cm}} \times \frac{1 \, \text{liter}}{10^3 \, \text{cm}^3} = 13 \times 10^{-9} \, \frac{\mu g \, As}{\text{cm}^2 \, \text{sec.}}$$

The entrie surface area of Puget Sound is about 2.5 x 10^{13} cm². Applying the diffusive flux calculated for Quartermaster Harbor to one-fifth of Puget Sound, we calculate an upper limit for the diffusive flux of arsenic out of sediments to the overlying seawater to be 0.2 x 10^7 g As/yr, small compared with the other major arsenic inputs summarized in Table 2.

Figure 7 shows the results of our studies of arsenic concentrations in seawaters in bell jars positioned on these Quartermaster Harbor sediments. The points for the arsenic concentrations with the bell jars on the sediments in the blank configuration are joined together. The amount of arsenic in solution in the sample configurations does not show large increases with time. Given the same error bars for each point as in the blank runs, it is questionable whether any significant increase in arsenic is observed.

For a 30-hour run with the bell jars covering 1,240 cm² of sediment surface we would expect the following As increase from the diffusive flux:

$$13 \times 10^{-9} \, \frac{\mu g \, As}{\text{cm}^2 \text{sec}} \times 1240 \, \text{cm}^2 \times 1.08 \times 10^5 \, \text{sec} = 1.7 \, \mu g \, As$$

In the 20-liter volume of seawater in the bell jars this corresponds to only a .08 ppb increase. The arsenic concentrations in the bell jars may not be increasing significantly with time because this diffusive flux is too small to be seen above the background concentrations of 1.7–2.0 ppb As already present in the bottom waters. The bell jars did show readily measurable increases in dissolved silica and ammonia, species with larger concentration gradients and hence larger diffusive fluxes than arsenic.

Surface sediments and interstitial waters at Quartermaster Harbor are oxygenated, and oxidation of the 1–9 ppm Fe^{+2} we observed in the surficial (0–10 cm) interstitial waters would lead to precipitation of hydrous ferric oxides, noted scavengers of dissolved arsenic. We postulate that this process is responsible for keeping the arsenic concentrations of the near-surface interstitial waters lower than we observed deeper in the sediments. This reduces the concentration gradient across the sediment/water interface and thereby limits the diffusive flux of arsenic.

These sediments do contain a moderately rich benthic macrofauna. Members of the polychaete family Cirratulidae were by far the most abundant, but numerous other conspicuous macrofauna were present as well (P. Jumars, pers. commun.). Activities of these organisms could in principle augment the diffusive arsenic flux by advecting arsenic and other species from the interstitial waters back to the overlying seawaters, but our bell jar studies did not detect any increased arsenic flux due to the activities of these organisms.

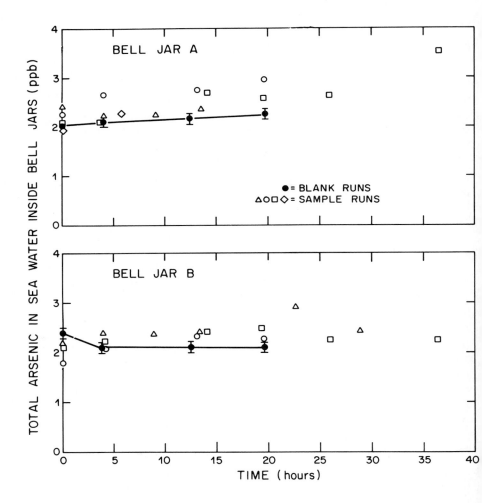

Figure 7. Results of in situ bell jar measurements of arsenic flux from Quartermaster Harbor sediments to overlying seawater.

Acknowledgment

We appreciate the financial support provided different parts of this research by National Science Foundation grant ENV 74-14649 and by U.S. Department of Energy contract AT(45-1)-2225-T24. This is Contribution No. 996 from the Department of Oceanography, University of Washington, Seattle.

References

1.   Anderson, M. A., J. F. Ferguson, and J. Gavis. 1976. Arsenate adsorption on amorphous aluminum hydroxide. J. Colloid. Interface Sci. 54:391-399.

2.   Atlas, E., C. Culberson, and R. M. Pytkowicz. 1976. Phosphate association with Na^+, Ca^{+2} and Mg^{+2} in sea water. Marine Chemistry 4:243-254.

3.   Barnes, C. A., and C. C. Ebbesmeyer. 1978. Some aspects of Puget Sound's circulation and water properties, pp. 209-228. *In* B. Kjerfve (ed.), Estuarine Transport Processes. Univ. of South Carolina Press, Columbia.

4.   Braman, R. S., D. L. Johnson, C. C. Foreback, J. M. Ammons, and J. L. Bricker. 1977. Separation and determination of nanogram amounts of inorganic arsenic and methylarsenic compounds. Analytical Chem. 49:621-625.

5.   Brinckman, F. E., G. E. Parris, W. R. Blair, K. L. Jewett, W. P. Iverson, and J. M. Bellama. 1977. Questions concerning environmental mobility of arsenic: needs for a chemical data base and means for speciation of trace organoarsenicals. Environmental Health Perspectives 19:11-24.

6.   Crecelius, E. A. 1974. The geochemistry of arsenic and antimony in Puget Sound and Lake Washington, Washington. Ph.D. dissertation, Univ. of Washington, Seattle. 133 pp.

7.   _____. 1975. The geochemical cycle of arsenic in Lake Washington and its relation to other elements. Limnol. Oceanogr. 20(3):441-450.

8.   Crecelius, E. A., M. H. Bothner, and R. Carpenter. 1975. Geochemistries of arsenic, antimony, mercury and related elements in sediments of Puget Sound. Environ. Sci. Technol. 9(4):325-333.

9.   Crecelius, E. A., C. J. Johnson, and G. C. Hofer. 1974. Contamination of soils near a copper smelter by arsenic, antimony and lead. Water Air Soil Pollut. 3:337-343.

10. DeGroot, A. J. 1973. Occurrence and behavior of heavy metals in river deltas, pp. 308-326. *In* E. D. Goldberg (ed.), North Sea Science, MIT Press, Cambridge, Mass.

11. Edzwald, J. K., D. C. Toensing, and M. Leung. 1976. Phosphate adsorption reactions with clay minerals. Environ. Sci. Technol. 10:485-490.

12. Friebertshauser, M. A., and A. C. Duxbury. 1972. A water budget study of Puget Sound and its subregions. Limnol. Oceanogr. 17:237-247.

13. Hingston, F. J., R. J. Atkinson, A. M. Posner, and J. P. Quick. 1968. Specific adsorption of anions on goethite. Ninth Int. Cong. Soc. Soil Sci., Transactions, Adelaide, Australia 1:669-678.

14. James, R. O., and T. W. Healy. 1972. Adsorption and hydrolyzable metal ions at the oxide-water interface. J. Colloid. Interface Sci. 40:42-81.

15. Lunde, G. 1977. Occurrence and transformation of arsenic in the marine environment. Environmental Health Perspectives 19:47-52..

16. Manheim, F. T. 1976. Interstitial waters of marine sediments, pp. 115-186. *In* J. P. Riley and R. Chester (eds.), Chemical Oceanography, Vol. 6, second edition. Academic Press, New York.

17. Muljadi, D., A. M. Posner and J. P. Quick. 1966. The mechanism of phosphate adsorption by kaolinite, gibbsite and pseudoboehmite. J. Soil Sci. 17:212-247.

18. Müller, G., and U. Förstner. 1975. Heavy metals in sediments of the Rhine and Elbe estuaries: mobilization or mixing effect. Environmental Geology 1:33-39.

19. Nelsen, F. M., and F. T. Eggertsen. 1958. Determination of surface area absorption measurements by a continuous flow method. Analytical Chem. 30:1387-1390.

20. Nelson, K. W. 1977. Industrial contributions of arsenic to the environment. Environmental Health Perspectives 19:31-34.

21. O'Connor. T. P., and D. R. Kester. 1975. Adsorption of copper and cobalt from fresh and marine systems. Geochim. et Cosmochim. Acta 39:1531-1543.

22. Parks, G. A. 1975. Adsorption in the marine environment, pp. 241-308. In J. P. Riley and R. Chester (eds.), Chemical Oceanography, Vol. 1, second edition. Academic Press, New York.

23. Penrose, W. R., H. B. S. Conacher, R. Black. J. C. Meranger, W. Miles, H. M. Cunningham, and W. R. Squires. 1977. Implications of inorganic/organic interconversion on fluxes of arsenic in marine food webs. Environmental Health Perspectives 19:53-60.

24. Ridley, W. P., L. Dizikes, A. Cheh, and J. M. Wood. 1977. Recent studies on biomethylation and demethylation of toxic elements. Environmental Health Perspectives 19:43-46.

25. Woolson, E. A. 1977. Fate of arsenicals in different environmental substrates. Environmental Health Perspectives 19:73-82.

CYCLING OF TRACE METAL AND CHLORINATED HYDROCARBON WASTES IN THE SOUTHERN CALIFORNIA BIGHT

David R. Young, Tsu-Kai Jan, and Theadore C. Heesen

Southern California Coastal Water Research Project
1500 East Imperial Highway
El Segundo, California

Abstract: Trace metals and chlorinated hydrocarbons are two important types of wastes released to the marine ecosystem off southern California. Municipal wastewater discharge is the dominant route of entry for most of the metals investigated. However, the use of vessel antifouling paints, primers, and corrosion-preventing anodes apparently can cause order of magnitude increases in metals levels for both harbor waters and mussels. Invertebrates living near highly-contaminated sediments around a major coastal municipal outfall concentrate certain metals up to ten times natural levels; in contrast, little abnormal uptake was measured in several species of fish from this region. In the past, municipal wastewater has also been the dominant source of chlorinated hydrocarbons to the Bight; however, between 1972 and 1975 these emissions decreased by an order of magnitude, and dry aerial fallout is now an equivalent input route. Despite these reductions, DDT and PCB levels in the highly-contaminated sediments and flatfish from the largest outfall zone decreased by only about a factor of 1.5 during the same period. This indicates that release of these synthetic organics to nearshore marine sediments can lead to persistent contamination of coastal ecosystems. Harbor mussels collected near sites of vessel activity in 1974 and 1977 were also contaminated by PCB's, containing up to twenty times the concentration found in coastal specimens.

Introduction

The marine ecosystem off southern California, known as the Southern California Bight, receives waste inputs via several different routes. More than ten million persons, approximately five percent of the nation's population, occupy the adjacent coastal plain, making this an important region for environmental pollution research. Here we summarize major findings made by our Project since 1970 on the inputs and cycling characteristics of two categories of wastes—trace metals and chlorinated hydrocarbons—in the Bight.

Study Area

Southern California is an arid region, typically receiving only 25–50 cm precipitation annually. The long-term mean flow of surface runoff to the sea is 0.56 x 10^{12} liter/year (Southern California Coastal Water Research Project, 1973), more than half of which occurs in the Los Angeles-Orange County Basin (between Pt. Dume and Newport, Figure 1). Most of this runoff occurs as pulse inputs carried by only a few storms each year. In contrast, during 1971–76 the average discharge rate of municipal (domestic and industrial) wastewater from the five major coastal treatment plants[1] was 1.3 x 10^{12} liter/year (Schafer, 1977), constituting more than 95 percent of such discharges to the Bight. Thus, these wastewater collection systems, whose outfall diffusers generally lie 3–8 km offshore at a depth of about 60 m (Figure 1), represent the major route by which freshwater is steadily carried to the adjacent marine ecosystem. As the 1971–76 average discharge rates for the JWPCP, Hyperion, OCSD, Pt. Loma, and Oxnard systems were 1.34, 1.31, 0.60, 0.39, and 0.04 x 10^9 liters per day, approximately 90 percent of this input comes from the Los Angeles-Orange County Basin.

This region also contains the major vessel activity in the Bight. In addition to the commercial and naval vessels served by Los Angeles-Long Beach Harbor, the largest southern California anchorage, approximately 70 percent of the 35,000 recreational vessels in the Bight are sheltered in marinas of the Los Angeles-Orange County Basin. A second major harbor is located in San Diego (Figure 1). We concluded from a 1973 Bight-wide survey that approximately 300,000 liters of antifouling paints, containing approximately 180 m tons of copper, are applied annually to vessel bottoms in southern California (Young *et al.*, 1973a).

Thermal effluents from electrical generating stations spread along the coast represent another potential source of chemical contaminants. The 1976 discharge rate for the eight stations of Southern California Edison Company (SCE) situated between Mandalay and San Clemente (Figure 1) was 6.8 x 10^{12} liters/year, roughly 70 percent of the total cooling water discharged to the Bight (Young *et al.*, 1977a). Finally, the severe atmospheric pollution which exists in the Los Angeles-Orange County and San Diego Basins constitutes another route of pollutant inputs to the adjacent marine ecosystem.

Trace Metal Inputs

Since 1971, utilizing atomic absorption spectroscopy (AAS), we have conducted a variety of surveys for eight trace metals (Ag, Cd, Cr, Cu, Hg, Ni, Pb, Zn) entering the Bight. Monitoring data for the relatively high levels found in

Figure 1. (opposite) The Southern California Bight.

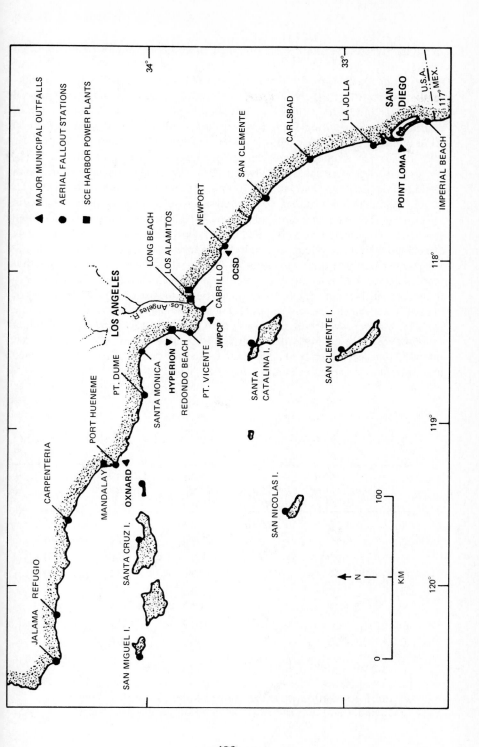

municipal wastewater have been obtained from the five major treatment plant laboratories (Schafer, 1977). Flow-weighted concentrations from a storm water survey conducted by the Project (Young *et al.*, 1973b) in 1971–72, an abnormally dry year (0.17 x 10^{12} liter/yr), were extrapolated to the following normal runoff year (0.57 x 10^{12} liter/yr). Estimated inputs from the SCE discharge of cooling water (excluding other waste streams added to the thermal effluents) were obtained from a recent Project study of the SCE system (Young *et al.*, 1977a). Dry aerial fallout inputs were estimated from a survey conducted during November 1975 at sites located between Carpinteria and Carlsbad, and on Santa Catalina Island (Young and Jan, 1977). Our findings are summarized in Table 1.

Although these studies have somewhat different spatial and temporal bases, it seems clear that municipal wastewater discharge is the dominant known route for trace metals entering the Bight. Only for lead are the inputs via atmospheric fallout and surface runoff comparable to those of the submarine wastewater outfalls; this is undoubtedly due to the extensive use of tetraethyl lead as an anti-knock additive in gasoline (Huntzicker *et al.*, 1975). The only other competitive input that has been quantified is the use of almost 200 m tons of copper in antifouling paints (versus 500 m tons via the outfalls). Although some of this is now removed with old paint scrapings to sanitary landfills, the fact that this relative large quantity of copper is specifically added to such paints and intended to be biologically available and toxic suggests its potential importance to harbor and nearshore coastal waters of the Bight.

Table 1. **Estimated annual inputs (m ton/yr) of trace metals to the Bight.**

	Municipal wastewater 1976	*Dry fallout*[1] *1975*	*Storm runoff*[2] *1972-73*	*Thermal discharge*[3] *1977*	*Sum*
Ag	20	0.06	2.6	--	23
Cd	45	0.84	2.8	0.3	49
Cr	593	6.6	60	0.6	660
Cu	507	31	42	2.1	760[4]
Hg	2.6	--	0.4	--	3
Ni	307	12	41	0.7	360
Pb	190	240	210	0.8	640
Zn	1,060	150	240	1.8	1,450

1. 100 km x 100 km off L.A. – Orange Co. Basin
2. Extrapolating flow-weighted results from 1971-72 survey
3. Southern California Edison cooling water (6.8 x 10^{12} 1/yr)
4. Includes 180 m tons/yr Cu used in vessel antifouling paints

Metals Contamination

To examine the extent of biological contamination resulting from the submarine discharge of copper wastes, in Figures 2 and 3 we compare distributions of copper measured in surface sediments and in livers of Dover sole flatfish (*Microstomus pacificus*) collected during 1970–71 from the monitoring zone of the JWPCP outfalls, the largest single point source of metals to the Bight. Between 1971 and 1976, the average annual mass emission rate of copper via

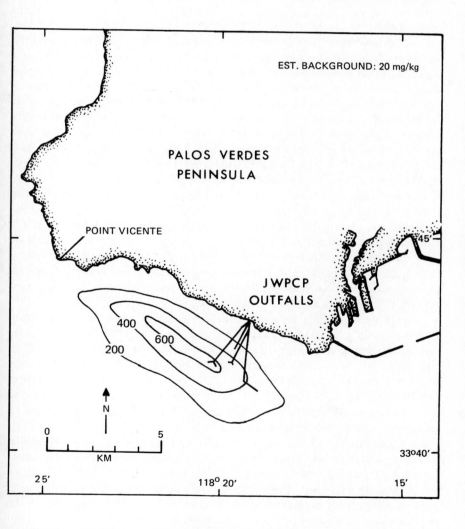

Figure 2. *Isopleths of bottom sediment copper concentrations (mg/dry kg) in the JWPCP outfall monitoring zone, May 1970.*

JWPCP was about 250 m tons/yr, and approximately 95 percent of this metal is associated with filterable (>0.4-micron) particulates (Young *et al.*, 1973b). As a result, the sediments off Palos Verdes Peninsula are highly contaminated; in 1970, concentrations measured by AAS in the upper few centimeters at the discharge depth (60 m) and within a 5 km zone downcurrent (northwest) of the diffusers exceeded 600 ppm Cu (mg/dry kg), more than 30 times the estimated natural background value of about 20 ppm (Galloway, 1972). Since then, the annual mass emission rate has decreased only to about 200 m tons/yr, and there has been no significant change in sediment concentrations (Hershelman *et al.*, 1977).

However, these high copper levels have not led to corresponding contamination of Dover sole known by their high DDE levels (Young, *et al.*, 1976a) and incidence of fin erosion disease (Mearns and Sherwood, 1974) to have occupied the contaminated sediments for an extended period. As seen in Figure 3, concentrations in livers of specimens from the JWPCP outfall zone were no higher than those from the uncontaminated sediments off Santa Catalina Island, both averaging about 2 ppm (mg/wet kg). These levels, determined by neutron activation analysis (NAA), were very similar to those found in specimens from the Hyperion and OCSD discharge zones. We found a corresponding lack of uptake in outfall zone flatfish above natural liver concentrations for several other toxic trace elements (de Goeij *et al.*, 1974). The following average ppm concentrations (± std. error) for Dover sole from "highly contaminated" (n=12) and "natural" (n=6) sediments were observed by NAA. As: 1.3 ± 0.2 vs. 3.1 ± 0.7; Cd: 0.2 ± 0.06 vs. 0.6 ± 0.3; Cu: 2.0 ± 0.4 vs. 2.2 ± 0.5; Hg: 0.11 ± 0.02 vs. 0.11 ± 0.04; Sb: 0.0029 ± 0.0009 vs. 0.0035 ± 0.016; Se: 0.65 ± 0.15 vs. 1.2 ± 0.3; Zn: 26 ± 3 vs. 27 ± 4. Corresponding estimated contamination (outfall: control) ratios for the sediments from which these fish were trawled were As: 15; Cd: 160; Cu: 23; Hg: 85; Sb: 13; Se: 14; and Zn: 17.

In September 1975 the 40-station JWPCP outfall monitoring zone (40 sq. km) was sampled with a Shipek grab and the top 5 cm of the high-organic sediments were analyzed for trace metals by AAS (Hershelman *et al.*, 1977). The ratios of the median concentration in this relatively large area to the estimated background value (Southern California Coastal Water Research Project, 1973) for Ag, Cd, Cr, Cu, Hg, Ni, Pb, and Zn were 9, 33, 5, 6, 25, 3, 13, and 4, respectively. (Comparison of 1970 and 1975 data indicates that no major changes in surface sediment contamination have occurred over this period.)

To determine whether the edible tissue of seafood organisms from this discharge region had become contaminated, three specimens each of five popular sportsfish were collected during 1975–76 from both the outfall and control zones. Muscle tissue was cleanly excised from these specimens and trace metal concentrations were measured by AAS (Jan *et al.*, 1977). Medians of the triplicate specimens were first determined, and then, for each metal, the median value of the five species medians was determined for both the outfall and control categories. The respective values are as follows. Ag: <0.01 vs. <0.01; Cd:

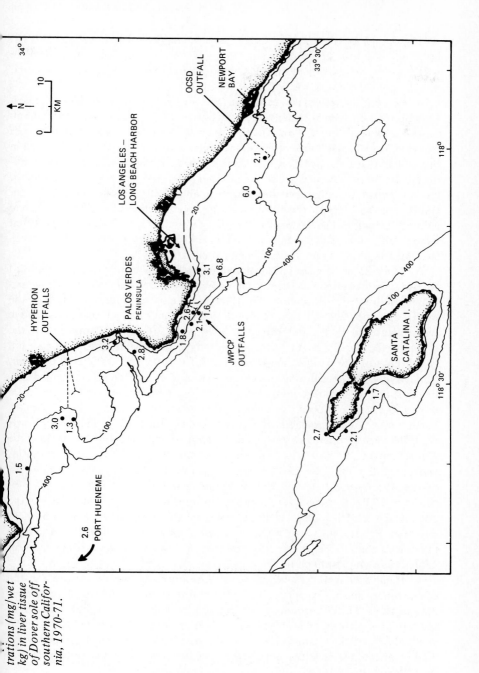

trations (mg/wet kg) in liver tissue of Dover sole off southern California, 1970-71.

<0.01 vs. <0.01; Cr: 0.03 vs. 0.02; Cu: 0.15 vs. 0.13; Hg: 0.10 vs. 0.22; Ni: 0.06 vs. 0.06; Zn: 3.6 vs. 1.9 ppm. Thus, of these seven metals, only for zinc was there any suggestion of muscle contamination in the outfall specimens, and then by only about a factor of 2.

Several invertebrates (sea urchin *Strongylocentrotus franciscanus;* black abalone *Haliotis cracherodii;* ridgeback prawn *Sicyonia ingentis;* yellow crab *Cancer anthonyi;* lobster *Panulirus interruptus*) were also sampled in triplicate from the outfall and control regions, and metal concentrations were measured in the edible tissue. In addition, 6-8 purple-hinged rock scallops (*Hinnites multirugosus*) were obtained from the two regions, and three tissues (adductor muscle, gonad, and digestive gland) were analyzed. The results indicate that, in contrast to the case for the fishes, certain invertibrates from the outfall zone exhibit distinct uptake of specific metals in muscle and gonadal tissues which were cleanly separated from the contaminated sediments or wastewater particulates to which the organisms had been exposed.

The greatest accumulations above natural levels (approximately tenfold) occurred for chromium in the muscle of two mollusks—the black abalone and the purple-hinged rock scallop. The three muscle tissue values measured in the outfall abalone (0.9, 1.0, and 2.2 ppm) were all an order of magnitude above those measured in the control specimens (0.04, 0.10, 0.10 ppm). For the scallops, the mean ($\pm$ std. error) values measured in the outfall (n=8) and island control (n=6) specimens were 0.35 $\pm$ 0.05 and 0.05 $\pm$ 0.02 ppm, respectively. Distinct chromium contamination of the scallop gonadal and digestive tissues was also observed; corresponding values for the gonads were 2.6 $\pm$ 0.3 vs. 0.39 $\pm$ 0.05 ppm; for the digestive gland, 41 $\pm$ 8 vs. 2.2 $\pm$ 0.4 ppm. Furthermore, silver appeared to be accumulated by the outfall zone scallops over control levels; comparative values for the adductor muscle, gonad, and digestive gland were 0.026 $\pm$ 0.008 vs. 0.008 $\pm$ 0.003, 0.080 $\pm$ 0.013 vs. 0.018 $\pm$ 0.006, and 2.3 $\pm$ 0.5 vs. 0.31 $\pm$ 0.06 ppm, respectively. Corresponding values for copper were 0.41 $\pm$ 0.1 vs. 0.16 $\pm$ 0.04, 3.2 $\pm$ 0.2 vs. 2.2 $\pm$ 0.5, and 190 $\pm$ 40 vs. 64 $\pm$ 15 ppm, respectively. Zinc levels appeared to be elevated only in the gonadal tissue of the outfall scallops; the comparative values were 46 $\pm$ 6 vs. 20 $\pm$ 6 ppm. Finally, the nickel values measured in the muscle of yellow crab from the outfall zone (0.22, 0.26, 0.51 ppm) were well above the available control values (<0.04, <0.05 ppm).

Relatively low concentrations of total mercury were measured in the edible tissue (muscle except for sea urchin gonads) of the outfall and control zone invertebrates. The corresponding median concentrations for sea urchin, abalone, scallop, prawn, crab, and lobster were 0.006 vs. 0.024, 0.011 vs. 0.009, 0.056 vs. 0.024, 0.080 vs. 0.046, 0.034 vs. 0.071, and 0.28 vs. 0.25 ppm, respectively. As was the case for the fishes, none of these median concentrations exceeded the 0.5 ppm limit established by the U.S. Food and Drug Administration.

During the past three years we have conducted a number of studies into the levels of "dissolved" (<0.4-micron) and "particulate" (>0.4-micron) metals in offshore, coastal, and harbor waters in the Bight (Young and Jan, 1975; McDermott and Heesen, 1975; Young *et al.*, 1977a; Jan and Young, 1977). The results indicate distinctly higher levels for dissolved cadmium, copper, nickel, and zinc in harbors, with the highest observed concentrations occurring near a vessel repainting facility in Newport Harbor. Compared to typical coastal background values for Cd, Cu, Ni, and Zn of 0.05, 0.1-0.2, 0.2-0.3, and <0.2 ppb (μg/1), median concentrations measured near the vessel repair yard at Newport were 0.35, 8.6, 1.1, and 22 ppb, respectively. In addition, overall median values of surveys conducted at the entrances of Newport, San Diego, and Los Angeles-Long Beach Harbors (Figure 1) for Cu, Ni, and Zn were 1.9, 1.3, and 4.0 ppb, respectively, each an order of magnitude above the estimated natural levels. Corresponding medians obtained for SCE thermal influent samples taken from Mandalay, Redondo, Long Beach, and Alamitos Harbors (Figure 1) were 1.5, 0.6, and 1.2 ppb. These elevated harbor water concentrations of dissolved metals appear to be due to vessel-related activities, such as the use of metal-based bottom primers and antifouling paints, and sacrificial zinc anodes.

Metals contamination of the harbor mussel *Mytilus edulis* collected during 1974 near sites of vessel activity have also been observed. Multi-element analyses were conducted by optical emission spectroscopy on freeze-dried tissues of this intertidal bioindicator in collaboration with George Alexander (University of California at Los Angeles). The highest values were measured in specimens collected near the Newport Harbor vessel repair yard discussed above (Young and Alexander, 1977). In Table 2 these concentrations are compared with corresponding values for coastal specimens collected at a station less than 0.5 km away across a sand spit, but situated approximately 5 km from the Harbor mouth. Because the only major anthropogenic activity in this harbor is the use and maintenance of recreational vessels, it appears that vessel-related activities can lead to distinct contamination of restricted marine waterways and their biota by a number of toxic trace metals.

Chlorinated Hydrocarbon Inputs

Chlorinated hydrocarbons are another important class of contaminants in the Southern California Bight. Prior to spring 1970, one of the worlds largest facilities for the manufacture of DDT released its wastes into the JWPCP wastewater stream for ultimate disposal off Palos Verdes Peninsula. Although reliable monitoring for these residues in JWPCP effluent did not begin until January 1971, during that year almost 22 m tons of total DDT in contaminated sewer sediments were discharged to the sea via this route. (Young *et al.*, 1976a). In the summer of 1971 we collected specimens (5 cm long) of the coastal mussel *Mytilus californianus* from throughout the Bight, and sent them to the laboratory of Dr. Robert Risebrough (University of California, Berkeley) for analysis of the whole soft tissues. The results are illustrated in Figure 4. The distribution clearly illustrates the dominance of this point-source DDT input, which was detectable

Table 2. *Mytilus edulis* mean concentration (± std. error) of metals (mg/dry kg) in digestive gland (n = 6), gonad (n = 2), adductor muscle (n = 2) and remainder tissues (n = 2) from Newport Harbor and Beach, 1974.

Metal	Tissue	Harbor	Beach	Harbor:Beach
Cadmium	Dig. Gland	10 ± 1.9	< 4.7	> 2.1
	Gonad	9.0 ± 9.0	< 2.8	> 3.2
	Muscle	7.1 ± 3.4	< 3.0	> 2.4
	Remainder	7.6 ± 0.8	< 4.8	> 1.6
Chromium	Dig. Gland	3.8 ± 0.6	3.7 ± 0.6	1.0
	Gonad	2.0 ± 0.4	0.3 ± 0.1	6.7
	Muscle	< 0.6	< 0.6	--
	Remainder	1.6 ± 0.1	1.0 ± 0.1	1.6
Copper	Dig. Gland	127 ± 18	16 ± 1.0	7.9
	Gonad	93 ± 15	9.6 ± 0.1	9.9
	Muscle	52 ± 10	5.7 ± 0.3	9.1
	Remainder	100 ± 14	11 ± 0.6	9.1
Lead	Dig. Gland	19 ± 2.7	5.5 ± 0.6	3.5
	Gonad	13 ± 4.6	< 0.9	> 14
	Muscle	< 1.3	< 1.2	--
	Remainder	10 ± 2.0	< 1.6	> 6.2
Tin	Dig. Gland	3.6 ± 0.8	1.4 ± 0.3	2.6
	Gonad	5.4 ± 1.4	< 0.3	> 18
	Muscle	< 0.5	< 0.7	--
	Remainder	3.4 ± 1.2	< 0.5	6.8
Zinc	Dig. Gland	240 ± 26	80 ± 11	3.0
	Gonad	360 ± 120	87 ± 3	4.1
	Muscle	210 ± 66	79 ± 3	2.7
	Remainder	280 ± 45	99 ± 16	2.8

Figure 4. (opposite) Total DDT concentrations (mg/wet kg) in whole soft tissues of Mytilus californianus *from the Bight, summer 1971.*

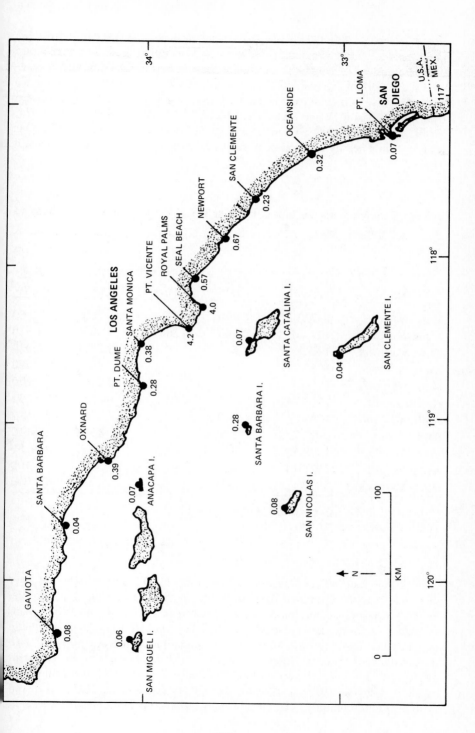

491

in the intertidal bioindicator for about 100 km in several directions from the outfall site.

Largely as a result of this gross contamination, and the growing concern over polychlorinated biphenyls (PCB) in the environment, in 1971 we initiated a comprehensive survey of chlorinated hydrocarbon inputs to the Bight (Southern California Coastal Water Research Project, 1973; Risebrough et al., 1974; Young and Heesen, 1975; Young et al., 1976b; Heesen and Young, 1977). Our findings, obtained by electron-capture gas chromatography, are summarized in Table 3.

Table 3. Estimated annual inputs (m tons/yr) of chlorinated hydrocarbons to the Bight.

| | | | | *kg/yr* | |
| | | *Total* | | *1242* | *1254* |
Route	*Year*	*DDT*	*Dieldrin*	*PCB*	*PCB*
Muni. Wastewat.[1]	1972	6,490	100	$\geq$ 19,200	$\geq$ 260
Muni. Wastewat.	1973	3,920	$\leq$ 280	$\geq$ 1,900	1,510
Muni. Wastewat.	1974	1,580	95	4,270	1,020
Muni. Wastewat.	1975	1,270	--	2,400	680
Muni. Wastewat.	1976	940	--	2,220	590
Harbor Indust.	1973-74	40	10	$\leq$ 70	30
Antifoul. Paint	1973	< 1	--	< 1	< 1
Surf. Runoff	1971-72	100	20	100-170	90-110
Surf. Runoff	1972-73	320	65	0-550	250-280
Aerial Fallout[2]	1973-74	1,400	--	--	1,100
Ocean Currents	1973	$\leq$ 7,000	--	--	$\leq$ 4,000

[1] 1971 JWPCP discharge of total DDT: 21,600 kg
[2] Inner coastal zone: 400 km x 50 km

These data indicate that, during the early 1970's municipal wastewater discharge was the dominant route of input for the DDT's, Dieldrin, and the PCB's, the principal chlorinated hydrocarbons detected at that time. Since then, restrictions on both the industrial discharge and general use of these synthetic organics has caused an order of magnitude reduction in their rate of injection to the coastal ecosystem via submarine outfalls. For example, between 1971 and 1975, JWPCP mass emissions of total DDT decreased from 22 to 1.2 m ton/yr; similarly, between 1972 and 1975 the JWPCP emissions of total PCB decreased from >12 to 0.6 m ton/yr. As a result, inputs of these contaminants to the Bight via aerial deposition are now as important as those via municipal wastewater discharge (Young *et al.*, 1976b; Young *et al.*, 1976c).

Chlorinated Hydrocarbon Persistence

Despite the reduced mass emission rates of DDT's and PCB's from the outfalls, relatively high levels of contamination persist in the benthic sediments and organisms around the JWPCP and Hyperion discharges. Based on a July 1972 survey conducted off Palos Verdes Peninsula, we concluded that approximately 200 m tons of DDT residues (mostly p,p'-DDE) were contained in the upper 30 cm of bottom sediments in a 50 sq km zone around the JWPCP outfalls (Young *et al.*, 1976a). The maximum concentration observed exceeded 200 ppm (mg/dry kg). When the surface sediments (0–5 cm) were resurveyed in September 1975, five and one-half years after the dominant industrial input to the sewers had ceased, sediment concentrations downcurrent of the outfall diffusers still exceeded 100 ppm.

This input has resulted in excessive levels of total DDT in several fishes living in the discharge zone. During 1972, approximately 50 and 75 percent, respectively, of the kelp bass *Paralabrax clathratus* and black perch *Embiotoca jacksoni* collected from this region exceeded the 5 ppm maximum allowed by the FDA, and muscle tissue concentrations ranged up to 65 ppm. In addition, the mean concentration ($\pm$ std. error) for 21 Dover sole captured there in May 1972 was 26 $\pm$ 5 ppm total DDT, more than five times the FDA limit (Young *et al.*, 1977b)

As shown above, the JWPCP inputs of DDT and PCB residues both fell by an order of magnitude in the early 1970's. However, when concentrations of chlorinated hydrocarbons in surface sediments were compared for 19 JWPCP stations sampled in both 1972 and 1975, the median total DDT and PCB 1254[2] values were found to have decreased by factors of only 1.6 (19 to 12 ppm total DDT) and 1.2 (1.0 to 0.81 ppm PCB 1254), respectively. Corresponding decrease factors for median levels in muscle of Dover sole trawled from this sediment sampling area were 1.5 (17 to 11 ppm total DDT) and 1.3 (1.0 to 0.76 ppm PCB 1254). These findings indicate that contamination of sediments by chlorinated hydrocarbons such as DDT and PCB can cause these synthetic organics to persist in bottom feeding fishes (and possibly other benthic organisms) long after major reductions have been made in the dominant inputs.

As a final example of the kinds of waste cycling that can occur in nearshore marine ecosystems, Figure 5 illustrates the distributions of total PCB we have measured in whole soft tissues of the intertidal mussel *M. edulis* collected during 1974 and 1977 from San Diego Harbor. Despite the facts that the "open" use of PCB has been restricted by the only U.S. manufacturer since 1971 (Environmental Protection Agency, 1976), and that major antifouling paints obtained in southern California during 1973 contained insignificant PCB concentrations (Young *et al.*, 1973a), the levels of this pollutant in the bay mussels collected during 1974 near large vessel repair yards in Commercial

Basin and near the Navy Moorings were approximately 20 times the coastal baseline. Although distinctly lower levels were found in 1977 specimens collected at nearby sites, the PCB contamination of earlier years is still clearly discernable in the ecosystem of this semi-enclosed bay.

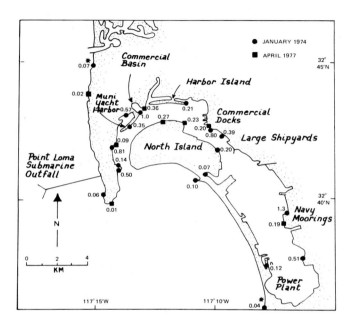

Figure 5. Total PCB concentrations (mg/wet kg) in whole soft tissues of Mytilus edulis *from San Diego Harbor.*

Acknowledgements

    We wish to thank G. Alexander, J. Galloway, J. Morgan, B. de Lappe, R. Risebrough, J. de Goeij, and V. Guinn for their part in the research which was conducted at several California universities. We also thank Project personnel A. Mearns, D. McDermott-Ehrlich, M. Moore, P. Hershelman, R. Eganhouse, and H. Schafer for their assistance. Support was provided in part by the U.S. Environmental Protection Agency (Grant R803707), the California State Water Resources Control Board (Contract No. 59H400), The San Diego Regional Water Quality Control Board (Agreement No. W609919), and the Southern California Edison Co. (Contract No. U0317016). Contribution Number 89 of the Southern California Coastal Water Research Project.

Notes

[1] Joint Water Pollution Control Plant (JWPCP) of Los Angeles County, Hyperion Treatment Plant of Los Angeles City, Orange County Sanitation District (OCSD) Treatment Plant, Point Loma Treatment Plant of San Diego City, and the City of Oxnard Treatment Plant.
[2] Characterized by electron-capture gas chromatography as most closely resembling Aroclor 1254.

References

1. de Goeij, J. J. M., V. P. Guinn, D. R. Young, and A. J. Mearns. 1974. Neutron activation analysis trace element studies of Dover sole liver and marine sediments, pp. 189-200. *In* Comparative Studies of Food and Environmental Contamination. International Atomic Energy Agency, Vienna.

2. Environmental Protection Agency, 1976. Production, usage, and distribution of PCBs, pp. 4-10. *In* PCBs in the United States Industrial Use and Environmental Distribution. EPA 560/6-76-005. Washington, D.C.

3. Galloway, J. N. 1972. Man's alteration of the natural geochemical cycle of selected trace metals. Ph.D. dissertation, Dept. of Chemistry, Univ. of Calif., San Diego, 143 pp.

4. Heesen, T. C., and D. R. Young. 1977. Halogenated hydrocarbons in wastewaters: knowns and unknowns, pp. 33-38. *In* SCCWRP Annual Report, 1977. NTIS PB 274463/AS. U.S. Dept. of Commerce, Springfield, Virginia.

5. Hershelman, G. P., T.-K. Jan, and H. A. Schafer. 1977. Pollutants in sediments off Palos Verdes, pp. 63-68. *In* SCCWRP Annual Report, 1977. NTIS PB 274463/AS. U.S. Dept. of Commerce, Springfield, Virginia.

6. Huntzicker, J. J., S. K. Friedlander, and C. I. Davidson. 1975. Material balance for automobile-emitted lead in Los Angeles Basin. Environ. Sci. Technol., 9:448-457.

7. Jan, T.-K., M. D. Moore, and D. R. Young. 1977. Metals in seafood near outfalls, pp. 153-157. *In* SCCWRP Annual Report, 1977. NTIS PB 274463/AS. U.S. Dept. of Commerce, Springfield, Virginia.

8. Jan, T.-K., and D. R. Young. 1977. Chromium speciation in municipal wastewater and seawater. J. Wat. Pollut. Control. Fed., in press.

9. McDermott, D. J., and T. C. Heesen, 1975. Inputs of DDT, PCB, and trace metals from harbors, pp. 133-138. *In* SCCWRP Annual Report, 1975. NTIS PB 274467/AS. U.S. Dept. of Commerce, Springfield, Virginia.

10. Mearns, A. J., and M. Sherwood. 1974. Environmental aspects of fin erosion and tumors in southern California Dover sole. Trans. Amer. Fish. Soc., 103 (4):799-810.

11. Risebrough, R., D. R. Young, T. Munson, M. Goodwin, and R. Parrish. 1974. Contamination of marine resources for human consumption—synthetic organic compounds, pp. 94-108. *In* Marine Bioassays Workshop Proceedings. Marine Technological Society, Washington, D.C.

12. Schafer, H. A. 1977. Characteristics of municipal wastewater discharges, pp. 19-23. *In* SCCWRP Annual Report, 1977. NTIS PB 274463/AS. U.S. Dept. of Commerce, Springfield, Virginia.

13. Southern California Coastal Water Research Project. 1973. The ecology of the Southern California Bight: implications for water quality management. SCCWRP Technical Report 104, 531 pp. NTIS PB 274462/AS. U.S. Dept. of Commerce, Springfield, Virginia.

14. Young, D. R., and G. V. Alexander. 1977. Metals in mussels from harbors and outfall areas, pp. 159-165. *In* SCCWRP Annual Report, 1977. NTIS PB 274463/ AS. U.S. Dept. of Commerce, Springfield, Virginia.

15. Young, D. R., and T. C. Heesen. 1975. Inputs of DDT and PCB, pp. 105-9. *In* SCCWRP Annual Report, 1975. NTIS PB 274467/AS. U.S. Dept. of Commerce, Springfield, Virginia.

16. Young, D. R., T. C. Heesen, D. J. McDermott, and P. E. Smokler. 1973a. Marine inputs of polychlorinated biphenyls and copper from vessel antifouling paints. SCCWRP Technical Memorandum 212, 20 pp. Southern California Coastal Water Research Project, 1500 E. Imperial Hwy., El Segundo, California.

17. Young, D. R., and T.-K. Jan. 1975. Trace metals in nearshore seawater, pp. 143-6. *In* SCCWRP Annual Report, 1975. NTIS PB 274467/AS. U.S. Dept. of Commerce, Springfield, Virginia.

18. _____. 1977. Fire fallout of metals off California. Mar. Pollut. Bull. 8 (5):109-112.

19. Young, D. R., T.-K. Jan, and M. D. Moore. 1977a. Metals in power plant cooling water discharges, pp. 25-31. *In* SCCWRP Annual Report, 1977. NTIS PB 274463/AS. U.S. Dept. of Commerce, Springfield, Virginia.

20. Young. D. R., D. J. McDermott, and T. C. Heesen. 1976a. DDT in sediments and organisms around southern California outfalls. J. Water Poll. Control Fed. 48:1919-28.

21. _____. 1976b. Marine inputs of polychlorinated biphenyls off southern California, pp. 199-208. *In* Proceedings of the National Conference on Polychlorinated Biphenyls. EPA 560/6-75-004. U.S. Environmental Protection Agency, Washington, D.C.

22. _____. 1976c. Aerial fallout of DDT in southern California. Bull. Envir. Contam. Toxicol. 16 (5):604-11.

23. _____. 1977b. Sediments as source of DDT and PCB. Mar. Pollut. Bull. 8 (11):254-257.

24. Young, D. R., C. S. Young, and G. E. Hlavka. 1973b. Sources of trace metals from highly urbanized southern California to the adjacent marine ecosystem, pp. 21-39. *In* M. G. Curry and G. M. Gigliott (eds.), Cycling and Control of Metals. National Environmental Research Center, Cincinnati, Ohio.

ESTUARY–NEARSHORE INTERACTIONS: ESTUARINE DEPENDENCE OF COASTAL WATERS

LOW-FREQUENCY RESPONSE OF ESTUARINE
SEA LEVEL TO NON-LOCAL FORCING

Björn Kjerfve, Jeffrey E. Greer, and Richard L. Crout

Belle W. Baruch Institute for Marine Biology
and Coastal Research
University of South Carolina
Columbia, South Carolina

Abstract: Variability in estuarine sea level and net flow on time scales longer than the predominant tidal cycle have long been ignored. However, recent work by Elliott (1976) focuses on the transient nature of estuarine circulation and its relation to local and far-field forcing with periods from 2 to 20 days. This forcing is well correlated with atmosphere variability, primarily wind events. North Inlet, South Carolina, is an ideal estuary for studies of non-local forcing because of the near absence of freshwater discharge and the small size of the winding estuarine creeks. One-year time series records of sea level, atmospheric pressure, and wind speed and direction indicate two important sea level responses. A 3.2 cm high 6.0-day sea level wave is attributable to atmospheric pressure, and a 6.4 cm high sea level fluctuation varies with the alongshore wind stress with a period of 9.2 days. In each case, it is believed that the forcing is transferred to the estuary from the coastal ocean via continental shelf waves. In addition, the yearly cycle of mean sea level, which is primarily due to changes in ocean and estuarine water temperature, causes the surrounding marshes to flood to a greater extent in the fall. This may be an important factor in facilitating material exchanges between estuary and marshes and could also be responsible for controlling net fluxes in or out of the estuary.

Classical Estuary

Estuaries are traditionally thought of as having a two-layered circulation with time-averaged outflow in the surface layer and net inflow in the bottom layer. This model was first proposed by D. W. Pritchard of the Chesapeake Bay Institute in a series of papers (e.g., 1952, 1954, 1956, and others), and verified by extensive sets of field data, primarily from the Chesapeake Bay and tributaries. However it was soon evident that the circulation in many estuaries deviated significantly from the traditional model. This was at first not reported in the literature (Pritchard, in press) as periods of reverse circulation were thought of as being just "unusual events."

The Six Circulation Types

It was not until after a year-long field study in the Potomac estuary that Elliott (1976) was able to put the classical estuarine circulation in reasonable perspective. He showed the importance of atmospheric events and variations in the coastal current field in causing shifts in the circulation structure over a few days. Elliott (1976) analyzed the records from a mooring of three digitally recording current meters and then defined six different circulation types for a single estuary:

1. Classical estuary: surface outflow and bottom inflow
2. Reverse estuary: surface inflow and bottom outflow
3. Three-layered: inflow at surface and bottom and outflow at mid-depth
4. Reverse three-layered: outflow at surface and bottom and inflow at mid-depth
5. Discharge: outflow at all depths
6. Storage: inflow at all depths

Type 1 occurred 43% of the time, with each period of classical estuarine circulation having an average duration of 2.5 days. Then followed type 6, occurring 22% of the time; type 2, 21%; type 4, 7%; type 5, 6%; and type 3, 1% of the time. Circulation types 2, 3, 4, 5 and 6 each had a mean duration of 1.0 to 1.6 days. In short, estuarine circulation is by no means a simple matter. Although the classical estuary circulation is most common in the Potomac, there occur at least an additional five circulation types. And still more complexity would arise if the estuary were considered to be three-dimensional so as to include net variations in the cross section (see Dyer, in press).

Forcing Mechanisms

Many forcing mechanisms act to control the circulation, including river discharge, wind stress, atmospheric pressure, water elevation, rate of change of water elevation, and water surface slope along the estuary (Elliott, 1976). The problem in analyzing for the importance of individual effects lies in the dependency between the forcing mechanisms. Through the use of empirical orthogonal function analysis, Elliott concluded that the response of the Potomac could be explained by two *modes*. The first *mode* accounted for 55% of the total variance and was best correlated with local effects such as wind stress and net surface slope. The second *mode* accounted for 25% of the total variance and was primarily correlated with far-field effects such as the time rate of change of the mean water surface.

Estuarine energetics are largely concentrated at the predominant tidal period, 12.42 hours for the east coast of the United States. However, Weisberg (1976a) showed that 48% of the current variance in a 51-day record from Narragansett Bay resided at subtidal frequencies. On a time scale of 4–5 days in particular these fluctuations were impeccably coherent with local winds. This response appears to correspond to Elliott's first *mode*. But all low frequency current and sea level variations are not due to local effects. Far-field effects, corresponding to Elliott's second *mode*, were discussed by Wang and Elliott (in press). They found current and sea-level fluctuations in the Chesapeake Bay due to non-local forcing with variance peaks at periods of 20 and 5 days. These far-field-driven fluctuations are probably largely the response of the estuary to continental shelf waves (CSW's) and fluctuations in the western boundary current (the Gulf Stream). CSW's with periods from 3 to 10 days have been found to propagate because of atmospheric forcing southward along the continental shelf off North Carolina (Mysak and Hamon, 1969). CSW's in the Florida Current have been measured to have periods from 7 to 14 days (Brooks and Mooers, 1977).

Meaningful Sampling Duration

In interpreting estuarine field data, it is usually necessary to consider sea-level and estuarine current variations on time scales longer than the predominant tidal period. Frequently reported measurements of reversed net currents are indicators of such current fluctuations at subtidal frequencies (frequencies longer than the tidal period). If a hydrographic study is conducted over too short a sampling period, it would be easy to make incorrect generalizations about the circulation and dynamics of a particular estuary. This point was stressed by Weisberg (1976b), who suggested that for typical wind and circulation conditions and a 20% error tolerance, it might be necessary to make measurements over 18 days in order to arrive at a meaningful estimate of the non-tidal mean flow. This estimate is in principle consistent with Elliott's (1976) results, which suggest a sampling time in excess of 9.5 days, the minimal possible duration in which all six estuarine circulation types can occur. However, if weighted according to the percentage of time each flow pattern prevailed, the required minimum sampling duration would be much longer. In reality, of course, few estuarine circulation studies have been conducted for more than four days.

Lack of Ocean-Estuary Coupling Studies

In the past, estuarine circulation has usually been treated separately from the dynamics of the coastal ocean. Although some emphasis has been placed on the influence of the estuarine outflow or plume on the coastal waters (e.g., Garvine 1974, 1975), the reverse coupling has largely been neglected. The salinity (density), for example, is commonly prescribed at the estuary-ocean boundary as a steady-state distribution. Tidal effects are lumped as viscosities and diffusivities in time-averaged mixing terms, but have also been shown to drive net currents (Cameron and Pritchard, 1963) and cause net material dispersion (e.g., Dyer, 1974) over a tidal cycle. Still, variations in circulation patterns and estuarine dynamics on time scales longer than the diurnal cycle have not been treated analytically. In fact, they have hardly been described prior to the studies by Elliott (1976) and Wang and Elliott (in press), although a large portion of the estuarine variance resides at sub-tidal frequencies.

Objectives

There are several objectives of this paper. The first one, already presented, is an argument for the need to consider low-frequency variations in estuarine responses to atmopsheric forcing and far-field effects.

Secondly, we wish to consider the low-frequency behavior of the North Inlet, South Carolina, sea level to identify periods of peak variance and response to far-field effects. North Inlet (Figure 1) is ideally suited for such an investigation, since this high-salinity estuary is too small to respond appreciably to local wind-forcing and has no measurable freshwater discharge; thus the sea level fluctuations in North Inlet may all be attributed to far-field ocean forcing. This

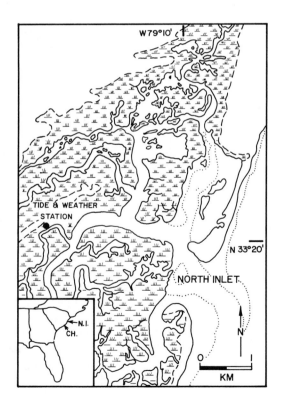

Figure 1.   Location map of North Inlet, S.C., with Charleston (CH.) and North Inlet (N.I.) indicated on the inset map.

removes some of the complexity encountered in the Chesapeake Bay studies (Elliott, 1976; Wang and Elliott, in press), where local and far-field effects were difficult to separate.

Thirdly, we wish to discuss some implications of low-frequency estuarine variability to material exchange between marshes, estuaries, and coastal waters.

Data Set and Analysis

The North Inlet data set consists of analog traces of water elevation, atmospheric pressure, wind speed, and wind directions for one year: 1 June 1974 to 31 May 1975. Water elevation was measured with a WeatherMeasure F551 tide gage, relevelled to a National Ocean Survey bench mark every two months. Atmospheric pressure was recorded with a WeatherMeasure B211 microbarograph, and a Climet CI-26 wind system was used for wind speed and direction measurements 15m above mean sea level.

The wind speed was used to compute the wind stress according to Wu (1969). The stress vector was then decomposed into orthogonal stress components for each 10° direction increment. This made it possible to determine the axis along which the stress variance was maximized (so that the covariance between the axes was minimum). This made it possible to determine the ocean response to winds from various directions.

A separate tide gage was installed at the mouth of North Inlet to assess the lag in water-level variations between the mouth and the estuarine gage. Based on a 3-week record, the estuarine gage lagged the tide at the mouth by less than 10 min for periods longer than the semi-diurnal tide. The semi-diurnal tide, with a mean range of 1.6 m, was 90° out of phase with currents, appearing to be a co-oscillating standing wave.

The tide, pressure, and stress component records were digitized at a rate of 1 sample per hour. To remove variability with periods shorter than one day and to avoid aliasing in the computed variance spectra, all records were low-pass filtered. A recursive Butterworth filter was chosen because of its superior gain characteristics (Ackroyd, 1973). It was designed with 3 db attenuation at 29 h, 20 db attenuation at 24 h, and 90 db attenuation at the semi-diurnal tidal period (Figure 2), which required a 12th-order filter. The filtered records were then resampled 12 hours, yielding a 1 cycle per day (cpd) cut-off frequency.

A fast Fourier transform (FFT) algorithm was used to compute variance spectra of all records and covariance spectra, phase, and coherence functions between the various filtered series. To permit making generalizations about the statistical processes, five adjacent spectral estimates were in all cases summed to yield 10 degrees of freedom for each resulting estimate. Confidence intervals were computed at the 90% level according to Rayner (1971).

Annual Sea Level Cycle

Fluctuations in the North Inlet sea level can be thought of as occurring over a continuum of frequencies with most of the variance concentrated at the

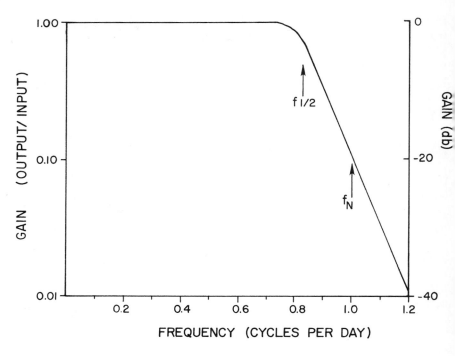

Figure 2. Gain characteristics of a 12th-order Butterworth filter with 3 db attenuation at 0.83 cpd and a 1.0 cpd cut-off frequency.

semi-diurnal period. Of course, if geologic time scales were considered, the sea
level variance associated with glacial and interglacial periodicities would be
dominant. However, on intermediate time scales, the seasonal variation of the
mean sea level (MSL) is the most noticeable feature.

Along with other locations in the temperate parts of the Northern hemisphere, North Inlet experiences a high MSL in October and low MSL in the
beginning of the year. The seasonal range in levels for South Carolina measures
26 cm and has been plotted for Charleston, S.C. over 26 years and compared to
the one-year record for North Inlet (Figure 3).

The annual cycle is due to a combination of effects. Steric sea level
variations associated with the annual temperature cycle appear to be the major
cause (Pattullo *et al.,* 1955). Annual fluctuations in the Gulf Stream strength or
location, probably due to changes in the atmospheric circulation, are another
likely source of MSL variation, whereas long-period astronomic tides have
negligible amplitudes (Pattullo *et al.,* 1955). It is surprising to find that the mean
atmospheric pressure at times correlates poorly with the mean sea level. From
hydrostatic considerations, the sea level is expected to be depressed 1 cm for
every 1 mb rise in atmospheric pressure. However, from Figure 4, it is seen that

the pressure variation is small compared to the sea level change (Figure 3). Also, the mean pressure and sea level at North Inlet both reach October highs, opposite to what is expected. On the other hand, the 10-year pressure record from Charleston indicates a better long-term agreement between low pressure and high sea level and v.v.

Effect of Annual Cycle

Whereas the annual sea level cycle probably has little direct effect on the estuarine circulation, it is likely to play a large role in the estuarine ecological cycles. *Spartina* marshes surround most of the U.S. east coast estuaries and are

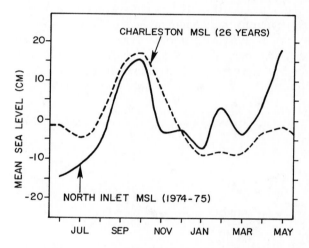

Figure 3. *Annual cycle of mean sea level for Charleston, S.C., for 26 years (from Pattullo et al., 1955) and for North Inlet, 1974-75. Monthly means, computed from hourly values, have been used to produce the plot.*

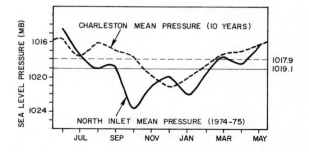

Figure 4. *Annual cycle of inverted mean atmospheric pressure for Charleston, S.C., 1951-60 (from U.S. Department of Commerce, 1965) and for North Inlet, 1974-75. Monthly means, computed from hourly values, have been used to produce the plot.*

inundated a larger percentage of the time when the MSL peaks. It is only when water covers the marsh surface that material exchanges between marsh and estuary are facilitated. This happens most frequently in October, when the North Inlet marsh is covered by water approximately 42% of the time as compared to a typical year low of 27% in January (Figure 5). Over the entire 1974–75 year the marsh was under water 30% of the time.

If the high autumn MSL is associated with at least some net water exchange between estuary and coastal ocean and flooding time of the marsh surface relates to dissolved and suspended constituent concentrations, it is likely that the annual MSL cycle is the mechanism controlling seasonal net material fluxes. The MSL cycle can be likened to circulation type 6 (storage) during summer and early autumn as MSL rises. Similarly, it is a low-frequency version of type 5 (discharge) during the late autumn and early winter as MSL decreases.

Fluxes of various classes of materials between estuaries and coastal waters have been poorly documented because of measurement difficulties. On the reasonable assumption that the marsh is maintaining its elevation relative to the yearly MSL, North Inlet experiences a net *inwelling* of materials, as long as the

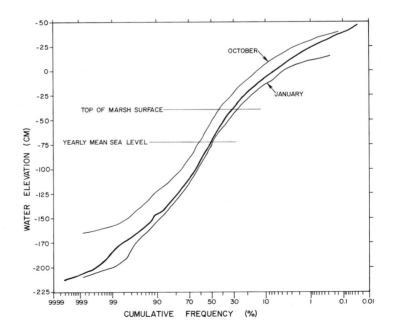

Figure 5.   *Cumulative frequency diagram showing percentage of time that the sea level in North Inlet exceeded a given elevation for the entire year (bold line) and for October and January separately. Yearly MSL was -72.5 cm (below a NOS benchmark) and corresponds to 0 cm in Figure 3. The hourly data were used to produce the plots.*

build-up of locally produced marsh material is less than the relative rise in MSL. This seems a reasonable assumption (data not yet available) in view of the rapid rise of MSL in South Carolina (Figure 6), on the average 0.361 cm y^{-1} in Charleston for more than half a century (Hicks and Crosby, 1974). Of course, whereas marsh building sediments may be accumulating in the system, other material classes may be *outwelled*, e.g., providing nutrients to the coastal ocean. This topic has recently been reviewed by Gardner and Kitchens (in press). The main point here is that low-frequency sea level fluctuations are important to the inwelling and outwelling of materials between estuaries and coastal ocean.

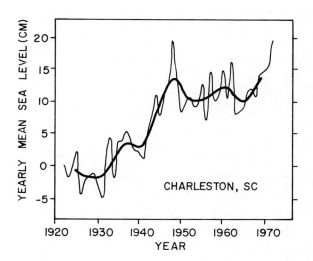

Figure 6. The change in the relative MSL in Charleston, S.C., 1922-72, (after Hicks and Crosby, 1974). The thin line represents the yearly means and the bold line the smoothed time series.

Sea Level and Atmospheric Pressure

Next, we will consider the possible effects of atmospheric pressure on sea level on a time scale greater than one day but less than the annual cycle. The sea level spectrum was computed on the filtered observed North Inlet data (Figure 7), the same data adjusted hydrostatically to a constant atmospheric pressure and then filtered (Figure 7), and on the filtered atmospheric pressure record (Figure 8).

The spectra of observed and hydrostatically adjusted sea level (Figure 7) show reasonable agreement for all frequencies. This indicates that hydrostatic sea level response to low-frequency atmospheric pressure fluctuations is only of minor importance, even though the sea level and atmospheric pressure are highly

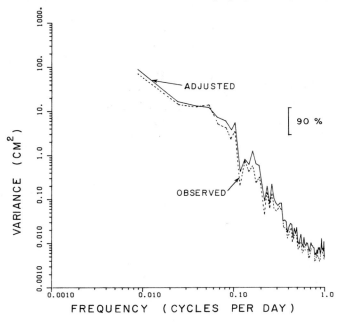

Figure 7.   *Variance spectrum of the low-pass filtered North Inlet sea level. The solid line is the barometrically adjusted spectrum, and the dotted line the measured sea level. Each spectral estimate has associated 10 degrees of freedom.*

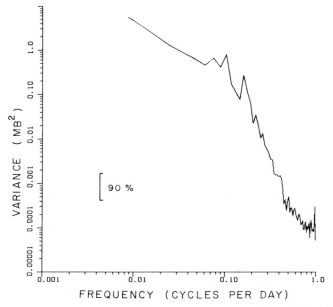

Figure 8.   *Variance spectrum of low-pass filtered North Inlet atmospheric pressure. Each spectral estimate has associated 10 degrees of freedom.*

coherent ($\gamma^2 = .9$) at 9.2 and 6.0 days, the two periods where the pressure spectrum (Figure 8) indicates signficant variance peaks. If pressure were the main excitation and this excitation were transmitted hydrostatically, the observed and hydrostatically adjusted sea level spectra would differ to a greater extent than indicated in Figure 7. The data show that only 25%–30% of the total sea level variance at these frequencies can be attributed to hydrostatic response of sea level to atmospheric pressure changes.

Because pressure and wind changes are highly interdependent, and because of possible non-hydrostatic sea level responses, it is difficult to separate pressure and wind stress effects; e.g., for the 9.2-day sea level peak, both atmospheric pressure and the along-shore wind stress have spectral peaks which are significantly coherent with the corresponding sea level variation. However, at 6.0 days, the wind stress has no spectral peak and the stress-sea level coherence is low. Thus, at this frequency, the atmospheric pressure is interpreted to be mainly responsible for the changing sea level, although primarily in a non-hydrostatic manner. The sine-wave height of the 6-day pressure wave is 1.5 mb, whereas the associated sea level has a sine-wave height of 3.2 cm, more than twice the expected value.

Because of the small size of North Inlet, it is not likely that the pressure effect is localized to the estuary. Rather, the coastal ocean responds to the pressure forcing that drives the 6-day sea level wave in or out of the estuary. Associated with this wave is a mass flux through the inlet mouth, pointing to the alternating storage (type 6) or discharge (type 5) of water in/from the system.

Lack of long-term inlet current data prevents us from testing the above hypothesis. However, numerous current measurements for several 2–5 tidal cycles over a 4-year period indicate that the net discharge through the inlet mouth may be either into or out of the estuary, consistent with the above hypothesis. Because of absence of much freshwater run-off, North Inlet typically has salinities from 30 to 34 ppt and lacks vertical salinity or velocity gradients. This in turn implies that circulation types 1, 2, 3, and 4 are unlikely events for North Inlet. However, Elliott's (1976) classification needs to be expanded to account for lateral circulation patterns, something shown to be a major factor in North Inlet (Kjerfve, in press).

Sea Level and Wind

Wind, local or synoptic, is the most probable mechanism for causing variability in the estuarine circulation structure and shifts from one circulation type to another. In the North Inlet case, because of the small scale of the narrowly winding marsh creeks, the synoptic wind-forcing of the coastal ocean is believed to have a much greater effect on sea level than the local wind stress. Variability in the estuarine sea level might therefore be interpreted to relate to the long CSW's, which are wind-forced and propagate southward (Brooks and Mooers, 1977). Here we will look for correlations between the estuarine sea level and wind, keeping in mind that the coastal ocean acts as an intermediary.

The hourly wind data for the 1974–75 year are shown as a frequency isopleth diagram (Figure 9). Winds from the southwest with speeds 3–4 ms^{-1} are by far most frequent. The strong winds from the southwest with speeds up to 25.2 ms^{-1} are associated with a series of frontal passages in March and April. The frequent winds (2–5 ms^{-1}) and peak winds (19 ms^{-1}) from the northwest, on the other hand, occurred during the late fall. Coastal sea breezes, with expected speeds from the east and southeast are surprisingly infrequent as judged from this data set. The vector stick diagram (Figure 10) breaks the data down into time increments, showing the resultant monthly wind vectors.

Rather than correlating sea level and wind speed, it seemed more appropriate to select the wind stress vector as the critical wind parameter because of its role in the equation of motion. We computed the mean and variance of the wind stress parallel to the coast, then along an axis at a 10° angle to the coast, then at a 20° angle, and so on for all directions in 10° increments. Obviously, the different estimates are not independent except for the decomposed stresses for any pair of orthogonal axes. The yearly resultant wind stress measured 0.10 dyne cm^{-2} and came from 220°. Variance, however, was maximized parallel to the coast along a compass direction 10°—190°, 0.083 dyne^2 cm^{-4}. Thus the least amount of stress variance was found normal to the coast and measured 0.021 dyne^2 cm^{-4}.

Variance spectra for the stress components parallel and normal to the coast (Figure 11) reveal numerous peaks. In general, the barometrically adjusted sea level and the two stress components are highly coherent. This indicates that the sea level does respond to both the along-the-shelf and cross-shelf wind forcing, a fact noted by Brooks and Mooers (1977) and Smith (1977). Because the total variance is much larger for the parallel stress component, the adjusted sea level response to this stress component is dominant.

The stress normal to the coast has four variance humps, with periods of 6.6, 4.2, 3.0, and 2.2 days. The coherence-squared values between the normal stress and the sea level are approximately .8 for each peak, but only at 4.2 days does the sea level respond. However, the response is weak as indicated by a corresponding insignificant sea level variance.

Figure 9.   *Frequency isopleth diagram (modified from Seppälä, 1977) of the hourly North Inlet wind data, showing percent frequency of the wind blowing from a given direction at a given speed. The data points were grouped into sectors 15° wide by 1 ms^{-1}, with the exception of the central area which corresponds to wind speeds less than 0.5 ms^{-1}, including all directions. It should be noted that the data sectors are smaller toward the center; thus it is important to consider data density rather than area on the diagram. The density is expressed as the average number of hourly observations per year for each 1° by 1 ms^{-1} sector. The frequency is expressed as the percentage of all observations corresponding to each density shading.*

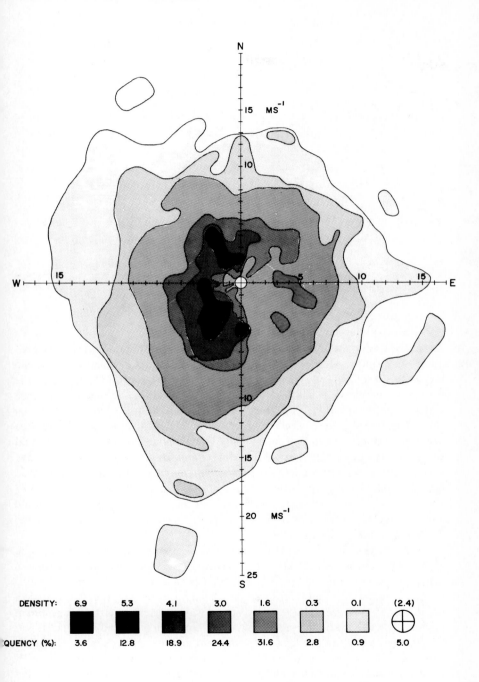

RESULTANT WIND VECTORS

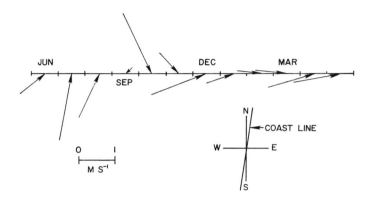

*Figure 10.   Vector stick diagram, indicating the resultant wind speed and direc-
tion for each month. The hourly North Inlet wind data were used to
produce the diagram.*

The along-shore wind stress spectrum (Figure 11) contains several variance peaks; those with periods of 19.3, 9.2, 6.6, 4.8, 3.7, and 2.9 days are
significant, or at least marginally significant. If a wave-form is assymetrical, the
fitting of sine-waves in the FFT procedure may result in a series of difference
waves with periods of 1/2, 1/3, 1/4, 1/6, and so on, of the period of the original
wave-form. This phenomenon is well known in tidal analysis and is referred to as
over-tides (Doodson and Warburg, 1941). Some of the above stress peaks could
be due to over-tides. However, this is not the case as only the 19.3 and 3.7-day
waves are maximized parallel to the coast. The maximum variances for the 9.2,
6.6, 4.8, and 2.9-day waves occur along different axes, the 20–200°, 50–230°,
170–250°, and 160–340° axes, respectively. If they were over-tides, they would
have to reach their maximum values along the same compass direction as the
fundamental period, in this case 19.3 days.

The adjusted sea level and along-shore stress are .95 and .92 coherent at
19.3 and 9.2 days, respectively. Although the 19.3-day sea level fluctuation was
identified as the dominant far-field effect in Chesapeake Bay (Wang and Elliott,
in press), in the adjusted North Inlet sea level spectrum (Figure 7) it is only a
broad ridge. However, the 9.2-day stress wave corresponds to a significant
pressure wave, has a highly significant cross-correlation with adjusted sea level,
shows up as a peak in the sea level spectrum, and has an associated sine-wave
height of 6.4 cm. As a rule, the sea level rises with NNE and falls with SSW
winds. On the average, the along-shore stress leads sea level by 3 h at this
frequency and is probably due to wind-forced continental shelf waves and

associated upwelling/downwelling. The higher frequency peaks are less coherent and contain much less variance.

In the absence of long-term current records, it is not possible to discuss the specific effects of these wind-forced sea level changes on the variability of the estuarine circulation. However, the 9.2-day sea level wave is quite energetic, has associated exchange of water between estuary and coastal ocean, and should be accounted for in hydrographic field studies.

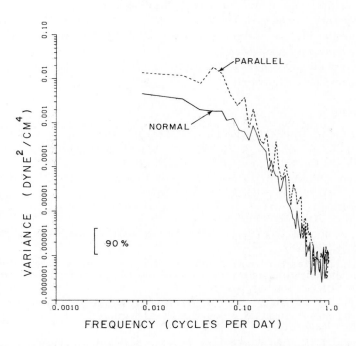

Figure 11. Variance spectra of the low-pass filtered North Inlet wind stress parallel and normal to the coast. Each spectral estimate has associated 10 degrees of freedom.

Conclusions

Year-long time series of sea level, atmospheric pressure, and wind in the North Inlet, S.C. estuary indicate that the estuarine sea level responds to forcing from the coastal ocean. In particular, a 3.2 cm high sea level wave at 6.0 days is highly correlated with changes in atmospheric pressure, and a 6.4 cm high sea level wave at 9.2 days is attributed to CSW's driven by the along-shore wind stress. These sea level changes may in turn relate to the variability in the estuarine circulation as described by Elliott (1976). Future studies of estuarine circulation, material fluxes, residence times, and dynamics certainly need to focus on the low-frequency variability of estuarine conditions.

Acknowledgments

Many people have helped in various phases of this work. M. S. Ivester and W. B. Sikora helped with field installations. M. L. Sloan and L. L. Vansant digitized and edited the data. S. J. Crabtree, E. K. Ritchie, and S. W. Stewart helped to reduce and analyze the data. L. Kjerfve helped with the drafting.

The work was supported by EPA Grant No. R-802928-01-0 from the U.S. Environmental Protection Agency and No. DEB76-83010 from the National Science Foundation, Ecosystems.

Contribution No. 209 from the Belle W. Baruch Institute for Marine Biology and Coastal Research.

References

1.   Ackroyd, M. H. 1973. Digital filters. Butterworth and Co., London. 82 pp.

2.   Brooks, D. A., and C. N. K. Mooers. 1977. Wind-forced continental shelf waves in the Florida Current. J. Geophy. Res. 82:2569-2576.

3.   Cameron, W. M., and D. W. Pritchard. 1963. Estuaries, pp. 306-324. *In* M. N. Hill (ed.), The Sea, Vol. 2.Interscience Publishers.

4.   Doodson, A. T., and H. D. Warburg, 1941. Admiralty manual of tides. Her Majesty's Stationary Office. London. 270 pp.

5.   Dyer, K. R. 1974. The salt balance in stratified estuaries. Estuarine Coastal Marine Science 2:273-281.

6.   _____ . In press. Lateral circulation effects in estuaries. *In* C. B. Officer (ed.), Estuaries, geophysics and the environment—overview, summary and recommendations. National Academy of Sciences.

7.   Elliott, A. J. 1976. A study of the effect of meteorological forcing on the circulation in the Potomac estuary. Special report 56. Chesapeake Bay Institute. The Johns Hopkins University.

8.   Gardner, L. R., and W. Kitchens. In press. Sediment and chemical exchanges between salt marshes and coastal waters. *In* B. Kjerfve (ed.), Estuarine transport processes. Seventh Belle W. Baruch Institute for Marine Biology and Coastal Research Symposium on "Transport processes in estuarine environment." 19-22 May 1976, Georgetown, S.C. Univ. of South Carolina Press.

9.   Garvine, R. W. 1974. Physical features of the Connecticut River outflow during high discharge. J. Geophys. Res. 79:831-846.

10. _____ . 1975. The distribution of salinity and temperature in the Connecticut River estuary. J. Geophys. Res. 80:1176-1184.

11. Hicks, S. D., and J. E. Crosby. 1974. Trends and variability of yearly mean sea level, 1893-1972. NOAA Technical Memorandum, NOS, 13 COM-74-11012, Rockville, Md. 16 pp.

12. Kjerfve, B. In press. Bathymetry as an indicator of net circulation in well-mixed estuaries. Limnol. Oceanogr.

13. Mysak, L. A., and B. V. Hamon. 1969. Low-frequency sea level waves off North Carolina. J. Geophys. Res. 74:1397-1405.

14. Pattullo, J., W. Munk, R. Revelle, and E. Strong. 1955. The seasonal oscillations in sea level. J. Mar. Res. 14:88-156.

15. Pritchard, D. W. 1952. Salinity distribution and circulation in the Chesapeake Bay estuarine system. J. Mar. Res. 11:106-123.

16. _____. 1954. A study of the salt balance in a coastal plain estuary. J. Mar. Res. 13:133-144.

17. _____. 1956. The dynamic structure of a coastal plain estuary. J. Mar. Res. 15:33-42.

18. _____. In press. What have recent observations for adjustment and verification of numerical models revealed about the dynamics and kinematics of estuaries? *In* B. Kjerfve (ed.), Estuarine transport processes. Seventh Belle W. Baruch Institute for Marine Biology and Coastal Research Symposium on "Transport processes in estuarine environments." 19-22 May 1976, Georgetown, S.C. Univ. of South Carolina Press.

19. Rayner, J. N. 1971. An introduction to spectral analysis. Pion Limited. London. 174 pp.

20. Seppälä, M. 1977. Frequency isopleth diagram to illustrate wind observations. Weather 32:171-175.

21. Smith, N. P. 1977. Near-bottom cross-shelf currents in the Northwestern Gulf of Mexico: a response to wind. J. Phys. Oceanogr. 7:615-620.

22. U.S. Department of Commerce. 1965. World weather records, 1951-60, vol. 1. North America. Washington, D.C. 535 pp.

23. Wang, D. -P., and A. J. Elliott. In press. Non-tidal variability in the Chesapeake Bay and Potomac River: evidence for non-local forcing. J. Phys. Oceanogr.

24. Weisberg, R. H. 1976a. The nontidal flow in the Providence River of Narragansett Bay: a stochastic approach to estuarine circulation. J. Phys. Oceanogr. 6:721-734.

25. _____. 1976b. A note on estuarine mean flow estimation. J. Mar. Res. 34:387-394.

26. Wu, J. 1969. Wind stress and surface roughness at air-sea interface. J. Geophys. Res. 74:444-455.

PHYSICAL TRANSFER PROCESSES BETWEEN
GEORGIA TIDAL INLETS AND NEARSHORE WATERS

J. O. Blanton and L. P. Atkinson

Skidaway Institute of Oceanography
P.O. Box 13687
Savannah, Georgia

Abstract: Nearshore continental shelf waters are directly influenced by the many tidal inlets which are spaced 10 to 20 km apart along the Georgia coast. Despite the highly variable and complex nature of the flow near inlets, there are recurring hydrographic features that typify the nearshore region.

An innermost zone, adjacent to inlet mouths, contains highly turbid waters ejected from the inlets and marshes along the sounds. Fresher waters override more saline waters in a more or less classic riverine plume, inside of which the water motion is nearly independent of the motion in the surrounding water.

Seaward of the zone containing the inlet plumes, a complex array of salinity and turbidity fronts is found that is probably a relict from preceding tidal cycles. The zone extends offshore 10 to 20 km and is defined here as the nearshore zone. In this zone, the fresher and more turbid waters are mixed horizontally and vertically with continental shelf water, resulting in a hydrographic structure similar to a partially mixed estuary.

Material from the many inlets enters the nearshore zone where the vertical and horizontal gradients inhibit the exchange in the onshore direction unless tidal and wind-generated currents induce transfer processes that overcome this inhibition. These transfer processes are investigated with a limited amount of time-series data at one point. It is shown that onshore salt fluxes have strong tidal components and are influenced by vertical shear accompanying the presence of vertically stratified water. While these transfer processes occur regularly over each tidal cycle, more efficient and dramatic exchange processes may be associated with the changes in alongshore current direction.

Introduction

The Georgia coast and the southern portion of the South Carolina coast consist of large expanses of salt marsh and regularly spaced (10–20 km) tidal inlets connecting the marshes to the sea. The marshes are a major source and sink of inorganic and organic material; thus the tidal inlets are the route through which the transfer of material must occur. The flow between marsh and ocean is heavily modulated by the semi-diurnal tide which reaches a range of 2–3 m. The maximum tidal range for the southeastern U.S. coast occurs in the region of the Savannah River.

Runoff into the coastal water is bimodal with a major peak in spring and a minor peak in late summer. The area receives runoff from many sources, but the Pee Dee, Cooper/Santee, Savannah and Altamaha Rivers provide over 80 percent of the total flow. The input of freshwater to the open shelf resembles a line source rather than a few point sources, since many smaller rivers also contribute to the flow. Rapid mixing due to the strong tides obscures the evidence of individual river plumes after one tidal cycle. Most of the freshwater on the open shelf is confined to depths less than 20 m. Monthly runoff between Cape Romain, South Carolina, and Fernandina Beach, Florida, varies between 1 and 5 km³/month (Atkinson, Blanton, and Haines, 1977).

The freshwater runoff onto the shelf acting in conjunction with the tides appears to be an important consideration in determining the dynamics of nearshore water motion and the consequent dispersion of water-borne materials. This paper reports the findings of a study to determine the physical processes that control the transfer of this material.

Nearshore Waters as an Estuary

Large tidal fluxes and freshwater runoff from the Georgia coast result in salinity regimes out to 10 or 20 km that are similar to those typified by a partially mixed estuary (Figure 1). The fresher waters in both regimes overrun the more saline oceanic water. A major difference is that the mixing of zero salinity (fresh) water takes place inside most estuaries, while zero salinity water is almost never found on continental shelves because it has been mixed with more saline water inside sounds and estuaries. Nevertheless, it seems appropriate to seek analogies between the mixing processes occurring within estuaries and those occurring in the nearshore waters of continental shelves that are characterized by frequent inputs of freshwater along their length.

Entrainment and diffusion act together to mix the open shelf waters with the fresher waters ejected from the tidal inlets. Entrainment occurs when one of the two adjacent water masses contains more turbulent energy than the other. The more turbulent water mass draws parcels of the less turbulent one into it, thereby increasing its volume. It is a one-way process. The erosion of thermoclines by wind mixing is a common example. The rate of entrainment increases as the velocity difference between the two water masses increases. Diffusion, on the other hand, is a two-way process in that equal volumes of water are exchanged between two adjacent water masses. The two processes are conceptually different but net effects are similar in so far as the transfer of salt is concerned. If tidal energy and wind stirring are greater in the shallower waters, these may entrain water and salt upward at the expense of the denser, more saline water below. On the other hand, there is no *a priori* reason to suppose that the overall energy levels between the nearshore water ejected from the inlets and the more

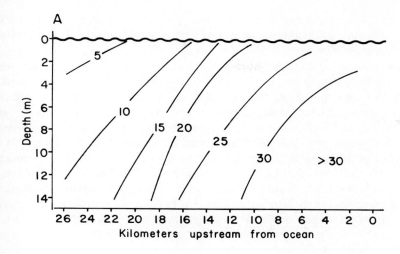

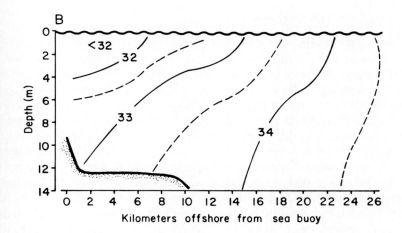

Figure 1. Vertical distributions of salinity ($^o/oo$), illustrating similarities of near-shore zone off Georgia with a partially mixed estuary. (A) Columbia River, Oregon, 10 September 1957 (from Burt and McAlister, 1959); (B) Wassaw Sound, Georgia, 15 October, 1976.

saline waters of the continental shelf are different. The two-way exchange of water parcels does not alter the relative volumes, but the salt content of the upper layer is increased at the expense of that of the lower layer.

As in estuaries, we assume that two important parameters affecting the transfer processes between the estuaries and the continental shelf are freshwater discharge along the coast and the dissipation of tidal energy. Wind stress is also likely to be important due to the fact that upwelling-downwelling cycles are thought to cause large mass exchanges between the nearshore waters and those farther offshore (Csanady, 1974).

In spite of all the complexities of the different inlet configurations, the hydrographic regimes show certain recurring features. Nearest the inlet mouths, highly turbid water is ejected during ebb flow and the well-defined turbidity plume is separated from surrounding water by strong vertical density gradients. Observations of floating debris confirm the presence of a strong convergence zone between the ebbing turbidity plume and the adjacent less turbid water. We suspect that the dynamics of water motion there are very similar to those observed in the Connecticut River plume (Garvine, 1977). Garvine's observations showed that (1) the motion of water inside the plume is essentially independent of the motion of the surrounding water; (2) the density structure and areal size of the plume at any particular time are controlled by the volume of freshwater discharged through the mouth during a particular half cycle of the tide (Garvine, 1974); and (3) that local wind stress has little bearing on water motion inside the plume.

Definition of nearshore zone

Beyond the tidal plume, aerial observations and satellite photos frequently show weaker turbidity fronts apparently left over from previous tidal cycles. Vertical density gradients may still be present, but a varying rate of vertical mixing with distance offshore creates horizontal density gradients to produce the salinity distribution shown in Figure 1B. This zone extends over distances as great as 20 km from the inlet mouth and is no longer influenced by single inlet plumes, but is generally a reflection of the discharge from several adjacent inlets. For example, turbidity plumes 5 or 10 km off Wassaw and Ossabaw Inlets are likely to contain material from the Savannah River as well as the closer Ogeechee River. The mixing of these river plumes must be influenced not only by tidal currents but by local wind stress that generates alongshore currents. We will concentrate our attention on this zone, hereafter called the nearshore zone, defined as the zone in which freshwater influence can be distinguished from open shelf conditions. Our analogy to estuaries is applied here.

Beyond 10 or 20 km from shore, no evidence of the fresher and turbid water is found. Most commonly, this water mass is well mixed vertically, but conditions that cause outer shelf water to intrude onshore along the bottom can vertically stratify this water (Blanton, 1971) making definition of a nearshore zone, as we define it, difficult.

Hydrographic Features of Nearshore Waters

We have conducted several hydrographic surveys of nearshore water structure off the Georgia coast during times of differing amounts of freshwater input. We report three such surveys during 15 October, 18 November 1976, and

21 April 1977 (Figure 2). The survey of 18 November included an anchor station off one of the inlets. Profiles of salinity and water velocity were measured hourly at the anchor station for one tidal cycle.

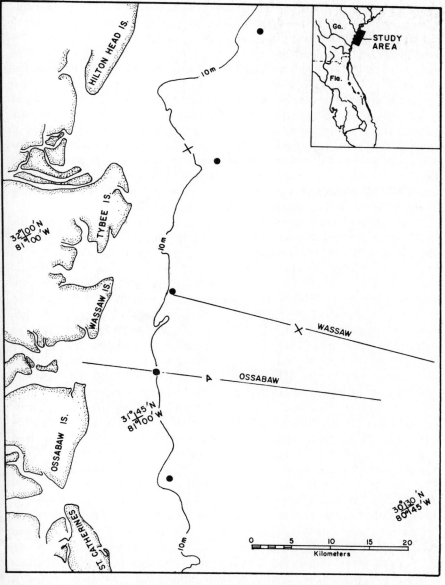

Figure 2.   Location of hydrographic sections off the Georgia coast. (●) denotes location of sea buoys at the termination of the inlet deltas from which offshore distances are measured. (A) denotes position of anchor station.

Discussion of data

A Plessey 9400 CTD system was used to obtain the salinity, temperature, and depth profile. The data are logged analog on a Hewlett-Packard XYY recorder and digitally on a Kennedy Incremental tape recorder. The digital data, the primary data source, is computer-processed, using a scheme similar to that of Scarlet (1975). The accuracy of salinity measurements is $\pm$ .03 ^{o}/oo except at depths of strong thermoclines, where the accuracy decreases. Temperature is accurate to $\pm$ .02° C. The depth accuracy is better than 1 m depending upon the ship's roll.

A profile of current velocity was obtained on 18 November 1976 (Figure 2) by hand-lowering a Bendix Model Q-15 ducted current meter. The cable was marked off in 1 m increments, and speed and direction were read at each meter of water depth. The average speed and direction were estimated at each meter from data recorded on a Rustrak Recorder for a period of 2 minutes. The manufacturer specifies accuracies in speed and direction of $\pm$ 5 cm/s and $\pm$ 10° for an individual reading. The 2-minute averages at each 1 m depth interval were recorded each hour for a period of 13 hours ($\sim$ 1 tidal cycle).

The October and November surveys (Figure 3) were conducted during low runoff conditions. The discharge from the Savannah River for the two surveys was 365 and 250 m^3/s respectively (Table 1). It is clear that fresher waters originating in the inlets and estuaries override the more saline continental shelf water. The nearshore zone contains vertical and horizontal salinity (density) gradients and is about 25 km wide in the October survey and about 10 km wide in the November survey (Table 1). Data from aerial surveys in November and data on suspended sediments show that surface water within the nearshore zone is highly turbid with a multiplicity of surface fronts. Not shown in Figures 3A and 3B is the highly stratified and turbid local inlet plume that was present inside the inlet mouth. Had the tide been ebbing at the time of observations, we would expect the plume to be visible near the surface between 0 and 5 km offshore.

About 6 km offshore of Ossabaw Sound (Figure 3B), we measured temperature, salinity and velocity profiles each hour for one tidal cycle. We were able to observe the tidal oscillation of the boundary between vertically mixed shelf water and the more turbid and stratified water inside 10 km. These measurements, together with the section data (Figure 3B), yielded an estimate of 8 $\pm$ 3 km for the distance offshore to the shelf water (Table 1).

The anchor station data were obtained at a position where we observed the passage of the front that separated shelf water from the fresher nearshore water (Figure 4). The profiles were begun on a rising tide. The water column was weakly stratified initially but became essentially isohaline after mid-tide on the flood cycle. At mid-tide on the ebb cycle, the water column became stratified. Concurrent velocity measurements indicated onshore flow up to an hour or so of high tide, after which flow became offshore. The alongshore component flowed mostly southwestward during the flood cycle. During ebb flow, near surface

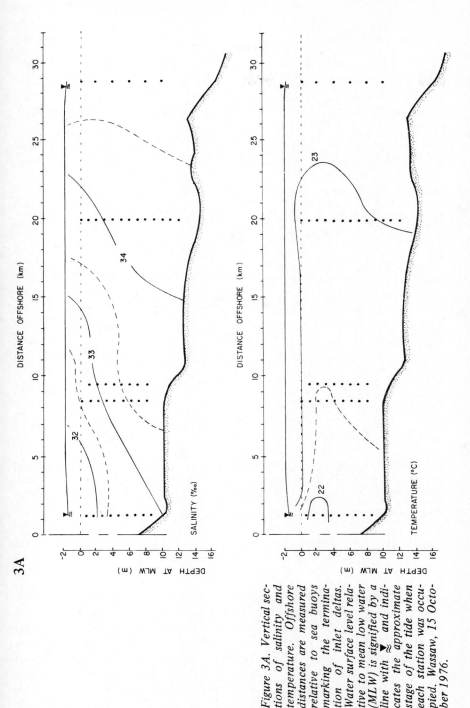

3A

DISTANCE OFFSHORE (km)

SALINITY (‰)

DISTANCE OFFSHORE (km)

TEMPERATURE (°C)

Figure 3A. Vertical sections of salinity and temperature. Offshore distances are measured relative to sea buoys marking the termination of inlet deltas. Water surface level relative to mean low water (MLW) is signified by a line with ≋ and indicates the approximate stage of the tide when each station was occupied. Wassaw, 15 October 1976.

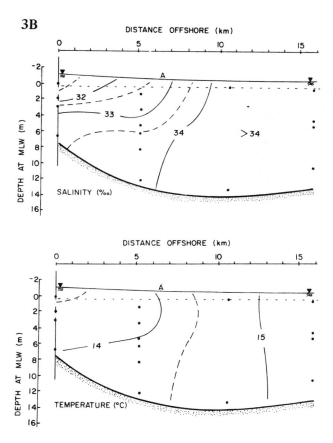

Figure 3B. Vertical sections of salinity and temperature. Offshore distances are measured relative to sea buoys marking the termination of inlet deltas. Water surface level relative to mean low water (MLW) is signified by a line with ≋ and indicates the approximate stage of the tide when each station was occupied. Ossabaw, 18 November 1976; "A" denotes position of anchor station.

alongshore currents ran northeastward until about two hours before low tide. The near bottom alongshore current oscillated slowly. Only the onshore-offshore component had an obvious correlation with the tide. The vertical shear in the onshore-offshore flow (indicated here by the difference between the 1 and 3 m average and the 8 and 10 m average) increased significantly after the salinity front passed the anchor station at about 0730 (EST). Also noteworthy is that the salt carried past the station was clearly asymmetrical over the tidal cycle, i.e., the flooding tide carried more salt than the ebbing tide. This would imply that the tidal oscillations may partially balance the salt advected out of the sounds by the salt-enriched estuarine discharge.

Wind stress during the October survey had a weak alongshore component northeastward with an even weaker offshore component (Table 1). During the November survey, wind stress was stronger by a factor of 2; the alongshore component was southwestward with an offshore component.

The April survey (Figure 3C and Table 1) shows a somewhat different picture. First, this section was begun on a falling tide and the inlet plume can be clearly seen as a zone with a salinity less than 30 $^o/oo$ and confined within 5 km of the inlet mouth. Secondly, the surface salinity was less than 31 $^o/oo$ out to as far as 30 km, where the survey was stopped. In contrast, the nearshore water out to "shelf water" was everywhere above 31.5 $^o/oo$ (Table 1) for the two autumn surveys. Thus, no nearshore zone bounded by well-mixed shelf water was observed in the April data. This is partially explained by the increased freshwater runoff (870 m^3/s, Savannah River) during the month of April. Moveover, a section, made two days earlier out to the Gulf Stream, revealed that diluted Gulf Stream water had intruded along the bottom across the entire width of the shelf. Strong solar insolation coupled with almost negligible winds 8 days prior to the cruise may also have created a thermocline which would confine the fresher water above it. All these factors—heavy runoff, intrusions from the outer shelf along the bottom, and strong solar heating—may have caused the high vertical density gradient observed in April inside the nearshore zone.

Discussion

Transfer Processes

Transfer processes that occur between shorelines or inlets and the open shelf must occur in the presence of tides, wind-driven currents and buoyancy forces that are induced by temperature and salinity gradients. The stresses induced by large tides along the Georgia coast are laterally variable. The magnitude of tidal currents is greatest off inlet mouths, where the tidal jets occur. Therefore, lateral maxima in onshore/offshore tidal currents occur at a spatial frequency equal to that of the inlets. The lateral shear, produced from tidal jet to tidal jet along the coast, must play a large, but as yet undetermined, role in balancing the salt transferred slowly outward by the freshwater flow. This conclusion is extrapolated from experimental results in estuaries (Fisher, 1972; Dyer, 1974; Murray and Siripong, 1977). Vertical shear in the shelf currents, in the presence of vertical salinity gradients, also must play a role, a hypothesis also extrapolated from experimental studies in estuaries (Bowden, 1963).

Wind-driven currents as a cause of salt flux are usually neglected in studies of estuaries, but should not be ignored in nearshore studies. Shelf currents in the proximity of tidal inlets have strong tidal components in directions perpendicular to shore, but alongshore currents clearly have energy at other frequencies (Figure 4). Thus the average salinity measured at a point offshore over several tidal

Table 1. Environmental data pertaining to hydrographic sections shown in Figure 3.

	Date		
	10/15/76 *Wassaw*	*11/18/76* *Ossabaw*	*4/21/77* *Ossabaw*
Nearshore Frontal Characteristics			
Salinity range, nearshore water (‰)	31.5-33.5	31.5-33.5	29.0-31.0
Salinity range, shelf water (‰)	34.5	34.2	33.0-35.0
Distance to shelf water (km)	25	8 ± 3	>30?
Max. observed vertical density gradient			
(kg/m^4)	0.40	0.90	3.9
Tidal Data			
Range (m)	1.8	2.4	1.9
Days before/after spring/neap	N+1	S-3	S+3
Wind Stress (previous 24-hour mean)			
Alongshore component (dynes/cm^2)	+0.05	−0.12	+0.20
Onshore component (dynes/cm^2)	−0.03	−0.08	+0.20
Savannah River Discharge (Clyo) (m^3/s)	365	250	870

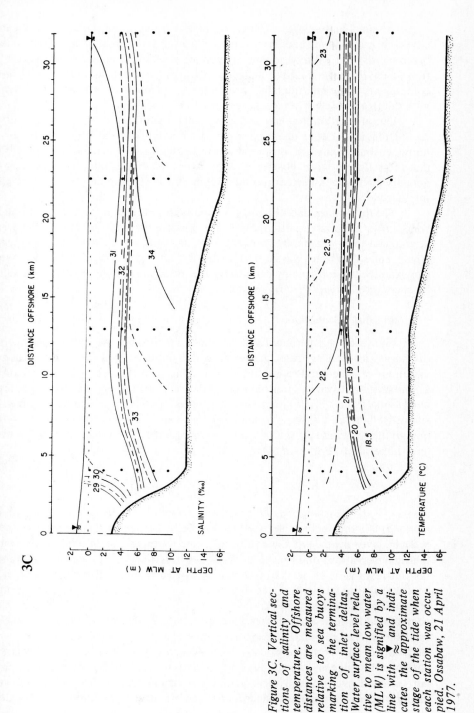

3C

SALINITY (‰)

TEMPERATURE (°C)

Figure 3C. Vertical sections of salinity and temperature. Offshore distances are measured relative to sea buoys marking the termination of inlet deltas. Water surface level relative to mean low water (MLW) is signified by a line with ▶ and indicates the approximate stage of the tide when each station was occupied. Ossabaw, 21 April 1977.

cycles is not likely to be constant, because varying alongshore currents can advect mixtures of salt and river water originating at different river locations. In other words, the salinity regime immediately offshore contains mixtures of freshwater from the nearby inlet *plus* mixtures from adjacent inlets, and the components of the mixture must surely vary with alongshore currents as well as with the rate of freshwater discharge.

Our anchor station data seems to contain evidence of this. The salinity regime (Figure 4) after one tidal cycle never returned to the almost vertically homogeneous conditions observed at the beginning. We can only conjecture that the salinity regime observed there toward the end of the series had components that were advected into the region by the alongshore current from an inlet farther south.

The time-series data (Figure 4) contain information on the transfer of salt, hence other materials, particularly in the onshore/offshore direction. There is strong tidal energy in this component as well as strong vertical shear induced by a frontal zone. The water was vertically stratified after the passage of the front. We can examine these fluxes by calculating the measurable components of the salt balance for onshore/offshore transfer.

Salt flux calculations

Fluxes of salt perpendicular to shore result from the mean freshwater discharge, as well as from mixing processes induced by lateral and vertical variations of speed and salt. Moreover, the fact that tidal currents are usually asymmetric (not strictly sinusoidal) near the coast also causes net salt transport over a tidal cycle. We will examine the fluxes resulting from conditions measured offshore at Ossabaw Sound. We must neglect lateral variations even though the frequent spacing of tidal inlets along the Georgia coast may dictate their importance. Following Dyer (1973),

$$\overline{Q} \;=\; \overline{h u s} \;+\; \overline{h U S} \;+\; \overline{h <u_1 s_1>} \;+\; \overline{h <u's'>}$$

where $\overline{Q}$ is the transport of salt through a unit width of a section oriented parallel to shore, h is the depth of the section, brackets $<>$ denote the averages of the products over depth, and the overbars denote averages over a tidal cycle. Our hourly observations of u (onshore speed) and s (salinity) are assumed to contain hourly means u_0 and s_0 so that, instantaneously, each observation can be written, $u = u_0 + u'$ and $s = s_0 + s'$, where primed quantities are the irregular turbulent fluctuations. Our observations do not measure these; therefore, $h <u's'>$ is neglected as in most other studies. In reality, they are concealed within the other three terms. The remainder of the derivation is explained by Dyer (1973).

Observations were taken at 1 m intervals to a depth of 12 m, which was at bottom at low tide and 2 m above bottom at high tide. This depth variation was not included even though the equation above includes it. We considered it negligible in view of other uncertainties. Subsequent calculations were made

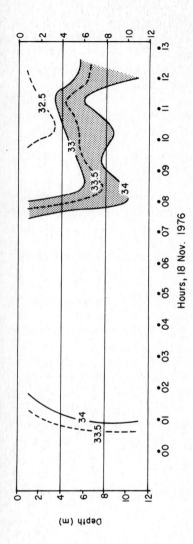

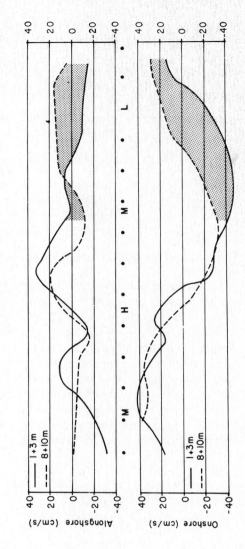

Figure 4. Time series of salinity and currents at an anchor station 6.1 km offshore of Ossabaw, 18 November 1976. Stippled zone marks the onset and configuration of the maximum salinity (and density) gradient. Note that maximum vertical shear in onshore currents occurs at this time. For simplicity, 1 and 3 m currents were averaged for near surface currents and 8 and 10 m currents were averaged for near bottom currents. H, M, and L denote the times of high, middle, and low water, respectively.

527

from pairs of u and s for each meter interval down to 12 m and each hour for 12 hours (tidal cycle = 12.48 hrs). The anchored ship severely influenced the velocity data in the first 2 m, and we chose to substitute the velocity observations at 3 m for the 1 and 2 m observations. With the fourth term neglected in the equation for $\bar{Q}$, the other three terms represent (see Dyer, 1973):

$\overline{\bar{h}\bar{u}\bar{s}}$ = the salt flux resulting from the mean flow presumably resulting from the offshore transport of freshwater;

$\overline{hUS}$ = the tidal variations in the means over depth of u and s;

$\overline{h <u_1\ s_1>}$ = the variation over depth of u and s; this is the gravitational circulation resulting from correlations of offshore flow and low salinity in upper layers and onshore flow and high salinity in lower layers.

The results of our calculations of the above three terms are presented in Figure 5 and Table 2.

The mean flow (averaged vertically and over the tidal cycle) is onshore at 0.6 cm/s and is presumed to represent a net onshore component induced by strong northwesterly winds which began during the previous day. The mean salinity ($\bar{s}$) is 33.9 $^0/_{00}$ and $\overline{\bar{u}\bar{s}}$ = 19.0 $^0/_{00}$ · cm·s^{-1} directed onshore. The cross-product, US, (Figure 5B) over the tidal cycle is onshore over most of the tidal cycle. S is above the average for more than half of the cycle. If the tide had been a pure standing wave and if S had been 90° out of phase with U (maximum S at flood slack and minimum S at ebb slack), the $\overline{US}$ correlation would be zero. Finally, $<u_1s_1>$ is always directed onshore and clearly contributes to the flux only when the salinity front passes the anchor station (Figure 4 compared with Figure 5B). In summary, we have

$$\overline{\bar{u}\bar{s}} = +19.0\ ^0/_{00}\cdot\mathrm{cm\cdot s^{-1}}\ \text{(onshore)}$$

$$\overline{US} = +5.3\ ^0/_{00}\cdot\mathrm{cm\cdot}\ ^{-1}\ \text{(onshore)}$$

$$\overline{<u_1s_1>} = +3.8\ ^0/_{00}\cdot\mathrm{cm\cdot s^{-1}}\ \text{(onshore)}$$

These results, taken at face value and assuming that $\bar{Q}$ = O (steady state), imply that a contribution of $-28.1\ ^0/_{00}\cdot$cm·s^{-1} must be directed offshore to balance our estimate of salt transported onshore. This could easily be supplied by contributions due to lateral variations in u and s, not measured by our study. The main portion of the tidal delta associated with the inlet between Ossabaw and Wassaw Islands was located several km southward. There the net onshore current could have been negative (offshore) because the freshwater discharge from the nearby sound could have been carried offshore through the main channel cutting through the delta. Very likely the steady state assumption is unjustified over one tidal cycle. During the experiment reported here, the overall transport at our anchor station was onshore. Thus an alternative interpretation

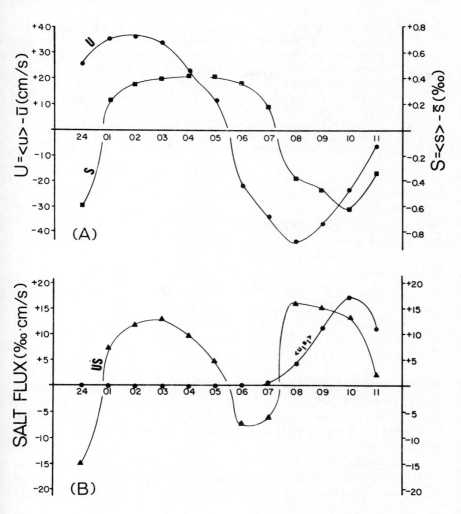

Figure 5. Variation over a tidal cycle (18 November 1976) of components of the salt flux, Q/h. Computations were based on data in Figure 4. Symbols are defined in the text.

would be that the nearshore zone during 18 November 1976 was storing water. This would result in a net buildup of sea level in response to the northwesterly to northerly winds blowing during 17–18 November.

Regardless of these interpretations, the calculations illustrate the importance of the tidal currents and the currents induced by the stratified waters

Table 2. Salt flux (Q/h) terms in (‰·cm·s⁻¹) for the onshore (u) and alongshore (v) flow off Ossabaw Sound, 18 November 1976. Flux values are positive toward shore in the onshore case, and positive northeastward in the alongshore case. The left-hand side of the flux equation (on page 526) is given at the bottom for comparison with the sum of the calculated terms. The vertical averages over the tidal cycle were $\bar{s}$ = 33.9‰, $\bar{u}$ = + 0.6 cm/s and $\bar{v}$ = 2.0 cm/s.

	Onshore	*Alongshore*
Mean flux ($\bar{u}\bar{s}$)	+19.0	+66.1
Tidal flux ($\overline{US}$)	+ 5.3	+ 1.5
Vertical shear flux ($<\overline{u_1 s_1}>$)	+ 3.8	+ 0.8
Sum of above terms	+28.1	+68.4
Total flux ($\overline{us}$)	+28.4	+68.5

nearshore in transporting salt shoreward. They play an important role in balancing the salt-enriched estuarine discharge occurring along the coast. Short-period turbulence occurring over an hour could contribute to the salt transport, but this is probably small compared to fluctuations of u and s over the tidal cycle and over depth.

Many uncertainties exist in our knowledge of the alongshore variations of u and s and whether a steady state in Q is ever justified. The values calculated here do not seem unrealistic in view of the high variability observed in estuaries between the relative contributions of the various terms in the salt balance (Dyer, 1973).

It is interesting to compare the flux calculations above with those for the alongshore component of flow (Table 2). Alongshore flux is primarily carried with the mean flow (northeast during 18 November). Tidal current fluctuations and those due to vertical shear account for only 3% of the total flux measured. The onshore fluxes account for more than 30%. We speculate that transfer of material alongshore is dominated by the mean alongshore flow, with tidal fluctuations and vertical shear playing a minor, perhaps negligible, role. By contrast, the dispersion or transfer of material across the nearshore zone is likely to result from competition between mean freshwater discharge, tidally induced fluxes, fluxes due to the gravitational circulation, and undoubtedly fluxes due to alongshore variations. The latter was neglected in this study.

Conclusions

We have dealt briefly with physical processes that transfer material across the nearshore zone bounded by tidal inlets and the open continental shelf, where hydrographic evidence of direct freshwater input disappears. This zone is 10–20 km wide off Georgia. Near tidal inlets, the mean freshwater discharge and onshore-offshore fluxes due to vertical variations in density and velocity and tidal fluctuations play large and probably competing roles in transferring material across the zone. Lateral variations were not included in calculations, but they are likely to be equally important. However, the alongshore transport of material appears to be predominantly influenced by the "mean" alongshore flow which changes slowly compared to a tidal cycle.

Our discussion has drawn heavily from estuarine studies and has obvious limitations. Varying amounts of freshwater input occur laterally, and this makes steady state conditions, insofar as salinity is concerned, highly unlikely. Salinity fluctuations over one tidal cycle may not repeat themselves, i.e., the mean salinity from tidal cycle to tidal cycle may change slowly. Alongshore variations in onshore-offshore velocity have been neglected. Only a long series of observations at several locations alongshore and offshore in the nearshore zone can provide convincing data on the transfer process.

For completeness, we must also consider wholesale "cleansing" of the nearshore zone by varying alongshore currents (Csanady, 1974). Winds that exert stress with the coastline to the right induce slow onshore flow at the surface due to the earth's rotation. The freshwater and suspended material in the nearshore zone are probably confined under such conditions to a narrower zone than would otherwise exist. Opposite wind stress produces the opposite result, and material is free to flow offshore. This may be expected to influence the width of the nearshore zone as defined by the distance to well-mixed shelf water. It is tempting to conclude that the difference in the alongshore wind stress accounts for the different widths of the nearshore zone (Table 1) in autumn, since freshwater discharge was relatively small, but our observations are too few to be convincing. However, reversing alongshore currents, due to large-scale weather patterns, often induce high lateral shears accompanied by increased turbulence (Blanton and Murthy, 1974). Rapid dispersion of the river and turbidity plumes can be expected under these conditions. This has been verified experimentally by Murthy (1972), measuring fluorescent dye plume concentrations during reversing alongshore currents. Non-tidal current reversals occur at time scales of several days and are essentially episodic in nature. These events are undoubtedly quite effective dispersive or transfer agencies and make predictive modelling of dispersion most difficult.

Acknowledgments

We appreciate the help of J. Singer and W. Chandler in obtaining and processing the CTD and current meter data used in this study. B. Blanton analyzed and plotted the hydrographic and current velocity data. We thank D. McIntosh for drafting the figures and P. Vopelak for typing the manuscript.

We appreciate the helpful comments of Dr. T. N. Lee of the University of Miami on an earlier version of the manuscript and thank Dr. Stephan Murray of Louisiana State University for pointing out an error in the flux calculations contained in the earlier version.

This work is a result of research sponsored by the U.S. Department of Energy (EY-76-S-09-0889) and by the Georgia Sea Grant Program, Office of Sea Grant, NOAA (R/EE-3).

References

1. Atkinson, L. P., J. O. Blanton, and E. Haines. 1977. Shelf flushing rates based on the distribution of salinity and freshwater in the Georgia Bight. Estuarine and Coastal Marine Science (in press).

2. Blanton, J. O. 1971. Exchange of Gulf Stream water with North Carolina shelf water in Onslow Bay during stratified conditions. Deep-Sea Res., 18:167-178.

3. Blanton, J. O., and C. R. Murthy. 1974. Observations of lateral shear in the nearshore zone of a Great Lake. Jour. Phys. Oceanogr., 4(4):660-663.

4. Bowden, K. R. 1963. The mixing processes in a tidal estuary. International Jour. Air and Water Pollution, 7:343-356.

5. Burt, W. V., and W. B. McAlister. 1959. Recent studies in the hydrography of Oregon estuaries. Res. Briefs, Fish Commission of Oregon, 7:14-27.

6. Csanady, G. T. 1974. Mass exchange episodes in the coastal boundary layer associated with current reversals. Rapp. Proc. -verb. Reun. and Conseil Internat. Explor. Mer, 167:41-45.

7. Dyer, K. R. 1973. Estuaries: A Physical Introduction. John Wiley and Sons, London and New York. 140 pp.

8. _____. 1974. The salt balance in stratified estuaries. Estuarine and Coastal Marine Science, 2:273-281.

9. Fischer, H. B. 1972. Mass transport mechanisms in partially stratified estuaries. Jour. Fluid Mechanisms, 53:672-687.

10. Garvine, R. W. 1974. Physical features of the Connecticut River outflow during high discharge. Jour. Geophys. Res., 79(6):831-846.

11. _____. 1977. Observations of the motion field of the Connecticut River plume. Jour. Geophys. Res., 82(3):441-454.

12. Murray, S. P., and A. Siripong. 1977. Role of lateral gradients and longitudinal dispersion in the salt balance of a shallow, well-mixed estuary. *In* B. Kjerfve (ed.), Estuarine Transport Process. University of South Carolina Press, Columbia, S. C. (in press).

13. Murthy, C. R. 1972. Complex diffusion processes in coastal currents of a lake. Jour. Phys. Oceanogr., 2:80-90.

14. Scarlet, R. I. 1975. A data processing method for salinity, temperature, depth profiles. Deep-Sea Res., 22:509-515.

DISTRIBUTION, COMPOSITION, AND MORPHOLOGY OF SUSPENDED SOLIDS IN THE NEW YORK BIGHT APEX

I. W. Duedall, R. Dayal, J. H. Parker

Marine Sciences Research Center
State University of New York
Stony Brook, New York

H. W. Kraner

Instrumentation Division
Brookhaven National Laboratory
Upton, New York

and

K. W. Jones, R. E. Shroy

Department of Physics
Brookhaven National Laboratory
Upton, New York

Abstract: Tidal and spatial changes in the morphology and concentrations of suspended solids, particulate carbon and nitrogen, the particulate metals Fe, Mn, Cu, and Zn, and chlorophyll *a* were determined over a tidal cycle at seven stations during 3 June 1975 on a transect between Sandy Hook, New Jersey and Rockaway Point, New York (the entrance to New York Harbor). Most of the particulate matter in the suspended solids consisted of diatom frustules which were present in relatively large abundances near Sandy Hook. Near Rockaway Point, both diatoms and dinoflagellates were found in the suspended matter. Other particulates included organic aggregates, mineral grains, and some opaque particles which were assumed to be anthropogenic in origin. The organic aggregates appeared as a large amorphous matrix containing a wide size range of mineral grains including some spherical and irregular opaque particles. Some of the opaque particles were reddish-brown in color and were therefore probably iron hydrous oxides. There was a strong correlation among the concentrations of Fe, Mn, Cu, and Zn, suggesting that these metals were associated with each other. Fine mineral grains were found attached to the surfaces and edges of phytoplankton cells.

Introduction

The waters surrounding the New York metropolitan region are a major source of suspended solids entering the apex of the New York Bight (Figure 1). There are, however, only a few reports which describe the character and elemental composition of these solids (Manheim *et al.*, 1970; Biscaye and Olsen, 1976). Knowledge of the composition of suspended solids is fundamental to our understanding of geochemical and sedimentary processes occurring in the Bight apex.

We have studied the concentration, distribution, composition, and morphology of suspended solids collected on 3 June 1975 at several stations on a transect at the mouth of the Hudson-Raritan estuary (Figure 2). The sampling was designed to examine the tidal and spatial distributions of total suspended solids, particulate carbon and nitrogen, phytoplankton biomass (chlorophyll *a*), and the particulate metals Fe, Mn, Cu, and Zn. In the present paper we describe (1) the physical oceanography in the study area, (2) the distribution, composition and morphology of suspended solids, and (3) the physical processes which could account for observations of particulate material. This work was carried out as part of our continuing research to determine the flux and fate of estuarine-derived dissolved and particulate material in the apex (Duedall *et al.*, 1977).

Sampling and Methods

The station locations, sampling sequence, and depths sampled were identical to our previous study (Duedall *et al.*, 1977). Briefly, the stations (Figure 2) were sampled sequentially (A through H) aboard the R/V *Onrust* from 0530 to 1732 h local time; station D, located at the center of Ambrose Channel, was not sampled because of the intense ship traffic into and out of the harbor. The sampling depths were 1, 4, 7, and 10 m, depth permitting.

Shipboard procedures

Water was pumped from depth using a submersible pump to a continuous recording salinometer and to a spigot. A thermistor, attached to the pump housing, permitted *in situ* temperature recording.

Samples for suspended solids (gravimetric analysis) were collected from the spigot in 500 ml glass bottles and brought back to the laboratory for filtering. Samples for particulate organic carbon and nitrogen were also collected from the spigot but filtered at sea, using pre-combusted glass fiber filters of 0.8 μm nominal porosity; the volume filtered varied between 50 and 100 ml. Chlorophyll *a* samples were obtained by onboard filtration using Millipore filters as described by Duedall *et al.* (1977).

To avoid contamination from the pumping system, samples for particulate metal analyses and microscopic identification were collected using 10 ℓ top-drop Niskin bottles. Here only stations A and H were sampled over the tidal cycle and only at surface and bottom. The filtering was done onboard by pressurizing the Niskin bottles with argon and forcing water through a 0.45 μm Millipore

Figure 1. Suspended sediment distribution map. ERIS scene No. 1636-15020, date 20 April 1974; ground truth provided by Duedall and O'Connors, 1976.

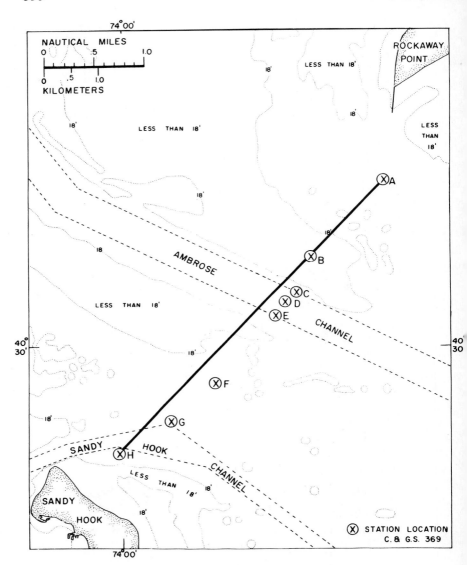

Figure 2. Station locations in the transect (see also Duedall et al., 1977).

filter contained in a Swinnex filter holder attached to each bottle. The volume filtered ranged between 500 and 1000 ml.

   In addition to particulate samples, water samples were taken for nutrient analyses using sampling and storage procedures already described (Duedall *et al.*, 1977). Knowledge of nutrient-salinity relations is useful in establishing mixing processes in the study area.

Laboratory methods

The water samples collected for gravimetric analysis of suspended solids were filtered using pre-weighed 0.8 μm Nuclepore (47 mm diameter) filters; the filters were dried in a desiccator and then reweighed. The coefficient of variation of the method, based on replicate sampling, is 10 percent.

The filters for particulate carbon and nitrogen analysis were analyzed using a CHN analyzer; the combustion temperature was 1140°C, and acetanilide was used as the standard. The coefficients of variation of the method, based on replicate sampling, are 30 and 20 percent for particulate carbon and nitrogen, respectively.

The concentration of chlorophyll a was determined trichromatically using acetone extracts of the collected pigment (Strickland and Parsons, 1972). In the extraction procedure an ultrasonic probe was used in a darkened room to rupture the collected cells. The coefficient of variation of the method, based on replicate sampling, is 6 percent.

The filtered samples for particulate Fe, Mn, Cu, and Zn were analyzed by X-ray fluorescence (Dzubay, 1977). Because this method of analysis is non-destructive, portions of each filter were also examined by scanning electron microscopy (SEM) to determine the morphology and nature of particles present on each filter.

The X-ray fluorescence analysis system used a 40 Kilovolt (Kv) tungsten target X-ray tube run at 30 Kv with molybdenum filtering, which gives a hardened distribution of incident X-ray energies peaked at 25 keV. The Millipore filters containing the suspended solids were placed in an evacuated 7.62 cm diameter aluminum chamber viewed by a Si(Li) X-ray detector 90° from the incident X-ray beam. The Millipore filter was held in a centerable lucite frame that did not itself intercept the X-ray beam. The frame also held a small piece of zirconium wire which produced 15.75 keV $K\alpha$ X-rays in the detected spectrum, and was used to measure the X-ray fluorescence for each run or sample. Characteristic fluoresced X-rays were observed in the range between 1 and 16 keV which includes K X-rays from lighter elements through the first transition group and L X-rays of very heavy metals. Observed X-ray spectra were analyzed by the computer program SAMPO (Routti and Prussin, 1969) to extract accurately the integrated characteristic X-ray counts for each element of interest from a variable background. Multielement standards on filter paper, obtained from Columbia Scientific Company, were used as primary standards to relate observed counts to μg cm^{-2}. All suspended solids samples were < 3 mg cm^{-2} in areal density which was sufficiently thin not to require a correction for self absorption for X-rays emitted by Fe, Mn, Cu, and Zn. The accuracy of the determinations is estimated to be about 15 percent which includes systematic and statistical errors of about equal proportion. Comparative measurements were also regularly made of National Bureau of Standards orchard leaf and bovine liver standards (SRM No. 1571 and 1577 for orchard leaf and bovine liver, respectively) as particulate samples on 0.45 μm Millipore filters. Areal densities were kept in the range of the filter samples and agreement was generally found within the above limits.

Nutrients were determined using Autoanalyzer methods (Strickland and Parsons, 1972).

Results and Discussion

Hydrographic properties and physical oceanography

The distribution of suspended solids along the transect (Figure 2) is dependent upon circulation. A brief summary of the physical oceanography in the study area will serve as a description of the important physical properties and the non-tidal flow.

Figure 3 shows tidally-averaged distributions of salinity, temperature, and density. For comparison, sections are also presented for the previous year. The tidal averaging procedure has been described by Parker (1976). The salinity sections reveal the presence of high salinity Bight waters near Rockaway Point and low salinity estuarine waters near Sandy Hook. The 3 June 1975 period showed considerable temperature stratification in the water column, and the density surfaces sloped upward toward Rockaway Point.

The distribution of salinity, and also other water properties, in the transect area is in large measure determined by nontidal currents which are primarily maintained by the seasonally variable inflow of the Hudson River and to a lesser extent the Raritan River. The seasonal impact of river flow on surface salinity in the Bight apex can be demonstrated by comparing river discharge with surface salinity. Figure 4 shows a six-year record of two-month running means of surface salinity at Ambrose Tower and total freshwater discharge from the Hudson and Raritan rivers. Peak river flows during the spring warming period correspond to rapidly decreasing salinities. Figure 5 shows the nontidal current structure in the transect. Inflow of salt water from the Bight apex occurs at depth within the Sandy Hook and Ambrose Channels and all depths on the Rockaway Point side of the transect. Thus in the 3 June 1975 period, salinities less than about 30 $^o/oo$ were associated with Bightward flow and extended at the surface from Sandy Hook to midway between Ambrose Channel and Rockaway Point; salinities greater than 30 $^o/oo$ were associated with the inflow of Bight water at depth.

According to Doyle and Wilson (1978), the nontidal current structure in the transect is well described by a lateral momentum balance between Coriolis acceleration due to nontidal flow, centripetal accelerations associated with tidal currents within the transect area, and the lateral pressure gradient due to the increase in density toward the Rockaway Point side of the transect.

Distribution of particulate material

Figure 6 shows tidally-averaged distributions of suspended solids, particulate carbon and nitrogen, and chlorophyll *a* (a measure of phytoplankton

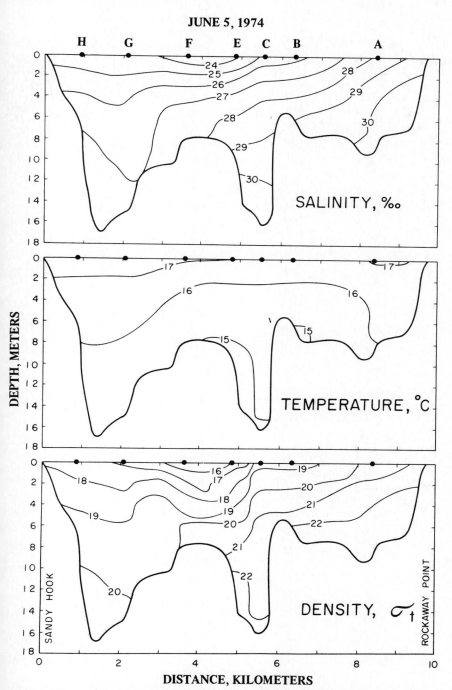

Figure 3A. Tidally-averaged distributions of salinity, temperature, and density [σ$_t$ = (density − 1) x 1000] for 5 June 1974.

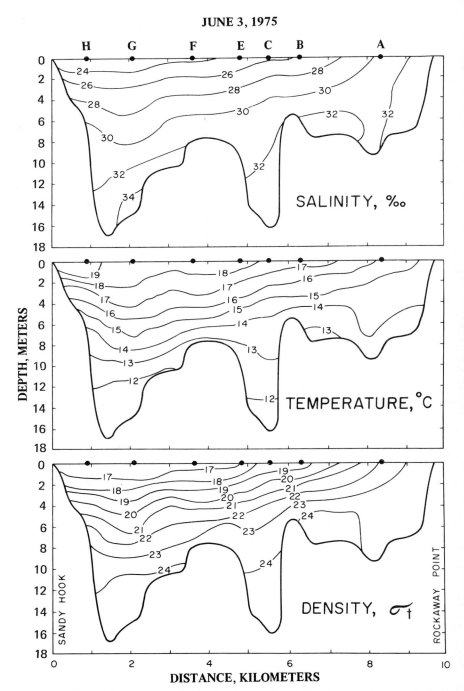

Figure 3B. *Tidally-averaged distributions of salinity, temperature, and density* $[\sigma_t = (density - 1) \times 1000]$ *for 3 June 1975.*

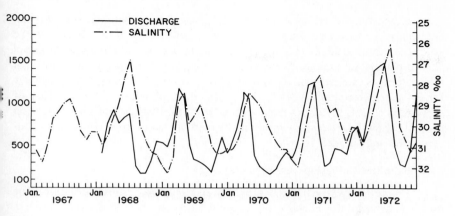

Figure 4. Variation in surface salinity and freshwater discharge in the New York Bight apex (from Duedall et al., in press).

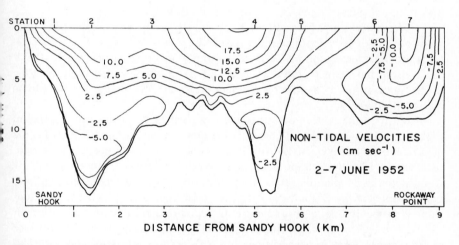

Figure 5. Non-tidal current velocities in the study area covering the period 2–7 June 1952. Positive sign velocities are seaward (from Kao, 1975).

biomass). During both the 3 June 1975 and 5 June 1974 sampling periods, highest concentrations of suspended solids were observed near Sandy Hook. Relatively high concentrations were also observed in the deeper samples collected in Ambrose Channel which probably receives strong bottom currents that scour the bottom and keep sediment in more or less continuous resuspension. The order-of-magnitude increase in suspended solids observed during the 5 June 1974 period demonstrates the variability that can be expected in this area.

Highest observed concentrations of particulate carbon and nitrogen and chlorophyll *a* were also found in the waters near Sandy Hook. Based on the nontidal current structure (Figure 5), one sees that there is a potentially large net flux of particulate organic matter being discharged to the Bight apex. Most of this material is carried out in the surface plume which moves south along the New Jersey shore (Ketchum *et al.*, 1951). The determination of the net flux of suspended solids, including the particulate organic carbon and nitrogen, must await a comprehensive study involving the simultaneous measurements of concentration and current.

Salinity relationships and tidal variations

Figure 7 shows the relationships between water properties and salinity. The nutrients behaved in a conservative manner with concentrations lying close to a straight line joining the two end members: low salinity estuarine water and high salinity Bight water. It is apparent from the curvature in the T-S diagram that a third water mass was also present in the transect during the sampling period. Parker *et al.* (1976) have suggested that the low salinity estuarine water comprises Raritan-Sandy Hook Bay water and Hudson River water.

The relationships between components in the suspended solids and salinity show a similar two-component mixing system; that is, high and low concentrations are associated with low and high salinity water, respectively. A similar relationship has been reported by Alexander *et al.* (1974) for particulate Fe in the same study area, and by Graham *et al.* (1976) for particulate Mn in Narragansett Bay.

Many of the bottom concentrations of particulate species represented in Figure 7, especially those of suspended solids and particulate Fe and Mn, are significantly above the conservative mixing line, indicating injection of particulate material from the bottom. Segar and Cantillo (1976) also observed relatively large increases in total dissolved and particulate Fe and Mn in the high salinity bottom water of the Bight apex. This particular feature in the salinity relationships is probably due to bottom currents which resuspend sediment (Schubel, 1971). The lack of any significant injection of particulate Cu and Zn near the bottom may be because these particulate metals are more associated with particulate carbon whose bottom concentrations show more or less conservative mixing behavior. Segar and Cantillo (1976) have suggested that the excess Fe concentrations in bottom waters may be due to a nepheloid layer containing high concentrations of fine particles that are enriched in Fe but contain less amounts of Mn and Cu. In our work, however, particulate Mn was also found to be significantly enriched in the bottom suspended solids.

Earlier we reported that water properties measured southwest of Ambrose Channel (Figure 2) exhibited considerably greater variation during a tidal cycle than those measured northwest of the channel (Duedall *et al.*, 1977). This variation was also observed during the 3 June 1975 period. Figure 8 shows, for example, that station A was dominated by Bight water during flood and slack

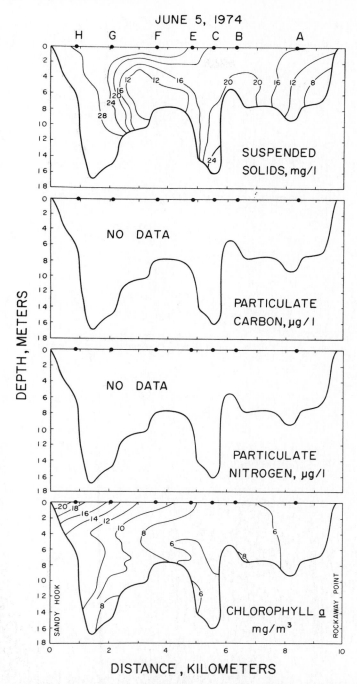

Figure 6A. *Tidally-averaged distributions of suspended solids, particulate organic carbon and nitrogen, and chlorophyll* a *for 5 June 1974.*

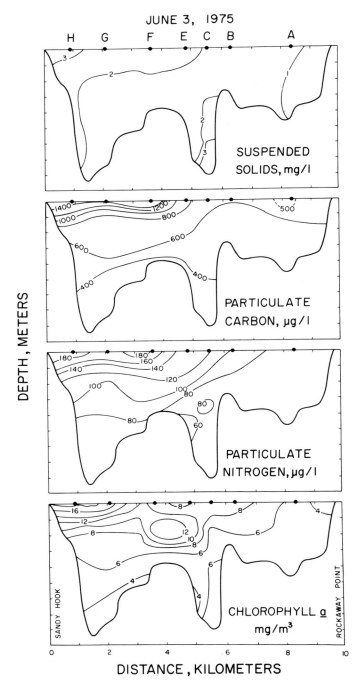

Figure 6B. *Tidally-averaged distributions of suspended solids, particulate organic carbon and nitrogen, and chlorophyll* a *for 3 June 1975.*

after flood; salinities were relatively high and concentrations of particulate carbon, suspended solids, and the particulate metals were low. At slack after ebb at station A, outgoing harbor water resulted in decreased salinities at this station and increased concentrations of all particulate species.

At station H we observed considerably more variation in water properties over the tidal cycle, especially in surface waters where concentrations of suspended solids were highest after slack after ebb and lowest during the period between flood tide and slack after flood (Figure 8). Relatively high concentrations of suspended solids were also observed in bottom waters at slack after ebb at this station but the lowest concentrations were observed at slack after flood rather than at peak flood as with the surface concentrations.

Concentrations of particulate metals in the surface waters at station H were extremely variable and often higher by a factor of three than the metals concentrations observed at station A. For the bottom samples, however, the tidal variation in the particulate metals concentrations was similar to that observed at station A, although the concentrations observed at station A were about half those found at station H. Alexander *et al.* (1974), based on their own data from the same area, explained the large variation in the particulate metals concentrations in surface waters as due to patches of water containing particulates with differing concentrations of heavy metals.

Although particulate metals concentrations would be expected to follow suspended solids, at station H we observed that the elevation in particulate metals concentrations in surface waters corresponded to particulate carbon rather than suspended solids which decreased in the surface waters. Microscopic examination of selected filters (Figure 9) from station H under plane polarized light revealed the presence of large organic aggregates with inclusions and opaque particles adhering to the surface. Under crossed-nicols, the presence of small ($< 1\mu$m) birefringent mineral particles incorporated in the aggregate structures was quite evident. Many of the larger, irregular opaque particles were reddish-brown in color, suggesting iron and manganese oxide phases. Wangersky and Gordon (1965) have shown that organic aggregates can concentrate Mn^{2+} into their structure. Very recently Hirsbrunner and Wangersky (1976) have demonstrated that naturally and artificially created organic aggregates in seawater are greatly enriched in Fe, as well as Mn, compared to seawater concentrations.

Also present in Figure 9 are numerous tiny opaque spherical particles which are either associated with or directly attached to organic aggregates. The size of these spherules is around 10μm, and in Figure 9(c) we count about 40 such particles which are attached to an organic aggregate. These particles may be fly ash or soot. The presence of fly ash particles and soot in suspended solids collected off the New Jersey coast and in the New York Bight has been reported (Biscaye and Olsen, 1976; Manheim *et al.*, 1970). Doyle *et al.* (1976) have recently demonstrated that opaque fly ash particles, identified as magnetite, are falling on the sea surface throughout a wide geographical area in the Gulf of

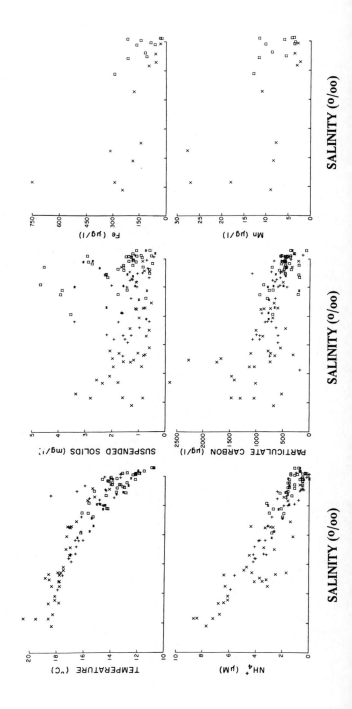

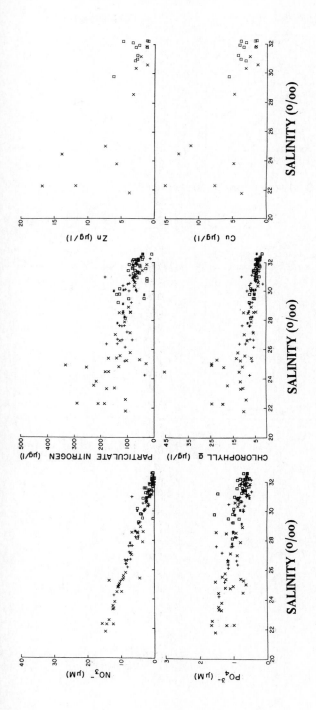

Figure 7. Variations of water properties with salinity: x = surface; + = 4 m; * = 7 m; and □ = bottom.

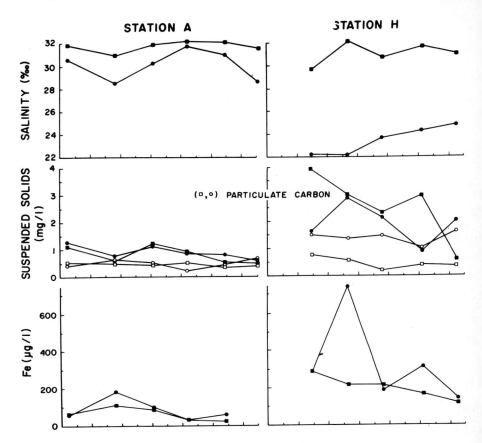

Figure 8. Tidal variation for salinity, suspended solids, particulate organic carbon, particulate Fe, Mn, Cu, Zn: ● = *and* ■ *= bottom.*

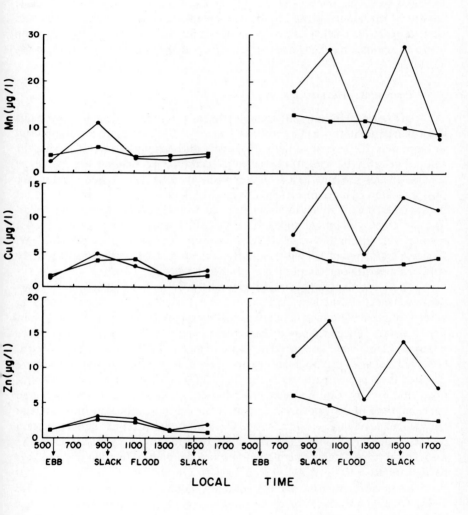

Mexico. Our future work on particulates will involve the determination and morphology of the small black particles shown in Figure 9.

Mineral particles were also observed on the arms of *ceratium tripos* (Figure 9(d)) and along the sides of a biogenic silica rod (Figure 9(a)). According to Esaias (pers. commun.; see also Postek and Cox, 1976), a sticky substance covers the thecal membrane of most phytoplankton cells. This substance could act to trap detrital particles onto the surface of cells. Thus sinking phytoplankton could be another mechanism for transporting detrital mineral particles to the sea floor.

Particulate relationships

In Figure 10, we present a compilation of particulate relations. The results show that particulate organic carbon is a major (>50 percent carbon) component in more than 50 percent of the suspended solids samples collected during the study. The ratio (by weight) of particulate carbon to particulate nitrogen in the organic matter present, based on composite data, is 5.9, a value typical for phytoplankton in nutrient-enriched waters (W. Esaias, pers. commun.) and for phytoplankton cells living in a prebloom environment (Platt and Irwin, 1973). The particulate carbon:chlorophyll *a* ratio, again based on composite data, is 41, a value well within the range of ratios observed for coastal phytoplankton (W. Esaias, pers.commun.). Thus a majority of the particulate carbon present in the study area during our sampling period was biogenic.

There are no clearly established relations between concentrations of particulate metals, particulate carbon, and suspended solids. Some trends are evident in particulate metals relations and were discussed earlier in this paper. For instance, concentrations of particulate metals in the surface waters were relatively higher when compared to bottom samples and appeared more related to observed increases in particulate organic carbon. Biscaye and Olsen (1976) have reported that organic particles in the Bight apex contain significant concentrations of Fe, Mn, Cu, Zn, and other heavy metals. Table 1 gives average concentrations of suspended solids, particulate carbon, particulate nitrogen, and the particulate metals Fe, Mn, Zn, and Cu. Additional data on the concentration of particulate metals in the study area are required to define more clearly the association of particulate metals with particulate carbon fraction and the suspended solids.

As in other estuarine and river systems (Gibbs, 1973; Trefry and Presley, 1976; Troup and Bricker, 1975), Fe and Mn are major components in the trace element composition of particulate matter in the New York Bight apex. We have already mentioned that one form of the Fe and Mn present in the suspended solids was probably the hydrous oxide. Gibbs (1973) has shown that Fe and Mn can also be present in relatively large amounts in the crystalline lattices of other minerals such as alumino-silicates. From our present work it is not possible to determine the composition of the major mineral phases present in the suspended solids; however our data suggests that the hydrous oxide form may be present in significant amounts because of the strong correlation we have found between Fe,

(2) Crossed-Nicols

(1) Plane Polarized Light

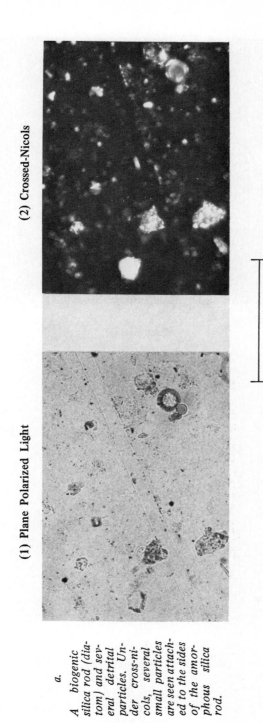

100μ

a.
A biogenic silica rod (diatom) and several detrital particles. Under cross-nicols, several small particles are seen attached to the sides of the amorphous silica rod.

Figure 9.   *(pages 551 - 553) Photomicrographs showing suspended solids at 10 m at station H, viewed under (1) plane polarized light and (2) crossed-nicols.*

(1) Plane Polarized Light

(2) Crossed-Nicols

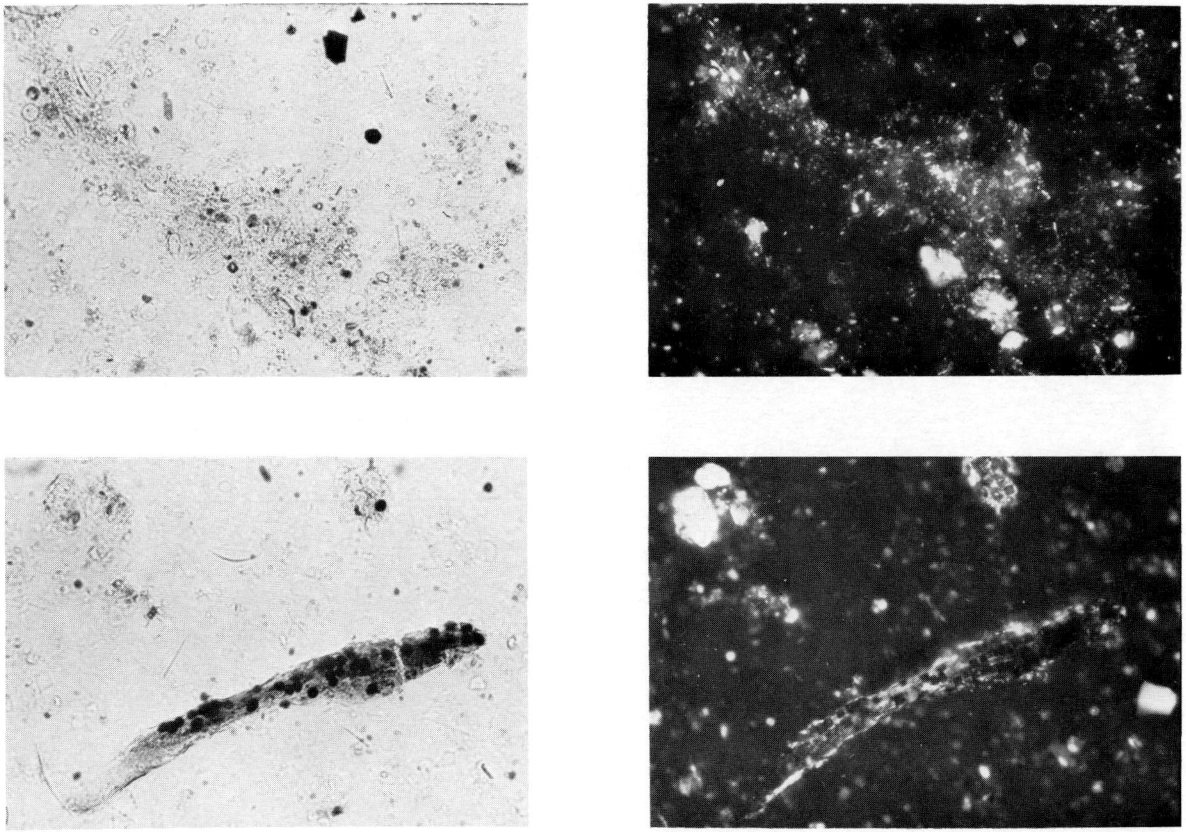

b.
*Very large or-
ganic aggregate
containing
many birefrin-
gent particles.
Also shown
are several
spherical and
irregular opa-
que particles.*

c.
*Elongated par-
ticle contain-
ing approxi-
mately 40
spherical opa-
que particles.*

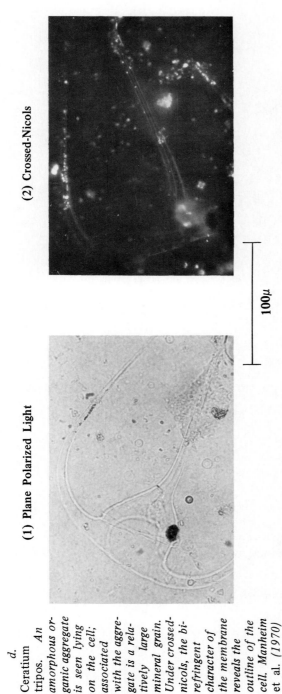

(1) Plane Polarized Light

(2) Crossed-Nicols

|← 100μ →|

d.
Ceratium tripos. An amorphous organic aggregate is seen lying on the cell; associated with the aggregate is a relatively large mineral grain. Under crossed-nicols, the birefringent character of the membrane reveals the outline of the cell. Manheim et al. (1970) have also reported that these cells have birefringent properties. The birefringence may be due to a fibrous cellulose present in the inner cell wall of the organism (Swift and Remsen, 1970). Note the concentration of small anisotropic particles on the arms of the cell.

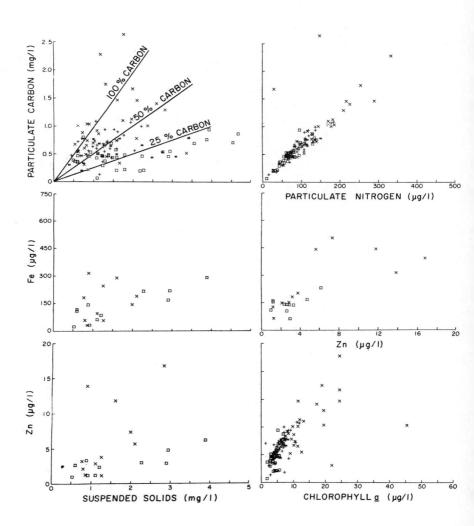

*Figure 10. Particulate relations: x = surface; + = 4 m; * = 7 m; and □ = bottom.*

Table 1. Average concentrations of suspended solids, particulate carbon, particulate nitrogen, and the particulate metals Fe, Mn, Zn, and Cu.

	Suspended Solids (mg/l)	Particulate Carbon (μg/l)	Particulate Nitrogen (μg/l)	Fe	Mn	Zn	Cu
					(μg/l)		
Surface[1]	1.33	918	121	214	11.0	6.3	6.3
Bottom[1]	1.53	456	68	133	7.5	2.8	3.3

[1] The average values given for suspended solids, particulate carbon, and particulate nitrogen were calculated based on corresponding available particulate metal data.

Mn, Cu, and Zn (Figure 11), Fe and Mn hydrous oxides have been shown to be very effective in scavenging other trace elements from seawater (Aston and Chester, 1973).

Particle morphology and size

Figures 12 and 13 are scanning electron photomicrographs showing the morphology and variety of particles that make up the surface and bottom suspended solids at station A and H, respectively. From these figures, it is obvious that a majority of the particles present were phytoplankton cells and broken cell fragments. Organic detritus, which is more clearly seen in Figure 9, was also present in relatively large abundances. Mineral grains and other inorganic particles represented a smaller but not an insignificant fraction of the particulate matter present in the suspended solids.

At station A, both diatoms and dinoflagellates, including the species *Ceratium linatum, C. tripos,* and *Dinophysis acuta* were prevalent throughout the water column. These dinoflagellates are typically found in coastal waters as opposed to the estuarine environment (W. Esaias, pers. commun.). Their presence at station A is consistent with our findings that Bight water is the principal water mass in this region of the sampling area.

At station H, however, only diatoms were observed in the suspended solids. The diatoms were mainly centric species and belonged to the genera *Cyclotella, Actinphtychus,* and *Thalasiossira* (E. Carpenter, pers. commun.). The suspended solids in the bottom samples at station H contained an abundance of diatom frustules with partially dissolved or totally missing valves. Additionally, we also observed several, 25–30 μm diameter, oil-like globules (Figure 14) in the bottom suspended solids. These globules are probably anthropogenic in origin.

Malone (1977) has summarized existing data on the systematics and distribution of plankton in the New York Bight and in the Hudson-Raritan estuary. His summary shows that in general there are greater numbers of phytoplankton cells near Sandy Hook than Rockaway Point. This is due to a combination of factors or processes, including increased nutrient availability, enhanced estuarine circulation due to the presence of the Hudson-Raritan plume, and nearby Raritan Bay which has been shown to be a principal source of phytoplankton (Patten, 1959; Parker *et al.*, 1976).

Conclusion

The present study has shown that suspended solids in the New York Bight apex are composed of a wide variety of particles. Because the samples we analyzed were collected during only one tidal cycle, it is not possible to generalize our results to include other time periods. During and after intense storm events, it is certain that concentrations and composition of suspended solids will differ dramatically from the results presented here. Additionally, seasonal effects will alter the composition of the particles present in the suspended solids.

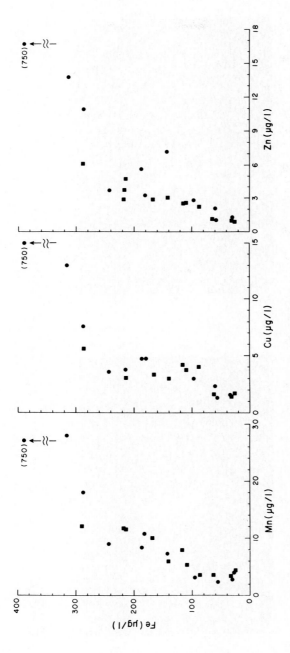

Figure 11. Relationships between particulate Fe, Mn, Cu, and Zn in suspended solids; ● = surface; ■ = bottom.

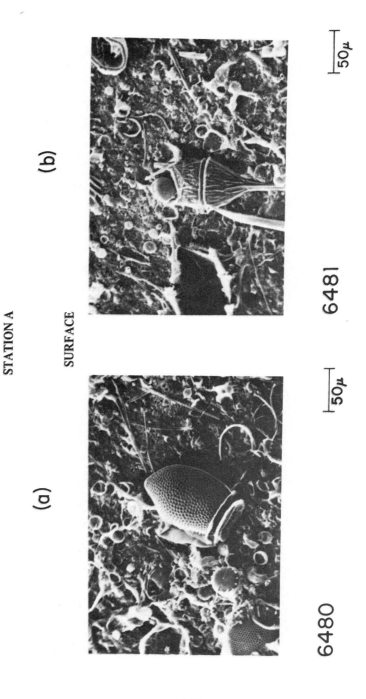

STATION A

SURFACE

(a)

(b)

6480

6481

50μ

50μ

Figure 12a and b. Photomicrographs (SEM) showing particle morphology of suspended solids collected at station A: (a) The large dinoflagellate is Dinophysis acuta; *(b)* Ceratium linatum.

STATION A

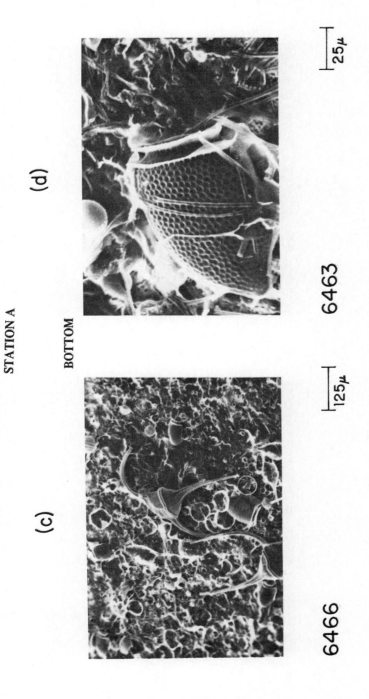

(d)

BOTTOM

25μ

6463

(c)

125μ

6466

Figure 12c and d. Photomicrographs (SEM) showing particle morphology of suspended solids collected at station A: (c) Ceratium tripos and diatom frustules; (d) large Dinophysis acuta.

STATION H

(b)

BOTTOM

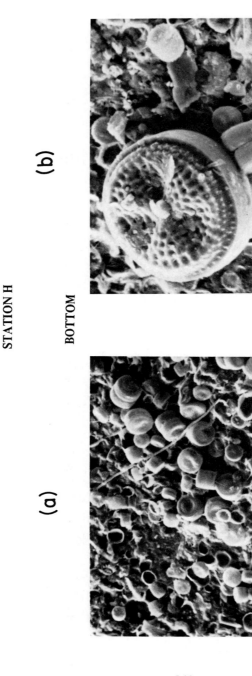

(a)

6472

|25μ

|12.5μ

6475

Figure 13a and b. *Photomicrographs (SEM) showing particle morphology of suspended solids at station H:* *(a) Relatively large abundance of centric diatoms, possibly* Cyclotella sp.; *(b)* Actinoptychus sp.

STATION H

(d)

BOTTOM

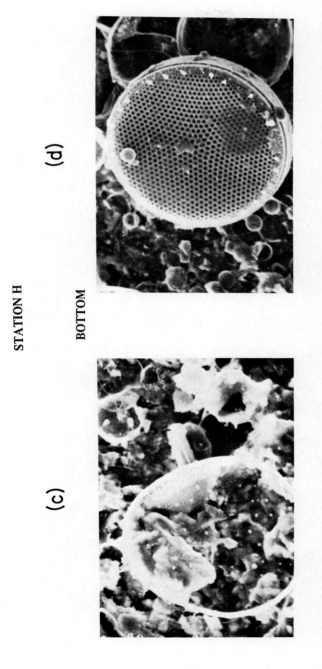

6581

25μ

(c)

6582

12.5μ

Figure 13c and d. Photomicrographs (SEM) showing particle morphology of suspended solids at station H: (c) dissolved diatom frustule; (d) Thalassiossira excentricus.

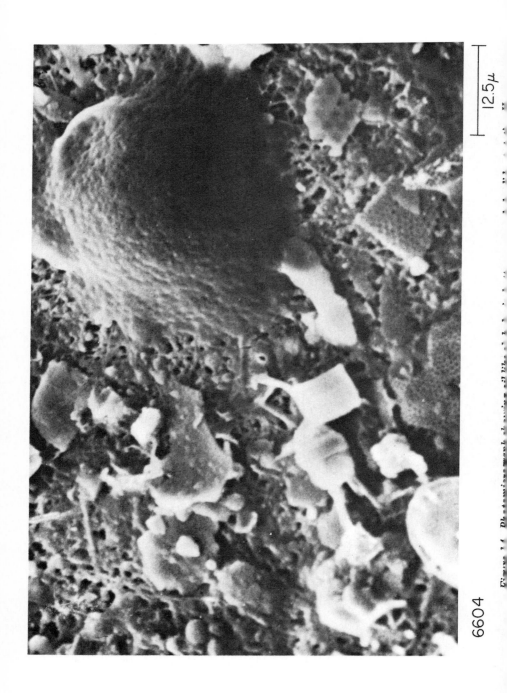

12.5 μ

6604

Figure 14. Photomicrograph showing... (caption illegible)

Our future work will focus on the seasonal variation in the composition of particulate matter present in the Hudson-Raritan estuary and the apex of the New York Bight.

Acknowledgments

Several people from the Marine Sciences Research Center (MSRC) and from Brookhaven National Laboratory (BNL) assisted in this work. In particular at MSRC, we gratefully acknowledge the assistance received from D. Bray, E. J. Carpenter, W. W. Esaias, P. J. Harder, K. Henricksen, S. A. Oakley, H. B. O'Connors, and J. M. Restivo. At BNL we are very thankful to C. Boulin and I. Still. A special note of sincere gratitude to the late Mr. J. J. Kelsch of the Instrumentation Division at BNL; his expert skill and enthusiasm on the SEM will always be remembered. We thank D. Suszkowski for Figure 1.

This work was supported by grants from the National Oceanic and Atmospheric Administration (MESA project), the Link Foundation, and the Energy Research and Development Administration (Grant No. EY-76-C-02-0016). We thank H. Stanford (MESA) for his help in the project.

Contribution 211 of the Marine Sciences Research Center of the State University of New York at Stony Brook

References

1. Alexander, J. E., R. Hollman, and T. White. 1974. Heavy metal concentration at the apex of the New York Bight. Final report No. 4-35212. New York Ocean Science Laboratory, Montauk, New York. 23 pp.

2. Aston, S. R., and R. Chester. 1973. The influence of suspended particles on the precipitation of iron in natural waters. Estuarine Coastal Mar. Sci. 1:225-231.

3. Biscaye, P. E., and C. R. Olsen. 1976. Suspended particulate concentrations and compositions in the New York Bight, pp. 124-137. *In* M. G. Gross (ed.), Middle Atlantic Continental Shelf and the New York Bight, Special Symposia Volume 2. American Society of Limnology and Oceanography, Inc., Lawrence, Kansas.

4. Doyle, L. J., T. L. Hopkins, and P. R. Betzer. 1976. Black magnetic spherule fallout in the Eastern Gulf of Mexico. Science 194:1157-1159.

5. Doyle, B. E., and R. W. Wilson. 1978. Lateral dynamic balance in the Sandy Hook to Rockaway Point transect. Estuarine Coastal Mar. Sci. 6:165-174.

6. Duedall, I. W., and H. B. O'Connors. 1976. Data report of cruises from November 1973 to June 1974, Final report part II. NOAA data report ERL MESA-20, National Oceanic and Atmospheric Administration, Boulder, Colorado. 456 pp.

7. Duedall, I. W., H. B. O'Connors, J. H. Parker, R. E. Wilson, and A. S. Robbins. 1977. The abundances, distribution and flux of nutrients and chlorophyll *a* in the New York Bight Apex. Estuarine Coastal Mar. Sci. 5:81-105.

8. Duedall, I. W., H. B. O'Connors, R. E. Wilson, and J. H. Parker. In press. The lower bay complex. MESA New York Bight Atlas Monograph 29. New York Sea Grant Institute, Albany, New York.

9. Dzubay, T. G. 1977. X-Ray Fluorescence Analysis of Environmental Samples. Ann Arbor Science Publishers, Inc., Ann Arbor, Michigan. 310 pp.

10. Gibbs, R. J. 1973. Mechanisms of trace metal transport in rivers. Science 180:71-73

11. Graham, W. F., M. L. Bender, and G. P. Klinkhammer. 1976. Manganese in Narragansett Bay. Limnol. Oceanogr. 21:665-673.

12. Hirsbrunner, W. R., and P. J. Wangersky. 1976. Composition of the inorganic fraction of the particulate organic matter in seawater. Marine Chemistry 4:43-49.

13. Kao, A. 1975. Current structure in the Sandy Hook to Rockaway Point transect. M.S. thesis. Marine Sciences Research Center, State University of New York, Stony Brook, New York. 82 pp.

14. Ketchum, B. H., A. C. Redfield, and J. C. Ayers. 1951. The oceanography of the New York Bight. Papers in Physical Oceanography and Meteorology 7 (No. 1), Massachusetts Institute of Technology and Woods Hole, Massachusetts.

15. Malone, T. C. 1977. Plankton systematics and distributions. MESA New York Bight Atlas Monograph 13. New York Sea Grant Institute, Albany, New York. 45 pp.

16. Manheim, F. T., R. H. Meade, and G. C. Bond, 1970. Suspended matter in surface waters of the Atlantic continental margin from Cape Cod to the Florida Keys. Science 166:371-388.

17. Parker, J. H. 1976. Nutrient budget in the lower bay complex. M.S. thesis. Marine Sciences Research Center, State University of New York, Stony Brook, New York. 30 pp.

18. Parker, J. H., I. W. Duedall, H. B. O'Connors, and R. E. Wilson. 1976. Raritan Bay as a source of ammonium and chlorophyll *a* for the New York Bight apex, pp. 212-219. *In* M G. Gross (ed.), Middle Atlantic Continental Shelf and the New York Bight, Special Symposia Volume 2. American Society of Limnology and Oceanography Inc., Lawrence, Kansas.

19. Patten, B. C. 1959. The diversity of species in net phytoplankton of the Raritan Estuary. Ph.D. dissertation. Rutgers University, New Brunswick, New Jersey. 111 pp.

20. Platt, T., and B. Irwin. 1973. Caloric content of phytoplankton. Limnol. Oceanogr. 18:306-310.

21. Posteck, M. T., and E. R. Cox. 1976. Thecal ultrastructure of the toxic marine dinoflagellate *Gonyaulax catenella*. J. Phycology 12:88-93.

22. Routti, J. T., and S. G. Prussin. 1969. Photopeak method for the computer analysis of gamma ray spectra from semiconductor detectors. Nuclear Instruments and Methods 72:125-1427.

23. Schubel, J. R. 1971. Tidal variation of the size distribution of suspended sediment at a station in the Chesapeake Bay turbidity maximum. Netherlands J. Sea Res. 5:252-266.

24. Segar, D. A., and A. Y. Cantillo. 1976. Trace metals in the New York Bight, pp. 171-198. *In* M. G. Gross (ed.), Middle Atlantic Continental Shelf and the New York Bight, Special Symposia Volume 2. American Society of Limnology and Oceanography Inc., Lawrence, Kansas.

25. Strickland, J. D. H., and T. R. Parsons. 1972. A Practical Handbook of Seawater Analysis. Bulletin 16-7 (2nd edition), Fisheries Research Board of Canada, Ottawa. 310 pp.

26. Swift, E., and C. C. Remsen. 1970. The cell wall of *Pyrocystis* ssp. (Dinococcales). J. Phycology 6:79-86.

27. Trefry, J. H., and B. J. Presley. 1976. Heavy metal transport from the Mississippi River to the Gulf of Mexico, pp. 39-76. *In* H. L. Windom and R. A. Duce (eds.), Marine Pollutant Transfer. D. C. Heath and Company, Lexington, Mass.

28. Troup, B. N., and O. P. Bricker. 1975. Processes affecting the transport of materials from continents to oceans, pp. 133-151. *In* T. M. Church (ed.), Marine Chemistry in the Coastal Environment. ACS Symposium Series 18, American Chemical Society, Washington, D.C.

29. Wangersky, P. J., and D. C. Gordon. 1965. Particulate carbonate, organic carbon, and Mn^{++} in the open ocean. Limnol. Oceanogr. 10:544-550.

COASTAL SOURCE WATERS AND THEIR ROLE
AS A NITROGEN SOURCE
FOR PRIMARY PRODUCTION IN AN ESTUARY IN MAINE

C. Garside, G. Hull, and C. S. Yentsch

Bigelow Laboratory for Ocean Sciences
West Boothbay Harbor, Maine

Abstract: The Sheepscot Estuary, located in central Maine, has been the subject of a survey study comprising eighteen cruises from July 1976. The lower 25 kilometers of the estuary had a seasonally varying salinity range from 20 to 26 $^\circ/_{oo}$ at Wiscasset to 33 $^\circ/_{oo}$ at the mouth and had a two-layered "structure" defined by a halocline and a seasonally coincident thermocline. The seasonal temperature range was from 0 to 15°C. The 1% light level was between 5 and 15 m, and production *versus* intensity curves show no light limitation. Inorganic nitrogen concentrations were high (>3 μg at N l^{-1}) throughout the year, and during the summer months primary production and chlorophyll *a* concentrations were high compared with adjacent ocean waters; ammonia and nitrate contributed to the inorganic nitrogen pool in the surface layer. The ultimate source of nitrogen for this estuary is the inflow of deep water from the Gulf of Maine; the drainage basin has neither large population centers nor a large area of agricultural land. That the phytoplankton population did not consume all the available inorganic nitrogen, phosphate, or silicate indicated that population size was limited by some "cropping factor." High ammonia concentrations and regeneration rates suggest a probable role of herbivorous filter feeders in cropping.

Introduction

This paper seeks to examine the inorganic nitrogen source supporting primary production in a Maine estuary. The Sheepscot River, located about 40 km "down east" from Portland, Maine, drains an area of 383 km². There are six towns along the 70-km river and estuary; the largest, Wiscasset (pop. 2,500), 20 km from the mouth, is the only one with a sewerage system and it discharges into the estuary. Only a small proportion of the basin is under agriculture and most of the area is mixed coniferous and deciduous forest. The potential terrigenous and anthropogenic input of inorganic nutrients to the river is small.

Materials and Methods

Eighteen one-day surveys of the lower Sheepscot Estuary were made between July 1976 and August 1977. Seven stations (numbered 10, 20, 30, . . . 70; Figure 1) were occupied at approximately two-week intervals during the summer, and monthly during the winter. Temperature and salinity profiles were measured, using a Beckman (model RS5-3) hand-lowered salinity temperature sensor to a maximum depth of 45 m. Light profiles were measured, using a Lambda model LI-192S quantum radiometer. Water samples were taken, using 1.7 or 4 l Niskin bottles. Oxygen was measured in the top of the bottle, using a YSI oxygen probe (model 54). Water samples for nutrient analysis were filtered through glass fiber filters into screw cap nalgene bottles and frozen. Ammonia samples were analyzed immediately on board on later cruises (Garside *et al.*, unpublished ms.). Nitrate, silicate and phosphate were measured, using standard Technicon manifolds on a modified Technicon AA I system. The sampler was rebuilt to take the sample bottles directly to minimize contamination, and the output was converted from transmittance to absorbance, using a Knobelsdorf Linearizer. Chlorophyll α (Chl α) samples were filtered onto glass fiber filters and stored frozen. They were analyzed, using the fluorometric technique of Yentsch and Menzel (1963). Primary production and photosynthesis versus light intensity were measured using ^{14}C uptake of water samples incubated under screens in an on-deck (natural light) incubator cooled with running seawater. Samples of 100 ml were incubated with 10 to 20 μCi sodium bicarbonate-^{14}C in "Whirl-Pak" bags for 2 to 4 h. After filtration through Gelman GF A/E filters, the filters were counted with a Beckman 100LS liquid scintillation spectrometer. One cruise (18 and 19 August 1977) was made to occupy station 40 for a period of two tidal cycles. In addition to the above measurements, with the exception of productivity, hourly STD profiles were made, using a Plessey model (9060). STD, and current meter measurements were made using the method of Pritchard and Burt (1951).

Results and Discussion

The seasonal cycle of runoff, and surface water temperature at station 30, is shown in Figure 2 (no interdependence is implied). The runoff data are 1967 to 1976, 10 year mean figures based on U.S.G.S. Water-Data Reports ME-67-1 through ME-76-1, from a gage located at North Whitefield (Figure 1). Maximum runoff occurs during the spring thaw (22.0 m^3s^{-1} in April). Winter flows are close to the annual mean of 7.6 m^3s^{-1} and are over twice the summer flow (June to October mean 3.1 m^3s^{-1}).

During the winter, runoff is predominantly from the frozen ground surface. This and surface cooling of the estuary contribute to the coldest temperatures (0.5 to 2.0°C) being found at the surface and toward the freshwater end of the estuary (Figure 3). The salinity distribution is typical of a "two-layered" estuary, that is, with salinities increasing downstream and with depth, and the

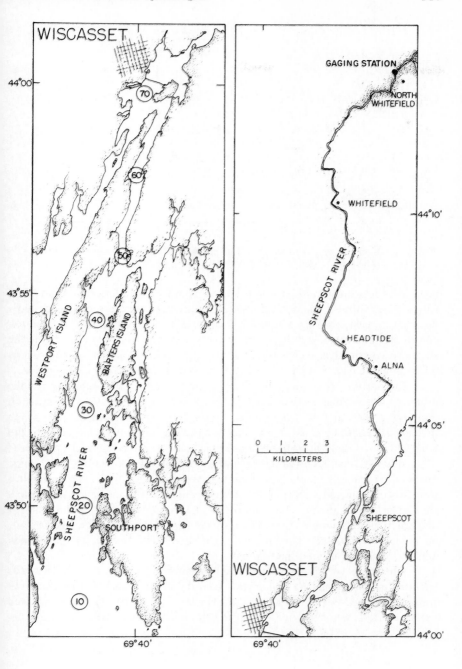

Figure 1. Lower Sheepscot Estuary showing station locations and U.S.G.S. gage.

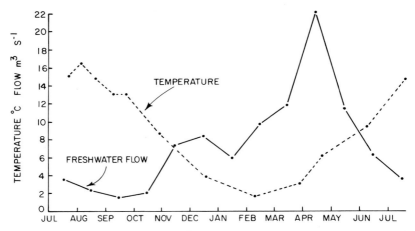

*Figure 2. Monthly temperature ($^\circ$C) at station 30 and freshwater flow (m^3 s^{-1})
at U.S.G.S. gage at North Whitefield.*

resultant density structure is stable with a pycnocline at between 5 and 15 m
(Figure 3). In the summer, the temperature structure is reversed; temperatures
decrease downstream and with depth from ~18°C, and the salinity distribution
contributes additional stability to the density distribution (Figure 4). Again the
structure has two layers separated by a sharp pycnocline. Oxygen concentrations
throughout the estuary over the entire year were within ± 20% of saturation.

During the winter months primary production was low throughout the
estuarine photic zone and was in the region of 0.1 g C $m^{-2}d^{-1}$ with assimilation
numbers in the range of 0.5 μg C μg Chl $\alpha^{-1}h^{-1}$. In the summer, production
increased to about 1 g C $m^{-2}d^{-1}$, production per unit chlorophyll varied from 2 to
8 μg Chl $\alpha^{-1}h^{-1}$ and total production for the study area reached about 50 tons C
d^{-1} and would have required a supply of 11.5 tons N d^{-1} assuming C:N atomic
ratios of 5:1 in the phytoplankton biomass. Seasonal variations in chlorophyll α
were less pronounced, with summer surface concentrations in the region of 2 to 8
μg Chl α l^{-1} (Figure 5). The location and concentration of the chlorophyll α
maximum varied, quite possibly as a result of tidal excursion alone (see below),
but regardless of biomass and production, inorganic nitrogen (nitrate) concentrations were always high in the estuary.

The source of this nitrate could be determined from a plot of nitrate versus
salinity for September, at which time primary production was low except at
station 10 (three low points on Figure 6). Under these conditions, nitrate showed
nearly conservative behavior, and if the three station 10 surface data are neglected, a relationship,

$$NO_3^- = 0.677 \text{ S } ^o/_{oo} - 12.81 \text{ (r = 0.83, n = 19)},$$

was obtained (Figure 6). The 95% confidence limits on the gradient are 0.677 ±
0.239. The relationship indicates that NO_3^- would have had zero concentration at

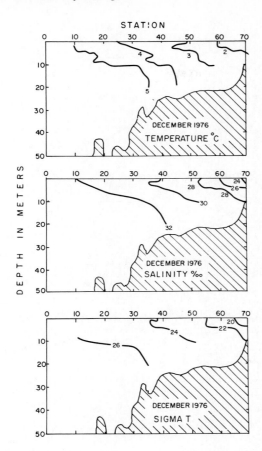

Figure 3. Longitudinal sections of temperature (°C), salinity (⁰/oo), and σₜ in December 1976.

S = 18.14 ⁰/oo, reflecting some biological uptake and insignificant input of nitrate to the lower estuary from the freshwater component. Consequently the source water for nitrate supply to the estuary was the saline end member of the mixing diagram, at S = 32.8 ⁰/oo and a nitrate concentration of 9+ μg at l^{-1} (Figures 5 and 6). This water has been described by Hopkins and Garfield (1977) as Maine Intermediate Water which is formed in variable volume during each winter cooling period. They characterize this water as having S = 32.75 ± 0.5 ⁰/oo, T = 4.5 ± 1.5°C (compare Figure 3).

The following considerations are interesting in corroborating the conclusion that anthropogenic and terrigenous sources are unlikely to be significant in supplying even that nitrogen required by phytoplankton for growth.

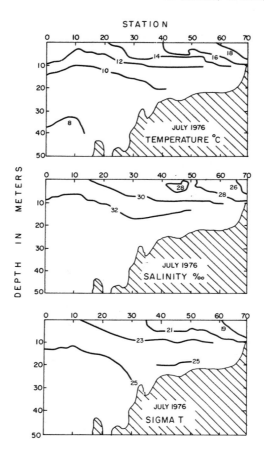

Figure 4. Longitudinal sections of temperature (°C), salinity (⁰/oo), and σ_t in July 1976.

If the 11.5 tons d^{-1} of nitrogen required by phytoplankton were to be supplied by domestic sewage, assuming a nitrogen excretion rate of 10 g N person $^{-1}d^{-1}$ (calculated from Garside *et al.*, 1976), a population of 1.15 x 10⁶ persons would be needed to supply this. The State of Maine has a population of only 0.9 x 10⁶ persons, most of whom do not live on the Sheepscot.

Alternatively, 11.5 tons N d^{-1} in the average annual freshwater flow of 7.6 $m^{-3}s^{-1}$ would mean that it would contain 1,250 μg at N l^{-1}. Such nitrogen concentrations have not been reported in any natural runoff and are equivalent to the national mean for secondary sewage effluent (Weinberger *et al.*, 1966).

The apparent failure of phytoplankton to reduce nitrate concentrations to zero may be explained by any or all of the following:

1. Production is light, not nutrient limited (analogous to a turbidostat).

2. Population growth is less than the dilution rate (analogous to a chemostat at washout).

3. The population size is limited by grazing.

Light limitation of populations in the surface layer seems unlikely because the 1% light level is always equal to or greater than the depth of the surface layer. Further, there is little turbidity in the water column while chlorophyll α concentrations in excess of 30 mg m^{-2} are unusual. This number should be compared with theoretical maximum concentrations of 300 mg m^{-2} (Steemann-Nielsen, 1957) under conditions which would result in self-shading.

To examine the second explanation, and somewhat indirectly the third, a 25 h (two tidal cycles) anchor station at station 40 was made, starting 1100 h, 18 August 1977. Flushing rate was to be estimated from salt fluxes in the surface layer and grazing was to be examined using diurnal cycles of surface layer ammonia, chlorophyll α and phaeopigment concentrations.

Vertical current and salinity profiles were measured at hourly intervals over the entire water column. Each profile was interpolated to 2 m intervals and the (salinity x velocity) products were calculated over the entire water column and the surface layer depth (estimated to be 12 m). Salt fluxes over two tidal cycles were calculated by intergration over time. The surface tidal excursion was 4.5 km with a non-tidal drift of 1 km per tide.

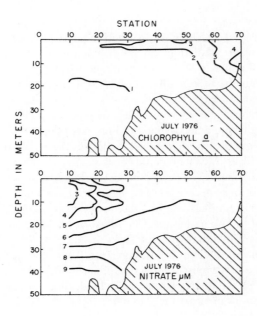

Figure 5. Longitudinal sections of chlorophyll a *(μg l^{-1}) and nitrate (μM) in July 1976.*

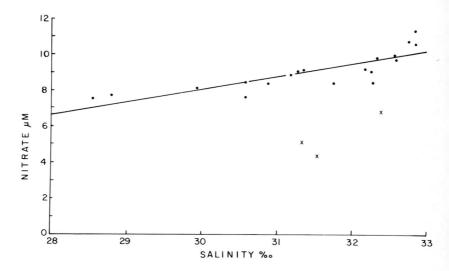

Figure 6.   Nitrate (μM) vs. salinity (°/oo) in September 1976. The regression line is computed on all points except those marked x.

Over the entire water column the upstream and downstream salt fluxes were equal within 5% of their mean. Within the limits of measurements this observation confirms a steady state circulation and a salt balance. In the surface layer the downstream (ebb) flux was 127% of the upstream (flood) flux. The surface layer was experiencing a daily dilution of about 25% which would require the phytoplankton to divide more rapidly than once every four days to overcome washout. Under summer light and nutrient conditions, such growth rates should be easily attained and washout should not potentially limit phytoplankton biomass.

The effect of grazing is reflected in the daily cycle of ammonia concentrations in the surface layer. Mean ammonia concentrations to 10 m are shown over two tidal cycles in Figure 7. During the daylight hours mean surface layer ammonia concentrations were generally between 1 to 2 μg at NH_3-N l^{-1}, although actual surface values reached the detection limit of the method employed (0.2 μg at l^{-1}). As ammonia is believed to be the preferred inorganic nitrogen substrate for phytoplankton uptake (Morris, 1974), it is likely that both nitrate and ammonia were being used by surface layer phytoplankton populations and that ammonia regeneration continued during daylight hours. With the onset of the dark period there was a rapid (and almost linear) increase in ammonia concentrations in the surface layer to 3.3 μg at NH_3-N l^{-1} over the first eight hours.

Whatever phytoplankton uptake of ammonia, if any, was occurring, the observed rate of accumulation of ammonia represents a minimum rate of excretion by grazing organisms. Chlorophyll α and phaeopigment distribution suggest that, in addition to potential temporal variability in ammonia production, there may also be considerable spatial variability in grazing. Although total pigments (chlorophyll and phaeopigments) show quite small variation ($3.76 \pm 0.96 \ \mu$g C^{-1}), chlorophyll ($2.26 \pm 1.3 \ \mu$g l^{-1}) and phaeopigments ($1.50 \pm 1.00 \ \mu$g l^{-1}) are individually more variable and also have more extreme ranges.

Nevertheless, if the observed production of ammonia is taken as a lower limit and it is assumed to occur in only 40% of the surface layer on any day (this based on the percentage of total pigments represented by phaeopigments), a lowest estimate of regeneration will be obtained. Thus, $2.2 \ \mu$g at l^{-1} or 308 mg m^{-2} of ammonia nitrogen will be produced in 40% of the 10 m water column in the estuary each day. Over the 50 km^2 of the estuary, this amounts to 6.16 tons of ammonia nitrogen regenerated daily or a little over half of the nitrogen required by phytoplankton each day. Zooplankton grazing of phytoplankton results in the excretion of only 74% of the ingested nitrogen as ammonia (Corner and Newell, 1967), so that 8.32 tons of nitrogen must be ingested daily. If this was principally phytoplankton nitrogen, grazing was forcing the phytoplankton to divide at 1.4 divisions per day. Since these are realistic minimum estimates, grazing pressure probably represents the controlling process on phytoplankton biomass and hence production.

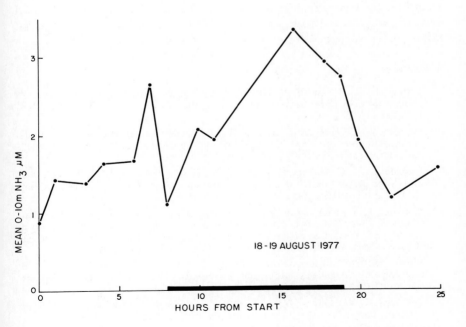

Figure 7. 0 to 10 m mean ammonia concentration at station 40 from 1100 h, 18 August 1977; the dark bar represents the period from sunset to sunrise.

Conclusions

Based on the foregoing discussion, the following conclusions are drawn:

The major source of inorganic nitrogen to the Sheepscot estuary is nitrate-rich Maine Intermediate Water, which enters in the upstream bottom layer flow of the two-layered estuarine circulation.

Phytoplankton production is dependent ultimately on this nitrogen supply, although regenerated ammonia is a significant component of the inorganic nitrogen used by phytoplankton. Terrigenous and anthropogenic inorganic nitrogen sources are probably insignificant to phytoplankton requirements. It is unlikely that eigher rapid dilution of phytoplankton populations or light limitation of photosynthesis play significant roles in limiting phytoplankton biomass, and high ambient nitrate concentrations eliminate the possibility of nutrient limitation. At the same time, high inorganic nitrogen concentrations do indicate some form of population limitation, and the rapid production of ammonia during the night suggests that grazing exerts the greatest pressure on phytoplankton standing stocks.

Acknowledgments

The authors wish to thank Jack Laird, who drove the boat, Jean Garside, who drove the computer, Jim Rollins, who drafted, and Toby Garfield, Carl Ketchum, and Charley Parker, who ran STD's and measured currents for 25 hours. This work was supported in part by NSF Grant #DES 75-15105.

References

1. Corner, E. D. S., and B. S. Newell. 1967. On the nutrition and metabolism of zooplankton. IV. The forms of nitrogen excreted by *Calanus*. J. Mar. Biol. Ass. U.K. 47:113-120.

2. Garside, C., G. Hull and S. Murray. 1977. The determination of sub-micromolar concentrations of ammonia in natural waters by a standard addition method using a gas sensing electrode. Submitted to Limnol. Oceanogr.

3. Garside, C., T. C. Malone, O. A. Roels, and B. A. Sharfstein. 1976. An evaluation of sewage-derived nutrients and their influence on the Hudson Estuary and New York Bight. Estuarine and Coastal Mar. Sci. 4:281-291.

4. Hopkins, T. S., and N. Garfield. 1977. The existence of the Maine Intermediate Water, p. 25. *In* R. C. Beardsley, B. Butman, and R. Wright (eds.), A Summary of an Informal Workshop of the Physical Oceanography of the Gulf of Maine and Adjacent Seas. Woods Hole Oceanographic Institution, Woods Hole, Mass.

5. Morris, I. 1974. Nitrogen assimilation and protein synthesis, chap. 21. *In* W. B. P. Steward (ed.), Algal Physiology and Biochemistry. Blackwell Scientific Publications, Oxford.

6. Pritchard, D. W., and W. V. Burt. 1951. An inexpensive and rapid technique for obtaining current profiles in estuarine waters. J. Mar. Res. 10(2):180-189.

7. Steeman-Nielsen, E. 1957. The chlorophyll content and the light utilization in communities of plankton algae and terrestrial higher plants. Physiol. Plant. 10:1009-1021.

8. Weinberger, L. W., D. G. Stephan, and F. M. Middleton. 1966. Solving our water problems—water renovation and re-use. Ann. New York Acad. Sci. 136:131-154.

9. Yentsch, C. S., and D. W. Menzel. 1963. A method for the determination of phytoplankton, chlorophyll, and phaeopigments by fluorescence. Deep-Sea Res. 10:221-231.

POSSIBLE EFFECTS OF GULF STREAM INTRUSIONS AND COASTAL RUNOFF ON THE BENTHOS OF THE CONTINENTAL SHELF OF THE GEORGIA BIGHT

Kenneth R. Tenore, Charles F. Chamberlain,
William M. Dunstan, Roger B. Hanson

Skidaway Institute of Oceanography
P.O. Box 13687
Savannah, Georgia

Barry Sherr

Department of Microbiology
University of Georgia
Athens, Georgia

and

John H. Tietjen

Department of Biology
City College of
The City University of New York

Abstract: The Georgia Bight has a broad shallow continental shelf. The major nutrient inputs are deepwater Gulf Stream intrusions along the shelf break and nearshore outwelling from *Spartina* salt marshes and river runoff. The middle portion of the shelf is not appreciably affected by either process. Nine stations off Georgia were sampled to detect possible differences in the benthos of these three regions.

All sediments were moderately- to well-sorted sand. A large coarse fraction occurred at the outer stations. Surface sediment carbon and nitrogen were extremely low at all stations ($< 0.1\%$ C and $< 0.01\%$ N dry wt). Sediment chlorophyll a values ranged from 29 to 142 μg m^{-2} (1 to 6 μg gm^{-1}).

Macrobenthic biomass at the inner three stations was significantly lower (3 to 9 grams wet weight m^{-2}) than middle and outer shelf regions (14 to 22) but all were lower than shelf environments in other areas. In contrast, meiofaunal densities (853 10 cm^{-2}) and biomass (543 μg 10 cm^{-2}) of the middle shelf regions were higher than inner and outer stations. Nematodes generally dominated the meiofaunal taxa.

ATP biomass (μg ATP cc^{-1}) ranged from 35 to 106 among the shelf stations with no apparent regional patterns. Microbial biomass was relatively constant along the coast but increased north to south along the shelf break. Interstitial glucose concentrations (57 to 100 ng cc^{-1}) and glucose uptake (6 to $19 \mu g^{-1}$ hr^{-1}) at the inner stations were similar to those observed at the outer stations. ATP biomass was positively correlated with glucose uptake but negatively correlated with denitrification rates. Nitrogen fixation (3 to 20 pmoles C_2H_4 cc^{-1} hr^{-1}) and denitrification (0.1 to 0.5 μg N_2O cc^{-1} hr^{-1}) decreased along the shelf break from north to south.

Preliminary results suggest that a combination of an unfavorable sedimentary regime and low nutrient input results in an impoverished benthos but that nitrogen-rich Gulf Stream intrusions may influence benthic processes on the outer regions of the continental shelf of the Georgia Bight. Microbenthos, with high metabolic rates and fast generation times, probably reflect more immediate nutrient effects, whereas the distribution of macrobenthos might reflect integrative effects of intrusion.

Introduction

The benthic community of the continental shelf of the Georgia Bight is dependent on nutrients brought into the system from various sources. It is generally assumed that the major inputs of these nutrients to coastal sediments are probably river discharge and tidal outwelling of marshes. However, estuaries along the Georgia Bight are not an important source of particulate organic matter or inorganic nitrogen to the outer coastal system and the organic carbon found in coastal waters is of autochthonous origin (Haines and Dunstan, 1975; Brokaw and Oertel, 1976). Along the Georgia coast there is a turbidity front about 20 kms offshore that causes most suspended materials originating inland to remain inshore. Thus, in the Georgia Bight, coastal runoff probably supplies very little, if any, nutrients to the outer shelf ecosystem except possibly during storms (Atkinson et al., in press). One major nutrient input to the outer shelf may be from nitrogen-rich Gulf Stream intrusions (Blanton, 1971; Stefansson et al., 1971; Dunstan and Atkinson, 1976; Atkinson et al., in press). The nutrients may be utilized for both autotrophic and heterotrophic processes in both the water column and sediments of the outer shelf region. Large phytoplankton blooms have frequently been observed in areas of intrusions (Dunstan and Atkinson, 1976).

Although there is good information available on the deep sea and nearshore benthos of the Georgia Bight (Rowe and Menzies, 1969; Rowe, 1971; Smith, 1971; Tietjen, 1971; Coull et al., 1977; Dorges, 1977), there are few studies of the benthos of the continental shelf proper off the southeastern United States. Especially lacking are functional studies combining microbial activity and the distribution of macro and meiobenthos. Cerame-Vivas and Gray (1966) and Day et al. (1971) studied the distributional patterns of the macrobenthos of the continental shelf off North Carolina. McNulty et al. (1962) studied benthic community structure off southern Florida. Smith (1971) and Frankenberg (1971) reported seasonal changes in species composition of the macrobenthos of nearshore stations off Georgia. However, none of these studies attempted to relate differences in benthic distribution to the hydrographic phenomenon described in this paper.

The study described here was initiated to determine any inshore-offshore effects of the different nutrient supplies on benthic communities of the continental shelf off Georgia.

General Methods

A sampling program was carried out in March 1976 aboard the R/V *Columbus Iselin* (Cruise CI-7604). Nine stations were located on the continental shelf off Georgia (Figure 1). The stations were spaced along three transects (off Wassaw Sound, St. Catherines Island, and Jekyll Island) to provide sampling in the inner (20 to 50 km), middle (50 to 90 km), and offshore (90 to 150 km) shelf regions. The station locations are:

Station Number	Latitude	Longitude
500	31°46′N	80°47′W
525	31°36′N	80°22′W
550	31°25′N	79°57′W
700	31°28′N	80°54′W
925	31°14′N	80°33′W
950	31°04′N	80°08′W
1000	31°00′N	81°08′W
1025	30°50′N	80°50′W
1050	30°42′N	80°22′W

Bottom sediments were collected with a box corer (10 x 20 cm core) similar to that described by Reineck (1958, 1963). Surface (1 m) and bottom (1 m above sediment) water samples were collected at each station with a 5 L PVC Niskin bottle. The sampling procedures and analytical techniques used by the various researchers are described in the following subsections.

Sediment and Suspended Particulate (Chamberlain and Tenore)

Methods

To determine the suspended sediment concentration of surface and near-bottom water, 1 to 3 liter samples were filtered through preweighed 45 μm pore size Millipore filters. The filter and the accumulated particulates were refrigerated in covered petri dishes until they could be dried and reweighed. Organic carbon determinations closely followed the procedure of weight loss after ignition described by Manheim *et al.* (1970).

A reversing thermometer on the Niskin bottle provided temperature information, and salinities were determined with a Baush and Lomb optical refractometer.

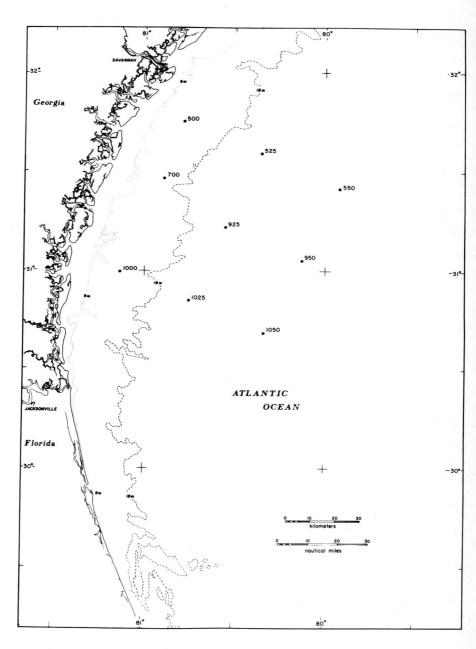

Figure 1. Bottom stations on the continental shelf off the Georgia coast.

The size distribution of the sediment was defined by sieve analysis (Folk, 1974) at $1/2\,\phi$ intervals ($\phi = -\log_2 d_{mm}$). The Folk mean, $M_z = (\phi16 + \phi50 + \phi94)/3$, and the inclusive graphic standard deviation, $\sigma\phi = (\phi84 - \phi16)/4 + (\phi95 - \phi5)/6.6$, were determined for all bottom samples.

Subsamples were taken with a 2.5 cm subcore and extruded in 2 cm sections for carbon-nitrogen analysis. The samples were frozen on board ship; were treated later with cold phosphoric acid to remove carbonate, and then dried at 90°C for 24 hrs. Carbon and nitrogen values were determined with triplicate samples on a Model 240 Perkin-Elmer Elemental Analyzer.

Results and Discussion

The size distribution of the bottom sediments, as characterized by mean diameter and sorting values, indicates that the predominant sediment type is a medium size, moderately sorted sand (Table 1). Gorsline (1963), Kingery (1973) and others have found a similar sediment type for this area. The sediments were composed principally of quartz with varying amounts of shell fragment, phosphorite, and minor amounts of unidentified accessory minerals.

Sediment carbon-nitrogen values for all stations were extremely low, below 0.09% C and 0.008% N (Table 2). Station 1000 sediment had the relatively high value of 0.09% C while all the other stations had surface values below 0.06%. There were no detectable vertical differences within 5 cm corers at any of the stations.

There was a general decrease in suspended particulate matter offshore, ranging from 1.2 mg/l to 0.2 mg/l. Suspended concentrations for nearshore samples averaged 0.9 mg/l while the offshore samples averaged 0.3 mg/l. These results agree with those of Manheim *et al.* (1970), and the reduction in suspended sediment concentrations in a seaward direction is attributed to seawater dilution of coastal-derived suspensoids.

The percent organic carbon of the suspended material showed no recognizable trends. The very low concentrations of suspended material offshore provided very little sample for analysis. A weight loss after ignition method for organic carbon determination proved inadequate for such small samples. A previous study by Brokaw and Oertel (1976) had indicated increasing percent organic carbon with increasing distance from shore.

Sediment and Water Column Chlorophyll a *(Dunstan)*

Methods

Water column chlorophyll *a* was measured fluorometrically (modified from Yentsch and Menzel, 1963) on water collected from surface and bottom. Sediment chlorophyll *a* was extracted with hot methanol and measured by a modification of the technique proposed by Tett *et al.* (1975). Samples were freeze dried and a period of shaking was added before methanol extraction (see McIntire and Dunstan, 1975).

Table 1. Sediment data of samples collected in March 1976 of the continental shelf of the Georgia Bight.

Station	Depth (m)	Salinity ‰ Surf.	Bottom	Bottom Temp. °C	Susp. Sed. Surf.	Bottom	% Organics Surf.	Bottom	Folk mean (M_z)* (ϕ/mm)	Sorting $(\sigma\phi)$†	Description	
500	13.0	30.2	30.5	16.2	1.2	0.9	66.7	33.3	1.5ϕ/0.35mm	0.99	Medium sand	Moderately sorted
525	28.5	31.0	31.2	—	1.0	0.6	80.0	66.7	1.45ϕ/0.38mm	0.87	Medium sand	Moderately sorted
550	44.0	31.4	31.5	19.2	0.4	0.4	100.0	50.0	1.03ϕ/0.50mm	0.75	Medium sand	Moderately sorted
700	14.5	30.2	30.0	16.8	0.8	1.0	87.5	80.0	2.18ϕ/0.23mm	0.60	Fine sand	Moderately well sorted
925	23.0	31.2	31.2	17.9	0.2	0.6	—	0.0	0.53ϕ/0.70mm	0.62	Coarse sand	Moderately well sorted
950	37.0	31.7	31.5	20.4	0.2	0.3	50.0	—	0.88ϕ/0.54mm	0.78	Coarse sand	Moderately sorted
1000	15.0	30.5	30.0	17.5	0.8	0.6	87.5	100.0	2.75ϕ/0.15mm	0.41	Fine sand	Well sorted
1025	26.0	31.0	31.0	17.1	0.4	0.8	10.0	87.5	1.25ϕ/0.42mm	0.72	Medium sand	Moderately sorted
1050	37.0	31.5	31.5	21.4	0.4	0.4	50.0	100.0	0.92ϕ/0.52mm	0.69	Coarse sand	Moderately well sorted

Table 2. Percent carbon-nitrogen values (by weight; corrected for carbonate) for samples from the March 1976 cruise of the continental shelf of the Georgia Bight.

Sediment depth (cm)		Station								
		500	525	550	700	925	950	1000	1025	1050
0-2	%C	.06	.05	.03	.11	.03	.03	.09	.06	.06
	%N	.005	.010	.004	.008	.004	.006	.008	.005	.004
	C/N	12.0	5.0	7.5	13.8	7.5	5.0	11.3	12.0	15.0
2-4	%C	.06	.05	0.4	.11	.03	.04	.09	.06	—
	%N	.006	.007	.004	.01	.006	.004	.008	.006	—
	C/N	10.0	7.1	10.0	11.0	5.0	10.0	11.3	10.0	—
4-6	%C	.05	.07	.03	.07	.02	.03	—	0.5	—
	%N	.007	.005	.004	.006	.004	.008	—	.005	—
	C/N	7.1	14.0	7.5	11.7	5.0	3.75	—	10.0	—

Results and discussion

Gulf Stream intrusions introduce substantial amounts of plant nutrients onto the shelf where utilization takes place when the nutrient-rich water upwells into the photic zone (Dunstan and Atkinson, 1976). We do not know if the resulting phytoplankton production is readily utilized by planktonic grazers or if it sinks out of the water column to be utilized by the benthos. If the intrusion-stimulated plant biomass sinks, we might expect that sediments and/or bottom water on the outer third of the continental shelf would be enriched or show higher chlorophyll levels.

The results from the present cruise indicate possible effects of both intrusions and river runoff. Water column chlorophyll was fairly uniform in the surface water while near-bottom samples were generally higher near the outer shelf (stations 550, 950 and 1050), indicating enhanced water column production along the outer shelf due to intrusions. However, sediments at stations 700, 925 and 1000 have two to three times as much chlorophyll *a* as the outer shelf stations.

Percent of degraded chlorophyll to total pigment shows slightly higher levels in the Savannah transect and near the shelf break.

Table 3. **Sediment and water column chlorophyll *a* distribution during March 1976 cruise of the continental shelf of the Georgia Bight.**

| Station | Sediment | | | Water Column | |
| | $mg\ m^{-2}$ | $\mu g\ gm^{-1}$ | % Pheo-pigment | $mg\ m^{-3}$ | |
				Surface	Bottom
500	29.0	.97	70	.67	.66
525	35.6	1.05	72	—	—
550	33.4	1.19	68	.34	.93
700	141.5	5.98	50	.53	.49
925	118.8	2.89	60	.55	.96
950	31.1	.94	68	.48	1.84
1000	118.9	2.55	65	.77	.62
1025	48.1	1.99	66	.55	.56
1050	39.9	1.59	67	.57	.82

Microbial Community (Hanson and Sherr)

Methods

Microbial processes and biomass were assayed to determine spatial variations on the shelf relative to potential nutrient inputs. Since nitrogen is generally considered as the limiting nutrient in most systems, nitrogen fixation and denitrification were measured to assess biological input and loss of nitrogen in the sediment. Glucose flux and ATP biomass were investigated to assess microbial productivity and metabolism in relation to potential organic and inorganic nutrient sources on the shelf.

At the first three stations, one subcore (PVC tubing, 3.2 cm dia.) was taken from each of the three box cores and the vertical distribution of the microbial community was measured. At the rest of the stations, the sediment from 0-5 cm was mixed together as one sample. Triplicate box cores were taken at all stations.

Heterotrophic Potential. The assay procedure described is a modification of methods described by Hobbie and Crawford (1969) and Christian and Hall (1976). Glucose in the form of uniformly-labeled $D-(U-{}^{14}C)$ glucose was diluted to 5 $\mu Ci/ml$ (3.96 $\mu g/ml$) for the assay.

Preliminary experiments using beach sand and marsh soil indicated that the uptake of ${}^{14}C$-glucose was linear for up to 20 minutes. Therefore, a reaction time of 10 minutes was used for these heterotrophy experiments. This was checked with sediment samples from station 550 and 950. The reaction time was also linear up to 20 minutes. Incubation of all samples was between 22 and 23°C.

To calculate glucose flux, glucose was determined by the enzymatic method of Hicks and Cary (1968). Interstitial water was collected from sediment cores by vacuum and filtered through a Whatman GF/C glass fiber filter. Bottom water was collected with a Niskin bottle and immediately filtered. All samples were frozen for onshore analysis.

Nitrogen Fixation Activity. Nitrogen fixation was determined by the acetylene reduction method (Stewart *et al.*,1967). Sediment cores (0-5 cm depth, 30 cc vol.) were taken and transferred by 50 ml syringe to 50 ml Erlenmeyer flasks that were then capped with a rubber serum stopper, injected with 5 ml of purified acetylene and 0.05 ml ethane (Matheson Co.) and excess pressure released. Gas samples were removed from the flasks with 2 ml Vacutainers after 10 hrs and 24 hrs of incubation. After each gas sample the pressure was released. Ethylene dilution was normalized to the ethane concentration. Ethylene and ethane were determined by gas chromatography (Hewlett-Packard, Model 5700A, with a Porapak N column). Ethylene and ethane peak areas were determined with a digital integrator (Autolab, Model 6300). Ethylene was not detected in any samples without acetylene. Controls containing 5 ml saturated NH_4Cl showed no ethylene production.

ATP Analysis. Extraction of ATP from the sediment was done by boiling $NaHCO_3$ buffer method of Bancroft *et al*. (1976). ATP was determined by the fly lucifern reaction, using a JRB photometer.

Denitrification Potential. The ability of shelf sediment slurries to reduce exogenously supplied nitrous oxide to nitrogen gas was determined quantitatively according to a modification of the method by Garcia (1974). The basic procedure for sediment samples is as follows: approximately 40 cc of sediment was obtained from a subcore (approximately 7.2 cm diameter and a depth of 1.0 cm); the sediment sample was transferred to an incubation bottle (120 cc capacity) and 40 ml of artificial seawater (ASW) (Lyman and Fleming, 1940; but excluding sodium sulfate) was added to yield a final slurry volume of 84 cc.

After ASW was added the bottle was sealed with a serum stopper and the stopper coated with silicone high vacuum grease. The head space was flushed with 99% pure helium (Matheson Co.) for six minutes. After an initial incubation period of one hour at between 22 to 23°C, 1000 μl of N_2O was added to the head space (1000 μl) and the system violently agitated for 30 seconds to establish quickly an equilibrium partitioning of the gas between the liquid and gaseous phases of the system. Three hundred μl aliquots of gas were then removed from the head space (36 cc volume) periodically with a gas tight syringe. These samples were quantitatively analyzed for N_2O using a thermal conductivity gas chromatograph equipped with a Carle microdetector and fitted with a column 10 ft x 1/8 in, packed with Porapak S (80-100 mesh).

Results and discussion

Table 4 summarizes the variables used to estimate microbial activity and biomass along the three transects in the Georgia Bight. Uptake of ^{14}C-glucose by benthic micro-heterotrophs significantly decreased ($r^2 = 0.98$; $p < 0.01$) with distance from shore along the Wassaw Island transect. However, along the St. Catherines Island transect, the uptake was significantly higher offshore than nearshore. A third pattern was observed within the Jekyll Island transect. ^{14}C-glucose uptake was greater at the inner and outermost stations than at the middle station.

The activity of the benthic nitrogen fixers showed the same trend along the three transects. Fixation rates were generally higher in the inner and outer stations than in the middle stations, and decreased north to south.

Reduction rates of exogenously supplied N_2O showed different trends between the three transects. Within the Wassaw Island transect the potential activity was lower in the coastal sediments than in the sediments near the shelf break. Along the St. Catherines Island transect N_2O reduction rates in the mid-shelf sediments were lower than in the coastal and shelf break regions. The potential activity within the Jekyll Island transect had a pattern opposite to that of the St. Catherines Island transect, i.e., the mid-shelf sediments had higher potential denitrification activity than either coastal or shelf break regions.

Sediment ATP concentrations had the same general trend as heterotrophic activity. The microbial biomass within the Wassaw Island transect decreased with distance from shore. Within the St. Catherines Island transect, however,

Table 4. Benthic microbial activities and biomass in the top 0-5cm of sediment from the March 1976 cruise of the continental shelf of the Georgia Bight. Correlations between inner, middle, and outer stations along each transect are given with level of confidence in ( ). All values are ± zone standard error.

Transect	Station Number	Heterotrophy		Nitrogen Fixation	Denitrification	ATP Biomass
		Flux μg glucose $g^{-1} h^{-1}$	Min.* (%)	(p mole $C_2H_4\,cc^{-1}\,h^{-1}$)	($\mu g\ N_2O\ cc^{-1}\ h^{-1}$)	($ng\ cc^{-1}$)
Wassaw Island	500	6.31 ± 1.87	8.24 ± 2.42	17.25 ± .36	.16 ± 0.02 (n=9)	101 ± 18.7
	525	5.26 ± 2.26	12.62 ± 1.27	14.90 ± 3.48	ND ±	76 ± 11.4
	550	4.78 ± .09	17.52 ± 2.07	21.07 ± 7.54	.46 ± 0.10	35.7 ± 9.54
		r = .978 (.01)		r = .602 (IS)		r = .991 (.01)
St. Catherines Island	700	5.87 ± .88	16.7 ± 9.25	9.40 ± 3.13	.29 ± 0.04	57.5 ± 18.5
	925	25.66 ± 3.65	1.06 ± .14	5.76 ± 2.80	.11 ± 0.04	106 ± 24.0
	950	22.75 ± 2.96	3.26 ± 1.04	10.40 ± 6.31	.40 ± 0.10	57.3 ± 19.6
		r = .793 (.05)		r = .205 (IS)	r = .376 (IS)	r = .004 (IS)
Jekyll Island	1000	18.49 ± 1.48	6.71 ± 1.99	7.92 ± 2.61	.20 ± 0.04	101 ± 13.2
	1025	10.06 ± 0.78	13.45 ± 6.60	3.12 ± 1.13	.39 ± 0.08	69.9 ± 6.2
	1050	20.78 ± 3.59	4.26 ± .39	9.24 ± 2.34	.26 ± 0.04	85.8 ± 12.4
		r = .204 (IS)		r = .205 (IS)	r = .309 (IS)	r = .489 (IS)

*Mineralization = ratio of ^{14}C glucose respired ($^{14}CO_2$) to total uptake.

microbial biomass was highest at the middle station and lowest at the inner and outer stations whereas along the Jekyll Island transect, microbial biomass estimates showed an opposite trend.

Interstitial and bottom water samples were analyzed for glucose (Table 5). The bottom water at all stations had lower glucose concentrations (15.5–24.1 μg l^{-1}) than the interstitial water (20.2–135.0 μg l^{-1}). The standing stock of glucose in the interstitial water of the mid-shelf stations was higher than in the coastal and shelf break interstitial water.

Along the southeastern United States, primary production usually decreases from the neritic to the oceanic zones (Thomas, 1966; Manheim *et al.*,1970; Haines, 1975; Haines and Dunstan, 1975). Because heterotrophic and autotrophic processes are coupled, benthic biomass and processes are controlled by primary production in the overlying water column. Hargrave (1973) found benthic oxygen uptake positively correlated with pelagic primary production and an inverse correlation between sediment respiration and depth of the water column mixed layer. This suggests that the benthic microbial activity and biomass should decrease offshore in the Georgia Bight. However, along the southeastern shelf break, the deep water intrusions onto the shelf and related increases in primary production (Dunstan and Atkinson, 1976) could significantly impact offshore pelagic and benthic communities. Thus if the intrusions are important, then the benthic microbial activity and biomass may be greater in

Table 5. **Glucose concentrations (μg l^{-1}) in bottom water (1m above sediment) and in interstitial water from the March 1976 cruise on the continental shelf of the Georgia Bight.**

Transect	*Station Number*		
Wassaw Island	500	525	550
Bottom water	18.5	24.1	17.6
Interstitial water	26.4	35.8	26.4
St. Catherines Island	700	925	950
Bottom water	15.5	16.0	15.8
Interstitial water	20.2	48.7	25.7
Jekyll Island	1000	1025	1050
Bottom water	22.0	19.2	19.9
Interstitial water	48.5	135.0	43.4

the outer shelf sediments than in the mid-shelf sediments of the Georgia Bight. Our preliminary findings suggest that intrusions indeed may influence the microbial community in diverse ways.

The uptake rates for the disturbed sediment (slurries) are several times higher than those for the undisturbed sediment (intact cores) (Hall *et al.*,1972; Christian and Hall, 1976). The rates so far obtained are relative rates (Wood, 1970; Harrison *et al.*,1971; Hall *et al.*,1972; Wood and Chua, 1973; Christian and Hall, 1976; and others). They only report of glucose uptake in sediments is that by Wood and Chua (1973) for Toronto Harbour. They diluted their samples 1:100 and expressed rates in mg $l^{-1} \cdot h^{-1}$. It is very difficult to compare their data (range 1-5 mg $l^{-1} \cdot h^{-1}$) with ours (5-25 μg $l^{-1} \cdot hr^{-1}$). The range of glucose mineralization (1–16%) on the shelf was similar to other systems (9–38%) (Hall *et al.*,1972; Wood and Chua, 1973). Although still preliminary, heterotrophic activity in the outer shelf sediments was greater in the two southern stations and the rates at these stations were greater than those at the inner stations. The high rates in the outer southern stations may have been attributed to intrusions.

Micro- and Meiobenthos. Measurements of ATP provide a reliable estimate of biomass in various communities (Paerl and Williams, 1976). The ATP concentrations found on the southeast continental shelf were several times lower than the values reported for the salt marsh soils (100-3000 ng/cc) (Christian *et al.*, 1975; Ferguson and Murdock, 1975) and estuarine sediments, and within the range for offshore sediments (10-500 ng/cc) (Ernst, 1970; Pamatmat and Skjoldal, 1974; Hodson *et al.*, 1976). The distribution of ATP biomass in the southeast shelf sediments suggests that intrusions of nutrient-rich deepwater onto the shelf may be important to the outer benthic systems as are estuarine and river inputs to the coastal benthic processes. ATP biomass along the shelf break increased southerly from the Wassaw to the Jekyll Island transects, whereas ATP biomass along a north-south transect of the inner and middle stations did not vary.

Benthic nitrogen fixation was investigated to determine its relationship to other biological and physical processes in coastal and offshore regions, since nitrogen has frequently been implicated in controlling carbon production, decomposition, and nutrient regeneration in marine systems (Ryther and Dunstan, 1971; Valiela and Teal, 1974; Sundström and Huss, 1975). Nitrogen fixation activity was low (0.003-0.021 nmoles $cc^{-1} h^{-1}$) compared to rates in other marine systems (0.031-4 nmoles $g^{-1} h^{-1}$) (Brooks *et al.*, 1971; Herbert, 1975; Marsho *et al.*, 1975; Hanson, 1977a, b). There have been no reports of benthic nitrogen fixation on continental shelves. If nitrogen-enriched intrusions are most frequent in the southern portion of the Bight (Atkinson, personal communication) then benthic nitrogen fixation might be lowest in this region. Our preliminary finding supports this hypothesis. Along a north-south line of outer stations, nitrogen fixation and denitrification activities decreased southerly toward the region where intrusions are most frequent.

"New" nitrogen input in the benthic community was estimated to illustrate the magnitude of the process. Although rather rough, the mean fixation rate (10 pmoles cc^{-1} h^{-1}) was extrapolated for the entire Georgia Bight. Based on a theoretical conversion factor of $3:1$ (Hardy *et al*., 1973) and a shelf area of 10^{10} m^2, a conservative estimate of 10^5 kg N_2 (0.1 kg N_2 • ha^{-1}) was calculated for March. If all this nitrogen was released to the overlying water, it would supply 0.4 to 4% of the daily primary production requirement (0.1 to 1 g C m^{-2} d^{-1}, Haines and Dunstan, 1975), assuming a phytoplankton C:N ratio of $10:1$. These estimates agree with Haines (1975) and Haines and Dunstan (1975) in that most of the phytoplankton nitrogen may be supplied by nitrogen regeneration from the benthic environment.

Infaunal Macrobenthos (Tenore)

Methods

Fifteen 10 x 20 cm cores (at least 15 cm depth) were collected at each station for the estimation of fauna biomass. The samples were sieved through a 0.5 mm mesh on board and preserved in 5% buffered formalin containing rose bengal stain. Appreciable amounts of sediment (about half of the volume of the core) remained on the screen. Back at the laboratory, under a dissecting microscope, the macrofauna were picked out of the remaining sediment, gently patted with absorbent paper to remove excess water, and the total wet weight biomass determined.

Results and discussion

Differences in macrobenthic biomass could reflect both sediment and intrusion effects. The biomass at the inner stations (500, 700 and 1000) was significantly lower than those of the middle and outer regions (excepting station 525) but all values were low compared to other east coast continental shelf areas (Table 6). There inner stations were located inside the turbidity front and presumably outside of the zone affected by oceanic intrusions. These inner stations also had a finer (all < 0.38 mm) mean grain size than middle and outer stations. Station 525, the only one of the middle and outer regions that exhibited a high sediment sorting 0ϕ, also had a low macrobenthic biomass. Thus the low macrobenthic biomass of these stations might also be due to adverse sedimentary conditions.

Meiofauna (Tietjen)

Methods

Samples for meiofauna were obtained by inserting 1.5 cm (inside diameter) plastic core tubes to a depth of 5 cm into sediment samples taken with the box corer. At each station three separate box cores were taken for meiofauna; three

Table 6. Biomass values for infaunal macrobenthos during the March 1976 cruise of the continental shelf of the Georgia Bight.

Station	Biomass grams wet wt m^{-2} $\bar{x} \pm 1$ s.d.
500	9.71 ± 6.83
525	6.29 ± 2.93
550	21.85 ± 16.04
700	7.33 ± 4.08
925	14.01 ± 10.39
950	15.87 ± 7.53
1000	2.99 ± 1.68
1025	15.73 ± 9.19
1050	13.23 ± 8.75

subsamples were taken from each box core, yielding nine samples for meiofauna at each station. The samples were preserved in a 5% buffered seawater formalin-rose bengal mixture. In the laboratory the samples were washed through a set of two sieves, the larger one with a mesh opening of 0.500 mm and the smaller one with a mesh opening of 0.044 mm. Animals that passed through the larger sieve and were retained on the smaller seive were considered meiofauna.

Dry weights of all taxa were obtained by weighing representative individuals from each taxon on a Mettler M5 Microbalance (± 1 μg) after they had been dried at 90°C to constant weight.

Results and discussion

Mean densities (number • 10 cm^{-2}) and biomass (μg dry weight • 10 cm^{-2}) of meiofauna (Tables 7 and 8) show that the dominant taxa, reported as percent of total individuals, were Nematoda, 60.0%; Copepoda (Harpacticoida), 16.4%; Foraminifera, 9.8%; and Gastrotricha, 3.6%. Nauplii comprised 6.3% of the individuals enumerated; all other groups collectively comprised only 3.9% of the meiofauna in the samples.

Although nematodes included 60.0% of the meiofauna individuals present, they constituted but 36.5% of total meiofauna biomass. Because the average copepod weighed about 1 μg more than the average nematode, the biomass of copepods was disproportionately large (33.0%) relative to their numbers.

Table 7. Mean meiofauna densities (No. 10cm⁻²) for the March 1976 cruise of the continental shelf of the Georgia Bight.

Taxon	500	525	550	700	925	950	1000	1025	1050
						Station			
Nematoda	870	56	281	863	288	274	475	275	197
Copepoda	110	164	124	98	118	98	6	179	102
Polychaete	14	23	11	7	7	11	5	7	14
Foraminifera	116	73	71	106	74	95	11	37	55
Gastrotricha	56	33	23	50	36	18	17	11	10
Kinorhyncha	2	8	2	6	5	5	<1	5	3
Ostracoda	3	3	3	3	1	2	1	<1	2
Tardigrada	25	11	8	18	4	7	1	6	1
Turbellaria	19	6	3	12	4	3	4	4	2
Bivalvia	2	2	1	1	4	3	1	0	1
Halacanda	1	1	1	3	1	2	<1	0	0
Hydrozoa	0	1	1	1	0	0	0	1	<1
Nauplii	72	75	55	34	43	51	4	50	25
Other	0	0	1	1	13	0	0	0	1
Total	1290	961	585	1203	598	569	527	576	413

Polychaetes, which comprised only 1.6% of total numbers of meiofauna, accounted for 15.0% of the biomass. All other groups collectively contributed 15.5% to the total meiofauna biomass.

There were north-south and inshore-offshore gradients in the density distribution of meiofauna. Mean meiofauna density (number of individuals • 10 cm⁻²) along the northern (500) transect was 945; along the middle (700, 925, 950) transect 790, and along the southern (1000) transect, 505. The difference between the northern and southern transects was significant ($p < .05$).

Longitudinally, mean density (organisms • 10 cm⁻²) along the inner series (stations 500, 700, 1000) was 1007; along the middle trio of stations (525, 925, 1025) 712, and along the outer trio of stations (550, 950, 1050), 522. Densities at the inshore series of stations were significantly ($p < .05$) higher than offshore; this was due entirely to significantly higher densities of nematodes at the inner trio of stations ($\bar{x} = 736$ • 10 cm⁻²) than at the outer trio of stations ($\bar{x} = 251$). Densities of nematodes at the middle series of stations (525, 925, 1025) ($\bar{x} = 374$ • 10 cm⁻²) were also significantly lower than inshore. While no statistically significant longitudinal differences in copepod distributions occurred, densities at the mid and outer shelf stations were consistently higher than inshore.

Table 8. Mean meiofauna biomass (μg dry weight 10cm^{-2}) for the March 1976 cruise of the continental shelf of the Georgia Bight.

Taxon	500	525	550	700	Station 925	950	1000	1025	1050
Nematoda	261.1	168.3	84.3	258.9	86.4	82.2	142.5	82.5	59.1
Copepoda	143.3	213.2	161.2	127.4	153.4	29.4	7.8	232.7	132.6
Polychaeta	72.5	115.0	55.0	35.0	35.0	55.0	25.0	35.0	70.0
Foraminifera	11.6	7.3	7.1	10.6	7.4	9.5	1.1	3.7	5.5
Gastrotricha	5.6	3.3	2.3	5.0	3.6	1.8	1.7	1.1	1.0
Kinorhyncha	6.0	24.0	6.0	18.0	15.0	15.0	1.5	15.0	9.0
Ostracoda	15.0	15.0	15.0	15.0	5.0	10.0	5.0	2.5	10.0
Tardigrada	1.2	0.6	0.4	0.9	0.2	0.4	<0.1	0.3	<0.1
Turbellaria	0.9	0.6	0.3	1.2	0.4	0.3	0.4	0.4	0.2
Bivalvia	10.0	10.0	5.0	5.0	20.0	15.0	5.0	0.0	5.0
Halacanda	1.5	1.5	1.5	4.5	1.5	3.0	1.0	0.0	0.0
Hydrozoa	0.0	0.5	0.5	0.5	0.0	0.0	0.0	0.5	0.2
Nauplii	7.2	7.5	5.5	3.4	4.3	5.1	0.4	5.0	2.5
Other	0.0	0.0	5.0	5.0	65.0	0.0	0.0	0.0	5.0
Total	535.7	566.8	349.1	490.4	397.2	226.7	191.4	378.7	300.1

Furthermore, the relative abundance of copepods at the inner shelf stations (5.7%) was significantly lower ($p < .05$) than at the mid shelf (22.5%) and outer shelf (21.0%) stations.

The increase in copepod densities offshore was not sufficient to balance the accompanying decrease in nematode densities; total meiofauna biomass, therefore, at the outer shelf stations ($\bar{x} = 292\ \mu$g $\cdot$ 10 cm^{-2}) was significantly lower than at the inner shelf stations ($\bar{x} = 405.8\ \mu$g 10 cm^{-2}).

The quantitative distribution of meiofauna in the present study was consistent with the distributions observed in sandy shelf sediments elsewhere (Wieser, 1960; Wigley and McIntyre, 1964; McIntyre and Murison, 1973; McLachlan *et al.*, 1977; Tietjen, in press). Nematodes were significantly negatively correlated ($r = -0.64$) and harpacticoid copepods significantly positively correlated ($r = +0.55$) with increasing mean grain size, a distribution which has been observed in other areas (Tietjen, 1969, 1971; Coull, 1970; McLachlan *et al.*, 1977). The majority of the copepods were interstitial forms, and their increased densities in the coarser (middle and outer shelf) sediments is due to the fact that such forms are able to move better through the larger interstices present in coarser sediments than through finer sediments (McLachlan *et al.*, 1977). With interstitial space removed as a stress factor, increased reproduction by the copepod populations probably occurs, resulting in increased competition for food resources between them and the nematodes, and a subsequent decline in the dominance of the latter taxon at the mid and outer shelf stations.

The copepod densities increased in coarser sediments despite the fact that the distribution of benthic plant material (as measured by chlorophyll a) decreased from the inner toward the outer shelf. This observation suggests that sediment granulometry may be the most important factor regulating meiofauna distribution on the Georgia shelf. The significantly higher numbers of nematodes at the inner shelf stations may be a reflection of the presence of more land-derived detritus in the sediments along the inner shelf, as indicated by the higher concentrations of chlorophyll a inshore.

The fact that meiofauna densities (and biomass), in contrast to the low macrobenthic levels, were consistent with those reported elsewhere, despite the extremely low concentrations of organic carbon and nitrogen in the sediments, suggests that they are effective in exploiting the meager resources available to them. For example, the average macrofauna-to-meiofauna biomass ratio was 6:1, a ratio more characteristic of harsh areas like exposed beaches (McIntyre, 1968) than of more benign areas like the New England continental shelf (Wigley and McIntyre, 1964), where the ratio is about 20:1. Thus it appears that on the shallow Georgia shelf, meiofauna compete successfully with macrofauna for the meager resources, significantly reducing the latter's biomass.

General Summary

The continental shelf off Georgia has an impoverished benthic community due to an unfavorable sedimentary regime and low nutrient input. The shallow depth of the shelf results in pronounced wind-induced and tidal scour of the sediments, especially at the inner stations. Most of the macrobenthos are small, mobile, surface forms that can survive in such an environment. The shelf receives a low nutrient input from coastal run-off, due to a salinity front existing approximately 20 kms offshore. Most suspended materials originating inland remain nearshore within this boundary. Because of low nutrient levels and concomitant low primary productivity there is little regular local input into the benthic system. Therefore biomass of macrobenthos and meiobenthos is generally low throughout the shelf, compared to other shelf communities.

Periodic intrusions of oceanic water along the shelf, however, might be influencing nutrient inputs into the benthic system, but differences in the time-scale response of different components of the benthos probably obscure results from a time-specific sampling period.

The generally higher biomass of macrobenthos in the middle and outer stations suggests nutrient enrichment due to intrusion-related biological production. Because macrobenthos have relatively longer generation times compared to meio- and microbenthos, these differences might reflect an integrated effect of the periodic intrusions. On the other hand, the microbial data showed no discernible inner-outer differences but the high biomass and heterotrophic activity and low N-fixation and denitrification in the southernmost outer stations. Microbenthos, because of their fast growth rate and generation time, respond rapidly to changes in nutrient enrichment. Therefore, they are excellent for detecting short-term nutrient fluctuations in environment.

Acknowledgments

We would like to thank the members of the technical staff at Skidaway Institute of Oceanography and the crew of the R/V *Columbus Iselin*, University of Miami, who made this work possible. This research was supported by the NSF Grants DES75-19065, DES74-21338, DES75-20847 and ERDA Grant E(38-1)-936 and NSF ship support for cruise CI-7604 of the R/V *Columbus Iselin*.

References

1. Atkinson, L. P., W. M. Dunstan, and G. Paffenhöfer. The chemical and biological effect of a Gulf Stream intrusion off St. Augustine, Florida. Bull. Mar. Sci. (in press).

2. Bancroft, K., E. A. Paul, and W. J. Wiebe. 1976. Extraction of adenosine triphosphate from marine sediments with boiling sodium bicarbonate. Limnol. Oceanogr. 21:473-480.

3. Blanton, J. 1971. Exchange of Gulf Stream water with North Carolina shelf water in Onslow Bay during stratified conditions. Deep-Sea Res. 18:167-178.

4. Brokaw, R. S., and G. F. Oertel. 1976. Suspended sediment data from nearshore waters of Georgia. Georgia Marine Science Center Technical Report No. 76-3, 42 pp.

5. Brooks, R. H., Jr., P. L. Brezonik, H. D. Putnam, and M. A. Keirn. 1971. Nitrogen fixation in an estuarine environment: The Waccasassa on the Florida Gulf Coast. Limnol. Oceanogr. 16:701-710.

6. Cerame-Vivas, M. J., and I. E. Gray. 1966. The distributional patterns of benthic invertebrates of the continental shelf off North Carolina. Ecology 47:260-270.

7. Christian, R. R., K. Bancroft, and W. J. Wiebe. 1975. Distribution of microbial adenosine triphosphate in salt marsh sediment at Sapelo Island, Georgia. Soil Sci. 119:89-97.

8. Christian, R. R., and J. R. Hall. 1976. Experimental trends in sediment microbial heterotrophy: Radioisotopic techniques and analysis, pp. 67-88. *In* B. Coull (ed.), Ecology of Marine Benthos. Belle Baruch Marine Symposium Volume 7, University of So. Carolina Press, Columbia.

9. Coull, B. C. 1970. Shallow water meiobenthos of the Bermuda platform. Oecologia 4:325-357.

10. Coull, B. C., R. L. Ellison, J. W. Fleger, R. P. Higgins, W. D. Hope, W. D. Hummon, R. M. Riger, W. E. Sterrer, H. Thiel, and J. H. Tietjen. 1977. Quantitative estimates of the meiofauna from the deep sea off North Carolina. Mar. Biol. 39:233-240.

11. Day, J. H., J. G. Field, and M. P. Montgomery. 1971. The use of numerical methods to determine the distribution of the benthic fauna across the continental shelf of North Carolina. J. Animal Ecol. 40:93-125.

12. Dorges, J. 1977. Marine macrobenthic communities of the Sapelo Island, Georgia region. pp. 399-422. *In* B. Coull (ed.), Ecology of Marine Benthos. Baruch Library in Mar. Sci., University of So. Carolina Press, Columbia.

13. Dunstan, W. M., and L. P. Atkinson. 1976. Sources of new nitrogen for the South Atlantic Bight, pp. 69-78. *In* M. L. Wiley (ed.), Estuarine Processes, Vol. 1, Academic Press, New York.

14. Ernst, W. 1970. ATP als indikator für die biomasse marine sedimente. Oecologia 5:56-60.

15. Ferguson, R. L., and M. B. Murdock. 1975. Microbial ATP and organic carbon in sediments of the Newport River estuary, North Carolina, pp. 229-250. *In* L. E. Cronin (ed.), Estuarine Research, Vol. 1, Chemistry, Biology and the Estuarine System. Academic Press, New York.

16. Folk, R. L. 1974. Petrology of sedimentary rocks. Hemphill Publ. Co., Austin, Texas.

17. Frankenberg, D. 1971. The dynamics of benthic communities off Georgia, USA. Thalassia Jugoslavica 7:49-55.

18. Garcia, J. L. 1974. Réduction de l'oxyde nitreux dans les sols de rizières du Senegal: mesure de l'activité dénitrifiante. Soil Biol. Biochem. 6:79-84.

19. Gorsline, D. S. 1963. Bottom sediments of the Atlantic shelf and slope off the southern United States, Jour. Geol. 71:422-440.

20. Haines, E. B. 1975. Nutrient inputs to the coastal zone: The Georgia and South Carolina shelf, pp. 303-324. *In* L. E. Cronin (ed.), Estuarine Research, Vol. 1, Chemistry, Biology and the Estuarine System. Academic Press, New York.

21. Haines, E. B., and W. M. Dunstan. 1975. The distribution and relationship of particulate organic material and primary productivity in the Georgia Bight, 1873-1974. Est. Coast. Mar. Sci. 3:431-441.

22. Hall, K., P. M. Kleeber, and I. Yesaki. 1972. Heterotrophic uptake of organic solutes by microorganisms in sediments. Mem. Inst. Ital. Idrobiol., Suppl. 29:441-471.

23. Hanson, R. B. 1977a. A comparison of the nitrogen-fixers in low and high *Spartina alterniflora* salt marsh soils. App. Environ. Microbiol. 33:596-602.

24. _____. 1977b. Nitrogen fixation (acetylene reduction) in a salt marsh amended with sewage sludge and organic carbon and nitrogen compounds. Environ. Appl. Microbiol. 33:846-852.

25. Hardy, R. W. F., R. C. Burns, and R. D. Holsten. 1973. Applications of the acetylene-ethylene assay for measurement of nitrogen fixation. Soil Biochem. 5:47-81.

26. Hargrave, B. T. 1973. Coupling carbon flow through some pelagic and benthic communities. J. Fish. Res. Bd. Canada 30:1317-1326.

27. Harrison, M. J., R. T. Wright, and R. Y. Morita. 1971. Method for measuring mineralization in lake sediments. App. Microbiol. 21:698-702.

28. Herbert, R. A. 1975. Heterotrophic nitrogen fixation in shallow estuarine sediments. J. exp. mar. Biol. Ecol. 18:215-225.

29. Hicks, S. E., and F. G. Carey. 1968. Glucose determination in natural waters. Limnol. Oceanogr. 13:361-363.

30. Hobbie, J. E., and C. C. Crawford. 1969. Bacterial uptake of organic substrate: new method of study and application to eutrophication. Verh. Int. Ver. Limnol. 17:725-730.

31. Hodson, R. E., O. Holm-Hansen, and F. Azam. 1976. Improved methodology of ATP determination in marine environments. Mar. Biol. 34:143-149.

32. Kingergy, F. A. 1973. Textural analysis of shelf sands off the Georgia coast. Unpubl. M.S. thesis, California State University, San Diego, 75 pp.

33. Lyman, J., and R. H. Fleming. 1940. Composition of seawater. J. Mar. Res. 3:134-146.

34. Manheim, F. T., R. H. Meade, and G. C. Bond. 1970. Suspended matter in surface waters of the Atlantic continental margin from Cape Cod to the Florida Keys. Science 167:371-376.

35. Marsho, T. V., R. P. Burchard and R. Fleming. 1975. Nitrogen fixation in the Rhode River estuary Chesapeak Bay. Can. J. Microbiol. 21:1348-1356.

36. McIntyre, A. D. 1968. The meiofauna and macrofauna of some tropical beaches. J. Zool. Soc. London 156:377-392.

37. McIntire, G. L., and W. M. Dunstan. 1975. Methods of analysis of *Spartina alterniflora* for carbohydrates, chlorophyll and iron. Georgia Marine Science Center Technical Report 75-4.

38. McIntyre, A. D., and D. J. Murison. 1973. The meiofauna of a flatfish nursery ground. J. Mar. Biol. Assn. U. K. 53:93-118.

39. McLachlan, A., P. E. D. Winter, and L. Botha. 1977. Vertical and horizontal distribution of sub-littoral meiofauna in Algoa Bay, South Africa. Mar. Biol. 40:355-364.

40. McNulty, J. K., R. C. Work, and H. B. Moore. 1962. Some relationships between the infauna of the level bottom and the sediment in South Florida. Bull. Mar. Sci. 12:322-332.

41. Paerl, H. W., and N. J. Williams. 1976. The relationship between adenosine triphosphate and microbial biomass in diverse aquatic ecosystem. Int. Revue ges. Hydrobiol. 61:659-664.

42. Pamatmat, M., and H. R. Skjoldal. 1974. Dehydrogenase activity and adenosine triphosphate concentration of marine sediments in Lindaspollene, Norway. Sarsia 56:1-11.

43. Reineck, H. E. 1958. Kastengreifer und Lotrohre "Schnepfe." Senckenbergiana Lethaea 39(1-2):45-48.

44. _____ . 1963. Der Kastengreifer. Natur Museum 93(2):58-65.

45. Rowe, G. T. 1971. Benthic biomass and surface productivity, pp. 441-454. *In* J. D. Costlow, Jr. (ed.), Fertility of the Sea, Vol. 2, Gordon and Breach.

46. Rowe, G. T., and R. J. Menzies. 1969. Zonation of large benthic invertebrates in the deep sea off the Carolinas. Deep-Sea Res. 16:531-537.

47. Ryther, J. H., and W. Dunstan. 1971. Nitrogen, phosphorus and entrophication in marine environment. Science 171:1008-1013.

48. Smith, K. L., Jr. 1971. Structural and functional aspects of a sublittoral community. Ph.D. dissertation, University of Georgia, 160 pp.

49. Stefansson, U., L. P. Atkinson, and D. F. Bumpus. 1971. Hydrographic properties and circulation of the North Carolina shelf and slope waters. Deep-Sea Res. 18:383-420.

50. Stewart, P., G. P. Fitzgeral, and R. H. Burris. 1967. *In situ* studies on N_2 fixation using the acetylene reduction technique. Porc. Nat. Acad. Sci., USA, 58:2071-2078.

51. Sundström, K.-R., and K. Huss. 1975. Effects of nitrogen fixing bacteria on mineralization in raw humus. Oikos 26:147-151.

52. Tett, P., G. K. Mahlon, and G. M. Hornberger. 1975. A method for the spectrophotometric measurement of chlorophyll *a* and pheophytin *a* in benthic microalgae. Limnol. Oceanogr. 20(5):887-895.

53. Thomas, J. P. 1966. The influence of the Altamaha River on primary production beyond the mouth of the river. M.S. thesis, University of Georgia, Athens, Georgia, 66 pp.

54. Tietjen, J. H. 1969. The ecology of shallow water meiofauna in two New England estuaries. Oecologia 2:251-291.

55. _____ . 1971. Ecology and distribution of deep-sea meiobenthos off North Carolina. Deep-Sea Res. 18:941-957.

56. _____ . Population distribution and structure of the free-living nematodes of Long Island Sound. Mar. Biol. (in press).

57. Valiela, I., and J. M. Teal. 1974. Nutrient limitation in salt marsh vegetation, pp. 547-563. *In* R. J. Reimold and W. H. Queen (eds.), Ecology of Halophytes. Academic Press, New York.

58. Wieser, W. 1960. Benthic studies in Buzzards Bay. II. The meiofauna. Limnol. Oceanogr. 5:121-137.

59. Wigley, R., and A. D. McIntyre. 1964. Some quantitative comparisons of offshore meiobenthos and macrobenthos south of Martha's Vineyard. Limnol. Oceanogr. 9:485-493.

60. Wood, L. W. 1970. The role of estuarine sediment microorganisms in the uptake of organic carbon under aerobic conditions. Ph.D. dissertation, Department of Zoology, North Carolina State University, Raleigh, 79 pp.

61. Wood, L. W., and K. E. Chua. 1973. Glucose flux at the sediment water interface of Toronto Harbour, Lake Ontario, with reference to pollution stress. Can. J. Microbiol. 19:413-420.

62. Yentsch, C. S., and D. W. Menzel. 1963. A method for the determination of phytoplankton chlorophyll and phaeophytin by fluorescence. Deep-Sea Res. 10:221-231.

INDEX